Lecture Notes in Compute 7

Commenced Publication in 1973
Founding and Former Series Editors:
Gerhard Goos, Juris Hartmanis, and Jan van

Michael Butler   Cliff Jones
Alexander Romanovsky   Elena Troubitsyna (Eds.)

Rigorous Development of Complex Fault-Tolerant Systems

 Springer

Volume Editors

Michael Butler
University of Southampton
School of Electronics and Computer Science
Highfield, Southampton SO17 1BJ, UK
E-mail: mjb@ecs.soton.ac.uk

Cliff Jones
Alexander Romanovsky
Newcastle University
School of Computing Science
Newcastle upon Tyne, NE1 7RU, UK
E-mail: {cliff.jones,alexander.romanovsky}@ncl.ac.uk

Elena Troubitsyna
Åbo Akademi University
Department of Computer Science
Lemminkäisenkatu 14 A, 20520 Turku, Finland
E-mail: etroubit@abo.fi

Library of Congress Control Number: 2006936100

CR Subject Classification (1998): C.2.4, D.1.3, D.2, D.4.5, F.2.1-2, D.3, F.3

LNCS Sublibrary: SL 2 – Programming and Software Engineering

ISSN   0302-9743
ISBN-10   3-540-48265-2 Springer Berlin Heidelberg New York
ISBN-13   978-3-540-48265-9 Springer Berlin Heidelberg New York

Springer is a part of Springer Science+Business Media

springer.com

© Springer-Verlag Berlin Heidelberg 2006
Printed in Germany

Typesetting: Camera-ready by author, data conversion by Scientific Publishing Services, Chennai, India
Printed on acid-free paper   SPIN: 11916246   06/3142   5 4 3 2 1 0

Foreword

Software is the fuel of the information society. Many of our systems and applications are today controlled and/or developed in software. It is also a well known fact that many software systems have reached a level of complication, mainly because of their size, heterogeneity and distribution (and hopefully not through bad programming), that results in faults appearing which cannot be traced back easily to the code. Some of these "faults" could also be unexpected program behaviour that appears as a result of interactions between the different parts of the program; this is commonly known as complexity. The problem is that sometimes is not easy to say whether a fault is traceable to the code or whether it is due to emergent unexpected behaviour from the complex software system. Testing the code for possible faults is also very costly.

New methods, approaches, tools and techniques are needed to cope with the increasing complexity in software systems; amongst them, fault tolerance techniques and formal methods, supported by the corresponding tools, are promising solutions. This is precisely the subject of this book, which is very much welcome.

The pervasiveness of software in today's information society makes it of paramount importance, and the main objective of the Software Technologies unit of the European Commission is to support the European software and services industry so that quality software and services are developed to compete in global markets. To help in reaching this objective, it is obvious that we need to maintain and contribute to the excellence in research from universities and research organizations in this specific area.

The volume has been prepared by the partners involved in the FP6 IST-511599 RODIN project (partly funded by the European Commission), "Rigorous Open Development Environment for Complex Systems". The book brings together papers focusing on the application of rigorous design techniques to the development of fault-tolerant, software-based systems.

In RODIN complexity is mastered by design techniques (specifically formal methods) that support clear thinking and rigorous validation and verification. Coping with complexity also requires architectures that are tolerant of faults and unpredictable changes in the environment; this side is addressed by fault tolerant design techniques. The sources of complexity under study in RODIN are those caused by the environment in which the software is to operate and from the poorly conceived architectural structure.

Who should read this book? Basically, the formal methods and fault tolerance communities. The formal methods people will learn more about (and probably be fired up by) the challenging issues in design for fault tolerance, while researchers on fault tolerance will better understand how formal methods can improve way in which their techniques are developed and applied.

The European Commission, through its successive framework programs, has supported work on methods and techniques to master system complexity and achieve dependable and trustworthy systems. Recently, specifically under the 6th Framework Programme, it has called, amongst other topics, for "Principles, methodologies and tools for design, management and simulation of complex software systems" and

"Foundational and applied research to enable the creation of software systems with properties such as self-adaptability, flexibility, robustness, dependability and evolvability".

It is clear that these issues are, by no means, fully resolved. Software systems are increasingly complex, and we will need increased efforts in research just to keep up with the pace of development (based on the reflection by the Red Queen in Lewis Carroll's *Through the Looking Glass*, "in this place it takes all the running you can do, to keep in the same place"). It is time, now, for renewed efforts; this book is a pointer in that direction.

August 2006   José-Luis Fernández-Villacañas Martín

Preface

There was, for several decades, a split between researchers who aimed to create perfect programs by using formal methods and those who pioneered techniques for fault tolerance. Of course, the approaches actually complement each other. Fault tolerance generally copes with failures of physical components (and might in specific cases be able to guard against some sorts of design mistakes). Formal reasoning is not just about proving (under assumptions) that a given program will function perfectly; the most productive use of formalism is early on in the design process to help clean up the architecture of a system. As systems have become larger and more intimately linked both to the physical world and to human users, the design task has become far more complex. One of the goals of design must always be to reduce unnecessary complexity in resulting systems.

The editors of this book are proud to be involved in an EU (FP-6) project which specifically brings together researchers from the fault tolerance and formal methods communities. We are aware that through abstraction, refinement and proof, formal methods provide design techniques that support clear thinking as well as rigorous validation and verification. Furthermore, good tool support is essential to support the industrial application of these design techniques.

In 2005 the RODIN (*Rigorous Open Development Environment for Complex Systems*) project organised a workshop on *Rigorous Engineering of Fault Tolerant Systems*. REFT 2005[1] was held in conjunction with the Formal Methods 2005 conference at Newcastle University. The aim of this workshop was to bring together researchers who were interested in the application of rigorous design techniques to the development of fault tolerant software based systems.

Such was the success of that event that the organisers decided to prepare a book on the same combination of topics by inviting the authors of the best workshop papers to expand their work and a number of well-established researchers working in the area to write invited chapters. This book contains the refereed and revised papers that came in response. Twelve of the papers are reworked from the workshop; nine of them are totally new. We have also included two provocatively different position statements from Abrial and Amey on the role of programming languages.

The organisers would like to thank the reviewers (some of whom work on RODIN, others are from outside the project): Jean-Raymond Abrial, Elisabeth Ball, Fernando Castor Filho, Patrice Chalin, Ernie Cohen, Joey Coleman, Neil Evans, Massimo Felici, Stefania Gnesi, Stefan Hallerstede, Michael Hansen, Ian Hayes, Alexei Iliasov, Dubravka Ilić, Maciej Koutny, Linas Laibinis, Annabelle McIver, Qaisar Ahmad Malik, César Muñoz, Simin Nadjm-Tehrani, Apostolos Niaouris, Ian Oliver, Patrizio Pelliccione, Mike Poppleton, Shamim Ripon, Colin Snook and Divakar Yadav.

---

[1] The proceedings are at http://www.cs.ncl.ac.uk/research/pubs/trs/papers/915.pdf

We should particularly like to thank José-Luis Ferández-Villacañas Martin who both gave his time to update the meeting on IST plans and has kindly contributed the Foreword to this volume; and Louise Talbot who has quietly and efficiently handled the collation of this book.

Both in organising REFT 2005 and in publishing this edited book we are aiming to build a network of researchers from the wider community to promote integration of dependability and formal methods research. It is encouraging to see that many of the papers address software based systems that impact peoples' everyday lives such as communications systems, mobile services, control systems, medical devices and business transactions. We hope that you enjoy reading this volume and encourage you to contribute to our aim of closer collaboration between dependability and formal methods research. We expect to organise another event in London in July 2007: details will appear on the project WWW site http://www.cs.ncl.ac.uk/research/projects/detail.php?id=219

August 2006   Michael Butler
                                                                  Cliff Jones
                                                       Alexander Romanovsky
                                                           Elena Troubitsyna

Table of Contents

Position Papers

Train Systems

Jean-Raymond Abrial

ETH Zurich, Switzerland
jabrial@inf.ethz.ch

Abstract. This chapter presents the modelling of a software controller in charge of managing the movements of trains on a track network. Some methodological aspects of this development are emphasized: the preliminary informal presentation of the requirements, the careful definition of a refinement strategy, the attention payed to the precise mathematical definition of the train network, and the modelling of a complete system including the external environment. A special attention is given to the prevention of errors and also (but to a less extend) to their tolerance. The modelling notation which is used in this presentation is Event-B.

Keywords: Event-B, Requirement, Refinement, Failure, Correct Construction.

1 Informal Introduction

The purpose of this chapter[1] is to show the specification and construction of a complete computerized system. The example we are interested in is called a *train system*. By this, we mean a system that is practically managed by a *train agent*, whose role is to control the various trains crossing part of a certain *track network* situated under his supervision. The computerized system we want to construct is supposed to help the train agent in doing this task.

Before entering in the informal description of this system (followed by its formal construction), it might be useful to explain the reason why we think it is important to present such a case study in great details. There are at least four reasons which are the following:

1. This example presents an interesting case of quite complex data structures (the track network) whose mathematical properties have to be defined with great care: we want to show that this is possible.
2. This example also shows a very interesting case where the reliability of the final product is absolutely fundamental: several trains have to be able to safely cross the network under the complete automatic guidance of the software product we want to construct. For this reason, it will be important to study the bad incidents that could happen and which we want to either completely avoid or safely manage. In this chapter however, we are more concerned by *fault prevention* than *fault tolerance*. We shall come back to this in the conclusion.

---

[1] This work has been partly supported by IST FP6 Rigorous Open Development Environment for Complex Systems (RODIN, IST-511599) Project.

M. Butler et al. (Eds.): Fault-Tolerant Systems, LNCS 4157, pp. 1–36, 2006.

3. The software must take account of the external environment which is to be carefully controlled. As a consequence, the formal modelling we propose here will contain not only a model of the future software we want to construct but also a detailed model of its environment. Our ultimate goal is to have the software working in perfect synchronization with the external equipment, namely the track circuits, the points, the signals, and also the train drivers. We want to *prove* that trains obeying the signals, set by the software controller, and then (blindly) circulating on the tracks whose points have been positioned, again by the software controller, that these trains will do so in a completely safe manner.

4. Together with this study, the reader will be able to understand the kind of methodology we recommend. It should be described, we hope, in sufficiently general terms so that he or she will be able to use this approach in similar examples.

We now proceed with the informal description of this train system together with its informal (but very precise) definitions and requirements. We first define a typical track network which we shall use as a running example throughout the chapter. We then study the two main components of tracks, namely points and crossings. The important concepts of blocks, routes, and signals are then presented together with their main properties. The central notions of route and block reservations are proposed. Safety conditions are then studied.This is followed by the complementary train moving conditions allowing several trains to be present in the network at the same time. We propose a number of assumptions about the way trains behave. Finally we present possible failures that could happen and the way such problems are solved.

The formal development (model construction) is preceded by the *refinement strategy* we shall adopt in order to proceed in a gentle and structured manner. This is followed by the formal model construction.

1.1   Methodological Conventions for the Informal Presentation

In the following sections, we give an informal description of this train system, and, together with this description, we state what its main *definitions and requirements* are. Such definitions and requirements will be inserted as separate labelled boxes in the middle of an explanatory text. These boxes must all together clearly define what is to be taken into account by people doing the formal development. The various definitions and requirements will be labelled according to the following taxonomy:

ENV	Environment		MVT	Movement
FUN	Functional		TRN	Train
SAF	Safety		FLR	Failure

- "Environment" definitions and requirements are concerned with the structure of the track network and its components.
- "Functional" definitions and requirements are dealing with the main functions of the system.
- "Safety" definitions and requirements define the properties ensuring that no classical accidents could happen.
- "Movement" definitions and requirements ensure that a large number of train may cross the network at the same time.
- "Train" definitions and requirements define the implicit assumptions about the behavior of trains.
- "Failure" definitions and requirements finally define the various failures against which the system is able to react without incidents.

Here is our first very general requirement:

The goal of the train system is to safely control trains moving on a track network	FUN-1

1.2 Network Associated with a Controlling Agent

Here is a typical track network that a train agent is able to control. In what follows, we are going to use that network as a running example:

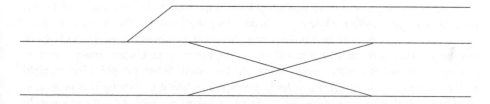

1.3 Special Components of a Network: Points and Crossings

Such a network contains a number of *special components*: these are the *points* and the *crossings* as illustrated in the following figure (five points and one crossing).

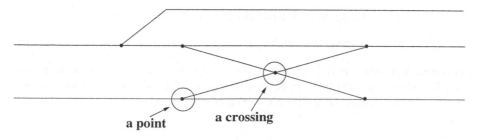

a point   **a crossing**

A point is a device allowing a track to split in two distinct directions. A crossing, as its name indicates, is a device that makes two different tracks crossing each other. In what follows we briefly describe points and crossings.

A train network may contain some special components: points and crossings	ENV-1

Point. A point special component can be in three different positions: left, right, or unknown. This is indicated in the following figure.

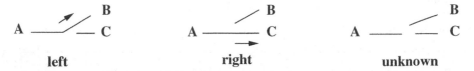

| left | right | unknown |

Note that the orientation from A to C is sometimes called the *direct track* whereas the one from A to B is called the *diverted track*. In what follows however, we shall continue to call them right and left respectively are there is no ambiguity in doing so.

In the first two cases above, the arrow in the figure shows the convention we shall use to indicate the orientation of the point. Note that these arrows do not indicate the direction followed by a train. For example, in the first case, it is said that a train coming from **A** will turn left, a train coming from **B** will turn right, and a train coming from **C** *will probably have some troubles*! Also note that a train encountering a point oriented in an unknown direction (third case) might have some trouble too, even more if a point suddenly changes position while a train is on it (we shall come to this in section 1.8).

The last case is the one that holds when the point is moving from left to right or vice-versa. This is because this movement is supposed to take some time: it is performed by means of a motor which is part of the point. When the point has reached its final position (left or right) it is locked, whereas when it is moving it is unlocked. Note however that in the coming development we shall not take this into account. In other words, we shall suppose, as a simplification, that a *point moves instantaneously and that it is thus always locked*. In other words, the unknown case is not treated, we then just require in this development that a point may have only two positions: left or right.

A point may have two positions: left or right	ENV-2

Crossing. A crossing special component is completely static: it has no state as points have. The way a crossing behaves is illustrated in the following figure: trains can go from **A** to **B** and vice-versa, and from **C** to **D** and vice-versa.

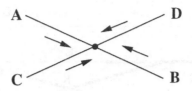

1.4 The Concept of Block

The controlled network is statically divided into a fixed number of *named blocks* as indicated in the following figure where we have 14 blocks named by single letters from A to N:

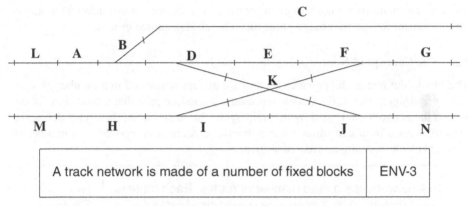

A track network is made of a number of fixed blocks	ENV-3

Each block may contain at most one special component (points or crossings).

A special component (points or crossings) is always attached to a given block. And a block contains at most one special component	ENV-4

For example in our case, block C does not contain any special component, whereas block D contains one point, and block K contains a crossing. Each block is equipped with a, so-called, *track circuit* which is able to detect the presence of a train on it. A block can thus be in two distinct states: unoccupied (no train on it) or occupied (a train is on it).

A block may be occupied or unoccupied by a train	ENV-5

In the following figure, you can see that a train is occupying the two adjacent blocks D and K (this is indicated in the figure by the fact that the blocks in question are emphasized).

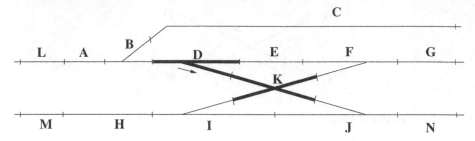

Notice that when a train is detected in a block we do not know a priori the precise position of the train in it, nor do we know whether the train is stopped or moving. Moreover, in the last case, we do not know in which direction the train is moving. But all such informations are not important for us: as will be seen in this development, it is only sufficient for our purpose to know that a block is occupied or not.

1.5   The Concept of Route

The blocks defined in the previous section are always structured in a number of statically *pre-defined routes*. Each route represents a possible path that a train may follow within the network controlled by the train agent. In other words, the routes define the various ways a train can traverse the network. A route is composed of a number of adjacent blocks forming an ordered sequence.

A network has a fixed number of routes. Each route is characterized by a sequence of adjacent blocks	ENV-6

A train following a route is supposed to occupy in turn each block of that route. Note that a train may occupy several adjacent blocks at the same time (even a short train). Also note that a given block can be part of several routes. All this is shown below in the following table where 10 pre-defined routes are proposed:

$R1$	$L\ A\ B\ C$	$R6$	$C\ B\ A\ L$
$R2$	$L\ A\ B\ D\ E\ F\ G$	$R7$	$G\ F\ E\ D\ B\ A\ L$
$R3$	$L\ A\ B\ D\ K\ J\ N$	$R8$	$N\ J\ K\ D\ B\ A\ L$
$R4$	$M\ H\ I\ K\ F\ G$	$R9$	$G\ F\ K\ I\ H\ M$
$R5$	$M\ H\ I\ J\ N$	$R10$	$N\ J\ I\ H\ M$

Besides being characterized by the sequence of blocks composing it, a route is also statically characterized by the positions of the points which are parts of the corresponding blocks. For example, route $R3$ $(L\ A\ B\ D\ K\ J\ N)$ is characterized as follows:

- the point in block B is positioned to right,
- the point in block D is positioned to right,
- the point in block J is positioned to right.

This is illustrated in the following figure where route $R3$ $(L\ A\ B\ D\ K\ J\ N)$ is emphasized. The little arrows situated next to the points of blocks B, D, and J indicate their position:

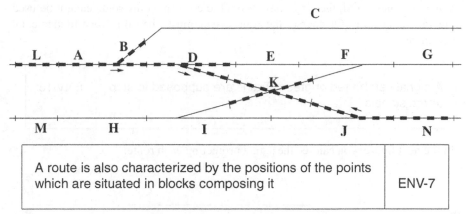

A route is also characterized by the positions of the points which are situated in blocks composing it	ENV-7

Routes have two additional properties. The first concern the first block of a route:

The first block of a route cannot be part of another route unless it is also the first block of that route	ENV-8

And the second one concerns the last block of a route :

The last block of a route cannot be part of another route unless it is also the last block of that route	ENV-9

At the end of the next section, we shall explain why the constraints we have presented just now are important. Finally, a route has some obvious continuity property:

A route connects its first block to its last one in a continuous manner	ENV-10

and it has no cycle:

A route contains no cycles	ENV-11

1.6   The Concept of Signal

Each route is protected by a *signal*, which can be red or green. This signal is situated just before the first block of each route. It must be clearly visible from the train drivers.

Each route is protected by a signal situated just before its first block	ENV-12

When a signal is red, then, by convention, the corresponding route cannot be used by an incoming train. Of course, the train driver must obey this very fundamental requirement.

A signal can be red or green. Trains are supposed to stop at red signals	ENV-13

In the next figure, you can see the signal protecting each route:

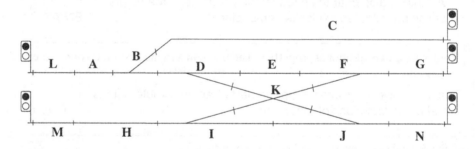

Notice that a given signal can protect several routes. For example, the signal situated on the left of block L protects route $R1$ (L A B C), $R2$ (L A B D E F G), and $R3$ (L A B D K J N): this is because each of these routes starts with the same block, namely block L.

Routes having the same first block share the same signal	ENV-14

In the previous figure and in the coming ones, we use the convention that a signal which is situated to the left of its pole protects the routes situated on its right and vice-versa. For example, the signal situated on the right hand side of block C protects route R6, namely (C B A L).

A last important property of a signal protecting the first block of a route is that, when green, it turns back automatically to red as soon as a train enters into the protected block.

A green signal turns back to red automatically as soon as the protected block is made occupied	ENV-15

The reason for the constraints defined at the end of section 1.5 must now be clear: we want a signal, which is always situated just before the first block of a route, to clearly identify the protection of that route. If a route, say r1, starts in the middle of another one r2, then the signal protecting r1 will cause some trouble for train situated in route r2. As very often the reverse of a route is also used as a route, the previous constraint applies for the last block of a route: it cannot be common to another route except if it is also the last block of that route.

1.7   Route and Block Reservations

The train agent is provided with a panel offering a number of commands corresponding to the different routes he can assign to trains traversing his "territory".

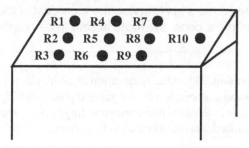

When a train is approaching the network, the train agent is told that this train will cross the network by using a certain route. The train agent then presses the corresponding command in order to *reserve* that route. Note that other trains might already be crossing the network while the train agent is pressing that command. As a consequence, the situation faced by the train agent is potentially dangerous: we shall come back to this very important fact in section 1.8. This is the reason why the forthcoming reservation process is entirely controlled by the software we want to construct.

A route can be reserved for a train. The software is in charge of controlling the reservation process	FUN-2

The reservation process of a route r is made of three phases:

1. the individual reservation of the various blocks composing route r is performed,
2. the positioning of the relevant points of route r is accomplished,
3. the turning to green of the signal protecting route r is done.

When the first phase is not possible (see next section), the reservation fails and the two other phases are then cancelled. In this case, the reservation has to be re-tried later by the train agent. Let us now describe these phases in more details.

Phase 1: Block Reservation. The block reservation performed during the first phase induces another state for a block (besides being occupied or unoccupied by a train, as seen in section 1.3): a block can be reserved or free.

A block can be reserved or free	FUN-3

Note that an occupied block must clearly be already reserved.

An occupied block is always reserved	FUN-4

At the end of this first successful phase, the route is said to be *reserved*, but it is not ready yet to accept a train.

Reserving a route consists in reserving the individual blocks it is made of. Once this is done, the route is said to be *reserved*	FUN-5

Phase 2: Point Positioning. When the reservation of all blocks of a route r is successful, the reservation process proceeds with the second phase, namely the positioning of the corresponding points in the direction corresponding to the route r. When all points of r are properly positioned, the route is said to be *formed*.

Once it is reserved, a route has to be *formed* by properly positioning its points	FUN-6

Note that a formed route remains reserved.

A formed route is always a reserved route	FUN-7

Phase 3: Turning Signal to Green. Once a route r is formed, the third and last phase of the reservation can be done: the signal controlling route r is turned green: a train can be accepted in it. A train driver, looking at the green signal, then leads the train within the reserved and formed route. We already know from requirement ENV-15 that the signal will then turn red immediately.

Once it is formed, a route is made available for the incoming train by turning its signal to green	FUN-8

1.8   Safety Conditions

As several trains can cross the network at the same time and as the train agent (or rather the software he uses) is sometimes re-positioning a point when forming a route, there are clearly some serious risks of bad incidents. This is the reason why we must clearly identify such risks and see how we can safely avoid them. This is, in fact, the main purpose of the software we would like to build in order to help the train agent in a systematic fashion. There are three main risks which are the following:

1. Two (or more) trains traversing the network at the same time hit each other in various ways.
2. A point may change position under a train.
3. The point of a route may change position in front of a train using that route. In other words, the train has not yet occupied the block of this point but it will do so in the near future since that block is situated on that route.

Case 1 is obviously very bad since the hit trains may derail. Case 2 would have the consequence to cut the train into two parts and, most probably, the train will derail too. Case 3 may have two distinct consequences: either to move the train outside its current route so that it can now hit another train (case 1), or to have the train derailing in case the point now disconnect the current route. We are thus going to set up a number of safety conditions in order to prevent such risks from happening. The first risk (train hitting) is avoided by ensuring two safety conditions:

1. a given block *can only be reserved for at most one route at a time*,

A block can be reserved for *at most one* route	SAF-1

2. the signal of a route is green *only* when the various blocks of that route are all reserved for it and are unoccupied, and when all points of that route are set in the proper direction.

The signal of a route can *only be green* when all blocks of that route are reserved for it and are unoccupied, and when all points of this route are properly positioned	SAF-2

As a consequence (and also thanks to requirement FUN-4 stating that an occupied block is always a reserved block), several trains never occupy the same block at the same time, *provided, of course, that train drivers do not overpass a red signal*. We shall come back to this important point in section 1.11.

The second and third risks (points changing direction under certain circumstances) are avoided by ensuring that a point can only be maneuvered when the corresponding block is that of a route which is *reserved (all its blocks being reserved) but not yet formed*.

A point can *only be re-positioned* if it belongs to a block which is in a reserved but not yet formed route	SAF-3

The last safety requirement ensures that no blocks of a reserved, but not yet formed, route are occupied by a train.

No blocks of a reserved, but not yet formed, route are occupied	SAF-4

A consequence of this last safety requirement is that the re-positioning of a point, done according to requirement SAF_3, is always safe.

1.9 Moving Conditions

In spite of the safety conditions (which could be preserved by not allowing any train to cross the network!) we want to allow a large number of trains to be present in the network at the same time without danger. For this, we allow each block of a reserved route to be freed as soon as the train does not occupy it any more.

Once a block of a formed route is made unoccupied, it is also freed	MVT-1

As a result, the only reserved blocks of a formed route are those blocks which are occupied by the train or those blocks of the route which are not yet occupied by the train.

A route remains formed as long as there are some reserved blocks in it	MVT-2

When no block of a formed route is reserved any more for that route, it means that the train has left the route, which can thus be made free.

A formed route can be made free (not formed and not reserved any more) when no blocks are reserved for it any more	MVT-3

1.10 Train Assumptions

Note that it is very important that a block once freed for a route (after being occupied and subsequently unoccupied) *cannot be made occupied again for this route* unless the route is first made free and then formed again. The reason for this is that the freed block in question can be assigned to another route. For achieving this, we must assume that trains obey two properties. First, a train cannot split in two or more parts while in the network.

A train cannot split while in the network	TRN-1

And second, a train cannot move backwards while in the network

A train cannot move backwards while in the network	TRN-2

This is so because in both cases a freed block can be made occupied again. Note that clearly trains do split and move backwards (for example, in Zurich main station): it simply means that the blocks where they do so are not within the network controlled by a train system.

Another important implicit assumption about trains is that they cannot enter "in the middle" of a route (it cannot land on a route!)

A train cannot enter in the middle of a route. It has to do so through its first block.	TRN-3

Likewise, a train cannot disappear in the middle of a route (it cannot take off!)

A train cannot leave a route without first occupying then freeing all its blocks	TRN-4

1.11   Failures

In this section, we study a number of abnormal cases which could happen. The fact that their probabilities are very low is not a reason to preclude these cases.

The first and most important case of failures is obviously the one where, for some reasons, the driver of a train does not obey the red signal guarding a route. In section 1.6 we said in requirement ENV_14 that "trains are supposed to stop at red signals". Now, is it always the case?

The solution to this problem is local to the train. This case is detected within the faulty train by a device called the Automatic Train Protection. As soon as this device detects that the train passes a red signal, it automatically activates the emergency brakes of the train. The distance between the signal and the first block of the route it protects is calculated so that we can be sure that the train will stop before entering that first block. Note that this protection is not certain as the Automatic Train Protection could be broken while the train does not stop at a red signal!

Trains are equipped with the Automatic Train Protection system, which guarantees that they cannot enter a route guarded by a red signal	FLR-1

In section 1.10, we claimed in requirement TRN_1 that "a train cannot split while in the network". Is it possible that it happens nevertheless by accident? The solution to this problem is again local to the train. Each train is now equipped with special bindings so that it forms a continuous body that cannot be mechanically broken. Here again, the solution is not certain but professionals claim that the risk is extremely low.

Trains are equipped with special bindings, which guarantee that they cannot be mechanically broken.	FLR-2

Another case raised in section 1.10 is requirement TRN_2 claiming that "a train cannot move backwards while in the network". Here again, the Automatic Train Protection system is used. It detects immediately any backward move and in that case it activates automatically the emergency brakes. But one has to be sure that the train nevertheless does not occupy again a block that it has freed recently. This is guaranteed by the fact that the transmission of the occupancy of a block by the track circuit is slightly delayed. As a consequence, when the train has physically left a block, this fact is not immediately transmitted to the controller, it is only done when the back of the train has moved to a certain distance. If the train slightly moves backwards then it does not occupy again the block since it did not left it (as "seen" from the software controller).

The Automatic Protection System and a slight delay observed by the track circuit guarantee that a train moving backward cannot occupy again a block which has been physically freed.	FLR-3

In section 1.10, we said in requirement TRN-3 that "a train cannot enter in the middle of a route". This is certainly the case for trains. The problem is that the software controller does not "see" trains. It only detects that a block is occupied or free by means of track circuits connections. As a consequence, it is possible that, for some reasons, a block is detected to be occupied by its track circuit because a piece of metal is put on the rail. The software controller can detect such a faulty occupancy. In that case the train agent can take some emergency action. But this is not always the case however. This risk is therefore accepted but not treated here.

The risk of a faulty detection of a block occupancy is not treated	FLR-4

In section 1.10, we said in requirement TRN-4 that "a train cannot leave a route without first occupying then freeing all its block". This is not always the case however in the very rare circumstance where a short train (say a single engine) derails and then falls down: it suddenly quits the block where it is situated! This case can certainly be detected by the software controller and some emergency action can be taken by the train agent. We do not treat this case here however.

The case where a short train derails and leaves its block is not treated here	FLR-5

Note that the last two cases of failure raise a difficult problem which is the one of restarting the system after an emergency. It seems that the only solution consists in carefully inspecting the network to decide whether a normal situation has been reached again.

2   Refinement Strategy

The summary of the various informal requirements we have seen in previous sections is as indicated below. We have all together 39 requirements. Of course, a real train system might have far more requirements than this: it must be clear that what we are presenting here is only a very simplified version of such a train system.

ENV	Environment	15	MVT	Movement	3
FUN	Functional	8	TRN	Train	4
SAF	Safety	4	FLR	Failure	5

The role of the formal phase which we start now is to build models able to take account of these requirements. As it is out of the question to incorporate all of them at ounce, we are going to proceed by successive approximations, which are called *refinements*. In this section, we define thus the refinement strategy we are going to follow. It is very important indeed to define the order in which we are going to extract the various requirements which have been exhibited in the previous phase.

1. In the initial model, the blocks and routes concepts are formalized. Blocks are defined from a logical point of view however
2. In the first refinement we introduce the physical blocks and thus start to formalize part of the environment. We establish the connection between the logical blocks

and the physical ones. This is done in an abstract way however as we do not introduce yet the points.

3. In the second refinement, we introduce the notion of readiness for a route. This corresponds to an abstract view of the green signals.
4. In the third refinement, we introduce the physical signals. We data-refine (implement) the readiness of a route by means of green signals.
5. In the fourth refinement, we introduce the points.
6. Some other refinements are needed in order to finalize details. Such refinements are not treated in this chapter however.

3   A Quick Introduction to Event-B

In this section, we give a very brief summary of Event-B [1]. This is the approach which we are going to follow in the remaining part of this chapter.

An Event-B development is made of a succession of *models* starting with an *initial model*, which is followed by a number of *refined models*. A *model*, be it the initial model or a refined model, is defined by a *state* and a number of *events*. The state contains a *constant part* and a *dynamic part*. The constant part of the state is made of a number of *basic sets* (also called carrier sets) and *constants*. These constants are made precise by means of a number of *named properties*. The dynamic part of the state is made of a number of *variables*. These variables are made precise by means of a number of *named invariants*. Properties and invariants are predicates (logical conditions) written using elementary logic and set-theoretic constructs (discrete mathematics concepts).

Each event defines a transition which can be observed. An event is made of four parts: the *name*, the (optional) *local variables*, the (optional) *guards*, and the *actions*. The guards are defined in terms of the local variables, the state variables and the constants. They all together express the necessary conditions for the event to be *enabled*. The actions define the state transitions that may occur for enabled events: they are made of parallel assignments to the state variables. Notice that non-mentioned variables in the action part of an event are supposed to be left unchanged.

A refined model N is supposed to refine a more abstract model M preceding it in the development sequence. Model M is called the *abstraction* of N, whereas model N is called a *refinement* of M. Model N contains events which are supposed to be refinements of events bearing the same name in M. But is is also possible for an abstract event to be split and thus be refined by two or more events. Model N may also contain some *new events*, which have no counterparts in the abstraction M. Such new events are supposed to refine abstract events doing nothing.

Various *proofs* can be performed on models. The main proofs are the *invariant proofs* and the *refinement proofs*. An invariant proof allows one to guarantee that an invariants is indeed kept unchanged when a transition occurs. A refinement proof allows one to guarantee that an event is indeed a correct refinement of its abstraction. The statements to be proved are not written explicitly by the people who define the models: they are generated by a tool called the *proof obligation generator* (also called the verification condition generator).

4   Initial Model

4.1   The State

The state is made of a number of carrier sets, constants and variables, which we study in the following sections.

Carrier Sets. The initial model is concerned with blocks and routes. We thus take account of requirement ENV-3 of section 1.4, and of requirement ENV-6 of section 1.5. We do not take account of points or signals for the moment, this will be done in further refinements. We have thus only two carrier sets, B and R, standing for blocks and routes. In what follows, we shall use the convention that carrier sets are named using single upper case letters.

$$\boxed{\textbf{carrier sets:} \quad B, R}$$

Constants. The organization of the track network, which is made of a number of routes, is formalized by means of two constant: $rtbl$ (pronounce "routes of blocks") relating routes to blocks and nxt (pronounce "next") relating blocks to blocks for each route.

$$\boxed{\begin{array}{ll} \textbf{constants:} & rtbl, \\ & nxt \end{array}}$$

The constant $rtbl$ is a total (all routes are concerned) and surjective (all blocks are concerned) binary relation from B to R (**prp0_1**). This is so because a route may have many blocks and a block can belong to several routes:

$$\boxed{\textbf{prp0\_1:} \quad rtbl \in B \leftrightarrow\!\!\!\rightarrow R}$$

The constant nxt denotes the succession of each blocks associated with a route (ENV-6). This succession forms an injective function from blocks to blocks (that is, a function whose inverse is also a function):

$$\boxed{\textbf{prp0\_2:} \quad nxt \in R \rightarrow (B \rightarrowtail B)}$$

For example, a route like route R3 comprising the following blocks $L\ A\ B\ D\ K\ J\ N$ in that order

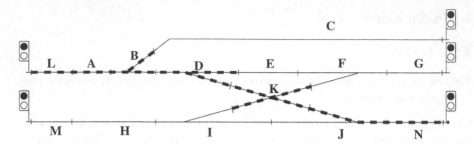

is represented as follows by the injective function $nxt(R3)$. As can be seen, the function $nxt(R3)$ establishes a continuous connection between the first block L and last block N of route R3:

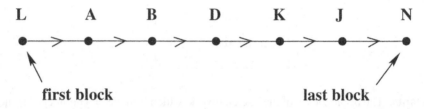

As the first and last block of a route will play a certain role in further properties, we have to introduce them explictely in our state by means of some new constants. We thus extend our set of constants by introducing the first and last block of each route r: fst and lst

$$
\begin{array}{ll}
\textbf{constants:} & \cdots \\
& fst, \\
& lst
\end{array}
$$

These first and last elements of a route enjoy the following obvious properties: they are defined for each route (**prp0_3** and **prp0_4**) and they are genuine blocks of the route (**prp0_5** and **prp0_6**). Moreover the first and last block of a route are distinct (**prp0_7**):

prp0_3: $fst \in R \to B$

prp0_4: $lst \in R \to B$

prp0_5: $fst^{-1} \subseteq rtbl$

prp0_6: $lst^{-1} \subseteq rtbl$

prp0_7: $\forall r \cdot (r \in R \Rightarrow fst(r) \neq lst(r))$

As illustrated in the previous figure, we want the connection represented by the function $nxt(r)$ for each route r, to be continuous as required by requirement **ENV-10** of section 1.5. In other words, we want to exclude cases like this, which do not make sense for a route:

first block   **last block**

Moreover, we want to express that the blocks of a route r which are present in the domain and range of the injection $nxt(r)$ are exactly the blocks of route r, namely $rtbl^{-1}[\{r\}]$. In order to express all this, we just say that the injection $nxt(r)$ is indeed a bijection from $rtbl^{-1}[\{r\}] \setminus \{lst(r)\}$ to $rtbl^{-1}[\{r\}] \setminus \{fst(r)\}$:

---

prp0_8: $\forall r \cdot (r \in R \;\Rightarrow\; nxt(r) \in s \setminus \{lst(r)\} \rightarrowtail\!\!\!\rightarrow s \setminus \{fst(r)\}$

where s is $rtbl^{-1}[\{r\}]$

But this is not sufficient, as the following pathological case can happen:

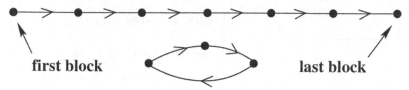

first block   **last block**

We have then to express that there is no such cycles in the connection. This corresponds to requirement **ENV-11** of section 1.5. This can be done by stating that the only subset S of B which is included in its image under $nxt(r)$, that is $nxt(r)[S]$, is the empty set (a genuine cycle is indeed equal to its image under $nxt(r)$):

---

prp0_9: $\forall r \cdot \left(r \in R \Rightarrow \forall S \cdot \left(\begin{matrix} S \subseteq B \\ S \subseteq nxt(r)[S] \\ \Rightarrow \\ S = \varnothing \end{matrix} \right) \right)$

A final property of the routes is that they cannot depart or arrive in the *middle* of another one. However several routes can depart from the same block or arrive at the same block. All this corresponds to requirements **ENV-8** and **ENV-9** of section 1.5. It is expressed by the following two properties:

---

prp0_10: $\forall r \cdot (r \in R \Rightarrow \mathrm{ran}(lst) \cap (\mathrm{dom}(nxt(r)) \setminus \mathrm{ran}(fst)) = \varnothing)$

prp0_11: $\forall r \cdot (r \in R \Rightarrow \mathrm{ran}(fst) \cap (\mathrm{ran}(nxt(r)) \setminus \mathrm{ran}(lst)) = \varnothing)$

Note that the previous properties do not preclude two routes to have the same first or last blocks.

Variables. In this initial model, we have four variables named $resrt$, $resbl$, $rsrtbl$, and OCC (see below, the box entitled **variables**). In what follows, we shall use the convention that *physical variables* are named using upper case letters only. By "physical variable", we mean a variable representing part of the external equipment (here OCC denotes the set of physical blocks which are occupied by trains). The other variables (named using lower case letters only) are called the *logical variables*: they represent variables which will be part of the future software controller. The invariants corresponding to all these variables can be seen on the right table below (these invariants are explained below):

variables:	$resrt$,
	$resbl$,
	$rsrtbl$,
	OCC

inv0_1: $resrt \subseteq R$

inv0_2: $resbl \subseteq B$

inv0_3: $rsrtbl \in resbl \rightarrow resrt$

inv0_4: $rsrtbl \subseteq rtbl$

inv0_5: $OCC \subseteq resbl$

Variable $resrt$ (pronounce "reserved routes") denotes the reserved routes (**inv0_1**): this is coherent with requirement **FUN-2** of section 1.7, which says that a route can be reserved for a train.

The second variable, $resbl$ (pronounce "reserved blocks"), denotes the set of reserved blocks (**inv0_2**): this is coherent with requirement **FUN-3** of section 1.7, which say that a block can be reserved for a route.

Our third variable, $rsrtbl$ (pronounce "reserved routes of reserved blocks"), relates reserved blocks to reserved routes: it is a *total function* from reserved blocks to reserved routes (**inv0_3**): this is coherent with requirement **SAF-1** stating that a block cannot be reserved for more than one route. Of course, this connection is compatible with the static relationship $rtbl$ between blocks and routes (**inv0_4**): a reserved block for a route is a block of that route.

Finally, variable OCC denotes the set of occupied blocks: this is coherent with requirement **ENV-5** stating that a block might be occupied by a train. Such occupied blocks are obviously reserved for some route (**inv0_5**): this is coherent with requirement **FUN-4** of section 1.7 stating that an occupied block is always reserved.

We have to define now more invariants corresponding to the way a train can occupy a reserved route. The general situation is illustrated on the following figure:

f r e e   **o c c u p i e d**   **u n o c c u p i e d**

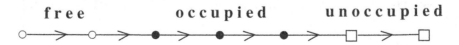

The blocks of a reserved route are divided in three areas:

1. In the first area (on the left, where the blocks are represented by white circles), the blocks are freed by that route because the train does not occupy them any more. They can readily be reused (and maybe they are already) for another reserved route.
2. In the second area (in the center, where the blocks are represented by black circles), the blocks are all reserved and occupied by a train.
3. In the third area (on the right, where the blocks are represented by white squares), the block are all reserved but not occupied yet by a train.

There are other situations corresponding to some special cases of the general situation depicted in the previous figure. In the first special case, areas 1 and 2 are empty: the route is reserved but the train has not yet entered the route:

The second special case is the one where area 1 is empty, but not areas 2 and 3. In fact, the train is entering the route as illustrated in the following figure:

A third special case is one where a (long) train occupies all blocks in a route:

The fourth special case it the one where the train is leaving the route:

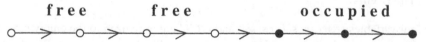

The last special case is the one where all blocks in the reserved route have been freed by that route. The route itself is then ready to be freed

More formally, let us call M the set of *free blocks* in a reserved route (those behind the train), N the set of *occupied blocks* in a reserved route, and finally P the set of reserved but *unoccupied blocks* of a reserved route (those situated in front of a train). Sets M, N, and P are formally defined as follows for a given reserved route r:

$$M = rtbl^{-1}[\{r\}] \setminus rsrtbl^{-1}[\{r\}]$$

$$N = rsrtbl^{-1}[\{r\}] \cap OCC$$

$$P = rsrtbl^{-1}[\{r\}] \setminus OCC$$

Note that M, N, and P partition $rtbl^{-1}[\{r\}]$. According to the previous presentation, the only transitions that are allowed are the following:

$$M \to M \qquad M \to N \qquad N \to N \qquad N \to P \qquad P \to P$$

This can be represented by the following conditions

$$nxt(r)[M] \subseteq M \cup N \qquad nxt(r)[N] \subseteq N \cup P \qquad nxt(r)[P] \subseteq P$$

Such conditions are equivalent to the following ones (since $nxt(r)[rtbl^{-1}[\{r\}]]$ is included in $rtbl^{-1}[\{r\}]$ according to **prp0_8**):

$$nxt(r)[M] \cap P = \varnothing \qquad nxt(r)[N \cup P] \subseteq N \cup P \qquad nxt(r)[P] \subseteq P$$

All this is eventually formalized in the following invariants:

---

inv0_6: $\forall r \cdot (r \in R \;\Rightarrow\; nxt(r)[rtbl^{-1}[\{r\}] \setminus s] \cap (s \setminus OCC) = \varnothing)$

inv0_7: $\forall r \cdot (r \in R \;\Rightarrow\; nxt(r)[s] \subseteq s)$

inv0_8: $\forall r \cdot (r \in R \;\Rightarrow\; nxt(r)[s \setminus OCC] \subseteq s \setminus OCC)$

where s is $rsrtbl^{-1}[\{r\}]$

These invariants are coherent with the train requirements TRN-1 to TRN-4 defined in section 1.10.

4.2   The Events

The four variables $resrt$, $resbl$, $rsrtbl$, and OCC are initialized to the empty set: initially, no trains are in the network and no routes or blocks are reserved. Besides the initialization event (which we do not present here), we have five normal events. Events define transitions which can be observed. In what follows, we shall use the convention that physical events corresponding to transitions occurring in the environment are named using upper case letters only. Here are the events of the initial model:

- route_reservation,
- route_freeing,
- FRONT_MOVE_1,
- FRONT_MOVE_2,
- BACK_MOVE.

Event route_reservation corresponds to the reservation of a route r. It is done on an unreserved route (i.e. $r \in R \setminus resrt$) whose blocks are not already reserved for a route (i.e. $rtbl^{-1}[\{r\}] \cap resbl = \varnothing$). Route r is then reserved together with its blocks.

This is coherent with requirement **FUN-5** which says that a route can be reserved as soon as all its blocks are themselves reserved.

```
route_reservation
  any  r  where
    r ∈ R \ resrt
    rtbl⁻¹[{r}] ∩ resbl = ∅
  then
    resrt := resrt ∪ {r}
    rsrtbl := rsrtbl ∪ rtbl ▷ {r}
    resbl := resbl ∪ rtbl⁻¹[{r}]
  end
```

```
route_freeing
  any  r  where
    r ∈ resrt \ ran(rsrtbl)
  then
    resrt := resrt \ {r}
  end
```

Event **route_freeing** makes a reserved route free when it does not contain reserved blocks any more. This is coherent with requirement **MVT-3** which says that a route can be made free when no blocks are reserved for it any more.

Event **FRONT_MOVE_1** corresponds to a train entering a reserved route r. The first block of r must be reserved and unoccupied. Moreover, the reserved route corresponding to the first block of r must be r itself. The first block is made occupied:

```
FRONT_MOVE_1
  any  r  where
    r ∈ resrt
    fst(r) ∈ resbl \ OCC
    rsrtbl(fst(r)) = r
  then
    OCC := OCC ∪ {fst(r)}
  end
```

```
FRONT_MOVE_2
  any  b, c  where
    b ∈ OCC
    c ∈ B \ OCC
    b ↦ c ∈ nxt(rsrtbl(b))
  then
    OCC := OCC ∪ {c}
  end
```

Event **FRONT_MOVE_2** corresponds to the occupancy of a block which happens to be different from the first block of a reserved route. Given a block b which is occupied and preceded (in the same route) by a block, say c, which is not occupied, then c is made occupied.

Finally, event **BACK_MOVE** corresponds to the move of the rear part of the train. This happens for a block b which is occupied and is the last block of a train. This is detected when block b has a follower in the route r reserved for b and that follower, if reserved, is not reserved for r. Moreover, when b has a predecessor, that predecessor must be occupied (so that the train does not disappear before reaching the end of route r). The action corresponding to that event makes b unoccupied and unreserved. This is coherent with requirement **MVT-1** which says that "once a block of a formed route is made unoccupied, it is also freed":

$$
\begin{array}{l}
\text{BACK\_MOVE} \\
\quad \textbf{any}\ \ b, n\ \ \textbf{where} \\
\qquad b\ \in\ OCC \\
\qquad n = nxt(rsrtbl(b)) \\
\qquad b\ \in\ \mathrm{dom}(n)\ \Rightarrow\ n(b)\ \in\ OCC \\
\qquad \left(\begin{array}{l}
b\ \in\ \mathrm{ran}(n)\ \wedge \\
n^{-1}(b)\ \in\ \mathrm{dom}(rsrtbl) \\
\Rightarrow \\
rsrtbl(n^{-1}(b)) \neq rsrtbl(b)
\end{array} \right) \\
\quad \textbf{then} \\
\qquad OCC := OCC \setminus \{b\} \\
\qquad rsrtbl := \{b\} \mathbin{\lhd\mkern-14mu-} rsrtbl \\
\qquad resbl := resbl \setminus \{b\} \\
\quad \textbf{end}
\end{array}
$$

Important Remark. It might seem strange at first glance (and even incorrect) to have physical events such as FRONT_MOVE_1, FRONT_MOVE_2, and BACK_MOVE using non-physical variables in their guards. Clearly, a physical event can be enabled under certain conditions depending on physical variables only: a physical event cannot magically "see" the non-physical variables. The reason for having non-physical variables in the guards here is that we are still in an abstract version where such abnormalities are possible. Of course, in the final refined version of physical events we have to check that it is not the case any more.

5   First Refinement

In this first refinement, we introduce the *physical tracks*. So that the movements of the train will correspond entirely on the physical situation of the track. Note however that we do not introduce yet the points and the signals.

5.1   The State

We do not introduce new carrier sets or new constants in this refinement.

Variables. In this refinement, we have three new variables named TRK (pronounce "track"), frm (pronounce "formed routes"), and LBT (pronounce "last blocks of trains"). Notice that the variables introduced in the initial models, namely $resrt$, $resbl$, $rsrtbl$, and OCC, are kept in this refinement.

$$
\begin{array}{ll}
\textbf{variables:} & \cdots , \\
& TRK, \\
& frm, \\
& LBT
\end{array}
$$

Variable TRK is a partial injection (**inv1_1**) from blocks to blocks defining the *physical succession of blocks*. It also contains the direction taken by trains following the tracks. Note that this last information is not "physical" (you cannot "see" it on the track), it corresponds however to the physical movements of trains on the physical tracks. Next is the invariant defining variable TRK as an injective function.

$$\textbf{inv1\_1:} \quad TRK \in B \rightarrowtail B$$

Here is an illustration of the variable TRK in a certain situation:

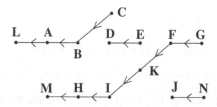

As can be seen, route $R9$ (G F K I H H M) is now established on the physical track. In section 5.2, we shall see how the event, which is positioning the points will modify this situation. Note that the crossing in block K is "broken" and that the physical track "remembers" the direction followed by trains circulating on it: of course, this is not what happen in the real tracks, but this is a convenient abstraction.

Finally, all pairs belonging to TRK also belong to $nxt(r)$ for some route r (**inv_2**):

$$\textbf{inv1\_2:} \quad \forall x, y \cdot (\, x \mapsto y \in TRK \;\Rightarrow\; \exists r \cdot (\, r \in R \;\wedge\; x \mapsto y \in nxt(r) \,) \,)$$

Variable frm represents the set of formed routes: it is a subset of the reserved routes (**inv1_3**) This is coherent with requirement **FUN-7** which says that "a formed route is always a reserved route". We have a number of invariants involving the formed routes. The reserved routes of occupied blocks are formed routes (**inv1_4**). A route r which is reserved but not yet formed is such that its reserved blocks are exactly the constant reserved blocks associated with r (**inv1_5**). The two previous invariants are coherent with requirements **SAF-4** which says that "no blocks of a reserved but not yet formed route are occupied"

$$\textbf{inv1\_3:} \quad frm \subseteq resrt$$

$$\textbf{inv1\_4:} \quad rsrtbl[OCC] \subseteq frm$$

$$\textbf{inv1\_5:} \quad \forall r \cdot \begin{pmatrix} r \in resrt \setminus frm \\ \Rightarrow \\ rtbl \rhd \{r\} = rsrtbl \rhd \{r\} \end{pmatrix}$$

Now comes the most important invariant (**inv1_6**): it relates the logical succession of blocks in a route (represented by the function $nxt(r)$ for each route r) to the physical tracks on the terrain (represented by the variable TRK). It says that for each formed route r, the logical succession of blocks (where the train is supposed to be and where it has to go when proceeding through route r) *agrees with the physical tracks on the terrain*. In other words, when a route r is formed, then the portion of the physical blocks where the train is or where it will be in the future when proceeding along this route, this portion of the physical blocks corresponds to what is expected in the logical blocks as recorded by the controller.

$$\textbf{inv1\_6:} \quad \forall r \cdot \left(\begin{array}{l} r \in frm \\ \Rightarrow \\ rsrtbl^{-1}[\{r\}] \lhd nxt(r) \;=\; rsrtbl^{-1}[\{r\}] \lhd TRK \end{array} \right)$$

Finally, variable LBT denotes the set of blocks occupied by the back of each train: this is also a "physical" variable like variable TRK. The first invariant (**inv1_7**) concerning this variable, quite naturally says that the last block of a train is indeed occupied by a train:

$$\textbf{inv1\_7:} \quad LBT \subseteq OCC$$

And now we state (**inv1_8**) that the last block b of a train, if it has a follower a on its route, then a, if reserved, is not reserved for the route of b.

$$\textbf{inv1\_8:} \quad \forall a, b \cdot \left(\begin{array}{l} b \in LBT \\ b \in \text{ran}(nxt(rsrtbl(b))) \\ a = nxt(rsrtbl(b))^{-1}(b) \\ a \in \text{dom}(rsrtbl) \\ \Rightarrow \\ rsrtbl(a) \neq rsrtbl(b) \end{array} \right)$$

Thanks to the introduction of the physical variables TRK and LBT we shall be able to define the movements of the train based only on what the train find on the terrain, namely the physical blocks. Notice that a train "knows" that the last part of it occupies a block belonging to LBT.

5.2 The Events

Event route_reservation is not modified in this refinement. Other events are modified as shown below. We also introduce two more events:

- point_positioning,
- route_formation

Event point_positioning is still very abstract in this refinement. It conveys however
the essence of the communication between the future software and the outside equipment: the physical TRK is modified according to the logical route $nxt(r)$. This event
is coherent with requirement SAF-3 which says that "a point can *only be re-positioned*
if it belongs to a block which is in a reserved but not yet formed route". In further refinements, this modification of the physical track will correspond to the controller action
modifying the point positions:

---

point_positioning
   any r **where**
      $r \in resrt \setminus frm$
   then
      $TRK := (\mathrm{dom}(nxt(r)) \lhd TRK \rhd \mathrm{ran}(nxt(r))) \cup nxt(r)$
   end

As can be seen, this logical event has an effect on the physical variable TRK. This
is due to the fact that this event is effectively changing (at ounce for the moment) the
physical position of the points of route r.

Next is an illustration of the physical situations just before and just after an occurrence of event point_positioning. As can be seen, after this occurrence we have three
properties: (1) route $R3$ (L A B K J N) is established on the physical track, (2)
the points have been modified accordingly, and (3) the crossing situated in block K has
been "reorganized":

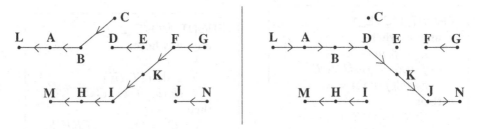

Event route_formation explains when a route r can be "formed", namely when the
physical and logical track agree, that is after event point_positioning has acted on
route r.

---

route_formation
   any r **where**
      $r \in resrt \setminus frm$
      $rsrtbl^{-1}[\{r\}] \lhd nxt(r) \ = \ rsrtbl^{-1}[\{r\}] \lhd TRK$
   then
      $frm := frm \cup \{r\}$
   end

It can be seen that this event refers to the physical variable TRK in its guard. This is due to the fact that this event is enabled when the controller detects (here at ounce for the moment) that all points of route r are correctly positioned.

Event route_freeing is slightly extended by making the freed route not formed any more. This is coherent with requirement MVT_2, which says that "a route remains formed as long as there are some reserved blocks in it" and MVT-3, which says that "a formed route can be made free (not formed and not reserved any more) when no blocks are reserved for it any more".

---

route_freeing
  any r **where**
    $r \in resrt \setminus \mathrm{ran}(rsrtbl)$
  then
    $resrt := resrt \setminus \{r\}$
    $frm := frm \setminus \{r\}$
  end

Event FRONT_MOVE_1 is only slightly modified for the moment as we have not introduced the signals yet: this will be done in further refinements. The present modification consists in extending the set LBT by adding to it the singleton $\{fst(r)\}$. As a matter of fact, when a train is entering a route, the last block of the train for that route is certainly the first block of the route until that block is freed when the back of the train will move in event BACK_MOVE.

FRONT_MOVE_1
  any r **where**
    $r \in frm$
    $fst(r) \in resbl \setminus OCC$
    $rsrtbl(fst(r)) = r$
  then
    $OCC := OCC \cup \{fst(r)\}$
    $LBT := LBT \cup \{fst(r)\}$
  end

FRONT_MOVE_2
  any b **where**
    $b \in OCC$
    $b \in \mathrm{dom}(TRK)$
    $TRK(b) \notin OCC$
  then
    $OCC := OCC \cup \{TRK(b)\}$
  end

Event FRONT_MOVE_2 is now following the physical situation on the real track. We shall have to prove that it refines its abstraction however. As can be seen, all guards are now defined in terms of physical variables.

Event BACK_MOVE is split into two events. Event BACK_MOVE_1 corresponds to the last block of the train leaving the route. Event BACK_MOVE_2 corresponds to the last block of the train progressing in the route.

BACK_MOVE_1
  any b **where**
    $b \in LBT$
    $b \notin \mathrm{dom}(TRK)$
  then
    $OCC := OCC \setminus \{b\}$
    $rsrtbl := \{b\} \lhd rsrtbl$
    $resbl := resbl \setminus \{b\}$
    $LBT := LBT \setminus \{b\}$
  end

BACK_MOVE_2
  any b **where**
    $b \in LBT$
    $b \in \mathrm{dom}(TRK)$
    $TRK(b) \in OCC$
  then
    $OCC := OCC \setminus \{b\}$
    $rsrtbl := \{b\} \lhd rsrtbl$
    $resbl := resbl \setminus \{b\}$
    $LBT := (LBT \setminus \{b\}) \cup \{TRK(b)\}$
  end

Remark 1. As can be seen, the guards of physical events FRONT_MOVE_2, BACK_MOVE_1, and BACK_MOVE_2 are all now involving physical variables only (remember our "important remark" at the end of section 4.2). It is still not the case for event FRONT_MOVE_1 however. Only wait until refinement 3 in section 7 where we shall see that event FRONT_MOVE_1 will be enabled as a consequence of a green signal, which clearly is a physical condition.

Remark 2. We notice that physical events BACK_MOVE_1 and BACK_MOVE_2 both make reference to some non-physical variables in their action part ($rsrtbl$ and $resbl$). We wonder whether this is allowed. It would seem obvious that a physical event cannot modify a controller variables. The reason to have some non-physical variables still present in the action parts of these events is because these events *have still to be decomposed* into two events: the "pure" physical event and a corresponding event in the controller. The reason can clearly be seen here: when the train does a physical back move, the controller has to react by freeing the corresponding logical block. The connection between the physical move and the (separate) logical reaction in the controller will be done later (in some refinement step to be done, but not presented in this chapter) by having the physical track circuit *sending a message to the controller* when it is physically made unoccupied. Upon receiving this message, the controller can then react.

Remark 3. Notice that both events FRONT_MOVE_1 and FRONT_MOVE_2 do not make any reference in their action part to some non-physical variables. It means that such events have no influence on the controller. This is quite understandable, when the front of the train proceeds, we have nothing to do in the controller whereas when the back of the train proceeds we have something to do (block freeing).

6   Second Refinement

In this refinement, we introduce the notion of *readiness* for a route. A route is ready when it is able to accept a new train. In the next refinement, we shall introduce the signals. As we shall see, the ready routes will have a green signal.

6.1   The State

We do not introduce new carrier sets or new constants.

Variables. In this refinement, we introduce the new variable rdy which denotes the set of ready routes.

$$\textbf{variables:} \quad \cdots,$$
$$rdy$$

Here are the basic properties of a ready route. A ready route is one which is formed (**inv2_1**), has all its blocks reserved for it (**inv2_2**), and has all its blocks unoccupied (**inv2_3**):

$$\textbf{inv2\_1:} \quad rdy \subseteq frm$$

$$\textbf{inv2\_2:} \quad \forall r \begin{pmatrix} r \in rdy \\ \Rightarrow \\ rtbl \rhd \{r\} \subseteq rsrtbl \rhd \{r\} \end{pmatrix}$$

$$\textbf{inv2\_3:} \quad \forall r \begin{pmatrix} r \in rdy \\ \Rightarrow \\ \mathrm{dom}(rtbl \rhd \{r\}) \cap OCC = \varnothing \end{pmatrix}$$

6.2   The Events

Events point_positioning, route_reservation, route_freeing, FRONT_MOVE_2, BACK_MOVE_1, and BACK_MOVE_2 are not modified in this refinement, they are thus not copied below. Event route_formation is extended by making the corresponding route ready besides being formed (this action was performed in the previous refinement).

route_formation
   any r **where**
      $r \in resrt \setminus frm$
      $rsrtbl^{-1}[\{r\}] \lhd nxt(r) \;=\; rsrtbl^{-1}[\{r\}] \lhd TRK$
   then
      $frm := frm \cup \{r\}$
      $rdy := rdy \cup \{r\}$
   end

The guards of event FRONT_MOVE_1 are simplified (and made stronger) by stating that the route r is a ready route (this event will be further simplified in the next refinement where we introduce the signals). We put the abstract version of this event next to the refined one to show the differences between the two guards:

(abstract-)FRONT_MOVE_1
   any r **where**
      $r \in frm$
      $fst(r) \in resbl \setminus OCC$
      $rsrtbl(fst(r)) = r$
   then
      $OCC := OCC \cup \{fst(r)\}$
      $LBT := LBT \cup \{fst(r)\}$
   end

(concrete-)FRONT_MOVE_1
   any r **where**
      $r \in rdy$
      $rsrtbl(fst(r)) = r$
   then
      $OCC := OCC \cup \{fst(r)\}$
      $LBT := LBT \cup \{fst(r)\}$
      $rdy := rdy \setminus \{r\}$
   end

7 Third Refinement

In this refinement, we define the signals. The role of a signal is to express, when green, that a route is ready.

7.1 The State

Carrier Sets. We introduce the new carrier set S defining the signals.

$$\textbf{carrier sets:} \quad B, R, S$$

Constants. In this refinement, we define one constant named SIG (pronounce "signal of first block"). This constant yields the unique signal associated with the first block of a route (**prp3_1**). This corresponds to requirements ENV-12 and ENV-14 of section 1.6. It is a bijection since every signal is uniquely associated with the corresponding first block of a route and vice-versa. Notice that routes sharing the same first block share the same signal.

$$\textbf{constants:} \quad \cdots \\ SIG$$

$$\textbf{prp3\_1:} \quad SIG \in \text{ran}(fst) \rightarrowtail\!\!\!\rightarrow S$$

Variables. In this refinement, we introduce the variable GRN denoting the set of green signals (**inv3_1**). This variable data-refines variable rdy which disappears. The connection between the two is established by saying that signals of the first blocks of ready routes are exactly the green signals (**inv3_2**). We have thus established a correspondence between the abstract notion of ready routes and the physical notion of green signals.

variables: $\cdots$ GRN	**inv3_1:** $GRN \subseteq S$ **inv3_2:** $SIG[fst[rdy]] = GRN$

7.2   The Events

The only two events that are modified in this refinement are events route_formation and FRONT_MOVE_1. Event route_formation is refined by turning to green the signal associated with the first block of the newly formed route. This is coherent with requirement FUN-8 which says that "once it is formed, a route is made available for the incoming train by turning its signal to green". This event is also coherent with requirement SAF-2, which says that "the signal of a route can *only be green* when all blocks of that route are reserved for it and are unoccupied". This is due to invariant **inv3_2** equating the blocks with green signal with ready routes, and invariants **inv2_2** and **inv2_3** telling that ready routes have all their blocks reserved and unoccupied.

> route_formation
>   **any** r **where**
> $r \in resrt \setminus frm$
> $rsrtbl^{-1}[\{r\}] \lhd nxt(r) = rsrtbl^{-1}[\{r\}] \lhd TRK$
>   **then**
> $frm := frm \cup \{r\}$
> $GRN := GRN \cup \{SIG(fst(r))\}$
>   **end**

This logical event acts on the physical variable GRN. It corresponds to the controller sending a command to turn the physical signal of the first block of route r to green.

Event FRONT_MOVE_1 now reacts to a green signal rather than to a ready route as in the previous refinement. We take at last account of requirement ENV-13.

> FRONT_MOVE_1
>   **any** b **where**
> $b \in \mathrm{dom}(SIG)$
> $SIG(b) \in GRN$
>   **then**
> $OCC := OCC \cup \{b\}$
> $LBT := LBT \cup \{b\}$
> $GRN := GRN \setminus \{SIG(b)\}$
>   **end**

As can be seen, the physical movement of trains follows the indication of green signals. Note that a green signal is *automatically turned red* when the train enters the corresponding block: this is coherent with requirement ENV-15.

8   Fourth Refinement

8.1   The State

In this refinement, we introduce the points from an abstract point of view for the moment. They are denoted by the set of blocks which contain points. We know from requirement ENV-4 that a block may contain at most one special component: point or crossing.

Constants. We introduce three constants in this refinement: $blpt$, lft, and rht. Constant $blpt$ (pronounce "blocks with points") denotes the set of blocks containing points (**prp4_1**). Each block b containing a point is connected to another block situated on the left of b and another block situated on its right. This is represented by two total functions lft and rht from $blpt$ to B (**prp4_2** and **prp4_3**). Notice that the two function lft and rht are disjoint (**prp4_4**) because a block cannot be situated simultaneously to the left and to the right of a point:

constants: · · ·
  $blpt$,
  lft,
  rht

prp4_1: $blpt \subseteq B$

prp4_2: $lft \in blpt \rightarrow B$

prp4_3: $rht \in blpt \rightarrow B$

prp4_4: $lft \cap rht = \varnothing$

Let us recall our usual example network:

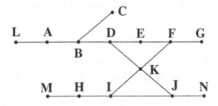

Next are the set $blpt$ and both functions lft and rht corresponding to this example:

$$blpt = \{\, B, D, F, I, J \,\}$$

$$lft = \{\, B \mapsto C,\ D \mapsto E,\ F \mapsto K,\ I \mapsto K,\ J \mapsto I \,\}$$

$$rht = \{\, B \mapsto D,\ D \mapsto K,\ F \mapsto E,\ I \mapsto J,\ J \mapsto K \,\}$$

Each point situated in a route is either in the "direct" or "inverse" direction of this route. This is illustrated in the following figure where you can see fragments of two routes: on the left, we have a point oriented "direct-right", and on the right we have a point oriented "inverse-right".

More precisely, a point is represented in a route by either the left or the right connection, and also on the direct direction of the route or the inverse one. For example, in route $R2$ (L A B D E F G), there are three points: in B, in D, and in F. The one in B is direct and represented by the pair $B \mapsto D$ which is a member of rht, the one in D is direct and represented by the pair $D \mapsto E$ which is a member of lft, and finally the one in F is inverse and represented by the pair $F \mapsto E$ which is a member of rht. The connection of each point-block to the next one in a route must be functional (since the point is either in the right or in the left position). This can be formalized as follows:

$$\textbf{prp4\_5:} \quad \forall r \cdot \begin{pmatrix} r \in R \\ \Rightarrow \\ (lft \cup rht) \cap (nxt(r) \cup nxt(r)^{-1}) \in blpt \nrightarrow B \end{pmatrix}$$

Notice that the position of each point relative to a given route r is the following: $(lft \cup rht) \cap (nxt(r) \cup nxt(r)^{-1})$.

We also have to add a technical property saying that there is no point in the first or last block of a route (**prp4_6** and **prp4_7**):

$$\textbf{prp4\_6:} \quad blpt \cap \mathrm{ran}(fst) = \varnothing$$

$$\textbf{prp4\_7:} \quad blpt \cap \mathrm{ran}(lst) = \varnothing$$

Variable. We have no new variable in this refinement, only a new invariant expressing that the point positioning is, as expected, functional in the real track. This is expressed by invariant **inv4_1** below

$$\textbf{inv4\_1:} \quad (lft \cup rht) \cap (TRK \cup TRK^{-1}) \in blpt \nrightarrow B$$

Notice that the function is partial only: this is due to the crossing. It is not difficult to prove that this invariant is maintained by event point_positioning, which is recalled below:

```
point_positioning
   any  r  where
      r ∈ resrt \ frm
   then
      TRK := (dom(nxt(r)) ◁ TRK ▷ ran(nxt(r))) ∪ nxt(r)
   end
```

A few additional refinements are clearly needed in order to complete this modelling development. It should contain the decomposition of events route_reservation, route_formation, and point_positioning in more atomic events so as to construct corresponding loops.

9   Proofs

The development which has been presented in previous sections has been entirely proved with the *Click'n'Prove* tool [2]. Here is the summary of these proofs:

	Number of proofs	Automatic	Interactive
Initial Model	40	24	16
1st Refinement	46	26	20
2nd Refinement	26	15	11
3rd Refinement	12	9	3
4th Refinement	10	8	2
Total	134	82	52

10   Conclusion

As was said in the introduction, this chapter contains more material on fault prevention than on fault tolerance. This is essentially due to the problem at hand were faults have to be avoided by all means. But faults can happen as was explained in section 1.11, so it is interesting to see how this could have been taken into account in the modelling process.

It would not have been difficult to incorporate the Automatic Train Protection System (alluded above in section 1.11) within the formal models because we have a global approach taking account of the environment. This would take care of requirements FLR-1 (drivers passing a red signal) and FLR-3 (trains moving backwards) which are protected by the Automatic Train Protection System.

As much as I understand form experts, the other failures are not treated simply because people consider that their probability is extremely low. However, such failures could sometimes be detected in the case of FLR-4 (wrong block occupancy) and that of FLR-5 (train leaving a block). In these cases, the controller has to stop the system by not allowing any signal to be turned green and by not doing any point positioning. This default phase is to last until the environment is inspected and the system is reset. It would be also very easy to model this.

What we have presented here is very close to similar studies done in [3] and [5]. The approach of [3] itself follows from original approaches done in the past by applying the "Action System" methodology [4]. The important lesson learned from Action System is the idea of reasoning at a global level by introducing not only the intended software into the picture but also its *physical environment*.

In the present study, we insisted on the preliminary informal phase consisting in presenting the structured "Definitions and Requirements" of the system we want to build. We think that it is extremely important from a methodological point of view as it is quite frequently a very weak point in similar industrial applications. It seems that we have also made a more complete mathematical treatment of the track network model.

Acknowledgements. I would like to give many thanks to Jacques Michaud who gave me lots of information about train systems. His immense knowledge of the subject makes it possible to write this chapter. Laurent Voisin, Michael Butler, and Dominique Cansell also provide numerous comments which allowed this chapter to be improved.

References

1. J.-R. Abrial and S. Hallerstede. *Refinement, Decomposition, and Instantiation of Discrete Models: Application to Event-B*. Fundamentae Informatica, to appear 2006.
2. J.-R. Abrial and D. Cansell. *Click'n'Prove: Interactive Proofs within Set Theory*. In Theorem Proving in Higher Order Logic, LNCS Volume 2758. Springer, 2003.
3. M. Butler. *A System-based Approach to the Formal Development of Embedded Controllers for a Railway.*. Design Automation for Embedded Systems, 2002.
4. M. Butler, E. Sekerinski, and K. Sere. *An Action System Approach to the Steam Boiler Problem*. In Formal Methods for Industrial Applications. LNCS Volume 1165. Springer, 1996.
5. A.E. Haxthausen and J. Peleska. *Formal Development and Verification of a Distributed Railway Control System*. FM'99, LNCS Volume 1709. Springer, 1999.

Formalising Reconciliation in Partitionable Networks with Distributed Services

Mikael Asplund and Simin Nadjm-Tehrani

Department of Computer and Information Science,
Linköping University SE-581 83 Linköping, Sweden
{mikas, simin}@ida.liu.se

1 Introduction

Modern command and control systems are characterised by computing services provided to several actors at different geographical locations. The actors operate on a common state that is modularly updated at distributed nodes using local data services and global integrity constraints for validity of data in the value and time domains. Dependability in such networked applications is measured through availability of the distributed services as well as the correctness of the state updates that should satisfy integrity constraints at all times. Providing support in middleware is seen as one way of achieving a high level of service availability and well-defined performance guarantees. However, most recent works [1,2] that address fault-aware middleware cover crash faults and provision of timely services, and assume network connectivity as a basic tenet.

In this paper we study the provision of services in distributed object systems, with network partitions as the primary fault model. The problem appears in a variety of scenarios [3], including distributed flight control systems. The scenarios combine provision of critical services with data-intensive operations. Clients can approach any node in the system to update a given object, copies of which are present across different nodes in the system. A correct update of the object state is dependent on validity of integrity constraints, potentially involving other distributed objects. Replicated objects provide efficient access at distributed nodes (leading to lower service latency). Middleware is employed for systematic upholding of common view on the object states and consistency in write operations. However, problems arise if the network partitions. That is, if there are broken/overloaded links such that some nodes become unreachable, and the nodes in the network form disjoint partitions. Then, if services are delivered to clients approaching different partitions, the upholding of consistency has to be considered explicitly. Moreover, there should be mechanisms to deal with system mode changes, with service differentiation during degraded mode.

Current solutions to this problem typically uphold full consistency at the cost of availability. When the network is partitioned, the services that require integrity constraints over objects that are no longer reachable are suspended until the network is physically unified. Alternatively, a majority partition is assumed to continue delivering services based on the latest replica states. When

M. Butler et al. (Eds.): Fault-Tolerant Systems, LNCS 4157, pp. 37–58, 2006.

the network is reunified the minority partition(s) nodes rejoin; but during the partition clients approaching the minority partition receive no service. The goal of our work is to investigate middleware support that enables distributed services to be provided at *all* partitions, at the expense of temporarily trading off some consistency. To gain higher availability we need to act optimistically, and allow one primary per partition to provisionally service clients that invoke operations in that partition.

The contributions of the paper are twofold. First, we present a protocol that after reunification of a network partition takes a number of partition states and generates a new partition state that includes a unique state per object. In parallel with creating this new state the protocol continues servicing incoming requests. Since the state of the (reconciled) post-reunification objects are not yet finalised, the protocol has to maintain virtual partitions until all operations that have arrived after the partition fault and provisionally serviced are dealt with.

Second, we show that the protocol results in a stable partition state, from which onwards the need for virtual partitions is no longer necessary. The proof states the assumptions under which the stable state is reached. Intuitively, the system will leave the reconciliation mode when the rate of incoming requests is lower than the rate of handling the provisionally accepted operations during reconciliation. The resulting partition state is further shown to have desired properties. A notion of correctness is introduced that builds on satisfaction of integrity constraints as well as respecting an intended order of performed operations seen from clients' point of view.

The structure of the paper is as follows. Section 2 i provides an informal overview of the formalised protocols in the paper. Section 3 introduces the basic formal notions that are used in the models. Section 4 describes the intuitive reasoning behind the choice of ordering that is imposed on the performed operations in the system and relates the application (client) expectations to the support that can reasonably be provided by automatic mechanisms in middleware. Section 5 presents the reconciliation protocol in terms of distributed algorithms running at replicas and in a reconciliation manager. Section 6 is devoted to the proofs of termination and correctness for the protocol. Related work are described in Sect. 7, and Sect. 8 concludes the paper.

2   Overview

We begin by assuming that middleware services for replication of objects are in place. This implies that the middleware has mechanisms for creating replica objects, and protocols that propagate a write operation at a primary copy to all the object replicas transparently. Moreover, the mechanisms for detecting link failures and partition faults are present in the middleware. The latter is typically implemented by maintaining a membership service that keeps an up to date view of which replicas for an object are running and reachable. The middleware also includes naming/location services, whereby the physical node can be identified given a logical address.

In normal mode, the system services read operations in a distributed manner; but for write operations there are protocols that check integrity constraints before propagating the update to all copies of the object at remote nodes. Both in normal and degraded mode, each partition is assumed to include a designated primary replica for each object in the system.

The integrity constraints in the system are assumed to fall in two classes: critical and non-critical. For operations with non-critical constraints different primary servers continue to service client requests, and provisionally accept the operations that satisfy integrity constraints. When the partition fault is repaired, the state of the main partition is formed by reconciling the operations carried out in the earlier disjoint partitions. The middleware supports this reconciliation process and guarantees the consistency of the new partition state. The state is formed by replaying some provisional operations that are accepted, and rejecting some provisional operations that should be notified to clients as "undone". It is obviously desirable to keep as many of the provisionally accepted operations as possible.

The goal of the paper is to formally define mechanisms that support the above continuous service in presence of (multiple) partitions, and satisfactorily create a new partition upon recovery from the fault. For a system that has a considerable portion of its integrity constraints classified as non-critical this should intuitively increase availability despite partitions. Also, the average latency for servicing clients should decrease as some client requests that would otherwise be suspended or considerably delayed if the system were to halt upon partitions are now serviced in a degraded mode.

Figure 1 presents the modes of a system in presence of partition faults. The system is available in degraded mode except for operations for which the integrity constraints are critical so that they cannot accept the risk of being inconsistent during partitions (these are not performed at all in degraded mode). The system is also partially available during reconciling mode; but there is a last short stage within reconciliation (installing state) during which the system is unavailable.

In earlier work we have formalised the reconciliation process in a simple model and experimentally studied three reconciliation algorithms in terms of their influence on service outage duration [4]. A major assumption in that work was that no service was provided during the *whole* reconciliation process. Simulations

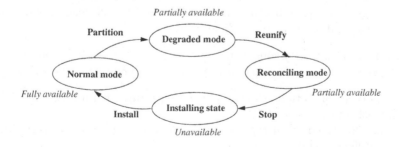

Fig. 1. System modes

showed that the drawback of the 'non-availability' assumption can be severe in some scenarios; namely the time taken to reconcile could be long enough so that the non-availability of services during this interval would be almost as bad as having no degraded service at all (thereby no gain in overall availability).

In this paper we investigate the implications of continued service delivery *during* the reconciliation process. This implies that we need to formalise a more refined protocol that keeps providing service to clients in parallel with reconciliation (and potential replaying of some operations). The algorithms are modelled in timed I/O automata, that naturally model multiple partition faults occurring in a sequence (so called cascading effects). More specifically, the fault model allows multiple partition faults in a sequence before a network is reunified, but no partitions occur during reconciliation. We also exclude crash faults during reconciliation in order to keep the models and proofs easier to convey. Crash faults can be accommodated using existing checkpointing approaches [5] with no known effects on main results of the paper. Furthermore, we investigate correctness and termination properties of this more refined reconciliation protocol. The proofs use admissible timed traces of timed I/O automata.

3 Preliminaries

This section introduces the concepts needed to describe the reconciliation protocol and its properties. We will define the necessary terms such as object, partition and replica as well as defining consistency criteria for partitions.

3.1 Objects

For the purpose of formalisation we associate data with objects. Implementation-wise, data can be maintained in databases and accessed via database managers.

Definition 1. *An* object *o is a triple $o = (S, \mathcal{O}, T)$ where S is the set of possible states, $\mathcal{O}$ is the set of operations that can be applied to the object state and $T \subseteq S \times \mathcal{O} \times S$ is a transition relation on states and operations.*

We assume all operation sets to be disjunct so that every operation is associated with one object.

Transitions from a state s to a state s' will be denoted by $s \xrightarrow{\alpha} s'$ where $\alpha = \langle op, k \rangle$ is an operation instance with $op \in \mathcal{O}$, and $k \in \mathbb{N}$ denotes the unique invocation of operation op at some client.

Definition 2. *An* integrity constraint *c is a predicate over multiple object states. Thus, $c \subseteq S_1 \times S_2 \times \ldots \times S_n$ where n is the number of objects in the system.*

Intuitively, object operations should only be performed if they do not violate integrity constraints.

A distributed system with replication has multiple replicas for every object located on different nodes in the network. As long as no failures occur, the existence of replicas has no effect on the functional behaviour of the system.

Therefore, the state of the system in the normal mode can be modelled as a set of replicas, one for each object.

Definition 3. *A replica r for object $o = (S, \mathcal{O}, T)$ is a triple $r = (L, s^0, s^m)$ where the log $L = \langle \alpha_1 \ldots \alpha_m \rangle$ is a sequence of operation instances defined over $\mathcal{O}$. The initial state is $s^0 \in S$ and $s^m \in S$ is a state such that $s^0 \overset{\alpha_1}{\rightsquigarrow} \ldots \overset{\alpha_m}{\rightsquigarrow} s^m$.*

The log can be considered as the record of operations since the last checkpoint that also recorded the (initial) state s^0.

We consider partitions that have been operating independently and we assume the nodes in each partition to agree on one primary replica for each object. This will typically be promoted by the middleware. Moreover, we assume that all objects are replicated across all nodes. For the purpose of reconciliation the important aspect of a partition is not how the actual nodes in the network are connected but the replicas whose states have been updated separately and need to be reconciled. Thus, the state of each partition can be modelled as a set of replicas where each object is uniquely represented.

Definition 4. *A partition p is a set of replicas r such that if $r_i, r_j \in p$ are both replicas for object o then $r_i = r_j$.*

The state of a partition $p = \{(L_1, s_1^0, s_1), \ldots, (L_n, s_n^0, s_n)\}$ consists of the state of the replicas $\langle s_1, \ldots, s_n \rangle$. Transitions over object states can now be naturally extended to transitions over partition states.

Definition 5. *Let $\alpha = \langle op, k \rangle$ be an operation instance for some invocation k of operation op. Then $\mathbf{s^j} \overset{\alpha}{\rightsquigarrow} \mathbf{s^{j+1}}$ is a partition transition iff there is an object o_i such that $s_i \overset{\alpha}{\rightsquigarrow} s_i'$ is a transition for o_i, $\mathbf{s^j} = \langle s_1, \ldots, s_i, \ldots, s_n \rangle$ and $\mathbf{s^{j+1}} = \langle s_1, \ldots, s_i', \ldots, s_n \rangle$.*

We denote by $Apply(\alpha, P)$ the result of applying operation instance α at some replica in partition P, giving a new partition state and a new log for the affected replica.

3.2   Order

So far we have not introduced any concept of order except that a state is always the result of operations performed in some order. When we later will consider the problem of creating new states from operations that have been performed in different partitions we must be able to determine in what (if any) order the operations must be replayed.

At this point we will merely define the existence of a strict partial order relation over operation instances. Later, in Sect. 4.2 we explain the philosophy behind choosing this relation.

Definition 6. *The relation $\rightarrow$ is a irreflexive, transitive relation over the operation instances obtained from operations $\mathcal{O}_1 \cup \ldots \cup \mathcal{O}_n$.*

In Definition 8 we will use this ordering to define correctness of a partition state. Note that the ordering relation induces an ordering on states along the time line whereas the consistency constraints relate the states of various objects at a given "time point" (a cut of the distributed system).

3.3 Consistency

Our reconciliation protocol will take a set of partitions and produce a new partition. As there are integrity constraints on the system state and order dependencies on operations, a reconciliation protocol must make sure that the resulting partition is correct with respect to both of these requirements. This section defines consistency properties for partitions.

Definition 7. *A partition state* $\mathbf{s} = \langle s_1, \ldots, s_n \rangle$ *for partition where*
$P = \{(L_1, s_1^0, s_1), \ldots, (L_n, s_n^0, s_n)\}$ *is* constraint consistent, *denoted* $cc(P)$, *iff for all integrity constraints c it holds that $\mathbf{s} \in c$.*

Next we define a consistency criterion for partitions that also takes into account the order requirements on operations in logs. Intuitively we require that there is some way to construct the current partition state from the initial state using all the operations in the logs. Moreover, all the intermediate states should be constraint consistent and the operation ordering must follow the ordering restrictions. We will use this correctness criterion in evaluation of our reconciliation protocol.

Definition 8. *Let* $P = \{(L_1, s_1^0, s_1), \ldots, (L_n, s_n^0, s_n)\}$ *be a partition, and let* $\mathbf{s}^k$ *be the partition state. The initial partition state is* $\mathbf{s}^0 = \langle s_1^0, \ldots s_n^0 \rangle$. *We say that the partition P is* consistent *if there exists a sequence of operation instances* $L = \langle \alpha_1, \ldots, \alpha_k \rangle$ *such that:*

1. $\alpha \in L_i \Rightarrow \alpha \in L$
2. $\mathbf{s}^0 \overset{\alpha_1}{\rightsquigarrow} \ldots \overset{\alpha_k}{\rightsquigarrow} \mathbf{s}^k$
3. *Every* $\mathbf{s}^j \in \{\mathbf{s}^0, \ldots, \mathbf{s}^k\}$ *is constraint consistent*
4. $\alpha_i \rightarrow \alpha_j \Rightarrow i < j$

4 Application-Middleware Dependencies

In Sect. 3 we introduced integrity constraints and an order relation between operations. These concepts are used to ensure that the execution of operations is performed according to the clients' expectations. In this section we will further elaborate on these two concepts, and briefly explain why they are important for reconciliation.

Due to the fact that the system continues to provisionally serve requests in degraded mode, the middleware has to start a reconciliation process when the system recovers from link failures (i.e. when the network is physically reunified). At that point in time there may be several conflicting states for each object since write requests have been serviced in all partitions. In order to merge these states into one common state for the system we will have to replay the performed operations (that are stored in the logs of each replica). Some operations may not satisfy integrity constraints when multiple partitions are considered, and they may have to be rejected (seen from a client perspective, undone). The replay starts from the last common state (i.e. from before the partition fault occurred) and iteratively builds up a new state. Note that the replay of an operation instance may potentially take place in a different state compared to that where the operation was originally applied in the degraded mode.

4.1   Integrity Constraints

Since some operations will have to be replayed we need to consider the conditions required, so that replaying an operation in a different state than that it was originally executed in does not cause any discrepancies. We assume that such conditions are indeed captured by integrity constraints.

In other words, the middleware expects that an application writer has created the needed integrity constraints such that replaying an operation during reconciliation is harmless as long as the constraint is satisfied, even if the state on which it is replayed is different from the state in which it was first executed. That is, there should not be any implicit conditions that are checked by the client at the invocation of the operation. In such a case it would not be possible for the middleware to recheck these constraints upon reconciliation.

As an example, consider withdrawal from a credit account. It is acceptable to allow a withdrawal as long as there is coverage for the account in the balance; it is not essential that the balance should be a given value when withdrawal is allowed. Recall that that an operation for which a later rejection is not acceptable from an application point of view should be associated with a critical constraint (thereby not applied during a partition at all). An example of such an operation would be the termination of a credit account.

4.2   Expected Order

To explain the notion of expected order we will first consider a system in normal mode and see what kind of execution order is expected by the client. Then we will require the same expected order to be guaranteed by the system when performing reconciliation. In our scenarios we will assume that a client who invokes two operations α and β in sequence without receiving a reply between them does not have any ordering requirements on the invocations. Then the system need not guarantee that the operations are executed in any particular order. This is true even if the operations were invoked on the same object.

Now assume that the client first invokes α and does not invoke β until it has received a reply for α confirming that α has been executed. Then the client knows that α is executed before β. The client process therefore assumes an ordering between the execution of α and β due to the fact that the events of receiving a reply for α precedes the event of invoking β. This is the order that we want to capture with the relation $\rightarrow$ from Definition 6. When the reconciliation process replays the operations it must make sure that this expected order is respected.

This induced order need not be specified at the application level. It can be captured by a client side front end within the middleware, and reflected in a tag for the invoked operations. Thus, every operation is piggybacked with information about what other operations must precede it when it is later replayed. This information is derived from the requests that are sent by the client and the received replies. Note that it is only necessary to attach the IDs of the immediate predecessors so the overhead will be small.

5   The Reconciliation Protocol

In this section we will describe the reconciliation protocol in detail using timed I/O automata. However, before going into details we provide a short overview of the idea behind the protocol. The protocol is composed of two types of processes: a number of replicas and one reconciliation manager.

The replicas are responsible for accepting invocations from clients and sending logs to the reconciliation manager during reconciliation. The reconciliation manager is responsible for merging replica logs that are sent during reconciling mode. It is activated when the system is reunified and eventually sends an install message with the new partition state to all replicas. The new partition state includes empty logs for each replica.

The reconciliation protocol starts with one state per partition is faced with the task of merging a number of operations that have been performed in different partitions while preserving constraint consistency and respecting the expected ordering of operations. In parallel with this process the protocol should take care of operations that arrive during the reconciliation phase. Note that there may be unreconciled operations in the logs that should be executed before the incoming operations that arrive during reconciliation.

The state that is being constructed in the reconciliation manager may not yet reflect all the operations that are before ($\rightarrow$) the incoming operations. Therefore the only state in which the incoming operation can be applied to is one of the partition states from the degraded mode. Or in other words, we need to execute the new operations as if the system was still in degraded mode. In order to do this we will maintain virtual partitions while the reconciliation phase lasts.

5.1   Reconciliation Manager

In Algorithm 1. the variable *mode* represents the modes of the reconciliation process and is basically the same as the system modes described in Fig. 1 except that the normal and degraded mode are collapsed into an idle mode for the reconciliation manager, which is its initial mode of operation.

When a reunify action is activated the reconciliation manager goes to reconciling mode. Moreover, the variable P, which represents the partition state, is initialised with the pre-partition state, and the variable *opset* that will contain all the operations to replay is set to empty. Now the reconciliation process starts waiting for the replicas to send their logs and the variable *awaitedLogs* is set to contain all replicas that have not yet sent their logs.

Next, we consider the action $receive(\langle \text{``}log\text{''}, L \rangle)_{iM}$ which will be activated when some replica r_i sends its operation log. This action will add logged operations to *opset* and to $ackset[i]$ where the latter is used to store acknowledge messages that should be sent back to replica r_i. The acknowledge messages are sent by the action $send(\langle \text{``}logAck\text{''}, ackset[i] \rangle)_{Mi}$. When logs have been received from all replicas (i.e. *awaitedLogs* is empty) then the manager can proceed and start replaying operations. A deadline will be set on when the next handle action must be activated (this is done by setting *last(handle)*).

The action *handle(α)* is an internal action of the reconciliation process that will replay the operation α (which is minimal according to → in *opset*) in the reconciled state that is being constructed. The operation is applied if it results in a constraint consistent state.

As we will show in Sect. 6.2, there will eventually be a time when *opset* is empty at which M will enable *broadcast("stop")$_M$*. This will tell all replicas to stop accepting new invocations. Moreover, M will set the mode to *installingState* and wait for all replicas to acknowledge the stop message. This is done to guarantee that no messages remain untreated in the reconciliation process. Finally, when the manager has received acknowledgements from all replicas it will broadcast an install message with the reconciled partition state and enter idle mode.

5.2   Replica Process

A replica process (see Algorithm 2.) is responsible for receiving invocations to clients and for sending logs to M. We will proceed by describing the states and actions of a replica process. First note that a replica process can be in four different modes, normal, degraded, reconciling, and unavailable which correspond to the system modes of Fig. 1.

In this paper we do not explicitly model how updates are replicated from primary replicas to secondary replicas. Instead, we introduce two global shared variables that are accessed by all replicas, provided that they are part of the same group. The first shared variable $P[i]$ represents the partition for the group with ID i and it is used by all replicas in that group during normal and degraded mode. The group ID is assumed to be delivered by the membership service.

During reconciling mode the group-ID will be 1 for all replicas since there is only one partition during reconciling mode. However, as we explained in the beginning of Sect. 5 the replicas must maintain virtual partitions to service requests during reconciliation. The shared variable $VP[j]$ is used to represent the virtual partition for group j which is based on the partition that was used during degraded mode.

During normal mode replicas apply operations that are invoked through the *receive(⟨"invoke", α⟩)$_{cr}$* action if they result in a constraint consistent partition. A set *toReply* is increased with every applied operation that should be replied to by the action *send(⟨"reply", α⟩)$_{rc}$*.

A replica leaves normal mode and enters degraded mode when the group membership service sends a partition message with a new group-ID. The replica will then copy the contents of the previous partition representation to one that will be used during degraded mode. Implicit in this assignment is the determination of one primary per partition for each object in the system (as provided by a combined name service and group membership service). The replica will continue accepting invocations and replying to them during degraded mode.

Algorithm 1. Reconciliation manager M

States

$mode \in \{idle, reconciling, installingState\} \leftarrow idle$
$P \leftarrow \{(\langle\rangle, s_1^0, s_1^0), \ldots, (\langle\rangle, s_n^0, s_n^0)\}$/* Output of protocol: Constructed partition */
$opset$ /* Set of operations to reconcile */
$awaitedLogs$ /* Replicas to wait for sending a first log message */
$stopAcks$ /* Number of received stop "acks"*/
$ackset[i] \leftarrow \emptyset$ /* Log items from replica i to acknowledge*/
$now \in \mathbb{R}^{0+}$
$last(handle) \leftarrow \infty$ /* Deadline for executing handle */
$last(stop) \leftarrow \infty$ /* Deadline for sending stop */
$last(install) \leftarrow \infty$ /* Deadline for sending install */

Actions

Input $reunify(g)_M$
Eff: $mode \leftarrow reconciling$
       $P \leftarrow \{(\langle\rangle, s_1^0, s_1^0), \ldots, (\langle\rangle, s_n^0, s_n^0)\}$
       $opset \leftarrow \emptyset$
       $awaitedLogs \leftarrow \{\text{All replicas}\}$

Input $receive(\langle\text{"log"}, L\rangle)_{iM}$
Eff: $opset \leftarrow opset \cup L$
       $ackset[i] \leftarrow ackset[i] \cup L$
       if $awaitedLogs \neq \emptyset$
         $awaitedLogs \leftarrow awaitedLogs \setminus \{i\}$
       else
         $last(handle) \leftarrow$
            $min(last(handle), now + d_{\text{han}})$

Output $send(\langle\text{"logAck"}, ackset[i]\rangle)_{Mi}$
Eff: $ackset[i] \leftarrow \emptyset$

Internal $handle(\alpha)$
Pre: $awaitedLogs = \emptyset$
       $mode = reconciling$
       $\alpha \in opset$
       $\nexists\beta \in opset \quad \beta \rightarrow \alpha$
Eff: if $cc(Apply(\alpha, P))$
         $P \leftarrow Apply(\alpha, P)$
         $last(handle) \leftarrow now + d_{\text{han}}$
         $opset \leftarrow opset \setminus \{\alpha\}$
         if $opset = \emptyset$
           $last(stop) = now + d_{\text{act}}$

Output $broadcast(\text{"stop"})_M$
Pre: $opset = \emptyset$
       $awaitedLogs = \emptyset$
Eff: $stopAcks \leftarrow 0$
       $mode \leftarrow installingState$
       $last(handle) \leftarrow \infty$
       $last(stop) \leftarrow \infty$

Input $receive(\langle\text{"stopAck"}\rangle)_{iM}$
Eff: $stopAcks \leftarrow stopAcks + 1$
       if $stopAck = mn$
         $last(install) = now + d_{\text{act}}$

Output $broadcast(\langle\text{"install"}, P\rangle)_M$
Pre: $mode = installingState$
       $stopAcks = m \cdot n$
Eff: $mode \leftarrow idle$
       $last(install) = \infty$

Timepassage $v(t)$
Pre: $now + t \leq last(handle)$
       $now + t \leq last(stop)$
       $now + t \leq last(install)$
Eff: $now \leftarrow now + t$

When a replica receives a reunify message it will take the log of operations served during degraded mode (the set L) and send it to the reconciliation manager M by the action $send(\langle\text{"log"}, L\rangle)_{rM}$. In addition, the replica will enter reconciling mode and copy the partition representation to a virtual partition representation. The latter will be indexed using virtual group-ID vg which will be the same as the group-ID used during degraded mode. Finally, a deadline will be set for sending the logs to M.

The replica will continue to accept invocations during reconciliation mode with some differences in handling. First of all, the operations are applied to a virtual partition state. Secondly, a log message containing an applied operation is immediately scheduled to be sent to M. Finally, the replica will not immediately reply to the operations. Instead it will wait until the log message has been acknowledged by the reconciliation manager and $receive(\langle ``logAck", L\rangle)_{Mr}$ is activated. Now any operation whose reply was pending and for whom a $logAck$ has been received can be replied to (added to the set $toReply$).

At some point the manager M will send a stop message which will make the replica to go into unavailable mode and send a $stopAck$ message. During this mode no invocations will be accepted until an install message is received. Upon receiving such a message the replica will install the new partition representation and once again go into normal mode.

6   Properties of the Protocol

The goal of the protocol is to restore consistency in the system. This is achieved by merging the results from several different partitions into one partition state. The clients have no control over the reconciliation process and in order to guarantee that the final result does not violate the expectations of the clients we need to assert correctness properties of the protocol. Moreover, as there is a growing set of unreconciled operations we need to show that the protocol does not get stuck in reconciliation mode for ever.

In this section we will show that (1) the protocol terminates in the sense that the reconciliation mode eventually ends and the system proceeds to normal mode (2) the resulting partition state which is installed in the system is consistent in the sense of Definition 8.

6.1   Assumptions

The results rely on a number of assumptions on the system. We assume a partially synchronous system with reliable broadcast. Moreover, we assume that there are bounds on duration and rate of partition faults in the network. Finally we need to assume some restrictions on the behaviour of the clients such as the speed at which invocations are done and the expected order of operations. The rest of the section describes these assumptions in more detail.

Network Assumptions. We assume that there are two time bounds on the appearance of faults in the network. T_D is the maximal time that the network can be partitioned. T_F is needed to capture the minimum time between two faults. The relationship between these bounds are important as operations are piled up

---

Algorithm 2. Replica r

Shared vars
$P[i] \leftarrow \{(\langle\rangle, s_1^0, s_1^0), \ldots, (\langle\rangle, s_n^0, s_n^0)\}$, for $i = 1 \ldots N$ /* Representation for partition i,
before reunification */
$VP[i]$, for $i = 1 \ldots N$ /* Representation for virtual partition i, after reunification */

States
$mode \in \{normal, degraded, reconciling, unavailable\} \leftarrow idle$
$g \in \{1 \ldots N\} \leftarrow 1$ /* Group identity (supplied by group membership service) */
$vg \in \{1 \ldots N\} \leftarrow 1$ /* Virtual group identity, used between reunification and install */
$L \leftarrow \emptyset$ /* Set of log messages to send to reconciliation manager M*/
$toReply \leftarrow \emptyset$ /* Set of operations to reply to */
$pending \leftarrow \emptyset$ /* Set of operations to reply to when logged */
$enableStopAck$ /* Boolean to signal that a stopAck should be sent */
$last(log) \leftarrow \infty$ /* Deadline for next $send(\langle\text{"}log\text{"}, \ldots\rangle)$ action */
$last(stopAck) \leftarrow \infty$ /* Deadline for next $send(\langle\text{"}stopAck\text{"}, \ldots\rangle)$ action */
$now \in \mathbb{R}^{0+}$

Actions

Input $partition(g')_r$
Eff: $mode \leftarrow degraded$
$P[g'] \leftarrow P[g]$
$g \leftarrow g'$

Input $receive(\langle\text{"}invoke\text{"}, \alpha\rangle)_{cr}$
Eff: $switch(mode)$
$normal \mid degraded \Rightarrow$
if $Apply(\alpha, P[g])$ is Consistent)
$P[g] \leftarrow Apply(\alpha, P[g])$
$toReply \leftarrow toReply \cup \{\langle\alpha, c\rangle\}$
$reconciling \Rightarrow$
if $Apply(\alpha, VP[vg])$ is Consistent)
$VP[vg] \leftarrow Apply(\alpha, VP[vg])$
$L \leftarrow L \cup \{\alpha\}$
$last(log) \leftarrow min(last(log), now + d_{act})$
$pending \leftarrow pending \cup \{\langle\alpha, c\rangle\}$

Input $receive(\langle\text{"}logAck\text{"}, L\rangle)_{Mr}$
Eff: $replies \leftarrow \{\langle\alpha, c\rangle \in pending \mid \alpha \in L\}$
$toReply \leftarrow toReply \cup replies$
$pending \leftarrow pending \setminus replies$

Input $receive(\text{"}stop\text{"})_{Mr}$
Eff: $mode \leftarrow unavailable$
$enableStopAck \leftarrow true$
$last(stopAck) \leftarrow now + d_{act}$

Input $receive(\langle\text{"}install\text{"}, P'\rangle)_{Mr}$
Eff: $P[g] \leftarrow P'$ /* g = 1 */
$mode \leftarrow normal$

Input $reunify(g')_r$
Eff: $L \leftarrow L_r$ where $\langle L_r, s_r^0, s_r\rangle \in P$
$mode \leftarrow reconciling$
$vg \leftarrow g$
$VP[vg] \leftarrow P[g]$
$g \leftarrow g'$
$last(log) \leftarrow now + d_{act}$

Output $send(\langle\text{"}log\text{"}, L\rangle)_{rM}$
Pre: $mode \in \{reconciling, unavailable\}$
$L \neq \emptyset$
Eff: $L \leftarrow \emptyset$
$last(log) \leftarrow \infty$

Output $send(\langle\text{"}reply\text{"}, \alpha\rangle)_{rc}$
Pre: $\langle\alpha, c\rangle \in toReply$
Eff: $toReply \leftarrow toReply \setminus \{\langle\alpha, c\rangle\}$

Output $send(\langle\text{"}stopAck\text{"}\rangle)_{rM}$
Pre: $enableStopAck = true$
$L = \emptyset$
Eff: $enableStopAck = false$
$last(stopAck) \leftarrow \infty$

Timepassage $v(t)$
Pre: $now + t \leq last(log)$
$now + t \leq last(stopAck)$
Eff: $now \leftarrow now + t$

---

during the degraded mode and the reconciliation has to be able to handle them during the time before the next fault occurs.

We will not explicitly describe all the actions of the network but we will give a description of the required actions as well as a list of requirements that the network must meet. The network assumptions are summarised in N1-N6, where N1, N2, and N3 characterise reliable broadcast which can be supplied by a system such as Spread[6]. Assumption N4 relates to partial synchrony which is a basic assumption for fault-tolerant distributed systems. Finally we assume that faults are limited in frequency and duration (N5,N6) which is reasonable, as otherwise the system could never heal itself.

N1 A receive action is preceded by a send (or broadcast) action.
N2 A sent message is not lost unless a partition occurs.
N3 A sent broadcast message is either received by all in the group or a partition occurs and no process receives it.
N4 Messages arrive within a delay of d_{msg} (including broadcast messages).
N5 After a reunification, a partition occurs after an interval of at least T_{F}.
N6 Partitions do not last for more than T_{D}.

Client Assumptions. In order to prove termination and correctness of the reconciliation protocol we need some restrictions on the behaviour of clients.

C1 The minimum time between two invoke actions from one client is d_{inv}.
C2 If there is an application-specific ordering between two operations, then the first must have been replied to before the second was invoked. Formally, admissible timed system traces must be a subset of $ttraces(C2)$. $ttraces(C2)$ is defined as the set of sequences such that for all sequences σ in $ttraces(C2)$:
$\alpha \rightarrow \beta$ and $(send(\langle \text{``}invoke\text{''}, \beta \rangle)_{cr}, t_1) \in \sigma \Rightarrow$
$\exists(receive(\langle \text{``}reply\text{''}, \alpha \rangle)_{r'c}, t_0) \in \sigma$ for some r' and $t_0 < t_1$.

In Table 1 we summarise all the system parameters relating to time intervals that we have introduced so far.

Table 1. Parameter summary

T_{F}	Minimal time before a partition fault after a reunify
T_{D}	Maximal duration of a partition
d_{msg}	Maximal message transmission time
d_{inv}	Minimal time between two invocations from one client
d_{han}	Maximal time between two handle actions within reconciliation manager
d_{act}	Deadline for actions

Server Assumptions. As we are concerned with reconciliation and do not want go into detail on other responsibilities of the servers or middleware (such as checkpointing), we will make two assumptions on the system behaviour that we do not explicitly model. First, in order to prove that the reconciliation phase ends with the installment of a consistent partition state, we need to assume that the state from which the reconciliation started is consistent. This is a reasonable assumption since normal and degraded mode operations always respect integrity constraints. Second, we assume that the replica logs are empty at the time when a partition occurs. This is required to limit the length of the reconciliation as we do not want to consider logs from the whole life time of a system. In practice, this has to be enforced by implementing checkpointing during normal operation.

A1 The initial state s^0 is constraint consistent (see Definition 7).
A2 All replica logs are empty when a partition occurs.

We will now proceed to prove correctness of the protocol. First we give a termination proof and then a partial correctness proof.

6.2 Termination

In this section we will prove that the reconciliation protocol will terminate in the sense that after the network is physically healed (reunified) the reconciliation protocol eventually activates an install message to the replicas with the reconciled state. As stated in the theorem it is necessary that the system is able to replay operations at a higher rate than new operations arrive (reflected in the ratio q).

Theorem 1. *Let the system consist of the model of replicas, and the model of reconciliation manager. Assume the conditions described in Sect. 6.1. Assume further that the ratio q between the minimum handling rate $\frac{1}{d_{\mathrm{han}}}$ and the maximum interarrival rate for client invocations $C \cdot \frac{1}{d_{\mathrm{inv}}}$, where C is the maximum number of clients, is greater than one. Then, all admissible system traces are in the set $ttraces(Installing)$ of action sequences such that for every $(reunify(g)_M, t)$ there is a $(broadcast(\langle \text{“install”}, P \rangle)_M, t')$ in the sequence, with $t < t'$, provided that $T_F > \frac{T_D + 7d}{q-1} + 9d$, where d exceeds d_{msg} and d_{act}.*

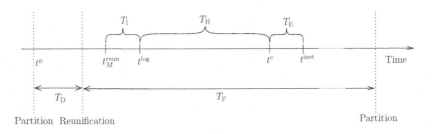

Fig. 2. Reconciliation timeline

Proof. Consider an arbitrary admissible timed trace γ such that $(reunify(g)_M, t_M^{\text{reun}})$ appears in γ. Let all time points t^i below refer to points in γ. The goal of the proof is to show that there exists a point t^{inst} after t_M^{reun}, at which there is an install message appearing in γ.

The timing relation between two partitions and the time line for manager M can be visualised in Fig. 2 (see N5 and N6). Let t_i^{reun} denote the time point at which the reunification message arrives at process i. The reconciliation activity is performed over three intervals: initialising (T_{I}), handling (T_{H}), and ending (T_{E}). The proof strategy is to show that the reconciliation activity ends before the next partition occurs, considering that it takes one message transmission for the manager to learn about reunification. That is, $d_{\text{msg}} + T_{\text{I}} + T_{\text{H}} + T_{\text{E}} < T_{\text{F}}$.

Let $t^{\log}$ be the last time point at which a log message containing a pre-reunification log is received from some replica. This is the time point at which handling (replaying) operations can begin. The handling interval (T_{H}) ends when the set of operations to replay (*opset*) is empty. Let this time point be denoted by t^e.

Initialising:

$$T_{\text{I}} = t^{\log} - t_M^{\text{reun}}$$

The latest estimate for $t^{\log}$ is obtained from the latest time point at which a replica may receive this reunification message (t_r^{reun}) plus the maximum time for it to react (d_{act}) plus the maximum transmission time (d_{msg}).

$$T_{\text{I}} \leq \max_r(t_r^{\text{reun}}) + d_{\text{act}} + d_{\text{msg}} - t_M^{\text{reun}}$$

By N4 all reunification messages are received within d_{msg}.

$$T_{\text{I}} \leq t_M^{\text{reun}} + d_{\text{msg}} + d_{\text{act}} + d_{\text{msg}} - t_M^{\text{reun}} \leq 2d_{\text{msg}} + d_{\text{act}} \tag{1}$$

Handling: The maximum handling time is characterised by the maximum number of invoked client requests times the maximum handling time for each operation (d_{han}, see Algorithm 1.), times the maximum number of clients C. We divide client invocations in two categories, those that arrive at the reconciliation manager before $t^{\log}$ and those that arrive after $t^{\log}$.

$$T_{\text{H}} \leq \left([\text{pre-}t^{\log} \text{ messages}] + [\text{post-}t^{\log} \text{ messages}]\right) \cdot C \cdot d_{\text{han}}$$

The maximum time that it takes for a client invocation to be logged at M is equal to $2d_{\text{msg}} + d_{\text{act}}$, consisting of the transmission time from client to replica and the transmission time from replica to manager as well as the reaction time for the replica. The worst estimate of the number of post-$t^{\log}$ messages includes all invocations that were initiated at a client prior to $t^{\log}$ and logged at M after $t^{\log}$. Thus the interval of $2d_{\text{msg}} + d_{\text{act}}$ must be added to the interval over which client invocations are counted.

$$T_{\text{H}} \leq \left(\frac{T_{\text{D}} + d_{\text{msg}} + T_{\text{I}}}{d_{\text{inv}}} + \frac{T_{\text{H}} + 2d_{\text{msg}} + d_{\text{act}}}{d_{\text{inv}}}\right) \cdot C \cdot d_{\text{han}} \tag{2}$$

using earlier constraint for T_I in (1). Finally, together with the assumption in the theorem we can simplify the expression as follows:

$$T_\mathrm{H} \leq \frac{T_\mathrm{D} + 5d_\mathrm{msg} + 2d_\mathrm{act}}{q - 1} \tag{3}$$

Ending: According to the model of reconciliation manager M an empty *opset* results in the sending of a stop message within d_act. Upon receiving the message at every replica (within d_msg), the replica acknowledges the stop message within d_act. The the new partition can be installed as soon as all acknowledge messages are received (within d_msg) but at the latest within d_act. Hence T_E can be constrained as follows:

$$T_\mathrm{E} = t^\mathrm{inst} - t^e \leq 3d_\mathrm{act} + 2d_\mathrm{msg} \tag{4}$$

Final step: Now we need to show that $d_\mathrm{msg} + T_\mathrm{I} + T_\mathrm{H} + T_\mathrm{E}$ is less than T_F (time to next partition according to N5). From (1), (3), and (4) we have that:

$$T_\mathrm{I} + T_\mathrm{H} + T_\mathrm{E} \leq 2d_\mathrm{msg} + d_\mathrm{act} + \frac{T_\mathrm{D} + 5d_\mathrm{msg} + 2d_\mathrm{act}}{q - 1} + 3d_\mathrm{act} + 2d_\mathrm{msg}$$

Given a bound d on delays d_act and d_msg we have:

$$d_\mathrm{msg} + T_\mathrm{I} + T_\mathrm{H} + T_\mathrm{E} \leq \frac{T_\mathrm{D} + 7d}{q - 1} + 9d$$

Which concludes the proof according to theorem assumptions.   □

6.3   Correctness

As mentioned in Sect. 3.3 the main requirement on the reconciliation protocol is to preserve consistency. The model of the replicas obviously keeps the partition state consistent (see the action under $receive(\langle\text{"invoke"}, \alpha\rangle)_{cr}$. The proof of correctness is therefore about the manager M withholding this consistency during reconciliation, and specially when replaying actions. Before we go on to the main theorem on correctness we present a theorem that shows the ordering requirements of the application (induced by client actions) are respected by our models.

Theorem 2. *Let the system consist of the model of replicas, and the model of reconciliation manager. Assume the conditions described in Sect. 6.1. Define the set ttraces(Order) as the set of all action sequences with monotonically increasing times with the following property: for any sequence $\sigma \in$ ttraces(Order), if $(handle(\langle\alpha\rangle), t)$ and $(handle(\langle\beta\rangle), t')$ is in σ, $\alpha \rightarrow \beta$, and there is no $(partition(g), t'')$ between the two handle actions, then $t < t'$. All admissible timed traces of the system are in the set ttraces(Order).*

Proof. We assume $\alpha \to \beta$, and take an arbitrary timed trace γ belonging to admissible timed traces of the system such that $(handle(\alpha), t)$ and $(handle(\beta), t')$ appear in γ and no partition occurs in between them. We are going to show that $t < t'$, thus γ belongs to $ttraces(Order)$. The proof strategy is to assume $t' < t$ and prove contradiction.

By the precondition of $(handle(\beta), t')$ we know that α cannot be in the *opset* at time t' (see the **Internal** action in M). Moreover, we know that α must be in *opset* at time t because $(handle(\alpha), t)$ requires it. Thus, α must be added to *opset* between these two time points and the only action that can add operations to this set is $receive(\langle ``log'', \ldots \rangle)_{rM}$. Hence there is a time point $t^l$ at which $(receive(\langle ``log'', \langle \ldots, \alpha, \ldots \rangle \rangle))_{rM}, t^l)$ appears in γ and

$$t' < t^l < t \tag{5}$$

Next consider a sequence of actions that must all be in γ with $t^0 < t^1 < \ldots < t_8 < t'$.

1. $(handle((\beta), t')$
2. $(receive(\langle ``log'', \langle \ldots, \beta, \ldots \rangle \rangle), t_8)_{r_1 M}$ for some r_1
3. $(send(\langle ``log'', \langle \ldots, \beta, \ldots \rangle \rangle), t_7)_{r_1 M}$
4. $(receive(\langle ``invoke'', \beta \rangle, t_6)_{cr_1}$ for some c
5. $(send(\langle ``invoke'', \beta \rangle, t_5)_{cr_1}$
6. $(receive(\langle ``reply'', \alpha \rangle, t_4)_{cr_2}$ for some r_2
7. $(send(\langle ``reply'', \alpha \rangle, t_3)_{r_2 c}$
8. $(receive(\langle ``logAck'', \langle \ldots, \alpha, \ldots \rangle \rangle, t_2)_{Mr_2}$
9. $(send(\langle ``logAck'', \langle \ldots, \alpha, \ldots \rangle \rangle, t_1)_{Mr_2}$
10. $(receive(\langle ``log'', \langle \ldots, \alpha, \ldots \rangle \rangle, t^0)_{r_2 M}$

We show that the presence of each of these actions requires the presence of the next action in the list above (which is preceding in time).

- $(1 \Rightarrow 2)$ is given by the fact that β must be in *opset* and that $(receive(\langle ``log'', \langle \ldots, \beta, \ldots \rangle \rangle), t_8)_{r_1 M}$ is the only action that adds operations to *opset*.
- $(2 \Rightarrow 3)$, $(4 \Rightarrow 5)$, $(6 \Rightarrow 7)$ and $(8 \Rightarrow 9)$ are guaranteed by the network (N1).
- $(3 \Rightarrow 4)$ is guaranteed since β being in $L = \langle \ldots, \beta, \ldots \rangle$ at r_1 implies that some earlier action has added β to L and $(receive(\langle ``invoke'', \beta \rangle, t_6)_{cr_1}$ is the only action that adds elements to L at r_1.
- $(5 \Rightarrow 6)$ is guaranteed by C3 together with the fact that $\alpha \to \beta$.
- $(7 \Rightarrow 8)$ Due to 7 α must be in *toReply* at r_2 at time t^3. There are two actions that set *toReply*: one under the normal/degraded mode, and one upon receiving a *logAck* message from the manager M.

  First, we show that r_2 cannot be added to *toReply* as a result of $receive(\langle ''invoke'', \alpha \rangle)_{cr_2}$ in normal mode. Since α is being replayed by the manager $((handle(\alpha), t)$ appears in γ) then there must be a partition between applying α and replaying α. However, no operation that is applied in normal mode will reach the reconciliation process M as we have assumed

(A2) that the replica logs are empty at the time of a partition. And since α belongs to *opset* in M at time t, it cannot have been applied during normal mode.

Second, we show that r_2 cannot be added to *toReply* as a result of $receive(\langle "invoke", \alpha \rangle)_{cr_2}$ in degraded mode. If α was added to *toReply* in degraded mode then the log in the partition to which r_2 belongs would be received by M shortly after reunification (that precedes handle operations). But we have earlier established that $\alpha \notin opset$ at t', and hence α cannot have been applied in degraded mode. Thus α is added to *toReply* as a result of a *logAck* action and ($7 \Rightarrow 8$).

- ($9 \Rightarrow 10$) is guaranteed since α must be in $ackset[r_2]$ and it can only be put there by $(receive(\langle "log", \langle \ldots, \alpha, \ldots \rangle \rangle, t^0)_{r_2 M}$

We have in (5) established that the received log message that includes α appeared in γ at time point t^l, $t' < t^l$. This contradicts that $t^0 = t^l < t'$, and concludes the proof.   □

Theorem 3. *Let the set ttraces(Correct) be the set of action sequences with monotonically increasing times such that if $(broadcast(\langle "install", P \rangle))_M, t^{inst})$ is in the sequence, then P is consistent according to Definition 8. All admissible timed executions of the system are in the set ttraces(Correct).*

Proof. Consider an arbitrary element σ in the set of admissible timed system traces. We will show that σ is a member of the set *ttraces(Correct)*. The strategy of the proof is to analyse the subtraces of σ that correspond to actions of each component of the system. In particular, the sequence corresponding to actions in the reconciliation manager M will be of interest.

Let γ be the sequence that contains all actions of σ that are also actions of the reconciliation manager M ($\gamma = \sigma | M$). It is trivial that for all processes $C \neq M$ it holds that $\sigma | C \in ttraces(Correct)$ as there are no install messages broadcasted by any other process. Therefore, if we show that γ is a member of *ttraces(Correct)* then σ will also be a member of *ttraces(Correct)*.

We will proceed to show that γ is a member of *ttraces(Correct)* by performing induction on the number of actions in γ.

Base case: Let P be the partition state before the first action in γ. The model of the reconciliation manager M initialises P to $\{(\langle \rangle, s_1^0, s_1^0), \ldots, (\langle \rangle, s_n^0, s_n^0)\}$. Therefore, requirements 1,2 and 4 of Definition 8 are vacuously true and 3 is given by A1.

Inductive step: Assume that the partition state resulting from action i in γ is consistent. We will then show that the partition state resulting from action $i+1$ in γ is consistent. It is clear that the model of the reconciliation manager M does not affect the partition state except when actions $reunify(g)_M$ and $handle(\alpha)$ are taken. Thus, no other actions need to be considered. We show that reunify and handle preserve consistency of the partition state.

The action $(reunify(g)_M, t)$ sets P to the initial value of P which has been shown to be consistent in the base case.

The action $(handle(\alpha), t)$ is the interesting action in terms of consistency for P. We will consider two cases based on whether applying α results in an inconsistent state or not. Let P^i be the partition state after action i has been taken.

(1) If $Apply(\alpha, P^i)$ is not constraint consistent then the if-statement in the action handle is false and the partition state will remain unchanged, and thus consistent after action $i + 1$ according to the inductive assumption.

(2) If $Apply(\alpha, P^i)$ is constraint consistent then the partition state P^{i+1} will be set to $Apply(\alpha, P^i)$. By the inductive assumption there exists a sequence L leading to P^i. We will show that the sequence $L' = L + \langle \alpha \rangle$ satisfies the requirements for P^{i+1} to be consistent.

Consider the conditions 1-4 in the definition of consistent partition (Def. 8).

1. By the definition of *Apply* we know that all replicas in P remain unchanged except one which we denote r. So for all replicas $\langle L_j, s_j^0, s_j \rangle \neq r$ we know that $\beta \in L_j \Rightarrow \beta \in L \Rightarrow \beta \in L'$. Moreover the new log of replica r will be the same as the old log with the addition of operation α. And since all elements of the old log for r are in L, they are also in L'. Finally, since α is in L' then all operations for the log of r leading to P^{i+1} is in L'.

2. Consider the last state $s^k = \langle s_1, \ldots, s_j, \ldots s_n \rangle$ where s_j is the state of the replica that will be changed by applying α. Let s_j' be the state of this replica in P^{i+1} which is the result of the transition $s_j \overset{\alpha}{\leadsto} s_j'$. By the inductive assumption we have that $s^0 \overset{\alpha_1}{\leadsto} \ldots \overset{\alpha_k}{\leadsto} s^k$. Then $s^0 \overset{\alpha_1}{\leadsto} \ldots \overset{\alpha_k}{\leadsto} s^k \overset{\alpha}{\leadsto} s^{k+1}$ where $s^{k+1} = \langle s_1, \ldots, s_i', \ldots s_n \rangle$ is a partition transition according to Definition 5.

3. By the inductive assumption we know that P^i is consistent and therefore $\forall j \leq k$ s^j is constraint consistent. Further since $Apply(\alpha, P^i)$ is constraint consistent according to (2), s^{k+1} is constraint consistent.

4. The order holds for L according to the inductive assumption. Let t be the point for $handle(\beta)$ in γ. For the order to hold for L' we need to show that $\alpha \not\rightarrow \beta$ for all operations β in L. Since β appears in L there must exist a $handle(\beta)$ at some time point t' in γ. Then according to Theorem 2 $\alpha \not\rightarrow \beta$ (since if $\alpha \rightarrow \beta$ then $t < t'$ and obviously $t < t'$).   □

7   Related Work

In this section we will discuss how the problem of reconciliation after network partitions has been dealt with in the literature. For more references on related topics there is an excellent survey on optimistic replication by Saito and Shapiro [7]. There is also an earlier survey discussing consistency in partitioned networks by Davidson et al. [8].

Gray et al. [9] address the problem of update everywhere and propose a solution based on a two-tier architecture and tentative operations. However, they do not target full network partitions but individual nodes that join and leave the system (which is a special case of partition). Bayou [10] is a distributed storage system that is adapted for mobile environments. It allows updates to occur in a

partitioned system. However, the system does not supply automatic reconciliation in case of conflicts but relies on an application handler to do this. This is
a common strategy for sorting out conflicts, but then the application writer has
to figure out how to solve them. Our approach is fully automatic and does not
require application interaction during the reconciliation process.

Some work has been done on partitionable systems where integrity constraints
are not considered, which simplifies reconciliation. Babaouglu et al. [11] present
a method for dealing with network partitions. They propose a solution that
provides primitives for dealing with shared state. They do not elaborate on
dealing with writes in all partitions except suggesting tentative writes that can
be undone if conflicts occur. Moser et al. [12] have designed a fault-tolerant
CORBA extension that is able to deal with node crashes as well as network
partitions. There is also a reconciliation scheme described in [13]. The idea is
to keep a primary for each object. The state of these primaries are transferred
to the secondaries on reunification. In addition, operations which are performed
on the secondaries during degraded mode are reapplied during the reconciliation
phase. This approach is not directly applicable with integrity constraints.

Most works on reconciliation algorithms dealing with constraints after network
partition focus on achieving a schedule that satisfies order constraints. Fekete et
al. [14] provide a formal specification of a replication scheme where the client can
specify explicit requirements on the order in which operations are to be executed.
This allows for a stronger requirement than the well-established causal ordering
[15]. Our concept of ordering is weaker than causal ordering, as it is limited to
one client's notion of an expected order of execution based on the replies that
the client has received. Lippe et al. [16] try to order operation logs to avoid
conflicts with respect to a *before* relation. However, their algorithm requires
a large set of operation sequences to be enumerated and then compared. The
IceCube system [17,18] also tries to order operations to achieve a consistent final
state. However, they do not fully address the problem of integrity constraints
that involve several objects. Phatak et al. [19] propose an algorithm that provides
reconciliation by either using multiversioning to achieve snapshot isolation [20]
or using a reconciliation function given by the client. Snapshot isolation is more
pessimistic than our approach and would require a lot of operations to be undone.

8 Conclusions and Future Work

We have investigated a reconciliation mechanism designed to bring a system
that is inconsistent due to a network partition back to a consistent state. As the
reconciliation process might take a considerable amount of time it is desirable
to accept invocations during this period.

We have introduced an order relation that forces the reconciliation protocol
to uphold virtual partitions in which incoming operations can be executed. The
incoming operations cannot be executed on the state that is being constructed.
Since the protocol would then have to discard all the operations that the client
expects to have been performed. However, maintaining virtual partitions during

reconciliation will make the set of operations to reconcile larger. Thus, there is a risk that the reconciliation process never ends.

We have proved that the proposed protocol will indeed result in a stable partition state given certain timing assumptions. In particular, we need time bounds for message delays and execution time as well as an upper bound on client invocation rate. Moreover, we have proved that the result of the reconciliation is correct based on a correctness property that covers integrity consistency and ordering of operations.

The current work has not treated the use of network resources by the protocol and has not characterised the middleware overheads. These are interesting directions for future work. Performing simulation studies would show how much higher availability is dependent on various system parameters, including the mix of critical and non-critical operations. Another interesting study would be to compare the performance with a simulation of a majority partition implementation.

An ongoing project involves implementation of replication and our reconciliation services on top of a number of well-known middlewares, including CORBA [3]. This will allow evaluation of middleware overhead in this context, and a measure of enhanced availability compared to the scenario where no service is available during partitions.

References

1. Szentivanyi, D., Nadjm-Tehrani, S.: Middleware Support for Fault Tolerance. In: Middleware for Communications. John Wiley & Sons (2004)
2. Felber, P., Narasimhan, P.: Experiences, strategies, and challenges in building fault-tolerant corba systems. IEEE Trans. Comput. **53**(5) (2004) 497–511
3. DeDiSys: European IST FP6 DeDiSys Project. http://www.dedisys.org (2006)
4. Asplund, M., Nadjm-Tehrani, S.: Post-partition reconciliation protocols for maintaining consistency. In: Proceedings of the 21st ACM/SIGAPP symposium on Applied computing. (2006)
5. Szentivanyi, D., Nadjm-Tehrani, S., Noble, J.M.: Optimal choice of checkpointing interval for high availability. In: Proceedings of the 11th Pacific Rim Dependable Computing Conference, IEEE Computer Society (2005)
6. Spread: The Spread Toolkit. http://www.spread.org (2006)
7. Saito, Y., Shapiro, M.: Optimistic replication. ACM Comput. Surv. **37**(1) (2005) 42–81
8. Davidson, S.B., Garcia-Molina, H., Skeen, D.: Consistency in a partitioned network: a survey. ACM Comput. Surv. **17**(3) (1985) 341–370
9. Gray, J., Helland, P., O'Neil, P., Shasha, D.: The dangers of replication and a solution. In: SIGMOD '96: Proceedings of the 1996 ACM SIGMOD international conference on Management of data, New York, NY, USA, ACM Press (1996) 173–182
10. Terry, D.B., Theimer, M.M., Petersen, K., Demers, A.J., Spreitzer, M.J., Hauser, C.H.: Managing update conflicts in bayou, a weakly connected replicated storage system. In: SOSP '95: Proceedings of the fifteenth ACM symposium on Operating systems principles, New York, NY, USA, ACM Press (1995) 172–182
11. Babaoglu, Ö., Bartoli, A., Dini, G.: Enriched view synchrony: A programming paradigm for partitionable asynchronous distributed systems. IEEE Trans. Comput. **46**(6) (1997) 642–658

12. Moser, L.E., Melliar-Smith, P.M., Narasimhan, P.: Consistent object replication in the eternal system. Theor. Pract. Object Syst. **4**(2) (1998) 81–92
13. Narasimhan, P., Moser, L.E., Melliar-Smith, P.M.: Replica consistency of corba objects in partitionable distributed systems. Distributed Systems Engineering **4**(3) (1997) 139–150
14. Fekete, A., Gupta, D., Luchangco, V., Lynch, N., Shvartsman, A.: Eventually-serializable data services. In: PODC '96: Proceedings of the fifteenth annual ACM symposium on Principles of distributed computing, New York, NY, USA, ACM Press (1996) 300–309
15. Lamport, L.: Time, clocks, and the ordering of events in a distributed system. Commun. ACM **21**(7) (1978) 558–565
16. Lippe, E., van Oosterom, N.: Operation-based merging. In: SDE 5: Proceedings of the fifth ACM SIGSOFT symposium on Software development environments, New York, NY, USA, ACM Press (1992) 78–87
17. Kermarrec, A.M., Rowstron, A., Shapiro, M., Druschel, P.: The icecube approach to the reconciliation of divergent replicas. In: PODC '01: Proceedings of the twentieth annual ACM symposium on Principles of distributed computing, New York, NY, USA, ACM Press (2001) 210–218
18. Preguica, N., Shapiro, M., Matheson, C.: Semantics-based reconciliation for collaborative and mobile environments. Lecture Notes in Computer Science **2888** (2003) 38–55
19. Phatak, S.H., Nath, B.: Transaction-centric reconciliation in disconnected client-server databases. Mob. Netw. Appl. **9**(5) (2004) 459–471
20. Berenson, H., Bernstein, P., Gray, J., Melton, J., O'Neil, E., O'Neil, P.: A critique of ansi sql isolation levels. In: SIGMOD '95: Proceedings of the 1995 ACM SIGMOD international conference on Management of data, New York, NY, USA, ACM Press (1995) 1–10

The Fault-Tolerant Insulin Pump Therapy

Alfredo Capozucca, Nicolas Guelfi, and Patrizio Pelliccione

Laboratory for Advanced Software Systems
University of Luxembourg
6, rue Richard Coudenhove-Kalergi
Luxembourg, L-1359 -Luxembourg
{alfredo.capozucca, nicolas.guelfi, patrizio.pelliccione}@uni.lu

Abstract. The "Fault-Tolerant Insulin Pump Therapy" is based on the Continuous Subcutaneous Insulin Injection technique which combines devices (a sensor and a pump) and software in order to make glucose sensing and insulin delivery automatic. These devices are not physically connected together and they come with the necessary features to detect malfunctions which they may have.

As the patient's health is the most important, the therapy has to be able to work despite the fact that hardware and/or software faults have or may ocurr.

This paper presents the development cycle for the Insulin Pump Therapy Control System case study, starting from requirements and reaching the implementation following a top-down approach. It will show how the Coordinated Atomic Actions (CAAs) structuring mechanism can be used for modelling Faul-Tolerant (FT) systems and how CAA-DRIP development environment is used to implement it.

1 Introduction

Software and hardware systems are being used increasingly in many sectors, such as manufacturing, aerospace, transportation, communication, energy and health-care. Failures due to software or hardware malfunctions and malicious intentions can not only have economic consequences, but can also endanger human life. In fact, if a health care system breaks down, the consequences for hospitals and patients could be huge. Dependability is vital in health care systems which must be available around the clock without exception.

One of the techiques used to achieve dependable systems is fault tolerance. This technique seeks to preserve the delivery of correct service even in the presence of active faults. It is implemented by error detection and subsequent system recovery. In the context of fault tolerance and distributed systems, a promising technique emerged in recent years named Coordinated Atomic Actions (CAAs) [14] is used to coordinate complex concurrent activities and support error recovery between multiple interacting objects. By using CAAs for designing and structuring these kinds of systems the necessary requirements of reliability and availability are met.

M. Butler et al. (Eds.): Fault-Tolerant Systems, LNCS 4157, pp. 59–79, 2006.
© Springer-Verlag Berlin Heidelberg 2006

The aim of this paper is to show how CAAs can be used successfully to design medical software with reliability and availability requirements. The code generation is delegated to the CAA-DRIP framework [4], which embodies CAAs in terms of a set of Java classes. The case study concerns a diabetes control system which aims at delivering insulin to patients in the correct manner. A tiny sensor checks the patient's status and a pump administers the insulin. Doctors have to set some parameters on the pump which are used by the software embedded on it. It is of primary importance, for the patient's health, that the whole application works properly 24 hours a day without interruption.

The case study is described following the *WRSPM* reference model [9]. It is a general methodology wich introduces the use of formal languages (no one in particular) early in the development software process. In particular, this methodology advocates a careful and explicit description of the environment that is independent of the presence and operations of the system to be constructed. Therefore W, the *world* or *domain knowledge*, has to provide presumed facts about the operational domain where the system to be built will be embedded. The other parts composing the methodology are: *requirements (R)*, which indicate what users need; *specifications (S)* which provide enough information for a programmer to build a system to satisfy the requirements, and *program (P)* which implements the specifications on the *Machine (M)*. W, R and S are described using formal languages.

The paper is organized as follows. In Section 2, some background information on the methodology, followed in order to reach the system specification, and details on the CAAs structuring mechanism are given. In Section 3, the CAA-DRIP framework will be presented, which provides support to implement specifications described in terms of CAAs. Section 4 provides a detailed description of the domain application (introducing basic terminology), requirements, specification, design and implementation of the considered case study. Finally, Section 5 will provide some conclusions and ongoing work.

2   WRSPM Methodology and Coordinated Atomic Actions (CAAs)

Software engineering methodology is aimed at guiding software system developers from user-level requirements until the code generation and execution. The WRSPM methodology does exactly that by putting special emphasis on the use of formal languages in order to capture the requirements as well as to describe the assumptions about the application domain.

The WRSPM methodology consists of five artifacts. W, the world, represents the presumed facts about the environment (domain knowledge) where the program P will be embedded. This program P will be running on a programming platform M and it has to satisfy the requirements R. S is the specification that provides enough information to programmers to build the program P.

To describe the application domain a primitive vocabulary, called *designate terminology*, needs to be available. It provides the terms used to described W,

R and S, and an informal explanation of their meaning to clarify the role that these terms may play. The designated terminology of the case study presented here can be found in the *Appendix* at the end of the paper.

The specification S is the intersection between the *system* (S,P,M) and its *environment* (W,R,S). The overlapping of these groups means that S lies in the common vocabulary of the environment and the system but, thanks to the domain knowledge W, S still has enough information to meet the requirements R. Since WRSPM does not impose a specific formal notation, statecharts [6] are used (with semantics as implemented in the STATEMATE system [10]) as the formal language for writing the descriptions.

In this paper, the purpose of using WRSPM methodology is to reach a specification (S) which, under the assumptions and constraints imposed by the "world" (or "domain knowledge") (W), is able to meet the requirements (R). Therefore, WRSPM is followed until the specification S is defined. Once S is determined, a new description of the system in terms of CAAs will be provided in order to meet the requirements of dependability, in particular, reliabilty, in spite of faults coming from the environment (external faults) and internal dormant faults which may be activated.

Coordinated Atomic Actions (CAAs) is a fault tolerance mechanism that uses concurrent exception handling to achieve dependability in distributed and concurrent systems. Thus, by using CAAs, systems that comply with their specification in spite of faults can be developed.

This mechanism unifies the features of two complementary concepts: *conversation* and *transaction*. Conversation [13] is a fault tolerance technique for performing coordinated recovery in a set of participants that have been designed to interact with each other in order to provide a specific service (cooperative concurrency). Objects that are used to achieve the cooperation among the participants are called **shared** objects. Transactions are used in order to deal with competitive concurrency on objects that have been designed and implemented separately from the applications that make use of them. These kinds of objects are referred to as **external** objects.

One CAA characterises an orchestration of actions executed by a group of roles that exchange information among them, and/or access to external objects (concurrently with others CAAs) to achieve a common goal. The CAA starts when all its roles have been activated and a pre-condition has been met. The CAA finishes when all of them have reached the CAA end and a post-condition is met. This behaviour returns a **normal** outcome to the enclosing context.

If for any reason an exception has been raised in at least one of the roles belonging to the CAA, appropriate recovery measures have to be taken. In that regard, a CAA provides quite a general solution for fault tolerance based on exception handling. It consists of applying both forward error recovery (FER) and backward error recovery (BER) techniques.

Basically, the CAA exception handling semantics says that once an exception has been raised the FER mechanism has to be started. At that point, the CAA can finish normally if the FER can meet the original request (**normal** outcome) or exceptionally if the original request is partially satisfied (**exceptional** outcome). Otherwise, if the same or another exception is raised during the FER, the FER mechanism is stopped and the BER is started. The BER's main task is to recover every external object to its last consistent state (roll back). If the BER is successful, the CAA returns the **abort** outcome. If for any reason the BER cannot be completed, then the CAA has failed and the **failure** outcome is signaled to the enclosing context.

Every external object that is accessed in a CAA must be able to be restored to its last consistent state (if BER is activated) and provide its own error recovery mechanism [15]. Therefore, when the BER takes place, it restores these external objects using their own recovery mechanisms. However, sometimes the designer/programmer might want to use an external object that does not provide any recovery mechanism (due to reasons of cost or physical constraints [2]). Therefore it would be necessary to allow designers/programmers to specify/implement a hand-made roll back inside the CAA. This can be achieved by refining the classic BER to deal with external objects that are restored using their own mechanism (called *AutoRecoverable* external objects) and also to deal with those that have to be restored by a hand-made roll back (called *ManuallyRecoverable*)

3   The CAA-DRIP Implementation Framework

A set of *Java* [1] classes and interfaces called CAA-DRIP has been defined using the DRIP framework [16] as a starting point. CAA-DRIP allows us to implement the CAAs concepts and behaviour described in Section 2 in a straightforward manner.

The core of this implementation framework is composed of *Manager, Role, Handler* and *Compensator* classes. The *Manager* class is the controller for *Role, Handler* and *Compensator* classes. Then, each role, handler and compensator object created is managed by a manager object. There is not a class to represent a CAA. It consists of a set of managers, roles, handlers and compensators linked together via a *leader* manager. This *leader* manager is one of the manager objects used to manage a role, handler and compensator. The *leader* manager is the responsible for synchronising roles upon entry and upon exit as well as handlers and compensators, in case the recovery process must take place.

Extending the CAA-DRIP framework classes
Some of the classes that are provided by CAA-DRIP implementation framework have to be extended by programmers. That is the case for *Role, Handler* and *Compensator* classes.

The definition of a role is made by creating a new class that extends the *Role* class. The programmer has to re-implement the *body* method. This method receives a list of external objects as input parameter and it does not return any value. The defined operations inside this method are executed by the participant which activated the role.

The other methods that have also to be redefined by the programmer are *preCondition* and *postCondition*. They return a *boolean* value and are used as guard and assertion of the role, respectively.

Once role classes have been created, it is necessary to define a handler for each CAA role in order to deal with exceptions (in this context, an exception means that a fault has been activated). This step is made by creating a new class that extends the *Handler* class. The programmer has to re-implement the *body* and the *postCondition* methods.

If the raised exception cannot be handled by FER, then the CAA has to undo all its effects on the external objects. This task is done by BER, which is composed of two phases, *Roll back* and *Compensation*. Compensation is used to execute specific tasks, in case there is at least one *external* object that needs manual recovery (see Section 2).

Compensation is achieved by defining a compensator for each CAA role. A compensator is made by creating a new class that extends the *Compensator* class. The *recovery* method has to be re-implemented by the programmer. This method receives, as input parameter, a list with the external objects that need hand-made recovery. The method has to contain the operations to leave these external objects in a consistent state.

Instantiating a CAA

Once roles, handlers and compensators classes have been created, the programmer has to make use of them to create the CAA itself. As said, a CAA consists of a set of managers, roles, handlers and compensators linked together via a *leader* manager. Thus, *Manager* framework class is used to create the manager objects.

When a *Manager* object is created it has to be informed of its name and the name of the CAA. Once the managers have been created it is necessary to create the role objects. Each role upon creation is informed of its name, which manager will be its controller and the manager that will act as the *leader*.

Each handler upon creation needs to know its name and the manager that will control this handler. The link between the exception to handle and each handler is implemented by a hash-table which has as key the exception and as value the handler object. The method *setExceptionAndHandlerList* is used to inform the manager about the relationships *exception-handler* that have been set before.

If the CAA has to handle manually recoverable objects (see Section 2), a compensator has to be created also. Then, analogously to a handler creation, each compensator upon creation is informed of its name and the manager that will drive its execution.

Executing a CAA

How classes are instantiated to create a CAA has been just shown. Now how these objects behave when the CAA is activated has to be explained. The CAA activation process begins when each participant starts the role that it wants to play. The *execute* method (belonging to the *Role* class) has to be used by a participant to start playing a role. When the *execute* method is called, the role passes the control to its manager.

The first activity a manager executes is to synchronise itself with all other managers that are taking place in the CAA. This is done by calling the *syncBegin* method. Remember that there is a leader manager which is responsible for this task. This method blocks until the *leader* determines that all the managers have synchronised and the CAA is ready to begin. Once the *syncBegin* method returns, the manager checks if the pre-condition of the role is valid.

The *preCondition* method receives all the external objects that will be passed to the role managed by this manager as parameters. If the pre-condition is not satisfied, then a *PreConditionException* will be thrown and caught by the *catch(Exception e)* block. If the pre-condition is met, then the manager will execute the role that is under its control by calling the *bodyExecute* method of the *Role* object.

After the role has finished its execution, the manager synchronises with all the other managers before testing its post-condition. If the post-conditions are satisfied, then the manager will synchronise with all the other managers and the CAA will finish successfully.

A *catch* block will be executed if an exception takes place during the execution of any role belonging to the CAA. In such situation, the role where the exception was raised notifies its manager. This manager passes the control to *leader* manager for interrupting[1] all the roles that have not raised an exception (exceptions can be raised concurrently). Once all the roles have been interrupted the *leader* executes an exception resolution algorithm to find a common exception[2] from those that have been raised.

When such an exception is found, the *leader* informs all managers about that exception and FER (for the found exception) is activated. If every handler completes its execution and the CAA post-condition has been satisfied, then the CAA can finish.

Now, if the exception resolution algorithm could not find a common exception, or other exceptions were raised in the FER (even *PostConditionException* exception could be possible if FER did not satisfy the post-condition), then the BER mechanism will be started.

BER calls *restoreExecution* method. This method uses the compensators objects, if any, to undo the CAA effects. Once this method has executed, the CAA finishs returnig *Abort*. If for any reason the BER process could not complete its execution, CAA will be finished returning *Failure*.

More details about CAA-DRIP implementation framework can be found in [4].

---

[1] Notice that a role will be interrupted in our framework only if the role is ready to be interrupted, i.e. the role is in a state that it can be interrupted.

[2] In the worst case, the common exception is *Exception*.

4   The Fault-Tolerant Insulin Pump (FTIP) Control System Case Study

In this section WRSPM methodology is used to describe the case study in details. Once the FTIP control system specification is reached, a new specification in terms of CAAs is introduced to improve the reliability of the control system.

4.1   The World (W): Regulation of Blood Glucose in a Non Diabetic and a Diabetic Person

According to WRSPM methodology it is essential to provide a careful and explicit description of the domain, which in this case corresponds to medical software systems for treatment of diabetes.

Normally, blood glucose (blood sugar) is maintained in a narrow range [8]. The hormones which assure this are insulin and glucagons. Both of them are secreted by the pancreas. If the blood glucose level is too low then the pancreas secretes glucagons. If the blood glucose level is too high then the pancreas secretes insulin.

Diabetes Mellitus [12,7] is an illness whereby the level of glucose in the blood is abnormally high. This can be caused by either an absolute deficiency of insulin secretion, or as a result of reduced effectiveness of insulin, or both. Therefore, our first approach in the domain is to understand how the body of a non diabetic person regulates increases in the glucose level. Figure 1 describes how the body reduces the glucose level when it is higher than normal.

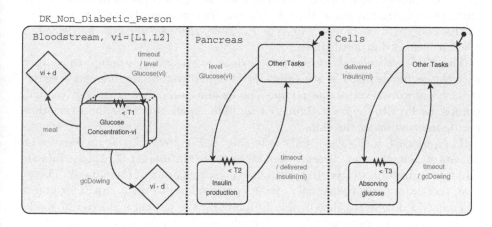

Fig. 1. Regulation of Blood Glucose in a non diabetic person

In a diabetic person this process does not succeed because of the lack of insulin secretion by the pancreas (event *deliverdInsulin(m$_i$)* is not present). Therefore, a diabetic person must make use of a insulin therapy to fulfil the process as in a normal person.

4.2   The Requirement (R)

Another artifact which has to be provided under WRSPM is *Requirements*, which is indication of what users need. The range of glucose in the blood of a person should be between **70 mg/dl and 110 mg/dl** (mg/dl means milligrams of glucose in 100 milliliters of blood). Therefore, the functional requirement which needs to be met for any diabetes therapy is that the glucose level be kept below of 110 mg/dl. Figure 2 describes this requirement formally (**T1** represents the time that the body takes to update the glucose concentrations in the bloodstream.)

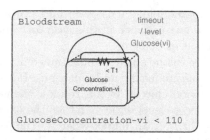

Fig. 2. The main requirement

4.3   The World (W): The Devices

The Continuous subcutaneous insulin infusion is typically called **insulin pump therapy** [12]. Insulin pump therapy is a way of continuously delivering insulin to the body at a controlled rate. For example, more insulin can be delivered when it is needed at meal times.

The FTIP control system uses two devices, a sensor and a pump, to comply with the requirements. The sensor is a piece of hardware that communicates the patient's glucose level to the pump. The insulin pump is a small device that pumps insulin into the body through a cannula (small, thin tube) or a very thin needle inserted under the skin.

The proposal in this case study is to join and improve the characteristics of sensors and pumps that currently can be found in the market [7,11] to achieve a **close loop insulin delivering** without any participation of the patient. Therefore, the sensor sends the actual patient's glucose level to the pump. This pump has embedded software that is able to maintain the patient's glucose in a safe level by delivering necessary doses of insulin (basal rate) day and night. Obviously, this basal rate, can be easily increased or decreased to match the actual patient's needs that can change because of physical activities, illness or, simply as a meals has been taken.

Any interruption in insulin delivery (loss of insulin potency, or sensor/pump malfunction) may result in *hyperglycemia* (high blood glucose). Therefore, both the hardware (sensors and pumps) and specially the software which take place in this therapy have to be built with special techniques to achieve highly reliable and safety operation.

As these devices are part of the "world" where the software system is embedded, according to WRSPM, their behaviour have to be described precisely.

The sensor

The sensor is an adaptation of one provided by [11] for glucose monitoring. The tiny sensor used in FTIP has an integrated small transmitter which wirelessly and continually communicates the patient's glucose level to the pump. Every $T_{SensorValue}$ ($T_{SensorValueTimeout} = T_{s2} + T_{s1}$) units of time the sensor sends an updated glucose value. This sensor behaviour is formally described in Figure 3 and it is part of the "world" W where the FTIP takes place.

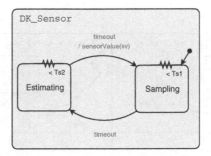

Fig. 3. Sensor behaviour description

The pump

The pump used by the FTIP control system is a fusion of two different pumps which can currently be found on the market [7,11], plus some special characteristics which have been added to allow it to work cooperatively with the sensor.

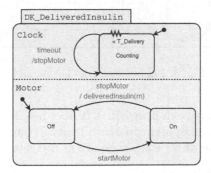

Fig. 4. Domain knowledge of the insulin delivering

The pump has an internal clock which provides the current time at any given moment. The FTIP control system starts the motor which is kept working for $T_{Delivery}$ units of time. The $T_{Delivery}$ value is defined by the control system according to the current patient's glucose value, which is sent by the sensor, and the individual settings defined by a doctor. The pump also contains a cartridge with fast-acting insulin which is supplied to the patient's body by a cannula that lies under the skin. The motor is connected to a piston rod which sends forward a plunger in order to deliver the insulin to the body.

Therefore, the necessary amount of insulin to keep the glucose at a safe level (**deliveredInsulin(m)** on Figure 1) is delivered as a result of the work of the motor. The relationship between the times at which the motor is in operation and the amount of insulin delivered, which is part of the domain knowledge that is accepted as true to develop the FTIP control system, is formally described in Figure 4.

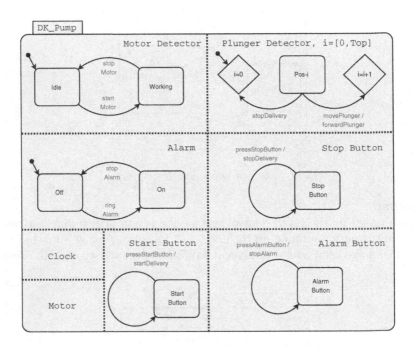

Fig. 5. Pump's elements behaviour

The plunger is built in such a way that it does not move unintentionally as a result of changes in atmospheric pressure. It moves only to its initial position (by pressing the **Stop** button) when the patient needs to fill the cartridge with fresh insulin.

The pump has also *infrared detectors* to check the correct movement of the plunger and the status of the motor. Both detectors help to determine whether the pump is delivering the insulin properly.

An alarm to alert the patient of abnormal situations is built-in to the pump. A button (**Alarm**) to allow the patient to switch it off when it rings and a button for starting the insulin delivery (**Start**) are also features of the pump.

Figure 5 shows how the physical elements which compose the pump behave. Their behaviour must be taken into consideration to specify the FTIP control system.

4.4   The Specification (S)

According to WRSPM methodology aspects introduced so far, a specification S has to be provide such as, S supplemented by the world W, must satisfy the requirements R. Formally, it means:

$$W\|S \Rightarrow R \text{ , where}$$
$$W = DK\_Sensor\|DK\_Pump\|DK\_Delived\|DK\_Diabetic\_Person$$

Meeting the requirements

To start receiving the insulin doses, the patient has to press *Start* button. Once this button has been pressed, FTIP control system starts its execution, which consists of performing repetitively a set of operations. This operations are spread over three processes running in parallel and cooperating each other. These processes are *Checking, Controller* and *Delivery*.

Checking is in charge of getting values from sensor device and to provide them to *Controller* process. Then, *Controller* uses these values to define how long the pump's motor has to work. The period of time in which the motor is working, according to the domain knowledge, represents the quantity of insulin that the patient needs. Once *Controller* process has defined how long the motor has to work, it sends this information to *Delivery* process. *Delivery* process uses this value to start and control the activity of the motor.

This sequence of steps defines a cyle that is executed repetitively to keep the patient's glucose level below 110 mg/dl (the requirement). While *Delivery* process is working with the pump's motor, *Checking* process is getting fresh values from the sensor to be used in the next loop of the cycle.

Safety

Because the insulin is delivered almost continuously, any interruption in the supplying may result in serious problems to the patient. Then, it is reasonable to make checks to ensure that the devices are working properly.

FTIP control system checks that each amount of insulin that has to be delivered does not drop out of the safe range programmed. The pump's detectors and the internal clock are used by the control system to check the correct movement of the plunger, to check the status of the motor and to check if the sensor is sending the values on time. Therefore, the control system is able to detect any of the following critical conditions:

- no values have been received from the sensor for the last T_{Sensor} units of time (**E1**),
- the current patient's glucose level is out of the safe range (**E2**),

  – the insulin that has to be delivered to keep the glucose in a safe level does
    not drop into the safe range programmed (**E3**),
  – the insulin is not being delivered properly by the pump (**E4**).

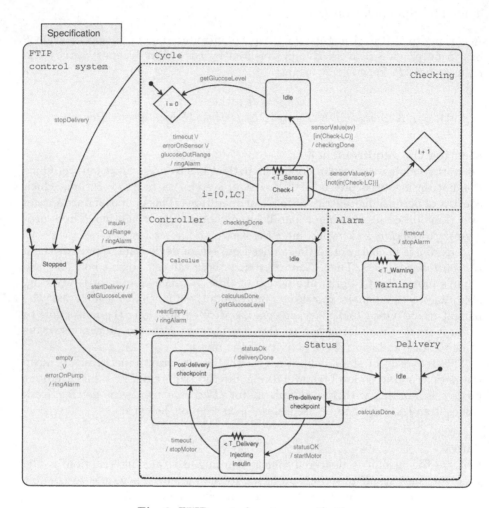

Fig. 6. FTIP control system specification

When, at least one of these critical conditions takes place, the control system
full stops the cycle execution and sounds the alarm to alert the patient about
the current situation. The alarm will remain ringing till the patient switches it
off. Instead, when the quantity of insulin in the cartridge is less than the *low
limit* parameter, the control system keeps executing the cycle and it rings the
alarm, as a warning, for only $T_{Warning}$ units of time.

Figure 6 shows the formal description of the aspects introduced before
concerning the functional requirement and safety.

For the moment nothing has been said about reliability, which is other of the atributes used to define dependability. Reliability is the ability of the system to keep on working in spite of unexpected circumstances (e.g. **E1,E2, E3, E4**). The next Section shows a new specification of the system in terms of CAAs in order to improve the reliabity of FTIP control system.

4.5   The Specification in Terms of CAAs

Both the specification presented in the previous section and the CAA conceptual framework, are used to reach a new specification to satisfy the requirements despite of the presence of potential faults. The reliabilty improvements concern *E1, E3* and *E4* critical conditions, which have been introduced in the previous section.

Instead of directly stop the control system execution if one of this critical conditions takes place, error recovery and redundancy have been added to tolerate *E1, E3* and *E4* critical conditions. In the following, details of how reliabilty has been met are shown.

- A possible reason why control system is not receiving values from the sensor (*E1*), could be because of it is being affected by an electronic "noise" that surrounds the patient. Usually, this type of problem represents a transient fault for its limited duration, so there is not need to stop the system. When the control system faces a situation as described before, a numerical method based on old received values is used to make an aproximation of the current glucose level. This alterative is used for the period that the sensor is not responding (forward error recovery). Nevertheless, if the sensor does not responde beyond of a such time limit, for safety reasons, the control system must stop its execution.
- Instead of rely on only one algorithm to define $T_{Delivery}$ (units of time that the motor has to work), **N-version programming** approach is used [3]. According to [2], *the semantics of N-version programming are as might be expected N-versions of a program (N > 1) which have been independently designed to satisfy a common specification is executed and their results compared by some form of replication check. Based on a majority vote, this check can eliminate erroneous results (**E3**) (i.e. the minority) and pass on the presumably correct results calculated by the majority to the rest of the system.*
- The infrared detectors are used in a combinated way to avoid false alarms. If really there is a problem on the plunger or the motor, then both detectors must report the abnormal situation (**E4**), since both devices are physically connected. Thus, the control system does not stop if only one detector reports a problem.

The new FTIP control system specification is described as a set of CAAs (Figure 7) that interact cooperatively among them to satisfy the functional requirement as well as those concenrnig safety and reliability.

The Cycle

CAA_Cycle is the outmost CAA. It is composed of four roles, *Sensor, Controller, Pump* and *Alarm* and its main task is to perform repetitively a set of operations: (1) getting current glucose level, (2) calculate $T_{Delivery}$, and (3) insulin delivering, which were described in the previous section.

The first step is carry out by *CAA_Checking*, the second step is done by *CAA_Calculus*. The last step is performed by *CAA_Delivery*.

Sensor, Pump and *Alarm* are the roles used to manage the access to the *SensorDev, MotorDev* and *AlarmDev* devices, respectively. The *Controller* role coordinates the others roles of *CAA_Cycle* to keep on executing these steps.

Once the *Controller* role has received the information from *CAA_Calculus*, the *CAA_Checking* and *CAA_Delivery* can be performed in parallel to improve the system performance. The *Controller* role synchronizes these CAAs in a way that it is always able to have the necessary information to perform the previous described steps.

The CAAs enclosed by *CAA_Cycle* were designed using **nesting** and **composing**.

Nesting

Nesting is defined as a subset of the roles that belong to the enclosing CAA (*CAA_Cycle*). These roles (*Sensor* and *Controller*) are the same roles that have been defined for *CAA_Cycle*, but they are used to define a new CAA (*CAA_Checking*). The operations that they are doing inside *CAA_Checking* are hidden for the other roles (*Pump* and *Alarm*) as well as for the others nested or composed CAAs that belong to *CAA_Cycle*. As said, *CAA_Checking* is in charge to carry out the first step and to handle **E1** and **E2** critical conditions.

If **E1** takes place, forward error recovery is applied to try to keep the control system running (reliability). In case that **E2** arrives or forward error recovery does not succeed for handling **E1**, the delivery of insulin has to be stopped (safety). It is achieved stopping the roles belonging to *CAA_Checking* and signaling an exception to the enclosing context (which is *CAA_Cycle*). When *CAA_Cycle* detects the exception, the control system is stopped and the alarm is rung to let the patient know about the abnormal situation.

Composing

Composing is different from nesting in the sense that CAAs can be used in other contexts. A composed CAA (*CAA_Calculus* and *CAA_Delivery*) is an autonomous entity with its own roles. The internal structure of a composed CAA (i.e., set of roles, accessed external objects and behaviour of roles) is hidden from the calling CAA (*CAA_Cycle*). For instance, when the role *Controller* which belongs to *CAA_Cycle* calls to the composed *CAA_Calculus* it synchronously waits for the outcome. The calling role, *Controller* in this case, resumes its execution according to the outcome of the composed *CAA_Calculus*. If the composed CAA (*CAA_Calculus*) terminates exceptionally, the calling role (*Controller*) raises an internal exception which is, if possible, locally handled. If local handling is not possible, the exception is propagated to all the peer roles of *CAA_Cycle* for coordinated error recovery.

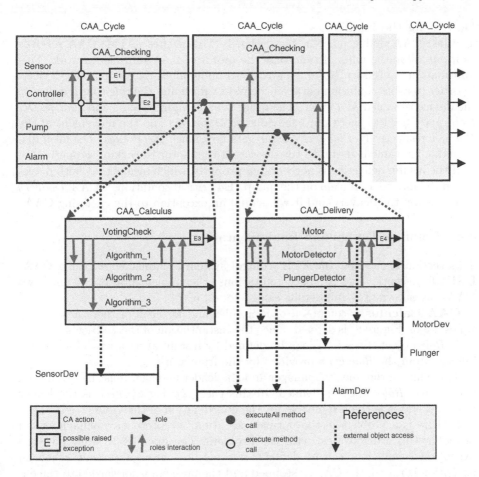

Fig. 7. CAA Design

N-version programming

CAA_Calculus has been specially defined to calculate $T_{Delivery}$ (step two). using N-version programming. The implementation of N-version programming requires a supervisor program (known as **driver program**) that is in charge for invoking each of the versions, waiting for the versions to complete their execution and comparing and taking a decision according to the N-results received. Even if the CAA technique was not thought to implement N-version programming, its features allow implementing this programming technique (N-version) easily. In this case, the *driver program* as well as each version of the algorithm used to calculate $T_{Delivery}$ has been implemented as roles belonging to *CAA_Calculus*. These roles are *VotingCheck*, which implements the driver program, and *Algorithm_1*, *Algorithm_2*, and *Algorithm_3*. Once the result has been defined by the majority, *VotingCheck* passes it to the enclosing CAA or, if the **E3** critical condition takes place, it will signal an exception.

Delivering the insulin

The last CAA taking place in the design is *CAA_Delivery*. This CAA receives as input value the units of time that the motor of the pump has to work. This information is used by *Motor* (the role) to manipulate the motor (the device). In order to avoid confusion between the motor itself and the role that handles it, the device is named *MotorDev*. The other roles (*MotorDetector* and *PlungerDetector*) are used to check the behaviour of *MotorDev* and the movement of the *Plunger* respectively. *PlungerDetector* gets how much the *Plunger* has been displaced. This value is useful to corroborate if the motor is working properly.

If the insulin delivering is not working properly, which means that both detectors have noticed a problem on the pump (**E4** critical conditions), *CAA_Delivery* will full stop the delivery and it will signal an exception to the enclosing CAA.

4.6   Detailed Design and Implementation

This section shows how the FTIP control system is implemented using CAA-DRIP framework. Due to space limitations, the implementation of only two CAAs are shown. The full details can be found in [5].

CAA_Calculus is composed of four roles and for each of them a *Manager* (lines 2-5 on Figure 8) is defined. Once the instantiation of these objects is done, each *Role* object (lines 8-15) can be defined by instantiating a new class, which inherits from the *Role* class provided by the framework.

The name of the role, its manager and the leader manager must be given each time a new *Role* object is defined. In this case, *mgrVotingCheck* is the leader manager and it is the responsible for the coordination of the CAA.

If there is a problem in the normal execution, an alternative behaviour can be defined in order to deal with the problem. The lines 18-37 show how the exceptional behaviour can be defined. If these lines are not present, when an exception is raised, the CAA is stopped and the problem is forwarded to the enclosing context. It means that the exception is signaled to the enclosing context.

The lines 18-21 correspond to the definition of the handlers that are only executed when the exception *E3* is raised. On Figure 7, error E3 represents the places where this exception could happen. Each defined handler object is an instance of a new class derived from *Handler* class, which belongs to the framework. For each exception that should be handled by the CAA, n handlers have to be defined, where n is the number of roles defined in the CAA. Each handler must be informed of its name and its manager.

The next step is the explicit definition of the binding between the considered exception, and the handlers that have been defined to manage it. Each binding is represented by a hash-table, which is controlled by a manager (lines 24-31). Each hash-table has to be set on the manager, which is controlling the handler (lines 34-37).

Each manager (e.g. *mgrVotingCheck*) coordinates the execution of a role (e.g. *roleVotingCheck*). The role represents the normal behaviour. In the case in which an exception is launched (*E3*), each manager stops the execution of its associated role and then it starts to execute its associated handler (e.g. *hndrE3_VC*).

CAA_Cycle is executed repeatedly until the patient stops manually the delivery (by pressing the *Stop* button) or a critical condition took place and it could not be handled. The *Controller* role works as a coordinator of the tasks that have to be carried out in *CAA_Cycle*. One of these tasks is to launch the composed *CAA_Calculus* that was described earlier.

```
1   //Managers
2   mgrVotingCheck = new ManagerImpl("mgrVotingCheck","CAA_Calculus");
3   mgrAlgorithm_1 = new ManagerImpl("mgrAlgorithm_1","CAA_Calculus");
4   mgrAlgorithm_2 = new ManagerImpl("mgrAlgorithm_2","CAA_Calculus");
5   mgrAlgorithm_3 = new ManagerImpl("mgrAlgorithm_3","CAA_Calculus");
6
7   //Roles
8   roleVotingCheck =
9       new VotingCheck("roleVotingCheck",mgrVotingCheck,mgrVotingCheck);
10  roleAlgorithm_1 =
11      new Algorithm_1("roleAlgorithm_1",mgrAlgorithm_1,mgrVotingCheck);
12  roleAlgorithm_2 =
13      new Algorithm_2("roleAlgorithm_2",mgrAlgorithm_2,mgrVotingCheck);
14  roleAlgorithm_3 =
15      new Algorithm_3("roleAlgorithm_3",mgrAlgorithm_3,mgrVotingCheck);
16
17  //Handlers for E3 exception
18  hndrE3_VC = new E3_VC("hndrE3_VC",mgrVotingCheck);
19  hndrE3_A1 = new E3_A1("hndrE3_A1",mgrAlgorithm_1);
20  hndrE3_A2 = new E3_A2("hndrE3_A2",mgrAlgorithm_2);
21  hndrE3_A3 = new E3_A3("hndrE3_A3",mgrAlgorithm_3);
22
23  //Binding between the Exception and the Handlers
24  Hashtable ehVC = new Hashtable();
25  ehVC.put(E3.class,hndrE3_VC);
26  Hashtable ehA1 = new Hashtable();
27  ehA1.put(E3.class,hndrE3_A1);
28  Hashtable ehA2 = new Hashtable();
29  ehA2.put(E3.class,hndrE3_A2);
30  Hashtable ehA3 = new Hashtable();
31  ehA3.put(E3.class,hndrE3_A3);
32
33  //Setting the binding on each Manager
34  mgrVotingCheck.setExceptionAndHandlerList(ehVC);
35  mgrAlgorithm_1.setExceptionAndHandlerList(ehA1);
36  mgrAlgorithm_2.setExceptionAndHandlerList(ehA2);
37  mgrAlgorithm_3.setExceptionAndHandlerList(ehA3);
```

Fig. 8. Definition of CAA_Calculus

The *Java* code in Figure 9 shows how the *body* method of the *Controller* role is implemented for the *CAA_Cycle*. The *Controller* role works as a coordinator of the tasks to be carried out in *CAA_Cycle*. One of these tasks is to launch the composed *CAA_Calculus* that was described earlier.

The first time that *CAA_Cycle* is called (lines 7-15) the *Controller* role starts to execute *CAA_Checking* (line 10) in order to get the information provided by the sensor. Once the role has got the information, it returns the value to the enclosing context (line 15). After *CAA_Cycle* has been executed once, the enclosing context is able to provide the *sv* value, which has been taken in the previous execution of *CAA_Cycle*. Thus, *Controller* role gets the *sv* value (line 18-19) and then passes it as an input parameter (line 23) to *CAA_Calculus*. The

CAA_Calculus execution (line 24) returns the period of time (*tDelivery* value) that the motor has to be working (line 26-27).

When the *tDelivery* value is known, it has to be passed to the *Pump* role (line 29). Next, the *Pump* role receives *tDelivery* and call *CAA_Delivery* to delivery the insulin. While *CAA_Delivery* is executing, *Controller* role launches *CAA_Checking* (line 33) to get information from the sensor that will be be used in the next iteration of *CAA_Cycle*.

When the information comming from *CAA_Checking* and *Pump* roles has been received (line 35-36 and 38 respectively), and passed to the enclosing context (lines 40 and 41), *Controller* role can finish its execution and pass the control to the enclosing context where *CAA_Cycle* is embedded.

```
1   public void body(ExternalObjects eos)
2     throws Exception, RemoteException {
3       try{
4         //Getting information from the enclosing context
5         Loop loop = (Loop)eos.getExternalObject("loop");
6         if(loop.isfirst()){
7           //launching nested CAA_Checking
8           ExternalObjects checking =
9                 new ExternalObjects("checking");
10          roleControllerChecking.execute(checking);
11          //getting outcome from CAA_Checking
12          SensorValue sv =
13                (SensorValue)checking.getExternalObject("sv");
14          //Sending information to the enclosing context
15          eos.setExternalObject("sv",sv);
16        }else{
17          //getting sensor value
18          SensorValue sv =
19                (SensorValue)eos.getExternalObject("sv");
20          //launching composed CAA_Calculus
21          ExternalObject calculusREOs =
22                new ExternalObjects("calculus");
23          calculus.setExternalObject("sv",sv);
24          roleVotingCheck.executeAll(calculus);
25          //getting outcome from CAA_Calculus
26          Time tDelivery =
27                (Time)calculus.getExternalObject("tDelivery");
28          //passing information to Pump role
29          pumpQueue.put(tDelivery);
30          //launching nested CAA_Checking
31          ExternalObject checking =
32                new ExternalObject("checking");
33          roleControllerChecking.execute(checking);
34          //getting outcome from CAA_Checking
35          SensorValue sv =
36                (SensorValue)checking.getExternalObject("sv");
37          //getting values from CAA_Delivery by Pump role
38          Status st = (Status)pumpQueue.get();
39          //Sending information to the enclosing context
40          eos.setExternalObject("sv",sv);
41          eos.setExternalObject("st",st);
42        }
43      }catch (Exception e) {
44        throw e; //Local handling for Controller exception;
45      }
46   }
```

Fig. 9. Body method of Controller class

5   Conclusions and Ongoing Work

In this paper a control system for a fault-tolerant insulin pump therapy has been described. In order to ensure the needed requirements of reliability, the system has been designed using the CAAs mechanism, which offers approaches for error recovery. The implementation of the control system has been made in Java, using an implementation framework called CAA-DRIP which fully supports the CAAs semantics. This work is part of the ongoing CORRECT project [5]. On the future work side, the plan is to apply the full CORRECT methodology, improving the design part and trying to automatically generate a skeleton code from the CAA design model, via transformation rules. Since it is usually impossible to generate a complete implementation, the expected result is to generate an implementation schema, with a set of classes and their methods and exceptions declaration. The role of a programmer will be then to write the body of the application methods, while the exception detection, resolution and propagation will be automatically managed by the other parts of the schema.

Acknowledgements. This work has benefited from a funding by the Luxembourg Ministry of Higher Education and Research under the project number MEN/IST/04/04. The authors gratefully acknowledge help from A. Campéas, B. Gallina, P. Periorellis, R. Razavi, A. Romanovsky and A. Zorzo.

References

1. Java 2 Platform, Standard Edition (J2SE). http://java.sun.com.
2. T. Anderson and P. Lee. Fault-tolerance: Principles and practice. *Prentice Hall*, 1981.
3. A. Avizienis. The n-version approach to fault-tolerant software. *IEEE Trans. Soft. Eng*, pages pp. 1491–1501, 1985.
4. A. Capozucca, N. Guelfi, P. Pelliccione, A. Romanovsky, and A. Zorzo. CAA-DRIP: a framework for implementing Coordinated Atomic Actions. *Laboratory for Advanced Software Systems Technical Report nr. TR-LASSY-06-05*, 2006.
5. Correct Web Page. http://lassy.uni.lu/correct, 2006.
6. David Harel. Statecharts: A visual formalism for complex systems. *Science of Computer Programming*, 8(3):231–274, June 1987.
7. DISETRONIC, A member of the Roche Group. www.disetronic.com.
8. Endocrine Disorders & Endocrine Surgery. *www.endocrineweb.com/insulin.html*.
9. C. A. Gunter, E. L. Gunter, M. Jackson, and P. Zave. A reference model for requirements and specifications. *IEEE Softw.*, 17(3):37–43, 2000.
10. D. Harel and A. Naamad. The statemate semantics of statecharts. *ACM Trans. Softw. Eng. Methodol.*, 5(4):293–333, 1996.
11. Medtronic. www.minimed.com.
12. National Institute for Health and Clinical Excellence. Guidance on the use of continuous subcutaneous insulin infusion for diabetes. *www.nice.org.uk*, (Technology Appraisal 57), February 2003.
13. B. Randell. System structure for software fault tolerance. *IEEE Transactions on Software Engineering. IEEE Press*, SE-1(2):220–232, 1975.

14. J. Xu, B. Randell, A. Romanovsky, C. M. Rubira, R. J. stroud, and Z. Wu. Fault Tolerance in Concurrent Object-Oriented Software through Coordinated Error Recovery. *Proceedings of the 25 International Symposium on Fault-Tolerant Computing*, pages 499–508, 1995.
15. J. Xu, B. Randell, A. B. Romanovsky, C. M. F. Rubira, R. J. Stroud, and Z. Wu. Fault tolerance in concurrent object-oriented software through coordinated error recovery. In *Symposium on Fault-Tolerant Computing*, pages 499–508, 1995.
16. A. F. Zorzo and R. J. Stroud. A distributed object-oriented framework for dependable multiparty interactions. In *OOPSLA '99: Proceedings of the 14th ACM SIGPLAN conference on Object-oriented programming, systems, languages, and applications*, pages 435–446. ACM Press, 1999.

Appendix: "Designated Terminology"

The World (W)

- *The body*
  - **L1** $\approx$ Lowest blood glucose concentration (in mg/dl) tolerated by a person (mg/dl means milligrams of glucose in 100 milliliters of blood) (**EC/U**).
  - **L2** $\approx$ Highest blood glucose concentration (in mg/dl) tolerated by a person (**EC/U**).
  - **d** $\approx$ positive value that represents the displacement of blood glucose concentration (**EC/U**).
  - **Meal** $\approx$ Carbohydrates (or sugars) which are absorbed from the intestines into the bloodstream after a meal (**EC/U**).
  - **gcDowing** $\approx$ the blood glucose level decreases (**EC/U**).
  - **T2** $\approx$ units of time required by the pancreas to produce insulin in order to decrease the detected blood glucose concentration (**EC/U**).
  - **deliveredInsulin**(m_i) $\approx$ **m** is the amount of insulin that has to be delivered to reach a normal level of glucose (**EC/U**).
  - **T3** $\approx$ units of time that the body's cells are absorbing glucose (**EC/U**).
- *The Sensor*
  - **sensorValue(sv)** $\approx$ **sv** is the blood glucose concentration detected by the sensor (**EC/S**).
  - **Ts1** $\approx$ units of time that the sensor is taking blood from the body (**EC/U**).
  - **Ts2** $\approx$ units of time required by the sensor to define the current (**sv**) blood glucose concentration (**EC/U**).
- *The Pump*
  - **startMotor** $\approx$ the motor is started (**MC/S**).
  - **stopMotor** $\approx$ the motor is stopped (**MC/S**).
  - **TOP** $\approx$ the plunger has reached its last position. It means that there is not insulin in the cartridge any more (**EC/S**).
  - **movePlunger** $\approx$ the plunger has moved one position forward (**EC/U**).
  - **forwardPlunger** $\approx$ the *plunger detector* has detected that the plunger moved one position forward (**EC/S**).

- **ringAlarm** ≈ sounds the alarm (**MC/S**).
- **stopAlarm** ≈ the alarm is stopped (**MC/S**).
- **pressStartButton** ≈ the patient presses the *Start* button (**EC/U**).
- **pressStopButton** ≈ the patient presses the *Stop* button (**EC/U**).
- **pressAlarmButton** ≈ the patient presses the *Alarm* button (**EC/U**).
- **startDelivery** ≈ the patient has pressed the *Start* button (**EC/S**).
- **stopDelivery** ≈ the patient has pressed the *Stop* button (**EC/S**).
- **stopAlarm** ≈ the patient has pressed the *Alarm* button (**EC/S**).

Requirements (R)

- **T1** ≈ units of time required by the body to update the blood glucose concentration (**EC/U**).
- **levelGlucose**(v_i) ≈ the blood glucose concentration in the body is vi (**EC/U**).

Specification (S)

- **LC** ≈ number of samples to take of the current patient's glucose level (**MC/U**).
- **getGlucoseLevel** ≈ the system asks to the sensor for number of samples to take of the current patient's glucose level (**MC/U**).
- $T_{Delivery}$ ≈ units of time that the motor will be working (**MC/S**).
- T_{Sensor} ≈ waiting limit time to get the current patient's glucose concentration from the sensor (**MC/U**).
- $T_{Warning}$ ≈ units of time that the alarm will be ringing to warn the patient about low insulin level in the cartridge (**MC/S**).
- **calculusDone** ≈ the FTIP system finds out the period of time that the motor has to work in order to supply the insulin into the patient (**MC/U**).
- **statusOk** ≈ the motor and the plunger have passed the checks made by the the FTIP system (**MC/U**).
- **errorOnSensor** ≈ malfunction detection on the sensor (**EC/S**).
- **errorOnPump** ≈ malfunction detection on the pump (**EC/S**).
- **glucoseOutRange** ≈ level of glucose out of safe range (**EC/S**).
- **insulinOutRange** ≈ dose of insulin to be delivered drops out of the safe range (**MC/S**).
- **nearEmpty** ≈ cartridge almost empty (**MC/S**).
- **empty** ≈ cartridge empty (**MC/S**).

Reasoning About Exception Flow at the Architectural Level*

Fernando Castor Filho**, Patrick Henrique da S. Brito***,
and Cecília Mary F. Rubira†

Instituto de Computação
Universidade Estadual de Campinas
Caixa Postal 6176. CEP 13083-970, Campinas, SP, Brazil
Phone/Fax: +55 (19) 3788-5842
{fernando, patrick.silva, cmrubira}@ic.unicamp.br

Abstract. An important challenge faced by the developers of fault-tolerant systems is to build reliable fault tolerance mechanisms. To achieve the desired levels of reliability, mechanisms for detecting and handling errors should be designed since early phases of software development, preferably using a rigorous or formal methodology. In recent years, many researchers have been advocating the idea that exception handling-related issues should be addressed at the architectural level, as a complement to implementation-level exception handling. However, few works in the literature have addressed the problem of describing how exceptions flow amongst architectural elements. This work proposes a solution to this problem to support the early detection of mismatches between architectural elements due to exceptions. Moreover, it makes it possible to validate whether the architecture satisfies some properties of interest regarding exception flow before the system is actually built. Our solution proposes a model for describing the architectural flow of exceptions which is precise and automatically analyzable by means of a tool.

1 Introduction

Exception handling [13] is a well-known mechanism for structuring error recovery in fault-tolerant software systems. Since exception handling is an application-specific technique, it complements other techniques for improving system reliability, such as atomic transactions [17], and promotes the implementation of sophisticated error recovery measures. Furthermore, in applications where backward error recovery is not possible, such as those that interact with mechanical devices, exception handling may be the only choice available.

---

* The authors are partially supported by FINEP/Brazil (1843/04), project Comp-Gov, which aims at developing a Shared Library of Components for e-Government.
** Supported by FAPESP/Brazil, grant 02/139960-2.
*** Supported by CAPES/Brazil.
† Partially supported by CNPq/Brazil under grant 351592/97-0, and by FAPE-SP/Brazil, under grant 2004/10663-8.

M. Butler et al. (Eds.): Fault-Tolerant Systems, LNCS 4157, pp. 80–99, 2006.
© Springer-Verlag Berlin Heidelberg 2006

Usually, a large part of a system's code is devoted to error detection and handling [13,25,31]. However developers tend to focus on the normal activity of applications and only deal with code responsible for error detection and handling at the implementation phase, in an ad hoc manner. Hence, this part of the code is usually the least understood, tested, and documented [13,25]. To achieve the desired levels of reliability, mechanisms for detecting and handling errors should be developed systematically from early phases of software development [27], starting from requirements, and passing by analysis, architectural design, detailed design, and, finally, implementation.

The concept of software architecture [29] has been recognized in the last decade as a means to cope with the growing complexity of software systems. According to Clements and Northrop [12], software architecture is the structure of the components of a program/system, their interrelationships and principles, and guidelines governing their design and evolution over time. It is widely accepted that the architecture of a software system has a large impact on its capacity to meet its intended quality requirements, such as reliability, security, availability, and performance, amongst others [5,11]. There are many proposals in the literature [2][16][22] of notations and techniques to formally describe software architectures to show how they achieve specific quality attributes, such as adherence to interaction protocols [2], and architectural styles [16]. These approaches are usually supported by tools that automatically or semi-automatically verify whether an architecture satisfies some previously-defined properties of interest.

An important challenge faced by developers of fault-tolerant systems is to build fault tolerance mechanisms that are reliable. If a system should be reliable and exception handling is one of the mechanisms that can be employed to achieve this goal, it may be beneficial to consider exception handling-related issues before the implementation phase; in particular during architectural design. This idea goes hand-in-hand with the notion that exception handling should be taken into account from early phases of software development, in order to define the exceptional activity of the system. However, to the best of our knowledge, there are currently no approaches for the specification and analysis of exception-related information at the architectural level. As pointed out by Bass and his coleagues [4], specifying how exceptions flow between architectural components is a real problem that appears in the development of systems with strict dependability requirements, such as air-traffic control and financial.

This paper proposes an approach for describing software architectures extended with information about exception flow based on a formal model that supports reasoning about exception flow-related properties of interest. Furthermore, our solution allows one to automatically verify whether an architecture satisfies these properties of interest. The ability to formally specify and verify the flow of exceptions in a system can help in the detection of ambiguities, mistakes, and incompletenesses, thus improving the system's overall reliablity. We present a model for reasoning about exception flow in software architectures. This model specifies the structuring of an architecture in terms of architectural components (loci of computation and data stores) and connectors (loci of interaction), as well as information relative to exception flow amongst these elements. We show how systems adhering to this model can be automatically verified using the Alloy [18] specification language and its associated tool set.

This work is organized as follows. Section 2 provides some background on exception handling and the Alloy design language. Section 3 describes the overall approach that we propose for extending architecture descriptions with exception flow-related information. Section 4 presents the proposed model for reasoning about the flow of exceptions at the architectural level. A mix of informal explanations and set theory notation is employed. Section 5 describes how the proposed model can be used to verify exception flow in architecture descriptions. Section 6 compares the proposed model with some related research. The last section rounds the paper and points directions for future works.

2   Background

2.1   Exception Handling

Exception handling [13] is a mechanism for structuring error recovery in software systems so that errors can be more easily detected, signaled, and handled. It is implemented by many mainstream programming languages, such as Java, Ada, C++, and C#. These languages allow the definition of exceptions and their corresponding handlers. The set of exceptions and exception handlers in a system define its abnormal or exceptional activity.

When an error is detected, an exception is generated, or *raised*. If the same exception may be raised in different parts of a program, different handlers may be executed, depending on the place where the exception was raised. The choice of the handler that is executed depends on the exception handling context (EHC) where the exception was raised. An EHC is a region of a program where the same exceptions are handled in the same manner. Each context has an associated set of handlers that are executed when the corresponding exceptions are raised. Typical examples of EHCs in object-oriented languages are blocks, methods, and classes [15]. At the architectural level, contexts are usually defined by architectural components and connectors [6].

The concept of *idealized fault-tolerant component* (IFTC) [3] defines a conceptual framework for structuring exception handling in software systems. An IFTC is a component (in a broader sense; an object, a software component, a whole system, etc.) in which the parts responsible for the normal and abnormal activities are separated and well-defined, within its internal structure. The goal of the IFTC approach is to provide means to structure systems so that the impact of fault tolerance mechanisms in the overall system complexity is minimized. This solution eases the detection and handling of errors. Figure 1 presents the internal structure of an IFTC and the types of messages it exchanges with other components in a system.

When an IFTC receives a service request, it produces a *normal response* if the request is successfully processed. If an IFTC receives an invalid service request, it *signals* an *interface exception*. If an error is detected during the processing of a

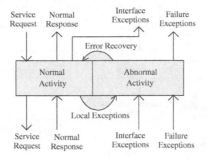

Fig. 1. Idealized Fault-Tolerant Component

valid request, the normal activity part of the IFTC *raises* an *internal exception*, which is received by the exceptional activity part of the IFTC. If the IFTC is capable of handling an internal exception properly, normal activity is resumed. If the IFTC has no handlers for an internal exception or is unable to handle an exception, it *signals* a failure exception. Interface and failure exceptions are collectively called *external exceptions*. An IFTC might also *catch* external exceptions signaled by other IFTCs and attempt to handle them. In this work, it is assumed that architectural elements behave like IFTCs. Hence, only external exceptions are taken into account, since internal exceptions are encapsulated inside components and connectors.

2.2 Alloy

Alloy [18] is a lightweight modeling language for software design. It is amenable to a fully automatic analysis, using the Alloy Analyzer (AA) [19], and provides a visualizer for making sense of solutions and counterexamples it finds. Similarly to other specification languages, such as Z and B [1], Alloy supports complex data structures and declarative models.

In Alloy, models are analyzed within a given scope, or size. The analysis performed by the AA is sound, since it never returns false positives, but incomplete, since the AA only checks things up to a certain scope. However, it is complete up to scope; the AA never misses a counterexample which is smaller than the specified scope. As pointed out by the Alloy tutorial [19], small scope checks are still very useful for finding errors.

3   Proposed Approach

The construction of robust fault-tolerant systems requires that developers take fault tolerance-related issues into account since the outset of software development [27]. Our ultimate goal is to devise a general approach for the rigorous development of dependable software systems that use exception handling to implement forward error recovery at the architectural level. This work addresses specifically the issue of verifying properties of interest related to exception flow

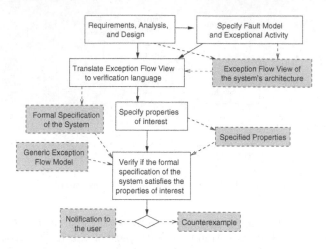

Fig. 2. Overview of the proposed approach. White rectangles represent activities and shaded rectangles with dashed borders represent artifacts.

in software architectures. Our solution is supported by the Aereal [8] framework. This framework aims to assist in documenting, analyzing, and validating exception flow in software architectures.

Figure 2 presents a schematic description of our solution. Developers start by performing traditional activities of a software development process, namely, requirements engineering, analysis, and design (both architectural and detailed) of the system. At the same time, they define the scenarios in which the system may fail (fault model), what exceptions correspond to each type of error, and where and how the exceptions are handled (exceptional activity). The specification of the system's fault model and exceptional activity can be conducted as prescribed by some works in the literature [27]. The result of these activities is an architecture description of the system that includes information about the exceptions that can be signaled by each architectural element and what elements are responsible for handling them. We refer to this specialized architecture description as the Architectural Exception Flow View [8]. *Architectural views* represent various aspects of the same architecture and each view shows how the architecture achieves a particular quality attribute [5]. In Aereal, exception flow views are specified using the ACME [16] architecture description language [23] (ADL).

To verify whether the exception flow view exhibits some properties of interest, it is necessary to translate this view to a formal language with adequate support for automated verification (*verification language*). The formal specification produced by this translation must adhere to a generic meta-model which specifies: (i) the elements that can be part of an architecture description; (ii) how exceptions flow amongst these elements; and (iii) how they relate to each other. Hereafter, we call this model *Generic Exception Flow Model*). Both the formal specification and the generic exception flow model are described in the verification language. Currently, we use Alloy to specify the generic exception flow model. A system is verified by providing its formal specification as input to a constraint solver for the verification language, together with the properties to be verified, and the definition of the generic exception flow model. We used the AA tool to verify formal specifications in Alloy. When a property of interest does not hold, the AA produces a counterexample.

In the rest of this paper, we focus on specifying the generic exception flow model. A detailed description of the general approach described in this section is available elsewhere [8].

4   Generic Exception Flow Model

In our model, special-purpose architectural connectors model exception flow between components. These connectors, called *exception ducts*, are unidirectional point-to-point links through which only exceptions flow. They are orthogonal to "normal" architectural connectors and do not constrain the way in which the architecture is organized [8]. Mehta and Medvidovic [24] argue that simple point-to-point connections are suitable general-purpose abstractions for modelling communication between architectural components independently of the architectural styles [29] to which an architecture adheres. We use this structural perspective on exception flow because it is intuitive to architects (who are used to thinking in terms of components and connectors), compatible with well-established views on what exception flow is [13], and it does not require the modeling of the complete activity of the application. Architectural elements are assumed to handle only one exception at a time. We address the case where an EHC might catch multiple exceptions concurrently elsewhere [9]. Upon receipt of an exception, the receiving element interrupts its execution and initiates exception handling. This is how exception handling works in most programming languages. Modeling issues such as data- and control-flow is beyond the scope of this work. Furthermore, we assume that the infrastructure supporting the exception handling mechanism (middleware, programming language, etc.) is correct. Therefore, exceptions are always delivered correctly and timely.

It is important to stress that exception ducts are not implementation-level connectors. They are just a high-level abstraction to describe exception flow. Architects often need to understand the architecture of a system from various perspectives, according to specific quality attributes. Since different architectural views target different aspects of an architecture, they usually employ different modeling constructs [21]. Hence, at the implementation level, exception flow is materialized by means of the constructs provided by the underlying programming language or infrastructure. For example, in a publisher/subscriber architecture, exception flow can be materialized as events flowing through a message bus.

4.1   Representation of Components, Ducts, and Exceptions

In our model, components, exception ducts, and exceptions are represented by objects of a certain type. The proposed model employs a notion of type that is adopted by some modern formal specification languages, such as Alloy [18]

Table 1. Elements of the proposed exception flow model

Set	Description
Element	The type of all architectural elements. Supertype of *Component* and *Duct*.
Component	The subtype of *Element* of which all components in a system are instances.
Duct	The subtype of *Element* of which all exception ducts in a system are instances.
RootException	The type of which all exceptions in a system are instances.

and B [1]. Moreover, it is compatible with the notion of types used in OO languages such as Java and C#. A type T is a set of instances and its subtypes $T_1, T_2, ..., T_N$ of T are disjunct subsets of T. Only single inheritance is allowed. An exception is any instance of a type that is subtype of type *RootException*. The same applies to components and exception ducts, and the types *Component* and *Duct*, respectively. In our model, types *Component* and *Duct* are subtypes of *Element* (and collectively called "elements"). Table 1 lists the basic elements of the proposed model. The sets in the table can also be seen as unary relations and are, therefore, subject to operations that apply to relations, such as composition.

We represent exceptions as objects, instead of using symbols or global variables, mainly because objects are more flexible and can be used to encode arbitrary information regarding the cause of an exception [15]. Moreover, many large and complex software systems are developed nowadays using object-oriented languages, such as Java and C++, which represent exceptions as objects.

The supertype of all exceptions is called *RootException*, instead of a more usual name, such as *Exception* or *Error*, in order to provide to developers the flexibility to organize exceptions as required, for instance, based on the adopted programming language. For example, considering the EHS of Java, a developer can define at least four exception types: (i) *Throwable*, subtype of *RootException*; (ii) *Exception*, subtype of *Throwable*; (iii) *Error*, subtype of *Throwable*; and (iv) *RuntimeException*, subtype of *Exception*. Application-specific exception types would then be subtypes of one of these types.

4.2   System Structure

We follow the general view of a system configuration as a finite connected graph of components and connectors [23]. We specialize this view, however, so that it can be used to reason about exception flow. In our model, a component is a structural architectural element that catches and/or signals exceptions and an exception duct is a structural element that represents flow of exceptions between two components. The structure of a system is defined in terms of connections between components and exception ducts. The relations *CatchesFrom* $\in$ *Element* $\leftrightarrow$ *Element* and *SignalsTo* $\in$ *Element* $\leftrightarrow$ *Element* specify these connections.

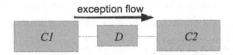

Fig. 3. A trivial software architecture

Given an element B, $\{B\}.CatchesFrom$ yields the set of elements that signal exceptions that B catches. Conversely, $\{B\}.SignalsTo$ yields the set of elements that catch exceptions that B signals. The "." operator represents relational composition (or join). Given two relations $A \subseteq T_1 \times T_2 \times ... \times T_n$ and $B \subseteq T_n \times T_{n+1} \times ... \times T_{n+m}$, $A.B$ yields a relation $C \subseteq T_1 \times T_2 \times ... \times T_{n-1} \times T_{n+1} \times ... \times T_{n+m}$. Relation C comprises all the tuples formed by combining tuples from A and B whenever the last element of a tuple from A is the same as the first element of a tuple from B. For example, given $A = \{(e_1, e_2), (e_2, e_3)\}$ and $B = \{(e_2, e_4), (e_2, e_5), (e_3, e_6), (e_7, e_8)\}$, $A.B$ yields $C = \{(e_1, e_4), (e_1, e_5), (e_2, e_6)\}$. Figure 3 illustrates relations $CatchesFrom$ and $SignalsTo$. The figure depicts two components, $C1$ and $C2$, connected by an exception duct D. Since exceptions flow from $C1$ to $C2$, passing through D, we can say that $C1 \in \{D\}.CatchesFrom$ and $D \in \{C2\}.CatchesFrom$. Conversely, $D \in \{C1\}.SignalsTo$ and $C2 \in \{D\}.SignalsTo$.

Table 2 lists some constraints on relations $CatchesFrom$ and $SignalsTo$. These constraints specify properties that a system specification adhering to our model should exhibit. Each one is identified by a name matching the pattern BPX, where "BP" stands for basic property and "X" is a positive integer. Properties $BP1$ and $BP2$ specify that the $CatchesFrom$ relation is not reflexive and it never associates elements of the same type, respectively. Properties $BP3$ and $BP4$ do the same for relation $SignalsTo$. Property $BP5$ states that exception ducts signal exceptions to exactly one element and catch exceptions from exactly one element. If B is a component, $\{B\}.CatchesFrom$ may yield an empty set, in which case B does not catch exceptions. If $\{B\}.SignalsTo$ yields an empty set, exceptions signaled by B, if any, are caught by an implicit component $OperatingSystem$. This is useful to model situations in which a system is not capable of handling a certain type of error and fails catastrophically by signaling an exception to the operating system. Properties $BP6$ states that the set of elements from which an element catches exceptions consists of all elements that signal exceptions to it. Property $BP7$ states that the set of elements to which an architectural element signals exceptions consists of all elements that catch exceptions from it, respectively. These two properties provide a link between $CatchesFrom$ and $SignalsTo$. Property $BP8$ specifies that the elements from which an architectural element catches exceptions are different from the ones to which it signals exceptions. For example, a configuration with only two elements, $C \in Component$ and $D \in Duct$, where $C \in \{D\}.CatchesFrom$ and $C \in \{D\}.SignalsTo$ is not valid.

For any valid system in the proposed model, the graph formed by using the components of the system as vertices and the ducts as edges is connected. More

Table 2. Contraints on the $CatchesFrom$ and $SignalsTo$ relations

Property	Constraint
$BP1$	$\forall B \in Element \bullet B \notin \{B\}.CatchesFrom$
$BP2$	$\forall B' \in Element \bullet (B, B') \in CatchesFrom \Rightarrow \neg(B \in Duct \wedge B' \in Duct) \wedge$ $\neg(B \in Component \wedge B' \in Component)$
$BP3$	$\forall B \in Element \bullet B \notin \{B\}.SignalsTo$
$BP4$	$\forall B' \in Element \bullet (B, B') \in SignalsTo \Rightarrow \neg(B \in Duct \wedge B' \in Duct) \wedge$ $\neg(B \in Component \wedge B' \in Component)$
$BP5$	$\forall D \in Duct \bullet |\{D\}.CatchesFrom| = 1 \wedge |\{D\}.SignalsTo| = 1$
$BP6$	$\forall B_1, B_2 \in Element \bullet B_1 \in \{B_2\}.CatchesFrom \Rightarrow B_2 \in \{B_1\}.SignalsTo$
$BP7$	$\forall B_1, B_2 \in Element \bullet B_1 \in \{B_2\}.SignalsTo \Rightarrow B_2 \in \{B_1\}.CatchesFrom$
$BP8$	$\forall B \in Element \bullet \{B\}.CathcesFrom \cap \{B\}.SignalsTo = \{\}$
$BP9$	$\forall C_1, C_2 \in Component \bullet C_1 \in$ $\{C_2\}. * ((SignalsTo \cup CatchesFrom).(SignalsTo \cup CatchesFrom))$

formally, let $G = (Component, Duct)$ be a graph, where $Component$ is the set of all vertexes and $Duct$ is the set of all edges. An edge $D \in Duct$ connects two vertexes $C_1 \in Component$ and $C_2 \in Component$ if $D \in \{C_1\}.CatchesFrom$ and $C_2 \in \{D\}.CatchesFrom$. In order for a graph to be connected, there must be a path between any two vertexes. Property $BP9$ specifies this constraint formally. It states that the reflexive transitive closure ($*$ operator) of any component with respect to the relation $(SignalsTo \cup CatchesFrom).(SignalsTo \cup CatchesFrom)$ contains all the other components of the system. In property $BP9$, the $*$ operator yields the set of all components reachable by composing component C_2 with $(SignalsTo \cup CatchesFrom).(SignalsTo \cup CatchesFrom)$ zero or more times.

4.3   Exception Interfaces and Exception Handling Contexts

As mentioned in previously, we consider a component to be a structural element that catches and signals exceptions. Exception ducts are similar, but simpler, as they catch exceptions from exactly one component and signal exceptions to exactly one component. A component includes (i) a collection of exception interfaces, which specify the exceptions the component signals; and (ii) a collection of EHCs, which define regions where exceptions are always handled in the same way. Exception interfaces are associated to components by the $SignalsTo$ relation and, for each exception duct in the set $\{C\}.SignalsTo$, there is a corresponding exception interface. The same applies for the $CatchesFrom$ relation and EHCs. This represents the fact that a component may signal different exceptions to (or catch different exceptions from) the various exception ducts to which it is connected. As imposed by property $BP5$ (Table 2), each exception duct has exactly one exception interface and one EHC.

Models for reasoning about exception flow at the programming language level do not have an explicit separation between exception interfaces and EHCs. This separation is not necessary because these models focus on fine-grained programming constructs, like methods and procedures, where multiple contexts are

Table 3. Contraints on the *PortMap* relation

Property	Constraint
BP10	$\forall B \in Element \bullet dom(\{B\}.PortMap) = \{B\}.CatchesFrom\wedge$ $ran(\{B\}.PortMap) = \{B\}.SignalsTo$

associated to a single exception interface. At the architectural level, however, this separation is very important, since a component can have multiple access points (ports) and the latter are explicit in the system description.

The *PortMap* $\in$ *Element* $\leftrightarrow$ *Element* $\leftrightarrow$ *Element* relation associates exception interfaces and EHCs. When an element catches an exception and does not handle it, the *PortMap* relation specifies the element to which the exception is signaled, based on the element that originally signaled it. *PortMap* associates architectural elements to EHCs and exception interfaces. Table 3 lists the single property associated to the *PortMap* relation. Property *BP*10 specifies that for every element B, *PortMap* associates all the elements from which B catches exceptions to some element to which it signals exceptions and vice-versa.

4.4 Exception Flow

Exception flow is specified in terms of five relations: *Signals* $\in$ *Element* $\leftrightarrow$ *Element* $\leftrightarrow$ *RootException*, *Generates* $\in$ *Element* $\leftrightarrow$ *Element* $\leftrightarrow$ *RootException*, *DoesNotMask* $\in$ *Element* $\leftrightarrow$ *Element* $\leftrightarrow$ *RootException* $\leftrightarrow$ *RootException*, *Catches* $\in$ *Element* $\leftrightarrow$ *Element* $\leftrightarrow$ *RootException*, and *Masks* $\in$ *Element* $\leftrightarrow$ *Element* $\leftrightarrow$ *RootException*. The first two concern the exception interfaces of an architectural element, whereas the last three are related to EHCs. In the rest of this section, we describe these relations in more detail.

The *Signals* relation defines the exception interfaces of an architectural element. This relation specifies which exceptions an architectural element signals and the elements that catch these exceptions. Let ES be a set of exceptions and B_1 and B_2 be architectural elements such that $B_2 \in \{B_1\}.SignalsTo$. If $\{B_2\}.(\{B_1\}.Signals) = ES$, we say that the element B_1 signals the exceptions in set ES to element B_2. Table 4 lists some properties associated to the *Signals* relation. Property *BP*11 specifies that elements only signal exceptions to elements to which they are connected, as specified by the *SignalsTo* relation.

Even though, for the sake of uniformity, we have called the second constraint on Table 4 a "property", it works more as a definition of the *Signals* relation. Property *BP*12 states that the *Signals* relation is derived from three other relations. Intuitively, the set of exceptions that a component signals depends on the exceptions it generates (raises) and on exceptions it catches that were signaled by other architectural elements. *Propagated* and *Unhandled* are auxiliary relations defined in terms of the relations that specify a component's EHCs (described in the following paragraphs). The *Generates* relation specifies the exceptions that components generate when erroneous conditions are detected. These conditions are dependent on the semantics of the application and on the assumed failure

Table 4. Contraints on the *Signals*, *Generates*, *Catches*, *Masks*, and *DoesNotMask* relations

Property	Constraint
$BP11$	$\forall B \in Element \bullet dom(\{B\}.Signals) \subseteq \{B\}.SignalsTo$
$BP12$	$Signals = Generates \cup Propagated \cup Unhandled$
$BP13$	$Generates \subseteq Signals$
$BP14$	$\forall B \in Element \bullet dom(\{B\}.Catches) \subseteq \{B\}.CatchesFrom$
$BP15$	$\forall B \in Element \bullet \forall B' \in \{B\}.CatchesFrom \bullet$ $\{B\}.(\{B'\}.Signals) = \{B'\}.(\{B\}.Catches)$
$BP16$	$\forall B \in Element \bullet dom(\{B\}.Masks) \subseteq \{B\}.CatchesFrom$
$BP17$	$\forall B \in Element \bullet dom((\{B\}.DoesNotMask).RootException) \subseteq$ $\{B\}.CatchesFrom$
$BP18$	$\forall B \in Element \bullet \forall B' \in \{B\}.CatchesFrom \bullet |\{B'\}.(\{B\}.DoesNotMask)| > 0$ $\Rightarrow (dom(\{B'\}.(\{B\}.DoesNotMask)) \cap \{B'\}.(\{B\}.Masks)) = \{\}$

model. For reasoning about exception flow, the fault that caused an exception to be raised is not important, just the fact that the exception was raised. Let ES be a set of exceptions and B_1 and B_2 be architectural elements such that $B_2 \in \{B_1\}.SignalsTo$. If $\{B_2\}.(\{B_1\}.Generates) = ES$, we say that the element B_1 raises exceptions ES to B_2. Property BP13 specifies that all the exceptions an element generates to another element are also signaled to the latter. This is coherent with the view that only external exceptions matter at the architectural level.

Exception handling contexts are defined in terms of three relations: *Catches*, *Masks*, and *DoesNotMask*. *Catches* specifies, for an arbitrary element B, the exceptions B receives from the elements in the set $\{B\}.CatchesFrom$. Let ES be a set of exceptions and B_1 and B_2 be architectural elements such that $B_2 \in \{B_1\}.CatchesFrom$. If $\{B_2\}.(\{B_1\}.Catches) = ES$, we say that the element B_1 catches exceptions ES from element B_2. Table 4 shows the basic properties associated with *Catches*, *Masks*, and *DoesNotMask*. Propety $BP14$ specifies that elements only catch exceptions from elements to which they are connected, as specified by the *CatchesFrom* relation. Property $BP15$ states that the exceptions that an element catches are the exceptions signaled to it.

The *Masks* relation specifies the exceptions that are masked by a component. By "masked", we mean that the component is capable of taking some action that stops the propagation of the exception and makes it possible for the system to resume its normal activity. Modeling the behavior of the exception handlers is beyond the scope of this work. We are just interested in the effect the handler has on the flow of exceptions. Let ES be a set of exceptions and B_1 and B_2 be architectural elements such that $B_2 \in \{B_1\}.CatchesFrom$. If $\{B_2\}.(\{B_1\}.Masks) = ES$, we say that the element B_1 handles exceptions ES from element B_2. Only property $BP16$ in Table 4 is directly associated to the *Masks* relation. This property states that elements only handle exceptions signaled by elements to which they are connected. We could also restrict *Masks* to be a subset of *Catches* just like *Generates* is a subset of *Signals*. We do

Table 5. Properties that define auxiliary relations *Unhandled* and *Propagated*

Property	Constraint
BP19	$Propagated = \{\ T \in Element \times Element \times RootException \mid s(T) \in \{f(T)\}.SignalsTo \wedge t(T) \in (((\{f(T)\}.PortMap).\{s(T)\}).(\{f(T)\}.Catches \backslash \{f(T)\}.Masks)). (((\{f(T)\}.PortMap).\{s(T)\}).(\{f(T)\}.DoesNotMask))\ \}$
BP20	$Unhandled = \{\ T \in Element \times Element \times RootException \mid s(T) \in \{f(T)\}.SignalsTo \wedge t(T) \in (((\{f(T)\}.PortMap).\{s(T)\}). (\{f(T)\}.Catches \backslash \{f(T)\}.Masks)) \backslash ((((\{f(T)\}.PortMap). \{s(T)\}).(\{f(T)\}.DoesNotMask)).(\{s(T)\}.(\{f(T)\}.Propagated)))\ \}$

not impose this restriction, however, because sometimes it is useful to specify general handlers, that is, handlers capable of dealing with any type of exception.

The *DoesNotMask* relation describes exception handlers that do not stop the propagation of exceptions. These handlers end their execution by signaling the same exception or a new one. *DoesNotMask* specifies a cause-consequence relationship between an exception that an element catches and an exception that it signals. Let E and E' be exceptions and B_1 and B_2 be architectural elements such that $B_2 \in \{B_1\}.CatchesFrom$. If $\{B_2\}.(\{B_1\}.DoesNotMask) = (E, E')$, we say that the element B_1 **explicitly propagates** (or simply "propagates") exception E' from E, signaled by B_2. The last two properties in Table 4 are directly related to the *DoesNotMask* relation. Property $BP17$ states that an element can only propagate exceptions signaled by an element from which it catches exceptions. Property $BP18$ specifies that an element can handle or propagate the exceptions it catches from another element, but not both.

Now we can go back to the definition of *Signals* and define *Propagated* and *Unhandled*. The $Propagated \in Element \leftrightarrow Element \leftrightarrow RootException$ relation specifies the subset of *Signals* comprising exceptions that are explicitly propagated by an element. It associates an element to the exceptions it propagates explicitly and the elements that catch these propagated exceptions. The $Unhandled \in Element \leftrightarrow Element \leftrightarrow RootException$ relation associates the set of exceptions that an architectural element **implicitly propagates** and the elements to which these exceptions are signaled. An exception is said to be implicitly propagated when an architectural element catches it but the element does handle it or explicitly propagate an exception from it. Such an exception ends up being signaled to some other architectural element. Table 5 presents formal definitions for relations *Propagated* and *Unhandled*. The constraints in Table 5 use three auxiliary functions, $f()$, $s()$, and $t()$, that take a triple as argument and return the first, second, and third elements of the triple, respectively.

4.5 Exception Propagation Cycles

An exception propagation cycle is a situation where an exception is propagated (implicitly or explicitly) indefinitely, without ever being handled, not even by the special *OperatingSystem* component, in an architecture that adheres to the basic properties $BP1 - BP20$. Furthermore, exceptions in an exception propagation cycle might potentially have never been raised. For these reasons, valid exception flow views should not have exception propagation cycles.

A conservative way of preventing the occurrence of exception propagation cycles is to completely disallow structural cycles in the graph formed by the components and exception ducts in a system. For most systems, this solution is sufficient without being overly restrictive. However, for software architectures where components are peers, like multi-agent and publisher-subscriber, this approach is not acceptable. At the implementation level, exception propagation cycles are not a problem, since in exception handling mechanisms such as Java's and Ada's, each EHC is kept in the stack, which is finite, and removed from it when controls returns from the EHC (possibly due to exception propagation). Therefore, in a language-level exception propagation cycle, eventually all the EHCs will be removed from the stack and exception propagation will stop. At the architectural level, however, this is not always the case, as an exception is not necessarily implemented as a language-level exception [6,8].

A simple way to avoid propagation cycles without removing structural cycles is to introduce a partial ordering on exceptions. This ordering could be introduced through additional information associated to each exception type. Then each element would be required to signal exceptions which are greater than the ones it catches. This solution has two shortcomings. The first is that it requires developers to be aware of this ordering, which is not required in any existing programming languages. The second problem is that it complicates the model and could have a negative effect on the performance of verification. Using the type hierarchy to represent the ordering of exceptions is also not adequate, since it also requires developers to be aware of the ordering and thus imposes constraints on the exception type hierarchy. Moreover, from a practical standpoint, this solution partially defeats the purpose of using different types of exceptions, as the topmost layers of a system would always receive general exceptions that do not provide accurate information about the specific error they represent. In the rest of this section, we propose an alternative solution that is a bit more complex, but avoids these shortcomings. We formalize the concept of exception propagation cycle and show how such cycles can be easily detected.

An **exception propagation** is a tuple $\phi = (B, E, E', B')$, with $B, B' \in Element$ and $E, E' \in RootException$. We use the functions $f()$, $s()$, $t()$, and $g()$ to obtain the first, second, third, and fourth elements of a propagation, respectively. Any propagation ϕ must satisfy the following well-formedness predicate:

$$(g(\phi) \neq f(\phi)) \wedge (g(\phi) \in \{f(\phi)\}.SignalsTo) \wedge (f(\phi) \in \{g(\phi)\}.CatchesFrom) \wedge$$
$$(t(\phi) \in \{f(\phi)\}.(\{g(\phi)\}.Catches)) \wedge (t(\phi) \in \{g(\phi)\}.(\{f(\phi)\}.Signals)) \wedge$$
$$\exists CF \in \{f(\phi)\}.CatchesFrom \bullet ((CF, g(\phi)) \in \{f(\phi)\}.PortMap) \wedge$$
$$(s(\phi) \in \{CF\}.(\{f(\phi)\}.Catches)) \wedge (s(\phi) \notin \{CF\}.(\{f(\phi)\}.Masks)) \wedge$$
$$(s(\phi) \in dom(\{CF\}.(\{f(\phi)\}.DoesNotMask)) \Rightarrow$$
$$t(\phi) \in \{s(\phi)\}.(\{CF\}.(\{f(\phi)\}.DoesNotMask)))$$

```
1  void computePropagations(Element B) {
2    foreach catchesP in B.Catches and not in B.Masks {
3    // catchesP is an (Element, RootException) pair
4      Propagation prop = new Propagation();
5      foreach portMapP in B.PortMap such that portMapP.f() == catchesP.f() {
6      // portMapP is an (Element, Element) pair
7        if(there is a Triple propagatesT in B.DoesNotMask such that
8          propagatesT.f() == catchesP.f() && propagatesT.s() == catchesP.s()) {
9        // propagatesT is an (Element, RootException, RootException) triple
10            prop.t = propagatesT.t();
11        } else { prop.t = catchesP.s(); }
12        prop.s = catchesP.s();
13        prop.f = B;
14        prop.g = portMapP.s();
15      }
16      B.propagations.add(prop);
17    }
18 }
```

Fig. 4. An algorithm to compute the exception propagations associated to an element

It is easy to compute the set of all exception propagations in a software architecture adhering to our model. Figure 4 presents an algorithm for computing all the exception propagations associated to an architectural element.

In order to impose a partial order between two exceptions propagations, we introduce the notion of consecutiveness. Two propagations ϕ_1 and ϕ_2 are said to be **consecutive** if they satisfy the following predicate:

$$(g(\phi_1) = f(\phi_2)) \wedge (f(\phi_1) \in \{f(\phi_2)\}.CatchesFrom) \wedge$$
$$(f(\phi_2) \in f(\phi_1).SignalsTo) \wedge (f(\phi_1) \neq f(\phi_2)) \wedge (t(\phi_1) = s(\phi_2)) \wedge$$
$$(t(\phi_1) \in \{f(\phi_1)\}.(\{f(\phi_2)\}.Catches)) \wedge (s(\phi_2) \in \{f(\phi_2)\}.(\{f(\phi_1)\}.Signals))$$

In this case, ϕ_1 is said to be the predecessor of ϕ_2 and ϕ_2 is the successor of ϕ_1. We indicate that propagations ϕ_1 and ϕ_2 are consecutive with the notation $\phi_1 \rightharpoonup \phi_2$. A **sequence of propagations** φ of length n is a set of propagations $\phi_1, \phi_2, \phi_3 ..., \phi_{n-1}, \phi_n$ such that $\phi_1 \rightharpoonup \phi_2, \phi_2 \rightharpoonup \phi_3, ..., \phi_{n-1} \rightharpoonup \phi_n$. For simplicity, we assume that all sequences of propagations are finite. A sequence of propagations $\varphi = \phi_1, \phi_2, ..., \phi_n$ forms an **exception propagation cycle** iff $\phi_n \rightharpoonup \phi_1$.

To verify if a software architecture has exception propagation cycles, it is necessary to build the directed graph formed by all the exception propagations of the architecture. This graph is constructed in two steps: (1) compute the exception propagations for all the elements in the architecture and use them as vertexes; and (2) create a directed edge between two propagations whenever they are consecutive, from the predecessor to the sucessor. Detecting exception propagation cycles in the resulting graph is only a matter of using a regular algorithm for finding cycles in directed graphs.

5 Materializing the Model

We have translated the generic exception flow model described in Section 4 to Alloy. In this section, we show how to specify systems based on this model and

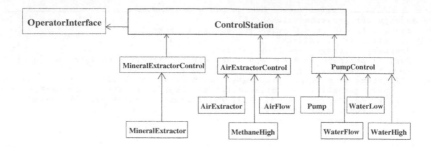

Fig. 5. Layered architecture of a mining control system

how to verify them. We use a well-known textbook example [30] to make the explanation more concrete. Addressing both the earlier (requirements definition and analysis) and later (detailed design, implementation, etc.) phases of software development is outside the scope of this paper.

Figure 5 shows the components and connectors view of a control system for the mining environment [27]. Rectangles represent architectural components and arrows represent exception flow. The extraction of minerals from a mine produces water and releases methane gas to the air. The mining control system is used to drain mine water from a sump to the surface, and to extract air from the mine when the methane level becomes high. The system consists of three control stations: one that monitors the level of water in the sump, one that monitors the level of methane in the mine, and another that monitors the mineral extraction. For safety reasons, the extraction of minerals should be interrupted when the amount of methane in the atmosphere exceeds a safety limit. The air extractor control station monitors the level of methane inside the mine, and when the level is high an air extractor is switched on to remove air from the mine. The whole system is controlled from the surface via an operator console.

The system can fail in several ways. For simplicity, we only consider the case where the AirExtractorControl component fails by signaling the exception `AirExtractorOffException`. This exception is caught and handled by the `ControlStation` component. The handler ends its execution by signaling the exception `EmergencyException`. A detailed description of the exceptional activity of the mining system is available elsewhere [27].

Figure 6 shows the Alloy specification of the mining system. In Alloy, a signature (`sig` keyword) specifies a type. The **one** keyword indicates that a signature has exactly one instance. We use signatures for modeling structural elements and exceptions. The **open** clause (Line 1) imports the definitions of the basic types of the generic exception flow model, `Element`, `Component`, `Duct`, and `RootException`. It also imports the predicates that specify the basic properties defined in Section 4. The relations defined in Section 4, such as *CatchesFrom*, *Masks*, etc., are explicitly instantiated by means of facts, predicates that the AA must assume to be true when evaluating constraints. For instance, the fact `SystemStructure` (Line 7) states, among other things, that component `ControlStation` catches exceptions from the exception duct `AEC_CS`. The latter connects `ControlStation` to the

```
 1  open ExceptionHandlingSystem
 2  one sig AirExtractorOffException, EmergencyException extends RootException{}
 3  one sig ControlStation, OperatorInterface, AirExtractorControl
 4      extends Component{}
 5  one sig CS_OI, AEC_CS extends Duct{}
 6  ...
 7  fact SystemStructure{ ...
 8    ControlStation.CatchesFrom = AEC_CS
 9    ControlStation.SignalsTo = CS_OI
10    AEC_CS.CatchesFrom = AirExtractorControl
11    AEC_CS.SignalsTo = ControlStation
12  } fact ExceptionFlow{ ...
13    AirExtractorControl.Signals = AEC_CS->AirExtractorOffException
14    AirExtractorControl.Generates = AEC_CS->AirExtractorOffException
15    AEC_CS.Catches = AirExtractorControl->AirExtractorOffException
16    AEC_CS.Signals = ControlStation->AirExtractorOffException
17    ControlStation.Catches = AEC_CS->AirExtractorOffException
18    ControlStation.Signals = CS_OI->EmergencyException
19    no ControlStation.Masks
20    ControlStation.DoesNotMask =
21        AEC_CS->AirExtractorControlOffException->EmergencyException
22  } fact PortMap{ ...
23    ControlStation.PortMap = AEC_CS->CS_OI
24  }
```

Fig. 6. Partial Alloy specification of the mining control system

`AirExtractorControl` component. Moreover, the fact `ExceptionFlow` (Line 12) states that component `ControlStation` catches the exception `AirExtractor-Control` (Line 17), signaled by the `AEC_CS` duct, and signals exception `Emergency-Exception` to the `CS_OI` duct (Line 18). `ControlStation` translates the former exception to the latter (Lines 20 and 21).

Verification consists in checking whether the Alloy specification of a system satisfies Alloy predicates corresponding to properties of interest. The properties of interest that a system must satisfy are split in three categories: basic, desired, and application-specific. Basic properties define the well-formedness rules of the model, that is, the characteristics of valid systems. These properties specify the functioning of the exception handling mechanism and how software architectures are structured. We have formally specified all the basic properties of the generic exception flow model in Section 4. Desired properties are general properties that are usually considered beneficial, although they are not part of the basic exception handling mechanism. They assume that the basic properties hold. Some examples are the following.

DP1. Architectural elements do not handle exceptions they do not catch.
DP2. All the exceptions caught by an architectural element are handled by it, even if some of its handlers end their execution by raising exceptions.
DP3. No unhandled exceptions.

Application-specific properties are rules regarding the flow of exceptions in a specific application. For the mining system, a possible application-specific property is one which guarantees that the OperatorInterface component does not receive domain-specific exceptions.

AP1. No architectural element signals to the OperatorInterface component an exception different from `EmergencyException`.

```
1  /* Basic property BP13 */
2  pred bp13() {  all C : Component | (C.Generates in C.Signals)  }
3  /* Desired property DP2 */
4  pred dp2() {
5   all C: Component | let nonHandled = (C.Catches - C.Masks)
6     | (all CF : C.CatchesFrom | #(CF <: nonHandled) > 0 =>
7        ((#nonHandled > 0 => #(C.DoesNotMask) > 0) &&
8         all E: CF.nonHandled | #(E.(CF.(C.DoesNotMask))) > 0))
9  }
10 /* Application-specific property AP1 */
11 pred ap1() {
12  all D: OperatorInterface.CatchesFrom |
13    OperatorInterface.(D.Signals) = EmergencyException
14 }
```

Fig. 7. Alloy specifications of properties $BP13$, $DP1$, $DP2$, and $AP1$

The Alloy definition of the generic exception flow model includes the specifications of several basic and desired properties that can be used "as-is". Developers only specify additional desired properties and application-specific properties, if any. The AA is employed to analyze exception flow. If a property of interest is violated, the AA generates a counterexample with a configuration of the system where the violated property does not hold. Otherwise it notifies the user that the system is valid.

Figure 7 defines four Alloy predicates named bp13, dp2, and ap1, formally specifying properties $BP13$, $DP2$, and $AP1$, respectively. Alloy predicates are logic sentences that must be checked by the AA. In the body of the predicates, Generates, Signals, Catches, DoesNotMask, Masks, and CatchesFrom are names of relations corresponding to the homonymous relations described in Section 4. Predicate bp13() states that the set of exceptions that a component raises is a subset of the exceptions it signals. Predicate dp2() selects, for each component in the Alloy specification, all the exceptions that the component catches but does not handle, and checks whether exceptions are propagated from them. The operators all, <:, &&, and in represent, respectively, universal quantification, domain restriction, logical conjunction, and subset. The operators -, =>, and # mean set subtraction, logical implication, and set cardinality, respectively, and the declaration let associates an alias to an expression. Predicate ap1() is a direct translation from the informal description of property $AP1$.

6   Related Work

Several works propose static analyses of source code that generate information about exception flow. Usually, this information consists in the exception propagation paths in a program and is used, for example, to identify uncaught exceptions in languages with polymorphic types, such as ML. Chang et al [10] present a set-based static analysis of Java programs that estimates their exception flows. This analysis is used to detect too general or unecessary exception specifications and handlers. Yi [32] proposes an abstract interpretation that estimates uncaught exceptions in ML programs. Fähndrich [14] and coleagues have employed their BANE toolkit to discover uncaught exceptions in ML. Schaefer and Bundy's [28] work describes a model for reasoning about exception flow in Ada programs. This model is used by a tool that tracks down uncaught exceptions and provides exception flow information to programmers. The JEX tool, proposed by Robillard and Murphy [26], analyzes exception flow in Java programs. The tool includes a GUI to display a program's exception propagation paths and detects handlers that are too general.

Our approach leverages previous proposals for exception flow analysis, most notably Schaefer and Bundy's [28], but it differs in focus. Out approach targets the early phases of development and is broader in scope. It describes how an architectural-level exception handling mechanism works and leverages existing verification tools to check for adherence to the rules prescribed by this mechanism. Furthermore, it supports the definition of new properties of interest and their automated verification. Moreover, as mentioned in Section 4.5, existing exception flow models do not take exception propagation cycles into consideration, as they are not a problem that occurs at the implementation level.

Jiang and coleagues [20] describe an approach for the analysis of exception propagation based on a data structure called exception propagation graph. The goal of the authors is to use exception propagation graphs as a basis for automatically generating structural tests. They do not address exception propagation cycles, as their work focuses on implementation-level exception flow analysis. Moreover, they do not show how the proposed approach can be employed to check whether a system exhibits some properties of interest, such as absence of useless handlers.

Several approaches for specifying software architectures so that they are passive to automated analysis have been proposed. Most of them define new ADLs that target specific aspects of a software system. These ADLs are usually based on some underlying formalisms that are well-supported by tools. Wright [2] specifications can be translated to CSP and analyzed for deadlock freedom and interface compatibility. Rapide [22] is based on partially-ordered event sets. The language supports simulation of architecture descriptions and analysis of the event patterns produced by components. We do not propose a new ADL. Instead, we use an existing ADL which supports extension, ACME, and a formal design language, Alloy, to specify and analyze exception flow at the architectural level. To the best of our knowledge, no ADLs currently available focus on the verification of properties related to exception flow.

In a previous work, Castor and coleagues [7] described an initial version of the model presented in this paper. This early work does not unify the definitions of components and ducts and is harder to use and less scalable. Furthermore, it does not take exception propagation cycles into account.

7   Concluding Remarks

This paper presented a model for reasoning about the flow of exceptions at the architectural level. This model is part of the Aereal framework and supports the specification of several properties of interest related to exception flow. We have described how systems adhering to it can be automatically analyzed using the AA, in order to verify whether they exhibit these properties. The main contributions of this paper are: (i) a formalization of exception flow in terms of elements that make sense at the architectural level; and (ii) a decomposition of this formalization in terms of a set of properties that can be easily verified through existing tools.

In another study [8], we assessed the scalability of the proposed model. We discovered that, for software architectures with a large number of exceptions (30+), it does not scale up well. Hence, our most immediate future work is to improve scalability. We envision two complementary approaches. The first is to optimize the system model by removing redundant information. The second is to implement a tool that checks if an Alloy specification satisfies all the basic properties of the EHS supported by Aereal. This would drastically reduce the complexity of the checks the AA performs, hence decreasing the amount of memory that verification requires. This change will not compromise the flexibility of the framework, since the basic properties do not change and any valid system must satisfy them.

Acknowledgments

The authors are partially supported by FINEP/Brazil (1843/04), project Comp-Gov, which aims at developing a Shared Library of Components for e-Government.

References

1. J. R. Abrial. *The B-Book Assigning Programs to Meanings*. Cambridge U. Press, 1995.
2. R. Allen and D. Garlan. A formal basis for architectural connection. *ACM Transactions on Software Engineering and Methodology*, 6(3):213–249, July 1997.
3. T. Anderson and P. A. Lee. *Fault Tolerance: Principles and Practice*. Springer-Verlag, 2nd edition, 1990.
4. L. Bass et al. Air traffic control: A case study in designing for high availability. In *Software Architecture in Practice*, chapter 6. Addison-Wesley, 2nd edition, 2003.
5. L. Bass et al. *Software Architecture in Practice*. Addison-Wesley, 2nd edition, 2003.
6. F. Castor Filho et al. An architectural-level exception-handling system for component-based applications. In *Proceedings of the 1st LADC*, LNCS 2847, pages 321–340. Springer-Verlag, October 2003.
7. F. Castor Filho et al. Modeling and analysis of architectural exceptions. In *Proceedings of the FM'2005 Workshop on Rigorous Engineering of Fault-Tolerant Systems*, pages 112–121, July 2005.
8. F. Castor Filho et al. Specification of exception flow in software architectures. *Journal of Systems and Software*, 2006.
9. F. Castor Filho et al. Verification of coordinated exception handling. In *Proceedings of the 21st ACM Symposium on Applied Computing*, pages 680–685, April 2006.
10. B.-M. Chang et al. Interprocedural exception analysis for java. In *Proceedings of the 16th ACM Symposium on Applied Computing*, 2001.

11. P. C. Clements et al. *Evaluating Software Architectures*. Addison-Wesley, 2003.
12. P. C. Clements and L. Northrop. Software architecture: An executive overview. Technical Report CMU/SEI-96-TR-003, SEI/CMU, February 1996.
13. F. Cristian. Exception handling. In T. Anderson, editor, *Dependability of Resilient Computers*, pages 68–97. Blackwell Scientific Publications, 1989.
14. M. Fahndrich et al. Tracking down exceptions in standard ml. Technical Report CSD-98-996, University of California, Berkeley, 1998.
15. A. Garcia et al. A comparative study of exception handling mechanisms for building dependable object-oriented software. *Journal of Systems and Software*, 59(2):197–222, November 2001.
16. D. Garlan et al. Acme: Architectural description of component-based systems. In *Foundations of Component-Based Systems*, chapter 3. Cambridge U. Press, 2000.
17. J. Gray and A. Reuter. *Transaction Processing: Concepts and Techniques*. Morgan Kaufmann, 1993.
18. D. Jackson. Alloy: A lightweight object modeling notation. *ACM Transactions on Software Engineering and Methodology*, 11(2):256–290, April 2002.
19. D. Jackson. Alloy home page, March 2006. Available at http://sdg.lcs.mit.edu/alloy/default.htm.
20. S. Jiang et al. An approach to analyzing exception propagation. In *Proceedings of the 8th IASTED International Conference on Software Engineering and Applications*, Cambridge, USA, November 2004.
21. P. Krüchten. The 4+1 view model of software architecture. *IEEE Software*, pages 42–50, November 1995.
22. D. Luckham and J. Vera. An event-based architecture definition language. *IEEE Transactions on Software Engineering*, 21(9):717–734, April 1995.
23. N. Medvidovic and R. N. Taylor. A framework for classifying and comparing architecture description languages. In *Proceedings of Joint 5th ACM SIGSOFT FSE/6th ESEC*, pages 60–76, September 1997.
24. N. R. Mehta and N. Medvidovic. Composing architectural styles from architectural primitives. In *Proceedings of Joint 9th ESEC/11th ACM SIGSOFT FSE*, pages 347–350, September 2003.
25. D. Reimer and H. Srinivasan. Analyzing exception usage in large java applications. In *Proceedings of ECOOP'2003 Workshop on Exception Handling in Object-Oriented Systems*, July 2003.
26. M. P. Robillard and G. C. Murphy. Static analysis to support the evolution of exception structure in object-oriented systems. *ACM Transactions on Software Engineering and Methodology*, 12(2):191–221, April 2003.
27. C. M. F. Rubira et al. Exception handling in the development of dependable component-based systems. *Software – Practice and Experience*, 35(5):195–236, March 2005.
28. C. F. Schaefer and G. N. Bundy. Static analysis of exception handling in ada. *Software: Practice and Experience*, 23(10):1157–1174, October 1993.
29. M. Shaw and D. Garlan. *Software Architecture: Perspectives on an Emerging Discipline*. Addison-Wesley, 1996.
30. M. Sloman and J. Kramer. *Distributed Systems and Computer Networks*. Prentice-Hall, 1987.
31. W. Weimer and G. Necula. Finding and preventing run-time error handling mistakes. In *Proceedings of OOPSLA'2004*, pages 419–433, October 2004.
32. K. Yi. An abstract interpretation for estimating uncaught exceptions in standard ml programs. *Science of Computer Programming*, 31(1):147–173, 1998.

Are Practitioners Writing Contracts?

Patrice Chalin

Dept. of Computer Science and Software Engineering,
Dependable Software Research Group, Concordia University
chalin@cse.concordia.ca

Abstract. For decades now, modular design methodologies have helped
software engineers cope with the size and complexity of modern-day industrial
applications. To be truly effective though, it is essential that module interfaces
be rigorously specified. Design by Contract (DBC) is an increasingly popular
method of interface specification for object-oriented systems. Many
researchers are actively adding support for DBC to various languages such as
Ada, Java and C#. Are these research efforts justified? Does having support
for DBC mean that developers will make use of it? We present the results of an
empirical study measuring the proportion of assertion statements used in Eiffel
contracts. The study results indicate that programmers using Eiffel (the only
active language with built-in support for DBC) tend to write assertions in a
proportion that is higher than for other languages.

Keywords: design by contract, program assertions, empirical study, Eiffel.

1 Introduction

It is generally accepted that there is no silver bullet and that there probably never will
be; the challenges faced by software engineers will be alleviated by a combination of
techniques. One of the effective ways that software engineers have found to manage
the size and complexity of modern-day software systems is to use a modular-design
methodology. An appropriate partitioning of a system into modules (e.g., libraries,
classes) offers an effective means of managing complexity while providing
opportunities for reuse. But when applied to large industrial applications in general
and fault-tolerant systems in particular, modular design methods can only be truly
effective if module interfaces are rigorously defined.

An increasingly popular approach to interface specification for object-oriented
software is design by contract (DBC) [19-21]. Support for DBC is built in to the
Eiffel programming language. Although Eiffel is the only active language with
integrated support for DBC, researchers are currently busy adding DBC support to
other languages. Generally, this added support is achieved by extending a subset of
the target language. For example,

- SPARK for Ada [1],
- Spec# for C# [2],
- JACK for JavaCard [5],
- Java Modeling Language (JML) [4], Jass [3], Jcontract [22] for Java.

M. Butler et al. (Eds.): Fault-Tolerant Systems, LNCS 4157, pp. 100–113, 2006.
© Springer-Verlag Berlin Heidelberg 2006

Are such research efforts justified? Does having built-in support for DBC mean that developers will write contracts? In an attempt to provide initial answers to these questions we undertook an empirical study of the use of contracts in Eiffel. More specifically, we sought to measure the proportion of source lines of code that are assertions because program assertions are the main ingredient of contracts, and they are easy to quantify. Why did we choose Eiffel programs as the subject of our study? Eiffel is the only active programming language with built in support for DBC, and this since its inception two decades ago. Hence, it is the only language for which there is a sufficiently large code base to sample.

In the next section, we explain the relationship between assertions, DBC and behavioral interface specifications. A brief review of Eiffel is also given, thus providing the necessary background for an understanding of the metrics used in the study. An introduction to the study and an explanation of the metrics are given in Section 3. Section 4 provides the study results, and Section 5 discusses threats to validity. We conclude in Section 6.

2 Design by Contract and Eiffel

2.1 Assertions, DBC and Behavioral Interface Specifications

Design by contract (DBC) refers to a *method* of developing object-oriented software defined by Bertrand Meyer [19, 20]. The main concept that underlies DBC is the notion of a precise and formally specified agreement between a class and its clients. Such an agreement, named a *contract* in DBC, is called a *behavioral interface specification* (BIS) in its most general form [26]. Contracts and BISs are built from class invariants, method pre- and post-conditions, (and other constructs) which are expressed by means of *program assertions*.

DBC as a programming language feature refers to a limited form of support for BISs where assertions are restricted to be expressions that are *executable*. Hence, for example, in Meyer's Eiffel programming language an assertion is merely a Boolean expression (that possibly makes use of the special old operator[1]). Meyer clearly identifies this as an *engineering tradeoff* in the language design of Eiffel [20]—a tradeoff that we believe is an important stepping stone from the current use of (plain) assertions in industry to the longer-term objective of the industrial adoption of verifying compilers [17]. It is understood that this engineering tradeoff imposes a limit on the expressiveness of Eiffel assertions (e.g. absence of quantifiers[2]) but, at the same time, we also believe that it is precisely this tradeoff that has kept them accessible to practitioners. We stress that it is the individual assertion expressions that are restricted to being executable, not the contracts. Hence, for example, a method contract might not be executable if its postcondition describes properties of the method result rather than how it can be computed.

---

[1] old e refers to the pre-state value of e, and can only occur in postconditions.
[2] This exclusion is due not to the quantifiers per se, but rather to the possibility of allowing quantified expressions with bound variables ranging over arbitrarily large or infinite collections.

How are contracts currently used in practice? A principal use for contracts, other than for documentation, is run-time assertion checking (RAC) [6]. All current systems supporting DBC also support RAC. When RAC is enabled, assertions are evaluated at run-time and an exception is thrown if an assertion fails to evaluate to true. Various degrees of checking can be enabled—e.g. from the evaluation of preconditions only, to the evaluation of all assertions, including preconditions, postconditions, invariants and inline assertions. Enabling RAC during testing, particularly integration testing, is an effective means of detecting bugs in modules and thus can help contribute to the increase in overall system quality.

Of course, for most applications, particularly fault-tolerant, safety- and security-critical systems, it is preferable to be able to guarantee the absence of assertion failures before a component is run. Extended Static Checking (ESC) [11] and Verified DBC (VDBC) [10, 25] tools can be used for this purpose. Such tools attempt to determine the validity of assertions by static analysis. ESC tools exist for Modula-3 and Java [9, 14], and one is currently under development for Eiffel. VDBC tools include Omnibus [25] and PerfectDeveloper [10].

2.2 Eiffel: A Brief Review

A sample Eiffel class taken from the Gobo Eiffel kernel library is given in Figure 1. Lines too long to fit on the page have been truncated and suffixed with ellipses ("..."). Classes optionally begin (and/or end) with an *indexing clause* that offers information about the class. In other languages this is often accomplished by using a comment block. Comments, like in Ada, start with a "--" and run until the end of the line. An Eiffel class generally declares a collection of *features* (attributes and "methods"). The given sample class declares only one feature, an *n*-ary exclusive or, nxor.

Of main concern to us here are assertions. An *assertion* in Eiffel is written as a collection of one or more optionally tagged assertion clauses. The meaning of an assertion is the conditional conjunction of its assertion clauses [12]. The tags can help readability and debugging since they can be output when the clause is violated [21]. Tags zero, unary and binary adorn lines 40, 41 and 42 of Figure 1, respectively.

An assertion clause is either a

- Boolean expression (as given in lines 40, 41 and 42) or a
- comment (e.g. line 43).

Such comments are called *informal assertions*. Eiffel's Boolean operators consist of the usual negation (not), conjunction (and) and disjunction (or) as well as conditional (i.e. short-circuited) conjunction (and then) and disjunction (or else). The implication, *a* implies *b*, is an abbreviation for (not *a*) or else *b*. Assertions can contain calls to methods identified as queries. A particular characteristic of a query is that it is not permitted to have side effects [21].

In Eiffel, an assertion can be used to express a

- precondition (introduced by the keyword require),
- postcondition (ensure),

```
1    indexing
2
3    description:
4
5        "Routines that ought to be in class BOOLEAN"
6
7    library: "Gobo Eiffel Kernel Library"
8    copyright: "Copyright (c) 2002, Berend de Boer and others"
...  Lines 9 to 11 have been removed.
12
13   class KL_BOOLEAN_ROUTINES
14
15   feature -- Access
16
17   nxor (a_booleans: ARRAY [BOOLEAN]): BOOLEAN is
18           -- N-ary exclusive or
19       require
20           a_booleans_not_void: a_booleans /= Void
21       local
22           i, nb: INTEGER
23       do
24           i := a_booleans.lower
25           nb := a_booleans.upper
26           from until i > nb loop
...                   Lines 27 to 37 have been removed.
38           end
39       ensure
40           zero: a_booleans.count = 0 implies not Result
41           unary: a_booleans.count = 1 implies Result = ...
42           binary: a_booleans.count = 2 implies Result = ...
43           -- more: there exists one and only one `i' in ...
44       end
45   end
```

Fig. 1. Sample Eiffel class (kl_boolean_routines.e)

- class invariant (**invariant**),
- loop invariant (**invariant**),
- inline assertion (**check**)

A sample precondition is given in line 20 of Figure 1. The sample postcondition (lines 40-43) illustrates the use of more than one assertion clause. Assertions in postconditions can contain occurrences of the special operator **old**. For example, the postcondition

ensure count = **old** count + 1

will be true when the post-state value of count is one more than the pre-state value of count. A check is equivalent to an **assert** statement in other languages such a C, C++ and Java.

There is only one looping construct in Eiffel, and it has the general form given in Figure 2. As was previously mentioned, an assertion can be used to express a loop invariant. Also, of interest is the loop variant: an integer expression that must decrease through every iteration of the loop while remaining nonnegative. That covers the basics of what we need to be able to explain the study metrics.

```
from
    init_instructions
invariant
    assertion
variant
    variant
until
    exit_condition
loop
    loop_instructions
end
```

Fig. 2. Eiffel loop instruction

3 Study

3.1 Objectives and Hypotheses

Given a language like Eiffel, with built-in support for DBC, our objective has been to measure the extent to which developers actually write contracts for their classes. Since program assertions are the basic ingredient of contracts and since it is relatively straightforward to count assertions, we chose this as a basic metric for our study. In addition to counting assertions we will also categorize them by kind—e.g. preconditions, postconditions, etc. vs. ordinary inline assertions. Our main study hypotheses are the following:

(H1) Developers using a programming language with built in support for DBC will write program assertions in a proportion that is higher than for languages not supporting DBC.

(H2) Furthermore, assertions will be used as part of contracts in a proportion that is higher than their use as inline assertions.

3.2 Projects

During the initial portion of our study we gathered metrics from free Eiffel software, consisting of both free commercial software (such as the sources distributed with EiffelStudio) as well as open source projects. This allowed us to conduct a pilot study during which we fine tuned our metrics gathering tool. This was essential before embarking on the second phase of the study in which we solicited the participation of industry.

In the second phase of our study, we posted announcements in the *EiffelWorld* newsletter [7]—published monthly by *Eiffel Software*, the makers of EiffelStudio— as well as Eiffel mailing lists and bulletin boards, inviting developers of commercial and open source Eiffel applications to contribute to the study. The invitation directed developers to a web site managed by our research group where the purpose of the study is explained and instructions for participation are given. After filling in a consent form, developers are provided with a script to run on their Eiffel code. The script generates a metrics file which participants subsequently upload to the study site. Finally, the identity of submitters is confirmed by means of an acknowledgement e-mail.

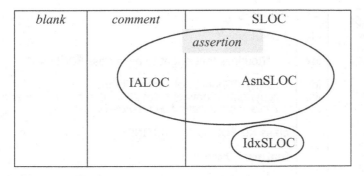

Fig. 3. Categorization of Eiffel LOC

3.3 Definition of Metrics

Our basic metric is a count of Lines of Code (LOC) per class file. As can be seen in Figure 3, each LOC is categorized at the top-level either as a

- blank line, containing at most white space
- comment line, containing a comment possibly preceded by white space
- (physical) Source Line of Code (SLOC) [23].

An illustration of the top-level categorization of the sample Eiffel class of Figure 1 is given in Figure 4.

One of our main statistics is a measure of the proportion of LOC that are assertions. The computation of this ratio is slightly complicated by the existence in Eiffel of informal assertions and index blocks, as we explain next.

An enumeration of the kinds of assertion that are supported by Eiffel is given in Figure 5. Note that we chose to include loop variant expressions as a kind of assertion, since it contributes, like the loop invariant, to the overall specification of the loop instruction.

As was explained in Section 2.2, an assertion can take the form of a source statement (**AsnSLOC**) or a comment. The latter is called an informal assertion (**IALOC**)—see line 43 of Figure 4 for an example. Hence,

$$\mathbf{AsnLOC} = \mathrm{AsnSLOC} + \mathrm{IALOC}$$

The lines in Eiffel indexing clauses (identified as **IdxSLOC** in Figure 3), though technically SLOC, merely provide documentation for a class in a manner that is handled by a comment block in other languages. We therefore define an "adjusted SLOC" metric as

$$\mathbf{AdjSLOC} = \mathrm{SLOC} - \mathrm{IdxSLOC} + \mathrm{IALOC}$$

so we can simply and accurately define the proportion of lines that are assertions as

$$\mathbf{AsnProp} = \mathrm{AsnLOC} \,/\, \mathrm{AdjSLOC}$$

1	SLOC	idx	**indexing**
2	blank		
3	SLOC	idx	description:
4	blank		
5	SLOC	idx	"Routines that ought to be in class BOOLEAN"
6	blank		
7	SLOC	idx	library: "Gobo Eiffel Kernel Library"
8	SLOC	idx	copyright: "Copyright (c) 2002, Berend de Boer and others"
...	...	...	*Lines 9 to 11 have been removed.*
12	blank		
13	SLOC		**class** KL_BOOLEAN_ROUTINES
14	blank		
15	SLOC		**feature** -- Access
16	blank		
17	SLOC		nxor (a_booleans: ARRAY [BOOLEAN]): BOOLEAN is
18	comment		-- N-ary exclusive or
19	SLOC		**require**
20	SLOC	req	a_booleans_not_void: a_booleans /= Void
21	SLOC		**local**
22	SLOC		i, nb: INTEGER
23	SLOC		**do**
24	SLOC		i := a_booleans.lower
25	SLOC		nb := a_booleans.upper
26	SLOC		**from until** i > nb **loop**
...	...	...	*Lines 27 to 37 have been removed.*
38	SLOC		**end**
39	SLOC		**ensure**
40	SLOC	ens	*zero*: a_booleans.count = 0 implies not Result
41	SLOC	ens	*unary*: a_booleans.count = 1 implies Result = ...
42	SLOC	ens	*binary*: a_booleans.count = 2 implies Result = ...
43	comment	ens	-- more: there exists one and only one `i' in ...
44	SLOC		**end**
45	SLOC		**end**

Fig. 4. LOC categorization for our sample (kl_boolean_routines.e)

Statement	Use to express ...	AsnLOC qualifier
`require`	preconditions	`Req`
`ensure`	postconditions	`Ens`
`invariant` (class)	class invariants	`Inv`
`invariant` (loop)	loop invariant	`invL`
`variant` (loop)	loop variant	`varL`
`check`	inline assertion	`chk`

Fig. 5. Kinds of assertion

We will keep separate $AsnLOC_a$ counts for each kind of assertion a (see Figure 5); we note that:

$$AsnLOC = AsnLOC_{req} + AsnLOC_{ens} + ... + AsnLOC_{chk}$$

Table 1. Number of projects, classes and LOC

Project Category	Number of projects	Number of classes	LOC (10^6)	% of total LOC
Proprietary	5	28 149	4.4	55%
Open Source	79	15 986	2.7	33%
EiffelStudio L&S	1	4 373	0.9	11%
Total	85	48 508	7.9	100%

3.4 Metrics Gathering Tool

At first we used the SLOCCount tool [24] as our base. This tool can count physical SLOC for over two-dozen languages—though initially not for Eiffel. Aside from its ability to process many different kinds of languages SLOCCount also does convenient house-keeping tasks such as determining the type of a file (by its extension or content), flagging duplicates and ignoring generated files.

Since our needs were specific to Eiffel source, we eventually chose to use a single Perl script to gather all metrics. The creation of the script did pose some challenges due, e.g., to the various flavors of Eiffel (as supported by different compilers) and inconsistent line endings (Unix, DOS or Mac) sometimes within the same file, as well as the variation in lexical rules used for multi-line string literals.

4 Results

4.1 General

As can be seen from Table 1, the study covered 85 projects totaling 48 508 Eiffel classes and 7.9 million lines of code (MLOC). The projects included applications from the areas of databases, developer tools, finance/HR, games, modeling, middleware, networking, scientific computing, systems software, utility library/toolkits, visualization and web applications. We divided the projects into three categories:

- proprietary (accounting for 55% of the code of the study),
- open source (33%), and the
- library and samples shipped with EiffelStudio 5.5 (11%).

Note that half of the files in the EiffelStudio category consist of open source samples (or what they call "free add-ons"), most of which are provided by GoboSoft—an important contributor of open source Eiffel libraries and tools. Nonetheless GoboSoft add-on files were counted in the EiffelStudio category only. We separated out EiffelStudio (libraries and samples) into its own category because we expected it to have the highest proportion of assertions.

The breakdown (partitioning) of LOC into SLOC, blank lines and comments is given in Table 2. We see that 74% of LOC are physical source lines of code. On average, the classes in our study contained 163 LOC (120 SLOC). The table also

Table 2. Breakdown of LOC into SLOC, blank and comment lines

	SLOC	blank	comment	Total	IdxSLOC	IALOC	AdjSLOC
LOC (10^6)	5.8	1.3	0.83	7.9	0.25	0.014	5.6
% of total LOC	74%	16%	10%	100%	3.2%	0.17%	71%
Average	120	26	17	163	5	0.3	115

Table 3. Assertion metrics by kind

	Assertion kind, $a \rightarrow$	require	ensure	class inv	loop inv	loop var	check	Total
(a)	$AsnLOC_a$	138 960	111 420	19 794	745	705	8 563	280 187
(b)	$AsnLOC_a$/AdjSLOC	2.5%	2.0%	0.35%	0.013%	0.013%	0.15%	5.0%
(c)	$AsnLOC_a$/AsnLOC	50%	40%	7.1%	0.27%	0.25%	3.1%	100%
(d)	max $AsnLOC_a$/AsnLOC	56%	49%	52%	11%	5%	33%	-
(e)	avg. $AsnLOC_a$ / file	2.9	2.3	0.4	0.0	0.0	0.2	5.8
(f)	no. of statements (stmt)	83 712	69 144	8 671	412	694	7 005	169 638
(g)	avg. $AsnLOC_a$ / stmt	1.6	1.6	2.3	1.8	1.0	1.2	-
(h)	max $AsnLOC_a$/ stmt	30	84	79	12	3	25	-
(i)	$IALOC_a$	1595	9 752	1 742	104	5	558	13 756
(j)	$IALOC_a$/AdjSLOC	0.03%	0.17%	0.03%	0.00%	0.00%	0.01%	0.25%
(k)	$IALOC_a$/AsnLOC	0.57%	3.5%	0.62%	0.04%	0.00%	0.20%	4.9%
(l)	count (e/=Void)	63 003	22 187	9 672	9	0	2 811	97 682
(m)	% (e/=Void)	45%	20%	49%	1.2%	0.00%	33%	35%

provides the value of AdjSLOC, namely 5.6 MLOC, which is defined to be the number of SLOC excluding indexing clause lines but including informal assertions (cf. Section 3.3). This adjusted SLOC count is the valued used in measuring the proportion of assertions.

4.2 Assertion Metrics

The metrics concerning assertions are summarized in Table 3. We highlight some of the most interesting results. For ease of reference, we have labeled the rows of the table from (a) to (m). Looking at the Total column for rows (a) and (b) we see that there were 0.28 MLOC of assertions. Hence, out of the 5.6 MLOC of adjusted SLOC previously mentioned, overall 5.0% of the LOC were assertions.

Row (c) of Table 3 gives the distribution of assertions by kind, which is also graphically illustrated in Figure 6. Assertions are mostly used to document preconditions (50%), postconditions (40%) and class invariants (7.1%). Few loop invariants and variants are given, though both of these appear almost as frequently relative to each other. The low frequency of loop invariants and variants may be a testimony to the high degree of challenge associated with writing useful loop invariants and variants. Remarkably only 3.1% of the assertions (0.15% of the overall AdjSLOC) were inline checks.

Recall that the various kinds of assertion statement can contain more than one assertion line. The average number assertion lines per statement (g) ranges from 1.0 to 2.3, while the average number of assertions per file (e) is 5.8. While preconditions occur most frequently, class invariants have the largest number of assertions

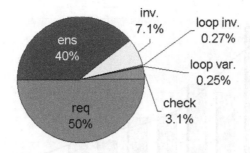

Fig. 6. Distribution of assertions by kind (all project categories)

per statement (2.3). This suggests that class invariants, when written, express more complex conditions since on average, it requires twice as many assertions to express a class invariant than a precondition. The maximum number of assertions per clause (h) can be fairly large, e.g. up to 79 LOC for a class invariant and 84 LOC for a postcondition.

We note that a very small proportion of assertions are given in the form of comments. Overall, only 0.25% of the AdjSLOC and 4.9% of assertion LOC are informal assertions (j), (k). Informal assertions are used most frequently in postconditions (3.5% of $AsnSLOC_{ens}$). We expect this to be the case either because (i) some aspect of the postcondition may be too complex to express as an assertion—e.g. it may require quantifiers—or, (ii) developers do not want the overhead of full postcondition evaluation during run-time checking and choose express as comments those predicates that would be too computationally intensive.

A noteworthy proportion of assertions include subexpressions of the form $e \mathrel{/=}$ void, stating that a given reference is not void (i.e. null). This number is close to 50% for class invariants and 35% overall (m). These figures provide some weight to the choice made by a number of language designers and static analysis tools (such as Splint [13]) which consider a reference type declaration to be non-null by default. In fact, we recently completed a more detailed study that indicates that well over 50% of reference type declarations in Java are meant to be non-null [8]. In the newly released ECMA Eiffel standard, the notions of attached and detachable types are introduced. An identifier of an attached type is guaranteed to always be bound to an object, i.e., it cannot be void/null. The standard mandates that types are attached by default; to indicate a detachable version of a type T one prefixes the type name with a question mark: $?T$ [12].

What was the distribution of AsnProp? A little over half (52.4%) of the classes in the study contained no assertions. We note that a class without assertions can still have a contract, since subclasses inherit contracts from their superclasses (but detecting and quantifying such implicit contracts is outside the scope of this study). The distribution of the files with a nonzero AsnProp is given in Figure 7. The highest proportion of files (11%) had an AsnProp in the range 2.5% to 5%. A third of the files had an AsnProp between 0 and 12.5%. Figure 8 shows the number of projects with an average proportion of assertions in a given range. Two projects had no assertions, while the majority of projects had between 1.5% and 7% of assertions per adjusted SLOC.

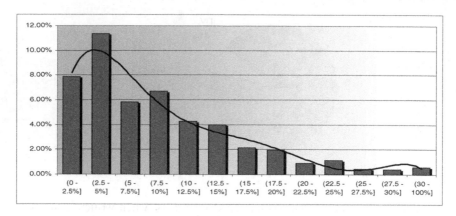

Fig. 7. Percentage of files with AsnProp in a given range

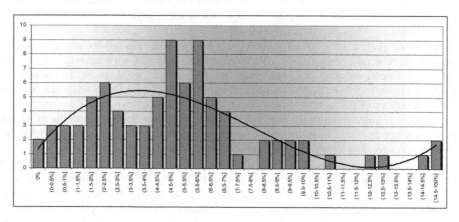

Fig. 8. Number of projects with AsnProp in a given range

Table 4 shows how the proportion of LOC that are assertions varies by project category. As might be expected, the EiffelStudio category has the highest proportion, 6.7%, followed by open source projects and proprietary code with 5.8% and 4.2%, respectively. (Recall that the open source category *excludes* GoboSoft software because it is counted in the EiffelStudio project category.)

Table 4. Proportion of AsnLOCs per project category

Project Category	SLOC (10^6)	AdjSLOC (10^6)	AsnLOC (10^6)	AsnLOC / AdjSLOC
Proprietary	3.3	3.2	0.13	4.2%
Open Source	1.9	1.8	0.11	5.8%
EiffelStudio L&S	0.62	0.59	0.04	6.7%
Total	5.8	5.6	0.28	5.0%

5   Threats to Validity

5.1   Internal Validity

The most significant potential source of error is in the measurement of metrics because the metrics are gathered by a script that uses keyword-based pattern matching rather than a true Eiffel parser. This was deemed the only practical approach because study samples were written in several different variants of Eiffel; with the variability being due to differences in the language as supported by different compilers or even to changes in the language introduced over time. Since none of the current Eiffel compilers support all variants, it seemed utterly impractical to attempt to build our own parser that would.

Due to the manner in which Eiffel makes use of keywords to delimit code blocks that can contain assertions, a keyword-based pattern matching approach turned out to be not only feasible but also (seemingly) quite accurate. Our confidence was boosted by the use of an inclusive test suite and by the fact that a comprehensive set of sanity checks have been build into the script—we have run the script on over 5 million LOC without it reporting errors.

Another aspect which could have biased the study results would be for a file's data to have been counted more than once. This would be likely to occur when the code of an open source library was used in multiple projects. To guard against this, the script used to compute the study metrics was also designed to generate a 32 bit hash code for each file based on the file content. In computing the final statistics we retained at most one file with the given hash code.

5.2   External Validity

Were the projects used in the study representative of typical Eiffel software? In the first phase of the study we obtained projects from SourceForge and other sites dedicated to open source Eiffel software. Our only selection criterion was for projects to appear to be active; we believe that this is reasonable. In the second phase of the study, we solicited contributions from the Eiffel community. This resulted in 10 submissions, half of which were proprietary, though this half contributed 55% of the LOC for the study. With respect to the threat to validity, our main concern is whether the volunteered projects would have a proportion of assertions that is higher than average, hence unfairly contributing support towards our hypothesis. This cannot be ascertained, but we note that the proportion of assertions for proprietary code (4.2%) was in fact less than that for open source code (5.8%) and that all but five of the open source projects were chosen by us in phase one. It is clear though, that the relatively small size of the Eiffel user community, as compared, say, to that of C or C++, may also have some bearing on the study results—e.g. lesser variability.

Could similar results be expected to hold for other languages supporting DBC? One might argue that those who write applications in Eiffel have chosen Eiffel over other programming languages precisely because of its built-in support for DBC. Hence, the proportion of developers who are willing to write contracts may be higher in the case of Eiffel than for another programming language. Even if this was the case, the results offer the promise that such developers may well choose to adopt another programming language if DBC support were adequate.

6 Conclusion

In previous work, we were able to establish that the industrial use of assertions is fairly widespread [6]. The present study focuses on the use of assertions in Eiffel, the only active language supporting the disciplined use of assertions in specifying contracts, i.e. Design by Contract (DBC). Overall, 5.0% of the studied code consisted of assertions. Ninety-seven percent of these assertions were used in contracts rather than inline assertions (confirming our hypothesis H2). We are not aware of any other empirical studies that measure the use of assertions, but *estimated* figures are available. For example, Hoare estimates that 1% of the Microsoft Office Suite LOC are assertions [15, 16]. Participants of a survey that we recently conducted offered estimates with a mean of 3.2% [6]. The results of the study reported here, allow us to confirm (H1) that Eiffel classes contain program assertions in a proportion that is higher than the use of assertions in programming languages not supporting DBC. In our opinion, this is good news for those researchers currently striving to add DBC support to other languages.

We expect that developers will be inclined to increase their use of assertions as other tools that process assertions and contracts become more mature and widely known—e.g. tools like JmlUnit that can automatically generate test oracles from JML specifications [18]. By design, DBC restricts the expressiveness of assertions by requiring that they be executable. We believe that this moderation in expressiveness is what will allow DBC to be more easily adopted by industry at large. It will then become a smaller step to reach the full expressiveness of behavioral interface specifications (BISs).

References

[1] J. Barnes, *High Integrity Software: The Spark Approach to Safety and Security*. Addison-Wesley, 2003.

[2] M. Barnett, K. R. M. Leino, and W. Schulte, "The Spec# Programming System: An Overview". In G. Barthe, L. Burdy, M. Huisman, J.-L. Lanet, and T. Muntean editors, *Proceedings of the International Workshop on the Construction and Analysis of Safe, Secure, and Interoperable Smart Devices (CASSIS'04)*, Marseille, France, 2004, vol. 3362 of *LNCS*. Springer, 2004.

[3] D. Bartetzko, C. Fischer, M. Moller, and H. Wehrheim, "Jass—Java with Assertions", *Electronic Notes in Theoretical Computer Science*, 55(2):103-117, 2001.

[4] L. Burdy, Y. Cheon, D. R. Cok, M. D. Ernst, J. R. Kiniry, G. T. Leavens, K. R. M. Leino, and E. Poll, "An Overview of JML Tools and Applications", *International Journal on Software Tools for Technology Transfer (STTT)*, 7(3):212-232, 2005.

[5] L. Burdy, A. Requet, and J.-L. Lanet, "Java Applet Correctness: A Developer-Oriented Approach". *Proceedings of the International Symposium of Formal Methods Europe*, 2003, vol. 2805 of *LNCS*. Springer, 2003.

[6] P. Chalin, "Logical Foundations of Program Assertions: What do Practitioners Want?" *Proceedings of the Third International Conference on Software Engineering and Formal Methods (SEFM'05)*, Koblenz, Germany, September 5-9, 2005. IEEE Computer Society Press, 2005.

[7] P. Chalin, "DbC and assertions in Eiffel: participants needed for quantitative research survey", *EiffelWorld Electronic Newsletter*, 32(2), 2006.

[8] P. Chalin and F. Rioux, "Non-null References by Default in the Java Modeling Language". *Workshop on the Specification and Verification of Component-Based Systems (SAVCBS'05)*, Lisbon, Portugal, Sept., 2005. ACM Press, 2005.

[9] D. R. Cok and J. R. Kiniry, "ESC/Java2: Uniting ESC/Java and JML". In G. Barthe, L. Burdy, M. Huisman, J.-L. Lanet, and T. Muntean editors, *Proceedings of the International Workshop on the Construction and Analysis of Safe, Secure, and Interoperable Smart Devices (CASSIS'04)*, Marseille, France, March 10-14, 2004, vol. 3362 of *LNCS*, pp. 108-128. Springer, 2004.

[10] D. Crocker, "Safe Object-Oriented Software: The Verified Design-By-Contract Paradigm". *Practical Elements of Safety: Proceedings of the 12th Safety-Critical Systems Symposium*, Birmingham, UK, February, 2004. Springer, 2004.

[11] D. L. Detlefs, K. R. M. Leino, G. Nelson, and J. B. Saxe, "Extended Static Checking", Compaq Systems Research Center, Research Report 159. December, 1998.

[12] ECMA International, "Eiffel Analysis, Design and Programming Language", ECMA-367. June 2005.

[13] D. Evans, "Splint User Manual", Secure Programming Group, University of Virginia. June 5, 2003.

[14] C. Flanagan, K. R. M. Leino, M. Lillibridge, G. Nelson, J. B. Saxe, and R. Stata, "Extended static checking for Java". *Proceedings of the ACM SIGPLAN Conference on Programming Language Design and Implementation (PLDI'02)*, June, 2002, vol. 37(5), pp. 234-245. ACM Press, 2002.

[15] C.A.R. Hoare, "Assertions: Progress and Prospects", http://research.microsoft. com/~thoare, 2001.

[16] C. A. R. Hoare, "Assertions: A Personal Perspective", *IEEE Annals of the History of Computing*, 25(2):14-25, 2003.

[17] C. A. R. Hoare, "The Verifying Compiler: A Grand Challenge for Computing Research", *JACM*, 50(1):63-69, 2003.

[18] G. T. Leavens, K. R. M. Leino, E. Poll, C. Ruby, and B. Jacobs, "JML: Notations and Tools Supporting Detailed Design in Java", in *OOPSLA 2000 Companion, Minneapolis, Minnesota*, 2000, pp. 105-106.

[19] B. Meyer, "Applying Design by Contract", *Computer*, 25(10):40-51, 1992.

[20] B. Meyer, *Object-Oriented Software Construction*, 2nd ed. Prentice-Hall, 1997.

[21] R. Mitchell and M. Jim, *Design by Contract, by Example*. Addison-Wesley, 2002.

[22] Parasoft, "Jcontract product page", www.parasoft.com, 2005.

[23] R. Park, "Software Size Measurement: A Framework for Counting Source Statements", CMU, Software Engineering Institute, Pittsburgh CMU/SEI-92-TR-20, 1992.

[24] D. A. Wheeler, "SLOCCount", www.dwheeler.com/sloccount, 2005.

[25] T. Wilson and S. Maharaj, "Omnibus: A clean language for supporting DBC, ESC and VDBC". *Proceedings of the Third International Conference on Software Engineering and Formal Methods (SEFM'05)*, Koblenz, Germany, September 5-9, 2005. IEEE Computer Society Press, 2005.

[26] J. M. Wing, "Writing Larch Interface Language Specifications", *ACM Trans. Program. Lang. Syst.* , 9(1):1-24, 1987.

Determining the Specification of a Control System: An Illustrative Example

Joey W. Coleman

School of Computing Science
University of Newcastle upon Tyne
NE1 7RU, UK
j.w.coleman@ncl.ac.uk

Abstract. Creating the specification of a system by focusing primarily on the detailed properties of the digital controller can lead to complex descriptions that are nearly incoherent. An argument given by Hayes, Jackson, and Jones provides reasons to focus first on the wider environment in which the system will reside. In their approach are two major ideas: pushing out the specification boundaries, and carefully distinguishing between the requirements of the system and the assumptions about the environment. Pushing out the boundaries of the system specification to include the pragmatic intent of the system being specified allows the specification to be understood relative to the environmental context, rather than remaining a mysterious black box in isolation. Clarifying the distinction between assumptions about the environment and requirements that the specification must meet increases the clarity of the specification, and has the potential to seriously reduce the complexity of the final specification. The example of a gas burner is explored in depth to illustrate this approach to system specification.

1 Overview of Approach

The general idea of the "Hayes/Jackson/Jones" (HJJ) approach [1] is simple: for many technical systems it is easier to derive their specification from one of a wider system in which physical phenomena are measurable. Even though the computer cannot affect the physical world directly, it is still worthwhile to start with the wider system. The message can be given as its converse: do not jump into specifying the digital system in isolation. If one starts by recording the requirements of the wider physical system, the specification of the technical components can then be *derived* from that of the overall system; assumptions about the physical components are recorded as rely-conditions for the technical components.

In order to be able to write this style of specification, some technical work derived from earlier publications of Hayes, Jackson and Jones has to be brought together. The process of deriving the specification of the software system involves recording assumptions about the non-software components. These assumptions are recorded as rely conditions because we know how to reason about them

M. Butler et al. (Eds.): Fault-Tolerant Systems, LNCS 4157, pp. 114–132, 2006.

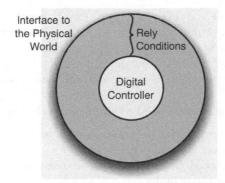

Fig. 1. Bridging from the physical world to a digital control system

from earlier work on concurrency (e.g. [2,3,4]). In most cases, we need to reason about the continuous behaviour of physical variables like altitude: earlier work by Hayes and Mahony provides suitable notation [5]. The emphasis on "problem frames" comes from Jackson's publications [6].

An example of the HJJ approach is a computer-controlled temperature system. One should not start by specifying the digital controller; rather, an initial specification in terms of the actual temperature should be written. In order to derive the specification of the control system, one needs to record assumptions (as rely-conditions) about the accuracy of sensors; there will also be assumptions about the fact that setting digital switches results in a change in temperature. Once the specification of the control system has been determined, its design and code can be created as a separate exercise. At all stages — but particularly before deployment — someone has to make the decision that the rely conditions are in accordance with the available equipment. Figure 1 gives an abstract view of the HJJ approach. The referenced [1] outlines this procedure on a "sluice gate" controller. The analysis includes looking at tolerating faults by describing weaker guarantees in the presence of weaker rely conditions.

Notice that it is not necessary to build a complete model of the physical components like motors, sensors and relays: only to record assumptions. But even in the simple sluice gate example of [1], it becomes clear that choosing the perimeter of the system is a crucial question: one can consider the physical phenomena to be controlled as the height of the gate, or the amount of water flowing; or the humidity of the soil; or even the farm profits. Each such scope results in different sorts of rely-conditions.

2 Examining the System

2.1 The Example

Our running example in this paper is the specification of a control program for a gas-burner. The gas-burner is very similar to the one used in [7]. A thermostat provides allows the whole system to react to its environment, and the rest consists of a gas-valve/nozzle assembly, a sensor to detect the flame, and an ignition transformer. The whole system also includes a computer and a thermostat. The requirements given in [7] include some detail for intended operation and safety, and there is also a requirement that the system must operate in an efficient manner [8].

We are presented with three initial requirements taken verbatim from [7]:

R1. In order to ensure safety the gas concentration in the environment must at all time be kept below a certain threshold

R2. The gas-burner should burn when heat request is on, provided the gas ignites and burns without faults

R3. The gas-burner should not burn when heat request is off

There is also a set of assumptions about the environment which will be touched on when we investigate the rely-conditions for this system.

So far we have presented almost no context for the gas-burner system, and our source for the example provides little other than what has been mentioned thus far. At this point, trying to generate a specification would be dangerous as our assumptions — still unrecorded — about the system would colour the requirements produced. First, then, we must consider the context and use of this system.

2.2   The Context

We know that this system reacts to its environment due to the signal provided by a thermostat. This implies an environment that is colder than the burn-temperature of the gas that will be used, as well as an environment that has the tendency to cool down — at least in the area of the thermostat. It would also seem reasonable to assume that the thermostat will turn the heat request signal on when the temperature crosses a low threshold, and off when it exceeds another threshold.

This leads to ruling out a larger set of possible uses: the gas-burner is not intended as a venting mechanism for something like a refinery. It seems unlikely that the need to vent gas would be triggered by a temperature (at least, high temperature gas would not be burnt because of a *need* for heat). There are also other usage scenarios that could be ruled out; we will not go into them here.

We also do not know why we are burning gas — perhaps the intention is to heat the pipes in a boiler, or the bottom of a pot on a gas hob, or just the air in a gas over or furnace.

For our investigation we will fix the system components to those mentioned at the beginning of Section 2.1, and assume that the gas-burner is intended to heat the air around it.

2.3   The Boundaries

The original development of a specification for the gas-burner in [7] starts by constructing a system model without fully examining the boundaries between the system and its surrounding environment. That development does provide an explicit model of an environment, but it provides little in the way of justification about the source and accuracy of that model. The definitions of the boundaries — and their subsequent extension — is not so much an exercise in specifying a larger system as it is one designed to help ensure that the specification encompasses all of the pertinent pieces.

Let us consider issues related to the gas itself. Our source gives the requirement (R1) that the concentration of gas in the atmosphere must be kept below a certain threshold for "safety". What does that mean? The first obvious concern is explosions, of course — it is likely that a high concentration of gas would explode if ignited. But there are other concerns, especially if people will be in the same environment as the gas-burner: while unlikely, it is possible that, for certain types of gas, asphyxiation or intoxication can be caused by a much lower concentration than is required for an explosion.

Considering the safety properties of the gas, there are also several deeper properties that should be examined. We are assuming a specific type of gas — possibly the same natural gas that is commonly piped into houses. What would happen if a different type of gas were to be used? If we look at the environment in which the gas-burner will be placed, what assumptions are there? Is it well-vented? Does it have a "standard" atmospheric gas mix (as opposed to a pure O_2 atmosphere)? These considerations — when decided upon — must be recorded as assumptions.

So much for the properties of the gas on its own; let us bring the gas valve and nozzle under consideration. We will assume that it is not possible for a flame to "hide" within the nozzle of the burner as it can with some varieties of oxyacetylene welding torches. Part of the justification for this assumption is to limit our system's boundaries such that we do not have to consider the gas delivery system. In that vein, we are also going to consider the gas valve to be an ideal component — its sealing mechanism never fails; it delivers a constant flow-rate of gas into the environment; and if it ever does fail, it will fail in such as was as to not release any further gas.

A physical nozzle typically delivers a varying rate of gas as it is turned on or off, however, the assumption in this example is that the nozzle's behaviour will appear binary, delivering either no gas to the environment, or a constant rate of flow. The development framework used is capable of modelling a variable flow-rate, but doing so would add little to this exposition.

The ignition transformer generates a spark to ignite the gas, but it is hardly the only way the gas could ignite. If a person were to hold a lit match near the gas nozzle, that would suffice to ignite the gas if the valve were opened. In an open environment there are many possible ignition sources: our specification must rely only on the ignition transformer.

On reflection, it seems that assuming that the ignition transformer is not the only source of ignition is a reasonable thing to do: if our specification is written such that the gas is only ever turned on when we actually want to burn it, then the source of ignition is irrelevant. If we do not want to burn gas then our usual behaviour is such that the ambient concentration of gas is being reduced. Note that there is no actual requirement from the source document to keep the gas off — just one not to burn it if the heat request signal is off (requirement R3).

The flame sensor is assumed to be able to detect a flame if one is present. The failure mode of the system, if it does not detect the presence of a flame, would be precisely the same as if the gas had failed to ignite in the first place — the gas would be shut off and the system would wait until the specified time for gas dissipation expired. If the sensor indicated the presence of a flame when there was none present, then, while it is possible to detect the fault, the system would be in a very dangerous state.

Now we hit an issue that falls firmly into the realm of fault tolerance, and is outside our given requirements: what should the system do if it cannot produce a flame, even after many attempts? (In this case, "cannot produce a flame" includes being unable to detect the presence of a flame.) Given our assumption that if the gas valve fails it will be closed, it is certainly safe to let the system continue to try to ignite the (possibly not present) gas, but that hardly fits the notion of an efficient gas-burner.

The thermostat in the system presents many opportunities to widen the scope of the system. The initial requirements and description suggest that the thermostat contains only a simple on/off switch (or, more precisely, the interface it presents to the controller will be a boolean value). What considerations are required for a thermostat that exports an interface that is a percentage of the maximum possible heat output? Can our gas-burner support that? One designed for a gas oven would certainly have to do so.

All of the components in the system — to varying degrees — need to be concerned with "value stutter". How quickly can the system produce flame; how quickly can it be extinguished; what sort of delay is required between those transitions? How often can we transition over a given period of time? Since it is the thermostat which controls the heat request signal, what are its transition properties? These questions push the specification boundaries in the temporal domain, helping determine the lowest granularity level that the specification is concerned with.

2.4   The Larger Context, Briefly

So, we have now investigated the components of the system and seen how they can affect the specification and requirements. Let us look at the larger context of the system. We have already identified some of the scenarios that we are not concerned with and identified a reasonable, immediate context for the burner: heating the air around it.

What is the larger context: what kind of larger system could this gas-burner be a component of? Could there be an unmentioned backup system that might be used if this gas-burner fails? If so, then the simplest — and possibly best — error-mode for this gas-burner would be to simply shut down. More important, however, is that a second gas-burner would invalidate all of the assumptions about the concentration of gas in the environment — we rely on this gas-burner being the only source of gas.

3   An Idealised Specification

Having now thoroughly considered the context that our system is in, we can finally begin its specification. To do so we are using the same notation as in [1]; systems are either implicitly specified using a **system** block, or built out of operators like **until/corrects**. The **system** block is an implicit specification, using keywords such as **external**, **input**, **output**, **rely**, and **guarantee**. The keywords mentioned here are not an exhaustive list as the notation can easily tolerate extension.

The **external** keyword is used to identify variables that are important to the behaviour of the system but are not actually a part of the system being specified. These variables are eventually eliminated from the specification of the control software through reification. The **input** and **output** keywords are similar to the VDM **rd** and **wr** keywords — they name the variables that the system can access.

At the heart of the behavioural notions are the **rely** and **guarantee** keywords. The rely-condition states the behaviour that the designer of the system expects of, and depends on, from the environment. As noted elsewhere, the system might be deployed in an environment that violates the rely-condition — it is the responsibility of the user of the system to ensure that the rely-condition holds. The guarantee-condition complements the rely-condition by describing the behaviour that the system must conform to in an environment which respects the rely-condition. Although the system is, formally, free of any behavioural constraints if the rely-condition is violated, we show some mechanisms to place constraints on a system under certain violations of the rely in Section 4.

Using this notation we can describe an idealised version of the gas-burner system as

$GasBurnerSystem0 \triangleq$
    system
    external *Concentration*
    inputs *Temperature*
    outputs *GasFlow, Spark, Flame*
    rely *PhysicalProperties* $\land$ *GluingAssumptions* $\land$ *Idealisations*
    guarantee *OperationalProperties* $\land$ *LowConcentrationLevel*

The idealised system is built under the assumption that everything is working properly. We will use structures such as **until/corrects** in Section 4 to add fault-tolerant features to the system.

In this version of the specification we have *Concentration* defined as an external variable as it is not possible for any part of this system to directly (or indirectly) measure the concentration of gas in the environment. Before the final specification could be handed off to be implemented all of the external variables must be removed. The presence of external variables in the initial specification serves to record the environmental factors: the details about why the system exhibits certain behaviours. This allows us to derive — and justify the derivation of — specifications that do not use these inaccessible external variables. The *Concentration* variable represents the concentration of gas in the environment immediately surrounding the nozzle of the gas-burner. We make the assumption that the gas diffuses evenly into the environment, and the *Concentration* variable is continuous in both domain (time) and range (percentage of gas in the environment).

The system only has *Temperature* as an input variable. This represents the temperature in the vicinity of the thermostat. The variable is continuous in both its domain (time) and range (temperature at the thermostat). We could easily put bounds on the range of the value, defining an operational temperature range, but they add little to the exposition here.

The output variables of the system — *GasFlow*, *Spark*, and *Flame* — are all boolean-valued and, respectively, represent whether or not the gas is on, whether or not the ignition transformer is producing sparks, and the presence of a flame caused by the combustion of gas.

Before moving on to the system's behaviour, note that all of the input and output variables will become external variables when the controller is specified. Because the controller is only able to interact through the signals it receives and emits, it will be unable to directly access the physical state of the overall system. So, in turn, the input and output variables of the overall system will not be present in the specification that is used to generate the controller's implementation.

The rely-condition for this system has been expressed as three conjuncts, each of which describes a class of assumptions about the environment. The *PhysicalProperties* is intended to record the physics that the system relies on, and is written in terms that are independent of the system itself. To relate the components of the system to the physical assumptions we use the *GluingAssumptions* conjunct. It makes the connection between things like the *IgnitionSource* of *PhysicalProperties* to the *Spark* output variable. It has been implicitly idealised, assuming that all transitions happen instantaneously; the extra complexity of modelling the delay in transition from one state to another is unnecessary for this illustration. The last portion, *Idealisations*, is a set of properties that allow the system at this level to ignore fault tolerance concerns.

The guarantee-condition of this system has two conjuncts: one of which expresses the actual desired behaviour; the other expresses a sort of behaviour we wish to exclude. The *OperationalProperties* gives the core behaviour that is desired from the gas-burner system. This portion is uncluttered by any notion of fault-tolerance, error detection/correction, or system constraints. The second conjunct, *LowConcentrationLevel*, deals with a particularly important safety condition that our system must respect: it must not cause the concentration of gas to exceed a certain level.

3.1   The Notation Used in Properties

The notation used to denote individual properties is essentially that developed by Mahony and Hayes [5] and used in [1]. The basic intuition is that all state variables can be treated as continuous functions over a time domain.

The time domain is usually denoted at T, and the expression **interval** T represents the set of all possible open, finite intervals of time within that time domain. It is of note that it is possible to consider T as an interval in its own right, and that given I as an interval in T, **interval** I simply represents all of the possible sub-intervals in I. The letters I, J, and K are typically used to stand for intervals.

Where they are defined, state variables map specific points in time to values, so they cannot be used directly with intervals. However, for an interval I and a predicate P, we write P **over** I to mean that the predicate holds for all points in I. This notation is shorthand for $\forall i \in I \cdot P(i)$.

Similar to the **over** operator, there is a form of integration that is used as in the Duration Calculus [9]. For some predicate, P, the expression $\int_I P$ gives the length of time that P was true in the interval I. There is also a shorthand notation that represents the total length of a duration, written $\#I$, that is equivalent to writing $\int_I$ **true**.

Two related predicates over intervals are **precedes** and **adjoins**. For the former, if I **preceeds** J, then we know that the supremum of I is less than or equal to the infimum of J. The latter, where I **adjoins** J, is the stronger case where the supremum of I is equal to the infimum of J.

3.2   Idealised Rely-Conditions

The *PhysicalProperties* conjunct contains a model of the physics that is important to the gas-burner. These properties do not so much have to be used to select the environment as verified themselves that they reflect the physics of the environment. These properties are specified in general terms, using the variable *Combustion* to represent any sort of gas combustion, including explosions. We will later relate the machine-specific *Flame* variable to the general environmental property of combustion represented by the *Combustion* variable.

One such property is the fact that gas, even in high concentrations, will not spontaneously combust without something to ignite it.

$$\forall I, J \colon \textbf{interval } T \cdot \left(\begin{array}{l} I \textbf{ adjoins } J \wedge \neg \ Combustion \textbf{ over } I \ \wedge \\ \neg \ IgnitionSource \textbf{ over } (I \cup J) \\ \Rightarrow \ \neg \ Combustion \textbf{ over } J \end{array} \right)$$

That is, given two adjoining intervals I and J, if the gas is not lit during I, and there is nothing to ignite the gas during either I or J, then the gas will not be lit during J. This holds for any adjoining pair of intervals. One thing to note about that formula is that *IgnitionSource* covers *anything* that could ignite the gas — the ignition transformer, a heating engineer with a match, and so on.

Directly related to that, we also need to record the physical property that lets the system ignite the gas:

$$\exists I\colon \mathbf{interval}\ \ T\cdot\left(\begin{array}{l}(IgnitionSource \wedge Concentration \geq IgnitionMin)\ \mathbf{over}\ I \\ \Rightarrow\ Combustion\ \mathbf{over}\ I\end{array}\right)$$

This formula is an existentially quantified predicate as it is entirely possible for the gas to not ignite, even in the presence of a spark.

More difficult to express is the notion that combustion reduces the amount of gas in the environment. Part of the difficulty is that a fully general statement of this has to talk about gas flow rates, combustion rates, and environmental dissipation, at the very least. The approach taken here is to codify three cases around the *GasSource* and *Combustion* variables in an attempt to create the outer bounds of a fully general statement.

$$\forall I, J\colon \mathbf{interval}\ \ T\cdot\left(\begin{array}{l}I\ \mathbf{adjoins}\ J \wedge \neg\ GasSource\ \mathbf{over}\ (I \cup J) \\ \Rightarrow\ \int_I Concentration > \int_J Concentration\end{array}\right)$$

This case is the simplest of the three: if there is no gas being added to the environment then the overall concentration of gas in the atmosphere will decrease.

$$\forall I, J\colon \mathbf{interval}\ \ T\cdot\left(\begin{array}{l}GasSource\ \mathbf{over}\ (I \cup J) \wedge \\ (\neg\ Combustion \wedge \neg\ IgnitionSource)\ \mathbf{over}\ (I \cup J) \wedge \\ (Concentration \leq EquilibriumLevel)\ \mathbf{over}\ I \\ \Rightarrow\ \int_I Concentration \leq \int_J Concentration\end{array}\right)$$

The above formula gives us the situation where gas is being added to the environment but it is not lit and there is nothing to ignite it. Here we have the overall concentration of gas increasing.

$$\forall I\colon \mathbf{interval}\ \ T\cdot\left(\begin{array}{l}(GasSource \wedge Combustion)\ \mathbf{over}\ I \\ \Rightarrow\ (Concentration \leq EquilibriumLevel)\ \mathbf{over}\ I\end{array}\right)$$

Finally, if the gas is on and lit, then the overall concentration of gas will not exceed a concentration where gas is being added at the same rate as it is being consumed (by dissipation and/or combustion).

The use of *EquilibriumLevel* in the past few paragraphs is a simplification made to prevent us from going into a long investigation of combustible gases, fluid dynamics, and dissipation rates in different environments. Its intended meaning is simply to act as a mechanism to allow us to note that, say, if the gas is on and burning then there will be a concentration of gas in the environment that will be maintained.

The last physical property that we will quickly look at in detail deals with the possibility of explosions.

$$\forall I\colon \mathbf{interval}\ \ T\cdot\left(\begin{array}{l}(Concentration < ExplosionMin)\ \mathbf{over}\ I \\ \Rightarrow\ \neg\ Explosion\ \mathbf{over}\ I\end{array}\right)$$

Simply put, if there is not enough gas to cause an explosion then we will not get one.

$$\exists I\colon \mathbf{interval}\ \ T\cdot\left(\begin{array}{l}(Concentration \geq ExplosionMin)\ \mathbf{over}\ I \\ \Rightarrow\ Explosion\ \mathbf{over}\ I\end{array}\right)$$

This property is permissive rather than mandatory as it is possible for the concentration of gas to exceed the minimum required for an explosion without actually causing the explosion. While it is not likely that a spark will fail to ignite a large concentration of gas, it is possible. And, since we have weakened the property into a permissive one, it is not necessary to add *IgnitionSource* to the formula.

There are, of course, other properties that could — and should — be included within *PhysicalProperties*; only a few of the more interesting are presented here.

The *GluingAssumptions* conjunct is a complement to the assumptions about the general physical properties of the environment. In them we make explicit what it is we assume that the physical components of our system do.

In some cases the state of our equipment implies that a property of the environment is true, for instance:

$$\forall I : \textbf{interval } T \cdot \left(\begin{array}{l} (GasFlow \ \Rightarrow \ GasSource) \ \wedge \\ (Spark \ \Rightarrow \ IgnitionSource) \ \wedge \\ (Flame \ \Rightarrow \ Combustion) \end{array} \right) \ \textbf{over } I$$

This formula relates variables in the *PhysicalProperties* to the output variables of the system. Specifically, if the gas is on in the system then we can conclude that there is a source of gas in the environment; when the ignition transformer is on then there is a means to cause ignition; and when the system is producing a flame then we have combustion. The formula does not, however, imply the converse, as it is not necessarily true that the only means of ignition is sparks from the ignition transformer; it is entirely possible that a person could be holding a lit match near the nozzle.

The *Idealisations* conjunct constrains the required scope of the specification, excluding failures from consideration. The properties expressed in *Idealisations* are, over long periods of time, certainly false in any real environment. They are, however, true most of the time, and are necessary to give the normal behaviour of the system.

One part of the *Idealisations* conjunct is essentially the converse of part of the *GluingAssumptions*:

$$\forall I : \textbf{interval } T \cdot \left(\begin{array}{l} (GasSource \ \Rightarrow \ GasFlow) \ \wedge \\ (IgnitionSource \ \Rightarrow \ Spark) \ \wedge \\ (Combustion \ \Rightarrow \ Flame) \end{array} \right) \ \textbf{over } I$$

This allows us to assume that there is nothing in the environment that can directly interfere with the operation of the gas-burner. For example, because of the formula above we can be certain that there are no other sources of gas that could help cause an explosion the next time the gas-burner tries to ignite a flame.

The rest of the *Idealisations* conjunct includes things to force some of the permissive parts of *PhysicalProperties* to become mandatory. For example,

$$\forall I : \textbf{interval } T \cdot \left(\begin{array}{l} IgnitionSource \ \wedge \\ Concentration \geq IgnitionMin \\ \Rightarrow \ Combustion \end{array} \right) \ \textbf{over } I$$

takes the physical property that *allows* gas to ignite if the concentration is high enough and there is a spark and adds the constraint that it *must* happen.

3.3   Idealised Guarantee-Conditions

The guarantee-conditions describe the behaviour that can be expected from a given system. In the case of the idealised gas-burner the behaviour is straight-forward.

The *OperationalProperties* conjunct of the guarantee-condition has a short definition:

$OperationalProperties \triangleq$
   $\forall I\text{: interval } T \cdot ((\textit{Temperature} \leq \textit{HeatThreshold}) \Leftrightarrow \textit{Flame}) \textbf{ over } I$

The operational behaviour is just that when the environmental temperature is less than a certain threshold then the system should be burning gas; otherwise, it should not be burning gas. The formula above has been simplified by the omission of any time delay between turning the gas on and igniting the gas, and it also does not consider stuttering when the value of *Temperature* is close to the value of *HeatThreshold*. We can, however, justify this development using the rely-conditions that we have written.

The *LowConcentrationLevel* conjunct is the formalisation of the condition that the concentration of gas in the environment must not exceed a certain safe threshold to avoid things like explosions.

$\forall I\text{: interval } T \cdot (\textit{Concentration} \leq \textit{SafeMax}) \textbf{ over } I$

The justification that satisfying this property prevents explosions relies directly on the physical property that they cannot happen if the concentration of gas in the environment is below a certain level, and that *SafeMax* is always below that level.

4   Adding Fault-Tolerance

One objection to the idealised specification is that it is impossible to find an environment that could satisfy the rely-conditions, not to mention equipment that never fails.

We need the system to have fault-tolerant properties then, and it is important to first consider how to add such properties to the system. Our approach to fault-tolerance — indeed, one of the major goals of it — is to keep the fault-handling behaviour separate from the ordinary behaviour as much as possible. This allows us the freedom to create idealised specification that are largely uncluttered by special cases.

These uncluttered specifications are then composed into a larger specification with provision to handle the faults. The additional material in the larger speci-fication does not have to deal with the system's ordinary behaviour and can be a clean description of what is required to deal with the fault.

There are two operators proposed in [1] for use when composing specifications: **until/allows** and **until/requires**, i.e.:

OrdinarySpec **until** *Condition* **allows** *FaultBehaviourSpec*

The particular example they use to explain the operators is related to fault detection and correction, although other uses of those structures can be imagined. Both operators result in a system that will behave as *OrdinarySpec* unless *Condition* is satisfied. In the case of **until/requires** the composed system immediately starts behaving as specified in *FaultBehaviourSpec*. For **until/allows**, the composed system can continue as it has been, and optionally change behaviour at any future time so long as *Condition* still holds. These operators do not have quite the right semantics for the purposes of our example, however, as neither of them allow a return to the ordinary behaviour specification.

We will here propose syntax for another, similar, structure:

OrdinarySpec **until** *Condition* **corrects** *FaultBehaviourSpec*

As with the two structures from [1], the composed system will initially behave as *OrdinarySpec* provides. And, as with **until/requires**, if the condition holds, this structure requires that the composed system's behaviour becomes that of *FaultBehaviourSpec*. The specification of *FaultBehaviourSpec* is limited to the precisely the same set of variables named in the **external**, **inputs**, and **outputs** keywords of the *OrdinarySpec* system. The composed system preserves the reification of the variables within the composition. Unlike either of the composition structures from [1], the specification of *FaultBehaviourSpec* must provide a test similar to a post-condition to indicate when the condition that triggered the fault behaviour has been corrected. Once that post-condition holds the composed system returns to behaving like *OrdinarySpec*. The intuition behind this composition operator is to segregate the ordinary behaviour of the system from the fault-correcting behaviour.

Returning to our idealised specification, we need to consider how to make the system more robust. The most obvious fault — touched on when the *Idealisations* conjunct was described — is the potential for the spark to fail to ignite the gas at the nozzle. If the gas fails to ignite it is unsafe to continue to attempt to ignite it as the concentration of unlit gas can quickly build up to unsafe levels. A desired safety property would be to ensure that in the face of repeated ignition failure the concentration of gas in the environment does not exceed some given level. This property would have the effect of preventing an explosive concentration of gas from occurring. The behaviour that satisfies this property, then, is that if the gas fails to ignite the system should shut off the valve and ignition transformer and wait until the concentration has reduced.

We can compose a system specification that handles an ignition failure using **until/corrects**:

GasBurnerSystem1 $\triangleq$
  GasBurnerSystem0 **until** *IgnitionFailure* **corrects** *PurgeWait0*

This composition creates a system, *GasBurnerSystem1*, that behaves like the *GasBurnerSystem0* system unless *IgnitionFailure* ever holds. If *IgnitionFailure* holds, then *GasBurnerSystem1* will behave as specified for the *PurgeWait0* system. The composed system will continue to behave as *PurgeWait0* even if *IgnitionFailure* ceases to be true. Only when the post-condition of *PurgeWait0* is satisfied can the composed system return to behaving as *GasBurnerSystem0*.

The definition of *IgnitionFailure* is given as a lambda function rather than a system, as the intention is to apply this over intervals during the operation of *GasBurnerSystem0*, rather than use it directly as a system specification.

IgnitionFailure $\triangleq$
  λI: **interval** $T \cdot \#I > MaxIgnitionWait \wedge (GasFlow \wedge \neg Flame)$ **over** I

This predicate will be true when the system has had the gas on, but not achieved ignition over a period longer than *MaxIgnitionWait*.

Our corrective system, *PurgeWait0*, is intended to turn off the gas and ignition transformer and wait for the gas level to dissipate.

PurgeWait0 $\triangleq$
  system
  external *Concentration*
  outputs *GasFlow, Spark, Flame*
  rely *PhysicalProperties* $\wedge$ *GluingAssumptions*
  guarantee *SystemOff*
  post *LowConcentrationRestored*

The rely-conditions of the system when it is just waiting for gas to dissipate are similar to *GasBurnerSystem0*, but the *Idealisations* conjunct is no longer needed or desired. The guarantee-condition is defined as

SystemOff $\triangleq \forall I$: **interval** $T \cdot (\neg GasFlow \wedge \neg Spark \wedge \neg Flame)$ **over** I

and, not surprisingly, requires that the system keep everything turned off.

The post-condition of this system is defined in terms of the environment

LowConcentrationRestored $\triangleq$
  $\exists I$: **interval** $T \cdot$
    $(Concentration \leq LowConcentrationThreshold)$ **over** I

This definition of the post-condition is unusual in that it allows the system to be considered finished whenever a suitable time interval is found. There is a semantic assumption that the system is done as soon as the post-condition can be satisfied, rather than at any arbitrary point after the post-condition has been satisfied.

5   Deriving the Controller

Up to this point we have been dealing with the specification of the overall system rather than that of the controller. The derivation of this controller's specification follows in two main steps: first, we establish a specification for the controller in terms of the system-level variables; and second, we reify that specification to cast it solely in terms of the signals that the controller can actually access.

A derivation step using this method is, conceptually, the process of moving from the specification of an overall system to that of a subsystem. This is, in a sense, the reverse of pushing out the boundaries of the overall system. When we were pushing out the boundaries we were attempting to bring more elements into consideration to understand the overall system. During the derivation we are shifting our focus back to the portion of the overall system which we must design, but in the process keeping the relevant elements of the overall system in the specification.

During a derivation step we allow existing variables given with the **input** and **output** keywords to be moved to the **external** keyword. New variables can be introduced into the specification as long as there is a part of the rely-condition that relates them to the external variables. The rely-conditions can be weakened to allow for a greater variety of behaviour on the part of the environment, and guarantee-conditions can be strengthened to give a tighter constraint on the behaviour of the system. Formally, the rely-condition of the original system must imply the rely-condition of the derived system, and the conjunction of the rely- and guarantee-conditions of the derived system must imply the guarantee-condition of the original system.

5.1 The Derivation

The first step is to derive an idealised controller directly from the idealised system.

$GasBurnerController0 \triangleq$
    system
    external $Concentration, Temperature, GasFlow, Spark, Flame$
    inputs $HeatRequest, FlameDetected$
    outputs $ValvePosition, IgnitionTransformer$
    rely $PhysicalProperties \wedge GluingAssumptions \wedge Idealisations \wedge$
        $SignalCorrespondences$
    guarantee $OperationalProperties \wedge LowConcentrationLevel$

The main differences between the controller and the system are in the input and output variables. In a sense we have just moved the boundary of the system that we are considering inwards from the whole gas-burner to just the processing unit, and this is precisely the approach we want to take. All of the input and output variables of the whole system are now considered external variables as the controller does not have access to them. The guarantee-condition can be taken directly from the overall system for this stage of the controller specification, as the external behavioural requirements are unchanged.

The rely-condition has a new conjunct that is required to relate the state of the variables that the controller can directly access to the external variables which it cannot. For brevity they are presented here under the assumption that the correspondence between the signals and reality is faultless, but a full specification would have to be sensitive to that.

$SignalCorrespondences \triangleq$
  $\forall I: \textbf{interval } T \cdot$
  $HeatRequest \Leftrightarrow (Temperature \leq HeatThreshold) \textbf{ over } I \wedge$
  $\forall I: \textbf{interval } T \cdot \begin{pmatrix} FlameDetected \Leftrightarrow Flame \wedge \\ ValvePosition \Leftrightarrow GasFlow \wedge \\ IgnitionTransformer \Leftrightarrow Spark \end{pmatrix} \textbf{ over } I$

Of itself, $SignalCorrespondences$ is just the straight mapping of a signal to the external state that it represents.

The idealised controller needs to be composed in a similar manner as the idealised system to gain a controller that can tolerate faults.

$FTGasBurnerController0 \triangleq$
  $GasBurnerController0 \textbf{ until } DetectionFailure \textbf{ corrects } PurgeWait1$

The $IgnitionFailure$ condition that was used in $GasBurnerSystem1$ becomes $DetectionFailure$ in this composition. We have defined it in terms of the signals that are available in $GasBurnerController0$:

$DetectionFailure \triangleq$
  $\lambda I: \textbf{interval } T \cdot \#I \geq MaxIgnitionWait \wedge$
  $\qquad\qquad (ValvePosition \wedge \neg FlameDetected) \textbf{ over } I$

In this definition we has used the signals $ValvePosition$ and $FlameDetected$ rather than the variables $GasFlow$ and $Flame$; from the $SignalCorrespondences$ conjunct of the rely-condition we can know $DetectionFailure$ and $IgnitionFailure$ will hold under the same conditions.

The corrective system $PurgeWait1$ bears the same relation to $PurgeWait0$ as $GasBurnerController0$ does to $GasBurnerSystem0$.

$PurgeWait1 \triangleq$
  $\textbf{system}$
  $\textbf{external } Concentration, GasFlow, Spark, Flame$
  $\textbf{outputs } ValvePosition, IgnitionTransformer$
  $\textbf{rely } PhysicalProperties \wedge GluingAssumptions \wedge SignalCorrespondences$
  $\textbf{guarantee } SystemOff$
  $\textbf{post } LowConcentrationRestored$

As with $GasBurnerController0$, all of the system-level variables have become external variables, and $SignalCorrespondences$ is introduced into the rely-condition to relate the signals the controller can access to the physical state external to the controller.

5.2   The Reification

The second phase of deriving the specification of the controller is the process of removing all of the references to external variables while retaining the system's behaviour. This involves specifying a new guarantee that — given the rely-condition of the unreified controller — implies the unreified guarantee-condition;

as well as recasting the unreified rely-condition purely in terms of the input and output variables.

The idealised, reified specification for the controller becomes:

$GasBurnerController1 \triangleq$
   system
   inputs $HeatRequest, FlameDetected$
   outputs $ValvePosition, IgnitionTransformer$
   rely $SignalProperties \land SignalIdealisations$
   guarantee $OperationalProperties1$

In this specification the external variables are completely eliminated, but the inputs and outputs are precisely the same as in $GasBurnerController0$. The rely- and guarantee-conditions are very different from the unreified controller specification.

To give the basis for how the signals work we have the $SignalProperties$ conjunct of the rely-condition. This is, essentially, a version of the original $PhysicalProperties$ expressed in terms of the input and output signals. Its justification is based on the use of $SignalCorrespondences$, such that

$$(PhysicalProperties \land SignalCorrespondences) \Rightarrow SignalProperties$$

To illustrate one particular part of $SignalProperties$, consider the physical property that allows combustion in the presence of both gas and an ignition source. This properties is defined in $SignalProperties$ as

$$\exists I: \textbf{interval } T \cdot \left(\begin{array}{c} ValvePosition \land IgnitionTransformer \\ \Rightarrow FlameDetected \end{array} \right) \textbf{ over } I$$

which states that if we turn on the $IgnitionTransformer$ and $ValvePosition$ signals then we might get the $FlameDetected$ signal turned on.

The idealisations that the reified version of the controller relies on are — unsurprisingly — semantically the same as those used by the unreified controller; they are, however, expressed in terms of the signals. Parallel to the permissive property on ignition, above, the idealisation that ignition is mandatory is expressed as:

$$\forall I: \textbf{interval } T \cdot \left(\begin{array}{c} ValvePosition \land IgnitionTransformer \\ \Rightarrow FlameDetected \end{array} \right) \textbf{ over } I$$

Fully specified, $SignalIdealisations$ plays the same role of removing the possibility of failures from the reified controller specification as $Idealisations$ does for the unreified controller and the whole system.

The reified controller cannot directly guarantee any behaviour relative to the whole system without the external variables, so its guarantee-condition, $OperationalProperties1$ must be written in terms of the input and output variables.

$OperationalProperties1 \triangleq$
   $\forall I: \textbf{interval } T \cdot$
$$\left(\begin{array}{l} HeatRequest \Leftrightarrow ValvePosition \land \\ (HeatRequest \land \neg FlameDetected) \Leftrightarrow IgnitionTransformer \end{array} \right) \textbf{ over } I$$

The first part of the quantified expression requires that the system will keep the *ValvePosition* signal on when the *HeatRequest* signal is on and off when there it is off; given the *SignalCorrespondences* we know that this will keep the gas on when there is a heat request and off when there is not.

The second part of the quantified expression controls the *IgnitionTransformer* signal, ensuring that it is on only when the *HeatRequest* signal is on and the *FlameDetected* signal is off. Again, given the *SignalCorrespondences*, we know that this will only engage the actual ignition transformer when the gas valve is open and there is a heat request.

Moving from the idealised to fault-tolerant version of the reified controller, we compose it in the same manner as before:

$FTGasBurnerController1 \triangleq$
    $GasBurnerController1$ **until** $DetectionFailure$ **corrects** $PurgeWait2$

Because we have already defined *DetectionFailure* in terms of the signals we do not need another version of it; the corrective specification, however, does require reification.

$PurgeWait2 \triangleq$
    system
    outputs *ValvePosition, IgnitionTransformer*
    guarantee *SignalsOff*
    post *MinPurgeTimeExceeded*

The lack of any input or external variables removes need for a rely-condition in the reified *PurgeWait2* specification. Recall that the reification is not attempting to preserve the description of what the whole system is doing, but rather is merely trying to preserve the observable behaviour of the system's input and output variables. The guarantee-condition is defined as

$SignalsOff \triangleq$
    $\forall I: \textbf{interval} \ T \cdot (\neg \ ValvePosition \wedge \neg \ IgnitionTransformer) \ \textbf{over} \ I$

which keeps the controller's output signals off during the period when the corrective behaviour is dominant. It is easy to see that this will be the same behaviour as *PurgeWait1*.

The post-condition of the reified corrective system is very different than the unreified version.

$$MinPurgeTimeExceeded \triangleq \exists I: \textbf{interval} \ T \cdot \#I \geq MinPurgeTime$$

The post-condition changes from being directly concerned with the concentration of gas in the environment to being concerned only with finding a duration of time that is sufficiently long. The justification for this comes from the selection of the length of *MinPurgeTime* and *PhysicalProperties*; the former must be shown to be long enough, using the dissipation properties in the latter, to reduce the concentration of gas so that *LowConcentrationRestored* is satisfied.

6 Conclusions

This example has been developed using a method that is still being actively developed by Hayes, Jackson, and Jones. Tackling these and similar further examples will inevitably refine the method described in [1]. Further effort includes creating a library of examples — including this one — to create a body of work that can serve as a guide to practitioners.

In the longer term, it should be possible to use such a library of examples to generate a set of "HJJ patterns", not unlike the design patterns [10] currently used by practitioners of object-oriented development. Even if a set of pattern-like structures cannot be developed, a full set of guidelines for using this method is required.

The composition of specifications given with this method, in senses of both subproblems and whole specifications, is a topic that remains to be fully explored. The task of creating a specification for a system's "normal" operation seems well understood, and creating the specification with weaker rely-conditions for the "abnormal" system behaviour is equally straightforward. However, the problem of combining such specifications is a problem that demands further study.

The basic ideas involved in the Jones' rely-conditions, while good at recording interference, leave gaps when it comes to notions such as ensuring that the system can make progress. Work such as Stølen's on wait-conditions [11] addresses some of these issues, and should be included in this method.

Acknowledgments. The author is supported in his research by EPSRC (UK) funding for the "Dependability IRC" (DIRC; see www.dirc.org.uk) and by EU-IST STREP funding for "RODIN" (see rodin.cs.ncl.ac.uk). The many discussions about this topic with Ian J. Hayes, Michael A. Jackson, Cliff B. Jones have been a wonderful source of insight into this material. The background material in Section 1 is a revision of some unpublished material drafted by Cliff B. Jones.

References

1. Hayes, I.J., Jackson, M.A., Jones, C.B.: Determining the specification of a control system from that of its environment. In Araki, K., Gnesi, S., Mandrioli, D., eds.: FME 2003: Formal Methods. Volume 2805 of Lecture Notes in Computer Science., Springer Verlag (2003) 154–169
2. Jones, C.B.: Development Methods for Computer Programs including a Notion of Interference. PhD thesis, Oxford University (1981) Printed as: Programming Research Group, Technical Monograph 25.
3. Jones, C.B.: Specification and design of (parallel) programs. In: Proceedings of IFIP'83, North-Holland (1983) 321–332
4. Jones, C.B.: Accommodating interference in the formal design of concurrent object-based programs. Formal Methods in System Design 8 (1996) 105–122
5. Mahony, B., Hayes, I.J.: Using continuous real functions to model timed histories. In Bailes, P., ed.: Engineering Safe Software, Australian Computer Society (1991) 257–270

6. Jackson, M.A.: Problem Frames: Analyzing and structuring software development problems. Addison-Wesley (2000)
7. Hansen, K.M., Ravn, A.P., Rischel, H.: Specifying and verifying requirements of real-time systems. In: SIGSOFT '91: Proceedings of the conference on Software for Critical Systems, New York, NY, USA, ACM Press (1991) 44–54
8. Ravn, A.P.: Private communication (2006)
9. Zhou, C., Hansen, M.R.: Duration Calculus. Springer-Verlag (2004)
10. Gamma, E., Helm, R., Johnson, R., Vlissides, J.: Design Patterns: Elements of Reusable Object-Oriented Software. Addison-Wesley (1995)
11. Stølen, K.: An attempt to reason about shared-state concurrency in the style of VDM. In: VDM '91: Proceedings of the 4th International Symposium of VDM Europe on Formal Software Development-Volume I, London, UK, Springer-Verlag (1991) 324–342

Achieving Fault Tolerance by a Formally Validated Interaction Policy

Alessandro Fantechi[1], Stefania Gnesi[2], and Laura Semini[3]

[1] Dip. di Sistemi e Informatica, Università di Firenze
`fantechi@dsi.unifi.it`
[2] ISTI, C.N.R., Pisa
`gnesi@isti.cnr.it`
[3] Dip. di Informatica, Università di Pisa
`semini@di.unipi.it`

Abstract. This paper addresses the rigorous validation of an integrity policy by means of the application of formal methods and related support tools. We show how the policy, which provides a flexible fault tolerant schema, can be specified using a process algebra and verified using model checking techniques. Actually, we show how this approach allows both the generic validation of a middleware based on such integrity policy, and the validation of an integrated application which internally uses this mechanism. In the first case, the fault tolerance of a system, possibly composed of Commercial Off The Shelf (COTS) components, is guaranteed by a validated resident interaction control middleware. The second case applies instead when the application is forced to use a given middleware, as it is the case of Web Services.

Keywords: Integrity policies, fault tolerance, process algebras, model checking.

1 Introduction

Design and analysis at the architectural level are considered as the most pertinent basis to support the development of complex computing systems. The software technology of fault tolerant systems is also moving in this direction.

As examples of complex systems where fault tolerance issues are of prominent importance, consider those for power plants or those for the transportation industry, be it automotive, avionic, or railway. These systems offer the customer several critical functions as well as non–critical ones.

For instance, a top range car is equipped with a multitude of sensors and actuators that provide the driver with both functionalities that assist in conducting the vehicle more safely (like ABS systems or vehicle stabilisation systems), and functionalities that provide travel information or even entertainment.

It is obvious that not all such functionalities have the same *criticality*: a component of a system is considered *critical* if its failure can seriously affect the ability of the overall system to fulfill its safety requirements.

M. Butler et al. (Eds.): Fault-Tolerant Systems, LNCS 4157, pp. 133–152, 2006.
© Springer-Verlag Berlin Heidelberg 2006

Then, an important issue is to limit failure propagation among communicating components. Preventing failure propagation is a way of guaranteeing the fault tolerance of a system, built as a set of communicating components. In particular, it is important to guarantee that a critical component (which should never fail – or should only fail with an extremely low probability) is not influenced by the failure of non critical ones.

One solution is to isolate critical components, dedicating to them, for instance, completely separated hardware resources with respect to those dedicated to the non critical ones, and to rigorously validate the critical components. However, complete isolation is not always possible because of the inevitable cooperation among the various parts of the system. In fact, the current trend is towards a greater integration of different functions on the same computer or network of computers.

Another solution is to treat all the components as critical. The advantage is that communications do not have to be limited, the drawback is that all components have to be rigorously validated making this approach not always feasible due to the large dimensions of systems and to the use of "COTS" (Commercial Off The Shelf) components. Moreover, usually only a few components are really critical.

The issue can be solved with a compromise between the non-effectiveness of the first solution, and the high cost of the second one, thanks to the definition of particular interaction policies among components, called *integrity policies* [2,6,8,25,26,13]. An integrity policy assigns a level of integrity to each component of an application and states the communication patterns among pairs of components, depending on the respective integrity levels. Once a valuable policy has been adopted, not all the components need to be rigorously validated with the same effort, but only those which accomplish a critical task and those which provide data for these critical components.

In particular, critical components may embed typical fault tolerance mechanisms (like majority voting) to fulfil their integrity level. Integrity policies can be considered as a fault tolerance mechanism at the intercomponent level, since they guarantee that critical components cannot be affected by the failure of non–critical ones.

This paper presents the rigorous verification of the *Multiple Levels of Integrity* (MLI) policy, defined in [25,26], which addresses an object–oriented framework. The original definition of the policy consists of a set of declarative rules. We show how the policy can be formally specified using a process algebra and verified using model checking techniques. Actually, we show how this approach allows both the generic validation of a middleware based on such integrity policy, and the validation of an integrated application which internally uses this mechanism. In a previous work [3] we have already addressed the formal validation of fault tolerance mechanisms by means of model checking techniques along the principles presented in [4]. The main difference between this paper and [3] is that in the previous work we addressed basic fault tolerance mechanisms, while here we address a communication scheme among components, which might include those fault tolerant mechanisms.

This paper is organized as follows: in Sect. 2 we describe the *Multiple Levels of Integrity* policy. In Section 3 we introduce the specification and verification approach we have adopted. In Sect. 4 we formally specify the integrity policy using the CCS process algebra. In Sect. 5 we present the model checking results and discuss the key points of the verification process over the generic communication scheme. In Sect. 6 we deal with the validation of applications which use the MLI mechanism. In Sect. 7 we consider a case study taken from [1]: a peer–to–peer system, where the MLI mechanism is integrated at the application level.

2   The Multiple Levels of Integrity Interaction Policy

Integrity policies are defined to prevent failure propagation from non critical to critical components: they assign a *level of integrity*, ranging over a finite set of natural values, to each system component, and they state the *communication patterns*.

The *Multiple Levels of Integrity* (MLI) policy [25,26] has been defined within an object–oriented framework, to provide flexible fault tolerant schemes. It permits some objects to receive low level data, by decreasing their integrity level by means of a set of general interaction rules.

The MLI policy builds on Biba's [6] and Clark and Wilson's [8] policies. Biba's policy, which is based on the Bell–LaPadula lattice model [2], forbids any flow of data from a low to a high integrity level components. The Clark-Wilson model defines a set of fine grained rules, based on commercial data processing practices, to maintain data integrity. Data can flow to a low level and go back, if it is possible to prove that they did not loose their integrity. The MLI policy is based on the following concepts:

Integrity levels (il) range on a discrete interval. Data are assigned the integrity level of the object which produced them.

Single Level Objects (SLO) are objects with a constant integrity level. Consequently, an SLO of level n is only allowed to receive data from objects of level greater or equal to n.

Multiple Level Objects (MLO) are the core of the policy: their integrity level can be dynamically modified, since they are allowed to receive low level data. To this purpose, an MLO is assigned three values:

maxil which represents the maximum integrity level that the MLO can have. It is also called the *intrinsic level* of the MLO, since it is assigned during the design of the application. It is a constant, and represents the integrity level at which the object is certified.

minil which represents the minimum value the integrity level of the MLO can reach while interacting with other objects. It is set at invocation time, on the bases of the invocation level. No memory of it is kept after the answer to the invocation is returned: *minil* is local to an invocation.

il which is the current integrity level. It is set at invocation time to a value ranging between *maxil* and *minil* and decreases if lower level data are received during the computation to serve the invocation. Also *il* is local to each invocation.

The policy requires a new MLO instance to be created every time the MLO is invoked. As a consequence, an MLO cannot be used to implement a component which has to store some data. This means that an MLO, from a functional point of view, is a stateless object: only SLOs can store data. Therefore MLO will typically refer to some SLOs to maintain their data. In Fig. 1, we provide an example of the evolution of an MLO in response to an invocation. When an MLO with *maxil* = 3 receives a read request of level 1, it sets its *minil* to 1, meaning that no answer with integrity level smaller than 1 can be returned. The value of *il* is set to *maxil*, since a read request does not corrupt the integrity level of the MLO. Suppose the MLO needs to delegate part of the answer construction, sending another read request to a third object. The level assigned to the request is set to *minil*, meaning that an answer is useless if lower than *minil*. Let the integrity level of the answer be 2, then the MLO can accept it but its *il* is decreased to level 2. Finally, an answer to the first request is provided, at level 2, that is the current *il*, and the MLO restores its initial state.

Validation Objects (VO) are used to extract reliable data from low level objects and to provide information at a fixed level of integrity. In real systems, it is sometimes necessary to get data from unreliable sources, such as sensors, and use them in critical tasks. However, this use could either lower the level of the entire system or violate the integrity policy. Validation Objects represent a safe way to upgrade the integrity level of these data. An example of Validation Object is the one that uses a redundant number of data sources, and filters them with appropriate algorithms. For instance, a majority voting can be used to filter out erroneous data from a set of redundant copies.

A set of **rules** is given, describing all the possible **communication patterns** among pairs of objects, depending on the respective integrity levels. We list them in Table 1: we call *A* and *B* the invoking and the invoked objects, respectively. The first part of the table considers invocation conditions. The invocation is refused if the specified condition is not satisfied. If it is accepted, the invoked

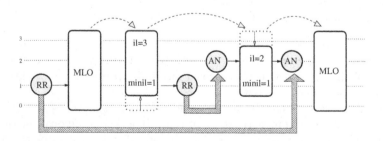

Fig. 1. Behaviour of an MLO: dotted arrows follow the MLO's evolution, thick arrows bind requests to the corresponding answers

object (if an MLO) might have to change its integrity level, as shown in the second part of the table, where invocation effects are considered. In the case of invoking MLO, the data returned at the end of a method execution may decrease the integrity level of the invoker, as shown in the third part of the table.

Table 1. Rules describing the communication patterns: conditions to be satisfied for a method invocation to be accepted, and the effect on the level of objects after acceptance and after method execution

Conditions	$A\&B$ SLOs	A SLO, B MLO	A MLO, B SLO	$A\&B$ MLOs
A reads B	$il(A) \leq il(B)$	$il(A) \leq maxil(B)$	$minil(A) \leq il(B)$	$minil(A) \leq maxil(B)$
A writes B	$il(B) \leq il(A)$	$always$	$il(B) \leq il(A)$	$always$
A r-w B	$il(A) = il(B)$	$il(A) \leq maxil(B)$	$minil(A) \leq il(B) \leq il(A)$	$minil(A) \leq maxil(B)$

Invocation effect	A SLO, B MLO	$A\&B$ MLOs
A reads B	$minil(B) := il(A);$ $il(B) := maxil(B)$	$minil(B) := minil(A);$ $il(B) := maxil(B)$
A writes B	$il(B) := min(il(A),\ maxil(B))$	$il(B) := min(il(A),\ maxil(B))$
A r-w B	$minil(B), il(B) := il(A)$	$minil(B) := minil(A);$ $il(B) := min(il(A),\ maxil(B))$

Return effect	A MLO, B MLO or SLO
A reads B A r-w B	$il(A) := min(il(A), il(B))$

The **communication model** is based on the notion of method invocation. Method invocations are assigned an integrity level too. In particular, *read, write* and *read–write requests* are considered as abstractions of any method, with respect to the effect on the state of objects. The level of a write request corresponds to the level of the data which are written, the level of a read request corresponds

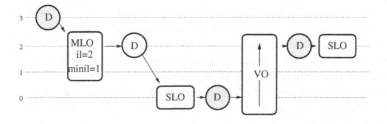

Fig. 2. A VO is able to (partly) restore the integrity of data

to the minimum acceptable level of the data to be read. Read–write requests are assigned two integrity levels, one for read and one for write.

The assignment of the integrity levels to an SLO or a VOs, or of the maxil value to an MLO should be done accordingly to the level of its trustiness. For instance, this value can be assigned by a certification authority. In a more decoupled world, we can foresee a model in which each application is designed in such a way that a component declares its own integrity level, which has to be accepted by the interacting parties.

3   Validation by Model Checking

It is worth noting that model checking algorithms [9] are successful formal verification techniques, and many efficient model checkers are currently available. They automatically check the truth of system properties, expressed as temporal logic formulae, on the finite state model representing the behavior of a system.

Model checking techniques have been already used to check the correctness of fault tolerant applications [3,4,7,18,24]. In this paper, we propose the formal validation of a mechanism implementing the MLI policy using model checking techniques. To do this we rely on a very simple and general specification and verification framework; we specify the behaviour of the mechanism using value–passing CCS [19], and describe the properties to be checked using an action-based branching time temporal logic, ACTL [10]. For verification purpose, we use the efficient on the fly model checker for ACTL FMC [14].

3.1   The CCS Process Algebra

Process algebras [15,19] are formalisms that can describe a system consisting of communicating objects at a high level of abstraction. They rely on a small set of basic operators, which correspond to primitive notions of concurrent systems, and on one or more notions of behavioral equivalence or preorder. Behavioral equivalences are used to study the relationships between descriptions of the same system at different levels of abstraction (e.g., specification and implementation).

Process algebras are particularly suited to describing an interaction policy and MLI in particular, since policies definition abstracts from the functionalities of the objects, and the relevant events to be described are the method invocations and method returns (the actions) which may change the object integrity level, which is our abstraction of the state.

Moreover, the original definition of the policy consists of a set of declarative rules (see Table 1). These rules cannot be formalized within a static framework, such as traditional type theory, due to the presence of dynamically changing integrity levels for MLOs. We rather need to associate a process to each object to model its dynamic behaviour with respect to the integrity level.

In CCS a system consists of a set of communicating processes. Each process executes input and output actions, and synchronizes with other processes to carry out its activities.

The syntax is based on a set *Act* of atomic actions. Actions are constituted by a name and one or more optional values. They are distinguished into output actions, terminated by "!", and input actions, terminated by "?". Moreover, τ denotes the special action not belonging to Act, representing the unobservable action (to model internal process communications). We assume $Act_\tau = Act \cup \{\tau\}$. In Table 2 we present the subset of the CCS operators we will use in the rest of the paper.

The semantic models of CCS terms are Labelled Transition Systems (LTS) which describe the behavior of a process in terms of states, and labelled transitions, which relate states. An LTS is a 4–tuple $\mathcal{A} = (Q, q_0, Act_\tau, \rightarrow)$, where: Q is a finite set of states; q_0 is the initial state; $\rightarrow \subseteq Q \times Act_\tau \times Q$ is the transition relation. The structural operational semantics of the considered CCS operators is given in terms of LTSs [19].

3.2 The ACTL Temporal Logic

The logic ACTL [10] is a branching-time temporal logic, which is the action based version of CTL [11]. ACTL is well suited to expressing the properties of a system in terms of the actions it performs at its working time. In fact, ACTL, whose interpretation domains are LTSs, embeds the idea of "evolution in time by actions" and is suitable for describing the various possible temporal sequences of actions that characterize a system's behavior.

The syntax of ACTL is given by the following grammar, where ϕ denotes a state property:

$$\phi ::= true \mid \sim\phi \mid \phi \& \phi' \mid [\mu]\phi \mid AG\phi \mid EG\phi \mid A[\phi\{\mu\}U\{\mu'\}\phi'] \mid E[\phi\{\mu\}U\{\mu'\}\phi']$$

In the above rules μ is an action formula defined by:

$$\mu ::= true \mid a \mid \mu \vee \mu \mid \sim\mu \qquad \text{for } a \in Act$$

We provide here an informal description of the semantics of ACTL operators. The formal semantics is given in [10].

Any state satisfies $true$. A state satisfies $\sim\phi$ if and only if it does not satisfy ϕ; it satisfies $\phi \& \phi'$ if and only if it satisfies both ϕ and ϕ'. A state satisfies $[\mu]\phi$ if for all next states reachable with μ, ϕ is true.

Table 2. A fragment of CCS

$a.P$	Action prefix	Action a is performed, and then process P is executed. Action a is in Act_τ
$P + Q$	Nondeterministic choice	Alternative choice between the behavior of process P and that of process Q
$P \parallel Q$	Parallel composition	Interleaved executions of processes P and Q. The two processes synchronize on complementary input and output actions (i.e. actions with the same name but a different suffix)
$P \setminus a$	Action restriction	The action a can only be performed within a synchronization

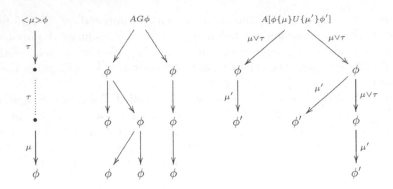

Fig. 3. Models and ACTL formulae

The meaning of $AG\,\phi$ is that ϕ is true now and always and anywhere in the future, i.e. in all states of all exiting paths. $EG\,\phi$ means that ϕ is true now and in all the states of an exiting path.

A state P satisfies $A[\phi\{\mu\}U\{\mu'\}\phi']$ if and only if in each path exiting from P, μ' will eventually be executed. It is also required that ϕ' holds after μ', and all the intermediate states satisfy ϕ; finally, before μ' only μ or τ actions can be executed. The formula $E[\phi\{\mu\}U\{\mu'\}\phi']$ has the same meaning, except that it requires one path exiting from P, and not all of them, to satisfy the given constraint.

A useful formula is $A[\phi\{true\}U\{\mu'\}\phi']$ where the first action formula is *true*: this means that any action can be executed before μ'.

Some derived operators can be defined: $\phi \vee \phi'$ stands for $\sim(\sim\phi \;\&\; \sim\phi')$; $<\mu>\phi$ stands for $\sim[\mu]\sim\phi$; finally, $EF\,\phi$ stands for $\sim AG \sim\phi$.

In Figure 3 we exemplify the truth of some formulae on some models.

4   Modeling the Integrity Policy

We formalize the MLI policy by specifying in value passing CCS the behaviour of SLOs, MLOs, and VOs.

We are interested in an abstraction of a system that only considers the effect of the interactions between objects on the objects integrity level. We thus model objects as interacting via the abstract methods read, write, and read–write, and abstract the objects state by the integrity levels. Also, we model method invocation through a remote procedure call, in which the invoking object waits for the method return event. In the following:

SLO(x), MLO(x), and VO(x) are process variables denoting the processes defining a SLO with integrity level x, a MLO with *maxil* value x, a VO providing data of level x, respectively.

read(x) is a read request action of level x. This means that the invocation was issued by an SLO with x as *il* or by an MLO with x as *minil*.

answer(x) is an answer action. Value x can be the current *il* of the object which is answering, or -1: answer(-1) means something like: "I cannot answer".

write(x) denotes a write request issued by an object with x as *il*. We call x the
  level of the write request. Write requests are not answered.
read_write(x,y) denotes a read–write request: variable x denotes the read level
  of the request, variable y denotes the write level.

4.1   Modeling the Behaviour of SLO(x)

We provide here the CCS specification of an SLO with integrity level equal to x.

```
SLO(x)=
   read(y)?.( [y≤x]SR(x) + [y>x]answer(-1)!.SLO(x) )                        +
   write(y)?.( [y<x]SLO(x) + [y≥x]SW(x) )                                   +
   read_write(y,z)?.([y≤z<x ∨ y>x]answer(-1)!.SLO(x) + [y≤x≤z]SR(x))
SR(x) =
   answer(x)!.SLO(x)                                                        +
   write(x)!.SR(x)                                                          +
   (read(x)! + read_write(x,x)!).answer(y)?.
                                    ( [y<x] answer(-1)!.SLO(x) + [y≥x] SR(x) )
SW(x) =
   SLO(x)                                                                   +
   write(x)!. SW(x)                                                         +
   (read(x)! + read_write(x,x)!).answer(y)?.([y< x]SLO(x) + [x≤y]SW(x))
```

When a read request of level y is received and $y \leq x$, then the SLO performs
the needed computation to serve the request, as described by SR, while if $y > x$
then the SLO has not the needed integrity level to supply an answer. When a
write request is received, a computation can be performed to serve the request
(see SW), but no answer is due. If the level of the request is smaller than x, then
it is ignored, and no computation is performed. A read–write request is dealt
with in the same way as the composition of a read and a write one.

   To serve a read or a read–write request, the SLO behaves as SR, it can: provide
the answer to the caller and end its duty (first choice); send a write request to
another object and continue (second choice); send a read or a read–write request,
wait for the answer (third choice). In this case, continuation depends on the level
of the answer received, if this is too low, then the computation is stopped, and
a "I cannot answer your request" message is sent.

   Note that the specification of SR is non–deterministic, and the SLO might get
into a loop and never send an answer back. Non–determinism is a consequence
of the abstraction from the object functionalities. In particular, whether the first
choice –the normal loop exit– is made or not depends on the functional behaviour
of the object. If it is correct, i.e. no integrity level violation occurs, then the
overall behaviour of the object only depends on its functional description[1].

---

[1] Static analysis can be used in some cases to determine termination, which is in
  general undecidable. When termination is not provable, it can be enforced by means
  of constrains on the functional behaviour (static bounds on the loops, finite state
  machine behaviour, fairness constrains, ...).

With SW(x) we represent an SLO(x) which serves a write invocation. Its description can be derived from SR(x), by removing all output actions of the type answer, since no answer is due to write requests.

4.2   Modeling the Behaviour of MLO(x)

Multiple Level Object can change their state (value of the integrity levels): the *il* is decreased in case of lower level write request, *minil* is raised when serving a higher level read request.

```
MLO(x) =
   read(y)?.( [y≤x]MR(y,x,x) + [y>x]answer(-1)!.MLO(x) )          +
   write(y)?.( [y≤x]MW(0,y,x) + [y>x]MW(0,x,x) )                  +
   read_write(y,z)?.
      ( [y≤z≤x]MR(y,z,x) + [y≤x≤z]MR(y,x,x) + [y>x]answer(-1)!.MLO(x) )
```

When a read request of level y is received and y≤x, then the MLO makes the necessary computation to serve the request taking y as its *minil* value, and x, its *maxil* value, as its value for *il*, and behaves like MR(y,x,x). On the contrary, a read request of level greater than x cannot be considered, since the MLO does not have the integrity level needed to supply an answer.

When a write request is received, the MLO takes 0 as *minil*, and the minimum among x (its *maxil*) and y (the level of the request) as *il*. A computation can then be performed to serve the requests, but no answer is due.

A read–write request is dealt with as the composition of a read and a write one. Depending on its read and write values, the object can refuse the invocation, and behave as MR(y,z,x) or as MR(y,x,x).

Process MR(min,il,max) represents an MLO which serves a read invocation, again characterized by the three values min, il, and max. Indeed, when serving a request, the MLO can interact with other objects and change these values. When the request has been served, the MLO forgets the min and il values and keeps only its intrinsic level max. This is possible since a new object instance is created every time the object is invoked, and thus the object keeps no memory of previous invocations.

```
MR(min,il,max) =
   answer(il)!.MLO(max)                                          +
   write(il)!.MR(min,il,max)                                     +
   (read(min)! + read_write(min,il)!). answer(x)?. (
   [x<min]answer(-1)!.MLO(max)+[min≤x≤il]MR(min,x,max)+[x≥il]MR(min,il,max)
                                                                 )
```

The behaviour of MW(min,il,max) is that of MR(min,il,max) where all output actions of the type answer are removed, as we have done in the case of SLOs. We omit the definition.

4.3   Modeling the Behaviour of VO(x)

A Validation Object provides data at a fixed integrity level, that is the level of integrity to which it is able to raise data. It can be modeled for our purposes as only accepting:

VO(x) = read(y)?. ([y≤x] VR(x) + [y>x] answer(-1)!. VO(x))

VR(x) = (answer(x)! + answer(-1)!). VO(x)

The Validation Object either tries to serve the request (VR), or it answers immediately that this is not possible. It can be that the request cannot be served. This is the case, for instance, if the VO cannot find all the (redundant) data it needs.

5   Verification of the Integrity Policy

The formal verification of the multi-level integrity policy can be addressed from two different points of view:

- looking at the generic mechanism itself: the interest is on a complete verification of the mechanism in all its possible utilization scenarios; this is especially useful when we want to propose the mechanism as a sort of certified integrity preserving middleware that mediates all inter-objects interactions enforcing the integrity policy. This point of view is addressed in this section;
- dealing with an application which internally uses the policy: in this case, an ad hoc formal verification should be carried on an integrated model of the application. This point of view is addressed in the next section.

The Multiple Levels of Integrity policy has to guarantee that the interaction among different components does not affect the overall confidence of the application, i.e that a non–critical component does not corrupt a critical one. In particular, data of a low integrity level cannot flow to a higher integrity level (unless through a Validation Object, which is the only kind of object authorized to break this rule). This condition should hold for isolated objects and in any schema of interaction among objects. In [12], we address object invocation, nested and concurrent invocations as verification cases, since in an object–oriented framework most interaction schemata can be reduced to combinations of these interaction patterns.

Here, we concentrate on the following properties:

Prop 1. An object with intrinsic level i cannot provide answers of level $j > i$.
Prop 2. An object with intrinsic level i does not accept read requests of level $j > i$.
Prop 3. If an MLO with intrinsic level i receives a read request of level $j \leq i$, and, to serve the request, it invokes with a read request a third object of intrinsic level *maxil* smaller than j, then it cannot answer the initial request. Indeed, its level is decreased to the *maxil* value of the third object because of the new data received.

We will check Prop 1 and Prop 2 against the model of an MLO, and Prop 3 against the model of a combination of MLOs based on nested invocation. Indeed, the most interesting cases are those involving MLOs, which can change their integrity levels during the computation.

The above properties are first formalized as ACTL formulae, then the FMC model checker is used to verify their satisfiability on the model of the selected subsystems. Since actual verification by model–checking requires non–parametric models, we will define particular instances of the considered validation cases which are sufficiently representative to be generalized. Hence, we will use these instances to prove the set of temporal logic formulae expressing the integrity properties above, and then we will discuss how model checking results can be generalized. In particular, in the following, we assume integrity levels to range from 0, the lowest, to 3, the highest.

5.1   Verifying Properties 1 and 2

We consider a system consisting only of the object A_2, which is formalized by MLO(2), i.e. it is an MLO with *maxil* equal to 2. In this case, properties 1 and 2 can be expressed by the following ACTL formulae[2]:

F1: $\sim EF \langle A_2\_answer(3)! \rangle\ true$
F2: $AG\ [A_2\_read(3)?]\ A\ [true\ \{false\}\ U\ \{A_2\_answer(-1)!\}\ true]$

i.e. A_2 cannot provide answers of level 3, nor serve read requests of level 3.

Formulae F1 and F2 have been proved true on the model of A_2 using the model checker FMC for ACTL.

For other values of *maxil*, we can repeat the verification using the corresponding formulae and processes. The general formulae formalizing properties 1 and 2, to be instantiated to the various cases, follow. The shorthand $\underset{j>i}{\&}\ \phi_j$ stays for $\phi_{i+1}\ \&\ \phi_{i+2}\ \&\ \ldots\ \&\ \phi_k$, where k is the highest integrity level of the concrete model (in our case, k=3).

Prop 1 and Prop 2 say that any A_i satisfies, respectively:

$$\underset{j>i}{\&}\ \sim EF\langle A_i\_answer(j)!\rangle true.$$

$$\underset{j>i}{\&}\ AG[A_i\_read(j)?]A[true\{false\}U\{A_i\_answer(-1)!\}true]$$

5.2   Verifying Property 3

We take into account here the case in which an MLO of a given level, in response to a read–request, invokes with a read–request another MLO of a lower

---

[2] In the following we rename requests and answers: requests carry the name of the object which is invoked to serve the request, answers take the name of the answering object.

integrity level. This is indeed the most complex case of nested invocations: all the other combinations (SLO vs. MLO, read–request vs. write–request or read/write–request, different levels of integrity) can be reduced to this one: in any case, a separate validation by model–checking of these other cases can be made following what is presented here.

We describe such a system with the parallel composition of the two objects: A_2 and B_0. A_2 is an MLO(2) that, to serve a read request of level 1, sends a further read request to B_0, defined by MLO(0) (see Fig. 4).

Prop 3 for this concrete system is expressed by the ACTL formula:

F3: $AG\,[A_2\_read(1)?]\,AG\,[\nu]\,A\,[true\,\{\mu\}\,U\,\{A_2\_answer(-1)!\}\,true]$

with $\mu =\sim (A_2\_answer(0)! \vee A_2\_answer(1)! \vee A_2\_answer(2)! \vee A_2\_answer(3)!)$ and $\nu = B_0\_read(0)! \vee B_0\_read(1)! \vee B_0\_read(2)! \vee B_0\_read(3)!$

i.e., if A_2 receives a read request of level 1 and then sends a read request to B_0, then the unique next visible answer has level -1.

Formula F3 has been proved true on the model of A2 $\parallel$ B0.

Generalization of the results. The generalization step deals with the integrity levels. We would consider all the models built with A_i, B_k, $read(j)$, for any i, j, k such that $i \geq j > k$ and integrity levels ranging from 0 to a maximum value M, and check the corresponding instances of the following general formula expressing Prop 3.

$$\underset{j\,\leq\,i}{\&}\ AG\,[A_i\_read(j)?]\,AG\,[\ \underset{\substack{k < j \\ m=0\ldots M}}{\vee}\ B_k\_read(m)!\,]$$

$$A\,[true\{\sim \overset{M}{\underset{m=0}{\vee}} A_i\_answer(m)!\}\,U\,\{A_i\_answer(-1)!\}true]$$

We can repeat the model–checking for any i, j, k, and it is easy to see that the result of model–checking will not change. The proved properties guarantee that data do not flow from a given level of integrity to a higher level of integrity through a pair of nested invocations.

A further generalization step can be made, to conclude that data do not flow from a given level of integrity to a higher one, through any number of nested invocations which include an invocation to an object with a lower level than the level of initial read invocation, as expressed by:

Prop G–3. If an MLO with intrinsic level i receives a read request of level $j \leq i$, and, to serve the request, it starts a chain of nested invocations to other objects, one of which has intrinsic level $k < j$, then it cannot answer the initial request.

We reason by induction. We consider n objects B^1 $\parallel$ B^2 $\parallel \ldots \parallel$ B^n , where B^1 is the first object of the chain, i.e. the one receiving the first read invocation. Let j be the integrity level of such an invocation. The inductive assumption guarantees that if any of the Bs has an integrity level lower that j, then the answer has level -1. Thus, we can safely simulate the behaviour of the parallel composition $B^1 \| B^2 \| \dots \| B^n$ with an MLO C_k with $k < j$. Hence, once we have proved that $A \| C_k$ behaves correctly, we can conclude that this is also true for $A \| B^1 \| B^2 \| \dots \| B^n$.

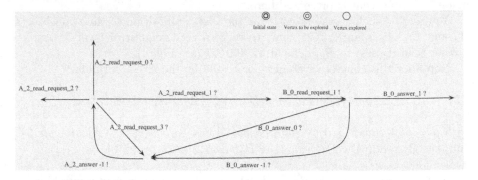

Fig. 4. A_2 behaviour in the case of nested invocations

6   Validation of Applications Instantiating the Policy

The model of an application which internally uses the policy will be an instance of the general model of Section 4 and its validation will inherit the proof results and techniques.

The computational units of an application will be objects, and behave as SLOs, MLOs, or VOs. Part of the design effort is indeed to decide, for each system component, which of the MLI policy objects has to be instantiated. An instance of the general model introduces the functional aspects of the application of interest, and reduces the number of possible behaviours, by limiting the non–determinism.

This way of applying the MLI policy in practice was presented in [1], where some case studies were considered, in the Web Services approach. Among them, the one discussed in Section 7, dealing with a peer–to–peer service where some peers may be untrusted.

As far as validation is concerned, in the case the application architecture is not an instance of the patterns already validated, then an ad hoc verification can be carried out, by stating the properties of interest in ACTL, and checking them with FMC.

Otherwise, if the application instantiates a pattern validated in the previous section or in [12], then the validation process can directly exploit some of the validation results for the pattern. In fact, the instantiation process preserves some of the properties holding in the general model.

Instances may, on the one side, prune some paths, on the other they may introduce new steps in a computation. Hence, not all the formulae holding in an interaction pattern also hold in the instances. The formulae which are maintained are those expressed in a fragment of ACTL which is fully abstract with respect to the weak trace equivalence. In [1] it has been shown this fragment to be:

$$\phi ::= true \mid false \mid \phi \,\&\, \phi' \mid [\mu]\phi \mid AG\,\phi \mid A[true\{\mu\}U\{\mu'\}true] \qquad (1)$$

Where μ is an action formula as defined in Section 3.2.

The proposed formalization and validation framework applies also to the case of Web Services. Conceptually, Web Services are stand-alone components that reside over the nodes of the network. Each Web Service has an interface which is network accessible through standard network protocols and describes the interaction capabilities of the service. Applications over the web are developed by combining and integrating together Web Services.

Web applications show the same verification problems of classical distributed systems. The modelling and validation techniques presented in the previous sections can be extended straightforwardly to Web Services. Indeed, interactions between Web Services are based on message exchange, and interactions can be one–way or follow a request–response pattern. The only added complexity is due to the fact that in most cases web applications operate in an open environment, instead of an environment where all the components and their relationships are known.

In an open system only a part of the system is known, while only some assumptions can be done on the nature and behaviour of the remaining components, whose set may also dynamically vary. A very weak assumption is to know only the interface of the remaining components (the environment) and to ignore their semantics.

For checking a property of a sub–system regardless of its environment, one can compose the sub–system with an abstraction of the environment. This can be thought of as the interface of the environment with respect to the specific sub–system, showing a non–deterministic behaviour. The result is a new system where more computations are allowed. The formal verification can be done by just observing the actions which involve the part of the system we are interested in. Since we allow more computations, i.e. more traces in the computation tree, the discussion above on the properties preserved by an instantiation process applies.

7   Case Study: Peer–to–Peer Validation Service

We describe a peer–to–peer service that a user can query to download a video [1]. This is a simplified instance of the concrete problem of identifying remote file content before downloading in peer–to–peer systems, where some or all of the peers are untrusted, or content-based access control has to be enforced. In the example we assume that two peers exist, at level 1 and 2 respectively. Moreover, the system includes two refutation lists which collect information of help to know whether the expected content of a file corresponds to the file name or not. The download is filtered by a Validation Object that first looks for the video with a `read_video` request, and then validates the answer by querying the refutation lists.

A peer's answer to a `read_video` request carries two values: the peer integrity level, and an integer holding -1 if the peer does not have the video, a different

value otherwise. If the video is not found from both peers P, the validator VO
sends a negative answer to the user, otherwise it validates the video content with
the help of the clauses of the agents VAL and VAL2. This involves querying one
or more of the refutation lists processes RL.

In the example, we abstract from actual validation algorithms in VAL and
VAL2, and show a completely non-deterministic behavior that can be refined
in any concrete solution. Our validation approach is compositional: to prove the
correctness of the final system, we only need to verify the refinement step. Indeed,
the abstract behavior of the VO specified here corresponds to the interface of any
actual Validation Object, with a specific validation algorithm demanded to the
VAL agent.

To complete the example description, we assume that peers perform a visible
action video when the video is available, and the user performs the visible
actions start at search beginning, then success, or failure. The last two
actions discriminate the cases where a valid video was found from the cases
where either no video was found, or the video content was not correct.

```
P(x) = ?read_video(y). ( ( [y <= x] (!video. !answer_video(x,x). P(x) +
                                      !answer_video(x,-1). P(x) )        ) +
                         ( [y > x] !answer_video(-1,-1). P(x)            ) )


RL(x) = ?query_video(y). ( ( [y <= x]   !query_answer(x). RL(x)  ) +
                           ( [y > x]    !query_answer(-1). RL(x) )  )


VO(x) = ?user_req(y). ( ( [y <= x]   !read_video(0). ?answer_video(z,w).
                              ( ( [z = -1]   !user_answer(-1). VO(x) ) +
                                ( [z >=0]     VAL(x,w)               ) ) +
                          ( [y > x]    !user_answer(-1).VO(x)          ) ) )


VAL(x,w) = [w = -1] !user_answer(-1). VO(x) +
           [w >= 0] ( !query_video(0). ?query_answer(y).
                                  ( !user_answer(x). VO(x)  +
                                    !user_answer(-1). VO(x) +
                                    VAL2(x)                 ) )


VAL2(x) = !query_video(0). ?query_answer(y). ( !user_answer(x). VO(x) +
                                               !user_answer(-1). VO(x)  )


User(x) = !start. !user_req(x). ?user_answer(y).
                ( ( [y < 0  ] !failure. User(x) ) +
                  ( [y >= 0 ] !success. User(x) )  )

net Net = ( VO(3) || P(1) || P(2) || RL(1) || RL(2) || User(1) )
          \read_video \query_video \user_req \answer_video \query_answer
          \user_answer
```

The properties of interest that have been checked state that each downloading
round leads either to a video or to a failure, and that it is not the case that

it always leads to the downloading of a video. We hence checked the following formulae, obtaining the expected results.

```
AG [ !start ] A [ true { ~ !start } U { !failure | !video } true ]
--        The formula is TRUE              --

AG [ !start ] A [ true { true } U { !video } true ]
--        The formula is FALSE             --
```

8   Conclusions

We have presented the application of a model–checking approach to specify and verify the Multiple Levels of Integrity policy defined in [25,26]. A formal description of the protocol has been provided, in CCS style, and a set of properties have been formally stated in the ACTL temporal logic. Property satisfaction has been proved by exploiting the FMC model checker.

We have found the use of process algebras as a natural way to describe the MLI policy. Anyway, a parallel formal specification and verification of the same policy has been made also using the popular PROMELA language and SPIN model-checker [16,17], but with no significant advantage in terms of modeling and verification effort.

The validation approach we have followed for the Multiple Levels of Integrity policy can be exported to other contexts where specific integrity or fault toler-ance properties of Object–Oriented distributed systems have to be guaranteed. Indeed, we have shown how the validation approach can apply both to "closed" systems, where ad hoc modeling of specific interactions within the system can be modeled, in order to check specific properties, and to "open" systems, in which components coming from different sources, and hence with different levels of integrity, interact.

The wide diffusion of Object–Oriented distributed middleware infrastructures and frameworks makes this issue a hot topic where our approach to validation may prove useful for the validation of the "interactional" aspects.

Indeed, since interaction policies can abstract from data and from functions, the description of a system adopting a policy can be reduced to the description of the possible interactions (method invocations) between the objects that make up the system.

Similar ideas are also used in the formalization and analysis of architectural styles in an operational framework [5]. The authors use a process algebra to formalize the interactional properties of components and connectors, abstracting from their functionalities. Similarly to us, they describe a component/connector with a term of a process algebra and interactions are specified through actions. They use the notion of bisimulation equivalence to reason on the properties of the architecture, with particular interest in architectural compatibility and conformance.

Abstraction from data and functional details, which maintains the behavioural information in a process algebraic style, has been adopted in the definition of the so called *behavioural type systems* [22,20,21]. These type systems associate to a component an abstraction of their behaviour in a suitable process algebra, aiming to check the compatibility of communicating concurrent objects, with regard to the matching of their respective behaviour.

The analogy with our approach lies in the interest to verification, though in the case of behavioural types the focus is in a verification of compatibility between components (which can be reduced to some form of equivalence or pre-order verification between two behaviours) while in our case the focus is on the verification of properties over a single behaviour, hence performed through model checking.

In an open system, the definition of a behavioural type for a component and the check of compatibility between components at the interaction level can again be seen as the enforcement of a specific interaction policy among components. It is an open research issue how these techniques can be efficiently adopted to guarantee the integrity of future open component–based applications, such as those based on the composition of web-services: indeed, the availability of "integrity preserving" middleware layers will require proving integrity properties in spite of failures of some of the components to respect their integrity constraints.

Actually, in open systems the integrity level of a remote component is often unknown or untrusted. In this case, we can envisage at least three solutions: give a very pessimistic estimate of the integrity level of the remote component; exploit a trust system; establish proper Validation Objects to be used as envelopes to guarantee the needed integrity level.

Acknowledgement

The work is supported by the Software Engineering for Service-Oriented Overlay Computers (SENSORIA) project, an IST project funded by the European Union as an integrated project in the FP6 GC initiative.

References

1. G. Amato, M. Coppola, S. Gnesi, F. Scozzari, and L. Semini. Modeling web applications by the multiple levels of integrity policy. In M. Falaschi M. Alpuente, S. Escobar, editor, *1st International Workshop on Automated Specification and Verification of Web sites (WWV 2005)*, pages 161–176, Valencia, Spain, Mar.14–15 2005. In ENTCS vol. 157, issue 2, Elsevier Science.

2. D.E. Bell and L.J. LaPadula. Security Computer Systems: Mathematical foundations and model. Technical Report Technical Report M74-244, MITRE Corp., Bedford, Mass., 1974.

3. C. Bernardeschi, A. Fantechi, and S. Gnesi. Formal Validation of the GUARDS Inter–consistency Mechanism. *Reliability, Engineering and System Safety (RE&SS)*, 71(3):261–270, Feb. 2001. Elsevier.

4. C. Bernardeschi, A. Fantechi, and S. Gnesi. Model checking fault tolerant systems. *Software Testing, Verification & Reliability (STVR)*, 12(4):251–275, December 2002. John Wiley & Sons Ltd.

5. M. Bernardo, P. Ciancarini, and L. Donatiello. On the Formalization of Architectural Types with Process Algebras. In *Proc. ACM SIGSOFT 8th Int. Symp. on the Foundations of Software Engineering (FSE-00)*, volume 25, 6 of *ACM Software Engineering Notes*, pages 140–148. ACM Press, 2000.

6. K. Biba. Integrity Considerations for Secure Computer Systems. Technical Report Tech. Rep. ESD-TR 76-372, MITRE Co., Apr. 1997.

7. G. Bruns and I. Sutherland. Model Checking and Fault Tolerance. In *Proc. 6-th International Conference on Algebraic Methodology and Software Technology*, volume 1349 of *Lecture Notes in Computer Science*, pages 45–59, Sydney, Australia, 1997. Springer-Verlag.

8. D.D Clark and D.R Wilson. Comparison of Commercial and Military Computer Security Policies. In *IEEE Symp. on Security and Privacy*, pages 184–194, Oakland, CA, 1987. IEEE Computer Society Press.

9. E.M. Clarke, O. Grumberg, and D.Peled. *Model Checking*. MIT Press, 1999.

10. R. De Nicola and F.W. Vaandrager. Action versus State based Logics for Transition Systems. In *Proceedings Ecole de Printemps on Semantics of Concurrency*, volume 469 of *Lecture Notes in Computer Science*, pages 407–419. Springer-Verlag, 1990.

11. E.A. Emerson and J.Y. Halpern. Sometimes and Not Never Revisited: on Branching Time versus Linear Time Temporal Logic. *Journal of ACM*, 33(1):151–178, Jan. 1986.

12. A. Fantechi, S. Gnesi, and L. Semini. Applications of formal methods for validating an interaction policy. Technical Report ISTI–2004–TR–59, ISTI–CNR, 2004.

13. T. Fraser. LOMAC: Low Water-Mark Integrity Protection for COTS Environments. In *IEEE Symposium on Security and Privacy*, pages 230–245, 2000.

14. S. Gnesi and F. Mazzanti. On the Fly Verification of Networks of Automata. In *Proc. Int. Conference on Parallel and Distributed Processing Techniques and Applications, PDPTA'99, special session on Current limits to automated verification for distributed systems.*, Las Vegas, Ne, June 1999. CSREA Pres.

15. C. A. R. Hoare. *Communicating Sequential Processes*. Series in Computer Science. Prentice Hall Int., 1985.

16. G.J. Holzmann. The Model Checker SPIN. *IEEE Transaction on Software Engineering*, 5(23):279–295, 1997.

17. G.J. Holzmann. *The SPIN model checker: Primer and reference manual*. Addison Wesley, 2004.

18. Z. Liu and M. Joseph. Specification and verification of fault-tolerance, timing, and scheduling. *ACM Trans. Program. Lang. Syst.*, 21(1):46–89, 1999.

19. R. Milner. *Communication and Concurrency*. International Series in Computer Science. Prentice Hall, 1989.

20. B.C. Pierce N. Kobayashi and D.N. Turner. Linearity and the Pi-Calculus. *ACM Transactions on Programming Languages and Systems*, 21(5):914–947, 1999.

21. E. Najm, A. Nimour, and J.-B. Stefani. Garanteeing liveness in an object calculus through behavioral typing. In *Proceedings of FORTE/PSTV'99*, Beijing, China, October 1999. Kluwer.

22. O. Nierstrasz. *Regular types for active object*, pages 99–121. Prentice-Hall, 1995.

23. D. Powell, editor. *A Generic Fault–Tolerant Architecture for Real–Time Dependable Systems*. Kluwer Academic Publishers, Jan. 2001.

24. W. Steiner, J. Rushby, M. Sorea, and H. Pfeifer. Model checking a fault-tolerant startup algorithm: From design exploration to exhaustive fault simulation. In *The International Conference on Dependable Systems and Networks*, pages 189–198, Florence, Italy, June 2004. IEEE Computer Society.

25. E. Totel, L. Beus-Dukic, J.-P. Blanquart, Y. Deswarte, V. Nicomet, D. Powell, and A. Wellings. Multi level integrity mechanism. Chapt. 6 of [23].

26. E. Totel, J.-P. Blanquart, Y. Deswarte, and D. Powell. Supporting Multiple Levels of Criticality. In *Proceedings 28th Int. Symp. on Fault-Tolerant Computing (FTCS-28)*, Munich, Germany, Jun. 1998. IEEE Computer Society Press.

F(I)MEA-Technique of Web Services Analysis and Dependability Ensuring

Anatoliy Gorbenko, Vyacheslav Kharchenko, Olga Tarasyuk,
and Alexey Furmanov

Department of Computer Systems and Networks (503)
National Aerospace University "KhAI"
17 Chkalov Str., Kharkiv, 61070 Ukraine
A.Gorbenko@csac.khai.edu, V.Kharchenko@khai.edu,
O.Tarasyuk@csac.khai.edu, A.Furmanov@csac.khai.edu

Abstract. Dependability analysis of the Web Services (WSs), disclosure of possible failure modes and their effects are open problems. This paper gives results of the Web Services dependability analysis using standardized FMEA- (Failure Modes and Effects Analysis) technique and its proposed modification IMEA- (Intrusion Modes and Effects Analysis) technique. Obtained results of FMEA-technique application were used for determining the necessary means of error recovery, fault prevention, fault-tolerance ensuring and fault removal. Systematization and analysis of WS intrusions and means of intrusion-tolerance were fulfilled by use of IMEA-technique. We also propose the architectures of the fault and intrusion-tolerant Web Services based on the components diversity and dynamical reconfiguration as well as discuss principles and results of dependable and secure Web Services development and deployment by use of F(I)MEA-technique and multiversion approach.

1 Introduction

The Web Services architecture [1] based on SOAP, WSDL and UDDI specifications is rapidly becoming a de facto standard technology for organization of global distributed computing and achieving interoperability between different software applications running on various platforms.

It is now extensively used in developing numerous business-critical applications for banking, hotel/flight/train reservation and booking, e-business, e-science, GRID-systems, etc. That is why analysis and dependability ensuring of this architecture are acute research issues [1–3].

Web Services dependability consists of several attributes: availability, reliability, security, performance/responsiveness, etc. For e-commerce, in particular, serviceability, describing user's satisfaction, and availability of the required services are important characteristics.

In this paper we focus on ensuring reliability, security, fault and intrusion tolerance of Web Services.

M. Butler et al. (Eds.): Fault-Tolerant Systems, LNCS 4157, pp. 153–167, 2006.
© Springer-Verlag Berlin Heidelberg 2006

To improve dependability of Web Services and ensure fault and intrusion tolerance it is necessary to take into account possible failures and intrusions modes, their causes and influence on the system. With this purpose we propose to use a standardized FMEA- (Failure Modes and Effects Analysis) technique [4].

The rest of the paper is organised as follows. Section 2 gives a result of the failure and intrusion modes and effect analysis of Web Services. In Section 3 we describe techniques of Web Services dependability ensuring, including means of error recovery, fault prevention, fault and intrusion tolerance and also fault removal. Section 4 discusses principles of dependable and secure Web Services development and deployment based on using multilevel diversity, dynamical adaptation and reconfiguration as well as application of regular updates. Finally, in section 5 we briefly outline the on-going work on implementation architectures of dependable and secure web services deployment and intrusion tolerance ensuring.

2   F(I)MEA-Approach to Web Services Dependability Analysis

2.1 Failure Modes and Effect Analysis

The FMEA is a standard formalized technique for the systems reliability analysis devoted to the specification of failure modes, their sources, causes and influence on the system operability [4]. The use of the FMEA-technique for the Web Services analysis allows to identify the typical failures and their influence on the Web Services dependability, and also to determine the necessary means for error recovery and fault-tolerance. FMEA-technique can be used in dependability guaranteeing program of Web Services.

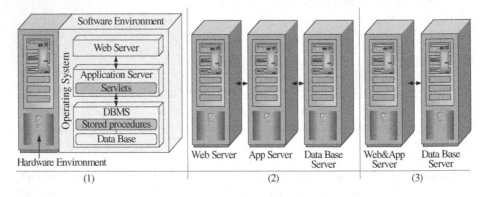

Fig. 1. Typical Web Services component architectures: (1) all components in the same host; (2) fully separated component architecture; (3) partially separated component architecture

Computer system providing some Web Services consists of hardware and specific software components (web server, application server, DBMS, and application software – servlets, stored procedures and triggers) and may have different architectures (Fig.1). These components must be taken into account during analysis of failure modes and effects.

The analysis of Web Services failures and intrusions modes, their causes and effects is obtained by using the FMEA-format (Tables 1, 2). To reduce scale of FMEA-tables we replaced duplicated rows by arrows and bus-lines.

To identify the Web Services failures modes new failure taxonomy was proposed (Fig. 2) taking into consideration variants described in [5–8]. The proposed taxonomy classifies possible failures from the point of view of publishers and end-users of Web Services, and takes into account failure domain, failure evidence and stability of occurrence, and also failures influence on system operability.

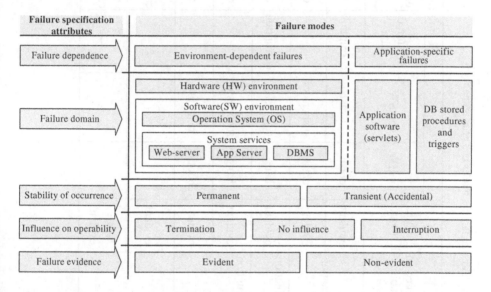

Fig. 2. Failure taxonomy

We performed the analysis of failure effects on data, system components, users and Web Services as a whole. Several failures modes can lead to the prolonged or short-term service aborting that affects on users as denial of service. Other failures may result in non-evident incorrect services. For many applications (e-commerce, e-science, etc.) such effect is more dangerous because it entails serious consequences, such as financial loss, calculation errors and, finally, service discrediting.

As it was found, the hardware design faults (faults in processors, chipsets, etc.) still remain one of the possible causes of the Web Services failures. Furthermore, a monthly Specification Update for Intel product series can contain up to several tens of errata, some of which, under certain circumstances, lead to unexpected program behavior, calculation errors or processor hang.

Table 1. Hardware failures modes end effects analisys

Failure Domain	Stability of Occurrence	Failure Cause	Influence on Operability	Failure Evidence	Failure Effect					
					on HW	on SW	on stored data	on session data & calculation	on web service as a whole	on user
HW environment	accidental failures	1) HW deterioration; 2) pernicious external influence	termination	evident	crash	Crash	corruption	data loss	service abort	deny of service
				evident	crash	suspension	–	data loss	service abort	deny of service
		non-pernicious external influence (interference)	termination	evident	hang	Crash	corruption	data loss	service abort	deny of service
			interruption	evident	hang	suspension	–	data loss	service abort	deny of service
				evident	rebooting	restarting	–	data loss	service abort	deny of service
	permanent failures	design faults	–	evident	–	–	–	data/calculation error	service exception	deny of service
				non-evident	–	–	–	data/calculation error	–	incorrect service

Bus-line

Table 2. Software failures modes end effects analisys

Failure Domain		Stability of Occurrence	Failure Cause	Influence on Operability	Failure evidence	Failure Effect					
						on HW	on SW	on stored data	on session data & calculation	on web service as a whole	on user
SW environment	OS	transient failures	design fault	termination	evident	hang	crash	corruption	data loss	service abort	deny of service
	Web Server			interruption	evident	hang	OS/Servers/DBMS/App suspension	–	data loss	service abort	deny of service
	App Server		malicious impact (hacker attack, viruses)	interruption	evident	rebooting	restarting	–	data loss	service abort	deny of service
Application SW	DBMS	permanent failures		–	evident	–	–	–	data/calculation error	service exception	deny of service
	Servlets		incorrect input data	–	non-evident	–	–	–	data/calculation error	–	incorrect service
	Stored procedures & triggers										

Bus-lines

Table 3. Intrusion modes and effects analysis

Intrusion /Attack mode	Attack nature	Attack cause	Influence on operability	Intrusion evidence	Intrusion effect					
					on HW	on SW	on transmitted /stored data	on session data	on web-service as a whole	on user
Sniffing	passive/ active	traffic broadcasting and retransmission	–	non-evident	–	–	privacy violation	data disclosure		user's data discrediting
Session hijacking	active	weak authentication	–	non-evident	–	exception		data disclosure and loss	service discrediting	user's data discrediting
Spoofing	active	lack of ARP searching mechanisms	interruption	evident	rebooting	restarting	privacy and integrity violation	–		user's data discrediting
Man-in-the middle	active	lack of DNS searching mechanisms	termination		hang	suspension		data disclosure		
	active	lack of routing mechanisms			hang	crash				
Direct intrusion	active	weak system guard, stack overflow, SW faults and vulnerabilities			hang	service emergency interruption		data loss	service abort	deny of service
DoS & DDoS	active	resource limitation			hang	resource exhaustion		–		deny of service

Bus-lines

However, the prevalent sources of Web Services failures are different software components. Besides, hacker attacks, viruses and other malicious impacts (Table 3) are becoming one of the dangerous sources of Web Services failures and require additional detailed consideration.

The reliability (probability of failure-free operation) of separated Web Services architectures presented in the Fig. 1 (2, 3) is lower than that of the centralized architecture (1) because of the increased a number of HW components that can fail. Thus, such architectures are more expedient to use in cluster systems.

Performed analysis will help in defining the necessary failure recovery and fault-tolerance means for specific failure modes. Set of the fault-tolerance means depends on failure modes and causes, whereas the required failure recovery means depend on failure effect on system and its components.

To address multiple faults all rows of F(I)MEA-tables should be weighted taking into account their severity and influence on system dependability. When multiply faults occur the several rows will be selected from the F(I)MEA-tables and top-priority fault-tolerant means will be chosen on the base of voting by faults severity.

2.2 The Analysis of Intrusion Modes and Effects

The network attacks and intrusions can be classified based on the following attributes: attack/intrusion mode, nature and cause of attack, intrusion evidence, influence on operability and effects on system, data and user.

The results of analysis of intrusion modes and effects are represented in Table 3. We consider such kinds of attacks and intrusions as "sniffing", "spoofing", "dummy embedding", "distributed denial of service" and "direct intrusions". They can be represented as IMEA table.

Direct intrusions are most dangerous because hackers can obtain a full control over attacked system with unpredictable dramatic consequences. The basic causes of direct intrusions are weak system guard, stack overflow, faults and many other vulnerabilities in the OS, Web & Application servers, DBMS and, finally, in the application software. When new malicious exploit occurs, all systems with the same security vulnerability become open to intrusions until the proper security patch is issued and applied.

3   Ensuring Web Services Dependability and Fault-Tolerance

3.1   Error Recovery

Common means of the error recovery for Web Services include: 1) replacement of crashed hardware components; 2) reinstallation of crashed software components; 3) data recovery; 4) system rebooting or restarting of the particular software services.

To achieve better availability system rebooting and restarting of the particular software services and applications must be performed in automatic mode with the help of hardware or software implemented watch-dog timers. Besides, it is preferable to have a secure way for remote system rebooting performed by the administrator. It is also very important for successful data recovery to perform regular data backup.

3.2 Fault Prevention

Fault prevention is attained, first of all, by quality control techniques employed during the design and manufacturing of hardware and software [5]. However, most of the hardware and software components of Web Services are the COTS- (commercial of the shelf) components developed by third parties.

Hence, service publisher has limited means for fault prevention:

- quality control techniques employed during the design of theown developed application software;
- procedures for input parameter checking;
- rigorous procedures for system maintenance and administration;
- firewalls, security guards and scanners to prevent malicious failures.

Besides, to prevent transient failures and performance reducing caused by software rejuvenation techniques based on forced restarting/reinitialization of the software components can be used [9].

3.3 Fault and Intrusion Tolerance

The development of fault tolerant techniques for the Web Services has been an active area of research over the last couple of years. The backward (based on rolling of the system components back to the previous correct state) and forward (which involves transforming the system components into any correct state) error recovery for the web on the basis of an application-specific exception handling is discussed in [10].

More generally, high dependability and fault-tolerance of the Web Services is ensured by using different kinds of redundancy and diversity at the different levels of the system structure (Fig. 3). HW redundancy may be partial (redundancy of processors, hard discs – RAID, network adapters, etc.) as well as complete with replication or diversification of SW.

Complete HW and SW redundancy is a foundation of cluster architectures and provides better performance and dependability.

Diversity is usually used to prevent software or hardware failures caused by design faults. But for tolerating transient failures a simple replication of SW environment with HW redundancy may be sufficient means, because of the individual behavior of even two replicated SW environments. To prevent non-evident failures the voting scheme must be used.

The 72-87% of the faults in open-source software are independent of the operating environment (i.e. faults in application software) and hence are permanent [6]. Half of the remaining faults is environment depended environment depended caused by transient conditions.

Hence, diversity is the most efficient method of providing fault-tolerance. It can be used for HW platform, OS, web and application servers, DBMS and, finally, for application software, both separately and in many various combinations.

However static diversity of Web Services can worsen the intrusion-tolerance and security (confidentiality and integrity) because it opens new potential ways for malicious intrusions. At the same time diversity brings additional protection against DDoS attacks.

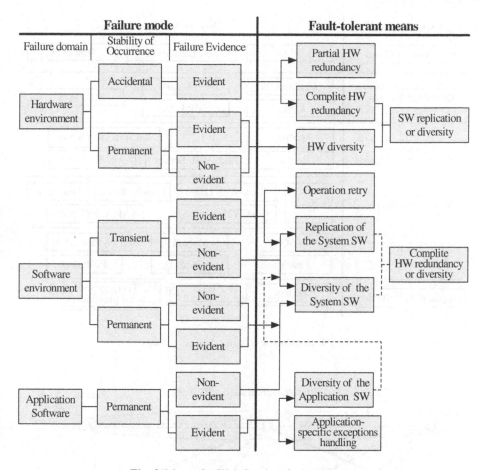

Fig. 3. Means for Web Services fault-tolerance

In this connection we propose to use dynamic system diversity. When new exploit occurs, it provides dynamic change of the current vulnerable system configuration to another one, which will be immune to this type of exploit.

In the Fig. 4 the set of possible diverse variants for different levels of the Web Services architecture is represented. For example, we can use Tomcat or BEA WebLogic or IBM Web Sphere as application server; Linux or Win2k or MacOS as operating system, etc.

It is well known that some software components may be incompatible with each other. Hence, it is very important to take into account this fact during multiversion system development. We propose to solve this problem with the help of diversity compatibility analysis at the different levels of Web Services architecture. Graph which represents such compatibility analysis is shown in the Fig. 5.

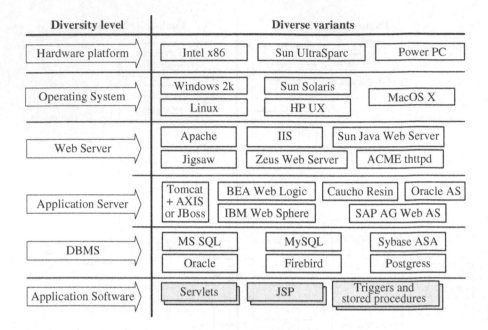

Fig. 4. Diversity levels and diverse variants

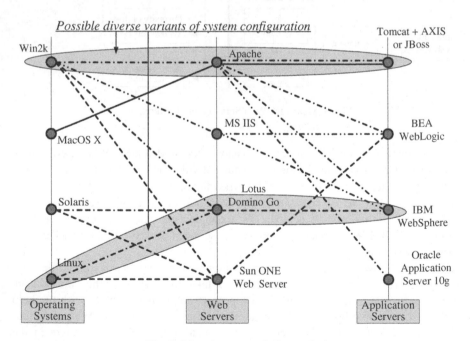

Fig. 5. Diversity compatibility analysis

Nodes correspond to the diverse variants at each of the diversity levels, whereas different types of arcs represent compatibility features. Types of arcs shading show which components are compatible and could be selected for particular configuration. As a result, all possible configurations of multiversion systems can be identified.

For example (see Fig. 5), we can choose following diverse Web Service configurations for multiversion system:

1. Win2k (OS), Apache (Web-server), Tomcat with AXIS (App server);
2. Linux (OS), Lotus Domino Go (Web-server), IBM WebSphere (App server).

3.4 Fault Removal

Fault removal of the Web Services is based, first of all, on the systematic application of the updates and patches for hardware (microcode updates) and software developed by third parties (OS, drivers, web and app servers, DBMS).

Fault removal from the own developed application software is performed both during the development phase and the maintenance. Technique, described in [11], provides cooperative and group testing of Web Services that can be performed on-line and just-in-time.

4 Dependable Web Services Development and Deployment

4.1 Using F(I)MEA-Technique for Dependable Web Services Development

To develop and deploy dependable Web Services the common FMEA- and IMEA-tables (see Tables 1-3) describing failures and intrusions modes and effects must be concretized taking into account actual hardware/software architecture of particular Web Service (Fig. 6).

Two different development strategies are possible. For business-critical applications it is necessary, as a rule, to provide the required dependability at the minimum cost, whereas for commercial applications it is important to provide the maximum dependability at the limited cost.

These goals can be achieved by solving optimization problem, taking into account failures criticality, probability of occurrence and cost of fault-tolerance means, their effectiveness and failures coverage. As a result the Web Service must be updated using chosen fault-tolerance means.

4.2 The Principles of Dependable and Secure Web Services Deployment

Fault and intrusion tolerance of the Web Services, their security and dependability as a whole could be improved using the following principles:

1. Defense in depth and diversity (D&D). Defense in depth implicates joint usage of existing intrusion and fault-tolerance facilities at the different levels of the Web Service architecture (HW platform, OS, System SW, etc.) to provide complex decision for dependability ensuring. Diversity (as it was shown in section 3.3) is one of the advanced techniques that can provide defense against both faults and intrusions.

2. Adaptability and update (A&U). The essence of this principle is in the dynamic changing of Web Service architecture and diversity modes according to the observed failures and intrusions. The intellectual monitoring means for detection of failures and intrusions, their analysis and the choice of better Web Services configurations could be used to achieve that. These means can include external alarm services, used to notify about recent Internet security vulnerabilities, novel viruses and to distribute security updates and patches.

The D&D and A&U principles are corresponding to the DIT (Dependable Intrusion Tolerance) architecture described in [12].

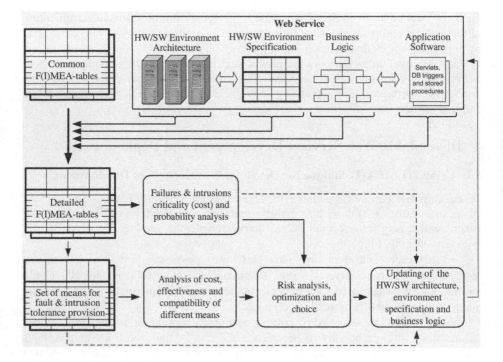

Fig. 6. Using FMEA-technique for dependable web services development

5 Implementation

In our previous work [8] we described solutions for dependable upgrading of Web Services with components upgraded on-line. It is based on using upgrading middleware, which includes monitoring and management tools and also database to store results statistics.

At the beginning, all versions of the same Web Service (or different divers Web Services with the identical functionality) are invoked concurrently and the final (composite) result forms by voting. All invocation results of the particular version are stored in the database as well as the composite results.

Afterwards, on the base of statistics analysis management tool switches from one versions of Web Service to another more reliable version.

Now we are extending this architecture according to the proposed principles of dependable and secure Web Services deployment (see Fig. 7). The new elements are:

- dynamically updated FMEA- and IMEA-tables and set of means for faults and intrusions tolerance provision;
- service resolver, that provides different customized strategies of the final result composition. For example, one strategy can provide better reliability/ trustworthiness of Web Service, whereas another one provides better performance/responsiveness.

Besides, the management tool implements Web Service configuration control.

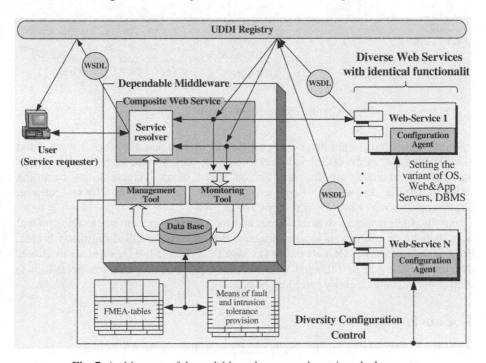

Fig. 7. Architecture of dependable and secure web services deployment

We also propose diverse architecture ensuring intrusion–tolerance of Web Systems and Services (Fig.8). This is the cluster architecture in which each host has *multiple-choice loading configuration*. It means that it is possible to load different OS after rebooting and start-up different web and application servers in the same host.

The main parts in this architecture are the Configuration Control Server (CCS) with Intrusion Detection System (IDS), and also Global Internet Security Alarm Service (GISAS). There are three main differences between proposed solution and DIT architecture, described in [12].

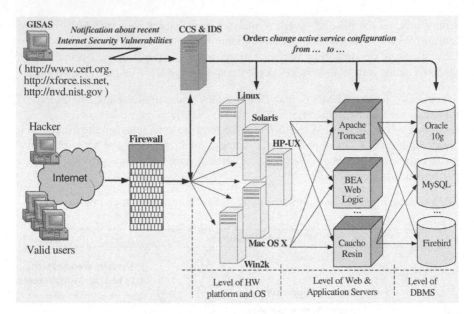

Fig. 8. Intrusion–tolerant Web service architecture

First, it provides deeper diversity level (levels of web and application servers and also DBMS). Secondly, IDS detects intrusions not only by scanning network traffic, but also by obtaining on-line information about recent vulnerabilities from the GISAS, which could be deployed on the base of http://www.cert.org, http://xforce.iss.net or http://nvd.nist.gov sites.

Finally, CCS performs dynamical reconfiguration of the current vulnerable channel with the help of configuration control agents that must be installed on the each host. For example, if new exploit attacking OS Win2k is detected, then all hosts in cluster that use Win2k will be rebooted with another alternative OS (for example, Linux) until proper update (security patch) is issued.

6 Conclusions

Publishers of Web Services have a limited possibility for fault prevention and fault removal of the most Web Services components, developed by the third parties. Thus, redundancy, in combination with diversity, is one of the basic means of ensuring dependability and providing tolerance to the majority failure modes. However, using diversity in Web Service architecture requires detailed research and additional solutions, because it can lead to additional security violations. Here, the cluster architecture with multilevel dynamic diversity and controlled configuration may be better solution providing high dependability, fault and intrusion tolerance.

Cluster architecture improves availability of Web Services. The additional adaptive reliable algorithms and means of voting, failures and intrusions diagnosis must be implemented to ensure tolerance to the non-evident failures and novel vulnerabilities. An important problem is the institution of the Global Internet Security Alarm Service.

The F(I)MEA is an effective technique, which can be used for the application of specific dependability analysis of Web Services, especially of composite WSs. The fulfilled analysis can be extended by taking into account the lack of required resources or services and unavailability of services due to network failures. Besides, the critical analysis of different failure modes can be performed.

FMEA- and IMEA-tables may be dynamically updated during Web Services operation. It allows (along with implementation of D&D and A&U principles) to increase the effectiveness of the employed means of dependability ensuring.

The estimates of the costs of performing F(I)MEA for an average web service as well as detailed compatibility analysis between different intrusion and fault-tolerant facilities and diversity modes will be the topics of our future research. We are also going to carry out a full-scale experiment with proposed intrusion-tolerant Web Service architecture.

References

1. W3C Working Group.: Web Services Architecture. http://www.w3.org/TR/ws-arch/ (2004)
2. Ferguson, D.F., Storey, T., Lovering, B., Shewchuk, J.: Secure, Reliable, Transacted Web Services: Architecture and Composition. Microsoft and IBM Technical Report. http://www-106.ibm.com/developerworks/webservices/library/ws-securtrans (2003)
3. Tartanoglu, F., Issarny, V., Romanovsky, A., Levy, N.: Dependability in the Web Service Architecture. In: Architecting Dependable Systems. Springer-Verlag (2003) 89–108.
4. IEC 812. Analysis Techniques for System Reliability – Procedure for Failure Modes and Effects Analysis (FMEA). International Electrotechnical Commission, Geneva (1985)
5. Avizienis, A., Laprie, J.-C., Randell, B., Landwehr, C.: Basic Concepts and Taxonomy of Dependable and Secure Computing. IEEE Transactions on Dependable and Secure Computing, Vol. 1(1) (2004) 11–33
6. Chandra, S., Chen, P. M.: Whither Generic Recovery From Application Faults? A Fault Study using Open-Source Software. Proc. Int. Conf. on Dependable Systems and Networks (2000) 97–106
7. Deswarte, Y., Kanoun, K., Laprie, J.-C.: Diversity against Accidental and Deliberate Faults. Proc. of Computer Security, Dependability, and Assurance (SCDA): From Needs to Solutions, York, England (1998) 171–181
8. Gorbenko, A., Kharchenko, V., Popov, P., Romanovsky, A.: Dependable Composite Web Services with Components Upgraded Online. In R. de Lemos et al. (Eds.): Architecting Dependable Systems III, LNCS 3549. Berlin, Heidelberg: Springer-Verlag (2005) 92–121
9. Vaidyanathan, K., Harper, R. et al.: Analysis and Implementation of Software Rejuvenation in Cluster Systems. Proc. Joint Intl. Conf. Measurement and Modeling of Computer Systems, ACM Sigmetrics and IFIP WG 7.3, Cambridge (2001) 62–71
10. Tartanoglu, F., Issarny, V., Romanovsky, A., Levy, N.: Coordinated Forward Error Recovery for Composite Web Services. Proc. 22nd IEEE Symposium on Reliable Distributed Systems (2003)
11. Tsai, Wei-Tek, Chen, Y., Paul, R., Liao, N., Huang, H.: Cooperative and Group Testing in Verification of Dynamic Composite Web Services. Proc. COMPSAC Workshops (2004) 170–173
12. Valdes, A., Almgren, M., Cheung, S., Deswarte, Y. et al.: An Architecture for an Adaptive Intrusion-Tolerant Server. Proc. 10th Int. Workshop on Security Protocols (2002), Lecture Notes in Computer Science, 2845 ed, Cambridge, UK: Springer (2004) 158–178

On Specification and Verification of Location-Based Fault Tolerant Mobile Systems

Alexei Iliasov, Victor Khomenko, Maciej Koutny, and Alexander Romanovsky

School of Computing Science, University of Newcastle
Newcastle upon Tyne, NE1 7RU, United Kingdom

Abstract. In this paper, we investigate context aware location-based mobile systems. In particular, we are interested how their behaviour, including fault tolerant aspects, could be captured using a formal semantics, which would then be suitable for analysis and verification. We propose a new formalism and middleware, called CAMA, which provides a rich environment to test our approach. The approach itself aims at giving CAMA a formal concurrency semantics in terms of a suitable process algebra, and then applying efficient model checking techniques to the resulting process expressions in a way which alleviates the state space explosion. The model checking technique adopted in our work is partial order model checking based on Petri net unfoldings, and we use a semantics preserving translation from the process terms used in the modelling of CAMA to a suitable class of high-level Petri nets.

Keywords: mobile systems, locations, LINDA, KLAIM, process algebra, Petri nets, fault tolerance, model checking.

1 Introduction

Mobile agent systems are increasingly attracting attention of software engineers. However, issues related to fault tolerance and exception handling in such systems have not yet received the level of attention they deserve. In particular, formal support for validating the correctness and robustness of fault tolerance properties is still under-developed. In this paper, we outline our approach to dealing with such issues in the context of a concrete system for description of mobility of agents (CAMA), and a concrete technique for verifying their properties (partial order model checking). Our overall goal in this paper is a formal model for the specification, analysis and model checking of CAMA designs. To achieve it, we will use process algebras and high-level Petri nets.

In concrete terms, our approach is first to give a formal semantics (including a compositional translation) of a suitably expressive subset of CAMA in terms of an appropriate process algebra and its associated operational semantics. The reason why we chose a process algebra semantics is twofold: (i) process algebras, due to their compositional and textual nature, are a formalism which is very close to the actual notations and languages used in real implementations; and (ii) there exists a significant body of research on the analysis and verification of process algebras. In our particular case, there are two process algebras which

M. Butler et al. (Eds.): Fault-Tolerant Systems, LNCS 4157, pp. 168–188, 2006.

are directly relevant to CAMA, viz. KLAIM [3,5] and π-calculus [14], and our intention is to use the former as a starting point for the development of the formal semantics.

The process algebra semantics of CAMA can then be used as a starting point for developing efficient model checking techniques aimed at verifying the behavioural correctness of CAMA designs. In our approach, we are specifically interested in model checking techniques which alleviate the state space explosion problem, and for this reason we adopted a partial order model checking based on Petri net unfoldings [13]. To be able to use it, we take advantage of a semantics preserving translation from the process terms used in the modelling of CAMA to a suitable class of high-level Petri nets based on [7,8].

2   Cama

CAMA is a middleware supporting rapid development of mobile agent software. It offers a programmer a number of high-level operations and a set of abstractions which help to develop multi-agent applications in a disciplined and structured way. CAMA is an extensible system. Its core functionality is concerned with inter-agent communication. Weak logical mobility, exception propagation and a number of other extensions are provided in the form of *plug-ins*. In this section, we briefly introduce the CAMA architecture and its core functionality.

CAMA inter-agent communication is based on the LINDA [9] paradigm which provides a set of language-independent coordination primitives that can be used for coordination of several independent pieces of software. Thanks to being language neutral, LINDA became quite popular and its coordination primitives have been implemented in many programming languages. It perfectly fits the domain of agent systems with its time and name decoupled communication style. In a nutshell, LINDA coordination primitives allow processes to put *tuples* (vectors of values) in a shared tuple space, remove them, and test for their presence. Input operations use special tuples called *templates*, where some fields are replaced with wildcards that can match any value. As a result, LINDA provides a mechanism for effective inter-process coordination, and other kinds of coordination primitives, like semaphores or mutexes, can be simulated using LINDA primitives in a straightforward way.

Mobile agent systems can be classified into two categories, according to the functionality of the nodes in a system. In one case, all the nodes carry the same functionality and have a capability for communicating with other nodes. A number of such nodes can create an ad-hoc network and start inter-process collaboration. Since all the nodes have similar functionality and capabilities, models of this kind are called *symmetric*. The other approach is to implement certain tasks, such as communication or migration, as additional services. This results in agents which depend upon service providers, but have a simpler structure and carry less functionality. This model is closer to the standard service provision architectures, and is often referred to as *asymmetric* as services and agents have complementary functionality.

The approach described in this paper is based on the asymmetric model of agent systems within the *location-based* paradigm of [1,12]. The main part of communication and control is implemented by a dedicated service, called *location*. The client part is lightweight, which facilities agent development for restricted platforms, such as PDAs and smart-phones. The approach supports large-scale mobile agent networks in a predictable and reliable manner, which is not the case with the symmetric approach [1]. Moreover, location-based architecture eliminates the need for employing complex distributed algorithms, such as voting or agreement. This allows one to guarantee atomicity of certain operations without sacrificing performance and usability. This scheme also provides a natural way of introducing context-aware computing, by defining location as a context of an agent.

The main disadvantage of the location-based scheme is that an additional infrastructure is required to support agent collaboration. However, in [1] it is argued that the current trends in wireless networks development are favourable with respect to the asymmetric model.

2.1   CAMA Basic Concepts

A CAMA system consists of a set of *locations*. The main role of a location is to provide an inter-agent communication service to its client agents. The communication service is based on a shared blackboard supporting LINDA operations.

One of the major contributions of CAMA is a novel mechanism to structure a shared blackboard so that groups of communicating agents can work in isolated sub-spaces, called *scopes*. Isolation of a communication space is only one of several roles of the scope construct; for example, it also provides a dynamic type-checking facility for multi-agent applications. Each agent carries attributes describing the functionality it implements, and the scoping mechanism only permits collaboration of agents with compatible functionality. It also acts as a service discovery mechanism. Agents look up for activities or services by analysing scope attributes. Scopes attributes are represented as a LINDA tuple and the discovery procedure is based on the LINDA tuple matching. This mechanism is both flexible and powerful.

The main structuring units of CAMA applications are *agents* which are pieces of software conforming to some formal *specification*. To distinguish between various functionalities of individual agents, and to match compatible agents, CAMA uses agent *roles* as units of functionality structuring. A role is also a structuring unit of an agent, and a part of the scoping mechanism. Role-based type-checking allows dynamic composition of multi-agent applications which ensures agent inter-operability and isolation.

Agents are executed on *platforms*, and several agents may reside on a single platform. Each platform provides an execution environment for the agents residing on it, and an interface to the location middleware.

2.2   CAMA Components

Scope is a dynamic container for tuples. It provides an isolated coordination space for compatible agents. It restricts visibility of tuples contained within the scope to the participants of the scope. A scope creation is initiated by an agent, however location controls the scope state depending upon the number and kind of the participants. When there are enough agents to instantiate a multi-agent application, the location allows participating agents to communicate. A scope is defined by a set of roles and restrictions on the roles. Scopes can be nested and scope participants may create new sub-scopes. Restrictions on roles dictate how many agents can play any given role of a scope. A restriction is a pair of natural numbers - the minimum required number of agents for a given role and the maximum allowed number of agents for a given role. The scope's state tracks the number of roles currently taken and determines whether the scope can be used for agent collaboration (see Figure 1).

R_1	R_1^{min}	R_1^{max}		
R_2	R_2^{min}	R_2^{max}	$R_i^{min} \le N_{R_i} \le R_i^{max}$	(roles taken)
...			n	(scope name)
R_k	R_k^{min}	R_k^{max}	A	(owner)

Fig. 1. Scope requirements (left), and scope state (right)

Role is an abstract description of agent's functionality. Each role is associated with some abstract scope model. An agent may implement a number of roles and can also take several roles within the same or different scopes. There is a formal relationship between a scope and its role. The latter is formally derived from an abstract model through decomposition process, while the former is a run-time instantiation of the model through the composition roles of individual agents (for more details see [10]).

Location is a container for *scopes*. It can be associated with a particular physical location. It is the core part of the system providing means of communication and coordination between agents. We assume that each location has a unique name. This roughly corresponds to IP addresses of hosts in a network which are often unique (at least within a local network). A location keeps track of the connected agents and their properties, in order to update the states of the scopes and ensure isolation properties. Location also provides additional services varying from location to location. These are made available to agents through what appears as a normal scope even though some roles are implemented by the location itself. As with all the scopes, agents are required to implement specific roles in order to connect to a location-provided scope. Few examples of such services include printing on a local printer, Internet access, making a backup to a location storage, and migration. In addition to supporting scopes as means of agent communication, locations may also offer support for logical mobility of agents, hosting of agents, and agent backup. Agent hosting allows autonomous agents to migrate from a location to location and participate in some activities on the locations. A location may play a role of a trusted third party in certain scope types. This facilitates implementation of various transaction schemes.

Platform provides an execution environment for agents. It is composed of a virtual machine for code execution, networking support, and client middleware for interacting with a location. A platform may be hosted by a PDA, smartphone, laptop or a location server. The notion of a platform is important to clearly differentiate between the concepts of a location providing coordination services to agents, and the middleware that only supports agent execution. In symmetric approaches no such distinction is made [4,15,16].

Agent is a piece of software implementing a set of roles which allows it to take part in certain scopes. All agents must implement some minimal functionality, called the default role, which specifies their activities outside of all the scopes.

2.3   CAMA Operations

We will now present a brief overview of the core operations provided by CAMA middleware. The operations can be seen as belonging to the following three groups: location engagement, scoping mechanism, and communication. Communication operations implement the standard LINDA coordination paradigm and so we will not discuss them here.

The location engagement operations associate or disassociate an agent with a location. There is one operation for each case:

- engage(ag)@ℓ - associates an agent ag with location ℓ. It also issues a new location-wide name a that is unique and unforgeable. This name is used as agent identifier in all other role operations. The name a is used by the agent to access other services of the location.
- disengage(a)@ℓ - disassociates agent a from location ℓ, and the previously issued name is no longer valid. After its execution, any operation invoked with the agent name a is ignored.

The scoping mechanism operations allow an agent to enquiry about the available scopes, create and remove scopes, join the existing scopes and control their visibility.

- create(a, R)@$\ell.s$ - creates a new scope s at location ℓ on behalf of agent a with the scope requirements R.
- destroy(a)@$\ell.s$ - destroys a scope s at location ℓ. This operation always succeeds if the requesting agent is the owner of the scope, and it is executed recursively for all the sub-scopes contained in the scope.
- join(a, r)@$\ell.s$ - if successful, it permits agent a to take role r in scope s at location ℓ. This operation succeeds if the scope $\ell.s$ exists and agent a is allowed to take the specified role in that scope.
- leave(a, r)@$\ell.s$ - disallows agent a to participate in the scope $\ell.s$ with role r. The calling agent must be already participating in the scope with the specified role.
- put(a, n)@$\ell.s$ - makes the scope $\ell.s$ available to other agents participating in the parent scope of $\ell.s$.

– get(a, r)@$\ell.s$ - enquires about the names of the scopes contained in scope $\ell.s$ and supporting the role(s) r.

An agent starts its execution by looking for available locations. Once it connects to a location it joins a scope, or creates a new one and waits for other agents to join it. When a scope requirements are satisfied, agents in a scope can start collaboration using the LINDA coordination primitives. After they finished using the scope, they leave it.

In the next section, we outline a formal description of various CAMA operations using a process algebra.

3   A Process Algebra for CAMA Systems

The semantical model of CAMA will be expressed using a process algebra which is basically the CKLAIM [3] extended with a few features taken from STOCK-KLAIM [6] (to model other useful constructs, we plan to use some elements of the π-calculus [14]). We now briefly outline the key aspects of this development which is strongly based on that presented in [7], with some features being omitted (i.e., those relating to location creation) and some added (i.e., simple conditionals, general data, and non-singleton tuples). We refer the reader to [7] for more details about the approach on which this section is based.

We assume that there is a set $\mathcal{L}$ of *localities* ranged over by $l, l', l_1, \ldots$ and a disjoint set $\mathcal{U}$ of *locality variables* ranged over by $u, v, w, u', v', w', u_1, v_1, w_1, \ldots$ (We also assume that a special locality self belongs to $\mathcal{L}$.) Their union forms the set of *locality names* ranged over by $\ell, \ell', \ell_1, \ldots$ In addition, $\mathcal{A} = \{A_1, \ldots, A_m\}$ is a finite set of *process identifiers*, each identifier $A \in \mathcal{A}$ having a finite arity n_A.

We further assume that $\mathcal{D}$ is a set of *data values* ranged over by $d, d', d_1, \ldots$ and $\mathcal{V}$ is a disjoint set of *data variables* ranged over by $h, h', h_1, h_1, \ldots$. Moreover, $\mathcal{E}$ is a set of *value expressions* ranged over by $e, e', e_1, \ldots$ constructed from values, value variables and suitable operators, some of which will be mentioned in the rest of the paper. We do not assume any specific syntax of the expressions except that they can always be evaluated if no variables are involved.

The process algebra we consider in this paper has the syntax given in Figure 2, where b is a boolean expression and e' an expression not involving variables. Moreover, for each $A \in \mathcal{A}$, there is exactly one definition $A(x_1, \ldots, x_{n_A}) \overset{\text{df}}{=} P_A$ (where the x_i's are variables), which is available globally. It is assumed that in a conditional **if** b **then** P **fi**. Q the process P uses only action prefixes and possibly other conditionals. Note that tuples can be represented either as finite sequences of elements or as comma-separated lists enclosed within angle brackets. The assumed order of precedence among the operators (from the weakest to the strongest binding) is as follows: '‖', '::', '|', '+' and '.'.

Networks are finite collections of computational nodes, where data and processes can be located. Each node consists of a locality l identifying it and a process or a datum. There can be several nodes with the same locality part. Effectively, one may think of a network as a collection of uniquely named nodes, each node

$$\mathfrak{N} ::= l :: P \mid l :: \langle \mathfrak{q} \rangle \mid \mathfrak{N} \parallel \mathfrak{N} \qquad \text{(networks)}$$

$$a ::= \mathbf{out}(\mathfrak{v})@\ell \mid \mathbf{rd}(\mathsf{t})@\ell \mid \mathbf{in}(\mathsf{t})@\ell \mid \mathbf{eval}(A(\mathfrak{v}))@\ell \qquad \text{(actions)}$$

$$P ::= \mathbf{nil} \mid A(\mathfrak{v}) \mid a . P \mid P + P \mid P|P \mid \mathbf{if}\ b\ \mathbf{then}\ P\ \mathbf{fi} . P \qquad \text{(processes)}$$

$$\mathsf{t} ::= \ell \mid e \mid !u \mid !h \mid \ell\,\mathsf{t} \mid e\,\mathsf{t} \mid !u\,\mathsf{t} \mid !h\,\mathsf{t} \qquad \text{(templates)}$$

$$\mathfrak{q} ::= l \mid d \mid l\mathfrak{q} \mid d\mathfrak{q} \qquad \text{(evaluated tuples)}$$

$$\mathfrak{v} ::= \ell \mid e \mid \ell\mathfrak{v} \mid e\mathfrak{v} \qquad \text{(tuples)}$$

$$\mathfrak{f} ::= l \mid \mathbf{self} \mid e' \mid \mathbf{self}\mathfrak{f} \mid l\mathfrak{f} \mid e'\mathfrak{f} \qquad \text{(variable-free tuples)}$$

Fig. 2. Process algebra syntax

comprising its own data space and a possibly concurrent process which runs there. This view is embodied in the rules for *structural equivalence* on nodes and networks, which is the smallest congruence such that the rules in Table 1 hold (note that $\{y_1/x_1, \ldots, y_{n_A}/x_{n_A}\}$ denotes substitution).

Table 1. Structural equivalence rules

(COM)	$\mathfrak{N}_1 \parallel \mathfrak{N}_2 \equiv \mathfrak{N}_2 \parallel \mathfrak{N}_1$
(ASSOC)	$(\mathfrak{N}_1 \parallel \mathfrak{N}_2) \parallel \mathfrak{N}_3 \equiv \mathfrak{N}_1 \parallel (\mathfrak{N}_2 \parallel \mathfrak{N}_3)$
(ABS)	$l :: P \equiv l :: (P|\mathbf{nil})$
(PRINV)	$l :: A(x_1, \ldots, x_{n_A}) \equiv l :: \{y_1/x_1, \ldots, y_{n_A}/x_{n_A}\}P_A$
(CLONE)	$l :: (P_1|P_2) \equiv l :: P_1 \parallel l :: P_2$
(IF1)	$\mathbf{if}\ 1\ \mathbf{then}\ P\ \mathbf{fi} . Q \equiv P . Q$
(IF2)	$\mathbf{if}\ 0\ \mathbf{then}\ P\ \mathbf{fi} . Q \equiv Q$

Actions are the basic (atomic) operations which can be executed by processes, as follows:

- $\mathbf{out}(\mathfrak{v})@\ell$ deposits a fresh copy of a tuple $\mathfrak{v}$ (after evaluation) inside the locality addressed by ℓ.
- $\mathbf{in}(\mathsf{t})@\ell$ retrieves an item matching the template t from the locality addressed by ℓ.
- $\mathbf{rd}(\mathsf{t})@\ell$ reads an item matching the template t at the locality addressed by ℓ.
- $\mathbf{eval}(A(\mathfrak{f}))@\ell$ instantiates a new copy of the process identified by A at the locality addressed by ℓ.

The special meaning of `self` is that it refers to the locality address at which an action is executed. Note that instantiating a process in an arbitrary locality allows one to model mobility.

Processes act upon the data stored at various nodes and spawn new processes. The algebra of processes is built upon the (terminated) process **nil** and recursive call $A(\mathfrak{v})$ as well as the composition operators: prefixing by an action $(a \,.\, P)$; simple conditional (**if** b **then** P **fi** $.\, Q$); choice $(P+Q)$; and parallel composition $(P|Q)$.

Binding is introduced by action prefixes like $\mathbf{in}(!z)@\ell \,.\, P$ or $\mathbf{rd}(!z)@\ell \,.\, P$ which *bind* the variable z within P, and we denote by $fn(P)$ the *free* names of P (and similarly for networks).[1] For the process definition, we assume that $fn(P_A) \subseteq \{x_1, \ldots, x_{n_A}\}$. Processes are defined up to the *alpha-conversion*, and $\{y/x, \ldots\}P$ will denote the agent obtained from P by replacing all free occurrences of x by y, etc., possibly after alpha-converting P in order to avoid name clashes. Note that self is a distinguished locality, not a variable, and so it is never free nor bound.

Given a network $\mathfrak{N}$, one can apply alpha-conversion to obtain a *well-formed* network definition. By this we mean that no variable across the network and process definitions generates more than one binding, and that there are no free variables in the network.

Recursive behaviour can be achieved in two ways. One is a kind of process instantiation, possibly at the current location. For example,

$$l :: \mathbf{eval}(A(l', \langle 5, 4 \rangle))@\mathtt{self} \,.\, \mathbf{nil}$$

with $A(u, d) \overset{\mathrm{df}}{=} \mathbf{out}(d)@u \,.\, \mathbf{eval}(A(u, d))@\mathtt{self} \,.\, \mathbf{nil}$ will be indefinitely depositing copies of the tuple $\langle 5, 4 \rangle$ from the locality with address l to the data space of the locality addressed by l'. Another way of effecting repetitive behaviour (at the current location) is through a declaration of the form $l :: A'(l', \langle 5, 4 \rangle)$ with:

$$A'(u, d) \overset{\mathrm{df}}{=} \mathbf{out}(d)@u \,.\, A'(u, d) \,.$$

In such a case, instantiating successive copies of $A'()$ will take place without executing any visible activating actions.

Operational semantics The operational semantics of networks and processes is detailed in Table 2. It is based on the structural equivalence defined above (see the STRUCT rule) and labelled transition rules:

$$\mathfrak{N} \xrightarrow{act} \mathfrak{N}'$$

where *act* is the record of an execution of a prefix. The *act* can be $\mathbf{o}(l, \mathfrak{q}, l')$, $\mathbf{r}(l, \mathfrak{q}, l')$, $\mathbf{i}(l, \mathfrak{q}, l')$ or $\mathbf{e}(l, A(\mathfrak{q}), l')$, where the initial symbol identifies the type of action, l is the locality where the action is executed, l' identifies the locality where the action takes effect, and $\mathfrak{q}$ is a parameter (argument of the action), which is in this case a tuple of data values and/or localities. For instance, action $\mathbf{e}(l, A(\mathfrak{q}), l')$ means that, from location l, an instance of process A is launched at location l' with an effective parameter $\mathfrak{q}$, while $\mathbf{i}(l, \mathfrak{q}, l')$ records the execution at l of an input of $\mathfrak{q}$ from location l'.

---

[1] It is assumed that the prefixes of P in a conditional **if** b **then** P **fi** $.\, Q$ do not generate any bindings within Q.

Table 2. Operational semantics rules

$$(\textsc{Par}) \quad \frac{\mathfrak{N} \xrightarrow{act} \mathfrak{N}'}{\mathfrak{N} \| \mathfrak{N}'' \xrightarrow{act} \mathfrak{N}' \| \mathfrak{N}'' \quad \text{and} \quad \mathfrak{N}'' \| \mathfrak{N} \xrightarrow{act} \mathfrak{N}'' \| \mathfrak{N}'}$$

$$(\textsc{Sum1}) \quad \frac{l :: P \xrightarrow{act} \mathfrak{N}'}{l :: P + P' \xrightarrow{act} \mathfrak{N}' \quad \text{and} \quad l :: P' + P \xrightarrow{act} \mathfrak{N}'}$$

$$(\textsc{Sum2}) \quad \frac{l :: P \| l' :: \langle \mathfrak{q} \rangle \xrightarrow{act} \mathfrak{N}'}{l :: P + P' \| l' :: \langle \mathfrak{q} \rangle \xrightarrow{act} \mathfrak{N}' \quad \text{and} \quad l :: P' + P \| l' :: \langle \mathfrak{q} \rangle \xrightarrow{act} \mathfrak{N}'}$$

$$(\textsc{Struct}) \quad \frac{\mathfrak{N} \equiv \mathfrak{N}_1 \quad \mathfrak{N}_1 \xrightarrow{act} \mathfrak{N}_2 \quad \mathfrak{N}_2 \equiv \mathfrak{N}'}{\mathfrak{N} \xrightarrow{act} \mathfrak{N}'}$$

$$(\textsc{Eval}) \quad \frac{l' = evaluate_l(\ell) \quad \mathfrak{q} = evaluate_l(\mathfrak{f}) \quad match_l(\mathbf{t}, \mathfrak{q}) = \rho}{l :: \mathbf{eval}(A(\mathfrak{f}))@\ell . P \xrightarrow{\mathbf{e}(l, A(\mathfrak{q}), l')} l :: P \| l' :: \rho P_A}$$

$$(\textsc{Out}) \quad \frac{l' = evaluate_l(\ell) \quad \mathfrak{q} = evaluate_l(\mathfrak{f})}{l :: \mathbf{out}(\mathfrak{f})@\ell . P \xrightarrow{\mathbf{o}(l, \mathfrak{q}, l')} l :: P \| l' :: \langle \mathfrak{q} \rangle}$$

$$(\textsc{In}) \quad \frac{l' = evaluate_l(\ell) \quad match_l(\mathbf{t}, \mathfrak{q}) = \rho}{l :: \mathbf{in}(\mathbf{t})@\ell . P \| l' :: \langle \mathfrak{q} \rangle \xrightarrow{\mathbf{i}(l, \mathfrak{q}, l')} l :: \rho P}$$

$$(\textsc{Rd}) \quad \frac{l' = evaluate_l(\ell) \quad match_l(\mathbf{t}, \mathfrak{q}) = \rho}{l :: \mathbf{rd}(\mathbf{t})@\ell . P \| l' :: \langle \mathfrak{q} \rangle \xrightarrow{\mathbf{r}(l, \mathfrak{q}, l')} l :: \rho P \| l' :: \langle \mathfrak{q} \rangle}$$

In Table 2 we use two special notations, for tuple evaluation and matching. To start with, for every variable-free component x of a tuple and locality $l \in \mathcal{L}$:

$$evaluate_l(x) \stackrel{\text{df}}{=} \begin{cases} l & \text{if } x = \mathtt{self} \\ d & \text{if } x \text{ is a value expresion evaluating to } d \\ x & \text{if } x \text{ is a locality} \end{cases}$$

Notice that $evaluate_l(x)$ is undefined if $x \in \mathcal{U}$, so that some of the rules may not be applicable if, for instance, a locality variable has not been substituted by an actual locality. The evaluation mapping is then extended to tuples, by setting

$$evaluate_l(\mathfrak{f}) \stackrel{\text{df}}{=} evaluate_l(f_1) \dots evaluate_l(f_r) ,$$

for every variable-free tuple $\mathfrak{f} = f_1 \dots f_r$. Another construct is needed to properly handle the input and reading of tuples residing at the tuple space.

Let $\mathbf{t} = t_1 \dots t_r$ be a template, $\mathfrak{q} = q_1 \dots q_r$ an evaluated tuple, and l a (non-$\mathtt{self}$) locality. Then we say that $\mathbf{t}$ and $\mathfrak{q}$ *match in* l if there exist disjoint subsequences $i_1 \dots i_p$ and $j_1 \dots j_m$ ($p + m = r$) of $1 \dots r$ such that the following hold:

- for each $z \leq p$ there is a variable x_z of the same type as q_{i_z} such that $t_{i_z} = !x_z$, and if for some g and h, $x_g = x_h$ then $q_{i_g} = q_{i_h}$;
- for each $z \leq m$, t_{j_z} is a data, locality or self and $evaluate_l(t_{j_z}) = q_{j_z}$.

If t and q match in l, then $match_l(t, q)$ is the substitution obtained from

$$\{q_{i_1}/x_1, \dots, q_{i_p}/x_p\}$$

by deleting all duplicates. It can be empty if none of the elements of t is of the form $!x$. For example, $match_{l_5}(!u\,\mathsf{self}\,!u\,l_3, l_4\,l_5\,l_4\,l_3) = \{l_4/u\}$.

Note that evaluated tuples are concrete lists of data values and/or locations which are deposited and removed from the data space, and templates are used to specify the composition of tuples being removed by processes.

4 Process Algebra Semantics of Cama

The semantics of CAMA operations is given using a straightforward adaptation of the process algebra outlined above. The semantics is based on the description of the scoping mechanism presented in [11].

The approach is based on simulating the scoping mechanism using a single shared tuple space and prefix-based tuple matching. The contents of a scope correspond to all tuples starting with some predefined prefix. Various attributes of agents and scopes are stored as tuples in the shared tuple space, and access to this information is restricted through the redefinition of the basic LINDA primitives.

All CAMA operations are initiated by a client and executed at a location. We specify actions for both the client and location as if they were operating on a single shared tuple space and we do not explicitly deal with the networking part of the middleware. The specification defines the CAMA scoping mechanism and actions of agents as well as the middleware. The latter controls the state of a location (tuple space) and provides a number of services, such as scope creation. Agents can synchronise using LINDA-style operations on scopes, and scopes may contain sub-scopes thus providing a hierarchy of nested agent activities (for brevity, in this paper we do not deal explicitly with the sub-scoping aspects).

We use locality variable argument as a reference to a location. In CAMA, locations are fixed network nodes and hence they do not appear or disappear during the system's lifetime. Thus the locality argument is often omitted and is assumed to be known from the context.

The specification uses prefix-based tuple matching. The notation $a\circ$ is used to match any tuple with size the same or greater than size of a and with the initial fields are matched by the template a. Prefixes can be concatenated in an obvious manner; for example, if $a = \langle f_1, f_2, \dots, f_k \rangle$ and $b = \langle g_1, g_2, \dots, g_m \rangle$ are two templates, then $a \circ b$ is the template $\langle f_1, f_2, \dots, f_k, g_1, g_2, \dots, g_m \rangle$ matching tuples with exactly $k+m$ fields. On the other hand, $a\circ b\circ$ would match any tuple whose initial $k+m$ fields are matched by $a \circ b$. In the same manner, prefixes can be concatenated with tuples.

In our model, a shared tuple space is the only available storage, and all the information about active agents and open scopes must be stored using tuples. In

Table 3. Prefixes used to partition the tuple space

tuple or prefix	description
$\mathfrak{L}\circ$	object locking
$\mathfrak{M}\circ$	requests to the middleware
$\mathfrak{A}\circ\langle A\rangle$	issued agent names
$\mathfrak{U}\circ\langle A'\rangle$	unused agent names
$\mathfrak{S}\circ\langle Sc\rangle$	names of active scopes
$\mathfrak{S}\circ s\circ\mathfrak{R}\circ\langle b\rangle$	status of scope s
$\mathfrak{S}\circ s\circ\mathfrak{P}\circ\langle param\rangle$	static parameters (requirements) of scope s
$\mathfrak{S}\circ s\circ\mathfrak{D}\circ\langle state\rangle$	dynamic state of scope s
$\mathfrak{S}\circ s\circ\mathfrak{C}\circ$	contents of scope s

addition, tuples are used for inter-agent communication inside a scope. Partitioning the tuple space into a number of disjoint parts makes it easy to manipulate records about scopes, agents and tuples. We introduce a unique prefix for each type of record used in the specification, as shown in Table 3. In the table, A and S are finite sets[2] which contain the currently issued agent names and the existing scopes, respectively (it is assumed that $A \subseteq Agents$ and $S \subseteq Scopes$, where $Agents$ and $Scopes$ are pre-defined finite sets). Moreover, A' is a set of unused agent names, disjoint from A. Initially, A is empty and A' non-empty.

The status of a scope, $\mathfrak{S}\circ s\circ\mathfrak{R}\circ\langle b\rangle$, can be either $\mathfrak{S}\circ s\circ\mathfrak{R}\circ\langle 0\rangle$, or $\mathfrak{S}\circ s\circ\mathfrak{R}\circ\langle 1\rangle$ which translates to the scope being available (1) for inter-agent communication or not (0). Whenever an agent wants to read or deposit a tuple in the scope, it checks the status and waits until it becomes 1.

Tuples with the prefix $\mathfrak{S}\circ s\circ\mathfrak{P}$ specify the set of roles supported by the scope s, and the restrictions on the number of agents for each role. Tuples starting with $\mathfrak{S}\circ s\circ\mathfrak{D}$ represent the current state of a scope, i.e., agents that are currently present in the scope and roles that are still available. This information is updated when an agent joins or leaves the scope. To make the notation more readable, we use the following:

- $param \overset{\mathrm{df}}{=} \langle rolesn, roles, min, max\rangle$ where: $rolesn \in \mathbb{N}$ is the number of different roles; $roles$ is a list of role names; $min : roles \rightarrow \mathbb{N}$ gives of the minimum number of required participants for each role; and $max : roles \rightarrow \mathbb{N}$ gives the maximum number of allowed participants for each role.
- $state \overset{\mathrm{df}}{=} \langle rolesr, rolesp, ag\rangle$ where: $rolesr \in \mathbb{N}$ is the number of roles still short of the minimal required number of participants; $rolesp : roles \rightarrow \mathcal{P}(A)$ is a list of the participants for each role of the scope; and $ag \in A$ is the name of the agent owning the scope.

We will now outline how we model the behaviour of a single CAMA location middleware which interacts with multiple agents. To avoid race conflicts on data

---

[2] We will often treat finite sets as though they were lists, and apply to them list operations. Also mappings with finite domains can be treated as finite lists.

produced and consumed by agents and the middleware, we introduce low-level synchronisation in the form of an advisory mutual exclusion (mutex). Two auxiliary operations, **lock**(3) and **unlock**(3) implement such locking by granting and releasing exclusive access to data associated with the prefix 3:

$$\mathbf{lock}(3) \ \overset{\mathrm{df}}{=} \ \mathbf{in}(\mathfrak{L} \circ 3 \circ \langle 1 \rangle)\mathbf{.out}(\mathfrak{L} \circ 3 \circ \langle 0 \rangle)$$
$$\mathbf{unlock}(3) \overset{\mathrm{df}}{=} \mathbf{in}(\mathfrak{L} \circ 3 \circ \langle 0 \rangle)\mathbf{.out}(\mathfrak{L} \circ 3 \circ \langle 1 \rangle)$$

In most cases, the associated data are tuples starting with the prefix 3. Being an advisory locking, it requires all the parties accessing a shared object to use this mechanism.

We model the location middleware as a set of cyclic event handlers activated by tuples of certain structure and always starting with the prefix $\mathfrak{M}$. The definition of a middleware process running at a location l has the following form:

$$\begin{aligned} Middleware \overset{\mathrm{df}}{=} \ &EngageLocation \mid DisenageLocation \mid CreateScope \mid \\ &DeleteScope \qquad \mid JoinScope \qquad \mid LeaveScope \end{aligned}$$

For each of the above processes, there is a corresponding agent code which generates requests and receives any results produced by the middleware. An agent process follows the standard process algebra syntax extended with the set of additional operations described below.

Engage location registers an agent in a given location and issues a name which is guaranteed to be location-wide unique. The name allows the recipient to request execution of other operations from the location middleware. The *AEngageLocation* operation is always the first one that an agent executes when it connects to a new location.

$$\begin{aligned} AEngageLocation \overset{\mathrm{df}}{=} \ &\mathbf{lock}(\mathfrak{M})\mathbf{.out}(\mathfrak{M} \circ \langle \text{ENGAGE} \rangle)\mathbf{.in}(\mathfrak{A} \circ \langle !a \rangle)\mathbf{.} \\ &\mathbf{unlock}(\mathfrak{M}) \end{aligned}$$

$$\begin{aligned} EngageLocation \overset{\mathrm{df}}{=} \ &\mathbf{in}(\mathfrak{M} \circ \langle \text{ENGAGE} \rangle)\mathbf{.in}(\mathfrak{A} \circ \langle !A \rangle)\mathbf{.in}(\mathfrak{U} \circ \langle !A' \rangle)\mathbf{.} \\ &\mathbf{out}(\mathfrak{A} \circ \langle A \cup \{first(A')\} \rangle)\mathbf{.out}(\mathfrak{U} \circ \langle tail(A') \rangle)\mathbf{.} \\ &\mathbf{out}(\mathfrak{A} \circ \langle first(A') \rangle)\mathbf{.}EngageLocation \end{aligned}$$

In the above, an agent acquires a lock for the prefix $\mathfrak{M}$, which is used to identify requests to the middleware. The agent produces the tuple $\mathfrak{M} \circ \langle \text{ENGAGE} \rangle$ to inform the middleware that there is a new agent connected to the location. The location middleware does not need to know any identifier of the agent since possible interference with other agents is avoided by locking of the prefix $\mathfrak{M}$. Note that the middleware does not have to do any locking since the requesting agent releases the lock only after it receives a name from the middleware. It is also implied that no other agent or middleware operations operate on tuples of the same structure.

The middleware reads the request which does not have any variable arguments and acts as a trigger for this operation. It then proceeds with reading in the set of issued agent names A, and yet unused names A'. A new agent name is allocated from the latter set, and both sets are updated accordingly. Note that $first()$ returns the first element of a list, and $tail()$ returns the list of remaining elements.

Disengage location removes the name of a connected agent from the set of issued names. This operation does not require locking because the interaction between an agent and the middleware is limited to a single tuple produced by the agent. In the request to the middleware, the agent passes its name (ag). The request triggers a handler in the middleware which updates the set of issued agent names.

$$ADisengageLocation \stackrel{\mathrm{df}}{=} \mathbf{out}(\mathfrak{M} \circ \langle \text{DISENGAGE}, ag \rangle)$$

$$DisengageLocation \stackrel{\mathrm{df}}{=} \mathbf{in}(\mathfrak{M} \circ \langle \text{DISENGAGE}, !a \rangle) . \mathbf{in}(\mathfrak{A} \circ \langle !A \rangle) .$$
$$\mathbf{out}(\mathfrak{A} \circ \langle A - \{a\} \rangle) . DisenageLocation$$

Create scope makes a new scope defined by a scope name (sc), scope requirements ($param$) and a role ($role$) that the requesting agent (ag) is going to play in the new scope. The middleware reads the requests and locks the part of the tuple space which contains description structures for all scopes ($\mathbf{lock}(\mathfrak{S})$). It then checks that the supplied agent name is one of the names issued by this location, and that the role it is going to take in the scope is one of the roles supported by the scope. If these conditions hold, the middleware creates records describing the new scope. The tuple $\mathfrak{S} \circ s \circ \mathfrak{P} \circ \langle param \rangle$ contains the requirements for this scope, i.e., the list of supported roles and the restrictions on number of agents for each role.

The initial state of the scope state needs the number of roles which require at least one agent. This is done by subtracting the number of roles with zero required agents from the total number of roles in the scope. The list of participants is left empty and is immediately populated by the $Update$ operation.

$$ACreateScope \stackrel{\mathrm{df}}{=} \mathbf{out}(\mathfrak{M} \circ \langle \text{CREATE\_SC}, ag, sc, param, role \rangle)$$

$CreateScope \stackrel{\mathrm{df}}{=} \mathbf{in}(\mathfrak{M} \circ \langle \text{CREATE\_SC}, !a, !s, !p, !r \rangle) . \mathbf{lock}(\mathfrak{S}) . \mathbf{rd}(\mathfrak{A} \circ \langle !A \rangle) .$
     if $a \in A \wedge r \in p.roles$
     then
         $\mathbf{out}(\mathfrak{S} \circ s \circ \mathfrak{P} \circ \langle p \rangle) . \mathbf{out}(\mathfrak{S} \circ s \circ \mathfrak{R} \circ \langle 0 \rangle) .$
         $\mathbf{out}(\mathfrak{S} \circ s \circ \mathfrak{D} \circ \langle p.rolesn - |p.min^{-1}(\{0\})|, \langle \rangle, a \rangle) .$
         $Update(r, a, s)$ **fi** .
     $\mathbf{unlock}(\mathfrak{S}) . CreateScope$

The $Update$ operation also determines whether all the required roles are present and the scope can be used for inter-agent communication. This is done by looking at the scope requirements and the current scope state:

$$Update(r, a, s) \overset{\text{df}}{=} \mathbf{rd}(\mathfrak{S} \circ s \circ \mathfrak{P} \circ \langle !rolesn, !roles, !min, !max \rangle) \,.$$
$$\mathbf{in}(\mathfrak{S} \circ s \circ \mathfrak{D} \circ \langle !rolesr, !rolesp, !agent \rangle) \,.$$
$$\mathbf{in}(\mathfrak{S} \circ s \circ \mathfrak{R} \circ \langle !b \rangle) \,.$$
$$\mathbf{out}(\mathfrak{S} \circ s \circ \mathfrak{D} \circ \langle rolesr', rolesp', agent \rangle) \,.$$
$$\mathbf{if}\ rolesr' = 0\ \mathbf{then}\ \mathbf{out}(\mathfrak{S} \circ s \circ \mathfrak{R} \circ \langle 1 \rangle)\ \mathbf{fi} \,.$$
$$\mathbf{if}\ rolesr' \neq 0\ \mathbf{then}\ \mathbf{out}(\mathfrak{S} \circ s \circ \mathfrak{R} \circ \langle 0 \rangle)\ \mathbf{fi}$$

If all the required roles are allocated, the scope is marked as ready with the tuple $\mathfrak{S} \circ s \circ \mathfrak{R} \circ \langle 1 \rangle$; otherwise, the communication is prevented by setting the readiness flag to zero. In the above,

$$rolesp' \overset{\text{df}}{=} \{(rolesp(r) + ag)/rolesp(r)\}rolesp$$

is a substitution which adds a new agent (the scope creator) to the list of participating agents and

$$rolesr' \overset{\text{df}}{=} \underline{if}\ |rolesp(r)| + 1 = min(r)\ \underline{then}\ rolesr - 1\ \underline{else}\ rolesr$$

The above expression tests whether the addition of an agent with role r would result in the fulfilment of the requirement for the minimum number of agents. If this the case, $rolesr$ is decremented to reflect the drop in the number of roles still short of required agents.

Delete scope destroys a scope previously created by the requesting agent. This operation starts with an agent issuing a deletion requests with two arguments: the agent's name and the name of the scope to be deleted. The middleware checks whether the requesting agent is the owner of the scope, and if it is so it removes all the information about the scope and updates the list of scope names. The affected structures are the scope state (prefix $\mathfrak{S} \circ s \circ \mathfrak{D}$), requirements ($\mathfrak{S} \circ s \circ \mathfrak{P}$), and readiness status ($\mathfrak{S} \circ s \circ \mathfrak{R}$).

$$ADeleteScope \overset{\text{df}}{=} \mathbf{out}(\mathfrak{M} \circ \langle \text{DELETE\_SC}, ag, sc \rangle)$$

$$DeleteScope \overset{\text{df}}{=} \mathbf{in}(\mathfrak{M} \circ \langle \text{DELETE\_SC}, !a, !s \rangle) \,.\, \mathbf{lock}(\mathfrak{M}) \,.$$
$$\mathbf{rd}(\mathfrak{S} \circ s \circ \mathfrak{D} \circ \langle !st \rangle))$$
$$\mathbf{if}\ a = st.ag$$
$$\mathbf{then}$$
$$\mathbf{in}(\mathfrak{S} \circ \langle !S \rangle) \,.\, \mathbf{in}(\mathfrak{S} \circ s \circ \mathfrak{D} \circ \langle !st \rangle) \,.\, \mathbf{in}(\mathfrak{S} \circ s \circ \mathfrak{P} \circ \langle !par \rangle) \,.$$
$$\mathbf{in}(\mathfrak{S} \circ s \circ \mathfrak{R} \circ \langle !b \rangle) \,.\, \mathbf{out}(\mathfrak{S} \circ \langle S - \{s\} \rangle)\ \mathbf{fi} \,.$$
$$\mathbf{unlock}(\mathfrak{M}) \,.\, DeleteScope$$

Join scope adds an agent to an existing scope provided that there is a vacant place for the requested role. In the request for this operation, the agent specifies the name of a scope it is wishing to join and the role it is going to assume. The middleware caries out a number of checks, such as whether the requested role is supported by the scope, and whether there are vacant places for the role.

$$AJoinScope \stackrel{\text{df}}{=} \textbf{out}(\mathfrak{M} \circ \langle \text{JOIN\_SC}, ag, sc, role \rangle)$$

$$JoinScope \quad \stackrel{\text{df}}{=} \textbf{in}(\mathfrak{M} \circ \langle \text{JOIN\_SC}, !a, !s, !r \rangle) \cdot \textbf{lock}(\mathfrak{S}) \cdot$$
$$\textbf{rd}(\mathfrak{S} \circ s \circ \mathfrak{P} \circ \langle !par \rangle) \cdot \textbf{rd}(\mathfrak{S} \circ s \circ \mathfrak{D} \circ \langle !st \rangle) \cdot$$
$$\textbf{rd}(\mathfrak{A} \circ \langle !A \rangle) \cdot \textbf{rd}(\mathfrak{S} \circ \langle !S \rangle) \cdot$$
$$\textbf{if } a \in A \wedge s \in S \wedge r \in p.roles \wedge |st.rolesp(r)| < par.max(r)$$
$$\textbf{then } Update(r, a, s) \textbf{ fi} \cdot$$
$$\textbf{unlock}(\mathfrak{S}) \cdot JoinScope$$

This operation also updates the *rolesr* value of the scope's state, and the readiness status. Note that the latter may have an important side effect if there were agents blocked due to the unavailability of agents for some roles, as the appearance of a new agent may change the readiness status to 1 unblocking the waiting agents.

Leave scope removes an agent from a scope. The agent leaves a particular role of the scope. The middleware checks whether the agent is currently participating in the relevant role and if this is the case, it removes it from the agent list.

$$ALeaveScope \stackrel{\text{df}}{=} \textbf{out}(\mathfrak{M} \circ \langle \text{LEAVE\_SC}, ag, sc, r \rangle)$$

$$LeaveScope \quad \stackrel{\text{df}}{=} \textbf{in}(\mathfrak{M} \circ \langle \text{LEAVE\_SC}, !a, !s, !r \rangle) \cdot \textbf{lock}(\mathfrak{S}) \cdot$$
$$\textbf{rd}(\mathfrak{S} \circ s \circ \mathfrak{D} \circ \langle !st \rangle)$$
$$\textbf{if } a \in st.roles(r)$$
$$\textbf{then } Update'(r, a, s) \textbf{ fi} \cdot$$
$$\textbf{unlock}(\mathfrak{S}) \cdot LeaveScope$$

where $Update'(r, a, s)$ is defined in the same way as $Update(r, a, s)$ except for the following:

$$rolesr' \stackrel{\text{df}}{=} \underline{if} \ |rolesp(r)|=min(r) \ \underline{then} \ rolesr+1 \ \underline{else} \ rolesr$$

Communication operations are LINDA operations that are suitably modified to include additional checks for the state of a scope. They differ from the standard LINDA primitives in that they may block if the target scope is not ready (or does not exists — this enables one to detect problems with the scoping mechanism through deadlock checking):

- $\textbf{in}(t)@s \stackrel{\text{df}}{=} \textbf{rd}(\mathfrak{S} \circ s \circ \mathfrak{R} \circ \langle 1 \rangle) \cdot \textbf{in}(\mathfrak{S} \circ s \circ \mathfrak{C} \circ t)$ checks if the specified scope exists and that it is ready, then it reads a tuple from the scope. If the scope is not ready then the operation blocks until the readiness status is changed to 1.

– $\mathbf{out}(t)@s \overset{\mathrm{df}}{=} \mathbf{rd}(\mathfrak{S} \circ s \circ \mathfrak{R} \circ \langle 1 \rangle) \,.\, \mathbf{out}(\mathfrak{S} \circ s \circ \mathfrak{C} \circ t)$ outputs a tuple after checking that the target scope is available and ready.

Other operations are defined in a similar way, each operation being prefixed by $\mathbf{rd}(\mathfrak{S} \circ s \circ \mathfrak{R} \circ \langle 1 \rangle)$ and its tuple or template argument by an appropriate prefix corresponding to the scope s.

5   Model Checking CAMA Systems

Mobile systems are highly concurrent causing the state space explosion when applying model checking techniques. We therefore use an approach which alleviates this problem, based on partial order semantics of concurrency and the corresponding Petri net unfoldings.

5.1   Verification of Behavioural Properties

A *finite and complete unfolding prefix* of a Petri net PN is a finite acyclic net which implicitly represents all the reachable states of PN together with transitions enabled at those states. Intuitively, it can be obtained through *unfolding* PN, by successive firings of transition, under the following assumptions: (i) for each new firing a fresh transition (called an *event*) is generated; (ii) for each newly produced token a fresh place (called a *condition*) is generated. If PN has finitely many reachable states then the unfolding eventually starts to repeat itself and can be truncated (by identifying a set of *cut-off* events) without loss of information, yielding a finite and complete prefix.

Efficient algorithms exist for building such prefixes [13], and complete prefixes are often exponentially smaller than the corresponding state graphs, especially for highly concurrent Petri nets, because they represent concurrency directly rather than by multidimensional 'diamonds' as it is done in state graphs. For example, if the original Petri net consists of 100 transitions which can fire once in parallel, the state graph will be a 100-dimensional hypercube with 2^{100} vertices, whereas the complete prefix will be isomorphic to the net itself. Since mobile systems usually exhibit a lot of concurrency, but have rather few choice points, their unfolding prefixes are often much more compact than the corresponding state graphs. Therefore, unfolding prefixes are well-suited for alleviating the state space explosion problem.

Our approach is suitable for verification of *reachability-like* (or *state*) properties, such as:

– The system never deadlocks (though it may terminate in a pre-defined set of successful termination states).
– Security properties, e.g., all sub-scope participants are participants of the containing scope.
– Proper using of the scoping mechanism: a scope owner does not attempt to leave without removing the scope; agents do not leave or delete a scope when other agents expect some input from the scope; the owner of a scope does not delete it while there are still active agents in the scope; etc.

- Proper use of cooperative recovery: all scope exceptions must be handled when a scope completes; all scope participants eventually complete exception handling; no exceptions are raised in a scope after an agent leaves it; etc.
- Application-specific invariants. (Note that the negation of an invariant is a state property, i.e., the invariant holds iff there is no reachable state of the system where it is violated.)

However, to apply net unfoldings, we first need to translate process algebra terms corresponding to CAMA systems into Petri nets.

5.2   From Process Algebra to Petri Nets

The development of a Petri net model corresponding to expressions of the process algebra for CAMA systems has been inspired by the box algebra [2] and by the rp-net algebra used in [8] to model π-calculus. It uses coloured tokens and read-arcs (allowing any number of transitions to simultaneously check for the presence of a resource stored in a place). Transitions can have different labels, such as **o** to specify outputting of data to tuple spaces, **i** to specify retrieving of data from tuple spaces, and **e** to specify process creation. The translation is described in detail in [7] and the modifications to the formal framework used there introduced in this paper to model CAMA can be easily accommodated. (Crucially, all the proofs that the translation preserves the equivalence of the underlying transition systems presented in [7] can be adapted for the framework used in this paper.) Hence we will only outline the main aspects behind the translation from the process algebra discussed in Section 3 to the domain of high-level Petri nets.

A key idea behind the translation is to view a system as consisting of a main program together with a number of procedure declarations. We then represent the control structure of the main program and the procedures using disjoint unmarked nets, one for the main program and one for each of the procedure declarations. The program is executed once, while each procedure can be invoked several times (even concurrently), each such invocation being uniquely identified by structured tokens which correspond to the sequence of recursive calls along the execution path leading to that invocation. With this in mind, we use the notion of a *trail* σ to represent in a unique way a finite (possibly empty) sequence of recursive calls. Places of the nets which are responsible for control flow will carry tokens which are simply trails. (The empty trail will be treated as the usual 'black' token.) Procedure invocation is then possible if, for example, each of the input places of a transition t labelled with **e** contains the same trail token σ, and it results in removing these tokens and inserting a new token σt in each initial (entry) place of the net corresponding to the definition of $A(\ldots)$, together with other tokens representing the corresponding actual parameters. Places are labelled in ways reflecting their intended role, as explained below.

- *Control flow places:* These are used to model control flow and are labelled by their status symbols (*internal* places by i, and *interface* places by e and x, for entry and exit, respectively).

- *Store places:* These are labelled by variables as well as `self`, and carry structured tokens representing data and localities known and used by the main program and different procedure invocations. Each such token, called a *trailed value*, is of the form $\sigma.y$ where σ is a trail and y is a data value or a locality other than `self`. Intuitively, its first part, σ, identifies the invocation in which the token is available, while the second part, y, provides the current value for the variable (or `self`) corresponding to the place. Note that store places labelled by `self` indicate localities where processes are being executed.
- *Tuple-place:* This is a distinguished place, labelled by $\mathbb{TS}$, used to represent data stored at various tuple spaces. It stores a multiset of structured tokens of the form $l :: \langle q \rangle$, as in the process algebra.

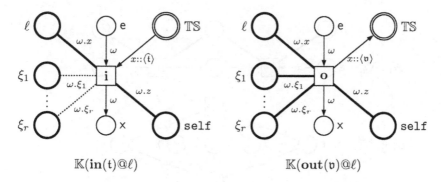

Fig. 3. Translation for output and input actions with data expressions. In the case of $\mathbb{K}(\mathbf{in}(t)@\ell)$, $\xi_1, \ldots, \xi_r$ are the variables used in t, including `self`. In the case of $\mathbb{K}(\mathbf{out}(v)@\ell)$, $\xi_1, \ldots, \xi_r$ are the variables used in v, including `self`. A dotted line between the transition and a place ξ_i indicates a directed arc from the former to the latter if $t_i =\,!\xi_i$, and a read arc otherwise. Transition labels are given in an abbreviated form: **i** stands for $\mathbf{i}(z, \hat{t}, x)$ and **o** stands for $\mathbf{o}(z, v, x)$, where $\hat{t}$ is t with all the !'s deleted.

Two example translations for the basic actions are given in Figure 3. In the first one, $\mathbb{K}(\mathbf{in}(t)@\ell)$, we do not assume that ℓ' and ℓ are distinct, and if that is the case, we collapse the corresponding store places, and gather together the annotations of the read arcs. In the second translation, $\mathbb{K}(\mathbf{out}(v)@\ell)$, we again do not assume that ℓ' and ℓ are distinct, and proceed similarly as before if they are.

The translation is syntax driven, and we use Petri net operators corresponding to those in the process algebra, allowing one to construct Petri nets *compositionally*. The operators we use are *prefixing* $(N . N')$, *choice* $(N + N')$ and *parallel composition* $(N|N')$; see Figure 4 for the illustration of these operations. Note that all three operators merge the store places with the same label.

- In the choice composition, the entry and exit places of N and N' are combined together. This has the following effect: if we start from a situation where each entry place contains a copy of a common trail token σ, then either N or N' can be executed under that trail.

- The prefixing operator combines the exit place of the prefix N with the entry places of N' into internal places, and the effect is that the execution of N after reaching the terminal marking, where the only exit place is marked, is followed by that of N'.
- The parallel composition of N and N' puts them side by side allowing to execute both parts in parallel.

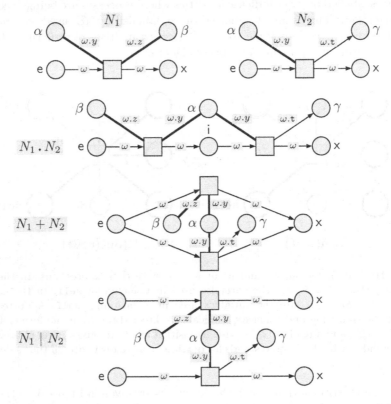

Fig. 4. Illustration of the various operators defined for Petri nets (transition labels are omitted as they are unaffected by the three operations)

To carry out the translation, we assume that the following well-formed network $\mathfrak{N}$ is given:

$$\left(\|_{i=1}^{h} l_i :: P_i\right) \ \| \ \left(\|_{j=1}^{k} l'_j :: \langle \mathfrak{q}_j \rangle \right)$$

together with the necessary process identifier definitions. We also assume that $l_i \neq l_{i'}$, for $i \neq i'$ (by the rules of the structural equivalence, we may always group all processes occurring in some location into a single, possibly parallel, process). Note that h or k may be 0, in which case the parallel composition in the middle is not present. The translation proceeds in the following three phases:

Phase I. Each process P_i is translated compositionally into a high-level net $\mathbb{K}(P_i)$ and during this process all store places with the same label are merged. Similarly, for each process definition $A(\mathfrak{v}) \stackrel{\mathrm{df}}{=} P_A$, we translate compositionally P_A into a high-level net $\mathbb{K}(A)$ and, again, during this process all store places with the same label are merged.

Phase II. For each network node $l_i :: P_i$, we take $\mathbb{K}(P_i)$ and add a store place labelled by $\mathtt{self}_i$ identifying it with the only $\mathtt{self}$-labelled place (if present) and give the merged place the label $\mathtt{self}_i$. The result is denoted by $\mathbb{K}(l_i :: P_i)$.

Phase III. We take the parallel composition of the $\mathbb{K}(A)$'s and $\mathbb{K}(l_i :: P_i)$'s, identifying all store places with the same label, and then suitably connect the nets to mimic process instantiation. After that we set the initial marking; in particular, for each $l'_j :: \langle \mathsf{q} \rangle$, we insert a single $l'_j :: \langle \mathsf{q} \rangle$-token into the $\mathbb{TS}$-labelled place.

It can be seen that the labelled transition system of the original process algebraic expression is behaviourally equivalent to that of the resulting net, and so the latter can be used for model checking instead of the former.

6 Conclusion

In this paper, we outlined an approach to dealing with context aware location-based mobile systems. In particular, we described a new formalism and middleware called CAMA, which provides a rich environment to test our approach. We sketched how to give CAMA a formal concurrency semantics in terms of a suitable process algebra, and then how to apply efficient model checking techniques to the resulting process expressions in a way which alleviates the state space explosion. The model checking technique adopted in our work is partial order model checking based on Petri net unfoldings, and we briefly described a semantics preserving translation from the process terms used in the modelling of CAMA to a suitable class of high-level Petri nets.

Acknowledgements. We would like to thank the anonymous referees for their useful comments and suggestions. This research was supported by the EC IST grant 511599 (RODIN) and the RAENG/EPSRC grant EP/C53400X/1 (DAVAC).

References

1. B.Arief, A.Iliasov and A.Romanovsky: On Using the CAMA Framework for Developing Open Mobile Fault Tolerant Agent Systems. Technical Report CS-TR-943, University of Newcastle (2006).
2. E.Best, R.Devillers and M.Koutny: *Petri Net Algebra*. EATCS Monographs on TCS, Springer (2001).
3. L.Bettini et al.: The KLAIM Project: Theory and Practice. Proc. of *Global Computing: Programming Environments, Languages, Security and Analysis of Systems*, Springer, LNCS 2874 (2003) 88–150.

4. C.Bryce, C.Razafimahefa and M.Pawlak: LANA: An Approach to Programming Autonomous Systems. Proc. of *ECOOP'02*, Springer, LNCS 2374 (2002) 281–308.
5. R.De Nicola, G.L.Ferrari, R.Pugliese: KLAIM: A Kernel Language for Agents Interaction and Mobility. *IEEE Trans. Software Eng* 24 (1998) 315–330.
6. R.De Nicola, D.Latella and M.Massink: Formal Modeling and Quantitive Analysis of KLAIM-Based Mobile Systems. Proc. of *Applied Computing*, Association for Computing Machinery (2005) 428–435.
7. R.Devillers, H.Klaudel and M.Koutny: A Petri Net Semantics of a Simple Process Algebra for Mobility. Technical Report CS-TR-912, University of Newcastle (2005).
8. R.Devillers, H.Klaudel and M.Koutny: Petri Net Semantics of the Finite π-calculus Terms. *Fundamenta Informaticae* 70 (2006) 203–226.
9. D.Gelernter: Generative Communication in LINDA. *ACM Computing Surveys* 7 (1985) 80–112.
10. A.Iliasov, L.Laibinis, A.Romanovsky and E.Troubitsyna: Towards Formal Development of Mobile Location-Based Systems (submitted).
11. A.Iliasov and A.Romanovsky: CAMA: Structured Coordination Space and Exception Propagation Mechanism for Mobile Agents. Proc. of *ECOOP-EHWS'05*, TR-05-050. Department of Computer Science, LIRMM, Montpellier-II University (2005) 75–87.
12. A.Iliasov and A.Romanovsky: Exception Handling in Coordination-based Mobile Environments. Proc. of *COMPSAC'05*, IEEE Computer Soc. Press (2005) 341–350.
13. V. Khomenko: *Model Checking Based on Prefixes of Petri Net Unfoldings*. PhD Thesis, School of Computing Science, University of Newcastle upon Tyne (2003).
14. R.Milner, J.Parrow and D.Walker: A Calculus of Mobile Processes. *Information and Computation* 100 (1992) 1–77.
15. G.P.Picco, A.L.Murphy, G.-C.Roman: Lime: LINDA Meets Mobility. Proc. of *ICSE'99*, ACM Press (1999) 368–377.
16. The Mobile Agent List. `http://reinsburgstrasse.dyndns.org//mal/preview`

Formal Development of Mechanisms for Tolerating Transient Faults

Dubravka Ilić[1], Elena Troubitsyna[1], Linas Laibinis[1], and Colin Snook[2]

[1] Åbo Akademi University, Department of Information Technologies
20520 Turku, Finland
[2] School of Electronics and Computer Science,
University of Southampton, SO17 1BJ, UK
{Dubravka.Ilic, Elena.Troubitsyna, Linas.Laibinis}@abo.fi,
cfs@ecs.soton.ac.uk

Abstract. Transient faults belong to a wide-spread class of faults typical for control systems. These are the faults that only appear for a short period of time and might reappear later. However, even by appearing for a short time, they might cause dangerous system errors. Hence, designing mechanisms for tolerating and recovering from the transient faults is an acute issue, especially in the development of the safety-critical control systems. In this paper we propose formal development of a software-based mechanism for tolerating transient faults in the B Method. The mechanism relies on a specific architecture of the error detection actions called the evaluating tests. These tests are executed (with different frequencies) on the predefined subsets of the analyzed data. Our formal model allows us to formally express and verify the interdependencies between the tests as well as to define the test scheduling. Application of the proposed approach ensures proper damage confinement caused by the transient faults. Our approach aims at the avionics domain by focusing on formal development of the engine Failure Management System. However, the proposed specification and refinement patterns can be applied in the development of control systems in other application domains as well.

Keywords: Transient faults, control systems, FMS, B Method, refinement.

1 Introduction

Nowadays software is a crucial part of many safety-critical applications. To guarantee *dependability* [1] of such systems, we should ensure that software is not only fault-free but also is able to cope with the faults of the other system components. In this paper we focus on designing a controller able to tolerate transient faults of system components. Transient faults are the temporal defects within the system [2]. They frequently occur in the hardware functioning. However, design of the mechanisms for tolerating transient faults is inherently complex. On the one hand, controlling software (further referred to as a controller) should not over-react on an isolated transient fault. On the other hand, it should ensure that even the isolated transient faults are not propagated further into the system. Moreover, if the fault persists, the controller should initiate the appropriate recovery actions. The algorithm for ensuring this was proposed in [3,4].

M. Butler et al. (Eds.): Fault-Tolerant Systems, LNCS 4157, pp. 189–209, 2006.
© Springer-Verlag Berlin Heidelberg 2006

In the complex fault-tolerant control systems, a controller largely consists of the mechanisms for implementing fault tolerance. This is often perceived as a separate subsystem dedicated to fault tolerance. In avionics, such a subsystem is traditionally called *Failure Management System* (further referred to as the FMS). The major role of the FMS is to mask the faulty readings obtained from sensors and hereby provide the controller with the correct information about the system state.

The requirements imposed on a specific engine FMS, which is typical in the avionics domain, are often changed as a result of simulation of the system behaviour under the failure conditions. These changes occur at the later development stages, which complicates the design of the FMS [4]. To overcome this difficulty, we propose a generic formal pattern for specifying and developing the FMS. The proposed pattern can be used in the product-line development [5].

Obviously, correctness of the FMS itself is essential for ensuring dependability of the overall system. Formal methods are traditionally used for reasoning about software correctness. In this paper we demonstrate how to develop the FMS by stepwise refinement in the B Method [6,7]. The B Method is a formal framework for the development of dependable systems correct by construction. AtelierB [8] – a tool supporting the method – provides a high degree of automation of the verification process, which facilitates better acceptance of the method in the industrial practice.

The paper is structured as follows: in Section 2 we describe the FMS by presenting its structure, the behaviour and the error detection mechanism. In this section we also give the graphical representation of the FMS relying on the data from a single sensor. In Section 3 we give a short introduction into our modelling framework – the B Method. Section 4 demonstrates the process of developing the FMS formally. We start from an abstract specification of the system and obtain the detailed specification by a number of correctness preserving refinement steps. In Section 5 we discuss the proposed approach.

2 Failure Management System

2.1 Structure and Behaviour

The Failure Management System (FMS) [3,4,9] is a part of the embedded control system as shown in Fig. 1.

The control system regularly reads data from its sensors. In this paper we consider multiple homogenous analogue sensors. The sensor readings are considered as the inputs to the FMS. The outputs from the FMS are forwarded to the controller. The task of the FMS is to detect erroneous inputs and prevent their propagation into the controller. Hence the main purpose of the FMS is to supply the controller of the system with the fault-free inputs from the system environment.

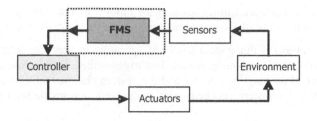

Fig. 1. Structure of an embedded control system

We assume that initially the system is error-free. The FMS operating cycle, defined as one FMS iteration step, starts by obtaining the readings from N sensors which become the inputs to the FMS. The FMS tests the inputs by applying a certain detection procedure. As a result, the inputs are categorized as fault-free or faulty. Then the FMS analyses the inputs to distinguish between recoverable and non-recoverable faulty inputs. This is achieved by assigning a status to each analyzed input. The status can be either *ok, suspected* or *confirmed failed*. The fault-free inputs are marked as *ok*, the recoverable inputs are marked as *suspected* and the non-recoverable inputs are marked as *confirmed failed*. After finishing analysis, the FMS takes the corresponding actions. These actions can be classified as healthy, temporary or confirmation[1]. The classification is adopted from [4].

In Fig. 2 we illustrate the general behaviour of the FMS, as proposed in [3]. For simplicity, here we assume that there is just one input (i.e., one single sensor) monitored by the FMS.

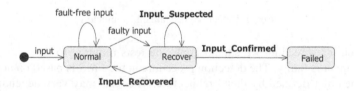

Fig. 2. Specification of the FMS behaviour

Healthy action. If the FMS is in the Normal state, i.e., a received input is fault-free (*ok*), then the input is forwarded unchanged to the controller and the FMS continues its operation by accepting another input from the environment.

Temporary action. If the FMS is in the Normal state and detects the first faulty input, it changes the operating state from Normal to Recover (Fig. 2). While in the Recover state, the FMS counts the number of faulty inputs in successive operating cycles. At the same time the status of the faulty input is marked as *suspected*. One of the requirements imposed on the FMS is to give a fault-free output even when the input is faulty. Hence, while operating in the Recover state, the FMS calculates the output using the last good value of this input obtained before entering the state Recover. Once a temporary action is triggered, it will keep the system in the state Recover until

---

[1] The confirmation action is an action taken when an input is confirmed as failed.

the counting mechanism determines whether the input (i.e., the corresponding sensor) has recovered. In this case, the system changes its state from Recover to Normal.

Confirmation action. If the system has been operating in the state Recover and the input fails to recover, the counting mechanism triggers the confirmation action. Then the input is marked as *confirmed failed* and the system changes the operating state to Failed. After this, the system proceeds with the control actions defined for the state Failed.

2.2 Error Detection

The detection mechanism is the most important part of the FMS. Its role is to determine whether the input is faulty or fault-free. In Fig. 3 we present the architecture of the detection mechanism.

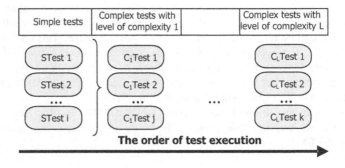

Fig. 3. Detection mechanism architecture

For each input reading we should apply the tests required to detect whether that particular input is faulty. The detection procedure in the FMS is based on applying the tests in the order defined by their architecture. The tests may vary depending on the application domain. For instance, the most commonly used tests for analogue sensors in avionics are the magnitude test, the rate test, and the predicted value test.

We differentiate between different kinds of tests. The basic category is the simple tests. An input reading may pass through several simple tests, which can be applied in any order. When triggered, a simple test runs using solely the input reading from the sensor. After the test is executed, it is marked as passed for the current input, which in turn may trigger the execution of some other associated test.

The second test category is the complex tests with the level of complexity 1. The complex tests may use input readings from several sensors. However, all the simple tests required for these sensors should be executed before any complex test is performed as shown in Fig. 3.

In general, there might be L+1 test categories, where the last test category is the complex tests with the level of complexity L. The execution of this kind of tests depends not only on the previous execution of the simple tests, but also on the execution of the complex tests with the level of complexity up to L-1. If the input requires several tests of the same complexity level, they can be executed in any order.

However, all the applicable tests of the lower levels should be already executed. Hence, the detection procedure operates in stages, first executing all the simple tests associated with a certain input and then all the complex tests of ascending complexity as shown in Fig. 3.

In general, sensors can be classified into analogue or switch-type sensors. Hence, the FMS inputs can be represented as numerical or Boolean values correspondingly. For both sensor types, the template of the detection mechanism is the same. However, different tests can be applied on the readings from analogue or switch-type sensor.

After executing all the required tests on received inputs, the FMS classifies the inputs as faulty or fault-free.

2.3   The FMS Pattern

The actions of the FMS described in Fig. 2 and the detection template presented on Fig. 3 constitute the generic FMS structure and behaviour pattern as summarized in Fig. 4. For simplicity, the pattern is presented for a single sensor.

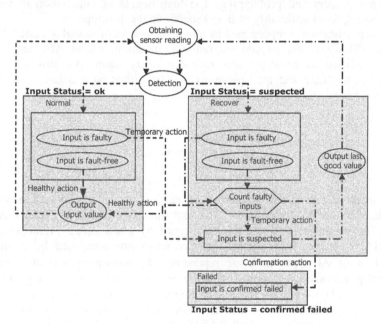

Fig. 4. The FMS pattern

Fig. 4. shows the flow of the detection decisions and the effect of FMS actions after the input is received from the system environment. The counting mechanism (described in detail later) is introduced to distinguish between the recoverable and unrecoverable transient faults. The system switches to the state Normal, if the input has recovered, or stays in the state Recover, if the input is still suspected. The system enters the state Failed, if the input has failed to recover.

The given pattern can also be applied for handling N multiple sensors. However, when handling N multiple sensors, the system failure state might be reached when several or all sensors have failed. Transition to the failure state corresponds to freezing the system or switching to a backup controller (if possible).

The pattern can be applied in the controlling software product line [5] for creating a collection of similar control systems that are tolerant against the transient faults, as proposed in [9].

3 Formal Modelling in the B Method

In this paper we have chosen the B Method [6,7] as our formal modelling framework. The B Method is an approach for the industrial development of highly dependable software that has been successfully used in the development of several complex real-life applications [10]. The tool support available for B provides us with the assistance for the entire development process with a high degree of automation in verifying correctness. For instance, Atelier B [8], one of the tools supporting the B Method, has facilities for automatic verification and code generation as well as documentation, project management and prototyping. The high degree of automation in verifying correctness improves scalability of B and speeds up the development.

In B, a specification is represented by a module or a set of modules, called Abstract Machines. The common pseudo-programming notation, called Abstract Machine Notation, is used to construct and formally verify them. An abstract machine encapsulates the state and the operations of a specification and has the following general form:

MACHINE	*name*
SETS	*Set*
VARIABLES	*v*
INITIALISATION	*Init*
INVARIANT	*I*
OPERATIONS	*Op*

Each machine is uniquely identified by its name. The state variables of the machine are declared in the **VARIABLES** clause and initialized in the **INITIALISATION** clause. The variables in B are strongly typed by constraining predicates of the **INVARIANT** clause. The constraining predicates are composed by conjunction (denoted as $\wedge$). All types in B are represented by non-empty sets and hence set membership (denoted as $\in$ expresses typing constraint for a variable, e.g., $x \in TYPE$. Local types can be introduced by enumerating the elements of the type, e.g., *TYPE = {element1, element2,...}* in the **SETS** clause. The operations of the machine are atomic and they are defined in **OPERATIONS** clause. To describe the computation in operations we use the B statements listed in the Table 1.

In this paper we adopt the event-based approach to system modelling [11]. The events are specified as the guarded operations of the form:

Event = SELECT *cond* **THEN** *body* **END**

Here *cond* is a state predicate, and *body* is a B statement describing how the state variables are affected by the operation. If *cond* is satisfied, the behaviour of the guarded operation corresponds to the execution of its *body*. If *cond* is false at the current state then the operation is disabled, i.e., its execution is blocked. The event-based modelling is especially suitable for describing reactive systems, typical examples of which are control systems. Then a **SELECT** operation describes the reaction of the system when a particular event occurs.

Table 1. List of B statements used in our operations

Statement	Informal meaning
$x := e$	Assignment
$x, y := e1, e2$	Multiple assignment
IF P **THEN** $S1$ **ELSE** $S2$ **END**	If P is true then execute $S1$, otherwise $S2$
$S1 ; S2$	Sequential composition
$S1 \parallel S2$	Parallel execution of $S1$ and $S2$
$x :\in T$	Nondeterministic assignment – assigns variable x arbitrary value from given set T
ANY x **WHERE** Q **THEN** S **END**	Nondeterministic block – introduces a new local variable x according to the predicate Q, which is then used in S
CHOICE S **OR** T **OR** ... **OR** U **END**	Nondeterministic choice – one of the statements S, T... U is arbitrarily chosen for execution

B also provides the structuring mechanisms for modularization, which allows us to express machines as compositions of other machines. For instance, if in the machine $M1$ we define that $M1$ **SEES** $M2$, where $M2$ is another machine, then the sets, the constants and the state of $M2$ are available to $M1$ for the reading in its own initialization and within preconditions and the bodies of operations. In particular, this allows us to define widely used sets and constants in a separate machine and then make it "seen" by all other machines where these sets and constants are needed.

The development methodology adopted by B is based on stepwise refinement [12]. The result of a refinement step in B is a machine called **REFINEMENT**. Its structure coincides with the structure of an abstract machine. A refinement machine contains the additional clause **REFINES**, which directly refers to the refined machine. Moreover, besides typing of variables, the invariant of a refinement machine includes the refinement relation (linking invariant) that describes the connection between the state spaces of the more abstract and refined machines.

Sometimes, it is useful to introduce user's own definitions as the abbreviations for certain complex expressions. Such definitions can be formulated in the **DEFINITIONS** clause.

To ensure correctness of a specification or a refinement, we should verify that initialization and each operation preserve the machine invariant. The verification can be completely automatic or user-assisted. In the former case, the tool generates the required proof obligations and discards them without user's help. In the latter case, the user has to prove the remaining proof obligations using the interactive prover provided by the tool.

In the next section we demonstrate how to formally specify the FMS system described in the previous section.

4   Formal Development of the FMS

4.1   The FMS Specification Pattern

Control systems are usually executed in an iterative manner. Their behaviour is essentially interleaving between environment stimuli and the controller reaction on these stimuli. The controller reaction depends on the results of error detection conducted by the FMS. The FMS, in turn, depends on the obtained inputs (i.e., stimuli). Because of these interdependencies, it is natural to consider the behaviour of the FMS in the context of the overall system.

The abstract specification pattern given in Fig. 5 is obtained from the informal FMS description represented graphically in Fig. 4. The abstract specification defines the behaviour of the FMS during one operating cycle (i.e., one FMS iteration step). The stages of such a cycle are modelled using the variable *FMS_State*. The type *STATES* of *FMS_State* is defined in the machine *Global*, as follows:

$$STATES = \{env, det, detloop, anl, anlloop, act, out, freeze\};$$

where the values of *FMS_State* define the phases of the FMS execution in the following way:

- *env* – obtaining inputs from the environment,
- *detloop* and *det* – performing tests on the inputs and detecting erroneous inputs,
- *anlloop* and *anl* – deciding upon the input status,
- *act* – setting the appropriate actions,
- *out* – sending output to the controller either by simple forwarding one of the obtained inputs or by calculating the output based on the last good values of the inputs,
- *freeze* – freezing the system.

The variable *FMS_State* models the evolution of the system behaviour in the operating cycle. At the end of the operating cycle the system either reaches the terminating (freezing) state or produces a fault-free output. In the latter case, the operating cycle starts again.

In our abstract specification the input values produced by the environment (i.e., the sensor data) are assigned nondeterministically in the operation **Environment**. The input values produced by the sensors are modelled by the variable *InputN*. The variable represents the readings of N multiple homogeneous sensors.

After obtaining the sensor readings from the environment, the FMS starts the operation **DetectionLoop**, which is at this development stage underspecified, and proceeds with the operation **Detection**. In the abstract specification we omit detailed representation of error detection and model only its result, which is assigned to the variable *Input_In_ErrorN*. Its value is **TRUE**, if an error is detected on the sensor reading of a particular input, and **FALSE** otherwise. Observe that the operation **Detection** produces the detection results for all sensors at once. In the further development, this will be done gradually in the operation **DetectionLoop**.

After the detection phase, the FMS performs the operation **AnalysisLoop**. In the abstract specification, this operation is underspecified, i.e., it nondeterministically chooses to remain in the current phase (*detloop*) or proceed with the next one (*det*). In the later development, the operation **AnalysisLoop** will be refined to include gradual analysis of the inputs. Now, however, the operation **Analysis** sets the results of the analysis for all the inputs at once. Based on the results obtained at the previous state, the FMS decides upon the status of an input – fault-free (i.e., ok), suspected or confirmed failed. The variable *Input_StatusN* is an array that for each of N inputs contains a value of the type:

$I\_STATUS = \{ok, suspected, confirmed\_failed\}$;

representing the status of this input. The nondeterministic assignment to *Input_StatusN* is bounded by the following conditions. If the input has successfully passed all required detection tests (*Input_In_ErrorN(ee)*=**FALSE**), its status can be either *ok* or *suspected*. However, if an error has been found for this input (*Input_In_ErrorN(ee)*=**TRUE**), the assigned status becomes either *suspected* or *confirmed_failed*. The assignment is then written as:

$Input\_StatusN :\in \{ff \mid ff \in Indx \rightarrow I\_STATUS \wedge$
$\qquad \forall ee.(ee \in Indx \wedge Input\_In\_ErrorN(ee)=\textbf{FALSE} \Rightarrow ff(ee) \in \{ok, suspected\}) \wedge$
$\qquad \forall ee.(ee \in Indx \wedge Input\_In\_ErrorN(ee)=\textbf{TRUE} \Rightarrow ff(ee) \in \{suspected, confirmed\_failed\}) \}$

where *Indx* is a set of *ok* or *suspected* inputs.

Upon completing analysis, the FMS applies the corresponding action. A healthy action is executed, if the input is fault-free, a temporary action, if the input is suspected, and a confirmation action, if the input is confirmed failed. While performing a healthy action, the FMS forwards its input to the system controller. As a result of a temporary action, the FMS calculates the output based on the information about the last good input values. In both cases the operating cycle starts again. If the FMS cannot properly function after the input has failed, the system enters the freezing state. Otherwise, it removes the input that has been confirmed failed from further observations. In the latter case, the output is calculated based on the last good input values (similarly as in a temporary action).

Since the controller of the system relies only on the input it obtains from the FMS, in our safety invariant we express the error confinement conditions:

$Safety\ Invariant ==$
$\quad (FMS\_State=act \Rightarrow$
$\qquad \forall (ee).(ee \in Indx \Rightarrow$
$\qquad (Input\_In\_ErrorN(ee)=\textbf{FALSE} \Rightarrow Input\_StatusN(ee) \in \{ok, suspected\}) \wedge$
$\qquad (Input\_In\_ErrorN(ee)=\textbf{TRUE} \Rightarrow Input\_StatusN(ee) \in \{suspected, confirmed\_failed\})))$
$\qquad \wedge$
$\quad (Indx=\varnothing \Rightarrow FMS\_State=freeze)$

The first predicate states that, whenever the FMS is in the state *act* and some input *ee* is detected fault-free, the value assigned to the variable *Input_StatusN* is either *ok* or *suspected*. Similarly, if an error is detected for some input *ee*, the value assigned to the variable *Input_StatusN* is either *suspected* or *confirmed_failed*. Finally, the last predicate states that, if the variable *Indx* is empty (i.e., all the inputs have failed), *FMS_State* is equal to *freeze* (i.e., the system is in the freezing state).

Our initial specification of the FMS abstractly describes the intended behaviour of the FMS. However, it leaves the mechanism for detecting errors and analysing the inputs underspecified. These details will be introduced by refinement.

```
MACHINE    FMS
SEES        Global
VARIABLES  Indx, InputN, Input_StatusN, Input_In_ErrorN, Last_Good_InputN, Output, FMS_State
INVARIANT
    Indx ⊆ 1 .. max_indx ∧
    InputN ∈ Indx → NAT ∧
    Input_StatusN ∈ Indx → I_STATUS ∧
    Input_In_ErrorN ∈ Indx → BOOL ∧
    Last_Good_InputN ∈ Indx → NAT ∧
    Output ∈ NAT ∧
    FMS_State ∈ STATES ∧ < safety invariant >

INITIALISATION                            /* Constants defined in the machine Global: */
    Indx := 1 .. max_indx ||              /* max_indx ∈ NAT ∧ max_indx ≥ 2 */
    InputN := ( 1 .. max_indx ) × { Good_Input } ||    /* Good_Input ∈ NAT */
    Input_StatusN := ( 1 .. max_indx ) × { ok } ||
    Input_In_ErrorN := ( 1 .. max_indx ) × { FALSE } ||
    Last_Good_InputN := ( 1 .. max_indx ) × { Good_Input } ||
    Output := Init_Output ||             /* Init_Output ∈ NAT */
    FMS_State := env
OPERATIONS

Environment =
    SELECT FMS_State = env
    THEN
            InputN :∈ Indx → NAT ||
            FMS_State := detloop
    END ;

DetectionLoop =
    SELECT FMS_State = detloop
    THEN
            FMS_State :∈ { detloop , det }
    END ;



Detection =
    SELECT FMS_State = det
    THEN
            Input_In_ErrorN :∈ Indx → BOOL ||
            FMS_State := anlloop
    END ;

AnalysisLoop =
    SELECT FMS_State = anlloop
    THEN
            FMS_State :∈ { anlloop , anl }
    END ;

                                                                            ...
```

```
Analysis =
    SELECT FMS_State = anl
    THEN
        Input_StatusN :∈ { ff | ff ∈ Indx → I_STATUS ∧
            ∀ee.(ee∈ Indx ∧ Input_In_ErrorN(ee)=FALSE ⇒ ff(ee)∈ {ok, suspected} ) ∧
            ∀ee.(ee∈ Indx ∧ Input_In_ErrorN(ee)=TRUE ⇒ ff(ee)∈ {suspected, confirmed_failed} ) } ||
        FMS_State := act
    END ;

Action =
    SELECT FMS_State = act ∧ confirmed_failed ∈ ran ( Input_StatusN )
    THEN
            CHOICE
                IF Input_StatusN⁻¹ [ { ok , suspected } ] ≠ ∅
                THEN
                    Indx := Input_StatusN⁻¹ [ { ok , suspected } ] ||
                    InputN := Input_StatusN⁻¹ [ { ok , suspected } ] ◁ InputN ||
                    Input_StatusN := Input_StatusN ▷ { ok , suspected } ||
                    Input_In_ErrorN := Input_StatusN⁻¹ [ { ok , suspected } ] ◁ Input_In_ErrorN ||
                    Last_Good_InputN := Input_StatusN⁻¹ [ { ok , suspected } ] ◁ Last_Good_InputN ||
                    FMS_State := out
                ELSE FMS_State := freeze END
            OR
                FMS_State := freeze
            END
    WHEN
        FMS_State = act ∧ confirmed_failed ∉ ran ( Input_StatusN ) ∧ Indx≠∅
    THEN
            FMS_State := out
    WHEN
        FMS_State = act ∧ confirmed_failed ∉ ran ( Input_StatusN ) ∧ Indx=∅
    THEN
            FMS_State := freeze
    END ;

Return =
    SELECT FMS_State = out
    THEN
            ANY in WHERE in = ( Last_Good_InputN ⩤ ( Input_StatusN⁻¹ [ { ok } ] ◁ InputN ) )
            THEN
                    Last_Good_InputN := in || Output :∈ ran ( in )
            END ||
            Input_In_ErrorN := Indx × { FALSE } || FMS_State := env
    END ;

TickTime =
    BEGIN
            skip
    END ;

Failed =
    SELECT FMS_State = freeze
    THEN
            skip
    END

END
```

Fig. 5. Excerpt from the abstract FMS specification pattern

4.2 Refining Input Analysis in the FMS

In our first refinement step we introduce a detailed specification of the input analysis procedure. In the initial FMS specification the input analysis was modelled by a nondeterministic assignment to the variable *Input_StatusN* in the operation **Analysis**. In the refined specification we calculate the current value of the input status based on the value of *Input_In_ErrorN* and the value of the input status obtained at the previous cycle of the FMS. Namely, if the analysed input was *ok* (fault-free), it becomes *suspected* (faulty) after an error on this input is detected. If the input was already *suspected* and an error is detected again, it can either stay *suspected* or become *confirmed_failed*. These properties are incorporated into the linking invariant as shown in Fig. 6.

In this refinement step we specify in detail the operation **AnalysisLoop**. The operation gradually performs the input analysis, considering inputs one by one until all the inputs are processed. The information about the input status of the processed inputs is correspondingly accumulated in the variable *Input_StatusN1*. After the operation **AnalysisLoop** is completed, the value of *Input_StatusN1* is assigned to *Input_StatusN* in the operation **Analysis**.

REFINEMENT   *FMSR1*
REFINES   *FMS2*
SEES   *Global*
VARIABLES   *..., Input_StatusN1, Processed*
INVARIANT
   $Input\_StatusN1 \in Indx \to I\_STATUS \wedge$
   $Processed \in Indx \to \textbf{BOOL} \wedge$

         /* Linking invariant */
   $(FMS\_State \in \{ env , detloop , det \} \wedge Indx \neq \varnothing \Rightarrow \textbf{ran} (Processed) = \{ \textbf{FALSE} \}) \wedge$
   $(FMS\_State \in \{ anl , act , out \} \Rightarrow \textbf{ran} (Processed) = \{ \textbf{TRUE} \}) \wedge$
   $(FMS\_State = det \Rightarrow Indx \neq \varnothing) \wedge$
   $(\forall ee.(ee \in Indx \wedge Processed(ee)=\textbf{TRUE} \wedge Input\_In\_ErrorN(ee)=\textbf{TRUE} \Rightarrow$
                                        $Input\_StatusN1(ee) \in \{suspected, confirmed\_failed\})) \wedge$
   $(\forall ee.(ee \in Indx \wedge Processed(ee)=\textbf{TRUE} \wedge Input\_In\_ErrorN(ee)=\textbf{FALSE} \Rightarrow$
                                        $Input\_StatusN1(ee) \in \{ok, suspected\})) \wedge$
   $(FMS\_State \in \{ act , out , env , detloop , det \} \Rightarrow Input\_StatusN = Input\_StatusN1) \wedge$
   $(FMS\_State \in \{ out , env , detloop , det \} \Rightarrow \textbf{ran} (Input\_StatusN) \subseteq \{ ok , suspected \}) \wedge$
   $(\forall ee.(ee \in Indx \wedge FMS\_State=anlloop \wedge Processed(ee)=\textbf{FALSE} \Rightarrow$
                                        $Input\_StatusN(ee)=Input\_StatusN1(ee))) \wedge$
   $(\forall ee.(ee \in Indx \wedge FMS\_State=anlloop \wedge Processed(ee)=\textbf{FALSE} \Rightarrow$
                                        $\textbf{ran}(Input\_StatusN) \subseteq \{ok, suspected\}))$
INITIALISATION

   $... \parallel Input\_StatusN1 := (1 .. max\_indx) \times \{ ok \} \parallel$
   $Processed := (1 .. max\_indx) \times \{ \textbf{FALSE} \}$

OPERATIONS

Environment = ...
DetectionLoop = ...
Detection = ...

                                                                    ...

```
AnalysisLoop =
   SELECT FMS_State = anlloop
   THEN
            ANY ii WHERE ii ∈ Indx ∧ Processed(ii)=FALSE
            THEN
              IF Input_In_ErrorN(ii)=FALSE
              THEN
                 IF Input_StatusN(ii)=suspected
                 THEN
                      ANY ch WHERE ch∈{ok, suspected} THEN Input_StatusN1(ii):=ch END
                 END
              ELSE
                      ANY ch WHERE ch∈{suspected, confirmed_failed} THEN Input_StatusN1(ii):=ch END
              END ‖
              Processed(ii):=TRUE
            END ;
            IF ran(Processed)={TRUE} THEN FMS_State:=anl ELSE FMS_State:=anlloop END
   END ;

Analysis =
   SELECT FMS_State = anl
   THEN
            Input_StatusN := Input_StatusN1 ‖
            FMS_State := act
   END ;

Action =
   SELECT FMS_State = act ∧ confirmed_failed ∈ ran ( Input_StatusN )
   THEN
            CHOICE
               IF Input_StatusN⁻¹ [ { ok , suspected } ] ≠ ∅
               THEN
                   ... ‖ Processed := Input_StatusN⁻¹ [ { ok , suspected } ] ◁ Processed
               ELSE FMS_State := freeze END
            OR
               FMS_State := freeze
            END ...
   END ;

Return =
   SELECT FMS_State = out
   THEN
            ... ‖ Processed := Indx × { FALSE } ‖
            FMS_State := env
   END ;

TickTime = ...
Failed = ...

END
```

Fig. 6. First FMS refinement – specifying input analysis

Our second refinement step (Fig. 7) aims at introducing a detailed procedure for determining the input status in the operation **AnalysisLoop**. The procedure is based on using a customisable counting mechanism which re-evaluates the status of the analyzed inputs at each FMS cycle.

```
REFINEMENT      FMSR2
REFINES         FMSR1
SEES            Global
VARIABLES       ..., cc, num
INVARIANT
    cc ∈ Indx ⇸ NAT ∧ num ∈ Indx ⇸ NAT
INITIALISATION
    ... ‖ cc := ( 1 .. max_indx ) × { 0 } ‖ num := ( 1 .. max_indx ) × { 0 }
OPERATIONS

Environment = ...
DetectionLoop = ...
Detection = ...

AnalysisLoop =
    SELECT FMS_State = anlloop
    THEN
            ANY ii WHERE ii ∈ Indx ∧ Processed ( ii ) = FALSE ∧
                            Config(yy)≤cc(ii) ∧ cc(ii)+Config(xx)≤max_int ∧ num(ii)+1≤max_int
            THEN
                    IF Input_In_ErrorN ( ii ) = FALSE
                    THEN
                        IF Input_StatusN ( ii ) = suspected
                        THEN
                            cc(ii):=cc(ii)-Config(yy); num(ii):=num(ii)+1;
                                IF (num(ii)<Limit ∧ cc(ii)=0) THEN Input_StatusN1(ii):=ok; num(ii):=0 END
                        END
                    ELSE
                        cc(ii):=cc(ii)+Config(xx); num(ii):=num(ii)+1;
                            IF (num(ii)≥Limit ∨ cc(ii)≥Config(zz))
                            THEN Input_StatusN1(ii):=confirmed_failed
                            ELSE Input_StatusN1(ii):=suspected END
                    END ‖
                    Processed(ii):=TRUE
            END ;
            IF ran(Processed)={TRUE} THEN FMS_State:=anl ELSE FMS_State:=anlloop END
    END ;
Analysis = ...

Action =
    SELECT FMS_State = act ∧ confirmed_failed ∈ ran ( Input_StatusN )
    THEN
            CHOICE
                    IF Input_StatusN⁻¹ [ { ok , suspected } ] ≠ ∅
                    THEN
                        ... ‖ cc := Input_StatusN⁻¹ [ { ok , suspected } ] ◁ cc ‖
                        num := Input_StatusN⁻¹ [ { ok , suspected } ] ◁ num
                    ELSE FMS_State := freeze END
            OR
                    FMS_State := freeze
            END ...
    END ;
Return = ...
TickTime = ...
Failed = ...

END
```

Fig. 7. Second FMS refinement – specifying error recovery

For each of N inputs, we introduce counters $cc_i (i \in 1..N)$, which contain accumulated values determining how trustworthy a particular input i is. If $cc_i=0$ then the input i is *ok*. If $0<cc_i<zz$, where zz is some predefined value, the input i is *suspected*. Otherwise, the input i is considered failed. At every cycle the counters cc_i are re-evaluated depending on the detection results. Each faulty input i increments the counter cc_i by a certain predefined value xx. Similarly, each fault-free input i decrements the corresponding counter cc_i by another predefined value yy. If at some point the value of cc_i reaches 0, the input i is declared *ok*. Similarly, if the value of cc_i exceeds zz, the input i is declared *confirmed_failed* and should be removed from the set of inputs used by the FMS.

The predefined values zz, xx and yy are set after observing the real performance of the FMS. By setting the value of xx higher then the value of yy, the counter cc is biased towards failure. However, such a specification is insufficient for guaranteeing termination of recovery. Observe that the input may behave in such a way that the counter cc is practically oscillating between some values but never reaches the limit zz or zero. To overcome this problem, we introduce the second counter num which counts the number of the consequent recovering cycles for each suspected input (i.e., when $0<cc_i<zz$). When a certain limit for num is exceeded, the recovery terminates and, if cc is different from zero, the input is *confirmed_failed*.

4.3 Refining Error Detection in the FMS

We continue the development of the FMS by refining the error detection procedure. This third refinement step aims at introducing a test architecture, which is then used by the refined error detection procedure.

The nondeterministic assignment to the variable *Input_In_ErrorN* in the operation **Detection** specifies only that each of N inputs can either be found in error or error free, without specifying in detail the detection procedure. This assignment is refined in the third refinement step by introducing the evaluation tests. Since we observe homogeneous multiple sensors measuring the same physical process in the environment, for each of N sensor readings the same series of tests can be applied as shown in Fig. 8.

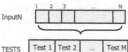

Fig. 8. Defining tests for homogeneous multiple sensors

The architecture of tests used for error detection follows the idea of test dependencies presented in Section 2.2. The set of all tests (modelled by the deferred set *TESTS*) is partitioned into two subsets:

$$S\_TEST \subseteq TESTS \land C\_TEST \subseteq TESTS$$

where *S_TEST* is the set of all simple tests and *C_TEST* is the set of all complex tests. Moreover, since each complex test depends on some simple tests, we define this dependency as the following constant function: $ComplexTest \in C\_TEST \to POW(S\_TEST)$.

To model the error detection performed gradually over a set of inputs, we refine the abstract operation **DetectionLoop**. The refined operation is presented bellow. Similarly as in the operation **AnalysisLoop**, the information about the failed inputs is gradually accumulated in the variable *Input_In_ErrorN1*. After **DetectionLoop** is completed, the value of *Input_In_ErrorN1* is assigned to *Input_In_ErrorN* in the operation **Detection**.

The evaluating tests enabled for execution in **DetectionLoop** are determined according to the following requirements obtained from the requirements document:

[req1]   each test can be executed at most once on a certain input;
[req2]   if the test is complex then all the simple tests it depends on have to be already executed;
[req3]   if some input has failed then no more tests on that input should be executed.

The condition of the nondeterministic block **ANY** of the operation **DetectionLoop** defines which tests are actually enabled for execution according to the requirements req1-3. To ensure req1, we introduce the relation *TestExecuted* that contains only those pairs (ii,te), where ii is an input and te is a test, such that the input ii has been tested by the test te. Then req1 can be expressed simply as the predicate $(ii,te) \notin TestExecuted$. Similarly, the requirement req2 can formally be expressed as the predicate $(te \in C\_TEST \Rightarrow \forall mm.(mm \in ComplexTest(te) \Rightarrow (ii,mm) \in TestExecuted))$. Finally, the requirement req3 is ensured by checking that the predicate $Input\_In\_ErrorN1(ii) = \textbf{FALSE}$ holds, i.e., an input has not failed yet.

When an enabled test is executed on a particular input, its result should be saved for later analysis. Therefore, we introduce the relation *TestPassed* that contains only those pairs (ii,te) such that the input ii has successfully passed the test te.

At the beginning of each FMS operation cycle both variables, *TestExecuted* and *TestPassed*, are initialised with the empty set (i.e., initially no tests have been executed and passed).

DetectionLoop =
SELECT *FMS_State=detloop* $\wedge$ *Counter>0*
THEN

        ANY *ii,te* **WHERE** *FMS_State=detloop* $\wedge$ *ii* $\in$ *Indx* $\wedge$ *te* $\in$ *TESTS* $\wedge$
        $(ii,te) \notin TestExecuted \wedge Input\_In\_ErrorN1(ii) = \textbf{FALSE} \wedge$
        $(te \in C\_TEST \Rightarrow \forall mm.(mm \in ComplexTest(te) \Rightarrow (ii,mm) \in TestExecuted))$
    THEN

        CHOICE *TestPassed:=TestPassed* $\cup$ $\{ii \mapsto te\}$ **OR skip END**;

        IF $(ii,te) \notin TestPassed$ **THEN**
            $Input\_In\_ErrorN1(ii):=\textbf{TRUE} \parallel$
            $TestExecuted:=TestExecuted \cup (\{ii\} \times TESTS)$
      ELSE

            $TestExecuted:=TestExecuted \cup \{ii \mapsto te\}$

      END
    END
WHEN   *FMS_State=detloop* $\wedge$ *Counter=0*
THEN
    FMS_State:=det
END ;

To ensure that the operation **DetectionLoop** terminates, we define its variant *Counter* as follows:

Counter ==
card ({*ii,te* | *ii*∈ *Indx* ∧ *te*∈ *TESTS* ∧ (*ii,te*)∉ *TestExecuted* ∧ *Input_In_ErrorN1*(*ii*)=**FALSE**
∧ (*te*∈ *C_TEST* ⇒ ∀*mm*.(*mm*∈ *ComplexTest*(*te*) ⇒ (*ii,mm*)∈ *TestExecuted*))})

Counter defines the number of tests enabled for execution. Each **DetectionLoop** decreases the number of enabled tests by increasing the number of tests that have been executed. When *Counter* reaches zero, the operation **DetectionLoop** finishes and the FMS operating cycle proceeds to the operation **Detection**.

The invariant of the third refinement step guarantees that, if any of the tests applied on a certain input has failed, the input is considered in error:

∀(*ii,te*).(*ii*∈ *Indx* ∧ *te*∈ *TESTS* ∧ (*ii,te*)∈ *TestExecuted* ∧ (*ii,te*)∉ *TestPassed* ⇒
Input_In_ErrorN1(*ii*)=***TRUE***)

However, this would be insufficient without additionally guaranteeing that, in order for some input to be error free, it should successfully pass all the executed tests:

∀(*ii*).(*ii*∈ *Indx* ∧ ∀(*te*).(*te*∈ *TESTS* ∧ (*ii,te*)∈ *TestExecuted* ⇒ (*ii,te*)∈ *TestPassed*) ⇒
Input_In_ErrorN1(*ii*)=**FALSE**)

The process of error detection can be graphically represented as shown in Fig. 9.

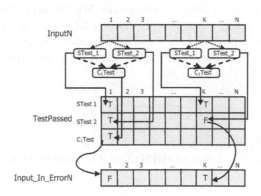

Fig. 9. Process of deciding upon the error detection

Let us observe the error detection procedure over the inputs (i.e., sensors) 1 and K, where K:2..N. Assume that the evaluating tests defined for these sensors are: simple tests – STest_1 and STest_2, and a complex test with the level of complexity 1 – C_1Test.

Both simple tests have successfully passed on the input 1, hence, the values in the matrix TestPassed for these tests on input 1 are T (i.e., true). After the simple tests have successfully passed on input 1, the complex test can be executed. Its result determines whether the input is in error or not. Since C_1Test has successfully passed on input 1, the input 1 is found error free, i.e., Input_In_ErrorN for input 1 is F (i.e, false).

Let us observe now error detection on the input K. The test STest_1 has successfully passed and the value in matrix TestPassed for this input is hence T. However, STest_2 has failed and hence the complex test C_1Test cannot be executed. Input K is considered in error, i.e., Input_In_ErrorN for input K is T.

The mechanism of error detection can be further refined. In particular, applicability of tests can depend not only on the requirements listed in req1-3 but also on some additional conditions on the required test frequencies and the internal state of the system:

[req4]   every test is executed with a certain frequency; The test frequency can be different for different tests;

[req5]   in order for some complex test to be executed, its frequency has to be divisible by the frequencies of all the simple tests required for its execution; This requirement is necessary in order to ensure the execution of all the required tests on the same data;

[req6]   the execution of each test may depend on the current internal state of the system.

To model this, we introduce the constant function *Freq*: *TESTS* → **NAT** that defines the frequency for each test. The state of the system is modelled as the variable *State*, whose values are assigned from the abstract set *STATE*.

With the new requirements in mind, we develop the fourth FMS refinement step. In order to apply tests according to the given frequencies, we introduce *time scheduling*. There is one global clock guaranteeing that the tests with the same frequency are executed at the same time instances. We model real time by introducing the event *TickTime* which increments the value of the current time (stored in the variable *Time*), whenever the event is enabled. In addition, the operation *TickTime* models possible change of the internal system state by nondeterministically updating the variable *State*.

TickTime=
SELECT *Clock_Flag=enabled*
THEN
        Time:=*Time*+1 ‖ *State* :∈ *STATE*;
        IF *Exist_Test_For_Execution* **THEN** *Clock_Flag*:=*disabled* **END**
END;

where the predicate *Exist_Test_For_Execution* is defined as:

Exist_Test_For_Execution ==
        ∃(*ii*,*te*).(*ii*∈ *Indx* ∧ *te*∈ *TESTS* ∧ (*ii*,*te*)∉ *TestExecuted* ∧ (*Time* **mod** *Freq*(*te*)=0) ∧
        Input_In_ErrorN1(*ii*)=**FALSE** ∧
        (*te*∈ *C_TEST* ⇒ ∀*mm*.(*mm*∈ *ComplexTest*(*te*) ⇒
                        (*ii*,*mm*)∈ *TestExecuted* ∧ (*Freq*(*te*) **mod** *Freq*(*mm*)=0)))

The progress of time is allowed in two situations:

- when one FMS operation cycle finishes and before the next one starts, or
- when there are no tests enabled for execution under given conditions.

In that case we allow time to progress and possibly update the internal system state until some tests become enabled.

The condition under which the tests are enabled combines now the given conditions on the internal state (modelled by the abstract function *Cond*) and the required frequency:

$$CONDITION(tt,ti,st)==(Cond(tt,st)=\textbf{TRUE} \wedge (ti \bmod Freq(tt)=0))$$

The above definition expresses that a particular test *tt* is enabled for execution at the time *ti* and the system state *st*. Using this definition, we strengthen the guard of the **ANY** block in the operation **DetectionLoop** so that it additionally implements the requirements req4-6.

With this refinement step we conclude our formal FMS development. The development can be instantiated by a domain-specific FMS. The developed specification and refinement patterns are designed specifically for N homogeneous multiple sensors. However, they can be easily extended to cover N heterogeneous sensors as well. In this case it would require to define tests for each one of N sensor readings separately, as shown in Fig. 10.

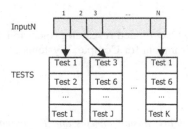

Fig. 10. Defining tests for heterogeneous multiple sensors

5 Conclusion

In this paper we proposed a formal pattern for specifying and refining the Failure Management System – a part of a safety-critical control system guaranteeing confinement of sensor errors. Our formal development of the FMS adopts system approach, i.e., we model the system together with its environment. The initial specification abstractly models the stages of the FMS execution cycle: input reading, error detection, input analysis, applying corresponding actions, calculating the output or freezing the system. Further formal development defines the input analysis procedure by introducing a customisable counting mechanism. Then we specify the error detection mechanism for N multiple homogeneous sensors by applying a certain architecture of tests.

In order to ensure application of tests on the same data, i.e., data collected at the same time instances, we introduced test scheduling. We defined a global clock and enabled the progression of time only when the whole FMS operating cycle finishes or when there are no enabled tests left for execution.

Laibinis and Troubitsyna have proposed a formal approach to the model-driven development of fault tolerant control systems in B [13]. However, they did not consider transient faults. Since we consider this type of faults our approach is an extension of the pattern proposed in their work.

Formal development of the FMS has also been undertaken in [3,9]. This work was focused on reusability and portability of the FMS modelled using UML-B [14]. However, the dependencies between tests of detection mechanism were not explicitly addressed. In our work we explicitly defined a hierarchical test architecture allowing us to tackle the input anomalies more efficiently.

A similar problem – design of software-implemented fault tolerance – was studied in [15,16,17]. This work focused on studying how to modify software at the code level to achieve fault tolerance. Our approach is complementary: we aimed at studying how to specify and develop software with fault tolerance mechanism integrated into it.

We verified our complete development with the automatic tool support – Atelier B. Around 70% of proof obligations have been proved automatically by the tool. The rest have been proved using the interactive prover.

Acknowledgments

This work is supported by EU funded research project IST 511599 RODIN (Rigorous Open Development Environment for Complex Systems).

References

1. Laprie, J.-C., *Dependability: Basic Concepts and Terminology*, Springer-Verlag, Vienna, 1991
2. Storey, N., *Safety-critical computer systems*, Addison-Wesley, 1996
3. Johnson, I., Snook, C., Edmunds, A., and Butler, M., "Rigorous development of reusable, domain-specific components, for complex applications", In *Proceedings of 3rd International Workshop on Critical Systems Development with UML*, Lisbon, 2004, pp. 115-129
4. Johnson, I., Snook, C., Rodin Project Case Study 2: Requirements Specification Document, *RODIN Deliverable D4 - Traceable Requirements Document for Case Studies*, Section 3, 2005, pp. 24-52
5. Bosch, J., *Design and Use of Software Architectures: Adopting and Evolving a Product-Line Approach*, Addison-Wesley, 2000
6. Abrial, J.-R., *The B Book: Assigning Programs to Meanings*, Cambridge University Press, 1996
7. Schneider, S., *The B Method. An introduction*, Palgrave, 2001
8. *Atelier B - User Manual*, Version 3.6, ClearSy, Aix-en-Provence, France, 2003
9. Snook, C., Poppleton, M., and Johnson, I., "The engineering of generic requirements for failure management", In *Proceedings of 11th International Workshop on Requirements Engineering: Foundation for Software Quality*, Oporto, 2005, pp. 145-160
10. MATISSE *Handbook for Correct Systems Construction*, EU-project MATISSE: Methodologies and Technologies for Industrial Strength Systems Engineering, IST-199-11345, 2003

11. Abrial, J.-R., "Event Driven Sequential Program Construction", 2001, available at: http://www.atelierb.societe.com/ressources/articles/seq.pdf
12. Back, R.J., and von Wright, J., *Refinement Calculus: A Systematic Introduction*, Springer-Verlag, 1998
13. Laibinis, L., and Troubitsyna, E., "Refinement of fault tolerant control systems in B", In *ComputerSafety, Reliability, and Security - Proceedings of SAFECOMP 2004* Lecture Notes in Computer Science, Vol. 219, Springer-Verlag, September 2004, pp. 254-268
14. Snook, C., and Walden, M., "Use of U2B for specifying B action systems", In *Proceedings of RCS'02 – International workshop on refinement of critical systems: methods, tools and experience*, Grenoble, France, 2002
15. Rebaudengo, M., Reorda, M.S., Torchiano, M., and Violante, M., "A Source-to-Source Compiler for Generating Dependable Software", *IEEE International Workshop on Source Code Analysis and Manipulation*, 2001, pp. 33–42
16. Reis, G.A., Chang, J., Vachharajani, N., Rangan, R., and August, D.I., "SWIFT: Software Implemented Fault Tolerance", *Proceedings of the Third International Symposium on Code Generation and Optimization*, March 2005, pp. 243–254
17. Oh, N., Mitra, S., and McCluskey, E.J., "ED4I: Error Detection by Diverse Data and Duplicated Instructions", *IEEE Transactions on Computers*, Vol. 51, No.2, 2002, pp. 180–199

Separating Concerns in Requirements Analysis: An Example

Daniel Jackson[1] and Michael Jackson[2]

[1] Computer Science and Artificial Intelligence Laboratory
Massachusetts Institute of Technology
Cambridge, MA
[2] Independent Consultant
London, England

Abstract. Often, a requirements document is structured as a long list of individual "requirements", each describing an anticipated function or user interaction. An alternative approach is to identify a collection of subproblems, each representing an aspect of the larger problem, and to describe each subproblem in isolation, deferring their composition to a later stage. This paper illustrates the approach by applying it to the requirements of the positioning functions of a proton therapy installation. It explains how a flaw in the design of the system can be isolated to a single subproblem, which can be formalized and subjected to automatic analysis.

1 Introduction

Many approaches to requirements analysis focus on the anticipated interactions between users and the system to be built. These interactions may be structured as a collection of representative scenarios or 'use cases'. Often the requirements document is just an elaborate informal narrative describing in detail the sessions of each class of user. By drawing attention to the experience of users, these approaches can be a useful kind of paper prototype.

A major flaw of such approaches is that, for many systems, they focus in the wrong place. The problem to be solved by the system usually exists not at the interface with the machine, but deeper in the environment [9]. The purpose of a traffic light system, for example, is not to control the lights but to ensure steady and safe flow of traffic. Its requirements analysis should therefore start with traffic and the expected and desired behaviours of drivers, rather than with the question of how the lights should be sequenced.

This paper addresses a different but related flaw of approaches based on user interaction: that enumerating and elaborating scenarios tends to conflate different concerns. A system must usually satisfy multiple properties, perform multiple functions simultaneously, and satisfy multiple purposes. The eventual design of its user interface brings these multiple concerns together. But to describe the interface be-

M. Butler et al. (Eds.): Fault-Tolerant Systems, LNCS 4157, pp. 210–225, 2006.
© Springer-Verlag Berlin Heidelberg 2006

fore the concerns have been identified and explored puts the cart before the horse. It can easily result in a development in which the individual concerns are never properly grasped, and are therefore inadequately addressed or made unnecessarily complicated.

This problem has special significance for systems that must be highly dependable. An inability to separate concerns makes it hard to pay more attention to the concerns that are more critical, and the resulting system may fail to satisfy its most critical requirements because their implementation is interwoven with the implementation of less critical requirements. In an earlier study, we found that the software control of the emergency stop feature of a radiotherapy machine was dependent on far less important features of the system; a signal to stop could be rejected, for example, if the disk were full so that a log record could not be written [12]. (Fortunately a redundant hardware interlock was in place.)

An alternative approach identifies the concerns at the outset. Instead of attempting to describe an interface that integrates the various concerns, each concern is considered independently, and only later is the composition of the concerns addressed [9]. This paper illustrates the approach with an example of a problem that arose in the development of the software for a proton therapy machine. The work is part of an ongoing collaboration between the Software Design Group at MIT and the Burr Proton Therapy Center (BPTC) at Massachusetts General Hospital whose aim is to find ways to improve the dependability of critical software.

The problem was known to the developers of the therapy system, and had been resolved before the writing of this paper, and it never posed a safety risk. But it is worth studying because it illustrates the pitfalls of the traditional approach to requirements analysis, some potential benefits of an approach based on problem decomposition, and is characteristic of problems that arise in many similar systems.

2 The Proton Therapy System

Proton therapy involves exposing a patient's tumour to a focused beam of protons. The positioning of the patient and the device issuing the beam is an intricate matter. At the BPTC, the positioning is carried out in two distinct phases. In the first phase, the patient and device are put in a "setup position" that is suitable for imaging. An X-ray image is taken to determine the exact position of the tumour, and a "delta" is obtained that captures the difference between the setup position and the position that would be required for the beam to be appropriately aligned. In the second phase, the patient and device are oriented in the "treatment position"; the delta obtained during setup is applied as a correction to the initial treatment position so that the proton beam will be aligned correctly.

Patient and beam position are adjusted in a number of ways. The beam follows a path along a fixed beamline from the cyclotron to the treatment room, and is bent by electromagnets to align with a snout mounted on a gantry that surrounds the patient couch and can rotate around one axis. The snout itself moves in and out (towards and away from the patient), and can also rotate. The patient is positioned, often on a firm cushion, on a robotic couch that has six degrees of freedom (lateral, longitudinal, vertical, roll, pitch and rotation). When the rotation of the couch is at 0 degrees, adjusting the roll of the couch and the angle of the gantry have the same effect, although the couch can only move plus or minus 3 degrees, so it tends to be used for making small adjustments only.

2.1 The Problem: Gantry Creep

In the initial design of the software, the therapist issued the command "gotoSetup" to move the patient into the recorded setup position. She then took X-rays, and adjusted the position of the gantry and couch until alignment was achieved. A single command "saveSetup" was then executed, whose effect was two-fold: to obtain the delta used to offset the treatment position, and to record a new setup position for subsequent treatment sessions.

The therapists observed that sometimes the gantry angle had deviated over the course of several treatment sessions quite considerably from its initial position, despite the fact that the therapist had made no adjustments to the gantry itself. This was not in itself a safety concern, since the unexpected movement of the gantry had been compensated by a corresponding adjustment of the couch. Eventually, however, the gantry had moved so far that it was no longer possible to compensate because of the limited freedom of movement of the couch.

The problem, it turned out, was that the "saveSetup" command would overwrite the gantry angle setting even when it had not been adjusted. Since the "gotoSetup" command only moved the gantry to within the recorded position by some tolerance, the effect of "saveSetup" was to change the gantry angle setting even when the therapist had not intended any change. In some cases, it seems that these small errors accumulated, resulting eventually in a significant change.

The solution that was implemented was simply to eliminate the ability to adjust the gantry angle during setup. The code of the "saveSetup" command was changed accordingly so that it never overwrites the gantry angle setting. This approach is acceptable because the adjustments that are typically needed are small, and can be achieved by adjustments to the couch position alone.

The solution suggested by the analysis based on subproblems is different. It distinguishes those "saveSetup" commands that follow "gotoSetup" commands, and insists that they make no change to the recorded setup position.

3 Decomposing into Subproblems

A decomposition into subproblems starts with an attempt to uncover the purpose behind the functions to be implemented. In this case, a discussion with the developers revealed two distinct purposes: (1) to save the setup position so that in a subsequent session the need for setup adjustment is eliminated or reduced; and (2) to

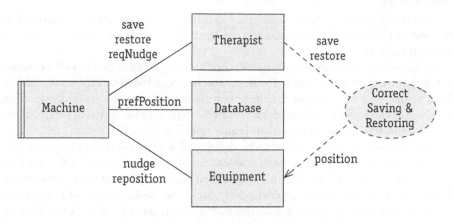

Fig. 1. Set/Restore subproblem

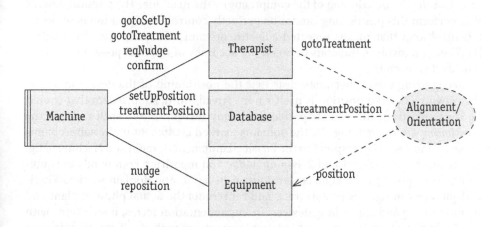

Fig. 2. Alignment subproblem

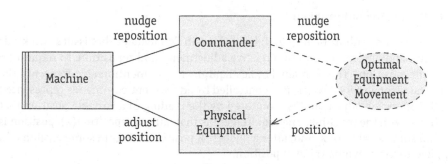

Fig. 3. Positioning subproblem

determine, with the help of an X-ray or some other imaging device, an adjustment to the relative positions of the patient and the beam that will ensure proper alignment during treatment.

An important clue that these purposes should be regarded as distinct subproblems is that they have different *spans*. The first, which we call the *Set/Restore subproblem*, has a span that encompasses multiple treatment sessions. The second, which we call the *Alignment subproblem*, involves only a single session. The two subproblems are shown in figs. 1 and 2 in Problem Frame notation [9]. In each figure the striped rectangle represents the *machine* to be developed for the corresponding subproblem. The other rectangles represent *problem domains* interacting with the machine at interfaces of shared phenomena; the dashed ellipse represents the *requirement*, which is a condition on the problem domains, expressed in terms of phenomena that may or may not be shared with the machine. An arrowhead indicates that the requirement expresses a constraint on the domain to which it points.

Before delving further into either subproblem, we notice that they share a common feature: the positioning of the equipment by the machine. The physical devices that perform this positioning cannot be perfectly controlled; a position is set using a control loop that makes repeated adjustments and measurements. The control loop's design involves tradeoffs between the accuracy of the final position and how quickly it is reached.

Recognizing this, it becomes clear that the positioning of the device in accordance with a desired position is itself a non- trivial, third, subproblem that should be separated from the two subproblems already identified. We shall call this the *Positioning subproblem* (fig. 3). The domains marked Equipment in the subproblems of figs. 1 and 2 now correspond to the PhysicalEquipment domain and Machine of fig. 3. The machines in figs. 1 and 2, issuing nudge and reposition commands to Equipment, correspond to the Commander domain in fig. 3. The domain marked PhysicalEquipment in fig. 3 is less abstract, and represents the actual physical plant and its monitoring and controlling devices. In implementation terms, interactions with the Equipment domain represent indirect interactions with the PhysicalEquipment domain mediated by the Machine in the Positioning subproblem.

Let's now examine each of the three subproblems in more detail.

3.1 Positioning Subproblem

The Positioning subproblem (fig. 3) has a domain Commander that issues two kinds of command: nudge, to request a relative adjustment, and reposition, to request an absolute position. The domain PhysicalEquipment, as mentioned, represents the physical plant and its devices; it is controlled by adjustment commands represented by the operation adjust, and is monitored by the reading of a variable position that is shared with the machine. The requirement is that, after a reposition(x), position is within some epsilon of x, and, after a nudge(d), position is within some epsilon of d applied to the previous value of position.

The details of the tolerance and the time taken to achieve the final position need not concern us here, and are standard issues in the design of a control loop for a physical device (such as a robot arm). A primary benefit of identifying such a subproblem is factoring out parts of the development that are complex and tricky when faced for the first time, but are conventional and easily handled by a specialist.

3.2 Set/Restore Subproblem

The Set/Restore subproblem is also an instance of a wider class. The setup protocol in our proton therapy setting is essentially the same as the protocol for adjusting the seat position in a fancy car. The car stores a preferred position for each driver, and has three principal commands: to adjust the seat position; to save a preference; and to restore the position to the last position saved for that driver.

In this subproblem, the domain Equipment has a shared variable position that reveals the current position of the equipment. Unlike the domain PhysicalEquipment in the Positioning subproblem, however, its phenomena include the more powerful commands nudge and reposition rather than just adjust. This subproblem therefore need not be concerned with how a particular positioning command is handled; it assumes that the equipment responds appropriately.

The Therapist issues three kinds of command: save(p) to save the current position as the preferred saved position for patient p, restore(p) to move to the position previously saved for patient p, and reqNudge(d) to request an adjustment by an amount d. The preferred positions are stored in a database represented by the Database domain, which offers a relation prefPosition mapping each patient to a preferred position.

A careful consideration of this subproblem in isolation reveals the creep problem. Since reposition only achieves an approximation to the desired position, issuing the command reposition (position) repeatedly can cause arbitrary changes in position; each request to set the position to the current recorded position may actually result in a change in position. A naive design in which every save(p) writes the current value of position to prefPosition[p] will exhibit this anomaly if a sequence of save/restore pairs is executed.

To avoid the problem, we can make save(p) have no effect if the preceding event was a restore(p). A full formalization of this subproblem is discussed below, with a more detailed explanation of this decision.

3.3 Alignment Subproblem

The Alignment subproblem is the hardest to handle, because it is more complicated, and because it seems to be unique to this domain. It can nevertheless be described fairly succinctly. Rather than representing the gantry and couch as distinct components with distinct positions, we regard the system as a whole as occupying a coordinate in some abstract space, just as we did with other subproblems.

In this space, some coordinates can be classified as *oriented*: these correspond to the gantry and couch positions in which the patient is oriented appropriately for treatment. Some coordinates, likewise, can be regarded as *aligned*: these are the coordinates in which the relative positions of the couch and the gantry will ensure that the beam is appropriately directed at the tumour. By viewing alignment and orientation as projections of a coordinate, we can define planes (isosurfaces) in the abstract space of coordinates that share a particular alignment or a particular orientation. Correct alignment (or orientation) means that the alignment (or orientation) projection has a particular value.

The Therapist issues four kinds of command: reqNudge to request a position adjustment, gotoSetUp to request the setup position, and gotoTreatment to request that the equipment move to the treatment position stored in the Database, and confirm to confirm that the equipment is well aligned in the current position. The Database holds a setup position and a treatment position for each patient p represented as shared variables setUpPosition[p] (assumed to be almost aligned) and treatmentPosition[p] (assumed to be oriented, and also almost aligned).

The procedure to be followed by the Therapist is first to request the setUpPosition with gotoSetUp; then, if adjustment is necessary to effect it by reqNudge commands; then to issue a confirm followed by gotoTreatment command.

The requirement is roughly that, following gotoTreatment, the equipment is both aligned and oriented. It will be established by a combination of assumed properties of the Therapist, Database and Equipment domains, and of the specification of the Machine, namely that (1) Therapist will issue the confirm command only when the equipment is shown to be aligned by the X-ray or other imaging technique; (2) the value of treatmentPosition[p] in Database is oriented; (3) in the Equipment domain, the command reposition(x), where x is aligned and oriented, results in a value of position that is also aligned and oriented.

4 Set/Restore Formalized

Decomposing into subproblems allows us to analyze each subproblem independently. In this section, we illustrate this by formalizing the Set/Restore subproblem in Alloy [8], and subjecting the formal model to an automatic analysis using the Alloy Analyzer [2].

An Alloy model begins with a module name, and imports for any modules that are used. In this case, we import a library module that imposes a total ordering on the set Event, to be declared later:

> **module** saveRestore
> **open** util/ordering [Event]

The import makes available functions which will be used later: next(e), nexts(s), prev(e), and prevs(s), which for an element e (or a set s) give respectively the next element, all subsequent elements, the immediately preceding element, and all preceding elements; and first() and last(), which give the first and last events in the ordering.

The set of positions is declared, with a relation near associating each position with the set of positions that are within some epsilon (the tolerance of the Positioning subproblem), along with a fact (a global assumption) that this relation is reflexive and symmetric:

> **sig** Position {near: **set** Position}

```
fact {
    Position <: iden in near
    near = ~near
}
```

It is significant that near is not transitive; its lack of transitivity is the source of the gantry creep problem.

A set of patients is likewise declared:

```
sig Patient {}
```

The states of the system are declared explicitly as a set also; Alloy has no built-in state machine idiom. Two relations are declared on states, one for the state of the Equipment domain that associates each state with a position – the physical position of the equipment – and one for the state of the Database domain that associates each state with a function mapping patients to preferred positions:

```
sig State {
    Equipment_position: Position,
    Database_prefPosition: Patient -> one Position
}
```

The Database_prefPosition relation is a total function: it maps each patient to exactly one position.

The various requests and commands are modelled as event objects. We start with a set of events declared to be abstract (indicating that it will be exhausted by the subsets that will be subsequently declared), and with relations associating each event with its pre-state (the state before its occurrence), its post-state (the state after its occurrence), and the patient to which the event applies:

```
abstract sig Event {
    pre, post: State,
    patient: Patient
}
```

The pre- and post-state relations must be constrained so that for any event e except the last event in a trace, the pre- state of e's successor event is the post-state of e:

```
fact {
    all e: Event - last () | next (e).pre = e.post
}
```

We declare a partition of the event set into subsets corresponding to the three commands issued by the therapist:

```
sig Therapist_save, Therapist_restore, Therapist_reqNudge extends Event {}
```

The Equipment domain has two event sets of its own; the use of the in keyword in their declarations allows these sets to overlap with the other event sets:

```
sig Equipment_reposition in Event {position: Position}
sig Equipment_nudge in Event {}
fact {no Equipment_reposition & Equipment_nudge}
```

Our plan is to have them overlap with the Therapist events, so that a reqNudge in the Therapist domain can be equated to a nudge in the Equipment domain. They will not overlap with each other, however, so an explicit fact is recorded to this effect.

Note that the reposition event has a position relation declared for it; this is in fact the only event in which a position must be made explicit. The commands of the Therapist domain are interpreted with respect to the current position in the Equipment domain, which is not communicated by the therapist.

It will be convenient to have two functions for describing temporal relationships between events. The function following takes an event e and a set of events s and returns either the first event that follows e that belongs to the set s or the empty set if there is none:

```
fun following (e: Event, s: set Event): lone Event {
    let succs = s & nexts (e) | succs - nexts (succs)
}
```

This defines succs as the intersection of s and the set of all events occurring after e. The difference between succs and the set of all events occurring after any of its members is then the singleton set containing its first member or the empty set if it has no first member. The lone keyword indicates that the function following may return a singleton or empty set of events; it can be read 'less than or equal to one'.

The function between takes two events and returns the set of events that occur between them:

```
fun between (from, to: Event): set Event {
    nexts (from) & prevs (to)
}
```

Now we can define the constraints: the requirements and the domain properties. There are two distinct requirements. The first says, roughly speaking, that a restore command returns the equipment to the position prior to the last save. More precisely, for any patient p and save command s associated with p, and for any restore command r following s, if there is no other save for p that intervenes between the two, the position after the restore is 'nearish' to the position before the save:

```
pred Memory_Requirement () {
    all p: Patient, s: Therapist_save & patient.p |
        all r: following (s, Therapist_restore &
        patient.p) |
            no Therapist_save & patient.p & between (s, r) implies
                nearish (r.post.Equipment_position, s.pre.Equipment_position)
}
```

The expression Therapist_save & patient.p denotes the set of Therapist_save events applying to patient p, and so on.

Two positions are 'nearish' if there is some position they are both near to:

pred nearish (p, p': Position) {**some** p": Position | p+p' **in** p".near}

(The need for this notion is explained below). The second requirements says, roughly speaking, that there is no creep. For any patient p, save command s associated with p, and restore commands r and r', also associated with p, that follow s without an intervening reqNudge command, the positions resulting from r and r' are nearish:

```
pred Consistency_Requirement () {
    all p: Patient, s: Therapist_save & patient.p, r: nexts (s), r': nexts (r) |
    (r + r' in Therapist_restore & patient.p and
    no between (r, r') & Therapist_reqNudge & patient.p) implies
        nearish (r.post.Equipment_position, r'.post.Equipment_position)
}
```

The two restore commands need not follow immediately, and can have other restore commands occurring between them.

The therapist positions each patient afresh, rather than using the position of the previous patient. We record this assumption as a predicate saying that if an event is associated with a different patient than its predecessor, it must be a restore command:

```
pred Therapist () {
    all e: Event | e.patient != prev(e).patient implies e in Therapist_restore
}
```

(Note that if e has no predecessor, then the expression prev(e).patient denotes the empty set: there are no undefined expressions or special values in Alloy.)

The specification of the machine links together the commands of the therapist with the reading and updating of the database, and the issuing of commands to the equipment:

```
pred Specification () {
    -- respond to a restore command from the therapist by issuing
    -- a reposition command to the equipment whose position argument
    -- is that position of this patient in the database
    all r: Therapist_restore |
        r in Equipment_reposition and
            r.position = r.pre.Database_prefPosition[r.patient]
    -- a reqNudge command from the therapist is matched to a nudge
    -- command to the equipment and a restore is matched to a reposition
    Therapist_reqNudge = Equipment_nudge
    Therapist_restore = Equipment_reposition
    -- when a save command is received from the therapist, the position of
    -- the associated patient is updated in the database with the current
```

-- equipment position, unless the previous command was a restore
-- for this patient
all s: Therapist_save | **let** p = s.patient |
    s.post.Database_prefPosition = s.pre.Database_prefPosition ++
      if some prev (s) & Therapist_restore & patient.p
        then none -> **none else** p -> s.pre.Equipment_position
-- for any event except a save, the database is not written
all e: Event - Therapist_save |
    e.pre.Database_prefPosition = e.post.Database_prefPosition
}

The assumptions about the equipment are that a reposition moves the equipment to a position near to the position requested, and that only reposition and nudge events result in a change in position:

pred Equipment () {
    all r: Equipment_reposition | r.post.Equipment_position **in** r.position.near
    all e: Event | e.post.Equipment_position = e.pre.Equipment_position
      or e **in** Equipment_reposition + Equipment_nudge
}

Finally, we can declare as assertions the key correctness properties, namely that the combination of the specification and domain properties implies each of the requirements:

assert CorrectnessM {
    Specification () **and** Equipment () **and** Therapist ()
      implies Memory_Requirement ()
}
assert CorrectnessC {
    Specification () **and** Equipment () **and** Therapist ()
      implies Consistency_Requirement ()
}

The Alloy language is undecidable, so an assertion cannot be checked automatically in an unbounded space. So Alloy's checking commands specify a *scope* indicating how many elements each set may have. For example, for an initial analysis, we might execute the command

check CorrectnessM **for** 3

which checks the assertion CorrectnessM for all scenarios involving up to 3 events, states, positions and patients. Because there are so many scenarios even within small scopes, they are often sufficient to detect interesting flaws.

For example, if the definition of nearish is replaced by

pred nearish (p, p': Position) {p **in** p'.near}

so that two points are nearish only when they are near the Alloy Analyzer finds a counterexample for this command in about 5 seconds (on a 1.67GHz Powerbook

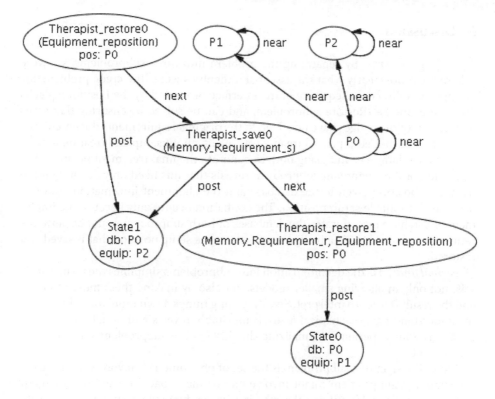

Fig. 4. A counterexample

G4 laptop), as shown in fig. 4. The large ovals linked by next show the chain of events for a particular patient. The first event is a restore; its pre-state, not shown in this particular visualization, associates position P0 with the patient in the database, so P0 is the argument to the reposition command. On receiving this command, the equipment is free to set the position to any that is near P0; it chooses P2. (The near relation amongst positions is shown in the upper right.) Now a save command occurs, which has no effect, since it is preceded by a restore. Then a second restore is performed. The database has not changed, but this time, the equipment chooses a different position near P0, namely P1. So although creep can't happen, since different restore commands can approximate the commanded position differently, the actual error margin is twice the tolerance of the equipment.

Replacing the definition of nearish by its original definition results in no counterexample. To gain further confidence, we can increase the scope. Checking the command for all scenarios involving 7 events, 7 states, 7 positions and 3 patients

check CorrectnessM **for** 7 **but** 3 Patient

gives no counterexamples, in a search that takes under 4 minutes.

5 Discussion

Separating concerns. By separating the problem into three subproblems, we were able to see more clearly what the essential difficulties were. The creep problem, for example, is a direct consequence of the interface presented by the Positioning subproblem to the Set/Restore subproblem, and can be solved by ensuring that saves that do not follow nudges have no effect. In the original requirements document, the description of the setup procedure involves reading both setup and treatment positions from a database, and using both to compute the final treatment position. Examination of the Alignment subproblem reveals that this need only depend on the treatment position given in the database and the alignment information obtained from any reasonable setup position. The conflation occurs only because the implemented database incorporates the databases of both subproblems, and because the setup position used to obtain alignment is the same setup position that is saved and restored.

Formal analysis. The decomposition into subproblems simplifies the formal analysis, not only in allowing smaller models, but also by making them more tractable and the results easier to interpret. Simply writing things down more formally reveals misunderstandings; mechanical analysis inevitably reveals additional, more subtle problems. Our experience formalizing the Set/Restore subproblem was typical in this respect.

Span. The span of a subproblem is the set of phenomena it involves. In this case, the span of a subproblem might involve one or many patients, and one or many treatment sessions. Identifying the span is a crucial first step in understand a problem, and the presence of requirements with different spans suggests a decomposition into subproblems.

Abstraction. A subproblem is easier to understand and analyze when the phenomena have been abstracted appropriately. In the original requirements document, for example, the discussion of positioning involves the many components of the gantry and patient couch position. This level of detail is not relevant to these subproblems.

Distinct phenomena. A scenario-based analysis encourages the developer to conflate phenomena, for example to assume that the saving of a preferred setup position and the confirmation of alignment are the same event. They happen to be performed by the same person at the same time, often for the same position, but there is no fundamental reason that they need to be equated. Arguably, a cleaner design would offer two separate commands, allowing the therapist to save a preferred position without confirming alignment, for example. In short, it is better to start with the assumption that phenomena are distinct and merge them than to start with a smaller set and try to split phenomena later.

Composing the Positioning subproblem. Analysis of a problem into distinct subproblems must be followed by recombination of the analysed subproblems to give a solution to the original problem. Recombining the Positioning subproblem with the other two is straightforward and entirely conventional. The span of the Positioning subproblem is receipt and execution of a single nudge or reposition command: the Machine in the Positioning subproblem has no need to save state from one command to the next, because the only significant state is held in the Physical Equipment. This Machine can therefore be easily implemented as a module that interfaces with the equipment on one side and offers the nudge and reposition commands on the other. This module is made available to the Set/Restore and Alignment subproblems.

Composing the Set/Restore and Alignment subproblems. Recombining the Set/Restore and Alignment subproblems demands more care. The composition task is to combine the subproblems by identifying phenomena that are common to both, and to ensure that the composition preserves the properties of each. The Therapist has, in principle, the full repertoire of both subproblems available, but each subproblem imposes its own restrictions on the acceptable command sequences. As has already been mentioned, it is appropriate to identify the Database field prefPosition in the Set/Restore subproblem with the setUpPosition field in the Alignment subproblem. The reqNudge commands in the two subproblems are evidently identical. The confirm command in the Alignment subproblem can be identified as a save command in the Set/Restore subproblem: responsibility for avoiding the creep problem belongs to the Set/Restore subproblem, where save will have no effect unless there has been a reqNudge since the most recent save. The databases are composed simply by merging their schemas. The two subproblem machines can be combined, in an object-oriented setting, by introducing a control layer that delegates commands issued by the Therapist to lower-level objects implementing the two machines.

Without hindsight? We have, of course, had the benefit of hindsight. The gantry creep problem had already been identified in the existing system, and we took that as our starting point. Would we have identified the problem if we had been doing an original design without the benefit of hindsight? We believe that we would. By our criteria the *Set/Restore* subproblem is clearly distinct from the *Alignment* subproblem, because the two have different spans: many sessions versus one session. Once these subproblems have been separated there is no reason to confuse the save action in the *Set/Restore subproblem* with the confirm action in the *Alignment subproblem*.

The confirm action need not, in principle, cause a database update, because the confirmed position will be used immediately to compute the delta and the treatment position. Only a later recognition that it, too, could involve saving a position in the database suggests the possibility that the two saved positions might be represented by the same database field in the patient's record. Such a design choice, in our approach, would be a conscious decision in an explicit composition task, and would demand careful examination of the circumstances in which the two actions could share a part of their implementation.

6 Related Work

Dijkstra coined the term 'separation of concerns'. In an early note [4], he advocated the idea of focusing on one aspect of a problem at a time. Since then, the notion of 'separating concerns' has become standard, although often only lip service is paid to it.

The insight that the requirements of a system to be built should be viewed as a collection of fairly independent subproblems is now also widely understood, although in practice the identification of subproblems is not made explicit in the requirements document, but arises only during design, when the subproblems emerge as design challenges. The idea that the requirements themselves should be structured around subproblems is the premise of the Problem Frames approach [9], which characterizes problems into archetypal classes, in the hope that most subproblems encountered will be instances of subproblems that have already been faced, and for which simple and effective solutions are well known.

Formal methods attempt to uncover the essence of the requirements problem, and to express it precisely and unambiguously in a formal notation. They do not tend, however, to give effective guidance or heuristics for decomposing problems into subproblems, although the presence of conjunction in declarative specification languages makes them well suited to such a decomposition [1, 7, 10].

Viewpoints [5] are a bit like subproblems, but they arise from the interests of different stakeholders, rather than from structure inherent to the problem itself.

Aspect-oriented programming [11] and subject-oriented programming [6] aim to achieve better separation of concerns by new implementation constructs. Work on 'early aspects' seems to focus not so much on separation of concerns in the early phases of development as on the early identification of features that can be implemented using the technology of aspect-oriented programming.

Failure to recognize that a problem is composed of multiple subproblems is likely to result in complicated and obscure implementation. An extreme programming approach [3] may well exacerbate the difficulties, by encouraging the coding of a complex composite machine before simpler submachines have been identified. The effort invested in an early decomposition into subproblems is likely to pay off, and an extreme programming approach in which individual submachines are implemented and evaluated prior to consideration of their composition might work well.

Acknowledgments

Dr. Jay Flanz, director of the Burr Proton Therapy Center, generously explained to us the details of the gantry creep problem; Dr. Hanne Kooy, radiation physicist, and Doug Miller and Nghia Ho Van, developers of the Therapy Control System were also very helpful. Robert Seater is developing a problem-frame- based analysis of the system, and shared his ideas and insights with us. This research was funded in part by grant 0325283 (Safety Mechanisms for Medical Software) from the ITR program of the National Science Foundation.

Any opinions, findings and conclusions or recommendations expressed in this material are those of the authors, and do not necessarily reflect the views of the National Science Foundation, or the Burr Proton Therapy Center.

References

1. M. Ainsworth, A.H. Cruickshank, L.J. Groves and P.J.L. Wallis. Formal Specification via Viewpoints. *Proc. 13th New Zealand Computer Conference*, New Zealand Computer Society, Auckland, New Zealand, 1993.
2. *The Alloy Language and Analyzer*, http://alloy.mit.edu.
3. Kent Beck. *Extreme Programming Explained*. Boston, Addison Wesley, 1999.
4. Edsger Dijkstra. On the role of scientific thought. EWD 447, 30th August 1974, Neuen, The Netherlands. Appears in: Edsger W. Dijkstra, *Selected Writings on Computing: A Personal Perspective*, Springer-Verlag, 1982. ISBN 0–387–90652–5, pp. 60–66. Available at http: www.cs.utexas.edu/users/EWD/.
5. A. Finkelstein, J. Kramer, B. Nuseibeh, L. Finkelstein and M. Goedicke. Viewpoints: A Framework for Integrating Multiple Perspectives in System Development. *International Journal on Software Engineering and Knowledge Engineering*, 2(1):31–57, World Scientific Publishing Company, March 1992.
6. William Harrison and Harold Ossher. Subject-Oriented Programming – A Critique of Pure Objects. *Proc. 1993 Conference on Object- Oriented Programming Systems, Languages and Applications*, September 1993.
7. Daniel Jackson. Structuring Z Specifications with Views. *ACM Transactions on Software Engineering and Methodology*, Vol. 4, No. 4, October 1995, pp. 365–389.
8. Daniel Jackson. *Software Abstractions: Logic, Language, and Analysis*. MIT Press, Cambridge, MA, March 2006.
9. Michael Jackson. *Problem Frames: Analyzing and Structuring Software Development Problems*. Boston, Addison Wesley Professional, 2000.
10. Daniel Jackson and Michael Jackson. Problem Decomposition for Reuse. *Software Engineering Journal*, Vol. 11, No. 1, January 1996, pp. 19–30.
11. Gregor Kiczales, John Lamping, Anurag Mendhekar, Chris Maeda, Cristina Lopes, Jean-Marc Loingtier and John Irwin. Aspect- Oriented Programming. *Proc. European Conference on Object- Oriented Programming*, 1997.
12. Andrew Rae, Daniel Jackson, Prasad Ramanan, Jay Flanz and Didier Leyman. Critical Feature Analysis of a Radiotherapy Machine. *Reliability Engineering and System Safety*, Elsevier Science, 2004.

Rigorous Fault Tolerance Using Aspects and Formal Methods

Shmuel Katz*

Department of Computer Science
The Technion, Haifa, Israel
katz@cs.technion.ac.il

Abstract. This paper examines the hypothesis that rigorous fault tolerance can be achieved by using aspect oriented software development in conjunction with formal methods of verification and analysis. After brief summaries on fault tolerance, aspect-oriented programming, and formal methods, some examples of aspects for fault tolerance are outlined. Then some recent research on applying formal methods to aspects is described, with the potential implications for rigorous fault tolerance using aspects.

Keywords: aspect orientation, fault tolerance, formal methods.

1 Introduction

This paper examines the hypothesis that rigorous fault tolerance can be achieved by using aspect-oriented software development in conjunction with formal methods of verification and analysis. It thus connects three largely disparate areas, each with an extensive literature of its own: fault tolerance, aspects, and formal methods.

Before considering a possible synthesis of these areas, some of the major objectives and accomplishments of each are briefly summarized. Then some examples of using aspects for fault tolerance are outlined, in Section 2. In Section 3 results on applying formal methods to aspects are surveyed. Finally, the potential mutual benefits of aspects, fault tolerance, and formal methods are considered.

1.1 Fault Tolerance

A variety of techniques and problems are combined under the heading of fault tolerance. Since most faults involve communications or processing units, the area largely deals with concurrent systems, usually distributed. The terminology and basic practices of the area are well established [38,37,39,26]. The treatment of processor faults is based on occasional checkpointing of a system state, detection of faults, and either rollback to a recent checkpoint for re-execution [9], or rollforward techniques [45] that use reserve processors to determine which processor is faulty when disagreement arises among multiple processors intended to be duplicating identical computations.

---

* This work was partially supported by the EU Network of Excellence AOSD-Europe.

M. Butler et al. (Eds.): Fault-Tolerant Systems, LNCS 4157, pp. 226–240, 2006.

Fault tolerance for communication faults has usually been treated as part of a layered view of communication. Even when configurable systems are needed, such a protocol stack view is possible, e.g., as seen in the x-kernel [25], that handles such issues transparently. However, in some contexts, it is much more natural to handle configurable fault-tolerance as a concern that interacts with the other system concerns in a more complex way. Such designs are seen in the Cactus system [22] and its predecessor Coyote [7]. The model assumes that services can have complex interactions. The modules within each service are called micro-protocols, and are activated by events that other services can raise.

On the practical system level considered above, the exact nature of the fault does not have to be analyzed, and, at least initially, is viewed as a transient problem that can be overcome by reactivation from a consistent state. In a more abstract context, the easiest faults to describe are known as crash faults, and involve the potential failure of a processing unit in a distributed system, often assumed to be executing a single process of such a system. On the level of a program, such a fault means that the code of that process simply is not executed from some point on. One of the major difficulties of treating such faults in an asynchronous system is that a crash occurs without an explicit announcement or warning. It thus is impossible [18] to distinguish this situation from one where the process is merely executing slowly relative to the others in an asynchronous system, unless time-outs or some other semi-synchronous mechanism is used.

Other forms of faults include those related to loss of messages in a distributed message-passing system. One form relates to "cutting a communication line", and means that from some point on, all communication stops. Other faults are more intermittent, such as occasionally losing messages, but with a guarantee that if sufficient messages are sent, some will get through [36].

All of the above relate to fault-events, that can be modelled as an augmented semantics where the fault can occur as an alternative to the regular successful instruction. Another form of fault tolerance relates to an occasional transient fault, that is followed by normal operation, but from an unexpected state. This is covered in the family of faults to be corrected by "self-stabilizing" algorithms [15]. The idea is that from time to time the system undergoes a traumatic "scrambling" of its state, and then continues execution from the resultant state that may be an inconsistent state in a distributed system, and otherwise unreachable. This type of fault could model, for example, a computer in space that is exposed to gamma radiation that could reverse some of the bits in memory arbitrarily from time to time. In its pure form, even the control counters can be arbitrarily reset, so that the code continues executing from unexpected locations, never having executed some of the preceding instructions. Such faults are modelled by viewing the system as if it begins in an abnormal and completely arbitrary state, often not reachable at all by normal computation. The goal of a self-stabilizing algorithm is to return the computation to a "normal" state that was previously reachable in the computations without faults.

Of course, many algorithms exist that are fault tolerant. Some work has been done on generic algorithms that add fault tolerance to a program that was correct relative to its specification but not fault-tolerant. However, more often the fault-tolerance is built into the algorithm along with its other functionality (because otherwise the loss in efficiency is too great), or is fixed in a hierarchy of system or communication levels. In these cases, it becomes difficult to apply various kinds of fault tolerance dynamically according to specific requirements or environments, to easily change the treatment of fault-tolerance, or to treat interactions of treatments for fault tolerance with other tasks. These questions are considered in greater detail later.

1.2 Aspects

Aspect-oriented programming [33] is an extension of the object oriented programming paradigm to treat what are known as cross-cutting concerns. A concern is a grouping of requirements, such as security, monitoring and debugging, preventing overflow of integer values, or fault-tolerance. The treatment of such concerns in traditional object-oriented systems often suffers from both *scattering*— the code treating the concern is scattered throughout the system— and *tangling*— the treatment is mixed together with the treatment of other concerns [43]. In this case it is said to cross-cut the primary decomposition of the system, and this is said to be inevitable for complex systems.

Aspects provide a new form of modularity to encapsulate the treatment of a concern. The approach was first developed for programming languages, and especially for extensions of Java such as AspectJ or Ceasar [41]. In such languages there is a way to define joinpoints (states or events where an aspect should be applied) using pointcuts (predicates or descriptors of groups of joinponts) and advice (portions of code to be executed at appropriate joinpoints). These appear within a separately declared, usually parametric, unit known as an aspect. The binding of an aspect declaration to an object system is known as weaving. This involves connecting the parameters of the aspect to actual elements in the classes to which the aspect is woven.

In recent years, the ideas of concerns and aspects have been extended to earlier stages of system development, such as requirements analysis and system design, and there are, for example, UML extensions to treat aspects [10,11,27].

Aspects have been shown particularly useful during the debugging stage of system development. Applying an aspect for tracing all changes to a variable that is suspect, or for recording the values each time a method is activated are natural debugging activities that are effectively done using aspects. In particular, by encapsulating the debugging activities in aspects, there is no need to disturb the original code, and the debugging can easily be deactivated, with the aspect code removed, when no longer needed.

Aspects have also proven useful in middleware components, where previously a series of flags were used to indicate how. e.g., security is to be handled in a version of a component. For example, the JBOSS middleware framework has been reimplemented in recent versions that are based on aspects. These show promise of adding flexibility and adaptability to Web-based components.

It should be noted that aspects were preceded by, and are closely related to, language constructs and reasoning for superimpositions of algorithms over distributed systems [29,3]. Connections between aspects and superimpositions are pointed out in [50].

1.3 Formal Methods

Formal methods for verification of programs have a long history and developed theory. Techniques include static code analysis, extended datatypes with predicates, model checking, bounded model checking, and inductive methods.

Several of these approaches have also gained practical acceptance in analysis and error detection for hardware designs, where the cost of errors in a relatively compact algorithm can be devastating. The infamous Pentium floating point error cost billions of dollar to correct and led to significant investment in using formal methods, and especially model checking. The formal techniques are used in addition to the more traditional simulation techniques for debugging algorithms that are ultimately implemented in firmware or hardware. Communication protocols and safety-critical software are two other areas where formal methods are considered and sometimes used.

Most model checking tools (see the excellent introduction to the subject by Clarke, Grumberg, and Peled [12]), such as SMV [40] or Spin [24], have specialized model description languages and treat key individual algorithms or protocols. Software model checkers, such as Bandera [20], Java Pathfinder [21], or Microsoft SLAM [5], work directly from high-level programs in Java or C with annotations. Such tools either have their own internal model checker, or translate to the notation of one of the earlier tools.

Although these methods are still not regularly applied to large software programs, due to their complexity and the limitations of the formal techniques, model checking and, more recently, tools based on satisfiability (SAT) solvers are beginning to gain acceptance as their capabilities are extended. For example, Microsoft routinely uses SLAM or the recent SDV extension [4] to help detect errors in their internal driver system software. NASA also has had excellent success detecting errors and improving quality of software with its Pathfinder model checker.

2 Aspects for Fault Tolerance

As seen, notations for aspects provide new expressive power in describing join points and types of changes to be made to underlying systems. This seems to promise renewed possibilities for defining fault tolerance generically for families of programs by using reusable parametric aspects. The notations allow identifying the key events in a system where changes must be made to guarantee different types of fault tolerance. The possibility of applying an aspect only when faults of a certain type are anticipated, and of dynamically deciding which faults and which algorithmic solutions are appropriate are additional attractive features of aspects. After showing a few examples of how aspects could be used to provide fault tolerance for different fault models, we will also show how formal methods for aspects can provide additional leverage for the approach.

2.1 Classic Fault-Tolerance Operations Using Aspects

The basic activities in dealing with processor faults using the classic techniques described in the Introduction are natural candidates for aspectization. The key task of recording consistent states in checkpoints is clearly appropriate for aspects since logging and recording values for purposes of debugging are well-know applications of aspects. Detecting faults, and activating a rollback or roll-forward strategy can also be expressed as aspects. A library of such aspects could be used to easily configure an underlying system with various forms of fault tolerance. Aspects can also be used to dynamically decide on which strategy to activate depending on the system state and history of execution, especially if another aspect has been used to gather relevant information on, for example, the frequency and location of previous faults.

Recent work [34] on using aspects to implement the ACID (atomicity, consistency, isolation, and durability) properties for transactional objects also anticipate some of the needed functionality of aspects for recovery from faults.

2.2 Communication Faults Using Aspects

Consider adding fault tolerance for communication faults over a network to a communication system that previously ignored this concern. As noted in the Introduction, such problems have usually been treated by a classic layered view of communication, which may be hard to configure easily.

The basic premise of treating fault tolerance and other network communication concerns in a flexible configurable way is that interactions among services can influence all layers. The analogy between micro-protocols used for fault tolerance and aspects is clear and has been analyzed in detail in [23]. That work includes suggestions to use the mechanisms of aspects to enhance the capabilities of configurable networks in general, and fault tolerance in particular. For example, even when an application level message is transmitted using an alternating-bit protocol (to treat occasional message loss at a lower layer), the implementation could interact with other services such as congestion control or security at both the application and transmission layers.

Similarly, a protocol for routing messages through nodes by using a routing table at each node could be made fault tolerant to node crash failures by sending each message twice, with disjoint routing tables, except source and final destination, and an indicator that the two represent the same message. Then at each sending point, the two messages are generated and sent, and at each receiving point, the first appearance of a message accepts the message, while the second receipt (if it occurs) is ignored. This can be encoded into an aspect, and is fault tolerant to a single crash fault of a communication node. Obvious questions of interactions among aspects, and their order of application, need to be treated and analyzed. For example, how would such an aspect interact with one treating the alternating-bit protocol, or with security concerns? Such issues are indeed the subjects of intense research in the aspect community, as will be shown later.

2.3   Self-stabilization Using Aspects

Several works have shown that self-stabilization can be added on to existing systems (rather than directly designed into the algorithm along with the other requirements of its functionality). As one example, in [31], a self-stabilizing distributed snapshot is added to algorithms with a variety of different tasks. In general such a snapshot [8] gathers information in the local state at one node about the global state of a distributed system, without stopping the execution of the system. The algorithm assumes reliable message passing in a FIFO channel, and gathers a state that is a possible descendant of the true (distributed) state when the algorithm begins, and a possible ancestor of the state when it finishes. Thus stable properties, which remain true in all descendants once they become true, will hold for the actual system state if they held for the local version obtained by the snapshot.

Many variations of this algorithm exist, but in a self-stabilizing context, most are incorrect. The difficulty is that the system could "awaken" after a traumatic fault in a state where a node has apparently just completed a snapshot, but the local state supposedly gathered might in fact have no relation to the actual state of the system. In the self-stabilizing version, repeated snapshots are taken even when it appear that none is needed, and the node resets the entire system to a correct "home" state when the snapshot seems to have detected an inconsistent global state. Even though this could lead to unnecessary resetting, it does guarantee that eventually an accurate snapshot is taken, and then the reset will correct any problems and no more resets will be necessary until the next traumatic fault.

2.4   Simulations to Ease Fault-Tolerance

A generic approach especially appropriate for aspects involves transformations of an algorithm designed to treat crash failures so that it can be used for stronger types of failures, up to Byzantine failures in synchronous systems. In [2] such simulations are divided into three concerns, each of which is a candidate for encoding as an aspect. First, the possibility of sending messages with different contents to different processors in the same round is treated. Second, a faulty processor can send an arbitrary message, even if it is the same to all neighbors, and finally, problematic behavior can persist over multiple rounds. In this and additional examples, the composition of relatively simple aspects to yield a more complex protocol is natural, again reflecting a central theme of AOSD.

3   Formal Methods for Aspects

3.1   Overview

Along with their flexibility and potential for reuse, aspects introduce new correctness issues that could reduce system reliability. Of course, there is the question of whether the aspect achieves the added functionality (in our case, the degree of fault-tolerance required) whenever it is woven to a system. Because the aspect is not a stand-alone program, and the definitions of the joinpoints are crucial, it is difficult to achieve a generic proof that an aspect adds fault tolerance, without considering a concrete underlying system. Moreover, it is important that the system augmented with an aspect does not violate desired properties that previously were already true of the system without the aspect. There is also the question of possible interference among multiple aspects: it is possible that each aspect individually woven is correct, but when applied together the augmented system violates the desired properties of either some of the aspects or of the underlying system.

Some work has been done on using modern testing techniques including model-based testing and testing frameworks for aspects [54,53]. However, there is still relatively little experience with testing for aspects.

Research on formal methods for aspects is also still at a relatively early stage. However, there are several results that show promise of practicality by exploiting the modularity of aspects. That is, instead of proving properties directly for a complex system including aspects, it may be possible to consider each aspect separately, and verify it relative to a generic specification. Below, we survey some of the major themes in using static code analysis and formal verification for systems with aspects. Many of the techniques are appropriate for the properties needed by fault-tolerance, but such specifications and verifications have not yet been investigated in terms of aspects.

The survey is not intended to be comprehensive, and is unlikely to be completely up-to-date, due to the considerable ongoing activity in this area. On some topics, there is also a greater description of work in which I personally participated and with which I am most familiar. However, the survey does provide a sampling of various approaches and tools for formal verification of systems with aspects.

3.2   Static Code Analysis

In static code analysis, standard categories of aspects are identified using type checking, dataflow analysis, or other code analysis techniques. For superimpositions of distributed algorithms, an informal classification was proposed in [29], and the same distinctions apply to aspects. Three categories of aspects are defined: *Spectative* aspects do not influence the values of underlying variables or conditions for underlying events, and only gather information in local variables. *Regulative* aspects can affect the control of the underlying system (e.g., by short-circuiting underlying computation sequences) in addition to the capabilities of spectative aspects. *Invasive* aspects can change the values of variables in the underlying system, and change the transformations (actions) of the underlying system.

In [30] the additional category of *weakly invasive* aspects is defined as those where the advice finishes in some previously reachable state of the underlying system. For each category, theorems are proven that automatically guarantee that some classes of properties of the underlying system will be maintained in the augmented system, or be such that new properties are easier to establish than for general aspects.

One intuitively clear theorem that can be proven is that all safety and liveness properties of the underlying system that do not involve a next-state temporal modality are maintained in an augmented system with a spectative aspect. Another is that for regulative aspects, all safety properties of the underlying system not containing a next-state operator are maintained in the augmented system (but liveness properties may not be automatically assumed to be maintained, and must be reproven for the augmented system).

In the influential work of Clifton and Leavens [13], the spectative aspects are called observers and a methodology for development is suggested to effectively modularize system development with aspects.

In the work of Rinard, Salcianu, and Bugrara [46], finer distinctions are defined, but the basic three above still appear. That work concentrates on determining the relations between an aspect and a method of the underlying system. If they are orthogonal, the two access disjoint fields, if they are independent neither writes to a field that the other may read or write (but both may read the same field), in an observation relation the advice may read fields that the methods may write, actuation means that the advice may write to a field that the method may read, but they are otherwise independent, and interference means that both may write to the same field.

As already noted, several works have concentrated on static code analysis, using typing and dataflow techniques. Although in the paper defining Observers [13] a tool was not developed, that work points out difficulties of aliasing that can complicate syntactic static analysis of code to determine whether an aspect is an observer. The code analysis system for a simplified aspect language by Sereni and de Moor [48] is intended primarily for code optimization, but the information gathered can also be (and has been) used by the authors to identify spectative aspects. Similarly, in the approach of Storzer and Krinke [52] an extensive interference analysis is made for real Java and AspectJ-like programs, emphasizing the complications introduced by inheritance and multiple instances. Again, the result is to effectively identify spectators/observers (which is there called interference-freedom).

The most extensive static code analysis tool to date is described in the system of Rinard, Salcianu, and Bugrara [46], where standard dataflow techniques are emphasized for AspectJ over Java, and numerous sample programs have been analyzed.

There is also considerable work on using well-known programming slicing techniques based on dataflow in order to identify the extent of influence of an aspect on the underlying system, and in order to identify potential conflicts among aspects . In effect, any potential interactions or conflicts are identified. Such techniques can also be used to reduce the size of the model that must be analyzed when model-checking techniques are to be applied. The first paper on slicing for aspects is by Zhou [55]. Recent work by Balzarotti, D'Ursa, Cavallaro, and Monga [6] includes an implemented slicing system for AspectJ to identify the influence of each aspect.

3.3 Assume-Guarantee Specification and Inductive Verification

A few works have begun to consider inductive proofs for aspects. The basic idea, first described by Devereux [14] and Sipma [51], is that an assume-guarantee paradigm is appropriate for aspect specification and verification. That is, each joinpoint is given an associated assumption of what must be true in the underlying system at that point, and using that assumption, the assertion guaranteed to hold when the appropriate advice has completed is proven to follow from the assumption and the advice code using an inductive proof system, such as PVS [47]. Clearly, it remains to show that the assumption indeed is true whenever the joinpoint is reached in the underlying system. For that task, the aspect advice can be assumed to have fulfilled its guarantee at all preceding return points. The assume-guarantee specification style is also seen in the aspect specifications by Sihman and Katz in [50], where semantic correctness criteria for aspects are also given, and collections of aspects are claimed to be the proper module for independent specification. Sipma also presented some initial ideas on using transition systems to represent aspects and their interactions with underlying systems.

In [30] the assume-guarantee paradigm is shown to allow extending an inductive invariant true of the underlying system to the augmented one (even for invasive aspects) without having to reprove anything for the code from the underlying system. An invariant is defined to be inductive if it only requires itself as a precondition to show that it is preserved by each step. When the invariant is not truly inductive on its own, new proofs may need to be done for the underlying code as part of extending the invariant.

3.4 Model Checking for Validation of Augmented Systems

Adapting model checking tools to treat aspects adds yet another level of complexity to the already-difficult task of model checking software and is still at a relatively early stage of research and development. In [32] a prototype system is described by Katz and Sihman that preprocesses collections of generic application aspects that have specifications themselves given as validation aspects. The idea is that each time the application aspects are woven to a system, the associated validation aspects, that express the specification, are used to generate automatically a series of model checking tasks. If all the tasks are completed successfully, then for the particular weaving of the application aspects over an underlying system, the properties described in the validation aspects are true in the augmented system. The generation of the model checking tasks, and the model checking themselves are in theory automatic and use the same bindings needed for the weaving of the application aspects into the underlying system. The approach is intended to encourage reuse through libraries of aspects, each with a specification given in validation aspects. However, because the entire augmented system is treated at once, there may be problems of scalability with this approach.

3.5   Modular Model Checking for Aspects

In order to have a more modular approach, some work has been done on conducting model checking only for the state machine generated by the aspect code. In the work of Krishnamurthi, Fisler, and Greenberg [35], CTL properties true of the original system are checked to see whether their extension to the augmented system is justified. That work separates finding the joinpoints-the states where new edges to the aspect state machine are to be added— from the analysis of the aspect state machine. The former task is done by a clever reversal of edges in the original state machine to discover states with a history satisfying the joinpoint description. It should be noted that this procedure detects potential pointcuts, in that some of the states identified may also have other paths that reach them but that do not satisfy the pointcut description.

The technique used to check the aspect state machine depends on the backwards marking of atomic formulas common in model checking. Unfortunately, this means that the aspect state machine must reconnect to the machine of the underlying program either at the state that was previously immediately following the added edge to the aspect from the underlying state machine or at one or two states later. These are not always realistic assumptions since the aspect often changes the values of fields, creating new states not in the underlying system at all. In particular, some of the aspects needed for fault tolerance do change the values of the system, and thus cannot be used with this approach, as given.

The first attempt to model check the aspect independently of a weaving to a particular base system is seen in [19]. An aspect is assumed to have an *assumption* about what any base system to which it may be woven should satisfy, and a *result* assertion that is then asserted to be true for an augmented system to which the aspect is woven, whenever the base satisfies the assumption. Both the assumption and result assertions are given in Linear temporal Logic (LTL). A single model is built by weaving the aspect into a state machine that is the tableau corresponding to the assumption. This provides a truly generic proof for the aspect, but there are still various restrictions. In particular, the approach has so far only been shown for weakly invasive aspects, where the state after the aspect advice completes was reachable in the original system. It should be noted that aspects for fault tolerance generally will be in this category, since a state is reached that could have occurred if there were no fault.

3.6   Scenario-Based Model Checking for Conformance

In a scenario-based specification of aspects, as presented in works by Araujo, Whittle, and Kim [1], the aspect is described as an added-on scenario activated at various states (that can depend on the history of computation to that point). In the actual system, the actions of the aspect scenario may be interleaved with other actions, and delayed, rather than executing all at once at each joinpoint. A system specification in this framework consists of regular scenarios and aspect scenarios that interrupt the regular ones when their joinpoint states are reached. The obviously significantly differs from specifications where temporal logic properties or invariants are used, and has a different correctness criterion. A system conforms to such a specification if every possible computation is equivalent to one where the aspects are applied immediately and as a block, interleaved with other scenarios. In [28] model checking is used to guarantee conformance in this sense, by automatically generating an extended model and a series of temporal logic assertions that can be checked using regular model checkers.

3.7   Interference and Conflict Among Aspects

In most of the work above, the relation between an aspect and an underlying system is considered. However, there has also been some work on detecting interference or conflicts among multiple aspects applied to a system. Especially when the entire system is seen as a collection of concerns or aspects, as in HyperJ [43], this approach is essential. As noted, aspects for fault tolerance can interact with aspects for other tasks, or for different forms of faults, and thus such analysis is also critical in this context. Of necessity, most such work concerns a particular composition and weaving (i.e., an augmented system), and is not generic for any weaving of an aspect.

General semantic criteria are described by Sihman and Katz in [49] for checking whether the specifications and applicability conditions of one distributed aspect (or superimposition) are interfered with by another, depending on how they are applied. Since this work depends on the existence of specifications it has not yet been implemented for realistic AOP languages. Using an abstract formalism with rules for composition, Douence, Fradet, and Sudholt present in [16] a framework and techniques to identify overlapping pointcuts and interfering advice. Strong (syntactic) independence, weak (semantic) independence, and an intermediate level based on requirements are defined and transformation rules for their detection are described. This work, like that above, provides a possible basis for analysis tools but has not yet been adapted or implemented for notations widely used in practice. Its main application so far has been in providing semantic foundations for aspect interactions.

In the framework of Compose*, in work by Bergmans, Nagy, and Aksit [42], there are implemented analysis tools which both influence the implementation of Composition Filters, and detect interference among the filters (which correspond to aspects). These tools are based on intercepting messages and then identifying types of filters such as Error (raising an exception), Wait (queueing the message until a condition is satisfied), or Substitute (replace elements of the message and continue). Some of the tools determine possible orderings of actions for a collection of filters and thus are part of the implementation engine, while others can identify impossible combinations, with conflicting message patterns or responses. They thus use static analysis to determine interference among composition filters. Some of the techniques analyze only the filters, while others also take advantage of user-provided requirements annotations.

In [44] Pawlak, Duchien, and Seinturier introduce a notation called CompAr to specify constraints on the application of multiple aspects with around advice (i.e., where advice code is added both before and after the activation of code from the underlying system). A compiler then checks conformance with the constraints, detecting conflicts in a way reminiscent of the Compose* approach, but for a more general context. This work provides an implemented static analysis for interference that seems common to a wide variety of aspect languages.

It should be noted that the tool described in [46] as well as some of the other static analysis tools also have capabilities of detecting interference among aspects. In particular, the tools described earlier based on program slicing (e.g., [6]) are applicable for detecting syntactic conflicts (i.e., potential semantic interference that should be further investigated).

3.8   Integrated Verification Tools for Aspects

Although considerable research has been undertaken on verification of aspects, most existing tools are in a preliminary prototype stage, and emphasize static code analysis. It is clear that a combination of tools will ultimately be necessary, combining static code analysis, model checking, and perhaps inductive proofs. The analysis and proofs will be complemented by reusable testing and simulation suites specific for the aspects. All of these techniques need to be connected through a comprehensive theory that justifies any conclusions on correctness by using formal semantic definitions. The choice of tool depends, among other factors, on the specifications available, on whether the aspect language is amenable to static analysis, and on the kind of properties.

As a first step in this direction, the Common Aspect Proof Environment (CAPE) framework is being developed. This integrated collection of tools for aspects is being designed and implemented as a project in the Formal Methods Lab of AOSD-Europe, an EU Network of Excellence. The architecture and design of the CAPE is available at the AOSD-Europe website [17], and several tools are currently being integrated in a preliminary implementation. The idea is to develop an extensible framework where different types of verification and analysis tools can be applied to systems with aspects, written in a variety of languages with constructs for aspect-oriented programming.

4   Conclusions

A gap has developed between the distributed algorithms community and language developers for systems, when fault-tolerance is considered. The algorithms community develops, reasons about, and evaluates complexity of various algorithms, but does not encapsulate them in language constructs. Moreover, only rarely do the algorithm developers consider how solutions for various kinds of fault tolerance interact with each other and with other parts of the system, or how to modularly express such algorithms so they can be reused. When fault-tolerance is hidden in a system or communication layer, the algorithms and treatment are often fixed, and cannot easily interact with other concerns of the system.

Aspects can be used to modularize many non-functional concerns of complex systems. Rather than attempting to develop language constructs or frameworks only for fault-tolerance, it seems advantageous to take advantage of the existing work on Aspect-Oriented Software Development to help in expressing fault-tolerant algorithms in a reusable configurable way. As seen, formal methods can be used to increase the reliability of such aspects. Interactions among multiple fault-tolerant algorithms, and with other concerns of the system can also be analyzed using known techniques from aspects.

References

1. J. Arajo, J. Whittle, and D. Kim. Modeling and composing scenario-based requirements with aspects. In *The 12th IEEE International Requirements Engineering Conference (RE2004)*, pages 58–67, Kyoto, Japan, September 2004.
2. H. Attiya and J. Welch. *Distributed Computing*. McGraw-Hill Publishing Company, UK., 1998.
3. R. Back and K. Sere. Superposition refinement for reactive systems. *Formal Aspects of Computing*, 8:324–346, 1996.
4. T. Ball, E. Bounimova, B. Cook, V. Levin, J. Lichtenberg, C. McGarvey, B. Ondrusek, S. Rajamani, and A. Ustuner. Thorough static analysis of device drivers. In *Proceedings of EuroSys2006*, pages 73–85. ACM, 2006.
5. T. Ball and S. Rajamani. Automatically validating temporal safety properties of interfaces. In *Proc. of SPIN Workshop on Model Checking of Software*, volume 2057 of *LNCS*, pages 103–122. Springer, 2001.
6. D. Balzarotti, A. D'Ursi, L. Cavallaro, and M. Monga. Slicing aspectj woven code. In *Proc. of Foundations of Aspect Languages Workshop (FOAL05)*, 2005.
7. N. Bhatti, M. Hiltunen, R. Schlichting, and W. Chiu. Coyote: A system for constructing fine-grain configurable communication services. *ACM Transactions on Computer Systems*, 16(4):321–366, 1998.
8. K. M. Chandy and L. Lamport. Distributed snapshots: determining global states of distributed systems. *ACM Transactions on Computer Systems*, 3(1):63–75, Feb 1985.
9. K.M. Chandy and C.V. Ramamoorthy. Rollback and recovery strategies for computer programs. *IEEE Transactions on Computers*, 21(6):546–556, June 1972.
10. R. Chitchyan, A. Rashid, and et al. Report synthesizing state-of-the-art in aspect-oriented requirements engineering, architectures and design. In *AOSD-Europe research report AOSD-Europe-ULANC-9*, pages 1–259, 2005. Available at http://www.aosd-europe.net.
11. S. Clarke. Extending standard UML with model composition semantics. *Science of Computer Programming*, 44(1):71–100, 2002.
12. E. M. Clarke, Jr., O. Grumberg, and D. A. Peled. *Model Checking*. MIT Press, Cambridge, MA, 1999.
13. C. Clifton and G. Leavens. Observers and assistants: a proposal for modular aspect-oriented reasoning. In *Foundations of Aspect Languages (FOAL)*, 2002. also, modified as Spectators and assistants: enabling modular aspect-oriented reasoning, Iowa State TR02-10, 2002.
14. B. Devereux. Compositional reasoning about aspects using alternating-time logic. In *Proc. of Foundations of Aspect Languages Workshop (FOAL03)*, 2003.
15. S. Dolev. *Self-Stabilization*. MIT Press, Cambridge, MA, 2000.
16. R. Douence, P. Fradet, and M. Sudholt. Composition, reuse, and interaction analysis of stateful aspects. In *Proc. of 3th Intl. Conf. on Aspect-Oriented Software Development (AOSD'04)*, pages 141–150. ACM Press, 2004.

17. E. Dror and S. Katz. The architecture of the CAPE. Technical Report AOSD-Europe-Technion-4, AOSD-Europe, February 2006. Available at www.aosd-europe.net.
18. M. Fischer, N. Lynch, and M/ Paterson. Impossibility of distributed consensus with one faulty processor. *Journal of the ACM (JACM)*, 32:374–382, 1985.
19. M. Goldman and S. Katz. Modular generic verification of LTL properties for aspects. In *Proc. of Foundations of Aspect Languages Workshop (FOAL06)*, 2006.
20. J. Hatcliff and M. Dwyer. Using the Bandera Tool Set to model-check properties of concurrent Java software. In K. G. Larsen and M. Nielsen, editors, *Proc. 12th Int. Conf. on Concurrency Theory, CONCUR'01*, volume 2154 of *LNCS*, pages 39–58. Springer-Verlag, 2001.
21. K. Havelund and T. Pressburger. Model checking Java programs using Java PathFinder. *International Journal on Software Tools for Technology Transfer (STTT)*, 2(4), Apr 2000.
22. M. Hiltunen, R. Schlichting, X. Han, M. Cardozo, and R. Das. Real-time dependable channels: Customizing QoS attributes for distributed systems. *IEEE Transactions on Parallel and Distributed Systems*, 10(6):600–612, 1999.
23. M. Hiltunen, F. Taiani, and R. Schlichting. Reflections on aspects and configurable protocols. In *Proc. of 5th Intl. Conf. on Aspect-Oriented Software Development (AOSD'06)*, pages 87–98. ACM Press, 2006.
24. G. J. Holzmann and D. Peled. The state of SPIN. In *Computer Aided Verification (CAV'96)*, volume 1102 of *LNCS*, pages 385–389. Springer-Verlag, 1996.
25. H. Hutchinson and L. Peterson. The x-kernel: an architecture for implementing network protocols. *IEEE Transactions on Software Engineering*, 17(1):64–76, 1991.
26. P. Jalote. *Fault Tolerance in Distributed Systems*. Prentice Hall, 1994.
27. M. Katara and S. Katz. Architectural views of aspects. In *Proc. of 2nd Intl. Conf. on Aspect-Oriented Software Development (AOSD'03)*, pages 1–10. 2003.
28. E. Katz and S. Katz. Verifying scenario-based aspect specifications. In *Proc. Formal Methods: International Symposium of Formal Methods Europe (FM05)*, volume 3582 of *LNCS*, pages 432–447. Springer, 2005.
29. S. Katz. A superimposition control construct for distributed systems. *ACM Transactions on Programming Languages and Systems (TOPLAS)*, 15:337–356, 1993.
30. S. Katz. Aspect categories and classes of temporal properties. *Transactions on Aspect Oriented Software Development (TAOSD)*, 1:106–134, 2006. LNCS 3880.
31. S. Katz and K. Perry. Self-stabilizing extensions for message-passing systems. *Distributed Computing*, 7:17–26, 1993.
32. S. Katz and M. Sihman. Aspect validation using model checking. In *Proc. of Intl. Symposium on Verification*, LNCS 2772, pages 389–411, 2003.
33. G. Kiczales, E. Hilsdale, J. Hugunin, M. Kersten, J. Palm, and W. G. Griswold. An overview of AspectJ. In *Proceedings ECOOP 2001*, LNCS 2072, pages 327–353, Jun 2001. http://aspectj.org.
34. J. Kienzle and S. Gelineau. Ao challenge–implementing the ACID properties for transactional objects. In *Proceedings of 5th Intl. Conference on Aspect-Oriented Software Development (AOSD06)*, pages 202–213, 2006.
35. S. Krishnamurthi, K. Fisler, and M. Greenberg. Verifying aspect advice modularly. In *Proc. of International Conference on Foundations of Software Engineering (FSE04)*, pages 137–146, 2004.
36. L. Lamport. Specifying concurrent program modules. *ACM Transactions on Programming Languages and Systems*, 5(2):190–222, April 1983.

37. J.C. Laprie. *Dependability: Basic Concepts and Terminology –in English, French, German, and Japanese.* Springer-Verlag, 1992. number 5 of Series on Dependable Computing and Fault Tolerance.

38. J.C. Laprie, J. Arlat, C. Beounes, K. Kanoun, and C. Hourtolle. Hardware and software fault-tolerance: definition and analysis of architectural solutions. In *FTCS-17*, pages 116–121, Jun 1987.

39. P.A. Lee and T. Anderson. *Fault Tolerance: Principles and Practice.* Springer-Verlag, 1990. second edition.

40. K. L. McMillan. *Symbolic Model Checking: An Approach to the State Explosion Problem.* Kluwer Academic Publishers, 1993.

41. M Mezini and K. Ostermann. Conquering aspects with Ceasar. In *Proceedings of 2nd Intl. Conference on Aspect-Oriented Software Development (AOSD)*, pages 90–99, 2003.

42. I. Nagy, L. Bergmans, and M. Aksit. Declarative aspect composition. In *Software Engineering Properties of Languages and Aspect Technologies (SPLAT) Workshop associated with AOSD04*, 2004.

43. H. Ossher and P. Tarr. Multi-dimensional separation of concerns and the hyperspace approach. In M. Aksit, editor, *Software Architectures and Component Technology.* Kluwer Academic, 2001.

44. R. Pawlak, L. Duchien, and L. Seinturier. Compar: ensuring safe around advice composition. In *Proc. International Conference for Open Object-Based Distributed Systems (FMOODS05)*, 20045.

45. D.K. Pradhan and N.H. Vaidya. Roll-forward checkpointing scheme: a novel fault-tolerant architecture. *IEEE Transactions on Computers*, 43(10):1163–1174, Oct. 1994.

46. M. Rinard, A. Salcianu, and S. Bugrara. A classification system and analysis for aspect-oriented programs. In *Proc. of International Conference on Foundations of Software Engineering (FSE04)*, 2004.

47. J. Rushby, S. Owre, and N. Shankar. Subtypes for specifications: Predicate subtyping in PVS. *IEEE Transactions on Software Engineering*, 24(9):709–720, September 1998.

48. D. Sereni and O. de Moor. Static analysis of aspects. In *AOSD*, pages 30–39, 2003.

49. M. Sihman and S. Katz. A calculus of superimpositions for distributed systems. In *Proc. of 1st Intl. Conf. on Aspect-Oriented Software Development (AOSD'02)*, pages 28–40. ACM Press, 2002.

50. M. Sihman and S. Katz. Superimposition and aspect-oriented programming. *BCS Computer Journal*, 46(5):529–541, 2003.

51. H. Sipma. A formal model for cross-cutting modular transition systems. In *Proc. of Foundations of Aspect Languages Workshop (FOAL03)*, 2003.

52. M. Storzer and J. Krinke. Interference analysis for aspectj. In *Proc. of Foundations of Aspect Languages Workshop (FOAL03)*, 2003.

53. T. Xie and J. Zhou. A framework and tool supports for generating test inputs of AspectJ programs. In *Proc. of 5th Intl. Conf. on Aspect-Oriented Software Development (AOSD'06)*, pages 190–201. ACM Press, 2006.

54. D. Xu and W. Xu. State-based incremental testing of aspect-oriented programs. In *Proc. of 5th Intl. Conf. on Aspect-Oriented Software Development (AOSD'06)*, pages 180–189. ACM Press, 2006.

55. J. Zhou. Slicing aspect-oriented software. In *IEEE International Workshop on Programming Comprehension*, pages 251–260, 2002.

Rigorous Development of Fault-Tolerant Agent Systems

Linas Laibinis[1], Elena Troubitsyna[1],
Alexei Iliasov[2], and Alexander Romanovsky[2]

[1] Åbo Akademi University, Finland
{Linas.Laibinis, Elena.Troubitsyna}@abo.fi
[2] University of Newcastle upon Tyne, UK
{Alexei.Iliasov, Alexander.Romanovsky}@ncl.ac.uk

Abstract. Agent systems are examples of complex distributed systems. Though agents operate in unreliable communication environment, often such systems have high reliability requirements imposed on them. Therefore, we need methods which allow us not only to ensure system correctness but also to integrate design of fault tolerance mechanisms in the development process. In this paper we present a formal approach for the development of fault tolerant location-based mobile agent systems. Our approach is based on stepwise refinement in the Event B framework. We start from an abstract system specification modelling agents together with their communication environment and gradually introduce implementation details in a number of correctness-preserving transformations. Such stepwise development allows us to specify complex system properties, such as fault tolerance, in a structured and rigorous way. Moreover, it enables a formal representation of essential abstractions used in the development of fault tolerant agent systems, including scopes, roles, locations, and agents. Application of the proposed approach results in designing fault tolerant agent systems in which inter-consistency and inter-operability of agents is ensured by construction.

1 Introduction

Mobile agent systems are complex distributed systems that are dynamically composed of independent agents. Usually agents are designed by different developers to perform individual computational tasks. The agent technology naturally solves the problem of partitioning complex software into smaller parts that are easier to analyse, design and maintain. However, to ensure interoperability of agents, the individual developments should adhere to a certain "standard", which would guarantee compatibility of constructed agents yet avoid over-constraining of the development process. Within IST RODIN project [17] we are working on creating a methodology allowing us to ensure correctness of the development of complex systems dynamically composed of individually developed agents.

In this paper we present a formal derivation of abstract patterns for specifying middleware for mobile location-based agent systems. We conduct the derivation

M. Butler et al. (Eds.): Fault-Tolerant Systems, LNCS 4157, pp. 241–260, 2006.
© Springer-Verlag Berlin Heidelberg 2006

in Event B [2,3] – a framework extending the B Method [1,20] to model complex distributed systems. Event B supports top-down development of systems correct by construction. We start from an abstract specification of the overall agent system, i.e., abstractly model agents together with the location supporting inter-agent communication. In a number of correctness preserving steps we incorporate various system properties, including fault tolerance, into the specification. Finally, we arrive at the specification of entire middleware, which can be decomposed into parts to be implemented by the location and by each individual agent.

In the independent development of individual agents the programmers merely need to augment this abstract part with an implementation of the desired agent functionality. Such an approach allows us to ensure inter-operability of individually developed agents and the correctness of the overall system. Moreover, since the proposed patterns contain abstract specifications of the means for detecting agent failures, such as disconnections and crashes, and the corresponding error recovery procedures, we can guarantee fault tolerance of an agent system developed according to the proposed approach.

Our work is based on an asymmetric model of the agent system within the *location-based* paradigm [12,11,4]. The asymmetric scheme is closer to the traditional service provision architectures. It can support large-scale mobile agent networks in a reliable manner. This scheme also provides a natural way of introducing context-aware computing by defining location as a context. The main disadvantage of the location-based scheme is that an additional infrastructure is required to support mobile agent collaboration. From fault tolerance point of view, this might seem to be disadvantageous, since it introduces additional point of failure in the system. However, since correctness of our middleware is formally verified we avoid this problem.

We proceed as follows: in Section 2 we describe our formal framework – the Event B formalism. In Section 3 we define the essential abstractions used in modelling of Context-Aware Mobile Agent systems – CAMA systems and demonstrate the system approach to specifying such systems in Event B. In Section 4 we show how to introduce the scoping mechanism by refinement in Event B. Finally, in Section 5 we discuss the proposed approach, give overview of the related work and outline future work.

2   Formal Modelling and Refinement in Event B

In this section we present the background for formal development of fault tolerant mobile agent systems in the EventB framework.

2.1   Modelling in Event B

A formal specification is a mathematical model of the required behaviour of a (part of) system. In B, a specification is represented by a collection of modules, called Abstract Machines. The pseudo-programming notation, called Abstract

Machine Notation (AMN), is used in constructing and formally verifying them. An abstract machine encapsulates a local state (local variables) of the machine and provides operations on the state. A simple abstract machine has the following general form:

$$
\begin{aligned}
&\textbf{MACHINE }\; AM \\
&\textbf{SETS }\; TYPES \\
&\textbf{VARIABLES }\; v \\
&\textbf{INVARIANT }\; I \\
&\textbf{INITIALISATION }\; INIT \\
&\textbf{EVENTS} \\
&\quad E_1 \;=\; \ldots \\
&\quad \ldots \\
&\quad E_N \;=\; \ldots \\
&\textbf{END}
\end{aligned}
$$

The machine is uniquely identified by its name AM. The state variables of the machine, v, are declared in the **VARIABLES** clause and initialised in $INIT$ as defined in the **INITIALISATION** clause. The variables in B are strongly typed by constraining predicates of the machine invariant I given in the **INVARIANT** clause. The invariant is usually defined as a conjunction of the constraining predicates and the predicates defining the properties of the system that should be preserved during system execution. All types in B are represented by non-empty sets. Local types can be introduced by enumerating the elements of the type, e.g., $TYPE \;=\; \{element1, element2, \ldots\}$, or by defining them as subsets of already existing types or sets.

In this paper we take the *event-based approach* to specifying mobile agent systems. The operations of event-based systems are called *events* and defined in the **EVENTS** clause. The events are atomic meaning that, once an event is chosen, its execution will run until completion without interference. An event is defined as follows:

$$E = \textbf{WHEN }\; g \;\textbf{ THEN }\; S \;\textbf{ END}$$

where the guard g is a predicate over the state variables v, and the body S is a B statement describing how v are affected by the event.

Several events can be grouped together in an *array of events*. It has the following syntax:

$$AE = \textbf{ANY }\; i \;\textbf{ WHERE }\; C(i) \;\textbf{ THEN }\; S \;\textbf{ END}$$

where i is a list of local distinct indices, $C(i)$ is a list of array conditions, and S is the body of the event.

The occurrence of events represents the observable behaviour of the system. The guard defines the conditions under which the body can be executed, i.e., the event is *enabled*. If several events are enabled simultaneously then one of them is non-deterministically chosen for execution. If no event is enabled (the guard of each event evaluates to *false*) then the system deadlocks, i.e., stops its execution.

B statements that we will use to describe the body of the events have the following syntax:

$$S \quad == \quad x := e \mid \textbf{IF } cond \textbf{ THEN } S1 \textbf{ ELSE } S2 \textbf{ END} \mid S1 \; ; \; S2 \mid$$
$$x \; :: \; T \mid \textbf{ANY } z \textbf{ WHERE } Q \textbf{ THEN } S \textbf{ END} \mid S1 \parallel S2 \mid \; \ldots$$

The first three constructs - an assignment, a conditional statement and a sequential composition have the standard meaning. Sequential composition is disallowed in abstract specifications but permitted in refinements. The remaining constructs allow us to model nondeterministic or parallel behaviour in a specification. Usually they are not implementable so they have to be refined (replaced) with executable constructs at some point of program development. We use two kinds of nondeterministic statements - the nondeterministic assignment and the nondeterministic block. The nondeterministic assignment $x \; :: \; T$ assigns the variable x an arbitrary value from the given set (type) T. The nondeterministic block **ANY** z **WHERE** Q **THEN** S **END** introduces the new local variable z which is initialised (possibly nondeterministically) according to the predicate Q and then used in the statement S. Finally, $S1 \parallel S2$ models parallel (simultaneous) execution of $S1$ and $S2$ provided $S1$ and $S2$ do not have a conflict on state variables. The special case of the parallel execution is a multiple assignment which is denoted as $x, y := e1, e2$.

The B statements are formally defined using the weakest precondition semantics [7]. Intuitively, for a given statement S and a postcondition P, the weakest precondition $wp(S,P)$ describes the set of all such initial states from which execution of S is guaranteed to establish P. The weakest precondition semantics is a foundation for establishing correctness of specifications and verifying refinements between them. To show correctness (consistency) of an event-based system, we should demonstrate that its invariant is *true* in the initial state (i.e., after the initialisation is executed) and that every event preserves the invariant:

$$wp(INIT, I) = true, \quad \text{and}$$
$$g_i \wedge I \Rightarrow wp(E_i, I)$$

2.2   Refinement of Event-Based Systems

The basic idea underlying formal stepwise development is to design the system implementation gradually, by a number of correctness preserving steps, called *refinements*. The refinement process starts from creating an abstract, albeit unimplementable, specification and finishes with generating an executable code. The intermediate stages yield the specifications containing a mixture of abstract mathematical constructs and executable programming artifacts. In general, refinement process can be seen as a way to reduce nondeterminism of the abstract specification, to replace abstract mathematical data structures by data structures implementable on a computer, and, hence, gradually introduce implementation decisions.

Formally, we say that the statement S is algorithmically refined by the statement S', written $S \sqsubseteq S'$, if, whenever S establishes a certain postcondition, so does S' [7]:

$$S \sqsubseteq S' \text{ if and only if for all postconditions } p: \; wp(S,p) \Rightarrow wp(S',p)$$

A more general form of refinement is data refinement. Assume S operates on variables a, u and S' operates on variables c, u. Let R be a predicate over a, c, u. We say that S is data-refined by S' via a relation R, written $S \sqsubseteq_R S'$ iff

$$\text{for all} \quad p: \; R \wedge wp(S,p) \Rightarrow wp(S', (\exists \, a \cdot R \wedge p))$$

In the AMN the results of intermediate development stages - the refinement machines - have essentially the same structure as the more abstract specifications. In addition, the refinement machine explicitly states which specification it refines.

Assume that the refinement machine AM' is a result of refinement of the abstract machine AM:

> **REFINEMENT** AM'
> **REFINES** AM
> **VARIABLES** v'
> **INVARIANT** I'
> **INITIALISATION** $INIT'$
> **EVENTS**
> $E_1 = \ldots$
> $\ldots$
> $E_N = \ldots$
> **END**

In AM' we replace the abstract data structures of AM with the concrete ones. The invariant of $AM' - I' -$ defines now not only the invariant properties of the refined specification, but also the connection between the newly introduced variables and the abstract variables that they replace. For a refinement step to be valid, every possible execution of the refined machine must correspond (via I') to some execution of the abstract machine. To demonstrate this, we should prove that $INIT'$ is a valid refinement of $INIT$, each event of AM' is a valid refinement of its counterpart in AM and that the refined specification does not introduce additional deadlocks, i.e.,

$$wp(INIT', \neg wp(INIT, \neg I')) = true,$$
$$I \wedge I' \wedge g'_i \Rightarrow g_i \wedge wp(S', \neg wp(S, \neg InvC)), \quad \text{and}$$
$$I \wedge \bigvee_i^N g_i \Rightarrow g'_i$$

While introducing implementation details into the abstract specifications we might need to refine granularity of events, i.e., split events. Such refinement is often called *atomicity* refinement. Let us consider the abstract machine AM_A and the refinement machine AM_AR:

	REFINEMENT AM_AR
MACHINE AM_A	**REFINES** AM
VARIABLES v	**VARIABLES** v'
INVARIANT I	**INVARIANT** I'
INITIALISATION $INIT$	**INITIALISATION** $INIT'$
EVENTS	**EVENTS**
E = **WHEN** g	E_1 ref E = **WHEN** g_1 **THEN** S_1 **END**
THEN S **END**	E_2 ref E = **WHEN** g_2 **THEN** S_2 **END**
	E_3 ref E = **WHEN** g_3 **THEN** S_3 **END**
END	**END**

Observe that the abstract event E is replaced by the events E_1, E_2 and E_3 in the refinement machine. To establish refinement between AM_A and AM_AR we should demonstrate that each of the events E_1, E_2 and E_3 is a valid refinement of E. Moreover, we should prove that AM_AR does not introduce additional deadlocks.

Often refinement process introduces new variables and the corresponding computations on them while leaving the previous variables and computations essentially unchanged. Such refinement is referred to as *superposition* refinement. Let us consider the abstract machine AM_S and the refinement machine AM_SR:

	REFINEMENT AM_AR
MACHINE AM_S	**REFINES** AM
VARIABLES a	**VARIABLES** a, b
INVARIANT I	**INVARIANT** I'
	VARIANT V
INITIALISATION $INIT$	**INITIALISATION** $INIT'$
EVENTS	**EVENTS**
E = **WHEN** g	E = **WHEN** g
THEN S **END**	**THEN** S **END**
	E_1 = **WHEN** g_1 **THEN** S_1 **END**
	E_2 = **WHEN** g_2 **THEN** S_2 **END**
END	**END**

Observe that the refinement machine contains the new events E_1 and E_2 as well as the new clause **VARIANT**. The new events define computations on the newly introduced variables b and, hence, can be seen as the events refining the statement *skip* on the abstract variables. Every new event should decrease the value of the variant. This allows us to guarantee that a new event cannot take the control forever, since the variant expression cannot be decreased indefinitely. For each newly introduced event, we should demonstrate that the variant expression is a natural number and execution of the event decreases the variant, i.e.,

$$V \in NAT, \text{ and}$$
$$I' \wedge g_i \Rightarrow wp((n := V;\ S_i),\ n < V)$$

Next we illustrate modelling and refining in Event B by formal development of a mobile agent system.

3   The System Approach to Modelling Agent Systems

3.1   CAMA Structure and Operations

Context-Aware Mobile Agents systems – CAMA systems – are defined via a set of abstractions and operations on them modelling inter-agent communication and operability. The primary goal of defining a CAMA system is to offer programmers a formally-verified basis for rapid development of mobile agent software in a disciplined and structured way.

One of the major contributions of CAMA is a novel mechanism to structure a shared blackboard so that groups of communicating agents can work in isolated coordination spaces, called *scopes* [12]. In addition to isolation of the coordination space, the scoping mechanism also provides a dynamic type-checking facility ensuring agent inter-operability for multi-agent applications. As a result, the scoping mechanism only permits collaboration of the agents with compatible functionality, which is defined by their attributes.

Let us now briefly describe the CAMA abstractions which we will use in our formal modelling. The detailed description of CAMA can be found in [15].

Scope is an abstraction designating an isolated coordination space for compatible agents. A scope creation is initiated by an agent. A scope is defined by a set of roles and restrictions on roles. The restrictions on roles dictate how many agents can play any given role in a scope. In particular, the restrictions for a role R_i are defined by R_i^{min} – the minimum required number of agents for a given role, and R_i^{max} – the maximum allowed number of agents for a given role. For any role R_i supported by a scope, we require that $R_i^{min} \le R_i^{max}$ and $R_i^{max} > 0$.

A location tracks the number of currently taken roles in all created scopes. On the basis of this information it determines the current state of a scope. There are three important states of a scope. Their summary is given in Fig. 1, where *Roles_S* designates a set of roles specific to the scope S and N_r stands for the current number of agents playing the role r in a scope.

A scope in the *pending* state does not allow agents to communicate because there are agents missing in some required roles. When the minimal number of all the required roles is taken, the scope becomes *expanding* or *closed*. In the *expanding* state, a scope supports communication among agents while still allowing other agents to join the scope. In the *closed* state, there are no free roles and no more agents may join the scope.

Scope state	Definition
pending	$\exists\, r \cdot (r \in \mathrm{Roles\_}S \,\wedge\, N_r < R_r^{min})$
expanding	$\forall\, r \cdot (r \in \mathrm{Roles\_}S \,\Rightarrow\, N_r \geq R_r^{min}) \,\wedge$
	$\quad \exists\, r \cdot (r \in \mathrm{Roles\_}S \,\wedge\, N_r < R_r^{max})$
closed	$\forall\, r \cdot (r \in \mathrm{Roles\_}S \,\Rightarrow\, N_r = R_r^{max})$

Fig. 1. States of a scope

Role is an abstract description of an agent functionality. Each scope supports a predefined number of different roles. An agent may implement a number of roles and can also take several roles within different scopes. In this paper we assume that an agent can play at most one role in each scope.

Location is an abstraction defining inter-agent communication. It is the core part of the system because it provides the means of communication and coordination between agents. We assume that each location can be uniquely identified. A location keeps track of the connected agents and their properties in order to update scope states and ensure isolation. A location by itself might also provide some additional services to agents. In addition to supporting scopes as means of agent communication, locations may also offer a support for logical mobility of agents, hosting of agent and agent backup.

Agent is a piece of software implementing a set of roles which allows it to participate in certain scopes. All agents must implement some minimal functionality which allows them to engage in or disengage from a location.

The CAMA operations can be grouped together into the following three categories: location engagement, scoping mechanism, and communication. The communication operations implement the standard LINDA [10] coordination paradigm. The location engagement operations associate or disassociate an agent with a location. The scoping mechanism operations allow an agent to enquiry for available scopes, create new scopes, destroy previously created scopes, join and leave existing scopes.

In a typical scenario, an agent connects to a location and then joins an existing scope. In a scope it can cooperate with agents participating in the same scope. When an agent leaves the scope, it either joins another scope or disconnects from the location.

One of the major challenges in designing agent systems lies in ensuring interoperability of agents. This problem can only be properly addressed if we define the essential properties of the overall agent system, derive the properties to be satisfied by the location and each agent, and ensure that they are preserved in the agent and location development. This goal can be achieved by adopting the system approach to developing agent systems, i.e., modelling the entire set of agents together with the location that provides the infrastructure for agent communication.

3.2 Specifying Fault Tolerant CAMA Systems

Next we present our approach to development of fault tolerant agent systems by refinement. The proposed development adopts the system approach. Indeed, our initial specification given in the machine *Cama* models the entire agent system, i.e., the agents and the location together. The variable *agents* represents the set of agents that joined the location. The operations *Engage* and *Disengage* model joining and leaving the location correspondingly. While an agent is in the location, it performs some computations as modelled by the operation *NormalActivity*. To express that these computations are performed locally within the agent and hence do not affect the abstract state of the system, we model them by the statement *skip*.

MACHINE *Cama*
SETS *Agents*
VARIABLES *agents*
INVARIANT *agents* ⊆ *Agents*
INITIALISATION *agents*:= ∅
EVENTS
   Engage = **ANY** *aa* **WHERE** $aa \in Agents \land aa \notin agents$
      THEN *agents* := *agents* ∪ {*aa*} **END**;
   NormalActivity = **ANY** *aa* **WHERE** $aa \in Agents \land aa \in agents$
      THEN skip END ;
   Disengage = **ANY** *aa* **WHERE** $aa \in Agents \land aa \in agents$
      THEN *agents* := *agents* - {*aa*} **END**
END

CAMA systems should operate in a volatile error prone environment and cope with abnormal situations typical for mobile agents. Hence, a methodology supporting development of CAMA should enable systematic integration of fault tolerance mechanisms into development of CAMA applications. The most typical faults that these applications encounter are temporal connectivity losses, which can cause failures of communication between cooperating agents or between an agent and the location. Since in our approach the agent and location software are developed from the corresponding B specifications, the fault tolerance features should be incorporated into these specifications.

For example, while modelling collaboration between agents in a scope, we have to define the agent behaviour in the presence of message losses, hardware failures, etc. Moreover, while developing agent roles from the corresponding scope specifications, the fault tolerance mechanisms should be distributed between all involved parties. Generally speaking, fault tolerance in CAMA is supported by a set of abstractions used by the application developers and a specialised middleware. The abstractions are developed to systematically separate the normal system behaviour from the abnormal one in a form of a specialised exception handling mechanism. The middleware detects disconnections and, when necessary, involves scope members into coordinated error recovery.

In our initial specification we abstracted away from explicit modelling of system behaviour in presence of faults. In our first refinement step we introduce an abstract representation of the most typical class of faults – a temporal loss of connection. Let us observe that in most cases an agent loses connection only for a short period of time. After connection is restored, the agent is willing to continue its activities virtually uninterrupted. Therefore, after detecting connection loss, the location should not immediately disengage the disconnected agent but rather set a deadline before which the agent should reconnect. If the disconnected agent restores its connection before the deadline then it can continue its normal activity. However, if the agent fails to do it, the location should disengage the agent.

Such a behaviour can be adequately modelled by the timeout mechanism. Upon detecting a disconnection the location activates a timer. If the agent reconnects before the timeout then the timer is stopped. Otherwise, the location forcefully disengages the disconnected agent. To model this behaviour, in the refinement step we introduce the variable *timers* representing the subset of agents that have disconnected but for which the timeouts have not expired yet. Moreover, we introduce the variable *ex_agents* to model the subset of agents that missed their reconnection deadline and should be disengaged from the location. Finally, we add the new events *Disconnect*, *Connect* and *Timer* to model agent disconnection, reconnection and timeout correspondingly.

To ensure that the refined system does not introduce additional deadlocks, we define variant, which limits the number of successive disconnections and reconnections. The constant *Disconn_limit* defines the maximal number of successive disconnections. The variable *disconn_limit* obtains the value *Disconn_limit* in the initialization. Each newly introduced events decreases the value of the variant either by decreasing the value of *disconn_limit* or by removing elements from the set *timers*. The value of the variant is restored by executing the *NormalActivity* event.

In our specification we assume that agent failure due to the loss of connection is detected by the location. However, an agent might by itself detect an error in its functioning and leave the location. Therefore, the agent might get disengaged from the location due to the following three reasons:

- because it has successfully completed its activities in the location,
- due to the disconnection timeout,
- due to a spontaneous failure detected by the agent itself.

In the refined specification we model all these different types of leaving by splitting the operation *Disengage* into three corresponding operations: *NormalLeaving*, *TimerExpiration* and *AgentFailure*. The result of this refinement step – the machine *Cama*1 is given below.

REFINEMENT *Cama1*
REFINES *Cama*
CONSTANTS *Disconn_limit*
PROPERTIES *Disconn_limit* $\in$ **NAT1**
INITIALISATION
 agents := $\emptyset$ || *timers* := $\emptyset$ ||
 ex_agents := $\emptyset$ || *disconn_limit* := *Disconn_limit*
VARIABLES *agents, timers, ex_agents, disconn_limit*
INVARIANT
 timers $\subseteq$ *agents* $\wedge$
 ex_agents $\subseteq$ *agents* $\wedge$
 timers $\cap$ *ex_agents* = $\emptyset$ $\wedge$
 disconn_limit $\in$ **NAT**
VARIANT
 card(*timers*) + *2*disconn_limit*
EVENTS
 Engage = **ANY** *aa* **WHERE** *aa* $\in$ *Agents* $\wedge$ *aa* $\notin$ *agents*
  THEN *agents* := *agents* $\cup$ {*aa*} **END**;
 NormalActivity = **ANY** *aa* **WHERE** *aa* $\in$ *agents*
  THEN *disconn_limit* := *Disconn_limit* **END**;
 NormalLeaving ref Disengage = **ANY** *aa* **WHERE**
   (*aa* $\in$ *agents*) $\wedge$ (*aa* $\notin$ *timers*) $\wedge$ (*aa* $\notin$ *ex_agents*)
  THEN *agents* := *agents* - {*aa*} **END**;
 TimerExpiration ref Disengage = **ANY** *aa* **WHERE**
   (*aa* $\in$ *agents*) $\wedge$ (*aa* $\in$ *ex_agents*)
  THEN *agents* := *agents* - {*aa*} || *ex_agents* := *ex_agents* - {*aa*} **END**;
 AgentFailure ref Disengage = **ANY** *aa* **WHERE**
   (*aa* $\in$ *agents*) $\wedge$ (*aa* $\notin$ *timers*) $\wedge$ (*aa* $\notin$ *ex_agents*)
  THEN *agents* := *agents* - {*aa*} **END**;
 Connect = **ANY** *aa* **WHERE** (*aa* $\in$ *agents*) $\wedge$ (*aa* $\in$ *timers*)
  THEN *timers* := *timers* - {*aa*} **END**;
 Disconnect = **ANY** *aa* **WHERE**
   (*aa* $\in$ *agents*) $\wedge$ (*aa* $\notin$ *ex_agents*) $\wedge$ (*aa* $\notin$ *timers*) $\wedge$ *disconn_limit* > 0
  THEN *timers* := *timers* $\cup$ {*aa*} || *disconn_limit* := *disconn_limit* - 1 **END**;
 Timer = **ANY** *aa* **WHERE** (*aa* $\in$ *agents*) $\wedge$ (*aa* $\in$ *timers*)
  THEN *ex_agents* := *ex_agents* $\cup$ {*aa*} || *timers* := *timers* - {*aa*} **END**
END

Our first refinement step is a combination of the superposition refinement and atomicity refinement. The resultant specification contains an abstract representation of both error detection and error recovery. Hence, already at a high level of abstraction we specify fault tolerance as an intrinsic part of the system behaviour.

4   Introducing Scopes and Roles by Refinement

4.1   Introducing Scoping Mechanism

In the abstract specification and the first refinement step we mainly focused on modelling interactions of agents with the location. Our next refinement step introduces an abstract representation of the scopes as an essential mechanism that governs agent interactions while they are involved in cooperative activities.

The creation of a scope is initiated by an agent, which consequently becomes the scope owner. The other agents might join the scope and become engaged into the scope activities. The agents might also leave the scope at any instance of time. The scope owner cannot leave the scope but might close it (this action is not permitted for other agents). When the scope owner closes the scope, it forces all agents participating in the scope to leave.

The introduction of the scoping mechanism also enforces certain actions to be executed when an agent decides to leave a location. Namely, an agent should first leave or close (if it is the scope owner) all scopes in which it is active.

The scoping mechanism also has a deep impact on modelling error recovery in agent systems. For instance, if a scope owner irrecoverably fails, then, to recover the system from this error, the location should close the affected scope and force all agents in this scope to leave.

While refining the machine *Cama*1, we introduce the variable *scopes*, which is defined as a relation associating the active scopes with the agents participating in them. Moreover, the variable *sowner* is introduced to model scope owners. It is defined as a partial function from the active scopes to agents.

We define the new events *Create, Join, Leave* and *Delete* to model creating a scope by the owner, joining and leaving it by agents, as well as closing a scope. In the excerpt from the refinement machine *Cama*2, we demonstrate introducing the new variables and events as well as the effect of the refinement on the events *AgentFailure* and *TimerExpiration*. The guard of the event *NormalLeaving* is now strengthened to disallow an agent to leave the location when it is still active in some scopes.

REFINEMENT *Cama2*
REFINES *Cama1*
SETS *ScopeName*
DEFINITIONS $activeAgent(aa) == (aa \notin ex\_agents \land aa \notin timers)$
VARIABLES ... , *scopes, sowner*
INVARIANT
   $scopes \in ScopeName \leftrightarrow agents \land sowner \in ScopeName \nrightarrow agents \land$
   $\mathbf{dom}(sowner) = \mathbf{dom}(scopes) \land sowner \subseteq scopes$
EVENTS
   ...
   Create = ANY *aa, nn* **WHERE** $(aa \in agents) \land (activeAgent(aa)) \land$
          $(nn \in ScopeName) \land (nn \notin \mathbf{dom}(scopes))$
          THEN CHOICE

$scopes := scopes \cup \{nn \mapsto aa\} \parallel sowner := sowner \cup \{nn \mapsto aa\}$
   OR skip END
  END;
Join = **ANY** aa, nn **WHERE** $(aa \in agents) \wedge (activeAgent(aa) \wedge$
   $(nn \in \mathbf{dom}(scopes)) \wedge ((nn \mapsto aa) \notin scopes)$
  THEN CHOICE $scopes := scopes \cup \{nn \mapsto aa\}$ **OR skip END**
  END;
Leave = **ANY** aa, nn **WHERE** $nn \in \mathbf{dom}(scopes) \wedge aa \in agents \wedge$
  $activeAgent(aa) \wedge (nn \mapsto aa) \in scopes \wedge aa \neq sowner(nn)$
  THEN $scopes := scopes - \{nn \mapsto aa\}$ **END**;
Delete = **ANY** aa, nn **WHERE** $nn \in \mathbf{dom}(scopes) \wedge aa \in agents \wedge$
  $activeAgent(aa) \wedge aa{=}sowner(nn)$
  THEN $scopes, sowner := \{nn\} \lhd scopes, \{nn\} \lhd sowner$ **END**;
NormalLeaving = **ANY** aa **WHERE** $aa \in agents \wedge aa \notin timers \wedge$
  $activeAgent(aa) \wedge aa \notin \mathbf{ran}(scopes) \wedge aa \notin \mathbf{ran}(sowner)$
  THEN $agents := agents - \{aa\}$ **END**;
TimerExpiration = **ANY** aa **WHERE** $aa \in agents \wedge aa \in ex\_agents$
  THEN
   $agents := agents - \{aa\}; scopes := scopes \rhd \{aa\};$
   $scopes := sowner^{-1}[\{aa\}] \lhd scopes;$
   $ex\_agents := ex\_agents - \{aa\}; sowner := sowner \rhd \{aa\}$
  END;
AgentFailure = **ANY** aa **WHERE** $aa \in agents \wedge activeAgent(aa)$
  THEN
   $agents := agents - \{aa\}; scopes := scopes \rhd \{aa\};$
   $scopes := sowner^{-1}[\{aa\}] \lhd scopes; sowner := sowner \rhd \{aa\}$
  END
 END

Note that the domain substraction $\lhd$ and the range substraction $\rhd$ operations
are used here to update the variables *scopes* and *sowner*. They allow us to remove
the data associated with the corresponding subsets of domains and ranges.

4.2 Introducing Failure Modes and Error Recovery

In our current specification the event *AgentFailure* treats any agent failure as an
unrecoverable error. Indeed, upon detecting an error, the failed agent is removed
from the scope and disengaged from the location. In our next refinement step we
distinguish between recoverable and irrecoverable errors. Namely, upon detecting
an error the agent at first tries to recover from it (probably involving some other
agents in the error recovery). If the error recovery eventually succeeds then the
normal operational state of the agent is restored. Otherwise, the error is treated
as irrecoverable.

 We introduce the variable *astate* to model the current state of the agent. The
variable *astate* can have one of three values: *OK, RE* or *KO*, designating a fault
free agent state, a recovery state, and an irrecoverable error correspondingly. We

introduce the event *AgentRecoveryStart* which is triggered when an agent becomes involved in an error recovery procedure. Observe that *AgentRecoveryStart* implicitly models two situations:

- when an agent itself detects an error and subsequently initiates its own error recovery,
- when an agent decides to become involved into co-operative recovery from another agent failure.

In both cases the state of the agent is changed from OK to RE.

The event *AgentRecovery* abstractly models the error recovery procedure. Error recovery might succeed and restore the fault free agent state OK or continue, i.e., leave the agent in the recovery state RE. Finally, error recovery might fail, as modelled by the event *AgentRecoveryFailure*. The event *AgentRecoveryFailure* enables the event *AgentFailure*, which removes the irrecoverably failed agent from the corresponding scopes and disengages it from the location.

While specifying error recovery procedure, it is crucial to ensure that the error recovery terminates, i.e., does not continue forever. To ensure this, we introduce the variable *recovery_limit*, which limits the amount of error recovery attempts for each agent. Each attempt of error recovery decrements *recovery_limit*. As soon as for some agent *recovery_limit* becomes zero, agent error recovery terminates and the error is treated as irrecoverable.

As in our previous refinement steps, we define the system variant to ensure that newly introduced events converge, i.e., do not take the control forever. Here we define the variant as the sum of *recovery_limit* of agents. However, in this refinement step the variant also allows us to express an essential property of the system – the termination of the error recovery procedure.

The introduction of agent states affects most of the events – their guards become strengthened to ensure that only fault free agents can perform normal activities, engage into location and disengage from it, as well as create and close scopes. In the excerpt from the refinement machine *Cama3*, we present only the newly introduced events and the refined event *AgentFailure*.

REFINEMENT *Cama3*
REFINES *Cama2*
SETS $STATE = \{OK, KO, RE\}$
DEFINITIONS $activeAgent(xx) == (xx \notin ex\_agents \wedge xx \notin timers)$
VARIABLES ..., *astate*, *recovery_limit*
INVARIANT
   ... $\wedge\ astate \in agents \rightarrow STATE \wedge recovery\_limit \in agents \rightarrow$ **NAT**
VARIANT $\sum aa.(aa \in agents \mid recovery\_limit(aa))$
EVENTS
   ...

  AgentFailure = **ANY** *aa* **WHERE**
      $aa \in agents \wedge activeAgent(aa) \wedge astate(aa) = KO$
    THEN
      $agents := agents - \{aa\};\ scopes := scopes \rhd \{aa\};$

$scopes := sowner^{-1}\,[\{aa\}] \lhd scopes;\ sowner := sowner \rhd \{aa\};$
$astate := aa \lhd astate;\ recovery\_limit := aa \lhd recovery\_limit$
END;

AgentRecovery $= \textbf{ANY}\ aa\ \textbf{WHERE}\ aa \in agents \wedge activeAgent(aa) \wedge$
$astate(aa) = RE \wedge recovery\_limit(aa) > 0$
THEN
$recovery\_limit(aa) := recovery\_limit(aa) \text{ - } 1\ \|$
$\textbf{ANY}\ vv\ \textbf{WHERE}\ vv \in \{OK,\ RE\}\ \textbf{THEN}\ astate(aa) := vv\ \textbf{END}$
END;

AgentRecoveryStart $= \textbf{ANY}\ aa\ \textbf{WHERE}\ aa \in agents \wedge activeAgent(aa) \wedge$
$astate(aa) = OK \wedge recovery\_limit(aa) > 0$
THEN
$recovery\_limit(aa) := recovery\_limit(aa) \text{ - } 1\ \|$
$astate(aa) := RE$
END;

AgentRecoveryFailure $= \textbf{ANY}\ aa\ \textbf{WHERE}\ aa \in agents \wedge activeAgent(aa) \wedge$
$astate(aa) = RE \wedge recovery\_limit(aa) > 0$
THEN
$recovery\_limit(aa) := recovery\_limit(aa) \text{ - } 1\ \|$
$astate(aa) := KO$
END

END

4.3   Defining Roles in a Scope

Each scope provides the isolated coordination space for compatible agents to communicate. Compatibility of agents is defined by their roles – abstract descriptions of agent functionality. To ensure compatibility of agents in a scope, each scope support a certain predefined set of roles. When an agent joins a scope, it chooses one of the supported roles. We assume that an agent can join a scope only in one role and this role remains the same while the agent is in the scope. However, an agent might leave a scope and join it in another role later.

The creator of the scope defines the minimal and maximal numbers of agents that are allowed to play each supported role. This is dictated by the logical conditions on the scope functionality. For instance, if the scope is created for purchasing a certain item on an electronic auction then there are must be only one seller and at least one buyer for a scope to function properly.

However, agent systems are asynchronous systems. Therefore, at the time of scope creation it cannot be guaranteed that agents will take all the required roles in the right proportions at once and the scope will instantly become functional. Since agents join and leave the scope arbitrarily, the scope can be in various states at different instances of time: *pending*, when the number of agents is still insufficient for normal functioning of the scope; *expanding*, when the scope is functional but new agents can still join it; *closed*, when the maximal allowed number of agents per each role is reached.

Though in our next refinement step we abstract away from representing the number of agents which has taken each of the supported roles, we introduce the function *role_status*, which returns the value

- *Pending*, if the minimal number of agents in this particular role is not yet reached,
- *Expanding*, if the minimal number of agents in this role has already joined the scope but the maximal number has not yet been reached,
- *Closed*, if the maximal allowed number of agent has already taken this role.

We introduce the variable *scope_roles*, that stores the information about which role an agent took when joining the scope. To model the state of the scope we introduce the variable *scope_status*, which takes the values from the set $\{Pending, Expanding, Closed\}$. The value of *scope_status* directly depends on the values of *role_status* for this particular scope. This conditions are defined as a part of the invariant as follows:

$$\forall\ ss.\ (ss \in ScopeName \land ss \in \mathbf{dom}(scope\_status) \Rightarrow$$
$$(scope\_status(ss)=Pending \Rightarrow Pending \in \mathbf{ran}(role\_status(ss)))) \land$$

$$\forall\ ss.\ (ss \in ScopeName \land ss \in \mathbf{dom}(scope\_status) \Rightarrow$$
$$(scope\_status(ss)=Closed \Rightarrow \mathbf{ran}(role\_status(ss))=\{Closed\})) \land$$

$$\forall\ ss.\ (ss \in ScopeName \land ss \in \mathbf{dom}(scope\_status) \Rightarrow$$
$$(scope\_status(ss)=Expanding \Rightarrow Pending \notin \mathbf{ran}(role\_status(ss)) \land$$
$$Expanding \in \mathbf{ran}(role\_status(ss))))$$

Let us observe that, when an agent fails, we need to update the states of all the scopes in which it has been active and all roles that it has been taking in them. We introduce the variable *affected_scopes* to model the scopes for which we need to re-evaluate their states and the event *StatusUpdate* that actually performs re-evaluation of status of each scope in *affected_scopes*. Moreover, when an agent joins or leaves a scope, we have to update the status of the taken role as well as re-evaluate the state of the scope. The events which are the most significantly affected by this refinement, as well as the newly introduced event *StatusUpdate* are presented below.

$\mathbf{Join} = \mathbf{ANY}\ aa,\ nn,\ rr\ \mathbf{WHERE}$
$\quad aa \in agents \land nn \in \mathbf{dom}(scopes)\ \land$
$\quad rr \in Role \land activeAgent(aa) \land (nn \mapsto aa) \notin scopes\ \land$
$\quad astate(aa) = OK \land role\_status(nn)(rr) \in \{Pending, Expanding\}\ \land$
$\quad \neg\ (nn \in affectedScopes)$
$\quad \mathbf{THEN}$
$\quad \mathbf{CHOICE}$
$\quad\quad scopes := scopes \cup \{nn \mapsto aa\};$
$\quad\quad scope\_roles(nn,aa) := rr;$
$\quad\quad \mathbf{ANY}\ rstatus\ \mathbf{WHERE}\ rstatus \in Status$

THEN
    $role\_status(nn)(rr) := rstatus$
END;
ANY new_st **WHERE** $new\_st \in scopeEval(nn)$
THEN
    $scope\_status(nn) := new\_st$
END
OR skip END
END;

AgentFailure = ANY aa **WHERE**
    $aa \in agents \wedge activeAgent(aa) \wedge astate(aa) = KO$
THEN
    $agents := agents - \{aa\}; \quad astate := \{aa\} \vartriangleleft astate;$
    $recovery\_limit := \{aa\} \vartriangleleft recovery\_limit;$
    $scopes := sowner^{-1}[\{aa\}] \vartriangleleft scopes ;$
    $affectedScopes := \mathbf{dom} (scopes \vartriangleright \{aa\}); \quad scopes := scopes \vartriangleright \{aa\};$
    $sowner := sowner \vartriangleright \{aa\}; \quad scope\_roles := scopes \vartriangleleft scope\_roles;$
    $scope\_status := \mathbf{dom}(scopes) \vartriangleleft scope\_status;$
    $role\_status := \mathbf{dom}(scopes) \vartriangleleft role\_status$
END;

StatusUpdate = ANY ss **WHERE** $ss \in affectedScopes$
THEN
    ANY new_st **WHERE** $new\_st \in scopeEval(ss)$
    THEN
        $scope\_status(ss) := new\_st$
    END;
    $affectedScopes := affectedScopes - \{ss\}$
END

Due to the lack of space, we omit presenting the B specifications in full length. The complete development can be found in the accompanying technical report [14].

We can continue the refinement process by introducing more low-level implementation details into our specification. For example, we can replace the variable *role_status* with the variables defining the minimal and maximal numbers of agents allowed to play a particular role in a created scope. Also, the presented error recovery mechanism can be further refined by introducing special messages (exceptions) that agents exchange when they cannot cope with some particular failure or erroneous situation.

The presented formal development has been completely verified by AtelierB [6] – an automatic tool supporting B. The use of AtelierB has significantly eased verification of the refinement process, since the tool generated all the required proofs and proved most of them automatically. Approximately

250 non-trivial proofs were generated and about 80 % of them were proved automatically by the tool. The remaining proof obligations have been discharged using the interactive prover provided by AtelierB. We observed that the most difficult to prove were the properties relating the scope status with the status of collaborating agents in the last refinement step. Also the later refinement steps required significant efforts for proving that newly introduced events converge, i.e., do not introduce additional deadlocks.

5   Conclusions

In this paper we have done two major technical contributions. First, we have defined the abstractions required to model behaviour of mobile location-based agent systems. Second, based on these abstractions we formally developed generic middleware for fault tolerant agent systems.

In our development we adapted the system approach, i.e., captured the behaviour of agents together with their communication environment. While carrying out the development of the system by refinement, we modelled the essential properties of agent systems and incorporated fault tolerance mechanisms into the system specification. We demonstrated how to define the mechanisms for tolerating agent disconnections typical for mobile systems as well as agent crashes.

The proposed approach provides the developers of agent systems with a formal basis for ensuring inter-operability of independently developed agents. Indeed, by decomposing the proposed formal model of the middleware into the parts to be implemented by the agents and by the location and ensuring adherence of their implementations to these specifications, we can guarantee agent inter-operability.

By straightforward translation of the proposed formal specification we obtained an implementation of the CAMA middleware in C [13]. The formal specification has significantly simplified the implementation process, which is usually cumbersome and error-prone due to distributive nature of the system.

Another paper [15] devoted to CAMA appearing in this book describes a method for verification of temporal properties of CAMA systems configurations. Configurations are made of a number of cooperating agents. The system evolution is constrained by a set of properties. Process algebra notation is used to describe configurations and Petri nets-based model checker is applied for the verification. The process algebra incorporates LINDA communication mechanism augmented with the scoping mechanism, which we formally specified in this paper. The range of verified properties includes deadlocks detection, proper use of the scoping mechanism and other application-specific properties. The formal development in B presented here can provide valuable inputs to model checking. For instance, the scope state invariants defined in out last refinement can be used by the model checker to verify that agents do not attempt to execute any illegal scope operations.

We believe that the approaches presented in these two papers well complement each other. Static verification with the B Method is used to develop a fine-grained model of the middleware. The model contains enough details to lay the foundation for an effective implementation. On the other hand, model checking approach uses a more abstract model of the middleware but permits analysis of system dynamics. Model checking helps to overcome the limitations of the static verification approach, while static verification is not prone to state explosion and thus suitable for modelling large systems.

A formalization of mobile agent systems has been proposed by Roman et al. [19]. In their approach agent systems are specified using the UNITY notation and then verified using the UNITY proof techniques. The latest extension, called ContextUNITY [18], also captures the essential characteristics of context-awareness in mobile agent systems. However, this approach focuses primary on specifying agent systems and leaves the gap between a formal specification and implementation. The use of refinement in our approach allows us to overcome this limitation.

Fisher and Ghidini have presented a formal logic for describing agent activities [9]. They proposed either to deduce agent correctness from an agent specification via a number of transformations or verify it using a model checker. In their work, communication is modelled very abstractly by representing a list of external messages for each agent. This restricts reasoning about agent interoperability, which is supported in our approach.

Model checking techniques have also been successfully employed for verifying agent systems. For example, [5] discusses model checking of a BDI-based formal agent model, [8] describes a verification of π-calculus based process algebra for mobile agents, and [16] presents modelling of fault-tolerant agents by stochastic petri nets. However, model checking approaches typically suffer from the state space explosion problem, which is especially acute for large systems. The major advantage of our approach that it avoids this problem.

In our future work we are planning to extend the proposed approach in two directions. On the one hand, it would be interesting to investigate the use of decomposition to derive role-structured agent software from the overall system specification. On the other hand, it would also be appealing to explore the formal specification of cooperative recovery as a basic mechanism for fault tolerance in agent systems.

Acknowledgments

This work is supported by IST FP6 RODIN Project.

References

1. J.-R. Abrial. *The B-Book*. Cambridge University Press, 1996.
2. J.-R. Abrial and L.Mussat. Introducing Dynamic Constraints in B. In *Proc. of Second International B Conference*, LNCS 1393, Springer-Verlag, 1998.
3. J.-R. Abrial. Event Driven Sequential Program Construction. Available at http://www.matisse.qinetiq.com, 2000.

4. B. Arief, A. Iliasov and A. Romanovsky. On Using the CAMA Framework for Developing Open Mobile Fault Tolerant Agent Systems. University of Newcastle, 2006.
5. R. H. Bordini, M.Fisher, W. Visser, and M. Wooldridge. Model checking rational agents. *IEEE Intelligent Systems, Special Issue on Dependable Agent Systems*, 19(5):46-52, 2004.
6. Clearsy. *AtelierB: User and Reference Manuals*. Available at http://www.atelierb. societe.com/index_uk.html.
7. E.W. Dijkstra. *A Discipline of Programming*. Prentice-Hall International, 1976.
8. G.-L. Ferrari, S. Gnesi, U. Montanari and M. Pistore. A model-checking verification environment for mobile processes. *ACM Transactions on Software Engineering Methodology*, 12(4):440-473, ACM Press, 2003.
9. M. Fisher and C. Ghidini. The ABC of Rational Agent Modelling. In *Proc. of the first international joint conference on autonomous agents and multiagent systems (AAMAS02)*. Bologna, Italy, July 2002.
10. D.Gelernter. Generative Communication in Linda. *ACM Transactions on Programming Languages and Systems*, 7(1): 80-112, 1985.
11. A. Iliasov and A. Romanovsky. Exception Handling in Coordination-based Mobile Environments. In *Proc. of the 29th Annual International Computer Software and Applications Conference (COMPSAC 2005)*, pp.341-350, IEEE Computer Society Press, 2005.
12. A. Iliasov and A. Romanovsky. CAMA: Structured Coordination Space and Exception Propagation Mechanism for Mobile Agents. Presented at *ECOOP 2005 Workshop on Exception Handling in Object Oriented Systems: Developing Systems that Handle Exceptions*, Glasgow, UK, 2005.
13. A. Iliasov. Implementation of Cama Middleware. Available online at http://sourceforge.net/projects/cama [Last accessed: 14 November 2005].
14. A. Iliasov, L. Laibinis, A. Romanovsky and E. Troubitsyna. *Rigorous Development of Fault Tolerant Agent Systems*. TUCS Technical Report No.762, March 2006.
15. A.Iliasov, V. Khomenko, M. Koutny, and A. Romanovsky. On Specification and Verification of Location-based Fault Tolerant Mobile Systems. In M.Butler, C.Jones, A.Romanovsky and E.Troubitsyna (Eds.) *Rigorous development of complex fault tolerant systems*. LNCS 4157, 2006.
16. M.R. Lyu, X. Chen, and T.-Y. Wong. Design and Evaluation of a Fault Tolerant Mobile Agent System. *IEEE Intelligent Systems, Special Issue on Dependable Agent Systems*, 19(5):32-38, 2004.
17. Rigorous Open Development Environment for Complex Systems, IST FP6 STREP project, online at http://rodin.cs.ncl.ac.uk/.
18. G.-C. Roman, C.Julien and J.Payton. A Formal Treatment of Context-Awareness. In *Proc. of FASE'2004*, LNCS 2984, Springer-Verlag, 2004.
19. G.-C. Roman, P.McCann and J.Plun. Mobile UNITY: Reasoning and Specification in Mobile Computing. *ACM Transactions of Software Engineering and Methodology*, July 1997.
20. S.Schneider. *The B Method. An Introduction*. Palgrave, 2001.

Formal Service-Oriented Development of Fault Tolerant Communicating Systems

Linas Laibinis[1], Elena Troubitsyna[1], Sari Leppänen[2],
Johan Lilius[1], and Qaisar Ahmad Malik[1]

[1] Åbo Akademi University, Finland
[2] Nokia Research Center, Finland
{Linas.Laibinis, Elena.Troubitsyna, Johan.Lilius, Qaisar.Malik}@abo.fi,
Sari.Leppanen@nokia.com

Abstract. Telecommunication systems should have a high degree of availability, i.e., high probability of correct and timely provision of requested services. To achieve this, correctness of software for such systems and system fault tolerance should be ensured. Application of formal methods helps us to gain confidence in building correct software. However, to be used in practice, formal methods should be well integrated into existing development process. In this paper we propose a formal model-driven approach to development of communicating systems. Essentially our approach formalizes and extends Lyra – a top-down service-oriented method for development of communicating systems. Lyra is based on transformation and decomposition of models expressed in UML2. We formalize Lyra in the B Method by proposing a set of formal specification and refinement patterns reflecting the essential models and transformations of the Lyra service specification, decomposition and distribution phases. Moreover, we extend Lyra to integrate reasoning about fault tolerance in the entire development flow.

Keywords: communicating systems, service-oriented development, fault tolerance, UML, B Method.

1 Introduction

Modern telecommunication systems are usually distributed software-intensive systems providing a large variety of services to their users. Development of software for such systems is inherently complex and error prone. However, software failures might lead to unavailability or incorrect provision of system services, which in turn could incur significant financial losses. Hence it is important to guarantee correctness of software for telecommunication systems.

Formal methods have been traditionally used for reasoning about software correctness. Nevertheless, they are yet insufficiently well integrated into current development practice. Unlike formal methods, Unified Modeling Language (UML) [18] has a lower degree of rigor for reasoning about software correctness but is widely accepted in industry. UML is a general purpose modelling language and, to be used effectively, should be tailored to a specific application domain.

M. Butler et al. (Eds.): Fault-Tolerant Systems, LNCS 4157, pp. 261–287, 2006.

Nokia Research Center has developed the design method Lyra [15] – a UML2-based service-oriented method specific to the domain of communicating systems and communication protocols. The design flow of Lyra is based on the concepts of decomposition and preservation of the externally observable behaviour. The system behaviour is modularised and organized into hierarchical layers according to the external communication and related interfaces. It allows the designers to derive the distributed network architecture from the functional system requirements via a number of model transformations.

From the beginning Lyra has been developed in such a way that it would be possible to bring formal methods (such as program refinement, model checking, model-based testing etc.) into more extensive industrial use. A formalization of the Lyra development would allow us to ensure correctness of system design via automatic and formally verified construction. The achievement of such a formalization would be considered as significant added value for industry.

In this paper we propose a set of formal specification and refinement patterns reflecting the essential models and transformations of Lyra. Our approach is based on stepwise refinement of a formal system model in the B Method [3] – a formal framework with automatic tool support. While developing a system by refinement, we start from an abstract specification and gradually incorporate implementation details into it until executable code is obtained. While formalizing Lyra, we single out a generic concept of a communicating service component and propose patterns for specifying and refining it. In the refinement process the service component is decomposed into a set of service components of smaller granularity specified according to the proposed pattern. Moreover, we demonstrate that the process of distributing service components between different network elements can also be captured by the notion of refinement.

To achieve system fault tolerance, we extend Lyra to integrate modelling of fault tolerance mechanisms into the entire development flow. We demonstrate how to formally specify error recovery by rollbacks as well as reason about error recovery termination.

The proposed formal specification and development patterns establish a background for automatic generation of formal specifications from UML2 models and expressing model transformations as refinement steps. Via automation of the UML2-based Lyra design flow we aim at smooth incorporation of formal methods into existing development practice.

2   Lyra: Service-Based Development of Communicating Systems

2.1   Overview of Lyra

Lyra [15] is a model-driven and component-based design method for the development of communicating systems and communication protocols. It has been developed in the Nokia Research Center by integrating the best practices and design patterns established in the area of communicating systems. The method covers all industrial specification and design phases from prestandardisation to final implementation. It has been successfully applied in large-scale UML2-based industrial software development, e.g., for specification of architecture for several network components, standardisation of 3GPP protocols, implementation of several network protocols etc.

Lyra has four main phases: Service Specification, Service Decomposition, Service Distribution and Service Implementation. The *Service Specification* phase focuses on defining services provided by the system and their users. The goal of this phase is to define the externally observable behaviour of the system level services via deriving logical user interfaces. In the *Service Decomposition* phase the abstract model produced at the previous stage is decomposed in a stepwise and top-down fashion into a set of service components and logical interfaces between them. The result of this phase is the logical architecture of the service implementations. In the *Service Distribution* phase, the logical architecture of services is distributed over a given platform architecture. Finally, in the *Service Implementation* phase, the structural elements are adjusted and integrated into the target environment, low-level implementation details are added and platform-specific code is generated. Next we discuss Lyra in more detail with an example.

2.2   Lyra by Example

We model a positioning system which provides positioning services to calculate the physical location of a given item of user equipment (UE) in a mobile network [1,2]. We consider Position Calculation Application Part (PCAP), which manages communication between two standard network elements. We assume that the PCAP functional requirements are correctly defined [1,2] and, hence, focus on the architectural decomposition and distribution decisions.

The Service Specification phase starts from creating the domain model of the system. It describes the system with included system level services and different types of external users. Each association connecting an external user and a system level service corresponds to a logical interface. For the system and the system level services we define active classes, while for each type of an external user we define the corresponding external class. The relationships between the system level services and their users become candidates for *PSAPs - Provided Service Access Points* of the system level services. The logical interfaces are attached to the classes with ports. The domain model for the Positioning system and its service PositionCalculation is shown in Fig.1(a) and PSAP of the Positioning system – *L_User PSAP* is shown in Fig.1(b). The UML2 interfaces *L_ToPositioning* and *L_FromPositioning* define the signals and signal parameters of *L_user PSAP*. We formally describe the communication between a system level service and its user(s) in the *PSAPCommunication* state machine as illustrated in Fig.1(c). The positioning request *pc_req* received from the user is always replied: with the signal *pc_cnf* in case of success, and with the signal *pc_fail_cnf* otherwise.

To implement its own services, the system usually uses external entities. For instance, to provide the *PositionCalculation* service, the positioning system

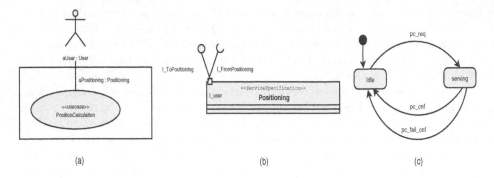

Fig. 1. (a) Domain Model. (b) PSAP of Positioning. (c) State diagram.

should first request Radio Network Database *(DB)* for an approximate position of User Equipment *(UE)*. The information obtained from *DB* is used to contact *UE* and request it to emit a radio signal. At the same time, one or more Reference Location Measurement Unit devices *(ReferenceLMU)* are contacted to provide additional measurements of radio signals. The radio measurements obtained from *UE* and *ReferenceLMU* are used to calculate the exact position of *UE*. The calculation is done by the Algorithm service provider *(Algorithm)*, which produces the final estimation of the *UE* location. Let us observe that the services provided by the external entities partition execution of the *PositionCalculation* service into the corresponding stages. In the next phase of the Lyra development - *Service Decomposition* - we focus on specifying the service execution according to the identified stages.

In the Service Decomposition phase, we introduce the providers of external services into the domain model constructed previously, as shown in Fig.2(a). The model includes the external service providers *DB, UE, ReferenceLMU* and *Algorithm*, which are then defined as the external classes. For each association between a system level service and the corresponding external class we define a logical interface. The logical interfaces are attached to the corresponding classes via ports called *USAPs – Used Service Access Points*, as presented in Fig.2(b).

Let us observe that the system behaviour is modularised according to the related service access points – PSAPs and USAPs. Moreover, the functional architecture is defined in terms of service components, which encapsulate the functionality related to a single execution stage or another logical piece of functionality.

In Fig.3(a) we present the architecture diagram of the *Positioning system*. Here *ServiceDirector* plays two roles: it controls the service execution flow and handles the communication on the PSAP. The behaviour of *ServiceDirector* is presented in Fig.3(b). The top-most state machine specifies the communication on PSAP, while the state submachine *Serving* specifies a valid execution flow of the position calculation. The substates of *Serving* encapsulate the stage-specific behaviour and can be represented as the corresponding submachines. In their

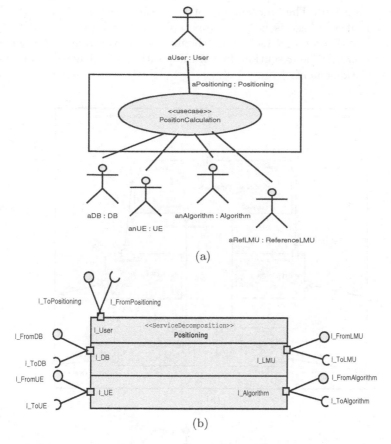

Fig. 2. (a) Domain Model. (b) PSAP and USAPs of Positioning.

turns, these machines (omitted here) include the specifications of specific PSAP-USAP communications.

The modular system model produced at the Service Decomposition phase allows us to analyse various distribution models. In the next phase – Service Distribution – the service components are distributed over a given network architecture. The signalling network protocols are used for communication between the service components allocated on distant network elements.

In Fig.4(a) we illustrate the physical structure of the distributed positioning system. Here *Positioning_RNC* and *Positioning_SAS* represent the predefined network elements called RNC and SAS correspondingly. The standard interface *Iupc* is used in the communication between them. We map the functional architecture obtained at the previous stage to the given network architecture by distributing the service components between the network elements. The functional architecture of the *Positioning_SAS* network element is illustrated in Fig.4(b). The functionality of *ServiceDirector* specified at the Service Decomposition phase is now decomposed and distributed over the given network. *ServiceDirector_SAS* handles the interface towards the RNC network element and controls the execution flow of the positioning calculation process in the SAS network element.

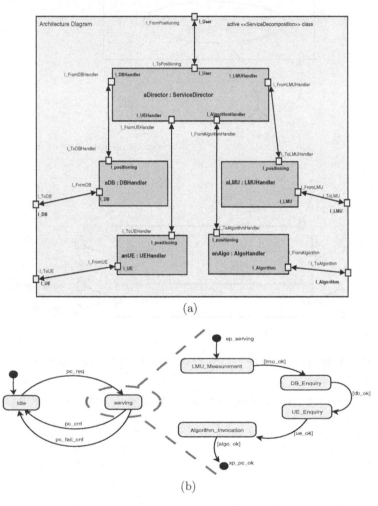

Fig. 3. (a) PositionCalculation functional architecture. (b) Service Director: PSAP communication and execution control.

Finally, at the *Service Implementation* phase we specify how the virtual communication between entities in different network nodes is realized using the underlying transport services. We also implement data encoding and decoding, routing of messages and dynamic process management. The detailed description of this stage can be found elsewhere [15,1,2].

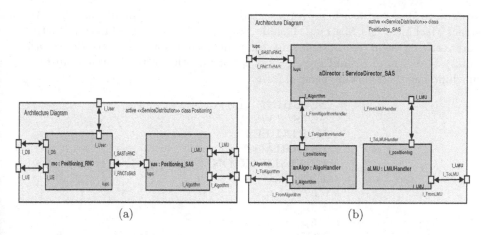

Fig. 4. (a) Architecture of service. (b) Architecture of Positioning_SAS.

In the next section we give a brief introduction into our formal framework, the B Method, which we will use to formalize the development flow described above.

3   Developing Systems by Refinement in the B Method

The B Method [3] is an approach for the industrial development of highly dependable software. The method has been successfully used in the development of several complex real-life applications [16]. Recently the B method has been extended by the Event B framework [4], which enables modelling of event-based systems. Event B is particularly suitable for developing distributed, parallel and reactive systems. In fact, this extension has incorporated the action system formalism [6] in the B Method. In the rest of the paper, we refer to the B Method together with its extension Event B simply as B.

The tool support available for B provides us with the assistance for the entire development process. For instance, Atelier B [9], one of the tools supporting the B Method, has facilities for automatic verification and code generation as well as documentation, project management and prototyping. It has a plug-in for integrating modelling in Event B. Atelier B provides us with a high degree of automation in verifying correctness that improves scalability of B, speeds up development and, also, requires less mathematical training from the users.

3.1   Modelling in B

The B Method adopts the top-down approach to system development. The development starts from creating a formal system specification. A formal specification is a mathematical model of the required behaviour of a system, or a part of a system. In B, a specification is represented by a collection of modules, called Abstract Machines. The Abstract Machine Notation (AMN), is used in constructing and verifying them. An abstract machine encapsulates a local state (local variables) of the machine and provides operations on the state. A simple abstract machine has the following general form:

$$
\begin{aligned}
&\textbf{MACHINE } AM \\
&\textbf{SETS } TYPES \\
&\textbf{VARIABLES } v \\
&\textbf{INVARIANT } I \\
&\textbf{INITIALISATION } INIT \\
&\textbf{EVENTS} \\
&\quad E_1 \; = \; \dots \\
&\quad \dots \\
&\quad E_N \; = \; \dots \\
&\textbf{END}
\end{aligned}
$$

The machine is uniquely identified by its name AM. The state variables of the machine, v, are declared in the **VARIABLES** clause and initialised in $INIT$ as defined in the **INITIALISATION** clause. The variables in B are strongly typed by constraining predicates of the machine invariant I given in the **INVARIANT** clause. The invariant is usually defined as a conjunction of the constraining predicates and the predicates defining the properties of the system that should be preserved during system execution. All types in B are represented by non-empty sets. Local types can be introduced by enumerating the elements of the type, e.g., $TYPE \; = \; \{element1, element2, \dots\}$, or by defining them as subsets of already existing types or sets.

The operations $E_1, \dots, E_N$ of the machine are defined in the **EVENTS** clause. The operations are atomic meaning that, once an operation is chosen, its execution will run until completion without interference. There are two standard ways to describe an operation in B: either by the preconditioned operation **PRE** cond **THEN** body **END** or the guarded operation **SELECT** cond **THEN** body **END**. Here cond is a state predicate, and body is a B statement. If cond is satisfied, the behaviour of both the precondition operation and the guarded operation corresponds to the execution of their bodies. However, these operations behave differently when an attempt to execute them from a state where cond is false is undertaken. In this case the precondition operation leads to a crash (i.e., unpredictable or even non-terminating behaviour) of the system, while the execution of the guarded operation is blocked. The preconditioned operations are used to describe the operations that will be turned (implemented) into procedures called by the user. On the other hand, the guarded operations are useful when we have to specify system behaviour in terms of its reactions on the occurrence of certain events. The operations of event-based systems are often called *events*.

The B statements that we will use to describe the bodies of events have the following syntax:

$$
\begin{aligned}
S \quad &== \quad x := e \mid \textbf{IF } cond \textbf{ THEN } S1 \textbf{ ELSE } S2 \textbf{ END} \mid S1 \; ; \; S2 \mid \\
&\quad\quad x \; :: \; T \mid \textbf{ANY } z \textbf{ WHERE } Q \textbf{ THEN } S \textbf{ END} \mid S1 \parallel S2 \mid \dots
\end{aligned}
$$

The first three constructs - an assignment, a conditional statement and a sequential composition have the standard meaning. A sequential composition is disallowed in abstract specifications but permitted in refinements. The remaining constructs allow us to model nondeterministic or parallel behaviour in a specification. Usually they are not implementable so they have to be refined (replaced) with executable constructs at some point of program development. We use two kinds of nondeterministic statements – the nondeterministic assignment and the nondeterministic block. The nondeterministic assignment $x \; :: \; T$ assigns the variable x an arbitrary value from the given set (type) T. The nondeterministic block **ANY** z **WHERE** Q **THEN** S **END** introduces the new local variable z which is initialised (possibly nondeterministically) according to the predicate Q and then used in the statement S. Finally, $S1 \parallel S2$ models parallel (simultaneous) execution of $S1$ and $S2$ provided $S1$ and $S2$ do not have a conflict on state variables. The special case of the parallel execution is a multiple assignment, which is denoted as $x, y := e1, e2$.

The B statements are formally defined using the weakest precondition semantics [10]. Intuitively, for a given statement S and a postcondition P, the weakest precondition $wp(S,P)$ describes the set of all such initial states from which execution of S is guaranteed to establish P. The weakest precondition semantics is a foundation for establishing correctness of specifications and verifying refinements between them. To show correctness (consistency) of an event-based system, we should demonstrate that its invariant is *true* in the initial state (i.e., after the initialisation is executed) and that every event preserves the invariant:

$$wp(INIT, I) = true, \quad \text{and}$$
$$g_i \wedge I \Rightarrow wp(E_i, I)$$

3.2   Refinement of Event-Based Systems

The basic idea underlying stepwise development in B is to design the system implementation gradually, by a number of correctness preserving steps called *refinements*. The refinement process starts from creating an abstract specification and finishes with generating executable code. The intermediate stages yield the specifications containing a mixture of abstract mathematical constructs and executable programming artefacts. In general, refinement process can be seen as a way to reduce nondeterminism of the abstract specification and replace abstract mathematical data structures by data structures implementable on a computer. Hence refinement allows us to introduce implementation decisions gradually.

Formally, we say that the statement S is refined by the statement S', written $S \sqsubseteq S'$, if, whenever S establishes a certain postcondition, so does S':

$$S \sqsubseteq S' \quad \text{if and only if for all postconditions } p: \; wp(S, p) \; \Rightarrow \; wp(S', p)$$

In the AMN the results of intermediate development stages – the refinement machines – have essentially the same structure as the more abstract specifications. In addition, a refinement machine explicitly states which specification it refines.

Assume that the refinement machine AM' given below is a result of refinement of the abstract machine AM:

> **REFINEMENT** AM'
> **REFINES** AM
> **VARIABLES** v'
> **INVARIANT** I'
> **INITIALISATION** $INIT'$
> **EVENTS**
> $\quad E_1 \;=\; \ldots$
> $\quad \ldots$
> $\quad E_N \;=\; \ldots$
> **END**

In AM' we replace the abstract data structures of AM with concrete ones. The invariant of AM', I', defines now not only the invariant properties of the refined specification but also the connection between the newly introduced variables and the abstract variables that they replace. For a refinement step to be valid, every possible execution of the refined machine must correspond (via I') to some execution of the abstract machine. To demonstrate this, we should prove that $INIT'$ is a valid refinement of $INIT$, each event of AM' is a valid refinement of its counterpart in AM and that the refined specification does not introduce additional deadlocks, i.e.,

$$wp(INIT', \; \neg wp(INIT, \neg I')) = true,$$
$$I \wedge I' \wedge g_i' \Rightarrow g_i \wedge wp(S', \neg wp(S, \neg I')), \quad \text{and}$$
$$I \wedge \bigvee_i^N g_i \Rightarrow g_i'$$

Often refinement process introduces new variables and the corresponding computations (new events) on them, while leaving the previous variables and computations essentially unchanged. Such refinement is referred to as *superposition* refinement [7]. Let us consider the abstract machine AM_S and the refinement machine AM_SR:

> **MACHINE** AM_S
> **VARIABLES** a
> **INVARIANT** I
>
> **INITIALISATION** $INIT$
> **EVENTS**
> $\quad E \;=\;$ **WHEN** g
> $\qquad\qquad$ **THEN** S **END**
>
>
>
> **END**

> **REFINEMENT** AM_SR
> **REFINES** AM_S
> **VARIABLES** a, b
> **INVARIANT** I'
> **VARIANT** V
> **INITIALISATION** $INIT'$
> **EVENTS**
> $\quad E \;=\;$ **WHEN** g
> $\qquad\qquad$ **THEN** S **END**
> $\quad E_1 \;=\;$ **WHEN** g_1 **THEN** S_1 **END**
> $\quad E_2 \;=\;$ **WHEN** g_2 **THEN** S_2 **END**
> **END**

Observe that the refinement machine contains the new events E_1 and E_2 as well as the new clause **VARIANT**. The new events define computations on the newly introduced variables b and, hence, can be seen as the events refining the statement *skip* on the abstract variables. Every new event should decrease the value of the variant. This allows us to guarantee that new events cannot take the control forever, since the variant expression cannot be decreased infinitely. For each newly introduced event, we should demonstrate that the variant expression is a natural number and execution of the event decreases the variant, i.e.,

$$V \in NAT, \ \text{ and}$$
$$I' \wedge g_i \Rightarrow wp((n := V; \ S_i), \ n < V)$$

In B, there are also mechanisms for structuring the system architecture by modularisation. The abstract machines can be composed by means of several mechanisms providing different forms of encapsulation. For instance, if the machine C **INCLUDES** the machine D then all variables and operations of D are incorporated in C. However, to guarantee internal consistency (and hence independent verification and reuse) of D, the machine C can change the variables of D only via the operations of D.

Next we illustrate modelling and refinement in B by presenting a formal development of fault-tolerant communicating systems according to the Lyra methodology.

4 Towards Formalizing and Extending Lyra

4.1 Modelling a Service Component in B

In Section 2 we have defined a service component as a coherent piece of functionality that provides its services to a service consumer via PSAP(s). We used this term to refer to the providers of external services introduced at the Service Decomposition phase. However, the notion of a service component can be generalized to represent the service providers at different levels of abstraction. Indeed, even the entire *Positioning* system can be seen as a service component providing the *Position Calculation* service. On the other hand, peer proxies introduced at the lowest level of abstraction can also be seen as the service components providing the physical data transfer services. Therefore, the notion of a service component is central to the entire Lyra development process.

A service component has two essential parts: functional and communicational. The *functional* part is a "mission" of a service component, i.e., the service(s) that it is capable of providing. The *communicational* part is an interface via which a service component receives requests to execute the service(s) and sends the results of service execution.

Execution of a service usually involves certain computations. We call the B representation of this part of a service component *Abstract CAlculating Machine (ACAM)*. The communicational part is correspondingly called *Abstract Communicating Machine (ACM)*, while the entire B model of a service component is called *Abstract Communicating Component (ACC)*. The abstract machine *ACC* below presents the proposed pattern for specifying a service component in B.

While specifying a service component, we adopt a *systemic* approach, i.e., model the service component together with the relevant part of its environment, the service consumer. Namely, when modelling the communicational *(ACM)* part of *ACC*, we also specify how the service consumer places requests to execute a service in the operation *input* and reads the results of service execution in the operation *output*. The input parameters *param* and *time* of the operation *input* model the parameters of a request and the maximal time allowed for executing the service. For instance, in the Positioning System example described in Section 2, an arrival of the position calculation request – the signal *pc_req* – can be represented as an instantiation of the operation *input*. Moreover, the request might have parameters – the precision of position calculation defined by the service consumer and the maximal execution time defined by the system, e.g., according to the current network load. The parameters of the request are stored in the internal data buffer *in_data*, so they can be used by *ACAM* while performing the required computations.

In our initial specification we abstract away from the details of computations required to execute a service, i.e., *ACAM* is modelled as a statement non-deterministically generating the results of service execution. These results are stored in the internal output buffer *out_data*. The service consumer obtains the results of service provision as the output parameter *res* of the operation *output*. Already in the abstract specification we model possibility of failure – *out_data* might contain values representing the results of not only successful service executions but also failed ones. In our example, in case of successful execution, the signal *pc_cnf* together with the calculated position are sent to the service consumer. Otherwise, the signal *pc_fail_cnf* is generated.

While executing the operation *output*, the input and output buffers are emptied and the service component becomes ready to accept a new service request. Here we reserve the abstract constant *NIL* to model the absence of data.

MACHINE *ACC*

SETS *DATA*

CONSTANTS *NIL, Abort_data*

PROPERTIES
  $NIL \in DATA \land Abort\_data \in DATA \land \neg (Abort\_data = NIL)$

VARIABLES *in_data, out_data*

INVARIANT
  $in\_data \in DATA \land out\_data \in DATA$

INITIALISATION
  $in\_data, out\_data := NIL, NIL$

EVENTS

$input(param, time) =$
  PRE $param \in DATA \land time \in \textbf{NAT1} \land \neg (param = NIL) \land in\_data = NIL$

THEN
  $in\_data := param$
END;

$calculate =$
  SELECT $\neg$ $(in\_data = NIL) \wedge out\_data = NIL$
  THEN
    $out\_data :\in DATA - \{NIL\}$
  END;

$res \leftarrow output =$
  PRE $\neg$ $(out\_data = NIL)$
  THEN
    $res := out\_data \parallel$
    $in\_data, out\_data := NIL, NIL$
  END

END

In Lyra, a service component is usually represented as an active class with the PSAP(s) attached to it via the port(s). The state diagram depicts the signalling scenario on PSAP including the signals from and to the external class modelling the service consumer. Essentially these diagrams suffice to specify a service component according to the ACC pattern. Namely, the UML2 description of PSAP is translated into the communicational (ACM) part of the machine ACC. The functional $(ACAM)$ part of ACC should be instantiated by the data types specific to the modelled service component. This translation formalizes the *Service Specification* phase of Lyra.

Let us observe that the machine ACC can be seen as a specification pattern, which can be instantiated by supplying the details specific to a service component under construction. For instance, the ACM part of ACC models data transfer to and from a service component very abstractly. We have shown how it can be instantiated for the Positioning system example. While developing a more complex service component, this part can be instantiated with more elaborated data structures and the corresponding protocols for transferring them.

Next we discuss how to extend Lyra with the explicit representation of the fault tolerance mechanisms and then show the use of the ACC pattern in the entire Lyra development process.

4.2 Introducing Fault Tolerance in the Lyra Development Flow

Currently the Lyra methodology addresses fault tolerance implicitly, i.e., by representating not only successful but also failed service provision in the Lyra UML models. However, it leaves aside modelling of mechanisms for detecting and recovering from errors – the fault tolerance mechanisms. We argue that, by integrating explicit representation of the means for fault tolerance into the entire development process, we establish a basis for constructing systems that are better resistant to errors, i.e., achieve better system dependability. Next we will discuss how to extend Lyra to integrate modelling of fault tolerance.

In the first development stage of Lyra we set a scene for reasoning about fault tolerance by modelling not only successful service provision but also service failure. In the next development stage – *Service Decomposition* – we elaborate on representation of the causes of service failures and the means for fault tolerance.

In the *Service Decomposition* phase we decompose the service provided by a service component into a number of stages (subservices). The service component can execute certain subservices itself as well as request other service components to do it. According to Lyra, the flow of the service execution is managed by a special service component called *Service Director*. It implements the behaviour of PSAP of a service component as specified earlier. Moreover, it co-ordinates the execution flow by enquiring the required subservices from the external service components.

In general, execution of any stage of a service can fail. In its turn, this might lead to failure of the entire service provision. Therefore, while specifying *Service Director*, we should ensure that it does not only orchestrates the fault-free execution flow but also handles erroneous situations. Indeed, as a result of requesting a particular subservice, *Service Director* can obtain a normal response containing the requested data or a notification about an error. As a reaction to the occurred error, *Service Director* might

- retry the execution of the failed subservice,
- repeat the execution of several previous subservices (i.e., roll back in the service execution flow) and then retry the failed subservice,
- abort the execution of the entire service.

The reaction of *Service Director* depends on the criticality of an occurred error: the more critical is the error, the larger part of the execution flow has to be involved in the error recovery. Moreover, the most critical (i.e., unrecoverable) errors lead to aborting the entire service. In Fig.5(a) we illustrate a fault free execution of the service S composed of subservices $S_1, \ldots, S_N$. Different error recovery mechanisms used in the presence of errors are shown in Fig.5(b) - 5(d).

Let us observe that each service should be provided within a certain finite period of time – the *maximal service response time Max_SRT*. In our model this time is passed as a parameter of the service request. Since each attempt of subservice execution takes some time, the service execution might be aborted even if only recoverable errors have occurred but the overall service execution time has already exceeded *Max_SRT*. Therefore, by introducing *Max_SRT* in our model, we also guarantee termination of error recovery, i.e., disallow infinite retries and rollbacks, as shown in Fig.5(e).

Next we demonstrate how to represent the extended Lyra development as refinement in B.

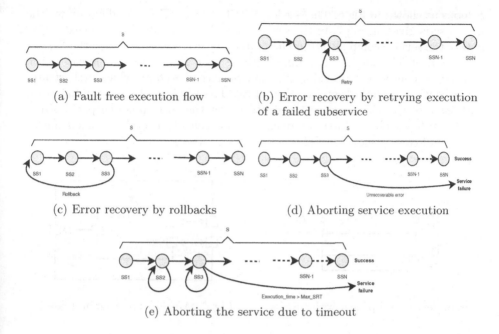

(a) Fault free execution flow

(b) Error recovery by retrying execution of a failed subservice

(c) Error recovery by rollbacks

(d) Aborting service execution

(e) Aborting the service due to timeout

Fig. 5. Service decomposition: faults in the execution flow

5   Service-Oriented Development by Refinement in B

5.1   Formalizing Service Decomposition

In the first stage of our formalized development we used the UML2 models produced at the *Service Specification* phase to specify a service component according to the *ACC* pattern. The next step focuses on modelling the service execution flow with the incorporated fault tolerance mechanisms. Namely, we introduce a representation of *Service Director* into the abstract specification of a service component. This is done by refining the machine *ACC* to capture the design decisions made at *Service Decomposition* and *Service Distribution* phases. Hence, to derive the specification of *Service Director*, we use UML2 diagrams modelling both the functional and the platform-distributed architectures. In general, we should consider two cases:

1. *Service Director* is "centralized", i.e., it resides on a single network element,
2. *Service Director* is "distributed", i.e., different parts of the execution flow are orchestrated by distinct service directors residing on different network elements.

Assume for simplicity that the set of subservices required in the execution of the service S consists of three elements: S_1, S_2 and S_3. At the *Service Decomposition* phase, in both cases the model of the service component providing the service

S looks as shown in Fig.6. The service distribution architecture diagram for the first case is given in Fig.7. In the second case, let us assume that the execution flow of the service component is orchestrated by two service directors: the *Service Director1*, which handles the communication on PSAP and communicates with the service component providing S_1, and *Service Director2*, which orchestrates the execution of the subservices S_2 and S_3. The service directors communicate with each other while passing the control over the corresponding parts of the execution flow. The architecture diagram depicting the overall arrangement for the second case is shown in Fig.9.

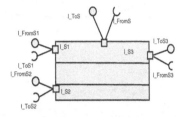
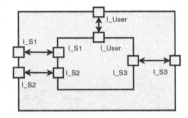

Fig. 6. Service component with USAPs   **Fig. 7.** Architecture diagram (case 1)

We model the decomposed service as a sequence over the abstract set *TASKS*. Each element of *TASKS* represents the individual subservice. Moreover, we introduce the abstract function *Next* to models the service execution flow. In case of the centralized *Service Director*, the subservices are executed one after another, i.e., the abstract representation of *Next* will be instantiated as follows:

$$Next(S_i) = S_{i+1}$$

for $i : 1..max\_sv$, where max_sv is the maximal number of subservices required to execute the service.

In the second case, the function *Next* describes the execution flow from the point of view of the main service director, i.e., it treats the groups of services managed by other service directors as atomic steps in the execution flow. In our example, the service S_1 is managed by *Service Director1*, while S_2 and S_3 are managed by *ServiceDirector2*. In this case the function *Next* treats the execution of S_2 and S_3 as one execution step the performance of which is delegated to *Service Director2*. Hence, in this example *Next* will be instantiated as follows:

$$Next(S_1) = S_2, \quad \text{and} \quad Next(S_2) = S_4$$

The result of refinement of the machine ACC – the machine ACC_DEC – is given below.

REFINEMENT ACC_DEC

REFINES ACC

SETS

$DATA$; $TASK$; $RESPONSE = \{OK,\ REPEAT,\ ROLLBACK,\ ABORT\}$

CONSTANTS $Service,\ Eval,\ Next,\ max\_sv$

PROPERTIES

$Service \in \mathbf{seq1}(TASK) \wedge \mathbf{size}(Service) = max\_sv \wedge$

$Eval \in TASK \times DATA \rightarrow RESPONSE \wedge$

$\forall\ dd.\ (dd \in DATA \Rightarrow \neg\ (Eval(Service(1),dd) = ROLLBACK)) \wedge$

$Next \in 1\ ..\ max\_sv \rightarrowtail 2\ ..\ max\_sv{+}1 \wedge$

$1 \in \mathbf{dom}(Next) \wedge (max\_sv{+}1) \in \mathbf{ran}(Next) \wedge$

$\forall ii.\ (ii \in \mathbf{dom}(Next) \wedge \neg\ (Next(ii){=}max\_sv{+}1) \Rightarrow Next(ii) \in \mathbf{dom}(Next)) \wedge$

$\forall ii.\ (ii \in \mathbf{dom}(Next) \Rightarrow ii{<}Next(ii)) \wedge \ldots$

VARIABLES

$in\_data,\ out\_data,\ time\_left,\ old\_time\_left,$

$curr\_task,\ resp,\ finished,\ results,\ curr\_data$

INVARIANT

$resp \in RESPONSE \wedge$

$results \in 1\ ..\ max\_sv \rightarrow DATA\text{-}\{NIL\} \wedge$

$curr\_data \in DATA \wedge$

$curr\_task \in 1\ ..\ max\_sv{+}1 \wedge$

$(finished = \mathbf{FALSE} \Rightarrow time\_left{>}0) \wedge$

$time\_left \leq old\_time\_left \wedge$

$\mathbf{dom}(results) \subseteq \mathbf{dom}(Next) \wedge$

$(finished = \mathbf{TRUE} \Rightarrow (resp{=}ABORT) \vee (curr\_task = max\_sv{+}1)) \wedge$

$(finished = \mathbf{FALSE} \Rightarrow curr\_task \in 1\ ..\ max\_sv) \wedge$

$(finished = \mathbf{FALSE} \Rightarrow curr\_task \in \mathbf{dom}(Next)) \wedge$

$(curr\_task = max\_sv{+}1 \Rightarrow \neg\ (resp{=}ABORT)) \wedge$

$(finished = \mathbf{TRUE} \wedge curr\_task = max\_sv{+}1 \Rightarrow$

$Next^{-1}\ (curr\_task) \in \mathbf{dom}(results)) \wedge \ldots$

INITIALISATION

$in\_data,\ out\_data := NIL,\ NIL\ ||$

$time\_left,\ old\_time\_left := max\_time,\ max\_time\ ||$

$curr\_task,\ resp := 1,\ OK\ ||$

$finished,\ results := \mathbf{FALSE},\ \emptyset\ ||$

$curr\_data := NIL$

EVENTS

$input(param,time) =$

  PRE $param \in DATA \wedge time \in \mathbf{NAT1} \wedge \neg\ (param{=}NIL) \wedge in\_data{=}NIL$

  THEN

    $in\_data,\ time\_left,\ old\_time\_left := param,\ time,\ time$

  END;

$handle =$

  SELECT $\neg\ (in\_data{=}NIL) \wedge finished{=}\mathbf{FALSE} \wedge (time\_left < old\_time\_left)$

  THEN

    $old\_time\_left := time\_left;\ curr\_data :\in DATA\text{-}\{NIL\};$

$resp := Eval(Service(curr\_task), curr\_data);$
CASE $resp$ **OF**
  EITHER OK **THEN**
    $results(curr\_task) := curr\_data;$
    $curr\_task := Next(curr\_task);$
    IF $curr\_task = max\_sv+1$ **THEN** $finished :=$ **TRUE END**
  OR $ROLLBACK$ **THEN**
    $curr\_task := Next^{-1}(curr\_task);$
    $results := \{curr\_task\} \lhd results$
  OR $REPEAT$ **THEN** skip
  OR $ABORT$ **THEN** $finished :=$ **TRUE**
  END
  END
END;

$timer =$
  SELECT $\neg\ (in\_data=NIL) \land finished=$**FALSE**$\land (time\_left = old\_time\_left)$
  THEN
    CHOICE
      $time\_left :\in \{xx \mid xx \in$ **NAT1** $\land\ xx < time\_left\}$
    OR
      $time\_left, resp := 0, ABORT\ ;$
      $finished :=$ **TRUE**
    END
  END;

$calculate =$
  SELECT $\neg\ (in\_data=NIL) \land out\_data = NIL \land finished =$ **TRUE**
  THEN
    IF $resp = ABORT$ **THEN** $out\_data := Abort\_data$
    ELSE
      $out\_data := results(Next^{-1}(curr\_task))$
    END
  END;

$res \leftarrow output =$
  PRE $\neg\ (out\_data = NIL)$
  THEN
    $res := out\_data\ ; in\_data, out\_data := NIL, NIL$
  END
END

The currently executed subservice is modelled by the variable $curr\_task$. The results of the current subservice execution are stored in the variable $curr\_data$. The results of all subservices already executed are accumulated in the variable $results$. The variable $finished$ indicates the end of service execution. The variable is set to $TRUE$ when the whole sequence of subservices has been executed or some unrecoverable error has occurred.

To model progress of time, we introduce the variable *time_left*. When a service request is received in the operation *input*, *time_left* is set to the maximal service response time *Max_SRT*, which is received as the second parameter of *input*. The variable *old_time_left* is used to force interleaving between progress of the execution flow and the passage of time. The operation *timer* decreases the value of *time_left*, disables itself and enables the operation *handle*, which specifies the service co-ordinating behaviour of *Service Director*.

In the operation *handle*, we model not only requesting a certain subservice and obtaining its response, but also handling notifications about errors. We introduce the abstract function *Eval*, which evaluates the obtained response from a requested subservice. The result of evaluation is assigned to the variable *resp*. If the subservice was successfully executed then the variable *resp* gets the value *OK*. In this case the next element from the sequence of subservices is chosen for execution according to the function *Next*. If a benign failure has occurred and error recovery merely requires to retry the execution of the failed subservice then the variable *resp* is assigned the value *REPEAT*. This situation is illustrated in Fig. 5(b). However, if a more critical error has occurred, i.e., the variable *resp* gets the value *ROLLBACK*, the execution of several subservices preceding the failed service should be repeated as well. This case is depicted in Fig. 5(c). The inverse of the function *Next* defines which subservices should be re-executed, i.e., to which subservice the execution flow should rollback. In this case, we also delete the results of executing these subservices from *results*. Finally, if an unrecoverable error has occurred, i.e., the value of *resp* becomes *ABORT*, then the execution of the service is terminated (i.e., the variable *finished* is assigned *TRUE*) as shown in Fig. 5(d).

Let us note, that the variable *resp* also obtains the value *ABORT* once the timeout has occurred. This is modelled in the operation *timer*. The system might be in a state where the value of *time_left* had already became zero, while the execution of the service has not yet been finished, as depicted in Fig. 5(e).

In the refined machine *ACC_DEC* the guard of the event *calculate* is strengthened to ensure that the final result of the service is computed only after the execution of all subservices is finished (or aborted), i.e., when *finished* = *TRUE*.

The performed refinement has affected the *ACAM* part of the *ACC* pattern. The newly introduced events allowed us to define the details of execution of the decomposed service. In the **VARIANT** clause of *ACC_DEC* we not only ensure that the newly introduced events do not take control forever but also that execution of the service terminates.

Let us observe that our approach to introducing fault tolerance can be seen as an abstract implementation of the rollback error recovery frequently used in distributed systems [11]. Indeed, the operation *handle* defines the rollback procedure by co-ordinating error recovery according to the check-points defined by the function *Next*. The stable data storage is modelled by the variable *results*. The operation *handle* ensures consistency of the system state by the appropriate updates of *results*.

While defining the execution flow over subservices in ACC_DEC, we abstracted away from modelling the details of the communication between *Service Director* and the external service providers – the USAP communication. Moreover, we omitted the explicit representation of the external service providers as such and modelled only the results of subservices provision. In our next refinement steps we decompose the obtained specification to introduce the detailed representation of the external service providers and the USAP communication.

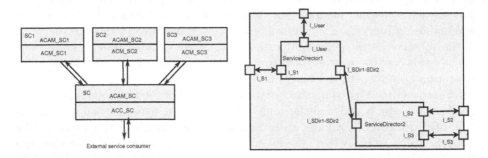

Fig. 8. Specification architecture (case 1)   **Fig. 9.** Architecture diagram (case 2)

5.2   Formal Modelling of Service Distribution

Let us first consider the case of a "centralized" service director shown in Fig. 7. It is easy to observe that the service component SC providing the service S plays a role of the service consumer for the service components $SC_1, \ldots, SC_N$ providing the subservices $S_1, \ldots, S_N$. We specify the service components $SC_1, \ldots, SC_N$ as the separate machines $ACC\_SC1, \ldots ACC\_SCN$ according to the proposed pattern ACC. The process of translating the UML2 models of $SC_1, \ldots, SC_N$ into B is similar to specifying SC at the *Service Specification* phase. The communicational parts of the included machines $ACC\_SC1, \ldots, ACC\_SCN$ specify the PSAPs of $SC_1, \ldots, SC_N$. To ensure the match between the corresponding USAPs of SC and PSAPs of the external service components, we derive USAPs of SC from PSAPs of $SC_1, \ldots, SC_N$.

To define the mechanism for communicating with $SC_1, \ldots, SC_N$, we refine the operation *handle* to specify the communication on USAPs. Namely, we replace the nondeterministic assignments modelling specific stages of the service execution by the corresponding signalling scenarios: at the proper point of the execution flow, a desired service is requested by writing into the input channel of the corresponding included machine, and later the produced results are read from the output channel of this machine. Graphically this arrangement is depicted in Fig.8.

Modelling the case of a distributed service director is more complex. Let us assume that the execution flow of the service component SC is orchestrated by two service directors: the *ServiceDirector1*, which handles the communication on PSAP of *SC* and communicates with *SC1*, and *ServiceDirector2*, which orchestrates the execution of the *SC2* and *SC3* services. The architecture diagram depicting the overall arrangement is shown in Fig.9.

The service execution proceeds according to the following scenario: via PSAP of *SC* *ServiceDirector1* receives the request to provide the service *S*. Upon this, via USAP of *SC*, it requests the component *SC1* to provide the service *S1*. When the result of *S1* is obtained, *ServiceDirector1* requests *ServiceDirector2* to execute the rest of the service and return the result back. In its turn, *ServiceDirector2* at first requests *SC2* to provide the service *S2* and then *SC3* to provide service *S3*. Upon receiving the result from *S3*, it forwards it to *ServiceDirector1*. Finally, *ServiceDirector1* returns to the service consumer the result of the entire service *S* via PSAP of *SC*.

This complex behaviour can be captured in a number of refinement steps. At first, we observe that *ServiceDirector2*, coordinating execution of *S2* and *S3*, can be modelled as a "large" service component *SC2-SC3*, which provides the services *S2* and *S3*. Let us note that the execution flow in *SC2-SC3* is orchestrated by the "centralized" service director *ServiceDirector2*. We use this observation in our next refinement step. Namely, we refine the B machine modelling *SC* defined according to the *ACC_DEC* pattern by including into it the machines modelling the service components *SC1* and *SC2-SC3* and introducing the required communicating mechanisms. The result of this refinement step – the machine *SDirector1* – is given below (the parts of *SDirector1*, which coincide with the corresponding parts of *ACC_DEC* are replaced with dots).

REFINEMENT *SDirector1*

REFINES *ACC_DEC*

INCLUDES *Comp1, SDirector2*

CONSTANTS
   boolnum , ...

PROPERTIES
boolnum $\in$ **BOOL** $\rightarrow$ 0 .. 1 $\wedge$
boolnum(**FALSE**) = 0 $\wedge$ *boolnum*(**TRUE**) = 1 $\wedge$
max_sv = 3 $\wedge$ *Next* = $\{1 \mapsto 2, 2 \mapsto 4\}$ $\wedge$
(*Service* = ([*C1_Service*] $\frown$ *SD2_Service*))

VARIABLES
   in_data, out_data, time_left, old_time_left,
   curr_task, resp, finished, results, curr_data, start_flag

INVARIANT
   start_flag $\in$ **BOOL**

VARIANT
   boolnum(*start_flag*)

INITIALISATION

... $\|$ *start_flag* := **TRUE**

ASSERTIONS

$Next \in 1 .. max\_sv \rightarrowtail 2 .. max\_sv+1 \land$
$1 \in \mathbf{dom}(Next) \land (max\_sv+1) \in \mathbf{ran}(Next) \land$
$\forall ii. (ii \in \mathbf{dom}(Next) \Rightarrow ii < Next(ii)) \land$
$\forall ii. (ii \in \mathbf{dom}(Next) \land \neg (Next(ii)=max\_sv+1) \Rightarrow Next(ii) \in \mathbf{dom}(Next))$

EVENTS

input(*param*,*time*) $= \dots$ **END**;

handle $=$
  SELECT $\neg (in\_data=NIL) \land$ *finished* $=$ **FALSE** $\land$
       ($time\_left < old\_time\_left$) $\land$
       (($curr\_task=1 \land C1\_out\_data \neq NIL$) $\lor$
       ($curr\_task=2 \land SD2\_out\_data \neq NIL$))
  THEN
    $old\_time\_left := time\_left$;

    CASE *curr_task* **OF**
      EITHER 1 **THEN** $curr\_data \leftarrow C1\_output$
      OR 2 **THEN** $curr\_data \leftarrow SD2\_output$
      END
    END;
    $resp := Eval(Service(curr\_task),curr\_data)$;
    CASE *resp* **OF**
      EITHER *OK* **THEN**
        results($curr\_task$) := $curr\_data$;
        $curr\_task := Next(curr\_task)$;
        IF $curr\_task = max\_sv+1$ **THEN** *finished* := **TRUE END**
      OR *ROLLBACK* **THEN**
        $curr\_task := Next^{-1} (curr\_task)$;
        $results := \{curr\_task\} \lhd results$
      OR *REPEAT* **THEN** **skip**
      OR *ABORT* **THEN** *finished* := **TRUE**
      END
    END;
    $start\_flag :=$ **TRUE**
  END;

starter $=$
  SELECT $\neg (in\_data=NIL) \land$ *finished* $=$ **FALSE** $\land$
       ($time\_left = old\_time\_left$) $\land$
       $start\_flag =$ **TRUE** $\land$
       (($curr\_task=1 \land C1\_in\_data = NIL$) $\lor$
       ($curr\_task=2 \land SD2\_in\_data = NIL$))
  THEN
    CASE *curr_task* **OF**
      EITHER 1 **THEN** $C1\_input(in\_data,time\_left)$

    OR 2 **THEN** $SD2\_input(results(Next^{-1}(curr\_task)), time\_left)$
    END
   END;
    $start\_flag :=$ **FALSE**
  END;
$timer = \ldots$ **END**;

$calculate = \ldots$ **END**;

$res \leftarrow output = \ldots$ **END**;
END

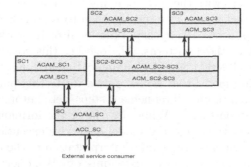

Fig. 10. Specification architecture (case 2)

The machine *SDirector1* includes the machines *Comp1* and *SDirector2* specifying the service components *SC1* and *SC2-SC3* correspondingly. They are defined according to *ACC* and *ACC_DEC* patterns respectively. Since these machines can be obtained by a simple instantiation of these patterns, we omit their representation here.

The Service Director of *SC* communicates with the service component *SC1* and the Service Director of *SC2-SC3* by placing the corresponding requests in their input channels and reading the responses from their output channels. The order of requests is defined by the function *Next*. The function is instantiated in the **PROPERTIES** close to represent the particular architecture given in Fig. 9. Requesting the services from *CS1* and *SC2-SC3* is modelled in the operation *starter*, reading the output channels of *SC1* and *SC2-SC3* in the operation *handle*. Note, that the operation *handle* have been refined to explicitly model obtaining a response from the requested component.

In our consequent refinement step we focus on decomposition of *SC2-SC3*. We single out separate service components *SC2* and *SC3* as before and refine *ServiceDirector2* to model communication with them. The final architecture of formal specification is shown in Fig.10. We omit the presentation of the detailed formal specifications – they are again obtained by recursive application of the proposed specification and refinement patterns.

At the further refinement steps we focus on particular service components and refine them (in the way described above) until the desired level of granularity is obtained. Once all external service components are in place, we can further decompose their specifications by separating their ACM and $ACAM$ parts. Such a decomposition will allow us to concentrate on the communicational parts of the components and further refine them by introducing details of the required concrete communication protocols.

5.3 Discussion

The proposed approach to formalizing Lyra in B allows us to verify correctness of the Lyra decomposition and distribution phases. This is done by introducing generic patterns for communicating service components and then associating the Lyra development steps with the corresponding B refinements on these patterns. In development of real systems we merely have to establish by proof that the corresponding components in a specific functional or network architecture are valid instantiations of these patterns. All together this constitutes a basis for automating industrial design flow of communicating systems.

The decomposition model that we have used for testing our approach is still relatively simple. As a result, all refinement steps were automatically proved by AtelierB – a tool supporting B. While describing the formalization of Lyra in B, we considered only the sequential model of service execution. However, parallel execution of services is also a valid interpretation of the considered UML2 models. We are planning to work on extending our B models to include parallel execution of services. We foresee that such extensions will make automatic proof of model refinements more difficult. However, by developing generic proof strategies, we will try to achieve high degree of automation in formal verification of our models.

Currently our approach can be implemented on a platform supporting the classical B Method and EventB. However, it can be adapted to the emerging RODIN platform [17] as well. The two major adjustments would need to be done. Firstly, we would need to replace the preconditioned operations modelling communication between service components by the events, which explicitly work with input and output buffers of communicating components. Consequently, in the operation *handle* and *starter*, the calls of preconditioned operations would be replaced by the assignments to the corresponding buffers. Secondly, we would need to eliminate sequential composition and other control structures (like conditional and *CHOICE* statements) extensively used in our specifications. This can be achieved by splitting the operations using these control structures into the corresponding sets of events. Obviously, it would lead to rather artificial proliferation of new events. However, we believe that in the future the RODIN platform will allow us to conservatively extend the language and, hence, keep the used control structures.

6 Conclusions

In this paper we proposed a formal approach to development of communicating distributed systems. Our approach formalizes and extends Lyra [15] – the UML2-based design methodology adopted in Nokia. The formalization is done within the B Method [3] and its extension EventB [4] – a formal framework supporting system development by stepwise refinement. We derived the B specification and refinement patterns reflecting models and model transformations used in the development flow of Lyra. The proposed approach establishes a basis for automatic translation of UML2-based development of communicating systems into the specification and refinement process in B. Such automation would enable smooth integration of formal methods into existing development practice. Since UML is widely accepted in industry, we believe that our approach has a potential for wide industrial uptake.

Lyra adopts the service-oriented style for development of communicating systems. We presented the guidelines for deriving B specifications from corresponding UML2 models at each development stage of Lyra and verified the development by the corresponding B refinements. The major model transformations aim at service decomposition and distribution over the given platform. The proposed formal model of communication between the distributed service components is generic and can be instantiated by virtually any concrete communication protocol. Moreover, we demonstrated how to extend Lyra to integrate reasoning about fault tolerance in the entire development flow.

The initial formalization of Lyra has been undertaken using model checking techniques [15]. However, since telecommunicating systems tend to be large and data intensive, this formalization was prone to the state explosion problem. Our approach helps to overcome this limitation.

Development of distributed communicating systems has been a topic of ongoing research over several decades. Our review of related work is confined to the consideration of the recent research conducted within B.

The pioneering work on formal development of distributed systems in Event B was done by Abrial et al. [5]. They demonstrated how to prove termination of a complex distributed protocol in Event B. In our work we use the principles defined in [5] to formalize the service-oriented development of complex communicating systems.

Yadav and Butler [22] used Event B to design fault tolerant transactions for replicated distributed database systems. They demonstrated how to formally verify by refinement that the design of a replicated database confirms to the one copy database abstraction. Similarly, in our work we use refinement to verify that the externally observable behaviour of distributed implementation of a service is equivalent to its centralized abstraction. However, our primary goal was not only formal verification of service development but also integration of modelling and refinement in B into the existing UML2-based development flow.

Treharne et al. [21] investigated verification of safety and liveness properties of communicating components by combining the B Method and the process algebra CSP. However, they do not consider service decomposition and distribution aspects of the communicating system development.

Boström and Walden [8] proposed a formal methodology (based on the B Method) for developing distributed grid systems. In their approach the B language is extended with grid-specific features and the system development is governed by B refinement. In our approach the system development is guided by the existing development practice, so that the refinement process is hidden behind the facade of UML2.

There is active research going on translating UML to B [12,13,14,19,20]. Among these, the most notable is research conducted by Snook and Butler [19] on designing the method and the U2B tool to support the automatic translation. In our future work we are planning to integrate our efforts with the U2B developers to achieve the automatic translation of Lyra into B. While doing this, we will focus specifically on translating models and model transformations used in Lyra to automate formalization of the entire UML-based development process in the domain of the communicating distributed systems. Moreover, we are planning to further enhance the proposed approach to address issues of concurrency.

Acknowledgments

This work is supported by IST FP6 RODIN Project.

References

1. 3GPP. Technical specification 25.305: Stage 2 functional specification of UE positioning in UTRAN. Available at http://www.3gpp.org/ftp/Specs/html-info/25305.htm.
2. 3GPP. Technical specification 25.453: UTRAN Iupc interface positioning calculation application part (pcap) signalling. Available at http://www.3gpp.org/ftp/Specs/html-info/25453.htm.
3. J.-R. Abrial. *The B-Book*. Cambridge University Press, 1996.
4. J.-R. Abrial. Extending B without Changing it (for Developing Distributed Systems). *Proceedings of 1st Conference on the B Method*, pp.169-191, Springer-Verlag, November 1996, Nantes, France.
5. J.-R. Abrial, D.Cansell, and D. Mery. A mechanically proved and Incremental development of IEEE 1394 Tree Identity Protocol. *Formal Aspects of Computing*, Vol.14, pp.215-227, 2003.
6. R. Back. Refinement calculus, Part II: Parallel and reactive programs. *Stepwise Refinement of Distributed Systems, Lecture Notes in Computer Science*, Vol.430, pp.67-93, Springer-Verlag, 1990.
7. R. Back and K. Sere. Superposition refinement of reactive systems. *Formal Aspects of Computing*, 8(3), pp.1-23, 1996.
8. P. Boström and M. Walden. An Extension of Event B for Developing Grid Systems. In *Proceedings of ZB 2005:Formal Specification and Development in Z and B, Lecture Notes in Computer Science*, Vol.3455, pp.142-161, Springer-Verlag, Guildford, UK, 2005.
9. Clearsy. *AtelierB: User and Reference Manuals*. Available at http://www.atelierb.societe.com/index_uk.html.
10. E.W. Dijkstra. *A Discipline of Programming*. Prentice-Hall International, 1976.
11. E.N. Elnozahy, L. Alvisi, Y. Wang, and D.B. Johnson. A Survey of Rollback-Recovery Protocols in Message Passing Systems. *ACM Computing Surveys*, Vol.34, No.3, 2002.

12. P. Facon, R. Laleau, H. Nguyen, and A. Mammar. Combining UML with the B Method for specification of database applications. Research report, CEDRIC laboratory, Paris, 1999.

13. K. Lano, D. Clark, and K. Androutsopoulos. UML to B: Formal Verification of Object-Oriented Models. In *Proceedings of ICM, Lecture Notes in Computer Science*, Vol.2999, Springer.

14. H. LeDang and J. Souquieres. Integrating UML and B specification techniques. In *Proceedings of Ninth Asia-Pacific Software Engineering Conference (APSEC'02)*, p.495, 2002.

15. S. Leppänen, M. Turunen, and I. Oliver. Application Driven Methodology for Development of Communicating Systems. *Forum on Specification and Design Languages*, Lille, France, 2004.

16. MATISSE. *Handbook for Correct System Construction.* Available at http://www.esil.univ-mrs.fr/ spc/matisse/Handbook/.

17. Rigorous Open Development Environment for Complex Systems (RODIN). IST FP6 STREP project, online at http://rodin.cs.ncl.ac.uk/.

18. J. Rumbaugh, I. Jakobson, and G. Booch. *The Unified Modelling Language Reference Manual.* Addison-Wesley, 1998.

19. C. Snook and M. Butler. U2B - A tool for translating UML-B models into B. *UML-B Specification for Proven Embedded System Design*, Springer, 2004.

20. C. Snook and M. Walden. Use of U2B for Specifying B Action Systems. In *Proceedings of International workshop on refinement of critical systems: methods, tools and experience (RCS'02)*, Grenoble, France, January 2002.

21. H. Treharne, S. Schneider, and M. Bramble. Composing Specifications Using Communication. In *Proceedings of ZB 2003: Formal Specification and Development in Z and B, Lecture Notes in Computer Science*, Vol.2651, Springer, Turku, Finland, June 2003.

22. D. Yadav and M. Butler. Application of Event B to Global Causal Ordering for Fault Tolerant Transactions. In *Proceedings of Workshop on Rigorous Engineering of Fault Tolerant Systems (REFT'2005)*, pp.93-102, Newcastle upon Tyne, UK, July 2005.

Programming-Logic Analysis of Fault Tolerance: Expected Performance of Self-stabilisation

C.C. Morgan[1] and A.K. McIver[2]

[1] Dept. Comp. Sci. and Eng., University of NSW, Sydney 2052 Australia
carrollm@cse.unsw.edu.au
[2] Dept. Computer Science, Macquarie University, Sydney 2109 Australia
anabel@ics.mq.edu.au

Abstract. Formal proofs of functional correctness and rigorous analyses of fault tolerance have, traditionally, been separate processes. In the former a programming logic (proof) or computational model (model checking) is used to establish that all the system's behaviours satisfy some (specification) criteria. In the latter, techniques derived from engineering are used to determine quantitative properties such as probability of failure (given failure of some component) or expected performance (an average measure of execution time, for example).

To combine the formality and the rigour requires a quantitative approach within which functional correctness can be embedded. Programming logics for probability are capable in principle of doing so, and in this article we illustrate the use of the probabilistic guarded-command language (*pGCL*) and its logic for that purpose.

We take self-stabilisation as an example of fault tolerance, and present program-logical techniques for determining, on the one hand, that termination occurs with probability one and, on the other, the the expected time to termination is bounded above by some value. An interesting technical novelty required for this is the recognition of both "angelic" and "demonic" refinement, reflecting our simultaneous interest in both upper- and lower bounds.

1 Introduction

Formal methods establishes correctness of a program (or system) by mathematical methods which have independently been proved sound. Ideally, a formal verification should cover as much of the system's construction as possible: beginning with a specification that is so clear the user can have no doubt of its meaning; and ending with an implementation that is so concrete the manufacturer can have no doubt of how to build it. With the caveat that there always is a gap at either end ("Is this the right specification?" — "Has the implementation been correctly transliterated?"), traditional formal methods concerns itself with so-called "absolute" correctness: a successful formal development ensures (modulo the caveats) that the program will satisfy its user *every time*.

Fault tolerance has a matching traditional form, where the unavoidable failures that reality serves up —in spite of all our efforts— are handled by backup

M. Butler et al. (Eds.): Fault-Tolerant Systems, LNCS 4157, pp. 288–305, 2006.
© Springer-Verlag Berlin Heidelberg 2006

mechanisms, redundancy, *etc.* whose aim is to make that so-called "absolute" correctness in fact as likely as possible. That is, independent of formal methods (and with a much longer history), the techniques of risk- and failure analysis are used to take account of statistical, that is *quantitative* information about possible component-failures and, from it, to derive an estimate about the reliability of the system as a whole.

Our recent work (about ten years [12,10]) has been to address that phrase "independent of formal methods", and the contribution of this article is to illustrate some of the progress that has been made. We choose self-stabilisation as a fault-tolerance paradigm, and show to what extent quantitative behaviour can be *included* in formal reasoning about correctness, rather than being independent of it or an adjunct to it.

Self-stabilisation is a compensating mechanism for systems prone to faults which are either too expensive or impossible to eliminate: when a fault occurs, and is detected, the system automatically takes steps to return itself to a state from which the fault has been removed. The "fault-free" state is considered *stable* in the sense that an absolute-correctness argument has established (or is supposed to have established...) that the system will not itself introduce faults through programming error.

The context for self-stabilisation is usually algorithms which are physically distributed, and "good style" generally dictates that the stabilisation process be symmetric and (hence) to some extent randomised deliberately. Symmetry is to avoid "weak links" whose failure on their own could bring down the whole system; but that symmetry itself introduces a problem because the stable configurations are asymmetric — and only randomisation can take a symmetric system to an asymmetric one.[1]

There are two especially important aspects of randomised algorithms: with what probability are they correct; and how long should we expect them to take. The technical theme of this paper is to show how to deal with those issues in a programming logic, *i.e.* formally. In particular, we investigate the following:

1. The theoretical foundations for reasoning *at the source-code level* about worst-case, *i.e.* upper bounds for expected performance of random algorithms;
2. A sound program-logic rule for estimating those bounds;
3. Practical techniques for using annotations to prove the bounds; and
4. Two case studies illustrating the techniques in action.

One case study deals with expected time to termination (where termination itself is obvious); the other, a more complicated situation, concentrates on showing termination itself.

A key methodological aspect is the prominent role of refinement in our analyses: rather than proving performance properties of "direct" representations of

---

[1] That is why coins are used in cricket matches: the symmetric state is that the two teams have equal right to bat first; but the outcome —where just one team does so— is asymmetric, and is brought about by the coin flip.

the algorithms, we prove properties of their abstractions. Working with abstractions makes the reasoning more tractable but, most importantly, relies on the properties' being preserved by refinement. That means of course that the refinement rules must be carefully formulated to do that, depending on the properties in question; in our case here, that accounts for our use of angelic nondeterminism when in Sec. 3 we are trying to preserve upper- (rather than the more usual lower) bounds.

We use the these notations. Function f applied to argument x is written $f.x$, where the dot "." is left-associative. This allows for example $f.g.x$ rather than $(f(g))(x)$.

A discrete probability distribution d over a set X is a one-summing function from X into $[0, 1]$, thus assigning probability $d.x$ to point x.

For some $x \in X$ the *point probability distribution* "x with probability one" is written $\overline{x}$; for a subset $X' \subseteq X$ the *characteristic function* taking 1 on X' and 0 on the remainder $X - X'$ is written $[X']$.

Under *abuses of notation* we collect the following: for the characteristic function of a point we write $[x]$ rather than $[\{x\}]$; for the probability of a set we write $d.X'$ rather than $\sum_{x \in X'} d.x$; for the expected value of a function over a distribution we write $d.f$ rather than $\sum_{x \in X}(d.x \times f.x)$.

Where context supplies unambiguously a predicate language for describing subsets, we write predicates directly for the subsets they denote. Thus for example if X is a state space and d a distribution over it, and (say) for some variables a, b the predicate $a > b$ denotes a subset of X' of X, then we write freely $a > b$ where X' might be expected — whence $d.[a>b]$ is the probability that $a > b$ holds in distribution d over X.

2   Performance-Style Properties in $pGCL$

When systems operate within random contexts their properties can no longer be guaranteed absolutely, but only up to some probability. The program fragment

$$x := 0 \; {}_{1/4}\oplus \; x := 1 \;, \tag{1}$$

for example, does not guarantee to set variable x to 0 under any (initial) condition — the probabilistic choice operator "${}_{1/4}\oplus$" describes the flip of a $(1/4, 3/4)$-biased coin, so that operationally *either* 0 or 1 will be observed, but it is impossible to predict which. The only guarantee is probabilistic, in this case that "with *probability* 1/4, x will be set to 0 if the program fragment is executed". What this means in practice is that over a large number of experiments, the ratio of recorded 1's and 0's will be approximately 3, up to statistical confidence measures [16].

A formal description of that behaviour —the operational semantics— takes the form of a transition-system model of programs combined with probability. The model characterises program execution as causing the state to change, though for probabilistic programs the precise state change can be decided by a coin flip. Thus an operational model for a probabilistic program is a function which maps an (initial) state to a (set of) *probability distributions* over final states. For example the program at (1) above maps any initial state s to a single result distribution d where $d.s_0 = 1/4$ and $d.s_1 = 3/4$. (Here s_0 and s_1 are states in which "$x = 0$" and "$x = 1$" respectively, but otherwise agree with s.) Given the details of the model we can, for example, determine the probability with which the above property "x is set to 0 finally" is established when the program executes: all we need do is evaluate $d.[x = 0]$, where d is the distribution of final states of the program, since from standard probability theory it is the probability that the predicate "$x = 0$" holds with respect to d. In this case the answer is $1/4$.

Although the operational semantics is indeed a faithful model of program behaviour, in practice —from a prover's perspective— it is too complicated to use as the basis for deriving properties of any intricacy. This becomes apparent when general program features are included in the the programming language, such as Boolean choice, nondeterminism, sequential composition and iteration. Better is to use the dual semantics —the so-called expectation transformers— which focusses directly on program properties, rather than on the details of the probabilistic transitions which imply them.

We use the *expectations* as a generalisation of predicates; they are defined to be the set of real-valued functions $\mathcal{E}S$ from the state space S to the reals $\mathbb{R}$, and they are ordered by lifting $\leq$ so that we say $A \Rightarrow A'$ if, for all $s \in S$, we have $A.s \leq A'.s$. They generalise Boolean predicates if the latter are considered as characteristic functions $S \to \{0, 1\}$ with false being zero and true one, in which case $\Rightarrow$ generalises $\Rightarrow$ as well.

To appreciate the duality we rationalise the above calculation, this time concentrating on properties rather than transitions. First of all, we use expectations to express properties rather than predicates. This immediately allows us to regard programs as *transforming* expectations consistent with their operational semantics. We write $\underline{wp}.(x := 0_{1/4} \oplus x := 1)$ for the expectation transformer associated with (1), which must now be defined in such a way that it *transforms* the *post-expectation* $[x = 0]$ to the *pre-expectation* $1/4$; more precisely we say that

$$1/4 \equiv \underline{wp}.(x := 0_{1/4} \oplus x := 1).[x = 0] .^2$$

In general, if Prog is a program, *PostE* a post-expectation, and s an initial state, then $\underline{wp}.\text{Prog}.PostE.s$ is defined to be the "greatest guaranteed expected value of *PostE* with respect to the result distributions of program Prog if executed from initial state s". We often make use of the familiar Hoare-triple format to say the same thing for all initial states at once; thus we would write equivalently

$$\{PreE\} \text{ Prog } \{PostE\} . \tag{2}$$

We say that Prog has been *correctly annotated* with a *pre-expectation PreE* and *post-expectation PostE* just when $PreE \Rightarrow \underline{wp}.\text{Prog}.PostE$.

The full definition of $\underline{wp}$, as a mapping from program texts to to expectation transformers, is set out at Fig. 1. We use the small programming language

---

[2] The underline is an indication that choice is interpreted demonically.

pGCL [11] an extension of *GCL* [3] with probabilistic choice. The definitions are almost identical to the Dijkstra's original predicate transformers, the difference being that we use a domain of expectations based on the $\Rrightarrow$ order, rather than predicates and implication. This means, conveniently, that the only apparent differences are that the definitions use arithmetical- rather than Boolean operators. Nondeterministic choice, for example, takes the minimum of its two arguments. The new operator *probabilistic choice* is parametrised by a real $0 \leq p \leq 1$ and takes the p-weighted average of its arguments.

skip	$\underline{wp}.\mathbf{skip}.A \mathrel{\widehat{=}} A$,
abort	$\underline{wp}.\mathbf{abort}.A \mathrel{\widehat{=}} 0$,
assignment	$\underline{wp}.(x := E).A \mathrel{\widehat{=}} A[E/x]$,
sequence	$\underline{wp}.(r;r').A \mathrel{\widehat{=}} \underline{wp}.r.(\underline{wp}.r'.A)$,
probability	$\underline{wp}.(r \mathbin{_p\oplus} r').A \mathrel{\widehat{=}}$ $p * \underline{wp}.r.A + (1-p) * \underline{wp}.r'.A$,
nondeterminism	$\underline{wp}.(r\|r').A \mathrel{\widehat{=}} \underline{wp}.r.A \sqcap \underline{wp}.r'.A$,
Boolean choice	$\underline{wp}.(\mathbf{if}\ B\ \mathbf{then}\ r\ \mathbf{else}\ r'\ \mathbf{fi}).A \mathrel{\widehat{=}}$ $[B] * \underline{wp}.r.A + [\neg B] * \underline{wp}.r'.A$,
iteration	$\underline{wp}.(\mathbf{do}\ B \to r\ \mathbf{od}).A \mathrel{\widehat{=}}$ $(\mu X \cdot [B] * \underline{wp}.r.X + [\neg B] * A)$.

A is an expectation, E is an expression in the program variables, and a term $(\mu X \cdot f.X)$ refers to the least fixed point of expectation-to-expectation function f with respect to $\Rrightarrow$. These definitions are dual to an operational model based on the state-to-distribution semantics [12]. We define (demonic) program refinement so that $\underline{wp}$-properties are preserved.

$$r \sqsubseteq r' \quad \text{iff} \quad (\forall A : \mathcal{ES} \mid \underline{wp}.r.A \Rrightarrow \underline{wp}.r'.A) .$$

Fig. 1. Structural definitions of $\underline{wp}$ for *pGCL*

Nondeterminism is distinguished from probabilility in the program model — unlike probability it represents truly *unquantifiable* uncertainty present in the system. This distinction leads to a logic of programs based on arithmetical properties of transformers, in which the presence of nondeterminism can be characterised by the failure to distribute addition. In Fig. 2 we set out the full transformer logic; the rules play the part of the "healthiness conditions" used by Dijkstra in his original presentation of the predicate transformers. Intuitively they characterise "legal computations" — mathematically they define the common rules satisfied exactly by $\underline{wp}$−images of programs [12]. For practical purposes this kind of "completeness" means that the prover is at liberty to appeal to any rule in Fig. 2 without disturbing the integrity of his proof.

$$subadditivity \quad \underline{wp}.\mathsf{Prog}.(A + B) \; \Lleftarrow \; \underline{wp}.\mathsf{Prog}.A + \underline{wp}.\mathsf{Prog}.B \;,$$
$$scaling \quad \underline{wp}.\mathsf{Prog}.(k * A) \; \equiv \; k * \underline{wp}.\mathsf{Prog}.A \;,$$
$$constants \quad \underline{wp}.\mathsf{Prog}.(A \ominus k) \; \Lleftarrow \; \underline{wp}.\mathsf{Prog}.A \ominus k \;.$$

A, B are expectations, k is a non-negative real, and Prog is a program. The function $\ominus$ is defined by

$$A \ominus k \quad \hat{=} \quad (A - k) \sqcup 0 \;.$$

Fig. 2. Axioms of the expectation transformer logic [12]

The decision to interpret nondeterministic choice as the minimum applies when lower bounds on guarantees are sought: one typically proves that a program establishes a postcondition with *at least* some probability. In standard logic this is reduces to the usual *total* correctness, where the postcondition is to be established with probability (at least) one.

For example the program

$$faultyFlip \quad \hat{=} \quad (x := 0 \;{}_{1/3}\oplus\; x := 1) \; [\!] \; (x := 0 \;{}_{2/3}\oplus\; x := 1) \;, \qquad (3)$$

represents the program that flips for the value of x with a probability that varies between the specified bounds, so that x is set to 0 with probability anywhere in the range $[1/3, 2/3]$. Thus we can regard *faultyFlip* as modelling a coin which does not behave like one which can exhibit an exact distribution of 0's and 1's (a feat which in any case is impossible to achieve in practice), but rather more realistically one which can approximate a probability distribution within error bounds. As suggested above, and from application of the definitions at Fig. 2, we have that $\underline{wp}.faultyFlip.[x = 0]$ is $1/3$, since all probabilistic transitions give a probability that x is set to zero of *at least* $1/3$ (even the right-most transition at (3)).

In some cases however we are interested in bounding the probabilistic properties from above, and for that we need to interpret the nondeterminism as maximum. Once we do that, refinement —corresponding to a reduction in the range of nondeterminism— means that upper bounds decrease.[3] The next definition supplies the details.

Definition 1. *The greatest possible expected value of A on execution of Prog is given by $\overline{wp}.\mathsf{Prog}.A$, where $\overline{wp}$ interprets all nondeterminism angelically: definitions in Fig. 2 remain the same except for nondeterminism which becomes*

$$\overline{wp}.(r [\!] r').A \quad \hat{=} \quad \overline{wp}.r.A \sqcup \overline{wp}.r'.A \;.$$

---

[3] This raises the question of whether "flipping" of nondeterminism from minimum to maximum should make us flip our fixed points from least- to greatest as well; we can do either, depending on how we want to interpret the performance metric in the case of non-termination. However when termination occurs with probability one (actually a slightly stronger condition [10, Sec. 2.11.1]) the fixed-points are the same, and that is the case here.

Angelic refinement decreases $\overline{wp}$-properties.

$$r \sqsubseteq r' \quad \textit{iff} \quad (\forall A : \mathcal{ES} \cdot \overline{wp}.r.A \Leftarrow \overline{wp}.r'.A) \ .$$

To see Def. 1 in action we can consider the upper bound on the probability that *faultyFlip* can establish $[x = 0]$.

$$
\begin{array}{lll}
& \overline{wp}.\textit{faultyFlip}.[x = 0] & \\
= & (x := 0 \ {}_{1/3}\oplus x := 1) \ \| \ (x := 0 \ {}_{2/3}\oplus x := 1).[x = 0] & (3) \\
= & \overline{wp}.(x := 0 \ {}_{1/3}\oplus x := 1).[x = 0] \sqcup \overline{wp}(x := 0 \ {}_{2/3}\oplus x := 1).[x = 0] & \text{Def. 1} \\
= & 1/3 \sqcup 2/3 & \\
= & 2/3 \ . &
\end{array}
$$

We write

$$\{\| \ \textit{PreE} \ \|\} \ \textsf{Prog} \ \{\| \ \textit{PostE} \ \|\} \ , \tag{4}$$

to mean that $\textit{PreE} \Leftarrow \overline{wp}.\textsf{Prog}.\textit{PostE}$, or "$\textit{PreE}$ is an upper bound on the greatest possible expected value of $\textit{PostE}$ after executing $\textsf{Prog}$".

As we shall see in the next section, for performance-style properties we are more interested in upper bounds.

3   Estimating Performance-Style Properties

The use of probability in many distributed algorithms and protocols is only to guarantee termination [5,14] — in these cases a proof of termination can often boil down to the behaviour of a finite-state probabilistic process, and techniques for proving termination *with probability 1* are explored in detail elsewhere [10]. The idea is to combine the notion of a standard program variant with probability theory, so that now a *termination variant* may either increase or decrease within some finite range of values provided that there is always some fixed probability with which it is guaranteed to decrease.

We summarise the main steps in a probabilistic proof rule [10, p.191]. Let V be an integer-valued expression in the program variables. Suppose further that

1. there are some fixed integer constants L (low) and H (high) such that $L \leq V \leq H$ is an invariant of the loop, and
2. for some fixed probability $\epsilon > 0$, and for all integers N we have

$$\epsilon[G \wedge (V = N)] \quad \Rightarrow \quad \underline{wp}.\textit{body}.[V < N] \ .$$

Then termination is certain everywhere.

Next we study the *expected time to termination*, and how to reason about it in a Hoare-style framework.

We begin with the simple case of *faultyFlip* inside a loop

$$
\begin{array}{l}
\textit{faultyLoop} \quad \hat{=} \\
\quad \textbf{do} \ \ x = 1 \rightarrow \ (x := 0 \ {}_{1/3}\oplus x := 1) \ \| \ (x := 0 \ {}_{2/3}\oplus x := 1) \ \textbf{od} \ ,
\end{array}
$$

and consider how to compute the expected number of times the loop body must iterate until x is set to 0. Using our definitions we see that, if we add a fresh variable n which is updated at the end of every iteration, so that

$$faultyLoop_n \quad \hat{=} \quad \textbf{do } x = 1 \rightarrow$$
$$(x := 0 \; _{1/3}\oplus \; x := 1) [] (x := 0 \; _{2/3}\oplus \; x := 1);$$
$$n := n + 1$$
$$\textbf{od} \; ,$$

we may compute the least expected number of iterations by evaluating

$$\underline{wp}.(n := 0; faultyLoop_n).n \; .$$

Here n, as a postcondition, is simply the expectation which returns the value of n in its current state. However, if we now imagine that $faultyLoop$ is used to guarantee termination in a distributed protocol, we would be more interested in the greatest expected number of iterations.

Definition 2. *The greatest expected time to termination of a loop with terminating body*
$$loop \quad \hat{=} \quad \textbf{do } B \rightarrow Prog \; \textbf{od} \; ,$$

is given by
$$\mathcal{T}(loop) \quad \hat{=} \quad \lim_{N \geq 1} (\overline{wp}.loop_N.n) \; ,$$

where

$$loop_N \quad \hat{=} \quad \textbf{do } (B \wedge n < N) \rightarrow Prog; n := n + 1 \; \textbf{od} \; .$$

In fact Def. 2 computes the longest expected execution path until termination.[4]
    Combining the above results reveals a rule for proving upper bounds on worst-case expected performance of programs.

Lemma 1. *Let loop be defined by*

$$loop \quad \hat{=} \quad \textbf{do } B \rightarrow Prog \; \textbf{od} \; .$$

If E is an expectation such that

$$\{| \; [B] \times (E - 1) \; |\} \quad Prog \quad \{| \; E \; |\},[5] \tag{5}$$

then $\mathcal{T}(loop)$ is bounded above by E. We call such an expectation a bounding *variant.*

---

[4] The reason we take an explicit limit is to avoid arithmetic with ∞ in Fig. 1's definition of loop semantics.

[5] Often in proving properties of a loop body it's convenient to assume truth of some predicate whose invariance is proved separately via standard (*i.e.* non-probabilistic) $\underline{wp}$ [10, Lem. 1.7.1]. That technique applies here also.

Proof. We show that $\overline{wp}.loop_N \Rrightarrow E + n$, and the result then follows from Def. 2 (where as before n is a fresh variable, so that E is independent of it). First we show that $[\neg B \vee n = N] \times n + [B \wedge n < N] \times \overline{wp}.Prog.(E + n) \Rrightarrow E + n$, as follows:

$$
\begin{array}{ll}
& [\neg B \vee n = N] \times n + [B \wedge n < N] \times \overline{wp}.Prog;(n := n + 1).(E + n) \\
\equiv & [\neg B \vee n = N] \times n + [B \wedge n < N] \times \overline{wp}.Prog.(E + n + 1) \\
\Rrightarrow & [\neg B \vee n = N] \times n + [B \wedge n < N] \times (E + n) \qquad \qquad (5), (4), arithmetic \\
\Rrightarrow & E + n \ . \qquad\qquad\qquad\qquad\qquad\qquad\qquad\qquad\qquad\qquad\qquad\qquad 0 \Rrightarrow E
\end{array}
$$

Appealing now to the least fixed point property, we see that $\overline{wp}.loop_N \Rrightarrow E + n$, as required.

To see Lem. 1 in action, we consider the expected number of iterations of *faultyLoop* above. We note that

$$\{\!| \ 2[x = 1] \ |\!\} \quad faultyFlip \quad \{\!| \ 3[x = 1] \ |\!\} \ , \tag{6}$$

since

$$
\begin{array}{lll}
& \overline{wp}.faultyFlip.(3 * [x = 1]) & \\
\equiv & 3 * \overline{wp}.faultyFlip.[x = 1] & \overline{wp} \text{ distributes scalars} \\
\equiv & 3 * 2/3 & \\
\equiv & 2 \ . &
\end{array}
$$

Thus we are able to deduce that, for any execution of the nondeterminism in *faultyLoop*, it must terminate after performing on average no more than 3 iterations.

In this section we have illustrated some general results for deducing the expected-performance-style properties of programs. Our approach is to analyse an *abstraction* of the program, then using program refinement to associate the results with a refinement.

Whether we use the program logic for demonic $\sqsubseteq$ or angelic $\sqsubseteq$ refinement depends on whether we are concerned with correctness (demonic: postcondition established with probability at least some p) or performance (angelic: expected iterations is at most some N). In either case, since refinement preserves program properties we see that if we prove termination with probability one of the abstraction, then any demonic refinement will also terminate with probability one. Similarly any upper bound or worst case behaviour of the abstraction is also an upper bound or worst case behaviour of any angelic refinement.

Note that "removing $[\!]$" achieves both forms of refinement simultaneously, as one would expect: our separation of the two is so that we do not have to calculate both if in fact we're interested in only one of them.

4   Case Study: Self-stabilisation Algorithms

We illustrate the above techniques on two case studies. The first is a leadership-election protocol, in which the stable states are those where exactly one of N

participants is the leader, allowed by convention then to take certain actions on behalf of the group; an unstable state is one where there is no leader or several (aspiring) leaders, perhaps due to hardware failure; and the stabilisation algorithm is to bring about the exactly-one-leader situation again. We analyse the expected time for the election to complete.

The second case study is a general network in which tokens circulate (an abstraction of many distributed algorithms); unstable states are those in which there are several tokens; stable states are those in which there is exactly one.

The difference between the two studies is that in the first, the communication pattern is regular (all-to-all) and the unstable state is presumed to be detected somehow, leading to the initiation of the stabilisation protocol. In the second, the network and communication patterns are so general that we can only hope to establish termination (and not expected time to it), and the stabilisation algorithm is running continuously, without any need to detect unstable states.

4.1   A Leadership-Election Protocol

Our first example is a leadership-election protocol [1, Sec. 8.5.4] for a totally connected network of processes; we show that its expected number of rounds to stabilisation is constant.[6]

We first give an informal description of the protocol.

Informal description and formalisation. A number N of processes are to elect a single leader. On each round, each process chooses a number k for itself, uniformly from $1..N$, and sends its choice to all other processes. Each process then separately acts as follows:

- If no process chose 1, then it enters a new round.
- If some processes chose 1, but it did not, then it drops out.
- If it and possibly other processes chose 1, it enters a new round.

The election is finished when only one process remains. We formalise the protocol in Fig. 3; more detailed descriptions would be angelic refinements of this one.

Rapid termination. We note first that the protocol of Fig. 3 terminates exponentially fast, that is the chance of its taking more than some number of steps M is exponentially small in M.

---

[6] The earlier example of cricket can illustrate rounds, and expected time to termination. The normal protocol is *not* symmetric, because one team flips and the other calls. But the time to termination is exactly one flip.

   A truly symmetric protocol would employ three coins, and both teams and the referee would flip all at once: the winning team would be the first to flip a face different from the other two. This protocol has constant *expected* time to termination of two rounds of three simultaneous flips each, assuming the coins are fair. (It still works if the players' coins are unfair —one never knows— but then it could take longer.)

1      $n := N$
2   **do** $n > 1 \;\rightarrow$
3          $n' :\in \{k: 0..n \;@\; \binom{n}{k} \times (n-1)^{n-k}/n^n\}$
4   **if** $n' \neq 0$ **then** $n := n'$ **fi**
       od

1— Initially all N processes participate; subsequently n is the number (still) participating at any point, and n decreases over time as processes drop out.
2— Termination occurs when only one process remains, and it becomes the leader. (Note that $1 \leq n \leq N$ is an invariant.)
3— Here with operator $:\in$ we choose n' from a distribution, indicated by a set-like comprehension (bound variable k) but containing an @ for "with probability" (instead of a | for "such that"), in which the probability of there having been being k processes that chose 1 (out of $1..n$) is explicitly given.
4— If no processes chose 1, then they all go on to the next round (and n is not changed); if at least one processor chose 1, then it and any others similarly go on to the next round. (Note therefore that they all go 'round again in *two* cases: all chose 1, or none did.)

Fig. 3. Leadership election protocol

Sufficient for that is a bounded-away-from-zero probability of termination on any single iteration. That is trivial, by inspection, as the probability of setting n' to 1 is just

$$\binom{n}{1} \times (n-1)^{n-1}/n^n \quad = \quad (n-1/n)^{n-1}$$

which, being anti-monotonic in n, is bounded below by $(N-1/N)^{(N-1)}$ no matter what value n has as the loop continues to execute.

Expected iterations. We now show that the expected number of iterations is constant. We assume that constant to be some E, and by a schematic proof find suitable conditions for it. Since termination occurs in zero steps when $n = 1$, we choose our bounding variant to be

$$E \times [n > 1] \;,$$

and from Lem. 1 we must show that $n > 1$ (the guard) implies

$$E \times [n > 1] \;-\; 1 \quad \Leftarrow \quad \overline{wp}. \text{``3;4 in Fig. 3''} . (E \times [n > 1]) \;.$$

Here is the calculation:

$$E \times [n - 1]$$

$$\cdot \equiv \quad \textbf{if } n' \neq 0 \textbf{ then } E \times [n' > 1] \textbf{ else } E \times [n > 1] \textbf{ fi} \qquad \text{applying } \overline{wp}.(4)$$

$$\cdot \equiv \quad \left(\sum k : 1..n \cdot E \times [k > 1] \times \binom{n}{k} \times (n-1)^{n-k}/n^n \right) \qquad \text{applying } \overline{wp}.(3)$$

$$+ E \times [n > 1] \times \binom{n}{0} \times (n-1)^n/n^n$$

$$\equiv \quad E \times \left(\sum k : 2..n \cdot \binom{n}{k} \times (n-1)^{n-k}/n^n \right) \qquad \text{arithmetic; assumption } n > 1$$

$$+ E \times \binom{n}{0} \times (n-1)^n/n^n$$

$$\equiv \quad E \times (1 - ((n-1)/n)^n - ((n-1)/n)^{n-1} \qquad \text{arithmetic}$$

$$+ E \times ((n-1)/n)^n$$

$$\equiv \quad E \times (1 - ((n-1)/n)^{n-1}) \qquad \text{arithmetic}$$

$$\Rightarrow \quad E \times [n > 1] \ - \ 1 \qquad \text{assume } n > 1 \text{ and } 1 \leq E \times ((n-1)/n)^{n-1}$$

Our assumption, rearranged, is that for $n \geq 2$ we have

$$(n-1/n)^{n-1} \ \geq \ 1/E \ ,$$

a property that holds for the "real" $e = 2.718 \cdots$

Thus we have shown that the protocol terminates in expected constant time no more than e, that is just under 3, rounds. If the rounds themselves cost time N each (for the exchange of N messages), then the expected time complexity of stabilisation is no more than $3N$.

A more severe abstraction. There is however an alternative approach, in which our initial description of the algorithm is "more severely abstracted" — we note merely whether $n = 1$ or not. Letting Boolean b record that abstraction, our algorithm is transformed into the one shown in Fig. 4.

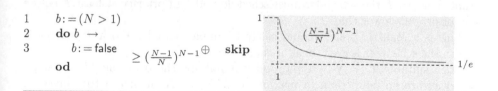

```
1    b := (N > 1)
2    do b →
3        b := false
     od
```
$\geq \left(\frac{N-1}{N} \right)^{N-1} \oplus$ **skip**

Fig. 4. Leadership election protocol, more severely abstracted

We justify the abstraction by noting that the only command that sets n to 1 in the original $(3; 4)$ does so with probability

$$\binom{n}{k} \times (n-1)^{n-k}/n^n \ = \ \left(\frac{n-1}{n} \right)^{n-1} \qquad \text{when } k = 1,$$

that we know $n \leq N$, and that the expression shown is anti-monotonic in n (tending to $1/e$ from above), so that the $n = N$ case —as appears in the abstracted algorithm— is indeed the most pessimistic value.

The expected number of rounds here is then no more than the inverse of that probability, which tends to e from below as N increases without bound.

But is this easier, really? The work to prove the soundness of the abstraction Fig. 4 is probably the same as required to do the earlier calculations anyway.

4.2   A Token-Graph Stabilisation Algorithm

As a second example we treat a more general situation whose exact behaviour is quite complex but for which, nevertheless, proof of termination is still possible using the techniques we have explained.

Informal description. There is a strongly connected directed graph with N nodes; each node is either full (contains a token) or empty (doesn't). An adversarial scheduler (but fair — see below) repeatedly selects some single node to take a step:

  – If the node is empty, nothing happens.
  – If the node is full then it chooses between keeping its token or passing it one step along an outgoing edge. The choice is made probabilistically, with a fixed non-zero lower bound applied to each alternative (including keeping). (Note that if the lower bounds sum to less than one, the node can itself act demonically — thus we have demonic choice potentially in both the scheduling and in the nodes' actions.)

Any node receiving a token becomes full (but never "over-full" — multiple tokens reduce to one).

The adversarial scheduler. We allow the scheduler to choose nodes demonically, except for the following fairness constraint. Say that a node's *priority* is the number of steps since it was last scheduled: we require that for some fixed constant (trigger) T the scheduler must schedule nodes of priority at least T before any of priority lower than T.

This is a realistic policy (could easily be implemented), and if T is large it allows the scheduler a great deal of choice.

With suitable $T \geq N > 1$ the policy maintains the invariant ($I1$) that all priorities are no more than (a maximum) $M = T+N$, which in turn gives an easy variant to show that no node is forever overlooked. To prove the invariant we need a subsidiary invariant ($I2$), that

> if there is a node with priority p satisfying $T \leq p \leq M$, then there are at least $p-T$ nodes with priority below $p-N$.

Truth of $I1$ is immediate from $I2$ and the fact that there are only N nodes: assume for a contradiction that some "high" node has priority p more than M;

then from $I2$ there would be more than $M - T = (T + N) - T = N$ nodes with priority below $p - N$. Since there are only N nodes overall, that is a contradiction.

Preservation of $I2$ is argued as follows. Suppose a step has just been taken, and consider all nodes in turn, just after a step has been taken: all nodes will have "new" priority one more than their "old" priority, except for the one scheduled, whose new priority will be 0.

If a node's new priority p satisfies $p < T$, then $I2$ is true trivially (false antecedent); if it satisfies $p = T$ then $I2$ is again trivial (there are at least zero nodes satisfying anything).

In the remaining case where the new priority p satisfies $T < p \le M$ then —because $p - T$ has increased by one— we must show there to be one more node prioritised below $p - N$ after the step than there were below $(p-1) - N$ before the step. Since all not-scheduled nodes below $(p-1) - N$ before are (still) below $p - N$ now, and also the just-scheduled node is below $p - N$ now with its new priority 0 satisfying $0 < p - N$ (because $p > T \ge N$), we need only show that the just-scheduled node was *not* below $(p-1) - N$ before.

Suppose the just-scheduled node had priority p' before. Since $T < p$ now, we know that $T \le p'$, since otherwise by the policy p' would not have been scheduled instead of p. We reason

$$
\begin{array}{lll}
 & p' \not< (p-1) - N & \\
\text{iff} & p' \ge (p-1) - N & \\
\text{if} & T \ge (p-1) - N & p' \ge T \\
\text{if} & T \ge (M-1) - N & p \le M \\
\text{iff} & T \ge (T+N-1) - N & M = T+N \\
\text{iff} & T \ge T-1 \,, &
\end{array}
$$

which concludes the argument for maintaining $I2$.

Formalisation of the protocol. Say that a *full cover* of the nodes is a directed path in which all full nodes appear; its *size* is the number of nodes in it (including of course any empty ones along the way). A *minimal* full cover (MFC) is a full cover of minimum size; and the *minimum cover size* (MCS) is the size of a minimal full cover.

We say that a node is a *straggler* if it is the trailing node of some MFC. The importance of stragglers is that, if scheduled, they will with non-zero probability decrease the MCS by choosing to move one edge along the MFC they are at the end of.

Let NId be a set of (unique) node identifiers, so that $\#NId = N$. Function $pr\colon NId \to \mathbb{N}$ gives the priority of each node, zeroed whenever it is scheduled and incremented otherwise.

The set $sgs\colon \mathbb{P}NId$ contains the NId's of the stragglers. Natural number $mcs\colon \mathbb{N}$ is the minimum cover size; note that if $mcs = 1$ then there is only one full node, and the algorithm should terminate.

In Fig. 5 is a program giving the behaviour of these variables; more detailed descriptions would be demonic refinements of this one. It turns out, surprisingly, that we do not have to keep track of which nodes are full: information about sgs is enough.

```
    pr: = 0;                        // All nodes' priorities initially zero.
    do mcs > 1 →
       // — Book-keeping of priorities; selection of token; fairness constraint. —
1      pr: = pr + 1;                // Increment all priorities...
       n :∈ NId;                    // ...but then choose one node...
       pr.n: = 0;                   // ...and schedule it.
       [pr ≤ M];                    // Require for fairness that no priority is too large.

       // — Movement of selected token: straggler, or not? —
       if n ∈ sgs  →                // If the scheduled node is a straggler...
2              ( mcs :<₁ mcs        // ...then it might decrease mcs...
                ≥ₚ⊕                 // ...but if it moves the wrong way...
3                mcs :≤₁ N );       // ...then anything goes.
4          sgs :⊆₁ NId             // Either way, the stragglers can change.

       ▯ n ∉ sgs  →                 // If it's not a straggler...
5              ( skip               // ...then it might stay where it is...
                ≥ₚ⊕                 // ...but, if not, again...
                mcs :≤₁ N;          // ...anything goes...
                sgs :⊆₁ NId)        // ...and stragglers can change if it moved.
       fi
    od
```

Assignments and tests to pr as a whole operate pointwise: thus $(pr + 1)$ increments all priorities, and $(pr \leq)$ bounds all priorities.

The "coercion" $[pr \leq M]$ acts as a miracle (in theory causing backtracking) if its predicate is false, having the effect thus of forcing earlier nondeterminism —if possible— never to *make* it false. The nondeterminism in this case is the selection $n{:}{\in}NId$ of the node to schedule, and our earlier argument establishing *I1* simply shows that there are non-backtracking implementations of the nondeterminism which make the scheduling feasible.

The assignments $:<_1$, $:\leq_1$ and $:\subseteq_1$ are nondeterministic choices according to the relation given, but requiring that the result be at least 1, or non-empty, as appropriate.

Note that in the $n \in sgs$ alternative the assignment to sgs occurs unconditionally; in the $n \notin sgs$ alternative, it occurs only with probability $< p$.

Fig. 5. Stabilisation of token network: abstraction

Termination of the algorithm. Define *V0* to be the maximum over all $n \in sgs$ of $pr.n$; this cannot exceed M. Define *V1* to be mcs. Then the termination variant overall is lexicographic, with *V0* ascending and *V1* descending:

$$V0 \;\;\widehat{=}\;\; (\sqcap n\colon sgs \cdot pr.n)$$
$$V1 \;\;\widehat{=}\;\; mcs$$

$$V \;\;\widehat{=}\;\; V1 \times (M+1) - V0 \,.$$

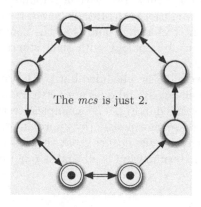

The directed network is connected as shown; note the uni-directional arc at bottom right. Nodes in a minimal cover are shown double-bordered, and the cover's arcs are double-arrowed.

On the left, the *mcs* is just two, and the algorithm is "near" termination: both full nodes are min-stragglers. We suppose the right-hand min-straggler is selected but — unfortunately— the probabilistic choice $\geq_p \oplus$ goes against us, and Statement 3 is executed for that node.

As a result the small minimal full cover is replaced by a very large one, and the variant V has *increased* substantially, by approximately $5M$ (where M, recall, is the fairness parameter for scheduling).

The virtue of the probabilistic variant is that these complex situations *do not matter* for termination —they can be ignored— as long as their probability of occurrence is bounded away from one.

Fig. 6. A straggler moves "the wrong way"

This variant is bounded below by zero because $V1$ is at least 1 (loop guard) and $V0$ never exceeds M (invariant $I1$, enforced by the coercion).

Thus for termination with probability one it is sufficient to show that on each iteration V strictly decreases with non-zero probability. Informally we argue that there are two cases:

- A straggler is scheduled, in which case with probability at least p the sub-variant $V1$ decreases by at least one (Statement 2). Sub-variant $-V0$ can increase (Statement 4), but not by more than M. Hence overall V decreases by at least 1.
- or a non-straggler is scheduled, in which case with probability at least p sub-variant $V1$ is unchanged (Statement 5), but sub-variant $-V0$ has (already) decreased by 1 (Statement 1). Again, V must decrease with non-zero probability.

Those two cases are sufficient to establish termination with probability one.

Illustration of the complexity avoided. Once the termination variant is found, the termination argument (as usual) is very straightforward. Recall however that we are illustrating novel *probabilistic* variant techniques, and that the control of complexity they provide was "designed in" by analogy with their standard versions, and we are taking advantgage of it.

Consider for example the case where a straggler is scheduled but (with probability $< p$) it moves "the wrong way" (Statement 3) and does not act to reduce the minimum cover size: this situation is illustrated in Fig. 6 for a simple directed ring topology. Although the variant can increase enormously (by approximately $5M$ in the figure), the probabilistic-variant technique ensures that those situations need not be analysed if probability-one termination is all that is required.

5   Conclusions

We have illustrated how the expectation-transformer approach to verification can be used to calculate both correctness and performance-style properties of probabilistic programs by reasoning at the source-code level. The fact that refinement is an integral part of the expectation transformers means that we may transfer proved properties of the abstraction to any refinement, a feature which separates us from other approaches to program verification, such as model checking [13,6,8]. This effectively allows us to use "lightweight" methods, leaving the bulk of the formality to a proof of refinement, and techniques for expediting that are addressed elsewhere [10], some of which have mechanised support [7].

In standard program semantics the use of a program variant is sufficient to supply both an upper bound on performance (number of iteration of a loop) as well as termination. In the probabilistic systems, it appears at first that the two must be separated — but in fact the bounding variant is the more general [2], although the termination variant is rather easier to use.

Other systems using refinement for performance include Hallerstede *et al.* [4] and Sere *et al.* [15].

Acknowledgements

We thank the reviewers for their helpful comments.

References

1. G. Brassard and P. Bratley. *Fundamentals of Algorithmics.* Prentice-Hall, 1996.
2. O. Celiku and A. McIver. Compositional specification and analysis of cost-based properties in probabilistic programs. In *Proceedings of Formal Methods 2005*, number 3582 in LNCS, 2005.
3. E.W. Dijkstra. *A Discipline of Programming.* Prentice Hall International, Englewood Cliffs, N.J., 1976.
4. S. Hallerstede and M. Butler. Performance analysis of probabilistic action systems. *Formal Aspects of Computing*, 16(4):313–331, 2004.

5. T. Herman. Probabilistic self-stabilization. *Inf. Proc. Lett.*, 35(2):63–7, 1990.
6. J. Hillston. *A Compositional Approach to Performance Modelling.* Cambridge University Press, 1996.
7. TS Hoang, Z Jin, K Robinson, A McIver, and C Morgan. Development via refinement in probabilistic B. In *Proc. of ZB 2005*, number 3455 in LNCS, 2005.
8. J.-P. Katoen, J. Meyer-Kayser, and M. Siegle. A Markov-chain model checker. In *Tools and Algorithms for the Construction and Analysis of Systems (TACAS 2000)*, volume 1785 of *LNCS*, pages 347–362. Springer Verlag, 2000.
9. A.K. McIver, C.C. Morgan, J.W. Sanders, and K. Seidel. Probabilistic Systems Group: Collected reports. `web.comlab.ox.ac.uk/oucl/research/areas/probs`.
10. Annabelle McIver and Carroll Morgan. *Abstraction, Refinement and Proof for Probabilistic Systems.* Technical Monographs in Computer Science. Springer Verlag, New York, 2004.
11. C.C. Morgan and A.K. McIver. *pGCL*: Formal reasoning for random algorithms. *South African Computer Journal*, 22, March 1999. Available at [9, key PGCL].
12. C.C. Morgan, A.K. McIver, and K. Seidel. Probabilistic predicate transformers. *ACM Transactions on Programming Languages and Systems*, 18(3):325–53, May 1996. `doi.acm.org/10.1145/229542.229547`.
13. PRISM. Probabilistic symbolic model checker. `www.cs.bham.ac.uk/~dxp/prism`.
14. M.O. Rabin. The choice-coordination problem. *Acta Informatica*, 17(2):121–34, June 1982.
15. Kaisa Sere and Elena Troubitsyna. Probabilities in action systems. In *Proc. of the 8th Nordic Workshop on Programming Theory*, 1996.
16. David Stirzaker. *Elementary Probability.* Cambridge University Press, 1994.

Formal Analysis of the Operational Concept for the Small Aircraft Transportation System

César Muñoz[1], Víctor Carreño[2], and Gilles Dowek[3]

[1] National Institute of Aerospace, 100 Exploration Way, Hampton VA 23666, USA
`munoz@nianet.org`
[2] NASA Langley Research Center, Hampton VA 23666, USA
`victor.a.carreno@nasa.gov`
[3] École polytechnique, 91128 Palaiseau Cedex, France
`Gilles.Dowek@polytechnique.fr`

Abstract. The Small Aircraft Transportation System (SATS) is a NASA project aimed at increasing access to small non-towered non-radar airports in the US. SATS is a radical new approach to air traffic management where pilots flying instrument flight rules are responsible for separation without air traffic control services. In this paper, the SATS project serves as a case study of an operational air traffic concept that has been designed and analyzed primarily using formal techniques. The SATS concept of operations is modeled using non-deterministic, asynchronous transition systems, which are then formally analyzed using state exploration techniques. The objective of the analysis is to show, in a mathematical framework, that the concept of operation complies with a set of safety requirements such as absence of dead-locks, maintaining aircraft separation, and robustness with respect to the occurrence of off-nominal events. The models also serve as design tools. Indeed, they were used to configure the nominal flight procedures and the geometry of the SATS airspace.

Acronyms	
AMM	Airport Management Module
FAF	Final Approach Fix
HVO	Higher Volume Operations
IAF	Initial Approach Fix
IF	Intermediate Fix
IMC	Instrument Meteorological Conditions
MAHF	Missed Approach Holding Fix
PVS	Prototype Verification System
SATS	Small Aircraft Transportation System
SCA	Self-Controlled Area

1   Introduction

The primary safety objective of an air traffic management system is to provide aircraft separation. This objective is achieved trough air/ground equipment and a set of flight rules and procedures, usually called *concept of operations*. Emerging

M. Butler et al. (Eds.): Fault-Tolerant Systems, LNCS 4157, pp. 306–325, 2006.

and more reliable surveillance and communication technologies have enabled new concepts where pilots and air traffic controllers share the responsibility for traffic separation. One of such concepts is NASA's *Small Aircraft Transportation System (SATS), Higher Volume Operation (SATS HVO)* [1].

The SATS project aims to increase access to small airports in the US during instrument approach operations. Currently, under poor weather conditions, small airports are restricted to *one-in/one-out* operations. The SATS HVO concept enables up to four simultaneous arrival approaches and multiple departures. A key aspect of the concept is that, under nominal operations, aircraft are *self-separated*, i.e., pilots are responsible for separation without assistance of an air traffic controller. To this end, the SATS HVO concept designs the airspace surrounding the airport as a *Self-Controlled Area (SCA)*. A centralized, automated system, called the *Airport Management Module* (AMM), serves as an arbiter to aircraft entering the SCA. In this concept, aircraft constantly broadcast their locations and receive traffic aircraft locations. Therefore, they have an updated view of the airspace.

The SATS HVO operational concept is a collection of rules and procedures to be followed by aircraft operating or transitioning in/out of the SCA. For instance, the concept of operations states when and how an aircraft is allowed to enter (or leave) the SCA, when an aircraft is allowed to initiate the approach, and how to perform a missed approach. In order to alleviate pilot workload and increase situational awareness, on board navigation tools provide advisories that assist pilots in following these procedures. An overview of the SATS HVO operational concept is given in Section 2.

Because the operational concept is a safety critical element of the SATS project, the task of showing that it satisfies safety requirements is accomplished using formal mathematical analysis. A discrete mathematical model of the SATS HVO operational concept for nominal operations is described in [11]. That model was mechanically checked for safety and liveness properties. The discrete model, and its limitations, is presented in Section 3.

In this paper, we extend the discrete model in [11] in two orthogonal ways. First, in Section 4, we include off-nominal procedures such as closing of the SCA and re-sequencing of aircraft. We verify that most of the safety properties are still maintained with minimal modifications to the operational concept. Second, in Section 5, we study spacing and separation issues in the Self-Controlled Airspace. To this end, we describe a *hybrid* model that extends the discrete model to take into account the geometry of the SCA and the aircraft speed performances. Using this new model, we formally verified that the SATS HVO operational concept *effectively* achieves self-separation, i.e., aircraft performing nominal approaches are safely separated according to minimum spacing criteria.

2   Higher Volume Operations

In the SATS HVO concept, pilots operating within the Self-Controlled Area (SCA) are required to fly by latitude/longitude points in the space, called *fixes*.

Similar to a GPS-T approach, fixes are arranged as a T (see Figure 1).[1] The fixes at the extremes of the T are called *initial approach fixes* (IAF's) and they are the entry points to the SCA. The IAF's also serve as *missed approach holding fixes* (MAHF's), i.e., fixes where aircraft will proceed in case they have to perform a missed approach. The holding areas are located at 2000 feet and 3000 feet above ground level at the IAF's.

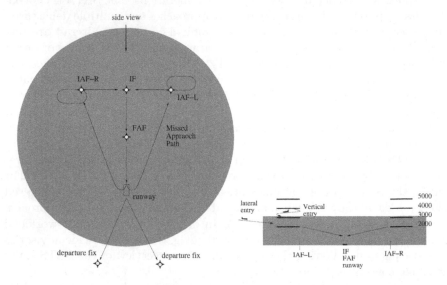

Fig. 1. Top and side view of SCA

There are two types of entry procedures: *vertical entry* and *lateral entry*. In a vertical entry, an aircraft at the IAF descends from 4000 feet to 3000 feet and holds at 3000 feet until it is enabled to descend to 2000 feet. In a lateral entry, an aircraft flies directly to its IAF at or above 2000 feet. When the aircraft is enabled to initiate the approach, it flies to the *intermediate fix* (IF), from there to the *final approach fix* (FAF), and finally to the runway threshold. In case of a missed approach, the aircraft flies to its assigned missed approach holding fix at the lowest available altitude (2000 or 3000 feet). Then, it re-initiates the approach and either follows a normal landing procedure or leaves the SCA. The linear segments between the IAFs and the IF are called *base segments*; the segment between the IF and the runway threshold is called the *final segment*. Henceforth, we say that an aircraft is *on final approach* if it is in the base or final segments.

The Airport Management Module (AMM) is an automated centralized system that resides at the airport grounds. It receives state information from aircraft in the vicinity of the airport and communicates with aircraft via data link. The AMM provides entry clearances (vertical or lateral) and assigns missed approach

---

[1] As it is usually depicted, right and left are relative to the pilot facing the runway, i.e., opposite from the reader's point of view.

holding fixes. When an entry is granted by the AMM, the aircraft receives a *follow notification* and a *missed approach holding fix assignment*. The follow notification is either *none*, if it is the first aircraft in the landing sequence, or the identification of a *lead* aircraft. Missed approach holding fixes are assigned by the AMM on an alternating basis. This technique ensures that consecutive aircraft on missed approach are not flying to the same missed approach holding fix.

For nominal arrival operations, self-separation is achieved by requiring an aircraft to hold at its IAF until it meets a spacing safety threshold with respect to its lead aircraft. The threshold guarantees a minimum separation during the approach and during a missed approach, in case of this eventuality.

The concept of operations also describes nominal departure operations. However, for simplicity, the analysis presented in this paper only considers arrival operations. This simplification does not affect the result of the formal verification as arriving aircraft are geographically separated from departing aircraft and an aircraft cannot depart if there is an aircraft on final approach. The fact that departing aircraft are separated was also verified using the techniques presented in this paper.

3   Discrete Model and Its Limitations

The discrete model described in [11] is a mathematical abstraction of the SATS HVO concept. A simple way to visualize that model is via an analogy with a board game where the board is a discretized SCA, the pieces that move across the board are the aircraft, and the rules of the game are given by the concept of operations. This analogy is illustrated in Figure 2.The places where an aircraft can be during an arrival operation are called *zones*. There are 12 zones:

- holding3 (left, right): Holding patterns at 3000 feet.
- holding2 (left, right): Holding patterns at 2000 feet.
- lez (left, right): Lateral entry zones.[2]
- base (left, right): Base segments.
- maz (left, right): Missed approach zones.
- final and runway: Final segment and runway.

An aircraft is always in one and only one zone, but several aircraft may be in the same zone. Aircraft leave the zones in the same order as they arrive. The arrows in Figure 2 are the valid moves and they represent 15 flight rules and procedures:

- Vertical entry (left, right): Initial move to holding3.
- Lateral entry (left, right): Initial move to lez.
- Descend (left, right): Move from holding3 to holding2.
- Approach initiation (left, right): Move from holding2 to base.
- Final approach (left, right): Move from base to final.

---

[2] Lateral entry zones start outside the SCA.

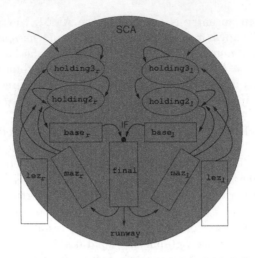

Fig. 2. Discrete view of SCA

- Landing: Move from `final` to `runway`.
- Missed approach initiation (left, right): Move from `final` to `maz`.
- Transition to lowest available altitude (left, right). Move from `maz` to either `holding3` or `holding2`.

The *state of the SCA* is then composed of the 12 zones, each one being a list of aircraft, the next available landing sequence (natural number), and the next alternating missed approach holding fix (left or right). Each aircraft is represented by its initial approach fix (left or right), landing sequence (natural number), and missed approach holding fix assignment (left or right). Aircraft identifications are implicit as aircraft can be distinguished from each other by their landing sequence.

The discrete model is conservative in the sense that it abstracts away the SCA geometry and physical performance parameters of the aircraft. Hence, it includes scenarios that may no physically occur in the real world. We argue that the model is complete, i.e., it includes all nominal operations. Indeed, the model has been extensively reviewed by the developers of the SATS HVO concept.

From a mathematical point of view, the discrete model is a state transition system where the states are snapshots of the zones at discrete times and the transitions describe how the states evolve when the flight procedures are applied. A priori, there are no bounds on the number of aircraft in each zone; therefore, the transition system is potentially infinite. However, an exhaustive exploration of the set of reachable states reveals that the transition system is finite. Indeed, the system was exhaustively explored [11] using an explicit model checker algorithm written and formally verified in the verification system PVS [12].

Using formal techniques, it has been shown in [11] that, under nominal operations, the concept satisfies the following safety properties:

- There are at most four arriving aircraft.
- There are no more than two aircraft assigned to a given missed approach holding fix.
- For an aircraft on missed approach, there is always an available altitude at the assigned MAHF.
- There are at most two aircraft on each side of the SCA.
- There is at most one aircraft holding at a given altitude of a holding fix.
- There are at most two aircraft on missed approach assigned to the same MAHF.
- There are no simultaneous lateral and vertical entries at a given fix.
- Aircraft land in order according to the landing sequence.

Furthermore, it has been verified that each reachable state evolves into an empty SCA when entry rules are inhibited, and that the concept of operations is free of dead-locks, i.e., all aircraft eventually land (or depart).

The rest of this section illustrates some limitations of the discrete model that are addressed by this paper.

3.1   Off-Nominal Operations

It is very difficult, if possible, to handle the occurrence of off-nominal events in a comprehensive way. For this reason, the operational concept for off-nominal SATS HVO operations [2] only addresses *pragmatic failures and operational errors*, i.e., conditions that have a practical expectation for occurrence. These conditions are further segregated in three categories:

1. *Routine non-normal conditions* due to pilot deviations from nominal operations.
2. *Equipment malfunction conditions* due to hardware failures.
3. *Emergency conditions* that cause a landing priority request.

In general, safety properties are not preserved under operations that are non-conforming to SATS HVO procedures. For example, if an aircraft returns to its incorrect missed approach holding fix, there is no guarantee that the aircraft will find an available altitude to hold. However, for this situation to occur, the pilot would have already ignored the information provided by the Multi-Function Display and the Pilot Adviser, which are components of the SATS HVO concept. Furthermore, the Conflict Detection and Alerting system provides an additional layer of safety to the overall system [4].

The discrete model presented in [11] does not include off-nominal operations. Given the complex nature of off-nominal events, a complete mathematical model of off-nominal operations is a major endeavor. In this work, we aim at a simpler objective. We extend the discrete SATS HVO model with procedures for SCA closing, re-sequencing, and re-assignment during a missed approach. These procedures are critical to several procedures for off-nominal conditions.

3.2 Self-separation Guarantees

Consider the two states depicted in Figure 3. Although these states do not satisfy the same separation requirements, they are indistinguishable by the discrete model. This behavior is due to the way the approach initiation procedure was written in the discrete model. The concept of operations states that an aircraft

(a) Aircraft A and B are separated   (b) Aircraft A and B are not separated

Fig. 3. Indistinguishable discrete states

may initiate the approach if (a) it is the first aircraft in the landing sequence or (b) it meets a safety threshold with respect to the lead aircraft, which is already on approach [1]. There are several ways a pilot can check whether the safety threshold is satisfied or not. In the most conservative case, the pilot has to delay the approach initiation until the lead aircraft is within 6 nautical miles from the runway. The value 6 is for a nominal SCA where the base segments are 5 nautical miles and the final segment is 10 nautical miles. In the general case, the initial distance between an aircraft and its lead aircraft is configurable and could be calculated by on-board tools according to the geometry of the SCA and the speeds of the aircraft involved. Since the geometry of the SCA and speeds of the aircraft are not considered in the discrete model, the approach initiation transition rule was simplified. The condition (a) rests the same. However, the discrete model uses a weaker condition (b) where an aircraft can initiate the approach as soon as the lead aircraft is already on the final approach (base or final segments). Because the safety threshold is not checked, spacing properties cannot be verified using the discrete model.

In order to verify spacing properties, we need a more detailed modeling of the approach initiation procedure. To this end, we extend the discrete model of the SATS HVO concept with continuous variables that encode the geometry of the SCA and the aircraft speed performances.

4   Off-Nominal Procedures

To model off-nominal procedures, the state of the SCA is extended with a new field *status* of an enumeration type { *OP,CLOSE,OFF* }. The value *OP* is used to indicate normal operations, the value *CLOSE* is used to indicate that the SCA is close, and the value *OFF* is used to indicate that the AMM is unavailable.

The status *CLOSE* and *OFF* differ in that in the former case the AMM is providing normal service to the aircraft already in the SCA but has inhibited new operations; in the latter case, the AMM is not providing any service. Transition rules are modified accordingly to cope with the extended state. For instance, entries are only allowed when *status* is *OP*, AMM services inside the SCA are provided only if *status* is different from *OFF*, etc.

4.1   SCA Closing

The following off-nominal conditions require the SCA to be closed to new operations:

- Change of approach direction.
- Loss of aircraft state data input/output on an arriving SATS aircraft.
- Loss of AMM.
- Loss of voice radio communication.
- Priority request from an aircraft on landing approach.

The SCA closing procedure is modeled as a transition rule that changes the status of the SCA to *CLOSE* and from *CLOSE* to *OP* in a non-deterministic asynchronous way.

4.2   Re-sequencing

Under normal operations, re-sequencing is only necessary for missed approach operations. In this case, the aircraft in the missed approach re-initiates the approach as the last aircraft in the landing sequence (or the first one, if it is the only aircraft in the SCA). Furthermore, if it is the first aircraft in the approach, it keeps its MAHF assignment. Otherwise, it gets an alternating MAHF with respect to its lead aircraft.

Off-nominal situations such as pilot cancellation of an approach request and priority request from an aircraft on approach, may require the AMM to remove one aircraft from the normal approach sequence and re-sequence the remainder aircraft. To handle these situations, the re-sequencing transition rule has been modified as follows. Assume that the removed aircraft had the landing sequence n:

- Aircraft with an approach sequence less than n keep their assigned approach sequence and MAHF.
- Aircraft with an approach sequence greater than n decrease their landing sequence by one. If $n \neq 1$, they get assigned to their opposite MAHF. Otherwise, they keep their MAHF.

4.3   Re-assignment During Missed Approach

Aircraft in missed approach get a new approach sequence and a MAHF assignment from the Airport Management Module. The concept of operations for off-nominal operations requires that, if the AMM output is lost, pilots use voice radio communication to complete the approach.

To support this procedure, we have designed a very simple transition rule for re-assignment during missed approach when *status* is *OFF*:

- Aircraft in a missed approach keep their relative landing sequence and their assigned MAHF.
- All other aircraft complete their normal approaches.

4.4   Verification of Off-Nominal Procedures

Exhaustive exploration of the discrete transition system extended with the previous off-nominal procedures shows that these procedures preserve all the safety properties in Section 3. In particular, it can be shown that in case of a AMM failure, aircraft in missed approach will always have a place to hold even if they perform a missed approach after the AMM has failed. However, in this case, MAHF are not necessarily assigned in an alternating way. We have not explored this issue further, but this may not be a major issue as, if the AMM is down, the SCA is closed for new operations and the probability of simultaneous consecutive missed approaches is relatively low.

5   Spacing Properties

The term *spacing* refers to linear separation of an aircraft with respect to the lead aircraft. If both aircraft are not flying the same approach, spacing is computed relative to the merging point of their linear trajectories. For instance, in a symmetric SCA, if the trail and lead aircraft are on opposite initial approach fixes their spacing is 0, although their Euclidean distance is twice the length of the of the base segments. Note that, independently of the initial Euclidean distance, if both aircraft start the approach at roughly the same time and speed, they will have a conflict at the merging point.

The geometry of the SCA is given by the lengths of the base segments, denoted $Lbase(s)$ where $s \in \{left, right\}$, the length of the final segment, denoted $Lfinal$, and the lengths of the missed approach zones, denoted $Lmaz(s)$ where $s \in \{left, right\}$. Henceforth, we write iaf_A and $mahf_A$ to denote, respectively, the initial approach fix and missed approach holding fix (*left* or *right*) of aircraft A.

We define $D_A(t)$ as the linear distance at time t of an aircraft A from its initial approach fix. In a symmetric SCA, i.e., $Lbase(left) = Lbase(right)$ and $Lmaz(left) = Lmaz(right)$, the spacing at time t between an aircraft A and its lead aircraft B is simply defined as $D_B(t) - D_A(t)$. However, in the general case, we must consider the difference in length of the base segments. Hence, if B is before A in the landing sequence, the spacing between A and B is defined as

$$S_{A \to B}(t) \equiv D_B(t) - D_A(t) + Lbase(iaf_A) - Lbase(iaf_B). \qquad (1)$$

Now, we specify the spacing requirements to be formally verified.

Proposition 1. *Under nominal operations, aircraft A and B on final approach at time t, such that B is the lead aircraft of A, satisfy the following spacing requirement:*

$$S_T \leq S_{A \to B}(t). \qquad (2)$$

Proposition 2. *Under nominal operations, A and B on final approach, on missed approach at the same fix at time t, such that B is before A in the landing sequence, satisfy the following spacing requirement:*

$$S_{MAZ} \leq S_{A \to B}(t). \tag{3}$$

The constants S_T and S_{MAZ} are the theoretical spacing that the concept guarantees on final approach and missed approach, respectively. These constants are determined by the geometry of the SCA, the minimum and maximum speed of the aircraft, v_{min} and v_{max}, and the initial spacing between the aircraft, S_0, as follows:

$$S_T \equiv S_0 - (L_{max} + Lfinal - S_0)\Delta_v, \tag{4}$$

$$S_{MAZ} \equiv \min(L_{min} + Lfinal - L_{maz}\Delta_v,$$
$$2S_0 - (L_{max} + Lfinal + L_{maz} - S_0)\Delta_v), \tag{5}$$

where

$$L_{min} \equiv \min(Lbase(left), Lbase(right)), \tag{6}$$

$$L_{max} \equiv \max(Lbase(left), Lbase(right)), \tag{7}$$

$$L_{maz} \equiv \max(Lmaz(left), Lmaz(right)), \tag{8}$$

$$\Delta_v \equiv \frac{v_{max} - v_{min}}{v_{min}}. \tag{9}$$

5.1   Hybrid Model

In order to verify Propositions 1 and 2, we extend the discrete model of the SCA with the following continuous variables:

- A current time t that evolves in a continuous way.
- For each aircraft A on final approach or missed approach, the linear distance from its IAF, $D_A(t)$. We assume that the speed of an aircraft may vary with time in the interval $[v_{min}, v_{max}]$. Therefore, the value of $D_A(t)$ is constrained by

$$(t_1 - t_0)v_{min} \leq D_A(t_1) - D_A(t_0) \leq (t_1 - t_0)v_{max}, \tag{10}$$

if $t_0 \leq t_1$ (t_0 and t_1 are measured in the same approach operation).

These continuous variables allow us to state the approach initiation rule in a more precise way:

- *Approach initiation for vertical and lateral entry (left and right)*: An aircraft A may initiate the approach when (a) it is the first aircraft in the landing sequence or (b) its lead aircraft B is already on the final approach (base or final segments) and

$$S_0 \leq S_{A \to B}(t). \tag{11}$$

Other transitions have to be modified to relate the continuous variables to the geometry of the SCA:

- *Merging*: An aircraft A in the base segment turns to the final segment when

$$D_A(t) = Lbase(iaf_A). \tag{12}$$

- *Missed approach initiation*: An aircraft A in the final segment may go to the missed approach zone when it is the first aircraft in the landing sequence and

$$D_A(t) = Lbase(iaf_A) + Lfinal. \tag{13}$$

- *Landing*: An aircraft A in the final segment may land if it is the first aircraft in the landing sequence, there is no other aircraft in the runway, and

$$D_A(t) = Lbase(iaf_A) + Lfinal. \tag{14}$$

- *Determination of lowest available altitude (left and right)*: An aircraft A on missed approach may go to the holding fix at the lowest available altitude when

$$D_A(t) = Lbase(iaf_A) + Lfinal + Lmaz(mahf_A). \tag{15}$$

We note that they hybrid transition system has been defined such that all the reachable states in the hybrid system are reachable in the discrete system (modulo the common discrete variables). Therefore, all the safety properties in Section 3 are satisfied on the hybrid transition system. Of course, the converse is not true: not all the reachable states of the discrete system are reachable in the hybrid system; in particular, those states violating the spacing requirement expressed by Formula (11) are not reachable in the hybrid system.

5.2   Mechanical Verification

The discrete model of the SATS HVO concept was written in PVS and verified using a state exploration PVS tool called Besc [11]. Roughly speaking, Besc is a basic explicit model checker, written and formally verified in PVS.[3] Early attempts to analyze the hybrid transition system described in this paper, using a hybrid model checker, e.g., HyTech [6], failed mainly due to the number of variables of the SATS HVO model. We tried a different approach: we encoded the hybrid transition system as a discrete one and explored it using Besc.

If we take all the reachable states in the discrete system and eliminate those that do not satisfy the continuous behavior expressed by Formulas (11)–(15), we have a valid abstraction of the SATS HVO concept. Instead of physically eliminating states during the state exploration, which would require a hybrid model checker, we collect for each state a set of constraints yielded by Formulas (11)–(15). Afterward, we process the set of reachable states and use the constraints

---

[3] Besc is available from http://research.nianet.org/~munoz/Besc

to discharge the spacing properties expressed by Propositions 1 and 2. As we will see, this process can be done using a discrete explicit model checker.

A *hybrid constrained state* of the SCA is a tuple $(\mathcal{D}, \mathcal{C})$, where $\mathcal{D}$ is the discrete state of the SCA and $\mathcal{C}$ is a set of constraints of the form $e \leq f$, where e and f are expressions described by the following grammar:

$$A, B ::= 1, 2, \ldots$$
$$s ::= left \mid right \mid iaf_A \mid mahf_A$$
$$T ::= t \mid T_A$$
$$e, f ::= T \mid D_A(T) \mid Lbase(s) \mid Lfinal \mid Lmaz(s) \mid S_0 \mid$$
$$Lmin \mid Lmax \mid Lmaz \mid S_{A \to B}(T) \mid e + f$$

Informally, a hybrid constrained state $(\mathcal{D}, \mathcal{C})$ represents an infinite set of hybrid states where all the constraints in $\mathcal{C}$ are satisfied.

A *hybrid constrained transition* is a rule that transforms a state $(\mathcal{D}, \mathcal{C})$ into a state $(\mathcal{D}', \mathcal{C}')$, i.e., in addition to modify the value of the discrete variables, a transition may also add or remove constraints from the previous state.

The continuous behavior described by Formulas (11)–(15) is expressed by hybrid constrained transitions. These transitions are discretized by encoding the constraints in a symbolic way. This is possible because the constraints only relate continuous variables.

- *Approach initiation for vertical and lateral entry (left and right)*: Let A be the aircraft that initiates the approach. The following symbolic constraints are added:
  - The fact that A is in the base segment:

$$T_A \leq t, \tag{16}$$
$$D_A(t) \leq Lbase(iaf_A). \tag{17}$$

  - If B is the lead aircraft of A, the fact that the aircraft are spaced at time T_A:

$$T_B \leq T_A, \tag{18}$$
$$S_0 \leq S_{A \to B}(T_A). \tag{19}$$

  - For all aircraft C on missed approach, the fact that C was ahead of A:

$$Lbase(iaf_A) + Lfinal \leq D_C(T_A). \tag{20}$$

- *Merging*: Let A be the aircraft that goes into the final segment. Constraint(17) is removed from the constraints. But, the fact that A is in the final segment is added to the constraints:

$$D_A(t) \leq Lbase(iaf_A) + Lfinal. \tag{21}$$

– *Missed approach initiation*: Let A be the aircraft that initiates the missed approach. Constraint (21) is removed from the constraints. But, the fact that A is on missed approach is added to the constraints:

$$D_A(t) \leq Lbase(iaf_A) + Lfinal + Lmaz(mahf_A). \tag{22}$$

– *Landing*: Let A be the aircraft that is landing. All constraints related to A are removed from the constraints, except instances of Constraints (18) and(19) when B, the previous lead aircraft of A, is on missed approach.
– *Determination of lowest available altitude (left and right)*: Let A be the aircraft that goes to the lowest available altitude. All constraints related to A are removed from the constraints.

Finally, to verify Propositions 1 and 2, we explicitly generate the set of reachable constrained states and for each state $s = (\mathcal{D}, \mathcal{C})$, we formally prove the following invariant properties.

Invariant 1. *For each pair of aircraft A and B in s such that A and B are on final approach at time t, and B is the lead of aircraft A,*

$$\mathcal{C} \vdash S_T \leq S_{A \to B}(t), \tag{23}$$

i.e., the minimum spacing S_T holds for A and B under the constraints $\mathcal{C}$.

Invariant 2. *For each pair of aircraft A and B in s such that they are on missed approach to the same fix at time t, and B is before A in the landing sequence,*

$$\mathcal{C} \vdash S_{MAZ} \leq S_{A \to B}(t), \tag{24}$$

i.e., the minimum spacing S_{MAZ} holds for A and B under the constraints $\mathcal{C}$.

We remark that, for the explicit model checker, the constraints $\mathcal{C}$ are just data without logical meaning. Thus, the invariant properties cannot be checked on the fly during the state exploration process. The mechanical verification proceeds in three different stages. In the first stage, the hybrid constrained transition system is fully explored in PVS using the explicit model checker Besc. In order to get a finite system, the constraints are implemented as a set rather than a list to avoid repetitions. Besc reports a total of 2768 reachable states and a diameter, maximum length of a path, of 27 states.

In the second stage, we process the set of reachable hybrid constrained states using an external tool called PVSio[4] and generate a PVS file where there is a lemma for each possible instance of Invariant 1 or Invariant 2. Without counting repetitions, 117 spacing lemmas were generated. From those, 73 lemmas are instances of the first invariant and the remaining 44 lemmas are instances of the second one.

---

[4] PVSio enhances the PVS ground evaluator with input/output operations. It is available from http://research.nianet.org/~munoz/PVSio

In addition to the spacing lemmas, proof scripts, which automatically discharge these lemmas, are also generated. In the final stage of the mechanical verification task, all 117 proof scripts are successfully checked in batch mode via the utilities provided by ProofLite.[5]

The proof scripts that are automatically generated are based on three lemmas. One lemma, called *T*, takes care of instances of Invariant 1. The other two lemmas, called *Maz1* and *Maz2*, handle particular cases of Invariant 2. These lemmas were checked in PVS. Afterward, they were integrated into a PVS strategy that mechanically discharges the automatically generated spacing lemmas. For completeness, the lemmas *T*, *Maz1*, and *Maz2* are included in the appendix.

The SATS HVO formal development, excluding the PVS tools Besc, PVSio and ProofLite, is about 2800 lines of PVS specification and lemmas and 6500 lines of proofs. From these, 1600 lines of lemmas and 5900 lines of proofs were automatically generated using the PVS tools.

6   Conclusion

Several air traffic management systems have been previously specified and analyzed using formal notations and tools. For instance, the collision avoidance system TCAS II, which is required on commercial aircraft with more than 30 seats, was formally specified in the Requirements State Machine Language (RSML) in [7]. A portion of this specification was translated to SMV and several general properties were studied using model checking [3]. Examples of these properties included identification of non-deterministic transitions, function consistency, and termination. In [9], reachability analysis is used to find optimal conflict-free trajectories for aircraft in a distributed air traffic management environment. A runway incursion monitoring algorithm is analyzed using the SMART model checker in [13]. This analysis resulted in the identification of suspicious scenarios that were not considered by the algorithm. All these works use discretized finite models of the airspace. Hence, the verification techniques are based on model checking.

Continuous infinite models that enable the verification of timing and spacing properties are used in [10] and [8]. The former work studies the minimum time prior to a collision after an alarm is issued by an alerting algorithm for parallel landing. The later one describes the formal proof of the correctness of a conflict detection and resolution algorithm for distributed air traffic management. In both cases, the verification effort was performed using the PVS verification system.

Another example of the use of formal methods in air traffic management is presented in [14]. In this case, components written in C++ of an aeronautical information systems are specified using pre- and post-conditions. The experience discovered ambiguities in the formal specification, but no major logical errors were found.

The work presented in this paper extends a previous work [11] in two orthogonal aspects: off-nominal procedures and spacing properties. The overall approach

---

[5] ProofLite is a PVS tool for non-interactive proof checking. It is available from http://research.nianet.org/~munoz/ProofLite

is novel in several aspects. First, it is not related to a particular piece of software but to a more general system: a concept of operations that defines the expected interactions beetween multiple components of an air traffic management system. Second, the analysis involves general safety properties, which are expressed using discrete variables, and precise spacing requirements, which are expressed using continuous variables. The complete approach is developed in PVS, but it involves both model checking and theorem proving techniques. Finally, the models presented in this paper served as design tools. Indeed, the verification effort resulted in the identification of 9 issues, including one major flaw, in the original concept. Ten recommendations were made to the concept development working group [5]. All the recommendations were accepted and incorporated into the final concept of operations, which was successfully demonstrated on a flight experiment.

The model of off-nominal procedures proposed in this paper does not capture all abnormal conditions described in [2]. One such model is a major endeavor. A hazard analysis may help to determine which conditions are the most critical. If these conditions are handled in a procedural way, they can be modeled using the formal techniques described in this paper.

From a practical point of view, the spacing analysis presented in this paper, e.g., Formulas (4) and (5), can be used to configure a nominal SCA and the parameters of the baseline procedure for self-separation. For instance, consider a symmetrical nominal SCA where $Lbase(left) = Lbase(right) = 5$ nm, $Lfinal = 10$ nm, and $Lmaz(left) = Lmaz(right) = 13$ nm. If the initial separation S_0 is 6 nm and $v_{min} = 90$ kt, $v_{max} = 120$ kt, then

$$L_{min} = L_{max} = 5 \text{ nm}, \tag{25}$$

$$L_{maz} = 13 \text{ nm, and} \tag{26}$$

$$\Delta_v = \frac{120 - 90}{90} = \frac{1}{3}. \tag{27}$$

The value of S_T is computed using Formula (4):

$$S_T = 6 - \frac{5 + 10 - 6}{3} = 3 \text{ nm}. \tag{28}$$

This configuration of the SCA satisfies Formula (60). Therefore, the value of S_{MAZ} can be computed using Formula (59):

$$S_{MAZ} = 12 - \frac{5 + 10 + 13 - 6}{3} = 4.66 \text{ nm}. \tag{29}$$

Hence, if the initial spacing of the trail aircraft with respect to the lead aircraft is 6 nm, the SATS HVO concept of operations guarantees a minimum spacing of 3 nm on final approach and 4.66 nm on missed approach.

The work presented demonstrates that the formal analysis can be used to show compliance with safety requirements and also to explore design decisions concerning the concept of operation. The mechanical verification is necessary to make sure that no cases were forgotten. Formal proofs are the ultimate guarantee that the mathematical development presented here is correct.

References

1. T. Abbott, K. Jones, M. Consiglio, D. Williams, and C. Adams. Small Aircraft Transportation System, High Volume Operation concept: Normal operations. Technical Report NASA/TM-2004-213022, NASA Langley Research Center, NASA LaRC Hampton VA 23681-2199, USA, 2004.
2. B. Baxley, D. Williams, M. Consiglio, C. Adams, and T. Abbott. The Small Aircraft Transportation System (SATS), Higher Volume Operations (HVO) off-nominal operations. In *Proceedings of the AIAA 5th Aviation, Technology, Integration, and Operations Conference, AIAA-2005-7461*, Arlington, Virginia, 2005.
3. W. Chan, R. Anderson, P. Beame, S. Burns, F. Modugno, D. Notkin, and J. Reese. Model checking large software specifications. *IEEE Transactions on Software Engineering*, 24(7):498–520, 1998.
4. M. Consiglio, V. Carreño, D. Williams, and C. Muñoz. Conflict prevention and separation assurance method in the Small Aircraft Transportation System. In *Proceedings of the AIAA 5th Aviation, Technology, Integration, and Operations Conference, AIAA-2005-7463*, Arlington, Virginia, 2005.
5. G. Dowek, C. Muñoz, and V. Carreño. Abstract model of the SATS concept of operations: Initial results and recommendations. Technical Report NASA/TM-2004-213006, NASA Langley Research Center, NASA LaRC,Hampton VA 23681-2199, USA, 2004.
6. T. Henzinger, P.-H. Ho, and H. Wong-Toi. HyTech: A model checker for hybrid systems. *Software Tools for Technology Transfer*, 1:110–122, 1997.
7. N. Leveson, M. Heimdahl, H. Hildreth, and J. Reese. Requirements specification for process-control systems. *IEEE Transactions on Software Engineering*, 20(9):684–707, September 1994.
8. J. Maddalon, R. Butler, A. Geser, and C. Muñoz. Formal verification of a conflict resolution and recovery algorithm. Technical Report NASA/TP-2004-213015, NASA Langley Research Center, NASA LaRC,Hampton VA 23681-2199, USA, April 2004.
9. M. Massink and N. De Francesco. Modelling free flight with collision avoidance. In *Proceedings 7th IEEE International Conference on Engineering of Complex Computer Systems*, pages 270–280, 2001.
10. C. Muñoz, V. Carreño, G. Dowek, and R.W. Butler. Formal verification of conflict detection algorithms. *International Journal on Software Tools for Technology Transfer*, 4(3):371–380, 2003.
11. C. Muñoz, G. Dowek, and V. Carreño. Modeling and verification of an air traffic concept of operations. *Software Engineering Notes*, 29(4):175–182, 2004.
12. S. Owre, J. M. Rushby, and N. Shankar. PVS: A prototype verification system. In Deepak Kapur, editor, *11th International Conference on Automated Deduction (CADE)*, volume 607 of *Lecture Notes in Artificial Intelligence*, pages 748–752, Saratoga, NY, 1992.
13. R. Siminiceanu and G. Ciardo. Formal verification of the NASA runway safety monitor. *Electronic Notes Theoretical Computer Science*, 128(6):179–194, 2005.
14. R. Yates, J. Andrews, and P. Gray. Practical experience applying formal methods to air traffic management software. In *Proceedings of the 8th Annual International Symposium of the International Council on Systems Engineering*, Vancouver, Canada, 1998.

Appendix

The lemmas described here were mechanically checked in PVS. Afterward, they were integrated into a PVS strategy that mechanically discharges the automatically generated spacing lemmas.

First, we present some auxiliary properties. The time when an aircraft A initiates the final approach, i.e., when it enters the base segment, is denoted T_A. Hence, by definition,

$$D_A(T_A) = 0. \tag{30}$$

Therefore, Constraint (19) is equivalent to

$$S_0 + Lbase(iaf_B) - Lbase(iaf_A) \leq D_B(T_A). \tag{31}$$

Furthermore, if A is on final approach at time t, Constraint (17) and Constraint (21) yield

$$D_A(t) \leq Lbase(iaf_A) + Lfinal. \tag{32}$$

Lemma 1 (T). *Let A and B be aircraft on final approach at time t such that B is the lead of aircraft A. It holds that*

$$S_0 - (L_{max} + Lfinal - S_0)\Delta_v \leq S_{A \to B}(t), \tag{33}$$

under the hypotheses

$$T_A \leq t \tag{34}$$
$$S_0 + Lbase(iaf_B) - Lbase(iaf_A) \leq D_B(T_A), \tag{35}$$
$$D_B(t) \leq Lbase(iaf_B) + Lfinal. \tag{36}$$

(Formula (34) is the Constraint (16), Formula (35) is the spacing constraint from Formula (31), and Formula (36) is the instantiation of Formula (32) on aircraft B, which is on final approach.)

Proof. Subtracting Formula (35) from Formula (36), we get

$$D_B(t) - D_B(T_A) \leq Lbase(iaf_A) + Lfinal - S_0. \tag{37}$$

Using Formula (10) on A and B,

$$(t - T_A)v_{\min} \leq D_B(t) - D_B(T_A), \tag{38}$$
$$D_A(t) - D_A(T_A) \leq (t - T_A)v_{\max}. \tag{39}$$

Formula 39 yields

$$D_A(t) \leq (t - T_A)v_{\max}. \tag{40}$$

From Formulas (37) and (38),

$$t - T_A \le \frac{Lbase(iaf_A) + Lfinal - S_0}{v_{\min}}. \tag{41}$$

Hence,

$$
\begin{aligned}
S_{A \to B}(t) &= D_B(t) - D_A(t) + Lbase(iaf_A) - Lbase(iaf_B) \\
&= D_B(T_A) + (D_B(t) - D_B(T_A)) - D_A(t) + Lbase(iaf_A) - Lbase(iaf_B) \\
&\ge S_0 + (D_B(t) - D_B(T_A)) - D_A(t), \quad \text{by Formula (35),} \\
&\ge S_0 + (t - T_A)v_{\min} - (t - T_A)v_{\max}, \quad \text{by Formulas (38) and (40),} \\
&\ge S_0 - (Lbase(iaf_A) + Lfinal - S_0)\frac{v_{\max} - v_{\min}}{v_{\min}}, \quad \text{by Formula (41),} \\
&\ge S_0 - (L_{max} + Lfinal - S_0)\Delta_v, \quad \text{by Formulas (7) and (9).}
\end{aligned}
$$

Lemma 2 (Maz1). *Let A and B be aircraft on missed approach at time t such that B is before A in the landing sequence. Furthermore, assume that when A initiated the approach, B was on missed approach. It holds that*

$$L_{min} + Lfinal - L_{maz}\Delta_v \le S_{A \to B}(t), \tag{42}$$

under the hypotheses

$$T_A \le t \tag{43}$$
$$D_B(t) \le Lbase(iaf_B) + Lfinal + Lmaz(mahf_B), \tag{44}$$
$$Lbase(iaf_B) + Lfinal \le D_B(T_A). \tag{45}$$

(Formula (43) is the Constraint (16), Formula (44) is the instantiation of Constraint (22) on aircraft B, and Formula (45) is the additional assumption about aircraft A and B.)

Proof. Subtracting Formula (45) from Formula (44), we get

$$D_B(t) - D_B(T_A) \le Lmaz(mahf_B). \tag{46}$$

Formulas (38)–(40) are derived as in Lemma 1. From Formulas (38) and (46),

$$t - T_A \le \frac{Lmaz(mahf_B)}{v_{\min}}. \tag{47}$$

Hence,

$$
\begin{aligned}
S_{A \to B}(t) &= D_B(t) - D_A(t) + Lbase(iaf_A) - Lbase(iaf_B) \\
&= D_B(T_A) + (D_B(t) - D_B(T_A)) - D_A(t) + Lbase(iaf_A) - Lbase(iaf_B) \\
&\ge Lbase(iaf_A) + Lfinal + (D_B(t) - D_B(T_A)) - D_A(t), \quad \text{by Formula (45),} \\
&\ge Lbase(iaf_A) + Lfinal + (t - T_A)v_{\min} - (t - T_A)v_{\max}, \\
&\qquad\qquad\qquad\qquad\qquad\qquad \text{by Formulas (38) and (40),} \\
&\ge Lbase(iaf_A) + Lfinal - Lmaz(mahf_B)\frac{v_{\max} - v_{\min}}{v_{\min}}, \quad \text{by Formula (47),} \\
&\ge L_{min} + Lfinal - L_{maz}\Delta_v, \quad \text{by Formulas (6), (8), and (9).}
\end{aligned}
$$

Lemma 3 (Maz2). *Let A and B be aircraft on missed approach at time t such that B is before A in the landing sequence. Furthermore, assume that when A initiated the approach, aircraft B and X where on final approach, B was the lead of aircraft X, and X was the lead aircraft of A. It holds*

$$2S_0 - (L_{max} + Lfinal + L_{maz} - S_0)\Delta_v \le S_{A \to B}(t), \qquad (48)$$

under the hypotheses

$$T_A \le t \qquad (49)$$

$$T_X \le T_A \qquad (50)$$

$$D_B(t) \le Lbase(iaf_B) + Lfinal + Lmaz(mahf_B), (51)$$

$$S_0 + Lbase(iaf_B) - Lbase(iaf_X) \le D_B(T_X), \qquad (52)$$

$$S_0 + Lbase(iaf_X) - Lbase(iaf_A) \le D_X(T_A). \qquad (53)$$

(Formula (49) is the Constraint (16), Formula (50) is the instantiation of Constraint (18) on aircraft X and A, Formula (51) is the instantiation of Constraint (22) on aircraft B, and Formulas (52) and (53) are the additional assumptions about aircraft A, B, and X.)

Proof. Subtracting Formula (52) from Formulas (51), we get

$$D_B(t) - D_B(T_X) \le Lbase(iaf_X) + Lfinal + Lmaz(mahf_B) - S_0. \qquad (54)$$

Formula (40) is derived as in Lemma 1. From Formula (30), $D_X(T_X) = 0$. Therefore, using Formula (10) on X,

$$D_X(T_A) \le (T_A - T_X)v_{\max}. \qquad (55)$$

From Formulas (49) and (50), $T_X \le t$. Using Formula (10) on B,

$$(t - T_X)v_{\min} \le D_B(t) - D_B(T_X). \qquad (56)$$

From Formulas (54) and (56),

$$t - T_X \le \frac{Lbase(iaf_X) + Lfinal + Lmaz(mahf_B) - S_0}{v_{\min}}. \qquad (57)$$

Hence,

$$
\begin{aligned}
S_{A \to B}(t) &= D_B(t) - D_A(t) + Lbase(iaf_A) - Lbase(iaf_B) \\
&= D_B(T_X) + (D_B(t) - D_B(T_X)) - D_A(t) + Lbase(iaf_A) - Lbase(iaf_B) \\
&\ge S_0 + Lbase(iaf_A) - Lbase(iaf_X) + (D_B(t) - D_B(T_X)) - D_A(t), \\
&\quad \text{by Formula (52),} \\
&\ge S_0 + Lbase(iaf_A) - Lbase(iaf_X) + (t - T_X)v_{\min} - (t - T_A)v_{\max}, \\
&\quad \text{by Formulas (40) and (56),} \\
&= S_0 + Lbase(iaf_A) - Lbase(iaf_X) - (t - T_x)(v_{\max} - v_{\min}) + \\
&\quad (T_A - T_X)v_{\max}
\end{aligned}
$$

$$\geq S_0 + Lbase(iaf_A) - Lbase(iaf_X) - (t - T_x)(v_{\max} - v_{\min}) + D_X(T_A),$$
by Formula (55),
$$\geq 2S_0 - (t - T_x)(v_{\max} - v_{\min}), \quad \text{by Formula (53)},$$
$$\geq 2S_0 - (Lbase(iaf_X) + Lfinal + Lmaz(mahf_B) - S_0)\frac{v_{\max} - v_{\min}}{v_{\min}},$$
by Formula (57),
$$\geq 2S_0 - (L_{max} + Lfinal + L_{maz} - S_0)\Delta_v,$$
$$\text{by Formulas (7), (8), and (9).}$$

Note that the conclusions of Lemmas 2 and 3 could be replaced by

$$\min(L_{min} + Lfinal - L_{maz}\Delta_v, 2S_0 - (L_{max} + Lfinal + L_{maz} - S_0)\Delta_v) \leq$$
$$S_{A \to B}(t). \quad (58)$$

Furthermore,

$$S_{MAZ} = 2S_0 - (L_{max} + Lfinal + L_{maz} - S_0)\Delta_v, \quad (59)$$

when

$$1 + \frac{v_{\min}}{v_{\max}} \leq \frac{L_{min} + Lfinal}{S_0}, \quad (60)$$

and

$$S_t \leq S_{MAZ}, \quad (61)$$

when

$$L_{maz}\Delta_v \leq S_0. \quad (62)$$

Towards a Method for Rigorous Development of Generic Requirements Patterns

Colin Snook[1], Michael Poppleton[1], and Ian Johnson[2]

[1] School of Electronics and Computer Science,
University of Southampton, Highfield,
Southampton SO17 1BJ, UK
{cfs, mrp}@ecs.soton.ac.uk
[2] AT Engine Controls, Portsmouth
IJohnson@atenginecontrols.com

Abstract. We present work in progress[1] on a method for the engineering, validation and verification of generic requirements using domain engineering and formal methods. The need to develop a generic requirement set for subsequent system instantiation is complicated by the addition of the high levels of verification demanded by safety-critical domains such as avionics. Our chosen application domain is the failure detection and management function for engine control systems: here generic requirements drive a software product line of target systems.

A pilot formal specification and design exercise is undertaken on a small (two-sensor) system element. This exercise has a number of aims: to support the domain analysis, to gain a view of appropriate design abstractions, for a B novice to gain experience in the B method and tools, and to evaluate the usability and utility of that method. We also present a prototype method for the production and verification of a generic requirement set in our UML-based formal notation, UML-B, and tooling developed in support. The formal verification both of the structural generic requirement set, and of a particular application, is achieved via translation to the formal specification language, B, using our U2B and ProB tools.

1 Introduction

The need for generic approaches to support reuse in systems engineering is well known; in the avionics industry, for example, [16, 11] describe the reuse of generic sets of requirements in engine control and flight control systems. The need for reuse arises in many contexts, such as in system evolution, adaptation, or component-based construction. In this paper we are concerned with formal, generic requirements engineering to address the need for software product lines in the failure management domain in avionics.

A *software product line* (SPL) is a collection of variant implementations of a generic software requirement specification, to meet a variety of platform, environmental, functional, or other requirements. In avionics, the generic requirement specification for an engine control system is implemented in a different variant in each manufacturer airframe; [Op.Cit.] describe SPL solutions. The notion of software product line engineering became well established [18], after Parnas' prescient proposal [22] in the 70's.

---

[1] This work is part of the EU funded research project IST 511599 - RODIN (Rigorous Open Development Environment for Complex Systems).

M. Butler et al. (Eds.): Fault-Tolerant Systems, LNCS 4157, pp. 326–342, 2006.
© Springer-Verlag Berlin Heidelberg 2006

Domain analysis and object oriented frameworks are among numerous vehicles proposed to support product line development. In Domain-Specific Software Architecture [29] for example, the production of a set of generic, domain-specific requirements through domain engineering is followed by its successive refinement, in a series of system engineering cycles, into specific product instance requirements. On the other hand [12] describes the Object-Oriented Framework as "a reusable, semi-complete application that can be specialized to produce custom applications". Here the domain engineering produces an object-oriented model that must be instantiated, in some systematic way, for each specific product required. In this work we combine object-oriented and formal techniques and tools in the domain analysis and engineering of generic requirements.

It is widely recognized that formal methods (FM) technology makes a strong contribution to the verification required for safety-critical systems [19]. It is further recognized that FM will need to be integrated [3] in as "black-box" as possible a manner in order to achieve serious industry penetration. The B method of J.-R. Abrial [1, 23] is a formal method with good tool support [2, 9] and a good industrial track record, e.g. [10]. At Southampton, we have for some years been developing an approach of integrating formal specification and verification in B, with the UML [8]. The UML-B [26] is a specialisation of UML that defines a formal modelling notation combining UML and B. It is supported by the U2B tool [24], which translates UML-B models into B, for subsequent formal verification. This verification includes model-checking with the ProB model-checker [17] for B. These tools have all been developed at Southampton, and continue to be extended in current work.

1.1 Failure Detection and Management for Engine Control

A common functionality required of many systems is to detect and manage the failure of its inputs. This is particularly pertinent in aviation applications where lack of tolerance to failed system inputs could have severe consequences. The failure manager filters inputs from the controlled system, providing the best information possible and determining whether a transducer or system component has failed or not.

Inputs may be tested for magnitude, rate of change and consistency with other inputs. When a failure is detected it is managed in order to maintain a usable set of input values for the control subsystem and provide 'graceful degradation'. To prevent over-reaction to isolated transient values, a failed condition must be confirmed as persistent before irreversible action is taken. Failure detection and management (FDM) in engine control systems is a demanding application area, see e.g. [7], giving rise to far more than a simple parameterizable product line situation.

Our approach contributes to the failure detection and management domain by proposing a method for the engineering, validation and verification of generic requirements for product-line engineering purposes. The approach exploits genericity both within as well as between target system variants. Although product-line engineering has been applied in engine and flight control systems [16, 11], we are not aware of any such work in the FDM domain. We define generic classes of failure-detection test for sensors and variables in the system environment, such as rate-of-change, limit, and multiple-redundant-sensor, which are simply instantiated by parameter. Multiple instances of these classes occur in any given system. Failure confirmation is then a generic abstraction over these test classes: it constitutes a configurable process of execution of specified tests over a number of system cycles, that will determine whether a failure of the component under test has occurred. Our approach is focussed on the genericity of this highly variable process.

1.2 Fault Tolerance

This application domain (and our approach to it) includes fault tolerant design in two senses: tolerance to faults in the environment, and in the control system itself. The FDM application is precisely about maximizing tolerance to faults in the sensed engine and airframe environment. The control system (including the FDM function) is supported by a backup control system in a dynamically redundant design. This backup system with dissimilar hardware/software design, with a reduced-functionality sensing fit can be switched in by a watchdog mechanism if the main system has failed.

In the narrower (and more usual) sense, we will be examining various schemes for designing fault tolerance into the FDM software subsystem. Work to date has specified and validated a generic requirements specification for FDM. As we apply refinement techniques and technology to construct the design, we will consider various relevant approaches, such as driving the specification of a control system from environmental requirements [13], or the use of fault-tolerant patterns for B specifications [14] and their refinements [15].

1.3 The Paper

We present the results of a pilot formal specification and design exercise. This was undertaken on a small (two-sensor) element of a typical system from our partner ATEC's domain. This exercise was intended to support the domain analysis, and to gain a view of appropriate design abstractions for the full exercise of developing and validating the generic requirements. Furthermore, since the ATEC engineer (and co-author of this paper) was a novice to the B method, the exercise would also enable him to gain experience in the B method and tools, and to evaluate the usability and utility of that method to an engineer in the target domain.

The pilot exercise took place in the context of our development of a prototype method for the specification and verification of generic requirements sets for systems of this type. The method is briefly presented here; for a fuller discussion see [27, 28]. We also report briefly on tooling subsequently developed to support the method.

The paper proceeds as follows. The pilot study and its evaluation is presented in section 2. Sections 3 and 4 review our prototype method and our domain analysis activity. Section 5 describes the domain engineering of the generic model, followed by the engineering of a sample application instance in section 6. A brief taxonomy of validation/verification problems is then presented in section 7. Section 8 concludes.

2   Pilot Study

To explore the FDM domain in more detail we carried out a pilot study that modeled and verified in B a very small example consisting of two sensors used to measure one environment variable. The aim of the pilot study was to gain a better understanding of the stages and processes involved, before embarking on the search for generic re-usable modeling abstractions. The pilot study was carried out by our co-author, an engineer with our industrial partner company, who provided the domain expertise. Since he was a novice to formal specification and the B method, the pilot study also provided insight into the reaction we might expect from industrial users that adopt our method. Thus a secondary aim was to evaluate model development using B and the existing B tools from the point of view of adoption in an industrial setting.

The model was intended to be both analytical and specificational, i.e. the aim was to explore the requirements as well as develop a specification. The dual redundant engine speed (ES) functionality was selected as it includes behaviour representative of other control inputs and includes interaction between sensors. The ES value is normally taken from the ESa input but if this is not healthy, the ESb input is used instead. If both inputs are unhealthy the ES signal is not updated. The ES failure management requirements include input magnitude tests, comparative (difference) tests between two given inputs, and confirmation mechanisms that select appropriate output values and failure flag settings.

2.1 Approach

The engineer initially explored the requirements by developing the model as a series of specifications adding functionality and validating new behaviour in stages using the ProB animation tool. The stages were 'idealisations' rather than true abstractions because they omitted to allow for the effects of events added in later stages. Hence they give only an approximate indication of behaviour corresponding to that obtained by ignoring some of the details to be added later. (Analogous to idealisation in physics, such as ideal gases, where some phenomena that affect the system are simply ignored even if they effect the the variables of the model). This approach, although less rigorous than refinement, was chosen as it allowed a quick exploration of the requirements by avoiding the difficult process of finding useful abstractions and proving their refinements. The ProB model checker was used to check internal consistency within the requirements at each stage.

The next stage was to revise the specifications to achieve refinement consistency. The ProB model checker [17] and the prover tool Click'N'Prove/B4free [9] were used to verify the refinements. A final stage to refine the model towards code implementation is ongoing.

To obtain a refinement chain, sufficient abstract detail was added to the idealised specification to satisfy the proof obligations. In practice this meant that, when adding new events, the abstract versions in previous levels were not skip, but non-deterministic alterations to variables at that level. Informally, this is a generalisation of event refinement where the effect of new events is, in a loose sense, not significant to the old variables. It is interesting to note that a proven refinement chain can be constructed in this manner with little experience, using the proof obligations as a guide to find the weakest appropriate abstraction. However, the constructed refinement chain is only useful if it is used in some way to validate the refinements. Hence the abstract level was reconsidered to ensure that the effect of the new events on the old variables is acceptable and does not invalidate the model.

Hence, the approach utilises idealisation (which seems to be easier than abstraction), superimposing detail (which is easy because it is not required to refine anything) and 'upwards' addition of suitable detail to obtain refinement (which is fairly easy because it is led by the proof tools). We present a sanitized version of the final specifications with notes to explain the initial intentions from which they derived.

2.2 Abstract Model

The most abstract specification is shown below in machine Engine_speed_0. The intention of this stage was to represent the functionality as a 'black box' that allows given output combinations as a result of under-specified environment changes. The only constraint is that the outputs have some interlocking relationships. For example, if a flag indicates that the ESa signal healthy action was taken, then the output should be equal to the ESa sensor value until the environment changes the ESa sensor value. The idealisation is that the output is only the same as a snapshot reading of the sensor value. In later refinements we would like to introduce the read value of the sensor and specify that the output is equal to this.

Two sensors, esa and esb are defined. Each sensor has a change event which alters the sensor value non-deterministically. Each sensor has a flag which is set (by the outcome operations) to record when it has failed. There are four alternative outcome events corresponding to the health or failure combinations of the two sensors (e.g. hh is the outcome taken when both esa and esb are healthy). These outcomes take the appropriate failure action by setting the output to either esa, esb or its previous value. In this stage, the selection of the appropriate outcome, from those available, is left to chance and not related to the input values in any way. Initially all 4 outcomes are available but, since failed sensors are not allowed to recover, hh will be disabled thereafter if either of the sensors is subjected to a failing outcome. This 'latching out' of a possible outcome is represented by the latch flags esalatch and esblatch. Eventually only the ff outcome will be available. An invariant specifies the alternative properties that should be achieved on the output in terms of the sensor values (until the environment changes the sensor values again).

```
MACHINE Engine_speed_0
...
INVARIANT             ... &
      (newVal = TRUE or
      (esalatch = UNSET & output = esavalue) or
      (esblatch = UNSET & output = esbvalue) or
      output = previous)


OPERATIONS /*EVENTS*/
esaChange =
BEGIN
      esavalue :: NATURAL || newVal := TRUE
END;

hh =
      SELECT
            esalatch = UNSET & esblatch = UNSET
      THEN
            output , previous := esavalue, esavalue ||
            newVal := FALSE
      END;
...
ff =
```

```
BEGIN
     output := previous ||
     esalatch, esblatch := SET, SET ||
     newVal := FALSE
END
```

2.3 First Refinement

In the first refinement of this abstract model more detail is added by introducing the events, esavalidate and esbvalidate. These events are responsible for determining which of the alternative outcomes will be taken. They do this by setting the esaresult and esbresult flags, which are now used in the guards of the outcome events. The guards of the outcome events are also strengthed to ensure that both esa and esb sensors have been newly validated before the outcome is taken. The means by which validate decides which outcome to activate remains underspecified. This is a valid refinement because the outcome event guards are strengthened and new data (result) is superimposed. However, the specification of validation is idealised because it omits the difference test which, in the next refinement, is added as a new event that also modifies the variable esbresult. To satisfy the prover and achieve the next refinement we later revisit this stage to de-idealise it by adding an abstract version of the difftest event that non-deterministically alters esaresult and esbresult.

This refinement stage led to consideration of what types and level of failure detection should be addressed and whether they should indicate different actions. The ordering of the sequence of events from failure detections to actions was considered. The refinement raised the issue of test scheduling and input sampling and whether a series of tests could easily be accommodated in the design by an appropriate sequencing mechanism

```
REFINEMENT Engine_speed_1
REFINES Engine_speed_0
...
;
esavalidate =
     SELECT
             esavalidated=FALSE
     THEN
             esaresult :: PASS_FAIL ||
             esavalidated := TRUE
     END
;
hh =
     SELECT
             esavalidated = TRUE & esbvalidated = TRUE &
             esaresult = PASS & esbresult = PASS &
             esalatch = UNSET & esblatch = UNSET &
     THEN
             esavalidated, esbvalidated := FALSE, FALSE ||
             output, previous := esavalue, esavalue ||
             newVal := FALSE
     END;
hf =
     SELECT
             esavalidated = TRUE & esbvalidated = TRUE &
             esaresult = PASS & esbresult = FAIL &
             esalatch = UNSET
     THEN
             esavalidated, esbvalidated := FALSE, FALSE ||
             output, previous := esavalue, esavalue ||
             esblatch := SET ||
             newVal := FALSE
     END;
...
```

2.4 Second and Third Refinements

In the second refinement, a new event that can also affect the selected outcome, is added. This event, `difftest`, represents a comparison between the two sensor values. It must happen after both `esa` and `esb` have been validated and before an outcome event occurs. Note that it can only change sensor results from `pass` to `fail` not vice versa. Again the mechanism by which it decides this is left under-specified.

```
difftest =
      SELECT
              esavalidated = TRUE & esbvalidated = TRUE &
              esdiffvalidated = FALSE
      THEN
              IF    esaresult = PASS & esbresult = PASS
              THEN esbresult :: PASS_FAIL
              END ||
              esdiffvalidated := TRUE
      END;
```

Since this stage added a new event that alters a variable (`esbresult`) introduced in the previous refinement stage, an abstract version of this event must be added to the first refinement to allow the second refinement to be a refinement of the first. The most abstract version of the event would be a simple non-deterministic assignment of the variable to any value from its type (`esbresult :: PASS_FAIL`). However, although this would ensure the refinement, it would be a pointless exercise since the previous level would no longer describe a desired behaviour. That is, the `difftest` event could unlatch some failure results which is one of the main features that were embodied in the abstract level. A slightly more constrained abstract version is obtained by also retaining any conjuncts from guards or conditions that are based on variables in the previous level. This restricts the effect of the event in a way that corresponds with the refinement. Hence it stands a better chance of being an acceptable specification for the refinement. Its consistency and validity can then be examined using the ProB model checker and animator. In our case, this method produced abstract specifications that were consistent with the existing invariants and valid but we are not convinced that this will always be the case. It may be necessary to reconsider the way the feature is introduced if the abstract model does not behave as desired or violates the invariant.

```
difftest =
      SELECT
              esavalidated = TRUE & esbvalidated = TRUE
      THEN
              IF    esaresult = PASS & esbresult = PASS
              THEN esbresult :: PASS_FAIL
              END
      END;
```

Similarly, the previous level abstract model must have an even more abstract version of the new `difftest` event added to it. This is obtained by a similar process, retaining only the guards, conditions and non-deterministic versions of assignments that utilise variables in the abstract specification.

```
difftest =
      IF esaresult = PASS & esbresult = PASS
      THEN esbresult :: PASS_FAIL
      END;
```

In the third refinement, the details of how `validate` and `difftest` set result (and hence select an outcome) is provided. This entails comparing the sensor value against fixed limits and against each other. A confirmation counter mechanism was also introduced to model the requirement to not be oversensitive to sensor noise. This entailed adding a third, intermediate state `FAILING` to the possible values of result with corresponding new outcome events. The refinement was proven by adding a gluing invariant to match the states with the abstract version.

2.5 Evaluation

The pilot study was carried out and proven in B and the refinement chain was fully proven by automatic proof. Since choosing useful abstractions and appropriate refinements is difficult, requiring considerable experience and understanding of the refinement process, it surprised us that the novice engineer was able to achieve this, even for the simple example. To complicate matters, an event style of B (used in the Rodin project) was used but proof had to be achieved using the existing proof tools which are not event B based. For example, if a new event is added at a refinement, an abstract version of the event, with body `skip` (i.e. do nothing) must be added to all previous levels. The prover was able to automatically prove all of the proof obligations when the specifications were correct. This meant that the interactive prover was only used to identify corrections to the specifications.

The ease of proof was due to two factors. Firstly, only simple data types were used. We tried rewriting the specifications using a set of sensors with two elements `esa` and `esb` and relations from this set for the sensor data. With this data representation, the prover was no longer able to complete automatically. The almost exclusive use of superposition refinement (i.e. lack of data refinement) also probably assisted the prover.

The engineer recognised that it was difficult to find early abstract models that allowed for future refinements. The modeller's perception of what is important may change through experience with the model and understanding of the domain. The process is therefore iterative in nature. The novice engineer found the animation facility of the ProB tool particularly useful to quickly validate and explore model behaviour. He recognised that in larger scale problems the use of invariant checking with the tools will be an invaluable aid to verification and validation where it may be quite onerous to exercise the equivalent assurance using other methods. However the effectiveness of invariants in models relies on how well they can be created and it was recognised that weak or incorrect invariants can be generated by lack of experience, which may be a hindrance to development and verification.

The syntax of the B notation did not present significant difficulties in this development as functionality could be expressed using simple constructs. Most proof obligations were discharged automatically. Where they were not, the proof goals were used to identify where the specifications need to be corrected or enhanced to achieve automatic proof.

The pilot study provided a better understanding of several issues in the FDM domain. In particular, a better understanding of the reaction between sensor values, tests and outcomes was gained.

3   Methodology

The process for obtaining a generic model of requirements is illustrated in Fig. 1. The first stage is an informal domain analysis which is based on prior experience of developing products for the application domain of failure detection and management in engine control. A taxonomy of generic requirements found in the application domain is developed. For example, class INP includes generic requirements INP2, INP5 and their sample instances below:

INP2	The subsystem input variables represent either sensor values or other subsystem variables.
INP5	Some "other subsystem" input variables represent the controller state.

Ref	Name	Type	Range	Res	Description	Freq
INP2.5	ET5	digitised	-200 to 2000F	0.1F	Engine Temp. sensor 5	24
INP2.10	ESa	digitised	0-200 %	0.01	Engine Speed (main)	24
INP5.1	CYCLE_NO	digital	1..16	1	Execution cycle counter	24

The instance requirements in each generic requirement class are thus expressed as data in tabular form. Thus a *first-cut generic entity-relationship model* can be constructed by relating these generic requirement entities, or classes. This generic model is represented as a UML-B class diagram, and a corresponding B specification is generated.

The identification of a useful generic model is a difficult process warranting further exploration. This is done in the domain engineering stage where a more rigorous examination of the first-cut model is undertaken, using UML-B, U2B and ProB. The model is animated by creating typical instances of its generic requirement classes, to test when it is and is not consistent. This stage is model validation by animation, using the ProB and U2B tools, to show that it is capable of holding the kind of information that is found in the application domain. During this stage the relationships between the classes are likely to be adjusted as a better understanding of the domain is developed. This stage results in a *validated generic model* of requirements that can be instantiated for each new application.

For each new application instance, the generic requirement classes are instantiated from product instance data, producing an instance model. The relationship between the generic and the instance model is analogous to that between a class and and object model in UML. Instantiation is done by our prototype *Requirements Manager* tool, which reads instance requirement data from a database (see sec. 6), and uses that data to instantiate the generic UML-B model. The ProB model checker is then used to automatically verify that the instantiated application is consistent with the relationship constraints embodied in the generic model. This stage, producing a *consistent instance model*, shows that the requirements are a consistent set of requirements for the domain. It does not, however, show that they are the right set of requirements that will give the desired system behaviour.

Our aim in future work, therefore, is to add dynamic features to the instantiated model in the form of variables and operations that model the behaviour of the entities in the domain and to animate this behaviour so that the instantiated requirements can be

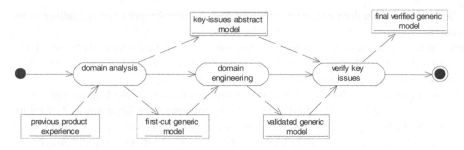

Fig. 1. Process for obtaining the generic model

validated. The ultimate goal is to specify this behaviour in the generic model in order to maximize reuse at the instantiation stage.

During the domain analysis phase we found that considering the rationale for requirements revealed key issues, which are properties that an instantiated model should possess. Key issues are higher level requirements that could be expressed at a more abstract level from which the generic model is a refinement. The generic model could then be verified to satisfy the key issue properties by proof or model checking. This matter is considered in [25] which gives an example of refinement of UML-B models in the failure management domain.

The final stage is to validate a specific, instantiated configuration. This would be done by providing actual values to generic behaviours when the generic model is instantiated. The resulting specific model could then be animated to validate its behaviour.

Finally, we recognize the need for tools to support uploading of bulk system instance definition data, as well as the efficient and user-friendly validation/ debugging of said data. The Requirements Manager prototype provides database storage and some validation; ProB could easily be enhanced to provide, for example, data counterexamples explaining invariant violations.

4 Domain Analysis

Domain analysis such as used by Lam [16] is the study of the application domain, with domain specialists, with the intention of capturing its characteristics, processes and requirements in textual and diagrammatic form. The first step was to define the scope of the domain in discussion with engine controller experts. An early synthesis of the requirements and key issues were formed, giving due attention to the rationale for the requirements. Considering the requirements rationale is useful in reasoning about requirements in the domain [Op.Cit.]. For example, the rationale for confirming a failure before taking action is that the system should not be generate false positive failure results from transient interference on its inputs. From the consideration of requirements rationale, key issues were identified which served as higher level properties required of the system. An example of such a property would be that the failure management system must not be held in a transient action state indefinitely. The rationale from which it has been derived is that a transient state is temporary and actions associated with this state may only be valid for a limited time.

A core set of requirements were identified from several representative failure management engine systems. For example, the identification of magnitude tests with variable limits and associated conditions established several magnitude test types; these types have been further subsumed into a general detection type. This type structure provided a taxonomy for classification of the requirements.

Domain analysis showed that failure management systems are characterised by a high degree of fairly simple similar units made complex by a large number of minor variations and interdependencies. The domain presents opportunities for a high degree of reuse within a single product as well as between products. For example, a magnitude test is usually required in a number of instances in a particular system. This is in contrast to the engine start domain addressed by Lam [16], where a single instance of each reusable function exists in a particular product. Our method is targeted at domains such as failure management where a few simple units are reused many times and a particular configuration depends on the relationships between the instances of these simple units. A first-cut entity relationship model was constructed from the units identified during the domain analysis stage. The entities identified during domain analysis were:

- **INP** Identification of an input sensor and its characteristics to be tested
- **COND** Condition under which a test is performed or an action is taken. (A predicate based on the values and/or failure states of other inputs)
- **DET** Detection of a failure state. A predicate that compares the value of an expression to be tested against a limit value. There are specialized versions of detection, e.g. **DET_MAG** for magnitude tests and **DET_RATE** for rate-of-change tests
- **CONF** Confirmation of a failure state. An iterative algorithm performed for each invocation of a detection, used to establish whether a detected failure state is genuine or transitory
- **ACT** Action taken either normally or in response to a failure, possibly subject to a condition. Assigns the value of an expression, which may involve inputs and/or other output values, to an output
- **OUT** Identification of an output to be used by an action

Figure 2 shows the final class diagram resulting from this early entity-relationship model of generic requirements.

5   Domain Engineering

The aim of the domain engineering stage is to explore, develop and validate the first-cut generic model of the requirements into a validated generic model, using suitable technology. At this stage this is essentially an entity relationship model, omitting any behaviours (except temporary ones added for validation purposes). The model indicates the necessary and permitted configurations of the various functional requirements without detailing the behaviour involved in those requirements. For example, that there must be one confirmation mechanism for each input and that a configuration must have at least one detection mechanism.

The first-cut model from the domain analysis stage was converted to the UML-B notation (Fig. 2) by adding stereotypes and UML-B clauses (tagged values) as defined in

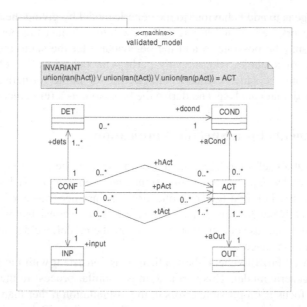

Fig. 2. Final UML-B version of generic model of failure management requirements

the UML-B profile [26]. This allows the model to be converted into the B notation where validation and verification tools are available. The model contains invariant properties, which constrain the associations, and ensures that every instance is a member of its class. As well as these diagrammatic invariants, additional textual invariants may be added where the diagram notation is unable to express constraints. For example, the invariant in Fig. 2 expresses the fact that every action (instance of class ACT) must be linked at least once to a confirmation (instance of class CONF) via one of the three associations, hAct, pAct and tAct. To validate the model we needed to be able to build up the instances it holds in steps. For this stage a constructor was added to each class so that the model could be populated with instances. The constructor was defined to set any associations belonging to that class according to values supplied as parameters.

The model was tested by adding example instances using the animation facility of ProB and examining the values of the B variables representing the classes and associations in the model to see that they developed as expected. ProB provides an indicator to show when the invariant is violated. Due to the 'required' (i.e. multiplicity greater than 0) constraints in our model, the only way to populate it without violating the invariant would be to add instances of several classes simultaneously. However, we found that observing the invariant violations was a useful part of the feedback during validation of the model. Knowing that the model recognises inconsistent states, is just as important as knowing that it accepts consistent ones. The model was rearranged substantially during this phase as the animation revealed problems. Once we were satisfied that the model was suitable, we removed the constructor operations to simplify the corresponding B model for the next stage.

The next stage is to add behaviour to the generic model by giving the classes operations. In future work we will investigate the best way to introduce this behaviour during the process. It may be possible to add the behaviour after the static model has been validated as described above. Alternatively, perhaps the behaviour will affect the static structure and should be added earlier. In either case, we aim to formalise the rationale described in the domain analysis and derive the behaviour as a refinement from this.

6   Requirements for a Specific Application

Having arrived at a useful model we then use it to specify the requirements for an instance application by populating it with instance requirements for each of the generic requirement classes. For a particular application, the instances are not created and destroyed dynamically but are defined as a static configuration consistent with the generic model. Thus we do not use constructors to populate the model; we define each class to have a fixed set of instances.

At first we used ProB to check the application is consistent with the properties expressed in the generic model. This verification is a similar process to the previous validation but the focus is on possible errors in the instantiation rather than in the model. The application is first described in tabular form. The generic model provides a template for the construction of the tables. Each class is represented by a separate table; foreign key links represent the associations owned by that class. The tabular form is useful as documentation of the application but is not directly useful for verification. To verify its consistency, the tabular form is translated into class instance enumerations and association initialisation clauses attached to the UML-B class model. We found that doing this manually was tedious and error prone. Therefore we automated the translation by implementing a 'Requirements Manager' tool. The tool was developed as an IBM eclipse plug-in by a student group[2]. The Requirements Manager (RM) tool loads application configuration data from an Excel file and populates the relevant fields in the UML-B class model.

Initially, we used ProB to check which conjuncts of the invariant are violated. For our FDM example, several iterations were necessary to eliminate errors in the tables before the invariant was satisfied. The ProB 'analyse invariant' facility provides information about which conjuncts of the invariant are violated but, in a data intensive model such as this, it is still not easy to see which part of the data is at fault. It would be useful to show a data counterexample to the conjunct (analogous to an event sequence counterexample in model checking). The RM tool verifies the application data against the class structure and association constraints of the UML-B class model, when that data is first loaded into the database. RM then reports any violations, identifying the specific data that caused the violation. Figure 3 is a screenshot of the RM tool in use, showing the generic requirements structure in two views, and two detail views (on lower right) of data verification errors. Note that a limitation of the tool (inherited from its underlying database representation) is that many to many associations cannot be represented. This is circumvented by inserting an intermediate class into the association (e.g. HACT, PACT and TACT). The RM tool is described in more detail in [28].

---

[2] See acknowledgements.

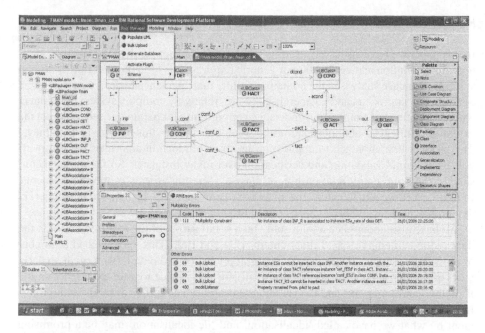

Fig. 3. Screenshot of Requirements Manager being used to populate the generic model

7 Classification of Problems

It is useful to classify the kinds of problems found during animation and verification in order to better understand the source of problems and improve the requirements engineering process. So far, we have found that problems can be classified on a methodological stage basis. Possible categories on this basis, some of which we have experienced, are as follows.

- Verification of generic model - the generic model is inconsistent or incorrect
- Validation of generic model - the generic model is correct and consistent but does not reflect the generic requirements
- Validation of generic requirement - the generic model works as expected but animation leads expert to review generic requirements
- Verification of instantiation - the instantiation is inconsistent with the generic model because of an incorrect instantiation
- Verification of instantiation (generic model) - the instantiation is inconsistent with the generic model because the generic model is inadequate
- Validation of instantiation - the instantiation is consistent with the generic model but does not reflect the specific requirements
- Validation of specific requirements - the instantiation is consistent with the generic model but animation leads expert to review specific requirements

In the future, when behavioural features are modelled, we expect to find other ways of classifying problems. For example we may be able to distinguish functional areas that are prone to incorrect specification.

8 Conclusion

In this paper we have discussed a formal, object-oriented approach to the rigorous engineering, validation and verification of generic requirements for a product line of critical systems. Our case study is in the domain of failure management and detection for engine control. The approach can be generalised to any relatively complex system component where repetitions of similar units indicate an opportunity for parameterised reuse but the extent of differences and interrelations between units makes this non-trivial to achieve. The product-line approach to application instance production amortises the effort involved in formal validation and verification over many instances. So far we have considered the static entity-relationship, or class-association aspects of the requirements. In future work we aim to extend the approach to consider also the detailed meaning (i.e. dynamic behaviour) of these classes of requirements.

We have also undertaken a pilot study on a small subset of the requirements, i.e. the dual redundant engine speed functionality ESa and ESb. This exercise had a number of aims: (i) to support the domain analysis at a level of fine detail, (ii) to gain an early view of appropriate design abstractions, (iii) for a B novice to gain experience in the B method and tools, (iv) and to evaluate the usability and utility of method and tools. In particular, the novice engineer's independent development of an approach to refinement by what we have called 'idealisation' and 'de-idealisation' may be a promising methodological contribution. Thus invaluable input has been provided to the ongoing exercise of developing the new Event-B method and tools.

Two broad areas of future work are indicated by the case study, both linking to related work on Product Line Engineering (PLE). The first concerns instance data management, the second variability vs. commonality in the generic model.

For a product family such as FDM at ATEC as currently envisaged, instance data management is in principle straightforward. This is because no system instance/variant requirements are defined at the generic level - all structure and behaviour is specified in terms of a single generic model. Instance/variant requirements are captured completely by instance-level data. This means that all instance data structures are defined in terms of the generic class definitions. Therefore, the data for a system instance is simply defined as a subset of the database of all required instance specifications; tooling is thus a straightforward database application, as we have demonstrated with our new Requirements Manager tool.

Instance management becomes more complex when variability is required in the generic model. This is the usual state of affairs in PLE. The mobile phone scenario of [20] is typical, where each system instance is defined by a distinct set of functional features, aimed at a specific market segment and target price. We might define a *feature* to be a small coherent group of requirements respresenting some system goal; examples in telephony include CH (call hold), CD (caller divert), CC (conference call). Features are not in general simply composable, and the totality of features cannot in general be specified in one generic model: variability specification is required in the generic model. To date approaches to this (such as [20]) have been in the obvious syntactic form: in ATEC for example, variants on the generic model for other engine manufacturers might be described as extra colour-coded classes, associations, states, events etc. A system variant (or sub-family) would thus be defined in terms of some colour-combination submodel. A more sophisticated metamodelling approach to variability specification, based on the Model-Driven Architecture of the OMG, has recently been proposed [21].

Future work will investigate developing such variability and tooling issues in the ATEC context, using the UML-B and refinement approaches and the RM tool discussed in this paper. The application of refinement approaches to PLE to date has been modest, e.g. [6, 30], and has, in our view, much potential. An obvious unit for modelling variabilities is the feature. Investigations are ongoing into the development of refinement decomposition and generic instantiation in Event-B, and their deployment on variability specification via features. Retrenchment, a generalizing theory for refinement, has been investigated in a feature engineering context [5], and may well also be useful in PLE.

Acknowledgements

We are grateful to ECS students Ledina Hido, Robert Stops and Martin Ross for their work developing the Requirements Manager tool, and to Ledina for her work on the tool specification and verification in B.

References

[1] J.-R. Abrial. *The B-Book: Assigning Programs to Meanings.* Cambridge University Press, 1996.

[2] J.-R. Abrial. http://www.atelierb.societe.com/index_uk.html, 1998. Atelier-B.

[3] P. Amey. Dear sir, Yours faithfully: an everyday story of formality. In F. Redmill and T. Anderson, editors, *Proc. 12th Safety-Critical Systems Symposium*, pages 3–18, Birmingham, 2004. Springer.

[4] K. Araki, S. Gnesi, and D. Mandrioli, editors. *International Symposium of Formal Methods Europe*, volume 2805 of *LNCS*, Pisa, Italy, September 2003. Springer.

[5] R. Banach and M. Poppleton. Retrenching partial requirements into system definitions: A simple feature interaction case study. *Requirements Engineering Journal*, 8(2), 2003. 22pp.

[6] D. Batory, J. Sarvela, and A. RauschMayer. Scaling step-wise refinement. *IEEE Transactions on Software Engineering*, 30(6):355–371, June 2004.

[7] C.M. Belcastro. Application of failure detection, identification, and accomodation methods for improved aircraft safety. In *Proc. American Control Conference*, volume 4, pages 2623–2624. IEEE, June 2001.

[8] G. Booch, I. Jacobson, and J. Rumbaugh. *The Unified Modeling Language - a Reference Manual*. Addison-Wesley, 1998.

[9] D. Cansell, J.-R. Abrial, et al. B4free. A set of tools for B development, from http://www.b4free.com, 2004.

[10] B. Dehbonei and F. Mejia. Formal development of safety-critical software systems in railway signalling. In M.G. Hinchey and J.P. Bowen, editors, *Applications of Formal Methods*, chapter 10, pages 227–252. Prentice-Hall, 1995.

[11] S.R. Faulk. Product-line requirements specification (PRS): an approach and case study. In *Proc. Fifth IEEE International Symposium on Requirements Engineering*. IEEE Comput. Soc, Aug. 2000.

[12] M. Fayad and D. Schmidt. Object-oriented application frameworks. *Communications of the ACM*, 40(10):32–38, Oct. 1997.

[13] I.J. Hayes, M. A. Jackson, and C. B. Jones. Determining the specification of a control system from that of its environment. In Araki et al. [4], pages 154–169.

[14] L. Laibinis and E. Troubitsyna. Fault tolerance in a layered architecture: a general specification pattern in B. In *Proc. 2nd Int. Conf. on Software Engineering and Formal Methods*, pages 346–355. IEEE Computer Society, Sep 2004.

[15] L. Laibinis and E. Troubitsyna. Refinement of fault tolerant control systems in B. In *Proc. SAFECOMP 2004*, volume 3219 of *LNCS*, pages 254–268. Springer, 2004.

[16] W. Lam. Achieving requirements reuse: a domain-specific approach from avionics. *Journal of Systems and Software*, 38(3):197–209, Sept. 1997.

[17] M. Leuschel and M. Butler. ProB: a model checker for B. In Araki et al. [4], pages 855–874.

[18] R. Macala, L. Jr. Stuckey, and D. Gross. Managing domain-specific, product-line development. *IEEE Software*, pages 57–67, May 1996.

[19] UK Ministry of Defence. Def Stan 00-55: Requirements for safety related software in defence equipment, issue 2. http://www.dstan.mod.uk/data/00/055/02000200.pdf, 1997.

[20] D. Muthig. GoPhone - a software product line in the mobile phone domain. Technical Report IESE-Report No. 025.04/E, Fraunhofer Institut Experimentelles Software Engineering, 2004.

[21] D. Muthig and C. Atkinson. Model-driven product line architectures. In G.J. Chastel, editor, *Proc. Software Product Lines, Second International Conference, SPLC 2002*, volume 2379 of *LNCS*, pages 110–129. Springer, 2002.

[22] D. L. Parnas. On the design and development of program families. *IEEE Transactions on Software Engineering*, SE-2, March 1976.

[23] S. Schneider. *The B-Method*. Palgrave Press, 2001.

[24] C. Snook and M. Butler. U2B - a tool for translating UML-B models into B. In J. Mermet, editor, *UML-B Specification for Proven Embedded Systems Design*, chapter 5. Springer, 2004.

[25] C. Snook, M. Butler, A. Edmunds, and I. Johnson. Rigorous development of reusable, domain-specific components, for complex applications. In J. Jurgens and R. France, editors, *Proc. 3rd Intl. Workshop on Critical Systems Development with UML*, pages 115–129, Lisbon, 2004.

[26] C. Snook, I. Oliver, and M. Butler. The UML-B profile for formal systems modelling in UML. In J. Mermet, editor, *UML-B Specification for Proven Embedded Systems*, chapter 5. Springer, 2004.

[27] C. Snook, M. Poppleton, and I. Johnson. The engineering of generic requirements for failure management. In E. Kamsties, V. Gervasi, and P. Sawyer, editors, *Proc. 11th Int. Workshop on Requirements Engineering: Foundation for Software Quality*, pages 145–160, Oporto, June 2005. Essener Informatik Beitrage.

[28] C. Snook, M. Poppleton, and I. Johnson. Rigorous engineering of product-line requirements: a case study in failure management. *submitted*, 2006.

[29] W. Tracz. DSSA (Domain-Specific Software Architecture) pedagogical example. *ACM Software Engineering Notes*, pages 49–62, July 1995.

[30] A. Wasowski. Automatic generation of program families by model restrictions. In R.L. Nord, editor, *Software Product Lines, Third International Conference, SPLC 2004, Proceedings*, volume 3154 of *LNCS*, pages 73–89. Springer, 2004.

Rigorous Design of Fault-Tolerant Transactions for Replicated Database Systems Using Event B

Divakar Yadav* and Michael Butler**

School of Electronics and Computer Science
University of Southampton
Southampton SO17 1BJ , U.K.
{dsy04r, mjb}@ecs.soton.ac.uk

Abstract. System availability is improved by the replication of data objects in a distributed database system. However, during updates, the complexity of keeping replicas identical arises due to failures of sites and race conditions among conflicting transactions. Fault tolerance and reliability are key issues to be addressed in the design and architecture of these systems. Event B is a formal technique which provides a framework for developing mathematical models of distributed systems by rigorous description of the problem, gradually introducing solutions in refinement steps, and verification of solutions by discharge of proof obligations. In this paper, we present a formal development of a distributed system using Event B that ensures atomic commitment of distributed transactions consisting of communicating transaction components at participating sites. This formal approach carries the development of the system from an initial abstract specification of transactional updates on a one copy database to a detailed design containing replicated databases in refinement. Through refinement we verify that the design of the replicated database confirms to the one copy database abstraction.

1 Introduction

A distributed system is a collection of autonomous computer systems that cooperate with each other for successful completion of a distributed computation. A distributed computation may require access to resources located at participating sites. A distributed transaction may span several sites reading or updating data objects. A typical distributed transaction contains a sequence of database operations which must be processed at all of the participating sites or none of the sites to maintain the integrity of the database [28]. Assuming that each site maintains a log and a recovery procedure, commit protocols [16,28] ensure that all sites abort or commit a transaction unanimously despite multiple failures. Several versions of commit protocols were proposed to improve performance dealing

---

* Divakar Yadav is a Commonwealth Scholar supported by the Commonwealth Scholarship Commission in the United Kingdom.
** Michael Butler's contribution is part of the IST project IST 511599 RODIN (Rigorous Open Development Environment for Complex Systems).

M. Butler et al. (Eds.): Fault-Tolerant Systems, LNCS 4157, pp. 343–363, 2006.

with various aspects such as site failures, blocking and even compensation. Distributed transaction execution within the framework of commit protocols ensures consistency and provides fault tolerance.

In this paper we formally develop an abstract model of transactions in B for a one copy database. The notion of replicated database is introduced in the refinement of abstract model. The replica control mechanism considered in the refinement allows both update and read-only transactions to be submitted at any site. In our abstract model, an update transaction modifies the abstract one copy database through a single atomic event. In the refinement, an update transaction consists of a collection of interleaved events updating each replica separately. The transaction mechanism on the replicated database is designed to provide the illusion of atomic update of a one copy database. Through our refinement proof we verify that this is indeed the case. A read-only transaction reads the values from a replica locally at the site of submission. Transaction failure is represented by sites aborting a transaction. A site may decide to abort an update transaction due to race conditions among conflicting transactions. We address the one copy equivalence consistency criterion through this refinement. By verifying the refinement, we verify that the design of the replicated database confirms to the one copy database abstraction despite transaction failures at a site.

The remainder of this paper is organized as follows: Section 2 contains background on the problem, Section 3 provides an introduction to the B Method, Section 4 describes the system model informally, Section 5 presents an abstract B model of transactions considering the database as a single logical entity, Section 6 presents a refinement of the abstract B model introducing details of replicated database, Section 7 present some properties of system given as gluing invariants detailing relationship between the single copy and the replicated database and lastly Section 8 concludes the paper.

2   Background

Replication improves availability in a distributed database system. It is advantageous to replicate data objects when the transaction workload is predominantly read only. However, during updates, the complexity of keeping replicas identical arises due to site failures and conflicting transactions. Several approaches has been proposed for management of replicated data using group communication primitives [5,17,18,25,29]. The application of formal methods to a replication algorithm is considered in [15]. Group communication has also been investigated in Isis [8], Totem [22] and Trans [20]. The protocols in these system use varying broadcast primitives and address group maintenance, fault tolerance and consistency services. The transaction semantics in the management of replicated data is also considered in [5,6,25]. In addition to providing fault tolerance, one of the important issues to be addressed in the design of replica control protocols is consistency. The *One Copy Equivalence* [7,23] criteria requires that a replicated database is in a mutually consistent state only if all copies of data objects *logically* have the same identical value.

The *One Copy Serializability* [7] is the highest correctness criterion for replica control protocols. It is achieved by coupling consistency criteria of *one copy equivalence* and providing *serializable* execution of transactions. In order to achieve this correctness criterion, it is required that interleaved execution of transactions on replicas be equivalent to serial execution of those transactions on one copy of a database. The one copy equivalence and serial execution together provide one copy serializability which is supported in a *read anywhere write everywhere* approach [26]. For example, consider any serial execution of a transaction produced by system in the *read anywhere write everywhere* replica control. A transaction which writes to a data item does so by writing data everywhere. Thus from the view point of a transaction which reads the values produced by an earlier transaction, all copies were written *simultaneously*. So no matter which copy a transaction reads, it reads the same value written by an earlier transaction [7]. Though serializability is the highest correctness criteria, it is too restrictive in practice. Various degrees of isolation to address this problem has been studied in [18].

The verification of distributed algorithms has long been an issue of study. Formal methods provide a systematic approach to the development and verification of dependable complex systems. They use mathematical notations to describe and reason about systems. The B Method [1,12] is a model oriented state based method developed by Abrial for specifying, designing and coding software-based systems. The development methodology supported in B Method is stepwise refinement. This is done by defining an abstract formal specification and successively refining it to an implementable specification through a number of correctness preserving steps. At each refinement step more concrete specifications of a system are obtained. The B Method requires the discharge of proof obligations for *consistency checking* and *refinement checking*. The B Tools Atelier B [30], Click'n'Prove [4], B-Toolkit [13] provide an environment for generation and discharge of proof obligations required for *consistency checking* and *refinement checking*. Applications of the B method to distributed system may be found in [3,9,10,11,24,31]. In this work we have used Click'n'Prove.

Our focus in this paper is on providing a formal analysis of *read anywhere write everywhere* replica control protocol for a distributed database system. An update transaction which spans several sites issuing a series of read/write operations is executed in isolation at a given site. The basic idea used in this paper is to allow update transactions to be submitted at any site. This site, called the coordinating site, broadcasts update messages to replicas at participating sites. Upon receipt of update requests, each site starts a sub transaction if it does not conflict with any other *active* transactions at that site. The coordinating site decides to commit if a transaction commits at all participating sites. The coordinating site decide to abort it if it aborts at any participating site.

3   B Method

The B Method provides a state based formal notation based on set theory for writing abstract models of systems. A system may be defined as an abstract machine. Abstract machines contains *sets, variables, invariants, initialization* and a set of *operations* defined on variables. The *sets* clause contains user defined sets that can be used in the rest of the machine. The variables describe the state of machine. The *invariants* are first order predicates and these invariants are to be preserved while updating the variables through the operations. The operations can have input and output parameters. Operation of machines are defined through generalized substitution which allow both *non deterministic* and *deterministic* assignments.

3.1   Event B

Event B [2,21] is an event driven approach to system modelling based on B for developing distributed systems. This formal technique consists of the following steps:

- Rigorous description of abstract problem.
- Introduce solutions or details in refinement steps to obtain more concrete specifications.
- Verifying that proposed refinements are valid.

In Event B operations are referred to as events which occur spontaneously rather then being invoked. The events are guarded by predicates and these guards may be strengthened at each refinement step. The state variables are modified by a set of events. The invariants state properties that must be *satisfied* by variables and *maintained* by activation of events. In refinement steps, variables may be replaced and new events may be introduced. Abstract and concrete variables are related through gluing invariants.

3.2   B Notations

In this section we present some B notation frequently used in our model (Table-1). A more detailed explanation of these may be found in [1,27].

Let A and B be two sets, then the relational constructor $\leftrightarrow$ defines the set of relations between A and B as,

$$A \leftrightarrow B = \mathbb{P}(A \times B)$$

where $\times$ is cartesian product of A and B. A mapping of element $a \in A$ and $b \in B$ in a relation $R \in A \leftrightarrow B$ is written as $a \mapsto b$.

Table 1. Some frequently used B Notations

$dom(\mathrm{R})$	domain of relation R	$ran(\mathrm{R})$	range of relation R
$\lhd$	domain restriction	$\mapsto$	mapping
$\lhd\!\!\!-$	domain anti restriction	$\times$	cartesian product
$\lhd\!\!\!-$	relational overide operator	R[A]	relational image of R over set A
$\mathbb{P}_1$	non empty power set	$\mathbb{P}$	power set
$\rightarrowtail$	partial function	$\rightarrow$	total function

The *domain* of a relation $R \in A \leftrightarrow B$ is the set of elements of A that R relates to some elements in B defined as,

$$dom(R) = \{a | a \in A \wedge \exists b.(b \in B \wedge a \mapsto b \in R)\}$$

Similarly, the *range* of relation $R \in A \leftrightarrow B$ is defined as set of elements in B related to some element in A :

$$ran(R) = \{b | b \in B \wedge \exists a.(a \in A \wedge a \mapsto b \in R)\}$$

A relation $R \in A \leftrightarrow B$ can be projected on a domain $U \subseteq A$ called *domain restriction*($\lhd$) defined as,

$$U \lhd R = \{a \mapsto b \mid a \mapsto b \in R \wedge a \in U\}$$

A domain anti-restriction $U \lhd\!\!\!- R$ removes all mappings whose first element is in U. The *domain anti-restriction* is defined as,

$$U \lhd\!\!\!- R = \{a \mapsto b \mid a \mapsto b \in R \wedge a \notin U\}$$

The *Relational image* $R[U]$ where $U \subseteq A$ is defined as,

$$R[U] = \{b \mid a \mapsto b \in R \wedge a \in U\}$$

If $R_0 \in A \leftrightarrow B$ and $R_1 \in A \leftrightarrow B$ are relations defined on set A and B, the *relational over-ride* operator $(R_0 \lhd\!\!\!+ R_1)$ replaces mappings in relation R_0 by those in relation R_1.

$$R_0 \lhd\!\!\!+ R_1 = (dom(R_1) \lhd\!\!\!- R_0) \cup R_1$$

A *function* is a relation having some special properties. A *partial function* from set A to B $(A \nrightarrow B)$ is a relation which relates an element in A to *at most* one element in B. A partial function $f \in A \nrightarrow B$ satisfies following,

$$\forall(a, b_1, b_2).(a \in A \wedge b_1 \in B \wedge b_2 \in B \Rightarrow (a \mapsto b_1 \in f \wedge a \mapsto b_2 \in f) \Rightarrow b_1 = b_2))$$

Similarly a *total function* $f \in A \rightarrow B$ is a partial function where $dom(\mathrm{f})=A$. Given $f \in A \nrightarrow B$ and $a \in dom(\mathrm{f})$, $f(a)$ represents the unique value that a is mapped to by f.

4   System Model

In this section we present an informal model of a distributed database. Our system model consist of a sets of sites and data objects. The distributed database consists of sets of objects stored at different sites. Users interact with the database by *starting transactions*. The data objects are assumed to be replicated across all sites. The *Read Anywhere Write Everywhere* [7,23] replica control mechanism is considered for updating replicas. We consider the case of full replication and assume all data objects are updateable. A transaction is considered as a sequence of read/write operations executed atomically, i.e., a transaction will either *commit* or *abort* the effect of all database operations.

Transaction Types

The following types of transactions are considered for this model of replicated database.

- *Read-Only Transactions* : These transaction are submitted locally to the site and *commit* after reading the requested data object locally.
- *Update Transactions* : These transactions update the requested data objects. The effect of update transactions are global, thus when committed, all replicas of data objects maintained at all sites must be updated. In case of abort, none of the sites update the data object.

To illustrate the two cases, consider Read Only transaction T_1 and Update transaction T_2 defined over set of data object O_1 and O_2 respectively. The read-only transaction T_1 issues a sequence of *read* operations over data objects in O_1 and update T_2 issues a sequence of *read* or *write* operation over data objects in O_2. A transaction is termed an update transaction if it issues *at least* one *write* operation.

Commitment of Transactions

Transactions in *Read Anywhere, Write Everywhere* replica control execute as follows. A read transaction may be submitted at any site and its execution remain confined to that site. However, an update transaction is executed globally and the global commit decision of an update transaction is determined by the commit decisions of the components of the update transaction at participating sites. Consider an update transaction T_i submitted at a site S_i called the *coordinator* site. Since T_i issues *write* operations, the coordinator site of T_i broadcasts its operations to all participating sites. Participating site S_j, upon receipt of request from coordinator S_i, begins a subtransaction T_{ij}. Each T_{ij} is executed following a two phase locking scheme at participating site S_j. Coordinating site S_i waits for the notification to commit or abort from each participating site. A notification to either *commit* or *abort* a sub transaction is sent by each S_j to coordinator S_i. The transaction may fail at a participating site due to race condition. The decision of a global commit or abort is taken at the coordinator site. Thus the decision of a global commit or abort of an update transaction is taken in the framework of a two phase commit protocol. The commit or abort decision of an update transaction T_i is taken as follows,

- T_i commits if *all* T_{ij} *commit* at S_j.
- T_i aborts if *some* T_{ij} *aborts* at S_j.

Degree of Isolation

We consider the situations where read-only and update transactions may be submitted to any site. In order to ensure correct serial execution of transactions they

MACHINE	*Replica1*
DEFINITIONS	*PartialDB* == (*OBJECT* $\rightarrow\!\!\!\!+$ *VALUE*) ;
	UPDATE == (*PartialDB* $\rightarrow\!\!\!\!+$ *PartialDB*) ;
	ValidUpdate (update,readset) == (*dom(update)= readset* $\rightarrow$ *VALUE*
	$\wedge$ *ran(update)* $\subseteq$ *readset* $\rightarrow$ *VALUE*)
SETS	*TRANSACTION; OBJECT; VALUE;*
	TRANSSTATUS={COMMIT,ABORT,PENDING}
VARIABLES	*trans, transstatus, database, transeffect, transobject*

INVARIANT	*trans* $\in$ $\mathbb{P}$*(TRANSACTION)*
	$\wedge$ *transstatus* $\in$ *trans* $\rightarrow$ *TRANSSTATUS*
	$\wedge$ *database* $\in$ *OBJECT* $\rightarrow$ *VALUE*
	$\wedge$ *transeffect* $\in$ *trans* $\rightarrow$ *UPDATE*
	$\wedge$ *transobject* $\in$ *trans* $\rightarrow$ $\mathbb{P}_1$ *(OBJECT)*
	$\wedge\forall t.(t\in$ *trans* $\Rightarrow$ *ValidUpdate (transeffect(t), transobject(t))*)

INITIALISATION	*trans* :=$\varnothing$ $\qquad\qquad$ $\parallel$ *transstatus* :=$\varnothing$
	$\parallel$ *transeffect* := {} $\qquad$ $\parallel$ *transobject* :={}
	$\parallel$ *database* :$\in$ *OBJECT* $\rightarrow$ *VALUE*

Fig. 1. Abstract Model of Transactions in B

must execute in isolation. Various degrees of isolation, e.g., *no isolation, read-write isolation* and *general isolation* are discussed in [14] in the context of replication. In order to meet the strong consistency requirement where each transaction reads the correct value of a replica, *conflicting* transactions need to be executed in isolation. Two transactions T_i and T_j are in *conflict* if the sequence of operations issued by T_i and T_j are defined on set of object O_i and O_j respectively and $O_i \cap O_j \neq \varnothing$. In our model, we ensure this property by not *issuing* a transaction at a site if there is a conflicting transaction that is *active* at that site.

5   Abstract Model of Transactions in B

The abstract data model of transactions is given in Fig.1 as a B machine. The operations of the machine are shown in Fig.2. The abstract model maintains a notion of a *central* or *one* copy database. The abstract database is modelled as a total function from objects to values :

$$database \in OBJECT \rightarrow VALUE$$

In practice a database will be partial, but for simplicity, in this paper, we avoid dealing with the errors caused by trying to read undefined objects and instead focus on errors caused by sites failing to commit a transaction. An individual transaction will involve a set of objects *readset* $\subseteq$ *OBJECT*. It will read from a partial projection of the database (*pdb*) on to *readset*, i.e.,

$$pdb = readset \lhd database$$

If it is an update transaction it will write to a subset of *readset* and the new values of the objects to be written may depend on the existing values of the objects in *readset*. Let the set of objects to be written be *writeset* where *writeset* ⊆ *readset*. So we model an update to a database as function that takes a partial database (representing the current values of the objects in *readset*) and yields a partial database (representing the new values of the objects in *writeset*). A transaction is a read only-transaction if its *writeset* = ∅. Thus for a read-only transaction, its update function maps a partial database defined over *readset* to an empty set. The update function is defined as below,

$$UPDATE \triangleq PartialDB \twoheadrightarrow PartialDB$$
$$where\ PartialDB \triangleq OBJECT \twoheadrightarrow VALUE$$

An update function *update* maps a partial database (*pdb1*) where *pdb1* = (*readset* ◁ *database*) to another partial database (*pdb2*) where *dom(pdb2)* = *writeset*. The update function *update* ∈ *UPDATE* updates the database as follows,

$$database := database \mathbin{\lhd\!\!\!-} update\ (pdb1)$$

We say that *update* ∈ *UPDATE* is valid with respect to a set of objects *readset* whenever,

$$dom(update) = readset \rightarrow VALUE$$
$$\wedge\ ran(update) \subseteq readset \twoheadrightarrow VALUE$$

Our model of database updates is sufficiently general to model atomic series of read-only and update transactions. A brief description of Fig.1 is given below.

- *TRANSACTION, SITE, OBJECT* and *VALUE* are defined as a deferred sets. The *TRANSSTATUS* is an enumerated set containing values *COMMIT,ABORT and PENDING*. These values are used to represent the global status of transactions.
- The database is represented by a variable *database* as a total function from *OBJECT* to *VALUE*. A mapping (o ↦ v) ∈ *database* indicates that object *o* has value *v* in the database.
- The variable *trans* represent a set of *started* transactions. The variable *transstatus* maps each started transaction to *TRANSSTATUS*.
- The variable *transobject* is a total function which maps a transaction to a set of objects. The set *transobject(t)* represents the set of data objects read by a transaction *t*. The set of objects written to by *t* will be a subset of *transobject(t)*.
- The variable *transeffect* is a total function which maps each transaction to an object update function *UPDATE* as previously described.
- A transaction *t* is a read-only transaction if *ran(transeffect(t))* = {∅}, i.e., each partial database is mapped to the empty partial database.

StartTran(*tt*∈ *TRANSACTION*) ≅
  ANY   *updates , objects*
  WHERE   *tt* ∉ *trans*
          ∧ *updates* ∈ *UPDATE*
          ∧ *objects* ∈ $\mathbb{P}_1$ *(OBJECT)*
          ∧ *ValidUpdate (updates,objects)*
  THEN   *trans* := *trans* ∪ *{tt}*   ‖ *transstatus(tt)* := *PENDING*
       ‖ *transobject(tt)* := *objects* ‖ *transeffect(tt)* := *updates*
  END ;

CommitWriteTran(*tt*∈ *TRANSACTION)* ≅
  ANY   *pdb*
  WHERE   *tt* ∈ *trans*
          ∧ *transstatus(tt)* =*PENDING*
          ∧ *ran(transeffect(tt))* ≠ {∅}
          ∧ *pdb* = *transobject(tt)* ◁ *database*
  THEN   transstatus(tt) := *COMMIT* ‖ *database* := *database* ◁ *transeffect(tt)(pdb)*
  END;

AbortWriteTran(*tt* ∈ *TRANSACTION)* ≅
  WHEN   *tt* ∈ *trans*
          ∧ *transstatus(tt)* = *PENDING*
          ∧ *ran(transeffect(tt))* ≠ {∅}
  THEN   *transstatus(tt)* := *ABORT*
  END;

val ← **ReadTran** *(tt*∈ *TRANSACTION*) ≅
  WHEN   *tt* ∈ *trans*
          ∧ *transstatus(tt)* = *PENDING*
          ∧ *ran(transeffect(tt))*= {∅}
  THEN   *val* := *transobject(tt)* ◁ *database* ‖ *transstatus(tt)* := *COMMIT*
  END;

Fig. 2. Operations of abstract transaction model

- The invariant $t \in trans \Rightarrow ValidUpdate(transeffect(t), transobject(t))$ indicate that all updates must be valid.

Starting a Transaction

The event *StartTran(tt)*, given in Fig.2, models starting a new transaction *tt*. The guard given in the *WHERE* statement ensure that *tt* is a fresh transaction. The *ANY* statement sets the variables *transobject(tt)* and *transeffect(tt)* so that *transobject(tt)* is a non empty set of objects and *transeffect(tt)* is some valid update on the objects. A transaction *tt* is considered as *read-only* if the *ran(transeffect(tt))* is set to an empty set and it is considered an *update transaction* if *ran(transeffect(tt))* contains *at least* one mapping of the form (o↦v). The status of transaction *tt* is set to *PENDING*.

REFINEMENT	*Replica2*
REFINES	*Replica1*

SETS   *SITE ;*
                 SITETRANSSTATUS={commit,abort,precommit,pending}

VARIABLES   *trans, transstatus, activetrans, coordinator, sitetransstatus,*
                 transeffect, transobject, freeobject, replica

INVARIANT   *activetrans ∈ SITE ↔ trans*
    ∧ *coordinator ∈ trans → SITE*
    ∧ *sitetransstatus ∈ trans ⇸ (SITE ⇸ SITETRANSSTATUS)*
    ∧ *replica ∈ SITE → (OBJECT → VALUE)*
    ∧ *freeobject ∈ SITE ↔ OBJECT*

INITIALISATION *trans := ∅ || transstatus := ∅ || activetrans := ∅*
    || *coordinator := ∅ || sitetransstatus := ∅ || transeffect := {}*
    || *transobject := {} || freeobject := SITE × OBJECT*
    || *ANY data WHERE data ∈ OBJECT → VALUE*
         THEN replica := SITE × {data} END

Fig. 3. Initial part of Refinement

Commitment and Abortion of Update Transactions

The event *CommitWriteTran(tt)* models *commitment* of an update transaction. As a consequence of the occurrence of this event, the abstract *database* is updated with the effects of the transaction and its status is set to *commit*.

The event *AbortWriteTran(tt)* models *abort* of an update transaction. As a consequence of occurrence of this event, the transaction status is set to *abort* and its effects are not written to the database. The B specification of these operations are given in Fig.2.

Commitment of Read Only Transactions

The event *ReadTran(tt)*, given in Fig.2, models *commitment* of a read-only transaction *tt*. A *pending* read-only transaction *tt* commits after reading the objects from the abstract database defined by variable *transobject(tt)*. A read-only transaction commits by returning the values of the objects as a partial database.

6   Refinement of Transactional Model

The initial part of the refinement of the abstract model is given in Fig.3. The B specification of events of the refinement are introduced later in this section. The abstract B model of transactions maintains a notion of an abstract *central database*. The variable *database* represents a *central database* in this model. In the refinement, the notion of *replicated database* is introduced. The abstract variable

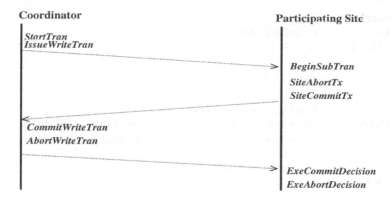

Fig. 4. Events of Update Transaction

database is replaced by a concrete variable *replica* in the refinement. It may be noted that in the abstract model given in Fig.2, an update transaction performs updates on an abstract central database whereas in the refined model, an update transaction updates replicas at each site separately. A read-only transaction reads the data from the replica at the site of submission of the transaction. A brief description of the refinement in Fig.3 is given below.

- The variables *coordinator, replica, activetrans,freeobject* and *sitetranstatus* are introduced in the refinement. The variable *coordinator* is defined as a total function from *trans* to *SITE*. A mapping of form $(t{\mapsto}s) \in coordinator$ implies that site s is a coordinator site for transaction t.
- Each site maintains a replica of the database. The variable *replica* is initialized to have the same value of each data object at each site. A mapping $(s{\mapsto}(o{\mapsto}v)) \in replica$ indicate that site s currently has value v for object o.
- Variable *activetrans* keeps a record of transactions running at various sites, i.e., it is in the state *pending* or *precommit*. A mapping $(s \mapsto t) \in activetrans$ indicates that site s is running transaction t. The variable *freeobject* keeps a record of objects at various sites which are *free*, i.e., those objects which are not *locked* by any *active* transaction.
- The variable *sitetransstatus* maintains the status of all started transactions at various sites. A mapping of form $(t{\mapsto}(s{\mapsto}commit)) \in sitetransstatus$ indicate that t has committed at site s.
- The new events such as *IssueWriteTran, BeginSubTran, SiteAbortTx, SiteCommitTx, ExeAbortDecision* and *ExeCommitDecision* are introduced in operations.

An informal logical ordering of the occurrence of various events of the refinement for an update transaction is given in Fig.4. These events are triggered within the framework of two phase commit protocol. These events are either coordinator site events or participating site event. A brief description of the events of the refinement is given below.

StartTran(*tt*) ≘
ANY   *ss, updates, objects*
WHERE   *ss* ∈ *SITE*
                 ∧ *tt* ∉ *trans*
                 ∧ *updates* ∈ *UPDATE*
                 ∧ *objects* ∈ $\mathbb{P}_1$ *(OBJECT)*
                 ∧ *ValidUpdate (updates,objects)*
THEN   *trans := trans* ∪ *{tt}* || *transstatus(tt) := PENDING*
                 || *transobject(tt) := objects* || *transeffect(tt) := updates*
                 || *coordinator(tt) := ss*
                 || *sitetransstatus(tt)(ss) := pending*
END;

IssueWriteTran(*tt*) ≘
WHEN   *tt* ∈ *trans*
                 ∧ *(coordinator(tt)* ↦ *tt)* ∉ *activetrans*
                 ∧ *transstatus(tt)=PENDING*
                 ∧ *ran(transeffect(tt))≠* {∅}
                 ∧ *transobject(tt)* ⊆ *freeobject[{coordinator(tt)}]*
                 ∧ ∀*tz.(tz* ∈ *trans* ∧ *(coordinator(tt)* ↦ *tz)*∈ *activetrans*
                                     ⇒ *transobject(tt)* ∩ *transobject(tz) =* ∅)
THEN   *activetrans := activetrans* ∪ *{coordinator(tt)*↦ *tt}*
                 || *sitetransstatus(tt)(coordinator(tt)):= precommit*
                 || *freeobject := freeobject - {coordinator(tt)}* × *transobject(tt)*
END;

Fig. 5. Refinement: Coordinator Site Events-I

Starting and Issuing a Transaction

Submission of a transaction *tt* is modelled by the event *StartTran(tt)*. The event *IssueWriteTran(tt)* models the *issuing* of an update transaction at the coordinator from a set of *started* transactions which are not in *conflict* with other *issued* transactions at the coordinator site. The guard of *IssueWriteTran(tt)* ensures that a transaction *tt* is issued by the coordinator when all active transactions *tz* running at the coordinator site of *tt* are not in *conflict* with *tt*, i.e.,

$$tz \in trans \wedge (coordinator(tt) \mapsto tz) \in activetrans$$
$$\Rightarrow transobject(tt) \wedge transobject\ (tz) = \varnothing$$

The B specification for events *StartTran(tt)* and *IssueWriteTran(tt)* of the refinement are given in Fig.5.

Commitment and Abortion of Update Transactions

Refined specifications for the commit and abort events of update transaction *tt* are given in Fig.6. An update transaction *tt* globally commits only if all participating sites are ready to commit it, i.e., it has status *pre-commit* at all sites.

CommitWriteTran(tt) $\hat{=}$
> **ANY** pdb
> **WHERE** $tt \in trans$
>> $\wedge\, pdb = transobject(tt) \lhd replica(coordinator(tt))$
>> $\wedge\, ran(transeffect(tt)) \neq \{\varnothing\}$
>> $\wedge\, (coordinator(tt) \mapsto tt) \in activetrans$
>> $\wedge\, transstatus(tt) = PENDING$
>> $\wedge\, \forall s.(\, s \in SITE \Rightarrow sitetransstatus(tt)(s) = precommit\,)$
>> $\wedge\, \forall (s,o) \cdot (s \in SITE \wedge o \in OBJECT \wedge o \in transobject(tt) \Rightarrow (s \mapsto o) \notin freeobject)$
>> $\wedge\, \forall s.(s \in SITE \Rightarrow (s \mapsto tt) \in activetrans)$
>
> **THEN** $transstatus(tt) := COMMIT$ $\|\, activetrans := activetrans - \{coordinator(tt) \mapsto tt\}$
>> $\|\, sitetransstatus(tt)(coordinator(tt)) := commit$
>> $\|\, freeobject := freeobject \cup \{coordinator(tt)\} \times transobject(tt)$
>> $\|\, replica(coordinator(tt)) := replica(coordinator(tt)) \Cleftarrow transeffect(tt)(pdb)$
>
> **END**;

AbortWriteTran(tt) $\hat{=}$
> **WHEN** $tt \in trans$
>> $\wedge\, ran(transeffect(tt)) \neq \{\varnothing\}$
>> $\wedge\, (coordinator(tt) \mapsto tt) \in activetrans$
>> $\wedge\, transstatus(tt) = PENDING$
>> $\wedge\, \exists s.\, (s \in SITE \wedge sitetransstatus(tt)(s) = abort)$
>
> **THEN** $transstatus(tt) := ABORT$ $\|\, activetrans := activetrans - \{coordinator(tt) \mapsto tt\}$
>> $\|\, sitetransstatus(tt)(coordinator(tt)) := abort$
>> $\|\, freeobject := freeobject \cup \{coordinator(tt)\} \times transobject(tt)$
>
> **END**;

$val \leftarrow$ **ReadTran**(tt,ss) $\hat{=}$
> **WHEN** $tt \in trans$
>> $\wedge\, transstatus(tt) = PENDING$
>> $\wedge\, transobject(tt) \subseteq freeobject[\{ss\}]$
>> $\wedge\, ss = coordinator(tt)$
>> $\wedge\, ran(transeffect(tt)) = \{\varnothing\}$
>
> **THEN** $val := transobject(tt) \lhd replica(ss)$ $\|\, sitetransstatus(tt)(ss) := commit$
>> $\|\, transstatus(tt) := COMMIT$
>
> **END**;

Fig. 6. Refinement: Coordinator Site Events - II

As a consequence of the occurrence of the *commit* event at the coordinator, the replica maintained at the coordinator site is updated with the transaction effects, data objects held for transaction tt are declared *free* and the status of the transaction at the coordinator site is set to *commit*. The *AbortWriteTran(tt)* event ensures that an update will abort if it has aborted at some participating site.

Further Refinement of Commit Event

The event *CommitWriteTran(tt)* can be further refined under the following observations.

- $sitetransstatus(t)(s) = precommit \Rightarrow (s \mapsto t) \in activetrans$
- $o \in transobject(t) \land (s \mapsto t) \in activetrans \Rightarrow (s \mapsto o) \notin freeobject$

These observations can be included as invariants in a further refinement allowing the guards of the *CommitWriteTran(tt)* event to be simplified. The simplified guards for the refined *CommitWriteTran(tt)* are given below.

$$[\ tt \in trans$$
$$\land\ ran(transeffect(tt)) \neq \{\varnothing\}$$
$$\land\ transstatus(tt) = PENDING$$
$$\land\ \forall s.(\ s \in SITE \land sitetransstatus(tt)(s) = precommit)\ ]$$

Read only Transactions

The specification of executing a read-only transaction is also given in Fig.6. A *pending* read-only transaction tt returns the value of objects in the set *transobject(tt)* from the replica at its coordinator. The necessary conditions for occurrence of this event are as follows.

$$[\quad transstatus(tt) = PENDING \quad \land\ ran(transeffect(tt)) = \{\varnothing\}$$
$$\land\ transobject(tt) \subseteq freeobject[\{ss\}]\ ]$$

As a consequence of the occurrence of this event, transaction tt reads the objects from the replica at site ss as,

$$val := transobject(tt) \lhd replica(ss)$$

It may be noted that in the abstract model given in Fig.2, a read-only transaction read the objects from abstract database as,

$$val := transobject(tt) \lhd database$$

In refinement checking, we need following invariant to show that the refinement is valid.

$$(ss \mapsto oo) \in freeobject \Rightarrow database(oo) = replica(ss)(oo)$$

A further explanation of this invariant is given in Section 6.

Starting a Sub-transaction

The *BeginSubTran(tt,ss)* event models starting a subtransaction of tt at participating site ss. The specification of this event is given in Fig.7. The guard of *BeginSubTran(tt)* ensures that a sub transaction of tt is started at site ss when all active transactions tz running at ss are not in *conflict* with tt and transaction tt has precommitted at the coordinator site of tt:

- $(ss \mapsto tz) \in activetrans \Rightarrow transobject(tt) \land transobject(tz) = \varnothing$
- $sitetransstatus(tt)(coordinator(tt)) = precommit$

As a consequence of the occurrence of this event, transaction tt becomes *active* at site ss and the *sitetransstatus* of tt at ss is set to pending.

BeginSubTran$(tt,ss)\widehat{=}$
WHEN	$tt \in trans$
	$\land\; sitetransstatus(tt)(coordinator(tt)) = precommit$
	$\land\; (ss \mapsto tt) \notin activetrans$
	$\land\; ss \neq coordinator(tt)$
	$\land\; ran(transeffect(tt)) \neq \{\varnothing\}$
	$\land\; transobject(tt) \subseteq freeobject[\{ss\}]$
	$\land\; transstatus(tt) = PENDING$
	$\land\; \forall tz.(tz \in trans \land (ss \mapsto tz) \in\; activetrans \;\Rightarrow\; transobject(tt) \cap transobject(tz) = \varnothing)$
THEN	$activetrans := activetrans \cup \{ss \mapsto tt\}$ $\parallel\; sitetransstatus(tt)(ss) := pending$
	$\parallel\; freeobject := freeobject - \{ss\} \times transobject(tt)$
END;	

SiteCommitTx$(tt,ss)\widehat{=}$
WHEN	$(ss \mapsto tt) \in\; activetrans$
	$\land\; sitetransstatus(tt)(ss) = pending$
	$\land\; ss \neq coordinator(tt)$
	$\land\; ran(transeffect(tt)) \neq \{\varnothing\}$
	$\land\; transstatus(tt) = PENDING$
THEN	$sitetransstatus(tt)(ss) := precommit$
END;	

SiteAbortTx$(tt,ss)\widehat{=}$
WHEN	$(ss \mapsto tt) \in activetrans$
	$\land\; sitetransstatus(tt)(ss) = pending$
	$\land\; ss \neq coordinator(tt)$
	$\land\; ran(transeffect(tt)) \neq \{\varnothing\}$
	$\land\; transstatus(tt) = PENDING$
THEN	$sitetransstatus(tt)(ss) := abort$ $\parallel\; freeobject := freeobject \cup \{ss\} \times transobject(tt)$
	$\parallel\; activetrans := activetrans - \{ss \mapsto tt\}$
END;	

Fig. 7. Refinement: Participating Site Events -I

Pre-commitment and Abortion of Subtransaction

A participating site ss can independently decide to either pre-commit or abort
a subtransaction. The events $SiteCommitTx(tt,ss)$ and $SiteAbortTx(tt,ss)$, given
in Fig.7, model pre-committing or aborting a subtransaction of tt at ss. Pre-
committing a transaction at a participating site is considered as a commit guarantee given to the coordinator by a participating site. In the case of abort, a site
sets all *objects* of transaction tt free and a subtransaction is removed from the
list of active transactions at that site.

Coordinator Decision of Global Commit

We have already seen how the refined *CommitWriteTran(tt)* and *AbortWrite-
Tran(tt)* model the global commit or abort decision. The event of *ExeCommit-
Decision(tt,ss) and ExeAbortDecision(tt,ss)* given in Fig.8 model commit and

ExeAbortDecision$(ss, tt) \cong$
    WHEN $tt \in trans$
           $\wedge \ (ss \mapsto tt) \in \ activetrans$
           $\wedge \ transstatus(tt) = ABORT$
           $\wedge \ ss \neq coordinator(tt)$
           $\wedge \ ran(transeffect(tt)) \neq \{\varnothing\}$
    THEN $sitetransstatus(tt)(ss) := abort$
           $\parallel activetrans := activetrans - \{ss \mapsto tt\}$
           $\parallel freeobject := freeobject \cup \{ss\} \times transobject(tt)$
    END;

ExeCommitDecision$(ss, tt) \cong$
    ANY pdb
    WHERE $tt \in trans$
           $\wedge \ (ss \mapsto tt) \in \ activetrans$
           $\wedge \ transstatus(tt) = COMMIT$
           $\wedge \ ss \neq coordinator(tt)$
           $\wedge \ ran(transeffect(tt)) \neq \{\varnothing\}$
           $\wedge \ pdb = \ transobject(tt) \lhd replica(ss)$
    THEN $activetrans := activetrans - \{ss \mapsto tt\}$
      $\parallel \ sitetransstatus(tt)(ss) := commit$
      $\parallel \ freeobject := freeobject \cup \{ss\} \times transobject(tt)$
      $\parallel \ replica(ss) := \ replica(ss) \lhd transeffect(tt)(pdb)$
    END;

Fig. 8. Refinement: Participating Site Events -II

abort of tt at participating site ss once the global abort or commit decision has been taken by the coordinating site. In the case of global commit, each site updates its replica separately.

In our model, messaging among the site is not dealt explicitly. A transaction may deadlock due to race conditions in a replicated database. It is our assumption that ordered delivery of messages may be used to prevent deadlock arising due to two simultaneous update requests on the same objects from two different sites. A formal development of causal ordering of messages for fault tolerant transactions and their implementation with logical clock has been proposed in [31].

7   Gluing Invariants

The *one copy equivalence* consistency criterion require us to prove that our refinement (replicated database) is a valid refinement of the abstract transaction model (abstract central database). We have replaced the abstract variable *database* in the abstract model by the variable *replica* in the refinement. An abstract machine is refined by applying the standard technique of data refinement. If a statement S that acts on variable a, is refined by another statement T that acts on variable b under invariants I then we write $S \sqsubseteq_I T$. The invariant I is called the gluing invariant and it defines the relationships between a

Table 2. Events Code

RT/ST	Read/StartTran	IWT	IssueWriteTran	CWT	CommitWriteTran
AWT	AbortWriteTran	BST	BeginSubTran	SAT	SiteAbortTx
SCT	SiteCommitTX	ECT	ExeCommitDecision	EAT	ExeAbortDecision

and *b*. Replacing the abstract variable *database* in machine *Replica1* by concrete variable *replica* in refinement *Replica2* results in proof obligations generated by the B tool. Initially, the only proof obligations that can not be proved involve the relationship between variables *database* and *replica*. These proof obligations were associated with the events *ReadTrans* and *CommitWriteTran*. In order to prove these we added the gluing invariants-I shown in Fig.9. The name of various events of our model and their corresponding event codes are given in Table 2.

The invariant Inv-1 means that a free object *oo* at site *ss* represents the value of *oo* in the abstract database. We have omitted the quantification over all identifiers (tt,ss,oo) to avoid clutter. When invariant Inv-1 is added to the refined machine, the B tool generates further proof obligations associated with several other events. Discharging these additional proof obligations required further invariants given by Gluing Invariants-II in Fig.10. A brief description of these invariants is given below.

- Inv-2 : If a transaction *t* is *active* at its coordinator then all transaction objects $o \in$ *transobject(t)* in the abstract database have the same value in the replica at the coordinator.
- Inv-3 : If two conflicting transactions t_1 and t_2 are active at a site *s*, they must represent the same transaction, i.e., $t_1 = t_2$. This also implies that two different conflicting transactions can not be *active* at the same time at the same site *s*.
- Inv-4 : For a committed transaction *t* which is *active* at one of the site *s*, the new values of objects defined by *transeffect(t)* reflects the value of those objects in the abstract database.

Following a similar approach, in order to preserve the invariants in Fig.10, we have to prove another set of invariants given by Gluing Invariants-III in Fig.11. The brief description of invariants in Fig.11 are given below.

- Inv-5 : For a committed transaction *t* which is still active at a participating site *s*, the value of any read-only objects of *t* is the same in replica(s) as in database.

Invariants		Required By
/*Inv-1*/ $(ss \mapsto oo) \in$ *freeobject* $\Rightarrow$ *database(oo)* = *replica(ss)(oo)*		RT,CWT

Fig. 9. Gluing Invariants-I

	Invariants	Required By
/*Inv-2*/	$(coordinator(t) \mapsto t) \in activetrans$ $\wedge\ o \in transobject(t)$ $\Rightarrow database(o) = replica(coordinator(t))(o)$	AWT,CWT,EAD,ECD
/*Inv-3*/	$(s \mapsto t1) \in activetrans$ $\wedge\ (s \mapsto t2) \in activetrans$ $\wedge\ transobject(t1) \cap transobject(t2) \neq \varnothing$ $\Rightarrow t1 = t2$	ST,IWT,BST
/*Inv-4*/	$transstatus(t) = COMMIT$ $\wedge\ (s \mapsto t) \in activetrans$ $\wedge\ o \in dom(transeffect(t)(transobject(t) \lhd replica(s)))$ $\Rightarrow database(o) = transeffect(t)(transobject(t) \lhd replica(s))(o)$	CWT,AWT,RT,SCT

Fig. 10. Gluing Invariants -II

	Invariants	Required By
/*Inv-5*/	$transstatus(t) = COMMIT$ $\wedge\ o \in transobject(t)$ $\wedge\ (s \mapsto t) \in activetrans$ $\wedge\ o \notin dom(transeffect(t)(transobject(t) \lhd replica(s)))$ $\Rightarrow database(o) = replica(s)(o)$	CWT,AWT,BST,ECD SAT,SCT
/*Inv-6*/	$transstatus(t) = ABORT$ $\Rightarrow sitetransstatus(t)(coordinator(t)) = abort$	AWT,EAD,ECD,ST
/*Inv-7*/	$transstatus(t) = COMMIT$ $\Rightarrow sitetransstatus(t)(coordinator(t)) = commit$	CWT,AWT,EAD,ECD,ST

Fig. 11. Gluing Invariants -III

	Invariants	Required By
/*Inv-8*/	$transstatus(t) \neq COMMIT$ $\wedge\ (s \mapsto t) \in activetrans$ $\wedge\ o \in transobject(t)$ $\Rightarrow database(o) = replica(s)(o)$	CWT,AWT,EAD, ECD,RT
/*Inv-9*/	$transstatus(t) \neq PENDING$ $\wedge\ ran(transeffect(t)) \neq \{\varnothing\}$ $\Rightarrow (coordinator(t) \mapsto t) \notin activetrans$	ST,IWT, SAT,SCT

Fig. 12. Gluing Invariants -IV

- Inv-6,7 : If a transaction t commits or aborts globally, it must have either committed or aborted locally at its coordinator.

Finally the B tool generates more proof obligations to preserve Invariant-III which in turns requires Gluing Invariants-IV shown in Fig.12. The brief description of Invariants-IV is given below.

- Inv-8: A transaction t which has not globally *committed* and is still *active* at some site s, then for all objects $o \in transobject(t)$, value of object o at *replica(s)* is the same as its value in abstract database. Since this refers to the situations where a transaction is not committed, therefore it also involves the situations where the transaction global status is either *PENDING* or *ABORT*.
- Inv-9: An update transaction whose global status is not *PENDING* must not be *active* at its coordinator site. This refers to situations where the global status of an update transaction is either *COMMIT* or *ABORT*.

We observe that at every stage new proof obligations are generated by the B tool due to the addition of new invariants. In this process at every stage we also discover further invariants to be expressed in our model. After four iterations of invariant strengthening, we arrive at an invariant that is sufficient to discharge all proof obligations. By discharging the proof obligations we ensure that refinement is a valid refinement of the abstract specification.

8   Conclusions

In this paper we have presented a formal approach to modelling and analyzing a distributed transaction mechanism for replicated databases using Event B. The abstract model of transactions is based on the notion of a single copy database. In the refinement of the abstract model, we introduced the notion of a replicated database. The replica control mechanism presented in the paper allows an update transaction to be submitted at any site. An update transaction commits atomically updating all copies at commit or none when it aborts. A read-only transaction may perform read operations on any single replica. The various events given in the B refinement are triggered within the framework of commit protocols which ensure global atomicity of update transactions despite site or transaction failures. The system allows the sites to abort a transaction independently and keeps the replicated database in a consistent state.

Distributed algorithms [19] are difficult to verify and their verification has long been an issue of study. The work reported in [15] applies formal modelling to a replica control strategy and considers proof of correctness. They use I/O automata to model an algorithm and then prove properties about all trace behaviors of the automation. Instead of proving trace properties, we prove that our model of the algorithm is a correct refinement of a abstract model of single copy database. Also [15] does not consider transaction failures at sites.

The system development approach considered is based on Event B, which facilitates incremental development of dependable systems. The work was carried out on the Click'n'Prove B tool. The tool generates the proof obligations for refinement and consistency checking. The majority of proofs were discharged using the automatic prover of the tool, however one third of the complex proofs required use of the interactive prover. These proofs helped us to understand the complexity of problem and the correctness of the solutions. They also helped us to discover new system invariants providing a clear insight to the system. Our experience with this case study strengthens our believe that abstraction and refinement are valuable technique for modelling complex distributed system.

Acknowledgements

Thanks to the REFT referees for the valuable comments which helped us improve the paper.

References

1. J R Abrial. *The B Book : Assigning Programs to Meaning*, Cambridge University Press,1996.
2. J R Abrial. *Extending B without changing it.* (For Distributed System).Proc. of 1st Conf. on B Method, pp 169-191, 1996.
3. J R Abrial, D Cansell, D Mery. *A Mechanically Proved and Incremetal development of IEEE1394 Tree Identify Protocol.* Formal Aspect of Computing, Vol 14, PP215-227, 2003.
4. J R Abrial, D Cansell : *Click'n'Prove - Interactive Proofs within Set Theory*,2003.
5. D Agrawal, G Alonso, I Stanoi. *Exploiting Atomic Broadcast in Replicated Database.* Proc. of Europar97, 1997.
6. O Babaoglu, A Bartoli, G Dini. *Replicated file management in large scale distributed system.* Proc. of 8th Intl. workshop on Distributed Algorithms. WDAG94,pp1-16,LNCS,Springer,1994.
7. P A Bernstein, V Hadzilacos, N Goodman. *Concurrency Control and Recovery in Database System.* Addision Wesley,1987.
8. K P Birman, A Schiper, P Stephenson. *Lighweight causal and atomic group multicast.* ACM Transaction on Computer System,Vol9,No 3,pp 272-314, 1991.
9. M Butler. *On the use of Data Refinement in the Development of Secure Communications Systems.* Formal Aspects of Computing, 14 : 2-34,2002.
10. M Butler. *An Approach to Design of Distributed Systems with B AMN.* Proc. 10th Int. Conf. of Z Users: The Z Formal Specification Notation (ZUM), LNCS 1212, pp. 223-241,1997.
11. M Butler, M Walden. *Distributed System Development in B.* Proc. of Ist Conf. in B Method, Nantes, pp155-168,1996.
12. D Cansell, D Mery. *Foundations of B Method.* Computing and Informatics, Vol 22,1-31,2003.
13. B Core UK Ltd. *B-Toolkit Manuals*,1999.
14. R Ekwall, A Schiper. *Replication : Understanding the advantage of atomic broadcast over quorum systems.* Journal of Universal Computer Science, Vol 11, No 5, pp 703-711, 2005.

15. A Fekete, M Frans Kaashoek, N Lynch. *Implementing Sequentiully Consistent Shared Objects using Broadcast and Point-To-Point Communication. Journal of the ACM*,Volume 45,Issue 1,pp 35 - 69, 1998.
16. J Gray, A Reuter. *Transaction Processing : Concepts and Technique*, Morgan Kaufmann, 1993.
17. J Holliday. *Replicated Database Recovery using Multicast Communication. IEEE Intl. Symposium on Network Computing and Application*, NCA2001, pp 104-107,2001.
18. B Kemme, G Alonso. *A New Approach to developing and implementing eager database replication protocols. ACM Transaction on Database System*, Vol 25, Issue 3, pp 333-379, 2000.
19. Nancy A Lynch. *Distributed Algorithms*, Morgan Kaughman,1996.
20. P Melliar, Y Amir, L Moser, V Agrawala. *Broadcast protocols for Distributed Systems*, IEEE Transactions on Parallel and Distributed System,1(1), pp17-25,1990.
21. C Metayer, J R Abrial, L Voisin. *Event-B Language*, RODIN Deliverables 3.2, 2005. (http://rodin.cs.ncl.ac.uk/deliverables/D7.pdf)
22. L Moser, P Mellier, D Agrawal, R Budhia, C Papadopoulos, *TOTEM : A fault tolerant multicast group communication*, Communication of ACM,39,4, PP 54-63, 1996.
23. M T Ozsu, P Valduriez. *Principles of Distribted Database Systems*. Prentice Hall, 1999.
24. A Rezazadeh, M Butler. *Some Guidelines for formal developement of web based application in B Method*. Proc. of 4th Intl. Conf. of B and Z users, Guildford, LNCS, Springer, pp 472-491, April 2005.
25. M. Patino-Martinez, R. Jimenez-Peris, B. Kemme, G. Alonso. *Consistent Database Replication at the Middleware Level*. ACM Transactions on Computer Systems (TOCS).no. 4, vol. 23, pp. 375-423, Nov. 2005.
26. B Silaghi, P Keleher, B Bhattacharjee. *Multi-Dimensional Quorum Sets for Red-Few Write-Many Replica Control Protocols*. In Proc. of the 4th CCGRID/GP2PC Chicago, IL, April 2004.
27. S Schneider. *The B-Method*. Palgrave Publications, 2001.
28. A Silberschatz, H Korth, S Sudarshan . *Database System Concepts*, McGrawHill, 2001.
29. I Stanoi, D Agrawal , A.El Abbadi. *Using Broadbast Primitives in Replicated Data*. Proceddings of 18 IEEE Intl. Conf. on Distributed Computing System,ICDCS98,pp 148-155,1998.
30. Steria- Atelier-B User and Reference Manuals, 1997.
31. D Yadav, M Butler. *Application of Event B to Global Causal Ordering for Fault Tolerant Transactions*. Proc. of REFT 2005, Newcastle upon Tyne, pp 93-103, 2005.(http://eprints.ecs.soton.ac.uk/10981/)

Engineering Reconfigurable Distributed Software Systems: Issues Arising for Pervasive Computing

Apostolos Zarras[1], Manel Fredj[2], Nikolaos Georgantas[2], and Valerie Issarny[2]

[1] Dept. of Computer Science, University of Ioannina, Greece
zarras@cs.uoi.gr
http://www.cs.uoi.gr/ zarras
[2] INRIA-Rocquencourt, France
{Manel.Fredj, Nikolaos.Georgantas, Valerie.Issarny}@inria.fr
http://www-rocq.inria.fr/arles/

Abstract. This chapter establishes a common base for discussing reconfigurability in distributed software systems in general and in pervasive systems in particular, by introducing a generic reconfiguration cycle. Following this cycle, we discuss in detail three former efforts on reconfigurable pervasive systems, and draw conclusions about the capacity of existing approaches to deal with open, dynamic, ad hoc environments. We, then, outline our approach towards uncontrolled reconfiguration targeting environments in which no centralized coordination or prior awareness between services being composed is assumed. Our solution supports awareness of service semantics and related service discovery, configuration change detection and state transfer, interface-aware dynamic adaptation of service orchestrations and conversation-aware checkpointing and recovery.

1 Introduction

Dynamic reconfiguration proved, along the years, to be a major issue towards the development of dependable distributed software systems. In principle, we may distinguish three basic types of reconfiguration situations based on the targeted needs [1]. First, we have *corrective* reconfiguration that aims at dealing with faults causing failures in the constituents of a system. Second, we have *perfective* reconfiguration that targets changes performed towards meeting the evolving functional and non-functional requirements of the system. Finally, we have *adaptive* reconfiguration aiming at the proper functioning of devices and their hosted applications that are dynamically integrated in a computing system without prior knowledge of the functional constraints (e.g., available functionalities and resources) imposed by this system. The first two types of reconfiguration were typically targeted by stationary distributed systems. On the other hand, the need for the last type of reconfiguration arose with the latest emergence of pervasive computing systems. An in between evolution with respect to these two system domains were nomadic computing systems, which added wide area

M. Butler et al. (Eds.): Fault-Tolerant Systems, LNCS 4157, pp. 364–386, 2006.

mobility to stationary distributed systems and were a precursor to pervasive computing systems. There, mobility makes the computing environment less predictable than in stationary systems, thus as well implying the need for adaptive reconfiguration, to a lesser extent, however, than in pervasive systems.

Reconfiguration in stationary distributed systems – architecturally modelled in terms of components and connectors [2] – concerns adding, removing or substituting components or connectors. Changes should take place at runtime to avoid compromising the availability of the overall system. The basic techniques to achieve this goal rely on a main authority that is often called *reconfiguration manager* [3]. This authority has knowledge of the changes that are going to take place and its main responsibility is to perform them, whilst not jeopardizing the overall system integrity. Techniques proposed for handling reconfiguration aim at isolating a component of the system that is to be removed or substituted by enforcing request blocking [3,4] or request redirection [5] on components that use this component. By request blocking, this component eventually reaches a state where it is not used, and reconfiguration can be safely performed. Request redirection supports immediate component replacement: a connector can direct all communication after a certain point in time from the old component to the new one. In this case and if the components are statefull, state transfer [4,6,7] from the old component to the new one enables a seamless transition.

Evolution to nomadic computing systems enabled users to be mobile and to carry around wireless devices. The key concept in such systems is that a client software entity resides on the user's device and is connected to some remote server software entity. Connectivity between client and server may be intermittent due to insufficient wireless network coverage or limited bandwidth shared between multiple users. However, it is assumed that eventually the client will reconnect to the same server or to some replica of the server. Then, the objective is to enable users to use their mobile devices even during periods of low or non-connectivity. The basic technique applied is to emulate locally at the client the remote server, e.g., by locally replicating server data [8,9] or code [10], or by just buffering client requests, and by synchronizing client and server upon reconnection [11]. Further attention may be required when a server is updated by multiple clients, or when clients connect to and disconnect from more than one server replica [8]. Data integrity should be maintained when data is replicated on multiple hosts. In terms of architectural modelling, connectors can handle transparently for components the disconnection, reconnection, or connection to replicated servers.

Being one step further, pervasive computing systems aim at making computational power available everywhere. Mobile and stationary devices will dynamically connect and coordinate to seamlessly help people in accomplishing their tasks. For this vision to become reality, systems must adapt themselves with respect to the constantly changing conditions of the pervasive environment: (i) the highly dynamic character of the computing and networking environment due to the intense use of the wireless medium and the mobility of the users; (ii) the resource constraints of mobile devices, e.g., in terms of CPU, memory and battery power; and (iii) the high heterogeneity of integrated technologies in terms of networks, devices and software infrastructures. In response to such challenges, the Service-Oriented Architecture (SOA) paradigm [12] provides an attractive solution. A service is a consistent piece of functionality made available over the network by a software entity and accessed by other – customer – software entities. A service is accessible at a specific network address, via a well-defined interface, i.e., a set of supported operations, and over a specific middleware communication protocol. Besides this generic definition, no restriction is imposed on the implementation of a service, which enables integration of diverse technologies and loose coupling between interacting services, making SOA suitable for dynamic, heterogeneous environments. Further, a service supports a set of valid service *conversations*, which are *processes* in the form of *workflow* that define the behavior of the service. All the above information concerning a service constitutes the service specification, which may be published on the network, thus, made discoverable by customers via a service discovery protocol. Discovering a service means matching a required service specification with a provided service specification. A direct matching technique constitutes in comparing – among others – the required and provided interface specifications syntax, assuming that two syntactically compatible interfaces imply semantically – i.e., concerning their meaning – compatible services. However, enforcing an agreement on a common syntax for denoting semantics is impossible to achieve in open environments, such as pervasive computing environments. Thus, the latest tendency is towards adopting semantic representation paradigms for specifying and matching services even when these differ in their syntactic interfaces. Such paradigms employ *ontologies* to represent concepts and related well-founded formalisms to enable machine reasoning about them [13]. Finally, services may be composed towards realizing complex functionalities. Two essential models for service composition are: (i) service *orchestration*, where a customer invokes a set of services in a coordinated way, and (ii) service *choreography*, where a set of services interact with each other in a peer-to-peer fashion.

Regarding reconfiguration, the distinctive feature of pervasive systems is that software entities making up a system may have no *a priori* knowledge of each other before their dynamic composition. Bindings between entities are ad hoc and temporary, which is served pretty well by the loosely coupled interaction model of SOA. However, unawareness not only concerns which concretely the entities are, but is further extended to the specification of entities, e.g., in terms of interfaces and conversations. This means that entities composing pervasive systems have not necessarily been developed to be syntactically compatible. In the same direction, after a disconnection, a client software entity will most likely not reconnect to the same server software entity or even a replica of it, but rather to another server. This new server should be semantically equivalent or similar to the old one, and thus compatible with the client, but it will not necessarily be syntactically compatible with it. Thus, semantic paradigms prove to be essential for pervasive systems. Semantic matching enables associating semantically compatible software entities, but this is not sufficient. To integrate such entities, adaptation is further needed in terms of interfaces and conversations. Furthermore, no central reconfiguration management can be established in such systems. We call such reconfiguration *uncontrolled*. Uncontrolled reconfiguration in pervasive systems distinguishes itself from the controlled one in stationary and nomadic systems, where prior awareness is a basic assumption.

Uncontrolled reconfiguration in pervasive systems presents numerous challenges as made clear in the above. In this chapter, we particularly contribute with an approach for reconfiguration in pervasive environments, which comprises syntactic and semantic dynamic service discovery, change detection, state transfer, interface-aware orchestration adaptation and conversation-aware checkpointint and recovery mechanisms. Before presenting our approach to uncontrolled reconfiguration in pervasive computing systems (Section 3), we examine in detail three related efforts on reconfigurable pervasive systems (Section 2), which gives a concrete view of ongoing research in the domain, and discuss goals, strong points and constraints in current approaches. We particularly examine the capacity of these approaches to deal with open, dynamic, ad hoc pervasive environments. In the beginning of the latter section, we introduce a general view of the reconfiguration procedure in distributed software systems, which establishes a common base for discussing both existing approaches and the proposed one. Finally, we conclude with a summary of this chapter, and point out open issues and future work (Section 4).

2   Reconfigurable Systems

In this section, we discuss in detail three former efforts related to dynamic reconfiguration of pervasive computing systems (Section 2.2). To allow comparative study of such systems, we introduce a *generic reconfiguration cycle*, which provides an abstract descriptive view of the reconfiguration procedure of a system; this cycle can pretty well apply to different distributed software systems – stationary, nomadic, pervasive – and related reconfiguration techniques (Section 2.1). Our detailed presentation of the three approaches allows a comprehensive view of the whole reconfiguration procedure, each time for a complete, consistent system.

2.1   Generic Reconfiguration Cycle

To allow a separation of concerns, we distinguish between the *Reconfigurable System (RS)*, its *Context* or *Environment (CE)*, and the *Reconfiguration Management System (RM)*, as depicted in Figure 1. CE is in constant interaction with RS, for example, affecting RS functioning or hosting some functional entity that may join RS as a result of reconfiguration. RM integrates all functionality necessary for RS reconfiguration, while RS should only hold some architectural and functional properties supporting its reconfiguration along with the capacity to respond to RM actions; otherwise, RS is not aware of its reconfiguration. We further assume that the architecture of RS, CE and RM can be described at a generic level in terms of components and connectors [2]. Based on that, we deal with architectural reconfiguration of RS in terms of adding, removing and substituting components [4] and connectors [6,7].

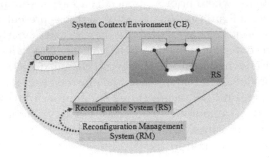

Fig. 1. Separation of concerns for reconfiguration

We call *reconfiguration cycle* a complete sequence of phases that takes place during the execution of RS and reconfigures it taking it from a consistent state to another consistent state, i.e., one from which RS can continue normally its execution rather than progressing towards an error state. We introduce the generic reconfiguration cycle depicted in Table 1, where lines are associated to phases succeeding one another in time in ascending order, and columns are associated to functional entities that may act or be acted upon concurrently, specifically RS, CE and RM. RM's activity is presented in two columns: the first one indicates RM's overall functions, while the second one is dedicated to RM's data processing concerning reconfiguration. Our reconfiguration cycle aims at enabling a common, abstract descriptive view of the reconfiguration procedure for a large variety of systems. Representing the exact state transitions of RS, CE and RM and the eventually complex interactions taking place between them for any of these systems with a single reconfiguration cycle is certainly not possible. Thus, we make no strict assumptions about the functional entities and phases of the reconfiguration cycle, other than the ones stated in the above. In the following, we introduce in detail the various phases of the reconfiguration cycle.

In Phase 1, RS executes normally, while RM monitors both RS and its CE. RM holds a set of data concerning RS, which were produced at RS development or deployment time. Thus, RS configuration description represents the current configuration of RS, which includes, for example, the functional dependencies between components. Further, the normal execution of the combination RS-CE is delimited by a set of execution constraints, for example, which components need to be up and running, or minimum communication bandwidth available to RS [14,15]. Definition of normal execution naturally directly defines as well abnormal execution. Along with this, enhanced execution may be identified, enabling automated perfective reconfiguration. Finally, a set of possible reconfiguration strategies and actions may be provided, specifying the scope of RM's role [14,15].

Table 1. Generic reconfiguration cycle

Phase	Reconfigurable system (RS)	System context/ environment (CE)	Reconfiguration management system (RM)	
			Function	**Data processing**
1	RS executes normally		RM monitors RS and CE	• Holds RS configuration description • Holds description of RS-CE constraints for normal, abnormal, enhanced execution • Holds set of reconfiguration strategies and actions • Produces RS and CE monitoring data • Periodically saves dynamic RS data
2	• RS executes normally/abnormally • RS generates cause for reconfiguration	CE generates cause for reconfiguration		
3			RM detects cause for reconfiguration	• Uses RS and CE monitoring data • Uses description of RS-CE constraints for normal, abnormal, enhanced execution
4			RM specifies reconfiguration	• Uses RS configuration description • Uses set of reconfiguration strategies and actions • Produces sequence of actual reconfiguration actions
5	RM prepares RS for reconfiguration	RM determines participation of CE to new configuration	RM applies reconfiguration	• Uses sequence of actual reconfiguration actions • Saves dynamic RS data
6	RM adapts RS to new configuration	RM adapts CE to new configuration		Uses saved dynamic RS data
7	RM reconfigures RS	RM reconfigures CE		Produces new RS configuration description

Moreover, during its execution, RM manages some dynamic RS data. Thus, it produces monitoring data concerning RS and CE. It may as well periodically save dynamic RS data, such as the state of RS components, thus checkpointing RS. Another example of such activity is the local caching or pre-fetching of remote server data by a client entity in nomadic systems [8,9].

In Phase 2, a cause for reconfiguration emerges, generated by either RS or CE. This cause may be accompanied by abnormal RS execution or not. An example of the first case may be the disconnection or failure of an essential component of RS, or the drop in the available bandwidth, while an example of the second case may be the availability of a new component that offers enhanced quality of service. In Phase 3, RM detects the emerging cause for reconfiguration after having observed current monitoring data and compared it with execution constraints. In Phase 4, RM decides its way of intervention to reconfigure RS. To this aim, RM uses the current RS configuration description and the set of possible reconfiguration strategies and actions in order to produce the sequence of actual reconfiguration actions that it will take. For example, based on dependencies between components, RM may identify components affected by the intended reconfiguration and take some preventive action before applying reconfiguration.

In Phases 5, 6 and 7, RM applies the sequence of actual reconfiguration actions. In Phase 5, RM prepares RS for reconfiguration. This preparation concerns components affected by the intended reconfiguration and may take several forms. For example, request blocking [3,4], request redirection [5] or request queuing may be enforced on components that interact with a component that is about to leave RS. RM may save the state of a leaving mobile component just in time if the component issues a warning before leaving; this provides a perfectly up-to-date state, which may not be the case for state saved by periodic checkpointing. A similar last minute action may be taken by a client entity in a nomadic system to locally pre-fetch remote server data just before disconection [9]. Further in the same phase, RM determines the participation of CE to the new configuration, i.e., whether some new components coming from CE will join RS. This task heavily depends on whether RM has *a priori* or not knowledge of the new components that will be introduced into RS. Such awareness may range: from concretely knowing already from the deployment of RS which these components are, to having to carry out dynamic component discovery based on syntactic or semantic descriptions of the interfaces and supported conversations of the components. In Phase 6, RM may have to adapt either one or both of RS and CE to the new configuration, so that their integration be possible. RS adaptation may involve coordination workflow adaptation to be compatible with a new component being introduced, or workflow rollback to cancel some interrupted transaction. CE adaptation may involve transferring the saved state of the leaving component to its substitute component [6,7,16]. In the case of a nomadic system upon reconnection, CE adaptation may involve synchronizing the remote server with updates maintained locally on the client, or submitting to the server all locally queued client requests [8]. Finally, in Phase 7, RM carries out the final reconfiguration action on RS, possibly integrating some new components coming from the CE. Now, the new RS configuration description is available, and RS may go back to normal execution (Phase 1).

In the next section, we study in detail three approaches to reconfigurable pervasive systems on the basis of the above discussion. We highlight the relation of the presented efforts to the introduced generic reconfiguration cycle by referencing specific phases of the cycle.

2.2   Reconfigurability in Pervasive Computing Systems

The first two reconfiguration approaches that we discuss in this section, *RAPID-ware* and *CASA*, focus on techniques enabling a smooth transition of the system from its initial to its target configuration, where no loss of component processing or data occurs during reconfiguration. RAPIDware calculates a safe reconfiguration strategy and employs request blocking based on dependencies between components, while CASA manages state transfer at object programming level for dynamically replaceable local objects. The third approach, *Polymorphic applications*, enables migration of distributed component-based applications between pervasive environments. The combined presentation of these three approaches allows looking into how well-established techniques coming from stationary distributed systems are applied to pervasive systems, as well as pointing out new requirements and solutions specific to pervasive systems.

RAPIDware. This project addresses perfective reconfiguration of component-based pervasive systems [17]. The reconfiguration approach is applied to a wireless video streaming application, which involves a video server multicasting video streams to clients residing on laptops and handheld devices. Streaming is secure via encryption of the wireless stream. Reconfiguration aims at enhancing system properties: in the specific application, encoder and decoder components are substituted by alternative ones in order to enforce a higher encryption scheme, thus enhancing security. All available encoder and decoder components are known before system execution and have been developed to directly fit together in terms of interfaces and behavior. Reconfiguration is executed by a central *reconfiguration manager (RM)*, which coordinates a set of *reconfiguration agents (RAs)* attached to system components involved in the reconfiguration.

RM holds the system configuration description, which is in terms of (Phase 1): (i) *dependency relationships* between components, i.e., the correct functionality of a component may require the correct functionality of other components; and (ii) *critical communication segments* between components, i.e., communication segments whose interruption may cause errors in the system. Further, the reconfiguration manager holds the set of all possible reconfiguration actions. A fixed cost is associated to each reconfiguration action, depending on associated system blocking time, delay of data delivery and resource usage.

Upon some external command, e.g., by the user, RM obtains the target configuration (Phases 2-3). A reconfiguration procedure is *safe* if (a) it does not violate dependency relationships and (b) it does not interrupt critical communication segments. Based on that, RM specifies reconfiguration in three steps (Phase 4):

1. Based on the source and target configurations and the dependency relationships, RM produces a set of safe configurations. A safe configuration is one that satisfies all the dependency relationships.
2. RM constructs a safe reconfiguration graph, where vertices are all safe configurations and edges are all possible reconfiguration actions connecting safe configurations. This graph can be deduced from available reconfiguration actions. To ensure a safe reconfiguration procedure, reconfiguration actions should not interrupt critical communication segments.
3. RM applies Dijkstra's shortest path algorithm on the graph to find a safe reconfiguration path with minimum weight, where the weight of a path is the sum of the costs of all the edges along the path.

Finally, RM applies the calculated reconfiguration path. For each reconfiguration action in the path:

1. RM sends block commands via RAs to affected components to enforce suspension of their functioning. Block commands are applied after waiting for the last critical communication segment to be completed (Phase 5).
2. RM/RAs carry out the actual reconfiguration action, e.g., replacing a component by another one. When the adaptation action is done, RM/RAs send resume commands to blocked components reactivating them (Phase 7).

The interest of the RAPIDware approach lies in the systematic way for calculating a safe reconfiguration path. Certainly, even if applied to a wireless mobile application, a well-controlled environment is required, where all information about component functionality and interaction, both for current and for new system components, is known in advance.

CASA (Contract-based Adaptive Software Architecture). This framework enables dynamic adaptation of a component-based software application executing on a mobile device in response to changes in contextual information such as user's location, or to changes in resource availability such as bandwidth [18]. A device hosting adaptive applications is required to run an instance of the CASA runtime system, which is responsible for monitoring the changes in the environment and adapt these applications accordingly. Components in CASA-enabled applications are objects in an object-oriented programming language. This reconfiguration approach is realized at object programming level and consequently inherits all restrictions coming from the strong coupling inherent in the object-oriented paradigm – which was relaxed in the descendant component-oriented and service-oriented paradigms. Nevertheless, it presents a number of features that can be of interest as well to reconfigurable systems based on the latter two paradigms.

Replaceability of objects is determined based on the notion of a *set of alternative classes*, which is a collection of classes whose instances can dynamically replace each other. This means that these classes: (1) conform to the same interface; (2) the pre- and post-conditions of the methods of their interfaces are the same; and (3) a valid *persistent* state of an instance of one such class can be mapped to a valid persistent state of an instance of another such class. To enable replacement, the *Bridge* software architectural pattern [19] is used, where every set of alternative classes is associated with a unique *Handle* class, which conforms to the same interface as the classes of the set. Clients of an object are actually bound to an instantiation of the Handle class, which allows hiding from them the fact that the object may be dynamically replaced.

CASA adaptation is based on an *application contract*, which is divided into *context elements*. Each context element represents a state of contextual information of interest to the application and contains a list of alternative configurations of the application, suited to the particular state of contextual information. Thus, reconfiguration is decided and carried out in order to respect the application contract (Phases 1-3). Regarding specification of reconfiguration (Phase 4), two replacement strategies are defined: (a) in *lazy replacement*, an already running component is allowed to complete its current execution before being replaced; (b) in *eager replacement*, the execution of a running component is suspended, and the execution resumes again from the point where it was suspended, after the component is replaced. To *eagerly replace* an object objA by an object objB, where both are handled by a Handle object objH, the following steps are taken:

1. objH starts queueing calls made to objA (Phase 5).
2. objA is notified to suspend execution of the current call. Suspension can be done only when execution of objA has reached one of the explicitly predefined *safe points* at which execution can be resumed correctly by objB. The information about the safe point where the call is suspended is passed to objH (Phase 5).
3. objH creates objB (Phase 5).

4. objH reinvokes the suspended call on objB, passing the information about the safe point where the call was previously suspended, in order to enable objB to resume the execution correctly (Phases 6-7).

A necessary condition for valid eager replacement is that the transferred state of objA can get transformed into a reachable state of objB. However, this may not be possible for a *transient* state of objA. In this case, lazy replacement is applied, where objA is not running at the time of replacement, and thus the state to be transferred is the *persistent* state of objA, which, as indicated above, can become a valid persistent state of objB.

As already indicated, even if the object-oriented architectural style may be restrictive, the interest of CASA lies in its management of state transfer which is a general issue concerning reconfiguration. As also observed for RAPIDware, reconfiguration in CASA requires as well a well-controlled local environment. Response to context changes based on an application contract is also worth noting in CASA, even if the alternative application configurations suited to a particular contextual state are pre-defined.

Polymorphic applications. This approach addresses application migration with the user across pervasive environments that may differ in terms of available devices and services as well as context [20]. Migration consists in suspending an executing application and resuming it later in a new environment. The targeted pervasive environment, called an *Active Space*, is situated in a physical space like a room or a building, and consists of various entities including users, applications, services and devices. An example polymorphic application is one that supports a user's slide show by integrating distributed resources, such as a PowerPoint viewer component, a wall-mounted display and a GUI component. Application structure is based on the Model-View-Controller framework [6], consisting of input (controller), output (view) and logic (model) components. Applications execute on top of Gaia, a CORBA-based meta operating system that manages all physical and digital entities in an Active Space.

Reconfiguration concerns three kinds of application adaptation: change in the type of components, change in the number of components, and change in the devices on which these components execute. These types of adaptation are based on the notion of *semantic similarity* of application components, stating that an application component can be substituted by another component if it allows the user to perform the same tasks in some manner. Thus, a PowerPoint viewer can be replaced by an Acrobat Reader viewer (if appropriate data transcoding is done) or by a Speech Engine that reads out the text in the slides. Certainly, Acrobat Reader is semantically closer to PowerPoint. Semantic similarity between components is determined with the help of ontologies that define a hierarchy of components based on the kinds of tasks that they help users to perform. Application migration between two Active Spaces is performed by two collaborating instances of the *Migration Service (MS)*, a central coordinating entity that controls an Active Space.

MS holds the current structure of an executing application stored in an *Application Customized Description (ACD)* file. Further, MS has access to the *Space*

Repository, which maintains information concerning all devices, components and services available in the Active Space (Phase 1). The migration procedure is triggered by the user through a GUI; the user specifies the Active Space to which the application is to be migrated (Phases 2-3). Then, MS saves the current state of the application along with its structure in the ACD file, and communicates the file to the new Active Space over the network. MS in the new Active Space takes the old ACD of the application and generates a new ACD for the application, after performing appropriate adaptation in three steps (Phases 4-6):

1. MS consults the Active Space ontologies to identify classes of components that are semantically similar to the components listed in the old ACD, as well as classes of devices that can host these component classes. Some additional components that should do, e.g., data transcoding, may be needed.
2. MS queries the Space Repository to get instances of the classes of devices obtained from the previous step that are available in the new Active Space.
3. For each identified component, MS decides the cardinality and the devices on which the components must be instantiated using rules involving the context of the new Active Space and preferences of the user. Context includes the location of the user in the room, the location of devices, the presence of other people in the room, the current activity of the user and so on.

Finally, once MS arrives at a new application structure, it instantiates this application in the new Active Space (Phase 7).

The approach of polymorphic applications is very interesting, as it highlights several issues of pervasive applications, such as mobility of users between pervasive environments, on-the-fly integration of available resources and adaptation to them, semantic similarity between resources, and context-awareness. Nevertheless, even if resources differ between Active Spaces, composition of resources within an Active Space is pretty direct in terms of interfaces, and only data encoding adaptation needs to be dealt with. While this is reasonable for stationary resources, it cannot be assumed for mobile resources present on devices of mobile users, which also make part of the pervasive environment.

Concluding this section, we point out that the presented efforts on reconfigurable pervasive systems largely assume a well-controlled environment: a central coordinating entity is responsible for reconfiguration, and has absolute control and, mostly, full *a priori* knowledge over available resources. In the next section, we deal with reconfiguration in *uncontrolled* environments, in an attempt to come closer to the realization of the concepts of pervasive and ubiquitous computing.

3   Uncontrolled Reconfiguration in Pervasive Computing Systems

In this section, we present our vision of *uncontrolled* reconfiguration targeting open, dynamic, ad hoc pervasive environments. Our approach adopts the SOA paradigm. To discuss in more detail the basic functional requirements for dealing with uncontrolled reconfiguration in SOA-based environments, we employ a motivating scenario inspired by [21] (Section 3.1). Based on this scenario, we introduce a service-oriented pervasive environment enhanced with awareness of semantics of services (Section 3.2), and we outline the essential mechanisms supporting reconfiguration in such an environment (Section 3.3). Throughout the present section, we relate our approach to the discussion of Section 2 by referencing specific phases of the generic reconfiguration cycle.

3.1   Scenario and Requirements

In our scenario, we are placed in the near territory of the island of Cyprus. Our pervasive environment consists of several services offering, e.g., tourist information, hotel reservation and car reservation. These services execute on stationary hosts located onshore. The environment that we consider further comprises mobile hosts located on cruise ships, yachts, and other boats. At a short distance from the island, software entities residing on mobile hosts may have access to the services located onshore through a wireless network. If moving further from the island, however, their only possibility to access the services is through satellite-based connections, which are usually expensive and inefficient (especially in the case of GEO networks). To confront this problem, the island's local authorities realized the following setup. The stationary software entities located onshore may actually recruit volunteer mobile entities that can serve as their proxies. Proxies provide indirect wireless access to the onshore services to mobile entities that do not have direct access to these services. As an exchange, the crew members and the tourists onboard may benefit from more favorable hotel, restaurant and car rental prices. Figure 2 gives three snapshots of our pervasive environment resulting from the mobility of the participating entities. In Figure 2(a), the mobile entity S4 is added to the pervasive environment. The entity requires using a hotel reservation service. Since S4 does not have direct access to the stationary services, it selects S5 as a proxy to the required service. In Figure 2(b), the geographical location of S5 obliges it to leave the pervasive environment. In Figure 2(c), S4 has to deal with the change triggered by the S5 entity. The removal of S5 may take place while S4 is trying to use the proxy services provided by S5.

Preserving the environment's consistency in the presence of the aforementioned changes involves dealing with the following issues. In Figure 2(a), the newly added entity should be able to execute its orchestration processes. Consequently, it should discover services suitable for the realization of these orchestration processes. In the open environment of the scenario, discovering services that are syntactically suitable should be considered as the exception rather than the rule. Thus, syntactic discovery of services is not sufficient; supporting semantic description and matching of services is an essential requirement. Then, to be able to use the discovered, semantically compatible services, adaptation is further needed in terms of interfaces and conversations. The newly added entity should adapt its orchestration processes to both the interfaces and

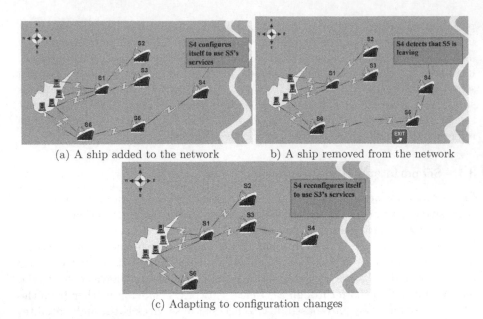

(a) A ship added to the network   b) A ship removed from the network

(c) Adapting to configuration changes

Fig. 2. A pervasive environment formed around the island of Cyprus

conversations of the discovered services. Getting to Figures 2(b) and (c), entities that use the leaving entity should detect its departure, so as to properly adapt their affected orchestration processes. The affected processes are distinguished into *pending* and *inactive*. Pending processes are ones whose execution started before the mobile entity decides to leave and involve the removed entity. Inactive processes are non-instantiated processes that involve the removed entity. In the case of a pending process, the affected entity should discover new services that can substitute the ones of the removed entity, semantically and, if possible, syntactically suitable, and adapt the process to the interfaces and conversations of the new services. Furthermore, the process should be rolled back to a point where it is possible to resume its execution, now with the new services in the place of the removed ones. State transfer between the old and the new services, if and whenever possible, could minimize rolling back or make it unnecessary. Finally, entities used by the leaving entity should also detect this incident so as to terminate all the pending conversations initiated by this entity.

The main outcome from the above discussion is that the effective support for dynamic reconfiguration in pervasive environments requires mechanisms for:

(1) semantic and syntactic service discovery; (2) configuration changes detection and state transfer; (3) process dynamic adaptation; and (4) checkpointing and recovery.

Apart from our motivating example, several other scenarios may involve the requirements we identified here. Consider for instance some of the scenarios identified by ISTAG (Information Society Technologies Advisory Group) for ambient intelligence (AmI) environments [22]. In the scenario that concerns AmI environments for business, employees who used to work at a fixed location, to-day change working locations and environments frequently. In such cases, the employees that are *added* in a new working environment would require access to location-specific, syntactically or semantically compatible services. Similarly, in AmI environments supporting E-Government, people may *migrate* from one country to another one. Different countries may employ semantically equivalent procedures for these people (e.g., for validating a driver's licence), supported by semantically compatible E-Government services offered by each community. Confronting the previous, involves transparently adapting the processes used by the immigrants with respect to the E-services of the new country that they visit. In AmI for intelligent transport systems the goal is to develop intelligent vehicles able to monitor traffic conditions using services offered either by the environ-ment or by other vehicles. *Moving* from one area to another implies adapting the processes used by intelligent vehicles with respect to the interfaces offered by the AmI environment that supports the new area.

In the following sections we concentrate on our sailing example. In particular, we introduce a semantics-aware service-oriented environment that can effectively represent the pervasive environment of our sailing scenario, and we outline the required mechanisms in the context of this environment.

3.2   Semantic Service-Oriented Pervasive Environment

Adopting the service-oriented architectural style in the context of pervasive com-puting systems implies employing a middleware infrastructure that supports it. SOA middleware infrastructures for pervasive environments should support the execution of services on top of resource-constrained devices. As an appropri-ate such middleware platform, we employ WSAMI [23], which is a lightweight Web Services middleware suitable for mobile devices with limited resources. A Web service is identifiable by a URI (Unified Resource Identifier), has its in-terface described in the XML-based WSDL language, and is accessible over the XML-based SOAP communication protocol on top of standard Internet protocols like HTTP.

To deal with dynamic reconfiguration in a pervasive environment, we intro-duce the notion of a pervasive configuration C, which consists of entities *avail-able* in the environment: a set ME of networked mobile entities, and a set SE of networked stationary entities, where an entity e (mobile or stationary) is a collection of software functionalities – which will be specified in the following – executing on a host over WSAMI. For the sailing scenario introduced in the previous section, *availability* is defined with respect to a specific entity e, i.e., $C.ME \cup C.SE$ are entities accessible to e thanks to network coverage; we also call them e's *neighboring* entities in the following. In terms of the generic recon-figuration cycle (Section 2.1), C is the union of the reconfigurable system (RS) and its context or environment (CE). We specify the addition (e.g., may apply to the case of an entity joining the environment) and removal (e.g., may apply to the case of an entity leaving the environment, or the case of an entity that fails) of an entity e as two actions that cause, respectively, the inclusion and exclusion of e in $C.ME$ ($C.SE$). The addition and the removal actions may be events generated by either the environment or the entities themselves.

An entity e (mobile or stationary) consists of: a set PS of provided application services ws, a set PR of orchestration processes pr, a service discovery service SD, a process execution engine PEE, a changes detection service D, a checkpointing service CH, a recovery service RE and possibly, a state transfer service ST. The $e.SD$, $e.D$, $e.CH$, $e.RE$ and $e.ST$ are system services, as well deployed over the WSAMI platform. In terms of the generic reconfiguration cycle, these system services, as well as part of the functionalities of $e.PEE$, constitute the reconfiguration manager (RM), which is completely distributed: there is an RM instance included in each entity of C. The $e.PS$ comprises concrete service specifications. A concrete service specification is a tuple consisting of the WSDL interface specification of the service, the URI identifying where the service is deployed, and the service conversations, which follow the standard, XML-based, Business Process Execution Language (BPEL) [24].

Orchestration processes are also defined in BPEL. Each process pr that belongs to $e.PR$ is a tuple that contains: a set of activities a, and a set of services ws required for the execution of these activities. Activities may be either simple ones, involving the invocation of an operation provided by a service, or complex ones, consisting of more than one constituent activity. Complex activities include *sequence* activities, comprising the sequential execution of two or more constituent activities; *while* activities, consisting of the iterative execution of a constituent activity; *flow* activities, involving the concurrent execution of two or more constituent activities; and *switch* activities, allowing the selection amongst two or more alternative activities. Required services ws are identified in terms of required WSDL interface specifications. URIs of concrete provided services that syntactically match these required services are resolved by service discovery. We assume that concrete services that provide interfaces syntactically compatible to the ones required by the orchestration process, also provide syntactically compatible conversations.

Finally, to enable semantic service specification and discovery, C is further characterized by an ontology O. The ontology O is defined for the purpose of this chapter as a graph whose nodes represent different semantic classes sc of services that may be provided by the entities of C. The edges between the nodes represent semantic relations between the classes. Currently, we assume *generalization* and *aggregation* relationships. Each semantic class aggregates the syntactic WSDL specifications of alternative standard interfaces which may be provided by different, semantically compatible, services ws that belong to this class; along with each service interface specification, the service conversations specification is also included. Different, semantically compatible, services that belong to the same semantic class provide alternative service conversations. Figure 3 gives an ontology that corresponds to the scenario discussed in the previous section. Specifically, we have the HotelReservation, CarReservation and TouristInformation classes,

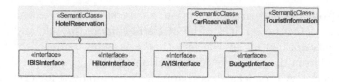

Fig. 3. An ontology for the sailing scenario

comprising services that may provide various kinds of interfaces (e.g., the IBIS-Interface and the HiltonInterface interfaces for the case of HotelReservation).

3.3 Mechanisms Supporting Reconfiguration

In the context of the semantic service-oriented pervasive environment introduced in the previous section, we now sketch the mechanisms elicited in Section 3.1.

Semantic and Syntactic Service Discovery. At the time when the entity e is added in a pervasive configuration C, e's service discovery $e.SD$ obtains information about services provided by e's (mobile and stationary) neighboring entities (i.e., $C.ME \cup C.SE$). More specifically, $e.SD$ periodically checks the environment for other instances of SD services hosted by neighboring entities, and maintains a related registry. This task is realized by multicasting a discovery request in a standard discovery protocol (e.g., the Service Location Protocol - SLP). Then, $e.SD$ provides two basic operations for syntactic and semantic service search.

The syntactic search takes as input the WSDL interface specification of a required service ws. When invoked by e, $e.SD$ makes corresponding calls to the SD services of e's neighbors. The replies of all neighbors concerning provided services that syntactically match ws are merged into a single set RES_{ws}, which is returned back to e. Caching the most recent replies enables optimizing service discovery latency and bandwidth consumption. The semantic search takes as input a required semantic class sc from the pervasive configuration ontology $C.O$, or the WSDL interface specification of a required service ws. In the second case, the semantic class sc to which ws belongs has to be resolved. The semantic search is executed in the same way as above discussed for the syntactic search. Now, replies contained in RES_{sc} or RES_{ws} concern provided services that belong to the semantic class sc. In the second case, this means that services contained in RES_{ws} semantically match ws. Optionally, to increase the possibility of discovering a provided service that can be employed, we may have supplementary semantic search calls for services that belong to *specializations* of the semantic class sc.

In our sailing scenario, a possible syntactic search could be for hotel reservation services which provide an interface that follows the IBISInterface WSDL specification (Figure 3). Similarly, a possible semantic search could be for any services belonging to the HotelReservation semantic class.

Configuration Changes Detection and State Transfer. The changes detection service (D) is a simple push-based notification service. When an entity e

is removed from a pervasive configuration, a corresponding event may be pushed in the change detection services of all of e's neighbors (mobile and stationary), which are thus notified about the fact that e is being removed or has already been removed from the pervasive configuration C (this depends on the particular network latency). A broadcast-based approach is employed for (D) instead of a unicast one that would involve only the entities that are affected by the removal, since it is not possible to know all of them in advance. Actually, the entity being removed knows only the entities that are engaged in a pending conversation with it. It can not possibly know the entities that intend to begin a conversation with it. Getting to our sailing scenario, at the time when S5 is leaving, notification events may be sent to all of S5's neighbors (including S4, who is actually using S5). Issuing a notification before departing or not may depend on the good will of the leaving entity or simply on its consciousness of its departure. In the case of no warning, pending connections with the leaving entity will be broken and new connection attempts will fail; thus, the changes detection services of affected entities will eventually be notified by the underlying middleware. Certainly, when applied, pre-departure notification enables detecting the change and dealing with it as early as possible. Moreover, it enables communicating the state of the removed entity. The state of e is the aggregate of the states of all services provided by e. When e is removed from a pervasive configuration C, its (current or logged) state may be exported with a corresponding event to the ST services of all of its neighbors. This information may be directly discarded or used afterwards so as to initialize compatible entities that are going to take e's place in the execution of orchestration processes that use e's services.

Process Dynamic Adaptation. The process execution engine PEE of an entity e has two main functionalities. The first one is to execute the orchestration processes of e. This execution may be triggered by a user in an application-dependent way (e.g., through a GUI). The second functionality amounts in adapting the orchestration processes dynamically in response to changes that occur in the pervasive configuration C that includes e. The first functionality of PEE is a typical one provided by various process execution engines that already exist for non-mobile service-oriented systems (e.g., ActiveBPEL[1]). On the other hand, the second functionality is introduced specifically to deal with the problem of dynamic reconfiguration in pervasive computing configurations. The realization of the second functionality involves the service discovery (SD), changes detection (D), state transfer (ST), checkpointing (CH) and recovery (RE) services.

We first consider the case of reconfiguration upon addition of an entity e to the pervasive configuration C. In terms of the generic reconfiguration cycle, this is actually an initial configuration of RS, which was not executing before. Upon entering in C and if triggered in an application-dependent way, e is requested to adapt its orchestration processes with respect to the services provided by the entities of C (Phases 2-4). Accordingly, e searches for syntactically compatible services required for the execution of its processes (Phase 5). If for every required

---

[1] http://www.activebpel.org/

ws_j service used in a process pr_i the syntactic search returns a non-empty set RES_{ws_j} of matching services, then one of them is selected. Following, e's process execution engine ($e.PEE$) should adapt pr_i with respect to the URI of the selected service (Phases 6-7). Suppose now that for a service ws_j, required by pr_i, the syntactic search returns an empty set of results. Following, e performs a semantic search, which may also return a set of alternative services (Phase 5). Suppose that a service ws_j^{sem} is selected. Following, $e.PEE$ should adapt pr_i with respect to the interface, the conversations and the URI of ws_j^{sem} (Phases 6-7). Achieving this step in a systematic manner involves using the concept of *refinement rules*.

In general, the refinement rules are a part of the overall reconfiguration policy/strategy [25] used upon an event that signals a configuration change (entity addition, removal). Specifically, a set of refinement rules is specified along with every pair of services (ws_j, ws_j^{sem}) which provide alternative standard interfaces that are aggregated by the same semantic class sc of the pervasive configuration ontology $C.O$. A refinement rule is a mapping relation between the activity a_i of a conversation process realized using ws_j and a corresponding activity a_j of a conversation process realized using ws_j^{sem}. In the simplest case, a refinement rule may directly map an invocation activity to another invocation activity. However, it is also possible that a refinement rule maps an invocation activity to a more complex activity (e.g., a sequence activity), or the inverse (e.g., a sequence activity to a simple invocation activity). We may envision even more complicated refinement rules, mapping complex activities (e.g., a sequence activity) to other complex activities (e.g., a while activity). Hence, to adapt the processes that use the ws_j service into corresponding ones that use the ws_j^{sem} one, $e.PEE$ uses the refinement rules defined for the (ws_j, ws_j^{sem}) pair.

Getting to our sailing scenario, let us assume that when S4 joins the environment (Figure 2(a)), it requires a service that provides the IBISInterface towards the realization of the orchestration process that is given in Figure 4(a). According to this process, the customer at some point confirms a reservation by executing a sequence of two invocations, involving the Book and the Pre-Payment operations. The PrePayment operation is required by IBIS hotels to deposit a percentage of the overall amount to pay for the room. Suppose now that there are no available proxies providing the IBISInterface and the semantic search returns among others a semantically compatible service that provides the HiltonInterface. The HiltonInterface provides operations that are semantically compatible with the operations of the IBISInterface, may differ, however, in terms of operation names and parameter names and data types. With regard to process structure, interaction with the service providing the HiltonInterface is simpler given that there is no need for advance payment. Consequently, to adapt S4's orchestration process to the conversation of the service providing the HiltonInterface, besides adapting semantically matching operations in terms of names and parameters, the sequence of the Book and the PrePayment operations should be reduced into a simple invocation that involves the Confirm operation of the HiltonInterface (Figure 4(b)).

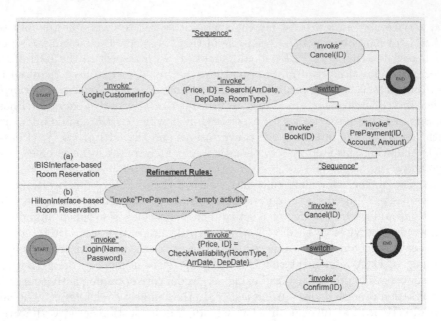

Fig. 4. Inactive process adaptation

We now consider the case of reconfiguration upon removal of an entity e' from the pervasive configuration C. As previously discussed, the changes detection service D of an entity e will receive a notification (either soft or hard) about entity e' removed from the pervasive configuration C (Phases 2-3). If e uses e' in some of its orchestration processes (i.e., the affected processes), these processes should be adapted as in the case where e is added to C (Phase 4). Specifically, for every affected process pr_i, a syntactic search, possibly followed by a semantic one, is performed for a substitute entity (Phase 5). Following, the affected process is adapted by $e.PEE$ in the way introduced earlier (Phase 6). At this point, the role of $e.PEE$ is done if pr_i is an inactive process. Otherwise, if pr_i is pending, the following steps are further followed (Phases 6-7): If the removed entity issues a notification before departing, and both the removed and the substitute entities provide state transfer capabilities and are *state-compatible*, then the part of the state of the removed entity that concerns pr_i is imported in the substitute entity. Then, the execution of pr_i resumes from a point that depends on the previous step. This particular step is realized based on the checkpointing and recovery mechanisms detailed in the following paragraph. In the worst case, all the activities of pr_i that involve the removed entity may have to be restarted.

Checkpointing and Recovery. The checkpointing and recovery mechanisms discussed here are primarily inspired by traditional mechanisms used in conventional distributed systems [26], adapted to the concepts of orchestrations and conversations. Specifically, the checkpointing and recovery mechanisms take charge of rolling back a pending orchestration process to a point that preserves the process *consistent* execution. These particular mechanisms are triggered if an entity e' is substituted by another one $e"$ and the entities do not provide any state transfer capabilities. As previously discussed, an orchestration process in BPEL consists of different types of activities executed using operations offered by Web services deployed in the environment. Moreover, a Web service specification comprises the service's interface (i.e., the operations provided), a service URI and the valid conversations that can be realized by invoking the service's operations (Section 1). Therefore, an orchestration process actually consists of a set of valid conversations executed over a set of Web services. Based on this observation, we define *consistency* for a pending orchestration process pr of e as follows: The execution of the pending orchestration process after reconfiguration is consistent if there exist no pending constituent conversations of this process that execute using data produced by conversations involving e'. Based on this definition, we discuss in the following the basic responsibilities of the checkpointing and recovery mechanisms.

The checkpointing mechanism is used on the side of Web services that participate in the execution of certain conversations. The checkpointing mechanism requires from a Web service to specify along with its valid conversations the decomposition of these conversations into atomic sub-conversations. An atomic sub-conversation is a subset of the activities of a conversation that must be rolled-back as a whole. Based on this specification, the mechanism checkpoints the state of the service at the beginning of each atomic sub-conversation triggered.

The recovery mechanism is used on the side of entities performing certain orchestration processes. Specifically, before the beginning of each orchestration pr performed by e that consists of conversations with a set of Web services, the orchestration is divided into atomic sub-conversations, based on the Web services specifications. Following, the mechanism discovers the possible data dependencies that exist between sub-conversations performed with Web services offered by different entities. A data dependency exists between two atomic sub-conversations spr_i and spr_j if the entity that performs the orchestration process uses data resulting from output messages of operations invoked during spr_i to construct input messages issued during the invocation of operations performed during spr_j.

Taking, now the case where e' is substituted by $e"$, the following actions are taken by the recovery mechanism of e. If pr is pending, the recovery mechanism locates every pending sub-conversation spr_j that depends on conversation spr_i performed with e'. Following, it notifies the checkpointing mechanism responsible for spr_i that spr_i must be rolled-back to the beginning of its execution. Regarding the overall orchestration pr, the recovery mechanism rolls it back to the beginning of the execution of the first sub-conversation performed with e'.

Getting back to our sailing scenario, suppose that S5 is leaving the environment and issues a related notification. S4's changes detection service will receive this notification. Suppose that at this time S4 is executing a pending orchestration process that consists of a flow of two conversations that execute concurrently (Figure 5). The first one is the HiltonInterface-based conversation of Figure 4(b)

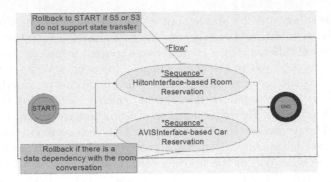

Fig. 5. Pending process adaptation

that executes on S5 and the second one is an AVISInterface-based car reservation conversation executed on S2. The syntactic search that follows the notification of S4 results in selecting S3 as S5's substitute. Suppose that both conversations are specified as being atomic. This means that before their beginning the states of S5 and S2 are saved by the checkpointing mechanisms deployed on the aforementioned entities. In the absence of state transfer, the whole HiltonInterface-based conversation should be restarted. Moreover, if there exists a data dependency between the two conversations the AVISInterface-based conversation must be rolled-back. Otherwise, the execution of the latter continuous normally.

4 Conclusion

In this chapter we established a common base for investigating reconfigurability in distributed software systems, by introducing a generic reconfiguration cycle. Based on this cycle, we investigated in detail former efforts on reconfigurable pervasive systems. The main outcome of this study was that these approaches are strongly influenced by principles, assumptions and techniques proposed in the context of stationary systems, where reconfiguration is *controlled* in the sense that a central reconfiguration manager is in control, *a priori* aware of entities currently present in the system and entities that are candidate to join the system. Finally, we discussed our approach towards uncontrolled reconfiguration targeting environments in which no centralized coordination or prior awareness between services being composed is assumed. The proposed solution comprises syntactic and semantic dynamic service discovery, change detection, state transfer, interface-aware orchestration adaptation and conversation-aware checkpointing and recovery mechanisms.

A number of issues are still open in our approach, which are to be dealt with in our current and future work. A language for specifying refinement rules and the process adaptation mechanism are currently under development. Particularly, we focus on an aspect-oriented approach that relies on our prior work in this field [27]. The development and global interconnection of ontologies proposed by paradigms such as the Semantic Web [28] may prove useful for our approach.

The issue of QoS-aware process adaptation is also an interesting direction for future research [29]. Finally, till now, we have considered service compositions in the form of orchestrated processes. Extending the proposed approach to deal with services choreography is challenging as it may possibly involve distributed coordination mechanisms for service discovery, changes detection, checkpointing, recovery, state transfer, and process adaptation.

References

1. Oreizy, P., Medvidovic, N., Taylor, R.N.: Architecture-based runtime software evolution. In: Intl. Conf. on Software Engineering, Kyoto, Japan (1998)
2. Garlan, D., Shaw, M.: An introduction to software architecture. Technical Report CMU-CS-94-166, Carnegie Mellon University (1994)
3. Kramer, J., Magee, J.: The evolving philosophers problem: Dynamic change management. IEEE Transactions on Software Engineering **16**(11) (1990) 1293–1306
4. Bidan, C., Issarny, V., Saridakis, T., Zarras, A.: A dynamic reconfiguration service for corba. In: ICCDS '98: Proceedings of the 4th IEEE International Conference on Configurable Distributed Systems. (1998) 35–42
5. Minsky, N., Ungureanu, V., Wang, W., Zhang, J.: Building reconfiguration primitives into the law of a system. In: ICCDS '96: Proceedings of the 3rd International Conference on Configurable Distributed Systems. (1996) 62–69
6. Blair, G.S., Blair, L., Issarny, V., Tuma, P., Zarras, A.: The role of software architecture in constraining adaptation in component-based middleware platforms. In: Proceedings of MIDDLEWARE'00. (2000) 164–184
7. Zarras, A.: Online upgrade of object-oriented middleware. Journal of Object Technology **3**(7) (2004) 121–140
8. Kistler, J.J., Satyanarayanan, M.: Disconnected operation in the coda file system. In: Thirteenth ACM Symposium on Operating Systems Principles. Volume 25., Asilomar Conference Center, Pacific Grove, U.S., ACM Press (1991) 213–225
9. Kuenning, G.H., Popek, G.J.: Automated hoarding for mobile computers. In: SOSP '97: Proceedings of the sixteenth ACM symposium on Operating systems principles, New York, NY, USA, ACM Press (1997) 264–275
10. Fuggetta, A., Picco, G.P., Vigna, G.: Understanding Code Mobility. IEEE Transactions on Software Engineering **24**(5) (1998) 342–361
11. Joseph, A.D., deLespinasse, A.F., Gifford, J.A.T.D.K., Kaashoek, M.F.: Rover: a toolkit for mobile information access. In: Proceedings of the 15th ACM Symposium on OperatingSystems Principles (SOSP '95), Copper Mountain Resort, Colorado (1995) 156–171
12. Papazoglou, P., Georgakopoulos, D., eds.: Service-oriented computing. In: Communications of the ACM. Volume 46. ACM Press (2003)
13. Martin, D., Paolucci, M., McIlraith, S., Burstein, M., McDermott, D., McGuinness, D., Parsia, B., Payne, T., Sabou, M., Solanki, M., Srinivasan, N., Sycara, K.: Bringing semantics to web services: The owl-s approach. In: First International Workshop on Semantic Web Services and Web Process Composition (SWSWPC 2004), San Diego, California, USA. (2004)
14. Cheng, S.W., Garlan, D., Schmerl, B.R., Sousa, J.P., Spitznagel, B., Steenkiste, P., NingningHu: Software architecture-based adaptation for pervasive systems. In: ARCS. (2002) 67–82

15. Garlan, D., Cheng, S.W., Huang, A.C., Schmerl, B., Steenkiste, P.: Rainbow: Architecture-based self-adaptation with reusable infrastructure. Computer **37**(10) (2004) 46–54
16. Soules, C., Appavoo, J., Hui, K., Silva, D., Ganger, G., Krieger, O., Stumm, M., Wisniewski, R., Auslander, M., Ostrowski, M., Rosenburg, B., Xenidis, J.: System support for online reconfiguration (2003)
17. Zhang, J., Cheng, B.H., Yang, Z., McKinley, P.K.: Enabling safe dynamic component-based software adaptation. In: Architecting Dependable Systems III, Springer Lecture Notes in Computer Science (2005)
18. Mukhija, A., Glinz, M.: Runtime adaptation of applications through dynamic recomposition of components. **16**(11) (2005) 124–138
19. Gamma, E., Helm, R., Johnson, R.: Design Patterns. Elements of Reusable Object-Oriented Software. Addison-Wesley Professional Computing Series. Addison-Wesley (1995) GAM e 95:1 1.Ex.
20. Ranganathan, A., Chetan, S., Campbell, R.: Mobile polymorphic applications in ubiquitous computing environments. In: Mobiquitous 2004 : The First Annual International Conference on Mobile and Ubiquitous Systems:Networking and Services, Boston, Massachusetts, USA (2004)
21. Pitkranta, T., Riva, O., Toivonen, S.: Designing and implementing a system for the provision of proactive context-aware services. In: CAPS '05: Proceedings of the Workshop on Context Awareness for Proactive Systems. (2005) 21–30
22. IST Advisory Group (ISTAG): Software Technologies, Embedded Systems and Distributed Systems - A European Strategy Towards Ambient Intelligent Environment. Technical report, IST (2002) http://www.cordis.lu/ist/istag.html.
23. Issarny, V., Sacchetti, D., Tartanoglu, F., Sailhan, F., Chibout, R., Levy, N., Talamona, A.: Developing ambient intelligence systems: A solution based on web services. Automated Software Engineering **12**(1) (2005) 101–137
24. IBM, Microsoft Corporation and BEA: Business Process Execution Language for Web Service (BPEL4WS) v.1.0. Technical report, IBM, Microsoft Corporation, BEA (2002) http://www.ibm.com/developerworks/webservices/library/ws-bpel/.
25. Porcarelli, S., Castaldi, M., Giandomenico, F.D., Bondavalli, A., Inverardi, P.: An Approach to Manage Reconfiguration in Fault Tolerant Distributed Systems. In: Proceedings of the ICSE 2003 Workshop on Software Architectures for Dependable Systems. (2003) 71–76
26. Babaoglu, O., Marzullo, K.: Consistent Global States of Distributed Systems: Fundamental Concepts and Mechanisms. In Mullender, S., ed.: Distributed Systems. Addison-Wesley (1993) 55–96
27. Zarras, A.: Applying Model Driven Architecture to Achieve Distribution Transparencies. Information and Software Technology **48**(7) (2006) 498–516
28. Berners-Lee, T., Hendler, J., Lassila, O.: The Semantic Web. In: Scientific American. (2001)
29. Mokhtar, S.B., Liu, J., Georgantas, N., Issarny, V.: Qos-aware dynamic service composition in ambient intelligence environments. In: ASE '05: Proceedings of the 20th IEEE/ACM international Conference on Automated software engineering, New York, NY, USA, ACM Press (2005) 317–320

Tools for Developing Large Systems (A Proposal)

Jean-Raymond Abrial

ETH Zurich, Switzerland
jabrial@inf.ethz.ch

Abstract. It is claimed, as a provocative thesis, that high level programming languages and corresponding compilers might not be the right tools to be used to construct large reliable software systems. An alternative is proposed which is based on the concept of a System Development Database.

Keywords: Correct Construction, Development System.

The subject mentioned in the title of this short article does not seem, at first glance, to be a genuine research subject. Although there are, from time to time, some famous breakdowns of large computerized systems (as, for instance, recently at SBB in Zurich), it seems nevertheless that these systems are working nowadays in a satisfactory fashion. As a consequence, their construction process must have been mastered otherwise such disasters would have occurred more frequently. This was clearly the case at the beginning of last century with an emerging technology such as avionics. There were lots of crashes due to the fact that people did not know how to construct good airplanes. The main reason for this was that they did not understood yet the theory of flight mechanics, which was in its infancy.

In our case, however, the situation is a bit different from that of early avionics in that there is no clear theory yet related to large computerized systems. The most obvious indication supporting this fact is that, most of the time, experts cannot clearly explain why such systems indeed work correctly. When a serious breakdown occurs, the corresponding superficial reason is normally found after some time (not always however), and it is usually repaired in a very ad-hoc fashion. But people are never sure that another breakdown will not occur some time later, precisely because they do not know the more profound reason for that earlier breakdown. It is my belief that such a state of the art is not satisfactory.

From almost the beginning of Informatics, the main tools used to develop computer systems were a High Level Programming Language and a corresponding Compiler. There has been many of them (far too many in fact) always proposing new features whose pretensions are to eventually solve the problem of constructing better programs than the previous generation of High Level Programming Languages and Compilers did. One can even regularly see in the literature the term "next generation of programming languages" being used. Unfortunately, it does not seem to solve the problem since, over the years, the famous software crisis is still with us.

An interesting research is then to investigate whether there could exist some other intellectual means and tools that could be used instead of High Level Programming

M. Butler et al. (Eds.): Fault-Tolerant Systems, LNCS 4157, pp. 387–390, 2006.

Languages and Compilers. It does not mean of course that we believe that we can replace final computer programs by something else. But, we would like to investigate whether we could invent some other ways to obtain such final programs.

When High Level Programming Languages were invented in the sixties (i.e. Algol), the idea was to make abstract programming patterns such as conditionals, loops, procedure calls, and the like be first class citizens in the programming methodology. In the more restricted realm of Assembly Code, such programming patterns did not exist explicitly but were all implemented by means of a single feature, namely the conditional goto instruction. The High Level Programming Language was then an abstraction of the more concrete Assembly Code. And the Compiler was the tool that allows us to move from this abstraction to a concrete implementation.

An interesting statistics that can be obtained from high level source programs is the ratio of the number of lines of code devoted to pure algorithms over the total number of lines of code excluding comments and the like. Of course, the figures differ from one application to the other but it is usually far less than 1/2. This means that such abstract relational features as components, classes, methods, inheritance, visibility, assertions and the like describing the objects, their properties, and their relationships are becoming far more important than pure algorithmic features such as conditionals, loops, and more generally computations. It is my belief that such abstract relational features are not well handled in a High Level Programming Languages, whereas pure algorithmic calculations are in my opinion still well handled in such languages.

In other engineering disciplines (i.e. mechanical construction) people do not hesitate to use languages when they are clearly needed and other means when they are not needed. For instance, they use the language Mathematica to define the formal computations related to their usage of the Calculus. But they do not use languages to describe the complex relationships between the components of their future system, their properties, their links, etc. In fact they store the various components of their product in one form or another and express the relationships that hold between them. We can consider that they thus build a Database of their future system. The engineering process is supported by the contents of this Database, its modification, and the tools that are disposed around it.

In our discipline, there is a frequent confusion between the two terms "assertion" and "specification", even if both of them are written using a mathematical notation. An assertion, is a *local predicate* that must always be true at some point in the *execution of a program*: it can be either checked dynamically while the program is running or better statically proved. But in no ways can such assertions represent the specifications of a large computerized system. For the simple reason that the specifications of a large computerized system essentially consist in the definition of a number of *global properties* by which it will be possible to state that the final system comprising software and external equipment (including users) works in a correct fashion. Clearly, when writing such properties the software part of the computerized system does not exist yet and even sometimes also the external equipment. In fact, such global properties are not associated with specific pieces of code in the final software, they are rather supposed to be globally maintained by the software in question together with its environment, which, most of the time, are both supposed to run for ever. Moreover, the specifications, as just described, are the point of departure of the *design* which has also to be defined first globally to end up eventually, *by architectural decomposition*, in some more local properties: the assertions then appear to correspond to the *final stage* of a long design process. It is quite clear that High Level Programming Languages (event "modern" ones) are not at all suited to be the place for writing such specifications.

What is wrong is to have the semantics of the High Level Programming Language being the medium defining the properties of the offered features. This is far more easily handled and modifiable as the invariant properties of a *System Construction Database*. It might still be useful to have some pretty printing of the contents of the Database. This would resemble a high level program but would be produced as an additional output of the construction process rather than as its input. In first approximation, the contents of the System Construction Data Base is made of the *various components* of the system in construction together with their *relationships*. These components are surrounded by a number of *tools* that can be used to *develop* them. The System Construction Database should not be confused however with what High Level Programming Language technology calls a "library". In fact, it is far more general as explained below. The System Construction Database approach offers quite a number of advantages over High Level Programming Languages. Here are a few of them:

1. The System Construction Database can be used not only to store future software components but also, more importantly, their various *abstract, and later refined, mathematical models*. And here the tools that replace the compiler and even the computer executing the final program are a *proof obligation generator* and a *prover*. Specification, and design, and corresponding tools, are put together with implementation and corresponding tools. In this respect, the System Construction Database contains the on-going design history of the software construction. It is important to note that the specification of a large system is not a monolithic text but rather a succession of more and more precise mathematical models taking account gradually of the requirements of the future system. High Level Programming Languages are not at all appropriate to handle this task: they suffer from their initial purpose, namely that of instructing a computer on the way to perform its computations. Specifications and design have nothing to do with instructing a computer, they rather record the thoughts and reasoning of the engineers.

2. The System Construction Database approach will also induce a rather more appropriate way of elaborating the final product than that given by the usage of a High Level Programming Languages and Compilers. Unless it is very small, you shall never write a program and subsequently submit it to the compiler. This sequential approach to construction will be replaced by a more reactive approach, which corresponds to the way engineers work. You rather interact with the Database by entering modeling elements, their properties, and their relationships. Such an interaction is permanently supported in the background by tools working in a *differential fashion* without being explicitly even invoked by the user.

3. The System Construction Database approach will also allow us to store and update components which can be quite different in nature from computer programs, namely models of pieces of equipments which might interact with the future software components. Such models will be able to be refined as other future software

models are. This will allow us to construct embedded systems by specifying and designing their software parts in strong relationships with some modeling of their environments.

4. Besides the formal tools we have already mentioned above in 1 (proof obligation generators and provers), the System Construction Database may contain other tools as well, being able to be applied to the various models, namely model checkers, informal modelling (UML) to corresponding formal modelling tools, model animators, abstract interpretation tools, even testing tools, etc. The reason for incorporating such tools is that clearly there is *no universal panacea*. The engineers need to have a large palette of possibilities at their disposal in order to construct their computerized systems in the most effective way. The System Construction Database offers the possibility to have all such tools working in an integrated fashion on all the models that are recorded in the Database.

5. Besides the components and their mathematical models (be they future software or environment components), it will be possible to also store in the System Construction Database a document related to the *requirements* of the future system. Such a document will take the form of natural language fragments intermixed with slightly more structured texts containing the concise and precise requirements of the system in construction. A useful analogy is that of a book of mathematics where definitions and theorems are labeled, numbered, and written using a different font from that used in the rest of the text corresponding to explanations and proofs: this will make the definitions and theorems immediately separable from the rest of the text. By structuring in this way the requirement document, the traceability of the requirements will be handled in an integrated fashion within the System Construction Database. This will be done by connecting each structured requirement to some parts of the abstract models dealing with that requirement. This traceability can then be pursued during the design phase and the final software and environment construction. It must be noted here that such requirement documents are usually very poor: either inexistent or far too verbose. As a consequence, the designers have often lots of difficulties in extracting from them the precise requirements. Experience shows that the famous, and said to be inevitable, syndrome of "specification changes during construction", appears to magically disappear when such a special attention is payed initially to writing and structuring the requirement document. Every large project must have an important initial phase devoted to this task: the System Construction Database will then be the natural repository for such requirement documents.

In conclusion, we question the present usage of High Level Programming Languages for constructing large computerized systems. We propose instead to partially replace it by defining and using a System Construction Database which will be far more appropriate as an engineering medium than the actual programming languages. As a matter of fact, this proposal is not really new: Eclipse is, among others, a proposal that has been made for a number of years and that goes clearly in that direction.

Why Programming Languages Still Matter

Peter Amey

Praxis High Integrity Systems, 20 Manvers St., Bath BA1 1PX, UK
peter.amey@praxis-his.com

Abstract. This paper examines some aspects of the aims and goals of the RODIN project and asks whether a successful outcome of the project will remove the need for us to worry about programming languages and the meaning of program source code. In common with some other currently ascendent approaches to software engineering, such as model-based development, RODIN is leading towards the construction of software models (in RODIN's case *precise* software models) from which we may hope to generate source or even object code. So, does this remove the need for us to be concerned with the form these automatically-generated, intermediate representations take? Perhaps rather surprisingly, I conclude that the need to show an unbroken chain of confidence from requirements to object code means that programming languages and their analysis, remain an extremely important topic. I hope to show that the ability to produce better specifications and designs, as promised by approaches exemplified by RODIN, is a *necessary precondition* for effective high-integrity software development rather than a *substitute* for approaches currently in use.

1 Introduction

RODIN [12] (or more fully Rigorous Open Development Environment for Complex Systems) is an EU funded research programme seeking to create a methodology and supporting open tool platform for the cost-effective, rigorous development of dependable complex software systems and services. For the purposes of this position paper I am focussing on one small aspect of this overall set of challenging and lofty goals: how will we *implement* a system that has been "cost-effectively and rigorously developed" using the RODIN methodology and tools?

Since the RODIN project is working towards formally-based, tool-supported methods for the construction of trustworthy, fault-tolerant systems. It seems obvious, at first glance, that these lofty goals, if achieved, will eliminate our concerns about programming languages and our need to reason about the meaning of program source code. After all, if we have a mathematically-sound specification which we can use in the following ways:

- to *prove* that certain safety or security properties are implemented and preserved;
- to *animate* so as to gain confidence that it meets the original user requirements; and
- as a basis for *automatic code generation* from which the implementation can be derived

then what role is left for conventional programming languages?

M. Butler et al. (Eds.): Fault-Tolerant Systems, LNCS 4157, pp. 391–402, 2006.

The answer to this conundrum can only be found by looking at the *totality* of the high-integrity software challenge and then seeing what parts of that challenge are addressed by RODIN and what parts are left to be dealt with by other means. The challenges for formally-based approaches are:

- handling mismatches between the logical model used to construct the specification and the real world in which the implementation lives;
- dealing with vital but non-functional requirements, such as performance or safety, that might be very hard to express formally; and
- showing an unbroken chain of integrity from the specification to the ones and zeroes on the hardware which implements it.

Adding the additional challenge of fault tolerance, a key objective of the RODIN project, can modify or amplify these challenges but does not fundamentally change them.

2   The Impact of Fault Tolerance

The building *fault-tolerant* systems is a major subgoal of the RODIN project so it is appropriate to consider how fault-tolerance affects the overall high-integrity software challenge. Fault tolerance is a *system level* property. We might achieve the goal of fault tolerance through some hardware means completely external to any software-controlled device we are building. For example, a plant operator might watch the plant operating on a closed-circuit TV screen and throw a large switch to turn on a backup control system if he sees that the plant has stopped working. These kinds of solution have *no* effect on the manner in which we construct high-integrity software.

Alternatively, and more likely, we will have to give some authority for fault tolerance to the software-controlled machines we are constructing. For example, part of the functionality of a control system might be to monitor the values read from a sensor and perform various tests to maintain confidence that the sensor is working correctly. The same system might select a chain of various fall-back options when it suspects that the sensor can no longer be trusted. These tests of trustworthiness and selection of fall back strategies are *software controlled* and so impose precisely the same challenges as the basic control functionality. So software-controlled fault tolerance does not *change* the nature of the high-integrity software challenge, it just means that there is *more of it!*

So I conclude that the need for fault tolerance does not fundamentally change the nature of the high-integrity software challenge[1]: we either provide it independently of the software, in which case it it out of scope; or provide it in software in which case it is just another requirement, specification and design item for us to worry about along with all the rest.

---

[1] There is one obvious counter example to this general argument and that is where fault tolerance can be moved to the operating system or even hardware level in a manner completely transparent to an application running on it; this approache is exemplified by high-reliability computing platforms such as those produced by Stratus Techologies. http://www.stratus.com

3   Boundaries of the Logical Model

3.1   Overview

All formal approaches to software construction work by creating a *model* of some aspect or aspects of the desired system. The model may be pictorial or textual. To be a *formal* model I would argue that it must have certain very specific properties. The model must have defined semantics such that it is possible, by mechanical means, to obtain *guarantees* that the model has certain specified properties. Different models may be used for different kinds of analysis and for the establishment of different properties. Comparisons between artefacts, for example specification and code, requires that a suitable model exists for each. Furthermore, a method can only be regarded as a *formal* method if its determination of the presence of a particular property is sound. Sound analysis means that the method never asserts a property to be true when it may not be true. Note that the converse case, the assertion that a property is false when it may be true, colloquially "the raising of false alarms", is a usability issue but not a soundness issue. Also note that these requirements do not imply that the method has to be complete: it is acceptable for a method to return "don't know" when trying to establish whether a property holds.

So far this discussion has been wholly about our formal *model*. What actually matters to us is the behaviour of our finished *system*. So a key property we need to establish is how well the model represents the behaviour of the finished system. My experience is that formal methods advocates, of which I am one, have a tendency to gloss over this rather awkward point, preferring to focus on the wonderful things they can prove about their model. It is perhaps also worth noting that this problem of equivalence between models and reality forms a major part of engineering disciplines other than software and that engineering failures frequently have causes that hide in the cracks between the two. The series of accidents involving metal fatigue in Comet airliner fuselages and, more recently, the wobbly Millenium Bridge, are both examples of the real world failing to conform to the behaviour of an engineering model.

Formal models have three important limitations:

1. Their ability to capture and express some key user requirements, especially non-functional ones.
2. The correspondence of the logic used in reasoning about the model with the behaviour of the real world.
3. The fidelity with which the model can be translated into binary object code on target hardware.

The Figure 1 below illustrates the first and second of these limitations.
I will now consider each of these potential problem areas in turn.

3.2   Beyond Simple Functional Behaviour

Formal notations provide an extremely powerful mechanism for capturing the desired functional behaviour of a system. We can unambiguously describe system state, inputs, outputs and the relationship between them. There is ample evidence (see for example

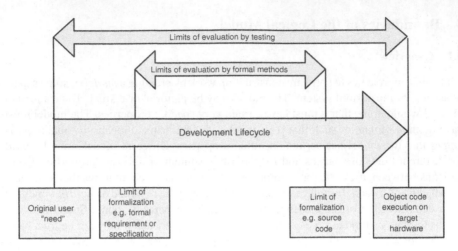

Fig. 1. The Limits of Formality

[1]) of the benefits of doing so, not least in the early resolution of requirements ambiguity and conflict that results from the *process* of writing the specification. Unfortunately many of the most complex challenges of software engineering are not readily expressed as functional behaviour. We may have key design concerns about integrity, reliability or security that are not about *behaviour* but rather *how that behaviour is delivered.*

As an example, consider the world's simplest aircraft stores management system. It comprises a single release button and a single weapon station. The functional requirement is simple: "when the button is pressed, the store falls off the weapon station". We can readily express this behaviour in any of our favourite formal notations and, indeed, implement it in any of our favourite programming languages. If we are interested in automatic code generation from our formal model then we can also readily define mapping rules from specification constructs to code constructs that will produce the desired functional result.

Unfortunately this is only a tiny part of the real problem because we also have a non-functional requirement: "when the release button is *not* pressed, the store will *not* fall off more often than once in 10^9 flying hours". Suddenly the problem looks rather harder! We now need to meet the original functional requirement but in a way which allows us to construct a credible engineering argument that our system will not malfunction in a dangerous way anytime in the next 114,000 or so years!

The Praxis "Correctness by Construction" (CbyC) approach (see [2]) tackles this problem by a deliberate separation of the specification process from the high-level design process. The former focusses on a complete, abstract description of the required behaviour while the latter concentrates on the design, architectural and structural approaches required to meet the non-functional challenges. For the stores management example, we might introduce multiple channels that need to agree before a weapon is released or dynamically generate a carefully-chosen "magic number" that has to exactly fit a hardware lock on the weapon station rather than just relying on control flow to enable release.

Without this conceptual separation, we are in a rather difficult position, especially if the goal is some form of automatic code generation from the formal model. How can the code generator know what *kind* of code to generate for the logical operation "button press"? The only sensible answer to this seems to be that the specification will have to have numerous levels of refinement which allow it to be transformed steadily from a *specification* into a *design*. We could, for example, express how our "magic number" weapon release key is generated at a sufficiently low level that very simple code generation rules would produce the desired result. We would then need to construct an argument that this chosen detailed specification was a valid refinement of the original abstract specification. Although this is clearly feasible, the approach does have some disadvantages. A strict refinement approach means that the detailed design can't be started until the abstract specification is complete whereas experience of CbyC suggests that abstract specification and high-level design can often be tackled in parallel because they address largely disjoint issues. Furthermore, a strict refinement approach is very vulnerable to requirement and consequential specification changes; these force us to roll back to the point of change and reconstruct all the refinements. Finally we have the problem that notations that are powerful and effective at one level of abstraction may not be so effective at another. Our store release "magic number", for example, may well be chosen so that the bit pattern of its representation does not match any op code of the target machine language (to reduce the chance that the weapon station might accidently be passed a piece of *code* that mimics a valid piece of *data*). That level of design detail is a very long way away from high level considerations of sets and partial functions.

In practice our experience is that suitable programming languages may be much more expressive than specification notations at this level of detail. SPARK [3,4], for example can be conceived as a detailed design and specification language which just happens to be compilable by any standard Ada compiler. Personally I would prefer to reason about the bit pattern of magic numbers in SPARK rather than say Z.

In case the reader thinks this example a little contrived, I can provide a real example. The SHOLIS system (see, *inter alia* [5]), which provides flight-critical guidance on ship's helicopter operating limits, had a system requirement that it should be possible to remove circuit boards from the system, while running, without it crashing or malfunctioning. You can be assured that this requirement needed considerable design activity; required SPARK code to handle it; and was completely impossible to specify in Z!

3.3 Logical Correspondence

The difficulties of the previous section are probably not insuperable provided we are willing to invest in suitably detailed notations and expend sufficient effort on constructing refinements.

Rather more challenging is the need to show that the logic used to reason about our formal specification is preserved in the resulting implementation. The challenge here is that the formal model is likely to inhabit a mathematically pure world of integer and Boolean values that only has a passing resemblance to the implementation domain. For example, our specification may refer to some integral input value and assert that a particular action results if the value exceeds a certain value, say $Temperature > 100 \rightarrow SystemOverheat$. This is a completely clear and precise abstract expression of

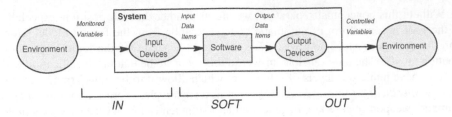

Fig. 2. The Four Variable Model

desired behaviour at the model level. In the real system things are rather different. What if the value of $Temperature$ obtained from the system's environment isn't actually any valid integer value at all? What does $Temperature > 100$ *mean* if $Temperature$ isn't an entity that has the integer-like properties being relied on in the model? This might sound rather esoteric but is a signficant problem in a real world of bent connector pins and other exotic hardware and sensor failures.

The usual response to these challenges is to wrap our formally-specified system in a layer of "device drivers" that deal with all these real-world inconveniences and deliver structurally valid values to the core application. We might need, for example, to read the sensor value into a machine word of a size chosen so that any bit pattern is a valid value and then check the actual bit pattern to ensure it represents a valid example of the type we have assumed in our specification model. These device drivers are rarely, if ever, formally specified because typical specification notations are not strong on the kind of 3-value logic (True, False, Unknown) needed to reason about them. So the correct behaviour of our formal model becomes dependent on a layer of hand written code on its boundaries. To misuse a rather famous diagram from [6], reproduced as Figure 2, we might say that our formal model is limited to the SOFT and, perhaps, OUT relations but that the IN relation has to be hand crafted.

The challenge this presents is for us to demonstrate, with the same rigour that we can reason about our formal model, that the composition of hand-written device drivers and other code, perhaps automatically generated from the formal model, has the required behaviour and integrity.

3.4   Fidelity of Translation

The Implementation Domain. Similar challenges arise when we attempt to translate the formal parts of our system description into code that we can either execute or, more likely, compile then execute. Again we face challenges from the fact the mathematically precise specification entity $Temperature + 1 > 100$ has a rather less precise meaning in the implementation domain. What if `Temperature + 1` overflows the valid range of machine representations for the type of the variable `Temperature`? We could capture, in the *specification*, the necessary information to avoid *implementation domain* problems of this kind, perhaps by adding side conditions to every operation in the specification. However, as with the issue of non-functional requirements, this greatly complicates the specification, blurs the distinction between specification and design, makes the specification less portable and places extra stress on our ability to reason about refinement.

Source Code Ambiguity. Other code generation issues are equally challenging. If we generate any of the commonly used programming languages we can only be sure that the generated code preserves properties we may have proved at the specification level if the generated code is wholly unambiguous. If a compiler can legally interpret our generated source code in a way that has a meaning different from that intended by the author of the specification *and* the author of the code generator then the link between model behaviour and system behaviour is broken. Ambiguity in programming languages can arise from many causes. A simple, and typical, example is freedom of expression evaluation order in the presence of expression side effects. The combination of these two creates a situation where a program statement may have different meaning when evaluated from left-to-right or from right-to-left. The compiler writer may be free, according to the language definition, to choose either order. If the code generator writer makes assumptions about the order then specification model properties may *not* be preserved in the generated code. I find it rather surprising how little this behaviour is understood and the naive confidence parts of the computing community seem to have in the precision of their source code![2]

Since the phenomenon is so widely unappreciated a tiny example (in Ada just to show that even well-designed languages suffer) is perhaps worthwhile.

```
with Text_IO; use Text_IO;
procedure Test1
is
   X, Y, Z, R : Integer;

   function F (X : Integer) return Integer is
   begin
      Z := 0;
      return X + 1;
   end F;

begin
   X := 10;
   Y := 20;
   Z := 10;
   R := Y / Z + F (X);        -- order dependency here.
   Put (Integer'Image(R));    -- R = 13 if L → R evaluation,
                              -- constraint error if R → L
end Test1;
```

This program exhibits an evaluation order dependency arising from a function side-effect, because function F updates the value of Z which is global to it. The evaluation

---

[2] An interesting corner of this naivety is the trust some mathematicians seem to have in computer-assisted proofs. When asked if the C code their proof depends upon has been compiled and run on different computer platforms using different compilers and whether that produces identical results, they often respond with blank incomprehension.

order dependency occurs in the assignment to R because evaluating F(X) before the division Y / Z is required to raise the predefined exception Constraint_Error. The expected, exception-free, result is obtained if the division is evaluated before the function call. It is worth noting that this program is defined as *erroneous* in Ada terminology. Erroneous here has the special meaning (or perhaps "cop out") that the program is wrong but the compiler is *not* required to detect the problem nor report it to the user.

Implementation issues such as this pose particular challenges for automatic code generation from formal specifications. We could, in principle, solve them by ensuring that our code generator never generated code that might have an implementation dependency concealed in it. For example, we could insist that function calls and operators with side effects are only used in simple assignment statements and only allow the use of simple variables in expressions. These are, however, rather draconian restrictions which may well impact on efficiency (important given that many high-integrity systems are also real-time systems). It is also, in practice, extremely hard to do because ambiguity is so easy to introduce. No amount of testing of simple specification constructs and the code they map to, can ensure that arbitrary *combinations* of such constructs will not produce code that exhibits ambiguous behaviour of the type illustrated above.

Resource Consumption. A more easily handled consideration for code generation is that of resource consumption. Many critical systems run for very long periods on devices with very limited resources. In such circumstances it is important that our method of code generation does not allow those limited resources to be consumed by such things as memory leaks. We should be able to ensure that is the case at the design level but it also needs to be considered at the intermediate code level; this issue will be revisisted in Section 4

Semantic Gaps. There remains one large problem with the generation of code from specifications: semantic gaps and our ability to reason across them. Let's assume for a moment that we solve all the problems outlined above and produce a code generator that produces binary object code for our target processor directly from our specification. We perform various rigorous analyses of our specification, press a button, and object code comes out. Can we deploy this in our critical application? The answer is clearly "no". We cannot readily *trace* the object code to the specification because the semantic gap between them is too large. What about *trusting* the code generator? Well, in current typical development processes we aren't always permitted to trust compilers yet the semantic gap between *source code* and *object code* is much smaller than between *specification* and *object code*, so it seems infeasible that we can take a complex and opaque code generator on trust for the kind of critical application for which we would choose formal methods in the first place. What about *testing* the output from the code generator. Well, yes, of course we should do that, but we also know that we cannot gain enough confidence for a critical application by this means alone (see [7,8,9]).

If we conclude that the semantic gap between specification and object code is too big then it follows that we need some kind of intermediate representation, presumably in the form of the source code of a suitable programming language. The consequences of this unavoidable design choice will be discussed in the next section.

4   Required Properties of Intermediate Representations

From the above, we have determined that some intermediate notation between our specification and object code is required, or at least highly beneficial. We have also identified
some of the challenges that our chosen notation must meet. An intermediate notation
that provides real value in a formal development chain would address the following
issues; it would:

- allow the rigorous generation of "device drivers" and other "glue" code required
  to handle those parts of the system that cannot sensibly be formally specified and
  facilitate the integration of that code with automatically-generated code;
- facilitate a demonstration that the logical rules used to formalize the behaviour
  described in the specification are preserved in the implementation;
- bridge the semantic gap between specification and object code by allowing precise reasoning showing the equivalence of the specification and the intermediate
  notation and the equivalence of the intermediate notation and the object code; and
- provide an alternative notation that may be more suitable than the specification
  notation for capturing specific design choices to deal with non-functional requirements such as safety, while still allowing formal equivalence with the specification
  to be proved.

These considerations have taken us rather a long way from our starting point. We
started with the strawman that: given a mathematically-sound specification which we can
animate for our end users; prove properties of; and generate code from, then it doesn't
matter what language the final code is generated in. The strawman is, I think, now thoroughly demolished. The intermediate notation, or programming language source code,
that bridges the gap between the specification and the deployed object code is not only
still essential but has to meet some very stringent requirements of its own. Furthermore,
ducking this issue very significantly undermines all the ultimate goals and ambitions of
the RODIN project. We should not, after all, be rather narrowly interested in whether
or not we can write better *specifications* because that goal, alone, is meaningless. Our
real goal is to produce better *systems* and better specifications are only of interest if they
contribute to that more important goal.

What properties might a suitable intermediate notation have? I think we can identify
the following requirements:

Logical soundness. This is fundamental. Logical soundness means freedom from the
  kinds of imprecise and ambiguous behaviour noted in section 3.4. We cannot begin
  to show correspondence between our formally verified specification and the code
  we obtain from it (both manually and automatically) without first achieving this
  goal. In practice, and as a minimum starting point, this means a language free from
  the possibility of undefined variable values; freedom from aliasing; and freedom
  from function and expression side effects.
Simplicity of formal language definition. Not essential, but a useful check. If we can't
  readily produce a formalization of the semantics of our intermediate notation then
  we are unlikely to have, or know that we have, a logically sound one.

Expressive power. The intermediate language must be rich and expressive enough to allow the efficient translation of our specifications into code and to allow the effective hand-crafting of those parts of the system for which this is appropriate. Clearly we could make a "safe" language by making it so small you couldn't write any programs in it; a rather unhelpful limiting case!

Security. Security here has the special meaning of "it shall be possible to detect all violations of the rules of the language". There is no point in imposing a language rule such as "functions are not permitted to have side effects" if there is no way of detecting those situations where the rule is broken. This consideration is especially important in the case of code generation from rigorous specifications because it provides protection from the difficult case where a combination of legal specification entities produces a collection of code entities that in combination violate the goal of logical soundness. The ability to check the generated code for such violations is essential and the principle of security makes it feasible.

Verifiability. Really a consequential property of logical soundness and security. A verifiable language allows us bind together both automatically-generated and hand-written code and demonstrate that the whole conforms to our formal specification. As noted in section 3.1, we can only formally compare two artefacts if we have a formalization of each of them. Even where nearly all of the code has been generated by a rigorous process of refinement, this independent verification path is of great value precisely because of its diversity and the extra confidence such redundancy brings. Verifiability also allows us to deal with the imperfect (in the pure mathematical sense) numerical behaviour of computers as noted in section 3.4. We may well do better to worry about these *implementation domain problems* in the *implementation domain* by a suitable proof of absence of run-time errors performed on our intermediate notation. See, for example, [10].

Bounded space and time requirements. This follows from the consideration noted in section 3.4. There is no point carefully devising a code generator that avoids such things as arbitrary heap allocations if the generated code is processed by a compiler that *does* do those unwanted things. We are likely to be equally concerned about *predicatability* of resource usage. For example, generating code in a language that relies on periodic garbage collection will lead to unpredictable execution timing which may be unacceptable in many critical applications. Our intermediate language must be designed to be free from such effects and so that the compilers we use to process it will preserve the desirable restrictions we have placed on the way the code is generated from the specification.

Compilable by standard tools. Long experience shows that, to gain acceptance, a language must provide access to a wide range of compilers targeted at a wide range of processors. The temptation to produce a custom intermediate notation for RODIN specifications is a strong but dangerous one. Essentially it would ensure that the application of all the advances generated by RODIN would be restricted to an extremely small subset of target processors and architectures. It follows from this consideration that any viable intermediate notation is likely to take the form of a *subset* of a mainstream programming language rather than being a completely new development.

Verifiability of compiled code. A rather grand requirement. Ideally we would devise an intermediate notation so that typical compilers for it produced machine code that was readily traceable to its source. If achieved, this would support the ultimate goal of traceability from specification to object code. Although there has been useful research in this area, it remains an area of considerable practical difficulty.

Minimal run-time system requirements. Finally, we need to remember that the machine code eventually deployed on our system will comprise that compiled from our intermediate notation (itself a mix of hand-crafted and automatically-generated) together with some underlying run-time library or support system. For the final system to be trustworthy, both components must be trustworthy. Unfortunately we are unlikely to have such strong evidence for the integrity of the compiler vendor's run-time as we hope to be able to generate for the code we produce using our RODIN-inspired tools. From this we conclude that a useful additional goal is that chosen intermediate language should be designed to require the smallest amount of run-time support that is possible. Ideally we should be able to generate code for a bare board target and trace every byte of machine code on it back to one of our design and specification artefacts.

The above is quite a daunting list. It has also been chosen quite deliberately because it is *identical* to the list of requirements from the original 1983 rationale for the SPARK programming language which can still be found in the introduction of [4]. This is not to suggest that SPARK represents the ultimate in programming language design but does at least provide existential proof that the properties we require in a notation that purports to bridge the semantic gap between a formal specification and a deployed system are actually achievable in practice.

5 Conclusions

So, far from programming languages being rendered obsolete by formal methods and code generation, they become *more* important! Fortunately, programs such as RODIN provide us with an opportunity here. Experience (some might say *bitter* experience) shows just how hard it is to wean programmers off error-prone and inadequate notations such as C. By moving the emphasis from *coding* to *specification*, and providing a rewarding development environment for the latter, RODIN may unblock some of these obstacles. Once users come to understand the benefits of a rigorous, formally-backed approach to specification, then persuading them to accept a more rigorous intermediate notation than C might just become a little more achievable. For large parts of a RODIN-specified system the code can be automatically generated and so we do not need to ask the C enthusiasts to write very much of our new and unfamiliar intermediate notation.

The idea that we might combine two different formal notations to both increase confidence in the verification we perform and also to widen the scope of that verification has been considered before in the context of the SCADE graphical notation and the SPARK programming language, see [11]. The combination of SCADE and SPARK illustrates many of the issues discussed in this paper and provides a practical demonstration of the benefits that come from combining different formal notations so as to spread rigour more widely across the entire development process.

The RODIN project, and follow-on work from it, offers us a unique opportunity to deploy these concepts more widely and to provide an unbroken chain of formal reasoning from requirements to (very nearly) object code. We shouldn't fumble that opportunity out of mistaken view that programming languages no longer matter: they do.

References

1. Peter Amey. *Dear Sir, Yours Faithfully: an Everyday Story of Formality.* "Practical Elements of Safety", Proceedings of the Twelfth Safety-critical Systems Symposium, Birmingham, UK, February 2004, pp3-15. Copyright Springer-Verlag 2004. ISBN 1-85233-800-8.[3]
2. Martin Croxford, Rod Chapman. *Correctness by Construction: A Manifesto for High-Integrity Software.* Crosstalk Journal, December 2005, pp5-8.[3]
3. John Barnes. *High Integrity Software - the SPARK Approach to Safety and Security.* Addison Wesley Longman, ISBN 0-321-13616-0. 2003
4. Finnie, Gavin et al. *SPARK 95 - The SPADE Ada 95 Kernel.* Praxis High Integrity Systems[3].
5. Steve King, Jonathan Hammond, Rod Chapman and Andy Pryor. *Is Proof More Cost Effective Than Testing?.* IEEE Transactions on Software Engineering Vol 26, No 8, August 2000, pp 675-686[3]
6. D L Parnas, J Madey. *Functional Documentation for Computer Systems,* "Science of Computer Programming". October 1995
7. Bev Littlewood, Lorenzo Strigini. *Validation of Ultrahigh Dependability for Software-Based Systems.* CACM 36(11): pp69-80 (1993)
8. Bev Littlewood. *Limits to evaluation of software dependability.* In Software Reliability and Metrics (Procedings of Seventh Annual CSR Conference, Garmisch-Partenkirchen). N. Fenton and B. Littlewood. Eds. Elsevier, London, pp. 81-110.
9. Ricky W. Butler, George B. Finelli. *The Infeasibility of Quantifying the Reliability of Life-Critical Real-Time Software.* IEEE Transactions on Software Engineering, vol. 19, no. 1, Jan. 1993, pp 3-12.
10. Rod Chapman, Peter Amey. *Industrial Strength Exception Freedom.* Proceedings of ACM SIGAda 2002[3]
11. Peter Amey, Bernard Dion. *Combining Model-Driven Design With Diverse Formal Verification.* Presented at ERTS2006, Embedded Real-Time Software, Toulouse 2006.[3]
12. Sixth Framework Programme for Research and Technological Development, Contract No. 511599. April 2004. The *Statement of Work* and other information can be found here: http://rodin.cs.ncl.ac.uk/index.htm
    See also: http://ec.europa.eu/research/fp6/index_en.cfm?p=0

---

[3] Also available from Praxis High Integrity Systems.

Author Index

Lecture Notes in Computer Science

For information about Vols. 1–4208

please contact your bookseller or Springer

Vol. 4252: B. Gabrys, R.J. Howlett, L.C. Jain (Eds.), Knowledge-Based Intelligent Information and Engineering Systems, Part II. XXXIII, 1335 pages. 2006. (Sublibrary LNAI).

Vol. 4251: B. Gabrys, R.J. Howlett, L.C. Jain (Eds.), Knowledge-Based Intelligent Information and Engineering Systems, Part I. LXVI, 1297 pages. 2006. (Sublibrary LNAI).

Vol. 4249: L. Goubin, M. Matsui (Eds.), Cryptographic Hardware and Embedded Systems - CHES 2006. XII, 462 pages. 2006.

Vol. 4248: S. Staab, V. Svátek (Eds.), Managing Knowledge in a World of Networks. XIV, 400 pages. 2006. (Sublibrary LNAI).

Vol. 4247: T.-D. Wang, X. Li, S.-H. Chen, X. Wang, H. Abbass, H. Iba, G. Chen, X. Yao (Eds.), Simulated Evolution and Learning. XXI, 940 pages. 2006.

Vol. 4246: M. Hermann, A. Voronkov (Eds.), Logic for Programming, Artificial Intelligence, and Reasoning. XIII, 588 pages. 2006. (Sublibrary LNAI).

Vol. 4245: A. Kuba, L.G. Nyúl, K. Palágyi (Eds.), Discrete Geometry for Computer Imagery. XIII, 688 pages. 2006.

Vol. 4244: S. Spaccapietra (Ed.), Journal on Data Semantics VII. XI, 267 pages. 2006.

Vol. 4243: T. Yakhno, E.J. Neuhold (Eds.), Advances in Information Systems. XIII, 420 pages. 2006.

Vol. 4242: A. Rashid, M. Aksit (Eds.), Transactions on Aspect-Oriented Software Development II. IX, 289 pages. 2006.

Vol. 4241: R.R. Beichel, M. Sonka (Eds.), Computer Vision Approaches to Medical Image Analysis. XI, 262 pages. 2006.

Vol. 4239: H.Y. Youn, M. Kim, H. Morikawa (Eds.), Ubiquitous Computing Systems. XVI, 548 pages. 2006.

Vol. 4238: Y.-T. Kim, M. Takano (Eds.), Management of Convergence Networks and Services. XVIII, 605 pages. 2006.

Vol. 4237: H. Leitold, E. Markatos (Eds.), Communications and Multimedia Security. XII, 253 pages. 2006.

Vol. 4236: L. Breveglieri, I. Korep, D. Naccache, J.-P. Seifert (Eds.), Fault Diagnosis and Tolerance in Cryptography. XIII, 253 pages. 2006.

Vol. 4234: I. King, J. Wang, L. Chan, D. Wang (Eds.), Neural Information Processing, Part III. XXII, 1227 pages. 2006.

Vol. 4233: I. King, J. Wang, L. Chan, D. Wang (Eds.), Neural Information Processing, Part II. XXII, 1203 pages. 2006.

Vol. 4232: I. King, J. Wang, L. Chan, D. Wang (Eds.), Neural Information Processing, Part I. XLVI, 1153 pages. 2006.

Vol. 4231: J. F. Roddick, R. Benjamins, S. Si-Saïd Cherfi, R. Chiang, C. Claramunt, R. Elmasri, F. Grandi, H. Han, M. Hepp, M. Hepp, M. Lytras, V.B. Mišić, G. Poels, I.-Y. Song, J. Trujillo, C. Vangenot (Eds.), Advances in Conceptual Modeling - Theory and Practice. XXII, 456 pages. 2006.

Vol. 4230: C. Priami, A. Ingólfsdóttir, B. Mishra, H.R. Nielson (Eds.), Transactions on Computational Systems Biology VII. VII, 185 pages. 2006. (Sublibrary LNBI).

Vol. 4229: E. Najm, J.F. Pradat-Peyre, V.V. Donzeau-Gouge (Eds.), Formal Techniques for Networked and Distributed Systems - FORTE 2006. X, 486 pages. 2006.

Vol. 4228: D.E. Lightfoot, C.A. Szyperski (Eds.), Modular Programming Languages. X, 415 pages. 2006.

Vol. 4227: W. Nejdl, K. Tochtermann (Eds.), Innovative Approaches for Learning and Knowledge Sharing. XVII, 721 pages. 2006.

Vol. 4226: R.T. Mittermeir (Ed.), Informatics Education - The Bridge between Using and Understanding Computers. XVII, 319 pages. 2006.

Vol. 4225: J.F. Martínez-Trinidad, J.A. Carrasco Ochoa, J. Kittler (Eds.), Progress in Pattern Recognition, Image Analysis and Applications. XIX, 995 pages. 2006.

Vol. 4224: E. Corchado, H. Yin, V. Botti, C. Fyfe (Eds.), Intelligent Data Engineering and Automated Learning - IDEAL 2006. XXVII, 1447 pages. 2006.

Vol. 4223: L. Wang, L. Jiao, G. Shi, X. Li, J. Liu (Eds.), Fuzzy Systems and Knowledge Discovery. XXVIII, 1335 pages. 2006. (Sublibrary LNAI).

Vol. 4222: L. Jiao, L. Wang, X. Gao, J. Liu, F. Wu (Eds.), Advances in Natural Computation, Part II. XLII, 998 pages. 2006.

Vol. 4221: L. Jiao, L. Wang, X. Gao, J. Liu, F. Wu (Eds.), Advances in Natural Computation, Part I. XLI, 992 pages. 2006.

Vol. 4220: C. Priami, G. Plotkin (Eds.), Transactions on Computational Systems Biology VI. IX, 247 pages. 2006. (Sublibrary LNBI).

Vol. 4219: D. Zamboni, C. Kruegel (Eds.), Recent Advances in Intrusion Detection. XII, 331 pages. 2006.

Vol. 4218: S. Graf, W. Zhang (Eds.), Automated Technology for Verification and Analysis. XIV, 540 pages. 2006.

Vol. 4217: P. Cuenca, L. Orozco-Barbosa (Eds.), Personal Wireless Communications. XV, 532 pages. 2006.

Vol. 4216: M.R. Berthold, R. Glen, I. Fischer (Eds.), Computational Life Sciences II. XIII, 269 pages. 2006. (Sublibrary LNBI).

Vol. 4215: D.W. Embley, A. Olivé, S. Ram (Eds.), Conceptual Modeling - ER 2006. XVI, 590 pages. 2006.

Vol. 4213: J. Fürnkranz, T. Scheffer, M. Spiliopoulou (Eds.), Knowledge Discovery in Databases: PKDD 2006. XXII, 660 pages. 2006. (Sublibrary LNAI).

Vol. 4212: J. Fürnkranz, T. Scheffer, M. Spiliopoulou (Eds.), Machine Learning: ECML 2006. XXIII, 851 pages. 2006. (Sublibrary LNAI).

Vol. 4211: P. Vogt, Y. Sugita, E. Tuci, C. Nehaniv (Eds.), Symbol Grounding and Beyond. VIII, 237 pages. 2006. (Sublibrary LNAI).

Vol. 4210: C. Priami (Ed.), Computational Methods in Systems Biology. X, 323 pages. 2006. (Sublibrary LNBI).

Vol. 4209: F. Crestani, P. Ferragina, M. Sanderson (Eds.), String Processing and Information Retrieval. XIV, 367 pages. 2006.